DATE DUE

D0397139

GAYLORD   PRINTED IN U.S A.

UPTON SINCLAIR:
American Rebel

UPTON SINCLAIR:
American Rebel

Leon Harris

THOMAS Y. CROWELL COMPANY

NEW YORK   ESTABLISHED 1834

PCHS Media Center
Grant, Nebraska

Copyright © 1975 by Leon Harris

Excerpts from the previously unpublished letters of Ezra Pound copyright © 1975 by the Trustees of the Ezra Pound Literary Property Trust, published by permission of New Directions Publishing Corporation, agent.

All rights reserved. Except for use in a review, the reproduction or utilization of this work in any form or by any electronic, mechanical, or other means, now known or hereafter invented, including xerography, photocopying, and recording, and in any information storage and retrieval system is forbidden without the written permission of the publisher. Published simultaneously in Canada by Fitzhenry & Whiteside Limited, Toronto.

Manufactured in the United States of America

Library of Congress Cataloging in Publication Data

Harris, Leon.
    Upton Sinclair, American rebel.

    Bibliography: p.
    Includes index.
    1. Sinclair, Upton Beall, 1878–1968.
PS3537.185Z64   813'.5'2 [B]   74-23582
ISBN 0-690-00671-3

1 2 3 4 5 6 7 8 9 10

All illustrations, except as otherwise noted, are courtesy of the Lilly Library.

Acknowledgement is made to the following for permission to quote brief excerpts: "The Confused Case of Upton Sinclair" by Howard Mumford Jones in *The Atlantic Monthly*, copyright 1946, copyright Renewed 1974 by The Atlantic Monthly Company, Boston, Mass. Reprinted by permission.
The Confident Years by Van Wyck Brooks. Copyright 1952 by Van Wyck Brooks. Reprinted by permission of the publishers, E. P. Dutton & Co., Inc.
The Van Wyck Brooks-Lewis Mumford Letters, The Record of a Literary Friendship, 1921–1963. Edited by Robert E. Spiller. Copyright © 1970 by E. P. Dutton & Co., Inc. and used with their permission.

4858

92
Si 62h

Acknowledgments   v

The Life of Emerson by Van Wyck Brooks. Copyright 1932 by E. P. Dutton & Co., Inc. Renewal © 1950 by Van Wyck Brooks. Reprinted by permission of the publishers, E. P. Dutton & Co., Inc.

Prejudices, Third Series by H. L. Mencken. Copyright 1922 by H. L. Mencken. Published by Alfred A. Knopf, Inc., and used with their permission.

The Floyd Dell Papers, courtesy of The Newberry Library and Mrs. Floyd Dell.

Letters from H. L. Mencken to Upton Sinclair, courtesy of The Mercantile-Safe Deposit and Trust Company (Baltimore, Maryland), Trustee U/W Henry L. Mencken.

A Radical's America by Harvey Swados, copyright 1961 by Harvey Swados. Published by Little Brown & Co. and used by permission of Mrs. Harvey Swados.

"The Survival of Upton Sinclair" by Granville Hicks in *College English*, copyright 1943 by The National Council of Teachers of English. Reprinted by permission.

"Warmakers and Peacemakers" by Granville Hicks in *The New Republic*, copyright 1940 by The New Republic, Inc. Reprinted by permission.

Letters from George Bernard Shaw to Upton Sinclair, used by permission of The Society of Authors on behalf of the Bernard Shaw Estate.

The author also wishes to thank all those who gave him permission to quote from unpublished letters and other material, among them: Robert Cantwell, Malcolm Cowley, Paul H. Douglas, the Dreiser Trust, Martin Esslin, James T. Farrell, Darley Fuller Gordon, Sheldon Harnick for the lyric line from "The Side of the Angels," © 1959 Sunbeam Music Corp., Sidney Hook, the Estate of Sinclair Lewis, the Estate of Perry Miller, Lewis Mumford, the Estate of Allan Nevins, Victor Reuther, Arthur Schlesinger Jr., and others.

For
Marina Svetlova
with love.

Contents

x   Contents

UPTON SINCLAIR:
American Rebel

Introduction

All biography . . . is concerned with the truth of life and the truth of experience . . . What is the essence of a life, and how do we disengage that essence from the eternal clutter of days and years. . . . And how tell, in especial, the life of the mind, which is what the literary life really is: the mind and the emotions—as distinct from the lives of generals and politicians . . . to take the base metals that are . . . disparate facts and turn them into the gold of human personality . . . a kind of alchemy of the spirit. LEON EDEL

UPTON SINCLAIR WAS BORN on September 20, 1878, and died November 25, 1968. Until 1905, he was an unknown failure. For forty years thereafter he was America's most important writer; that is, he was more responsible than any other writer for the changing view Americans had of themselves, their rights, and their reasonable expectations. But by the time he died, Sinclair was again virtually unknown.

Throughout history, writers have not proved demonstrably less vain than others. Simply being a writer implies a belief that one has something to say that is worthwhile for others to read. Nor has it been unknown for a biographer to exaggerate the importance of his subject, because the importance of his book is thereby increased and consequently his own. I have tried to avoid this. When I say that Sinclair is, to date, the most important writer in the history of the United States, it is because I believe the facts substantiate it.

I have not said that he was America's *best* writer, in the sense of having created the most enduring literature, although he was a better writer than he is presently taken to be, but the *most important*. By that I mean that the effects of his writing have been and still are more important than those of any other American professional writer.

Perhaps one at least partial definition of great art may be that art which lasts—which continues to be moving to succeeding generations. Art that is not great, even if it is thought so initially, eventually disappears from public view and interest.

Great propaganda, on the other hand, must be just the opposite; it must so convince the public that its ideas or attitudes become generally accepted; so commonplace, in fact, that they are taken for granted and the propaganda itself disappears from memory. When people attribute to their own good sense or to the natural order of things an idea that was first or best proposed by a propagandist—and have forgotten him—it was successful propaganda.

Sinclair originated *none* of the ideas for which he propagandized, nor did he claim to have. But he convinced millions of people all over the world of them. Other of his contemporary muckrakers played a greater role than he in effecting particular social change. But not one of them approached his total influence in regard to all the ideas he advocated. In the variety of his work and in his incomparable success in having it widely reprinted, discussed, attacked, and kept in print, Sinclair outweighed all other individual muckrakers.

When President Theodore Roosevelt in 1906 first called these reformers "muckrakers," he meant it to be derogatory, but they seized the name and used it themselves proudly. With the passing years it has, however, come to be vaguely synonymous with yellow journalists.

Nor did Sinclair only sit and write. He took courageous physical and political action to advance his causes, was used by Presidents and used them in turn. His own life was as exciting as that of most of his heroes.

When Sinclair became an important writer at the beginning of the century, there was no minimum wage, no maximum working hours, no employer liability for accidents, no pure food and drug laws, no right to bargain collectively, no strong unions, no votes and, as a practical matter, no rights for women, no education permitted on birth control or venereal disease, no effective anti-price-fixing activity, no health insurance or social security or unemployment compensation, and no supervision of banks or stock exchanges or insurance companies. These are only a few of the areas in which Sinclair's propaganda helped to bring about reform.

More important even than the lack of legislation were the attitudes of most Americans—might makes right, *caveat emptor*, the end justifies the means—simple social Darwinism and devil take the hindmost. By the end of Sinclair's ninety years, the attitudes of the majority of Americans had so changed that curative legislation had been enacted, was generally supposed to be enforced, and was, as a matter of fact, too much taken for granted.

Sinclair's was a time when writers were important, when America had no television. A single book or article of his could reach millions more people than would see and hear the most hard-working politician-lecturer, such as Eugene V. Debs, in his whole lifetime.

Because of the ephemeral nature of great propaganda, it is very difficult to assess a propagandist's direct influence on specific individuals through his own works; but it is even harder to identify his influence extended by others affected by him. Nevertheless, I have tried to trace his effect through other men and women who themselves have had an important influence of their own on this country and elsewhere. Because Sinclair believed that reform was possible in virtually every institution of America, he wrote about them all, and I have quoted throughout this book from specialists in each field regarding his influence on them. But in this Introduction, I quote a few merely to indicate the almost unbelievable breadth of that influence.

Eric Sevareid: "He was one of those figures from the great muckraking days . . . who excited me as a young student . . . to become a journalist."

Dr. Karl Menninger: "Sinclair's *Jungle*, read to me as a teenager, produced a profound effect, a kind of horror regarding the inhumanity of man to man."

Robert McNamara: "He did influence me in my thinking by identifying three or four decades ago many of the problems which because they remain unresolved are dividing our nation today."

Allen Ginsberg: "Sinclair influenced my family, i.e., 20's and thirties radicalism was sustained by his common sense & good heart. . . . Hindsight in the 60's made his economic & political activities seem charming prefigurations of present youth rebellion."

Daniel Patrick Moynihan: "Sinclair was much in my mind when I began to work on traffic safety problems in the late 1950's. . . . This development —I brought Ralph Nader to Washington to work on the subject when I became Assistant Secretary of Labor under Kennedy did, I think, lead to important legislation."

Norman Mailer: "Upton Sinclair had no particular influence on my life except in one way and that was not small. I read his novel, BOSTON, when I was 12 or 13 and hardly understood it, but for better or worse it moved me to the left. I still remember the portrait of Vanzetti."

Writers as unlikely as Moss Hart and George S. Kaufman, journalists with audiences as great as Walter Cronkite and William Shirer, politicians and political activists, blacks as well as whites, all attest to Sinclair's direct effect on their lives.

The indirect effects (those ever-expanding circles) of a propagandist on individuals are even harder to measure, but sometimes not impossible.

John Kenneth Galbraith: "I expect like others I was influenced by him but I am sure at second or third hand."

Ramsey Clark: "I have sensed a powerful influence of Upton Sinclair on many people whom I respect. . . . his influence on those who most strongly influenced us was undoubtedly great."

Outside of America, Sinclair's effect on those who influenced others is also traceable. Bertolt Brecht was clearly influenced by Sinclair and, in fact, was in touch with him through Elizabeth Hauptmann. The millions of copies of Sinclair's books published in the Soviet Union registered on its artists great and small from Sergei Eisenstein to Aleksandr Solzhenitsyn. And according to Herbert Marcuse: "I remember that I read almost all of Upton Sinclair's books, quite a few of them prior to my coming to the United States in 1934. I can say that they gave me a new and very powerful picture of this country."

Perhaps as significant as Sinclair's effect on august politicians and pundits is the fact that he first inspired Charlie Chaplin's interest in politics and made him a Socialist.

Whoever chooses to write conscientiously a biography of Sinclair must want to do so very much indeed, because the material available is excessive. In the Lilly Library at Indiana University alone, there are between eight and nine tons of material in the Sinclair Collection including more than 250,000 letters of Sinclair correspondence; to and from Krupskaya, Kennedy, Mencken, Mann, Gorki, Gandhi, Trotsky, Shaw, and both Presidents Roosevelt. Big numbers, like big casualty lists, being sometimes less easy to comprehend than small examples, I point out that even if one were able to read sixty letters an hour for eight hours a day, it would take five hundred working days just to read a quarter of a million letters. Sinclair also wrote thousands of articles, book reviews, letters to the editor, and essays, in addition to ninety books, on almost every imaginable subject, from economics to extrasensory perception to alcoholism to religion to politics to sex; so his biographer must read other works on all Sinclair's subjects, as well as on the world Sinclair lived in and sought to change from 1878 to 1968.

I chose to write Upton Sinclair's biography first because it was such an extraordinary life. But also, it seemed to me to indicate that within the American system, given enough energy, change for the better is possible. This I want to believe and to have others believe, even though 1975 is not 1905 nor even 1935. However, I have not tried to prove anything and so may quote, with Strachey: *"Je n'impose rien; je ne propose rien; j'expose."*

For I have tried to remember that as André Maurois observed: "Writing biography is an art, like portrait painting. . . . the aim of the biographer is to make a man (or woman) and his (or her) times come alive again. . . . a biographer, like a novelist, proves nothing if he wants to prove too much. . . . from no other type of book can one draw such fruitful moral lessons. But the moral must remain implicit. . . . the effect on men of works of art is better and greater than that of any story with a moral. . . . Most of the greatest in man comes from the imitation of great lives." Or, as Harold Nicolson has suggested: "biography is essentially a profane brand of literature; its triumphs do not proceed from theological convictions. . . . For biography is the preoccupation and the solace, not of certainty but of doubt."

But one may hope that the Republic will continue to produce writers like Sinclair, who will help keep its citizens from becoming short of breath or losing their good humor in the endless opposition to injustice. Such writers provide one of the answers to the question, "What can one person do?"

CHAPTER I

Childhood

Men always hate most what they envy most.   H. L. MENCKEN

"WE NEVER HAD BUT ONE ROOM AT A TIME, and I slept on a sofa or crossways at the foot of my parents' bed. . . . One adventure recurred; the gas-light would be turned on in the middle of the night, and I would start up, rubbing my eyes, and join in the exciting chase of bedbugs. They came out in the dark, and went scurrying into hiding when they saw the light; so they must be mashed quickly."

Those flat, reddish-brown, stinking bedbugs, along with the other many obscenities of poverty, explain why Upton Sinclair became a rebel. These vermin that feed only on human blood and can, unlike their poor victims, survive for many months without eating at all appear and reappear throughout Sinclair's work like a leitmotiv.

Upton was born in Baltimore in a boardinghouse on Biddle Street. What made his childhood experiences with poverty far worse than they would have been had he known nothing else was his constant moving back and forth between wretched boardinghouses and the homes of his rich relatives.

Sinclair's carefully wax-mustached, potbellied father, Upton Beall Sinclair, was a drunkard. Proud of his aristocratic ancestors and their distinguished naval careers, he was, like so many Southerners of his and later generations, unable to accept that reality differed from memories and pretensions. He was a drummer, selling at such times as sobriety coincided with good business, first wholesale whiskey, later men's straw hats, and finally men's clothing.

In *Life on the Mississippi*, Mark Twain blamed the Civil War on Sir Walter Scott, whose tales of chivalry so shaped the South's self-image. Of similar importance to young Upton were the ideas of duty, truth, and honor, incessantly droned into his ears. The chivalry and loyalty of Sinclair naval

7

officers were all the elder Sinclair could offer his son, and he recited endlessly the example of a cousin whose vessel was sunk and who himself drowned, because he gallantly gave his supporting oar to a comrade who had been slightly wounded.

Sinclair, Sr., was not a high liver or a womanizer. He loved his wife and son and desperately wanted their love and respect in return. But increasingly, with his lack of success in the commercial world, his craving for whiskey overwhelmed him. He would disappear for days, and although on his return he would tearfully promise both his wife and his son that he would reform, he could not.

Saloons being no place for a lady, Upton while still a boy went regularly to fetch his father home. "It was the Highway of Lost Men. . . . their faces . . . gaunt with misery, or bloated with disease . . . a policeman . . . swinging his club and watching . . . down this highway walked a lad . . . pale of face, and with delicate and sensitive features. . . . a girl in a doorway . . . nodded to him. . . . Her wanton black eyes haunted him, hinting unimaginable things. . . . At last, in a dingy bar-room . . . suddenly the boy sprang forward, with a cry: 'Father!' And a man . . . fell upon his shoulder, sobbing, 'My son!' . . . those words . . . they voiced all the terror and grief of a defeated life—'My son! My son!' "

In a style that today seems overwritten and sentimental, this and similar passages throughout Sinclair's work, in fact like Hogarth's work, understate the horror and terror. As the child repeatedly searched for and found his father and somehow got him home (except when *delerium tremens* made it necessary to take him for brutal treatment to a charity hospital), he must have had such mixed feelings of repugnance, loyalty, mortification, and love as he would be unable ever to express satisfactorily.

On the many nights when he could not find his father, Upton slept alone with his mother in the sordid single rooms that were all they could afford and that changed constantly because of the chronic shortage of rent money.

Sinclair never wrote, then or later, about any effect on himself, or on his outlook or writing, that might have been brought about by his sleeping in the same bed with his parents, much less, by sleeping alone with his mother. He was, however, not reluctant as an adult, when discussing a writer he didn't like, to assert the psychological and literary effects that sleeping arrangements could have on a boy's later life: "three boys sleeping in one bed as a source of abnormal sexual imaginings, which constitutes one of the original elements in Sherwood Anderson's books."

It is at least possible that similar informal sleeping arrangements in Sinclair's own boyhood were not totally unrelated to his extraordinarily close relationship with his mother in his youth, to his lifelong idealization of women, and to his lifelong prudery and puritanism.

A child's individual reaction to a common childhood experience may indicate, at least partially, an important characteristic of his personality. Once accused of being a girl, young Upton protested stoutly that he was not. Asked by the man teasing him how he knew that he was a boy, Sinclair replied, "Because my mother tells me so."

Upton's proof contrasts interestingly with that given by another small boy who was also destined to grow into an important American writer but who, even as a child, was not dependent on his mother for his sense of reality. When Thomas Wolfe was accused by older boys of being a girl, he opened his pants to disprove their contention.

Upton's tight-lipped, stern-faced mother, Priscilla Harden, was also a Southerner, the daughter of John S. Harden, the secretary-treasurer of the Western Maryland Railroad. She was a practical and proper woman who did not drink coffee or tea because they were "stimulants," and their use constituted the arch sin, self-indulgence. Not only a puritan, she was also a snob, and as her economic security lessened, her pathetic snobberies became increasingly insistent and essential.

When Upton was about ten, the family moved to New York City. Thereafter, when matters became too desperate with his parents, he was sent back to Baltimore, often for months at a time, where he lived either with his grandfather Harden or his "Uncle Bland," both of whom had houses on Maryland Avenue.

Priscilla Sinclair's older sister, Maria, had married John Randolph Bland, an astute banker who founded the United States Fidelity and Guaranty Company and was on his way to becoming one of the richest men in Baltimore. The ever increasing grandeur of the Blands' way of life contrasted bitterly with that of the Sinclairs.

John Bland was also quick to assert the superiority of his lineage to that of mere money-grubbers. He laid claim to relations and connections with members of the most famous families of Virginia, including John Randolph of Roanoke. The atmosphere created by that endless snobbery and talk about money in the Bland house outraged young Upton, whom it reminded of his parents' pathetic pretensions. "I do not know why I came to hate it, but I know that I did hate it from my earliest days. And everything in my later life confirmed my resolve never to 'sell out' to that class."

In Baltimore Upton experienced or heard discussed wondrous adult luxuries: terrapin soup as liberally laced with sherry as the plum puddings were with brandy; the Cotillon, the Assembly, the Supper Club, and the races. "I will spend my money for ball & torpedoes & fire-crackers. . . . Uncle B. took Howard [Bland's son] & me to a Turkish bath. We all went into the plunge . . . had lots of fun. . . . I certainly do have fine things to eat here."

Not very surprisingly, the boy both enjoyed and resented these luxuries that his cousins had by right and he only by favor, and he later wrote: "to explain the appearance of a social rebel in a conventional Southern family . . . I diagnose my psychology as that of a 'poor relation.' It has been my fate from earliest childhood to live in the presence of wealth which belonged to others. . . . all my life I was faced by the contrast between riches and poverty, and thereby impelled to think and to ask questions. 'Mamma, why are some children poor and others rich? How can that be fair?' I plagued my mother's mind with the problem, and never got any answer. Now I plague the ruling-class apologists of the world with it, and still get no answer."

The repeated injustices and humiliations in the boy's life with his parents, worsened by the constant trips to Baltimore, bred rebellion in his heart. "Readers of my novels know that I have one favorite theme, the contrast between social classes; there are characters from both worlds, the rich and the poor, and the plots are contrived to carry you from one to the other. The explanation is that as far back as I can remember, my life was a series of Cinderella transformations; one night I would be sleeping on a vermin-ridden sofa in a lodginghouse, and the next night under silken coverlets in a fashionable home. . . . No Cophetua or Aladdin in fairy lore ever stepped back and forth between the hovel and the palace as frequently as I."

It was, however, not the luxury of firecrackers and food in Baltimore that gave Upton the greatest pleasure and resentment there. It was the escape from his own unhappy world into the fantasy world of literature that the Blands' enormous, unused library gave the boy. His mother had read to him as far back as he could remember and with his photographic memory and near perfect recall, he stored away every image and often every word. He had asked what the various letters of the alphabet were, then memorized them and their sounds. Then he had taught himself to read with a book of rhymes he had been given for Christmas. By the time he was five he had learned to read before his elders realized what he was doing.

Reading became his refuge from both the world of New York and of

Baltimore. On a cold day when the icy wind swept off Chesapeake Bay, the boy could sit in front of the crackling, hospitable logs in one of the Blands' many fireplaces and be with Gulliver in Lilliput or on the way to the Celestial City with Christian. Upton had far more than an average child's time to read, because he was ten before he ever went to school. A doctor had told his mother that the delicate child's mind was outgrowing his body, so he was kept at home, where he taught himself more than he would have learned of academic subjects at school. In time he became, if not robust, at least adequately healthy, lean, active, and fleet of foot.

He later wrote of inheriting from his naval grandfather "that same predatory beak which I carry through life and have handed on to my son," but in fact he was handsome. The nose was aristocratic, the eyes big, blue-gray, and, by turn, piercing or poetic. Indeed, except for his upper lip being a bit long (or his lower lip too short), he was almost beautiful, with the pale, intense poet's face he almost invariably was to give to all the heroes of his novels. He only grew to be five feet seven and remained thin throughout his long life. Those who knew him at every age remarked on his sweetness and boyishness. Charlie Chaplin often entertained his friends by giving an imitation of Sinclair who, he said, always spoke through a smile.

When he was taken to public school in New York at ten, his previous education was found to be most satisfactory, except in arithmetic. "This branch of learning so essential to a commercial civilization, had shared the fate of alcohol and tobacco, tea and coffee; my mother did not use it, so neither did I." Humiliated at being in class with children younger than himself, he cured this deficiency in less than a month.

But it was his self-education that made him. He devoured books, any and everything he could lay hands on. When Upton was missing at mealtime, his cousins knew they might find him hidden anywhere—behind a couch, in the bushes, but always out of this world, lost in a book. He first read whole libraries of adventure thrillers, Henty and the like, graduating next to Cooper, Stevenson, and Scott. Then came more serious novels, *Don Quixote, Les Misérables*, George Eliot's, which he loved, and Dickens', whose social protest he would later say influenced him to fight for social justice. But it was Thackeray, whose work Upton said most molded his thought, who so clearly understood and delineated the greed and hypocrisy of the *haute monde* that Upton's Baltimore relatives worshipped.

The other important escape for Upton was religion. "I was an extraordinarily devout little boy; one of my earliest recollections—I cannot have been more than four years of age—is of carrying a dust-broom about the house as a choir-boy carried the golden cross every Sunday morning. I remember asking if I might say the 'Lord's Prayer' in this fascinating play." At thirteen, he insisted on attending services every single day during the forty days of Lent, and at fifteen was teaching Sunday school.

Even at church, however, or perhaps especially there, Upton was mortified, as in Baltimore, by his inferior position, because his mother insisted on taking him only to the most fashionable Episcopal churches, where the Sinclairs were too poor to be members. The Sinclair family had always been Episcopalian, Upton's father having been named for an Episcopal clergyman, the Reverend Upton Beall. But the boy's maternal grandparents were and remained Methodists even after their daughters decided that the Episcopal Church was more suited to their social standing. Such snobbery was a basic part of young Sinclair's early religious training. The more insecure her economic condition, the more insistent Priscilla Sinclair became that she and her son be seen at the most exclusive church. It was her way of proving their real social status.

But however poor the Sinclairs were, young Upton always wore new shoes, gloves, and a neatly brushed little derby hat, "supreme discomfort to the glory of God." Priscilla Sinclair had decided her only child was to become no less than a bishop.

Like visiting his rich relatives, going to rich men's churches was bound to wound the boy's pride. The best pews were reserved for the members of the church, whose fine clothes offended Upton less than what he judged to be their carefully cultivated manner of aloofness. He resented fiercely having to wait for the few seats that might or might not be left for hoi polloi. Much of the overstatement of his muckraking exposé of all organized religion, *The Profits of Religion*, which he published in 1918, was due to that anger, still burning. Only by his middle fifties could he finally say he did not want to destroy the churches, that his was a lover's quarrel with them, but he still wanted to drive the money changers from the front pews.

Nevertheless, on Easter-Even of 1892 at New York's Church of the Holy Communion, Upton B. Sinclair was confirmed in the Protestant Episcopal Church by the Bishop of Montana.

Perhaps because, unlike Priscilla Sinclair, her husband was born into the Episcopal Church, he did not share with her this particular snobbery, his being more in the political and sartorial areas. He succinctly summed up his political philosophy in 1888 when Harrison defeated Cleveland and he told young Upton who had been to the less than joyous torchlight parade of the defeated Democrats: "I'd rather vote for a nigger than for a Republican."

This Southern gentleman *manqué*, whose affection for whiskey deprived his small family of necessities, had, as his son observed and remembered, more important things than work to which he addressed his attention. "What was the size and flavor of Blue Point oysters as compared with Lynnhaven Bays. . . . where had the Vanderbilts obtained the fifty thousand dollar slab of stone which formed the pavement in front of their Fifth Avenue palace? Questions such as these occupied the mind of my little, fat, kind-hearted father. . . . He was a fastidious dresser . . . especially proud of his small hands and feet—they were aristocratic; he would gaze down rapturously at his tight little shoes, over his well-padded vest . . . the right kind of shoes and vests and hats and gloves . . . they were 'nobby,' they were 'natty,' they were 'neat'—such were the phrases by which he sold them to buyers. I heard much of these last-named essential persons, but cannot recall ever seeing one. They were Jews . . . and the social lines were tightly drawn; never would my father, even in the midst of drink and degradation, have dreamed of using his aristocratic wife to impress his customers. Nor would he use his little son, who was expected to grow up into a naval officer like his ancestors. 'The social position of a naval officer is the highest in the world,' pronounced my father. 'He can go anywhere, absolutely anywhere; he can meet crowned heads as their equals.' "

Far more likely than protecting his wife and son from contaminating contact with Hebrew tradesmen (who might not have been overwhelmingly impressed by the minimally aristocratic lady and the thin boy with the naval ancestors), the elder Sinclair was protecting the buyers and himself from two ardent prohibitionists, who would have stopped at least his own drinking. That Upton, four decades later still ascribed it to snobbery rather than guile may indicate his own guilelessness.

The salesman's anti-Semitism was probably chiefly rhetorical. Like the Populists imprecating the Rothschilds, it was less religious than symbolic, for it derived from the expression of the country man's hatred of the city man and his banks, very few of which were then or have been since under Jewish control or, in fact, willing even to hire Jews in important positions. It was not unrelated to the end of homogeneity in America, where the Protestants were feeling threatened by increasing waves of Irish, Jewish, and Middle European immigrants, an anti-Semitism that sadly was common to most non-Jewish, white Americans of the time.

The grand talk of meeting crowned heads, from a man chronically unable to meet his rent, was typical of a failure's dreams of glory, not only for his son but for himself as well. Especially he dreamed of eventual triumph over the vile men of business. "He worshipped General Lee and the old time 'Virginia gentlemen'; and those . . . for whose unclean profits he sold himself, never guessed the depths of his contempt for all they stood for. They had the dollars, they were on top; but some day the nemesis of Good-breeding would smite them—the army of the ghosts of Gentility would rise, and with 'Marse Robert' and 'Jeb' Stuart at their head, would sweep away the hordes of commercialdom."

The contempt of his father for business and its venalities had a great influence on Upton. As he grew older, there were other sources of his distaste for the vulgarity of big business and the *nouveau riche*, a distaste traditional among American writers and intellectuals, as seen in the work of Henry Adams, Herman Melville, Mark Twain, and Sinclair Lewis, among others. For the muckrakers, on the other hand, this would be more than merely a matter of taste. They would be revolted by business's brutalizing of its employees and the public, as well as its corruption of politics at all levels. Both kinds of repugnance were to move Sinclair, the first as well as the second.

Lessons in snobbery from Priscilla Sinclair were even more telling, however, because Upton worshipped her. But even she could lose stature in his eyes when her snobbishness was too ridiculous. When the boy's hero, "Gentleman Jim" Corbett, defeated John L. Sullivan, Upton's mother pointed out that " 'he is a gentleman for a prizefighter.' But I assured her, 'No, no, he is a real gentleman. The papers all say so.' This was in 1892, and I was fourteen, and still believed the papers."

But despite both his mother and father, young Upton was, at least in his own view, less and less taken in by the pretensions to Southern aristocracy he saw all about him. "His nursery had been haunted by such musty phantoms . . . but . . . in earliest childhood the fates had given . . . [him] the gift of seeing beneath the shams of things, and to him this dead Aristocracy cried out loudly for burial. . . . These people came and went, an endless procession of them . . . through the boy's life, and unconsciously he judged them, and hated them and feared them." In the summer, if there was a bit of money to spare, or as guests of the Blands, the boy and his mother "visited various Springs . . . where the broken down aristocracy took boarders without quite admitting it. . . . in one case they also took dope." It was at one of these that young Upton was impressed by that final flowering of Southern aristocracy, an idiot boy who gobbled food out of a tin plate like a dog. Years later Upton confided to the novelist Floyd Dell, "I could write a regular Dickens novel about it if I thought that the 'Old South' was worth muckraking."

That the reformer held this opinion was evidence of his insensitivity to the plight of the blacks, assimilated in his youth, an insensitivity common to most of the muckrakers. That he in fact never escaped entirely from his Southern heritage would become increasingly evident during his second marriage, to a woman whom he characterized as his "Southern Belle."

Walter Lippmann would later observe that the mere fact that muckraking was what America's citizens wanted to hear was possibly the most important revelation of the whole campaign, which also explained the quick approval won by the muckrakers. If this is true, the fact that the muckrakers did *not* want to deal with the black problem must mirror the same people's desire *not* to hear about it.

Had Upton wanted sufficiently to escape from those things that horrified him in his life with his parents, an easy means was at hand, for his rich relatives were more than willing to welcome the handsome and precocious boy as a permanent foster-son in their home. He was often tempted, but his feelings about one milieu were quite as mixed as about the other. And if there was one favorite story in the Sinclair collection of traditional family tales, it was the one about loyalty: Upton's grandfather, Lieutenant Commander Arthur Sinclair, and his old friend, fellow Virginian, and shipmate Captain David Farragut had stayed up and argued all night long in Sinclair's study, the day after Virginia had seceded. The next morning, Farragut had gone north, loyal to the Union. Sinclair, like Lee, had been loyal to Virginia and the lost cause.

Furthermore, resistance to temptation was a supporting pillar of Upton's life, second to no other, and this would become increasingly clear throughout his career. "In the most deeply significant of the legends concerning Jesus, we are told how the devil took him up into a high mountain. . . ." There are those who would find others "of the legends concerning Jesus," for example, the crucifixion or the resurrection, as significant, but to Sinclair, *the* most deeply significant was the temptation. Because of his father's weakness and his mother's puritanism, nothing so frightened Sinclair as the possibility of succumbing to temptation, of falling into the most terrible sin of self-indulgence. So whether what tempted him later was sex or an orgy of the ice cream he so loved but so rarely allowed himself, Sinclair usually resisted. He pretended to himself that one gains strength with each successful resistance. But, in fact, Sinclair only kept himself in line with self-terrorism, for consciously or unconsciously he knew with Mark Twain that of all protections against temptation, the surest is cowardice.

So Upton did not escape; "duty held him, and love and memory held him still tighter. For his father worshipped him, and craved his help. . . . he fought to keep his son's regard—he prayed for it with tears in his eyes . . . so the boy had to stand by. And that meant that he grew up in a torture house."

But no boy with Upton's remarkable reservoir of energy could be exclusively in a torture house or in books or in church. He had all the self-created adventures and fun of a child of the eighties and nineties and a good deal more spunk than many. "I had whooping cough, and the other children were forbidden to play with me; this seemed to me injustice, so I chased them and coughed into their faces, after which I had companions in misery." After these lines in his autobiography, Upton pointed out with such good humor as is extraordinary in a reformer, "I should add that this early venture in 'direct action' is not in accordance with my present philosophy." This sort of humor, often at his own expense and often, to his dismay, taken seriously by his critics, crops up throughout his writing, because although he was in many respects a puritan, he was never one of that dour variety who, in Macaulay's phrase, "hated bear-baiting, not because it gave pain to the bear, but because it gave pleasure to the spectators."

Especially after he moved to New York, young Sinclair had all the street adventures that are the birthright and the lifelong glory (when they are not the death) of poor big city boys. Most especially for those, like Sinclair, whose families are so poor that it is cheaper to move than to pay rent, accommodation is the most important lesson to be learned, because such moves mean the child constantly has new enemies before he has time to build up protective alliances. A child who survives frequent neighborhood changes in really poor neighborhoods must be one who can repeatedly find a *modus vivendi*.

Only a few years before Upton's arrival, New York had ten thousand street children. They had no parents who would have them, and spent all their time seeking, usually in vain, any sort of work however ill-paid or degrading. Many begged. Others, singly or in gangs, stole their livings. Death from starvation and even then preventable disease was so common as to attract no notice.

Children's games which are not formalized by tradition but are extempore imitation of adult conduct may serve to reveal what is commonplace in a society. Sinclair never forgot the story Sam DeWitt, the Socialist poet, told him of being raised in a tenement that contained a bordello, and at the age of five playing brothel with the little boys and girls who were his neighbors, as other children play hide-and-seek, and quarrelling as to whose turn it was to be the "madam." Adults believed that prostitution, like poverty, was quite as natural and inevitable a condition for some as holy orders for others.

Even Sinclair's photographic memory, however, could not retain all his different New York addresses, but a few were "a dingy lodging-house on Irving Place, a derelict hotel on East Twelfth Street, housekeeping lodgings over on Second Avenue, a small 'flat' in West 65th Street, one in West 92nd Street, one in West 126th Street. . . . Second Avenue was especially thrilling, because the 'gangs' came out from Avenue A and Avenue B, like Sioux or Pawnees in war paint, and well-dressed little boys had to fly for their lives. . . ."

Much as his mother would have loved him to be one, Upton was no Little Lord Fauntleroy. "Blasting and building were going on [on New York's Upper West Side], and the Italian laborers who did this hard and dangerous work were the natural prey of us young aborigines. We snow-balled them from the roofs . . . and when there was no snow we used clothes-pins. When they cursed us we yelled with glee. I can still remember the phrases—or at any rate what we imagined the phrases to be. 'Aberragotz!' and 'Chingasol!' . . . When these 'Dagoes' chased us, we fled with terror most delightful.

"Sometimes we would raid grocery stores on the avenue, and grab a couple of potatoes, and roast them in bon-fires on the vacant lots. I was a little shocked at this idea, but the other boys explained to me that it was not stealing, it was only 'swiping,' and the grocers took it for granted. . . .

"The Nietzscheans advise us to 'live dangerously,' and this advice I took without having heard it. . . . Riding down Broadway . . . the wheel of my bicycle slipped in the wet 'trolley-slot,' and I was thrown directly in front of an oncoming car. Quick as a cat, I rolled out of the way, but the car ran over my hat, and a woman bystander fainted. Again, skating on an asphalt street, I fell in the space between the front wheels and the rear wheels of a fast-moving express-wagon, and had to whisk my legs out before the rear wheels caught them. When I was seventeen I came to the conclusion Providence must have some special purpose in keeping me in the world, for I was able to reckon up fourteen times that I had missed death by a hair's breadth."

When not in the streets, it was in Central Park that Upton learned much of what was later important to him, especially tennis, which had been introduced to America about the time he was born and had become popular very quickly. The sport was to prove almost his only respite from work.

"In those days I was one of Nature's miracles, such as she produces by the millions in tenement streets—romping, shouting, and triumphant. . . . I was a perpetual explosion of energy, and I cannot see how anybody . . . tolerated me, yet they all liked me, all but one or two who were 'mean'. . . . My young mother would go out . . . leaving me snugly tucked in bed. . . . I would lie still until I heard a whistle, and then forth I would bound . . . sliding down the bannisters into the arms of the young men of the house. What romps I would have, all over that place, flying on bare feet, or borne aloft on sturdy shoulders! We never got tired of pranks; they would set me up in the office and tell me jokes and conundrums, teach me songs . . . take me to see the circus parade. . . . I remember a trick they played on one of these parade evenings; just after dinner they offered me a quarter if I would keep still for five minutes by the watch. . . . A couple of minutes passed, and I was still as any mouse, until one of the young men came running in at the front door, crying 'The parade is passing!' Of course I leaped up with a wail of despair."

The precocious boy was a delight to his elders, to whom it was early evident that he had the intelligence and the energy to take almost any role in life he chose, save only a silent one; that the parade of life would not pass him by, in fact, that he would lead it.

Even more than most children, Upton craved praise and almost as far back as he could remember he turned his considerable gifts of energy and memory and charm to that end. When still, in his phrase, "a tiny toddler," Upton was once told by his mother not to throw a piece of rag in a drain because although paper dissolves, rag does not. Treasuring this worldly wisdom, he sprang it on a duly impressed aunt, receiving what he would describe fifty years later as "My first taste of glory."

Had Sinclair had no father at all, it might have affected his life less strongly than having such a failed father. His horror of drink and his perpetual, proselyting prohibitionism would be but the most obvious effects and less important than his search for foster-fathers. But, in fact, his endless search for heroism, for recognition, for fame, were in no small part compensations for having had such a father. His furious efforts in so many directions to reform the world were paternal—he became his own father and tried to play father to the world, and so, ironically, had no time for his own son and was, in his turn, a bad father.

From his boyhood on, Upton was goal-driven, highly organized, in fact, obsessive, displaying the extraordinary self-discipline that characterized his whole life. Unlike most of those who find their place in the world too uncomfortable and fight merely to improve their own lot in it, Upton would try to change the world. He blamed the system for his poverty and even for his father's drunkenness, but his concept of the system changed over the years. At first the greed of the saloonkeeper seemed the major evil. Later he would come to see that the saloonkeeper and the brothelmaster were servants of the politicians and their police. And eventually he would conclude that the politicians too were but servants of the rich at the top of the capitalist system.

As a youth, Sinclair had many good times as well as bad. But Providence, which allegedly saved his life fourteen times, did not balance the fat and the lean with that remarkable evenhandedness He had demonstrated in Genesis. To a child, perhaps even more bitter than hunger is injustice, and not only in Upton's own view, but also in fact, his boyhood was full of injustice.

CHAPTER II

Youth and Ecstasy

The impulse to create beauty is rather rare in literary men. . . . Far ahead of it comes the yearning to make money. And after the yearning to make money comes the yearning to make a noise.   H. L. MENCKEN

ONE OF THE MOST IMPORTANT NEW INFLUENCES on Upton's life during his teens, and by his own estimate during his entire life, was that of the Reverend William Wilmerding Moir, of the Church of the Holy Communion at Sixth Avenue and Twentieth Street. Upton adopted the minister as his first of several foster-fathers. Moir's specialty was sexual abstinence, keeping his young male parishioners chaste. They reported to him monthly, or oftener if they were tempted sexually. Long after Moir had passed out of Upton's life, the minister's limited view as to what is acceptable and what is not in matters of sex continued to be Upton's gauge—to the amusement of many and the despair of others.

Floyd Dell, after completing his biography of Sinclair in 1927, made fun of "how you were saved from sin by having to report to the Rev. Willie" and further suggested, "(I suspect he was a fairy!)."

Sinclair was outraged by Dell's assumption and six years later in his first autobiography, *American Outpost*, he wrote pointedly: " 'Will' Moir was a young man of fashion who had gone into the church from genuine devoutness and love of his fellow-man. 'Spirituality' is out of fashion at the moment, and open to dangerous suspicions, so I hasten to say that he was a thoroughly wholesome person. . . ."

At the time of his association with Moir, Sinclair's ignorance of even the most elementary facts of heterosexuality was so nearly perfect as to defy belief today. His knowledge of homosexuality may therefore perhaps be assumed to have been zero and, in fact, almost four decades later, his ignorance of homosexuality was still such as to shock a visiting journalist. Consequently, Upton's defense of Moir was meaningless, and by 1939,

Sinclair himself had decided that this foster-father had probably been a sublimated homosexual.

At the time, however, Upton had needed any information on sex he could get because: "Childhood lasted long and youth came late in my life. I was taught to avoid the subject of sex . . . in Victorian fashion, by deft avoidance and anxious evasion. Apparently my mother taught me even too well; for one time when I was being bathed, I persisted in holding a towel in front of myself. Said my mother: 'If you don't keep that towel out of the way, I'll give you a spank.' Said I: 'Mamma, would you rather have me disobedient, or immodest?'

"The first time I ever heard of the subject of sex, I was four or five . . . playing on the street with a little white boy and a Negro girl, the child of a janitor. They were whispering about something mysterious and exciting; there were two people living across the street who had just been married, and something they did was the subject of snickers. I, who wanted to know about everything, tried to find out about this, but I am not sure if my companions knew what they were whispering about, at any rate, they did not tell me. But I got the powerful impression of something strange.

"It was several years later when I found out the essential facts. I spent a summer in the country with a boy cousin . . . and we watched the animals, and questioned the farm-hands. But I never did get one word of information or advice from either father or mother . . . only the notion of shrinking away from something dreadful. I recollect how the signs of puberty began to show themselves in me, to my great bewilderment; my mother and grandmother stood helplessly by, like the hen which hatches ducklings and sees them go into the water."

During his teens, despite Moir's earnest efforts, Upton was becoming increasingly agnostic, while teaching a Sunday school class of poor boys. "I taught them . . . Moses in the Bulrushes . . . Jonah and the Whale . . . Joshua blowing down the walls of Jericho . . . but they seemed to me futile . . . as practical as the procedure of the Fijians, blowing horns to drive away a pestilence . I followed the fates of my little slum-boys—and what I saw was that Tammany Hall was getting them. . . . when the boys got into trouble . . . it was the clergyman who consoled them in prison—but it was the Tammany leader who saw the judge and got them out. So these boys got their lesson, even earlier in life than I got mine—that the church was a kind of amiable fake, a pious horn-blowing; while the real thing was Tammany."

Speculative as well as practical matters were destroying Upton's faith. Early in his life he had been so horrified by Thomas Paine's *The Age of*

Reason that he had burned his copy. But the questions raised by the book haunted him increasingly as he tried to forget them. What would have happened physically in the universe if the sun had stood still? How many different pairs of animals would the ark have had to hold? If Jesus was really God, could he really have been tempted? Does not being God and man at the same time mean both knowing and not knowing simultaneously?

Moir was not at all shocked or surprised by such youthful apostasies and gave his Thomas several volumes of Episcopalian apologetics. This cure resulted in the illness proving fatal, because the apologetics stated anti-church positions, new to Upton, in order to refute them, but these raised new doubts not put to rest by the refutations. "Literally, I was made into an agnostic by reading the official defenses of Christianity.... .

"I no longer taught Sunday School, but remained under my friend's sheltering wing, and told him my troubles—up to the time when I was married, which was apparently regarded as a kind of graduation from the school of chastity."

Despite his disillusion with the church itself, Sinclair's two great heroes would always be Christ and Shelley. The impassioned words of Shelley, read in his uncle's library, were pulling the boy as rapidly away from organized religion as the tedious apologetics and the bruises to his pride caused by the rich pew holders. He had been for some time determined to become a hero, believing with the poet that "Man is soul and body, formed for deeds, of high resolve."

Upton always said it was Shelley's poetry that inspired him with the desire to become a great poet, and he was able to maintain the delusion that he had become one because what enthralled him was not the splendor of Shelley's imagery or style but rather his political visions. His notion that Justice, like Art, is an absolute set Upton afire, and although the poet's revolutionary fervor is now almost as forgotten as the Aspheterism and Pantisocracy of Southey and Coleridge, it would be almost impossible to exaggerate Shelley's political influence on Sinclair.

Increasingly the bishop's robes Upton's mother coveted for him seemed hardly the proper hero's costume as he learned from *Queen Mab* that: "The same means that have supported every popular belief have supported Christianity. War, imprisonment, assassination and falsehood; deeds of unexampled and incomparable atrocity have made it what it is."

To discover a man's character, the why as well as the what of his life, it is necessary to know the major influences in that life. Sinclair's views on business, on marriage, on politics, and even on diet were formed by Shelley quite as much as was his changing view of the church, and there was growing within him the terrible conviction that his call was to be one of that number Shelley had named the unacknowledged legislators of the world.

In his adult writings and letters Upton would frequently quote from the Bible to prove his revolutionary points, to exhort his fellow revolutionaries, or to incite his readers to join the ranks of the revolution, but no other single quotation appears so often as the young counter-culture poet's cry:

> Men of England, wherefore plough
> For the lords who lay you low?

Even after Sinclair finally discovered Socialism and read widely in it, he never lost his essentially Shelleyan vision that the ideal society was a kind of enlightened, middle-class utopia with poets, or at least intelligent, right-thinking, gifted people, like himself, leading mankind down a rational, healthy, and loving path of social virtue.

The poverty and injustice of Upton's childhood and youth were what made him a rebel, but what sustained him in rebellion and particularized his nonviolent rebellion was what he learned from the poet.

Most, or at least many, who suffer early from poverty direct their efforts only to improving their own individual lives rather than the lives of their fellow sufferers as well. Sinclair would choose a life of service to the poor and put upon rather than merely enriching himself, though he would obviously have both the capability and opportunity for the latter. Part of the reason for this choice was his having seen close up the life of the rich and having found it unhappy and repellent. But what made it repellent to him was in great part its contrast to the ideal life described by Shelley.

> A brighter dawn awaits the human day . . .
> When poverty and wealth, the thirst of fame,
> The fear of infamy, disease and woe,
> War with its million horrors, and fierce hell
> Shall live but in the memory of time

Shelley, whose thirty years ending in 1822 were lived in the echo of the American and French revolutions, put into words the very things Upton felt most passionately and had never before heard expressed. As the food Upton ate became part of his muscular reactions, the Shelley he ingested became part of his mental reactions. The boy who so needed a hero to compensate for his father had found a permanent one just at the moment when his first hero, Moir, was proving to have a mind of clay.

On September 15, 1892, five days before his fourteenth birthday, "a tiny chap in short pants and a shirtwaist, noisy and fond of jokes," Sinclair entered the College of the City of New York, an old brick building at Lexington Avenue and Twenty-third Street, to begin a five-year course, the first of which was really the last year of high school. There he discovered that one of his classmates, Simon Stern, had written a short story that was printed (with no payment) in a monthly magazine published by an orphan home. Not to be outdone, Upton wrote a story about a pet bird who proved the innocence of a Negro boy and sold it to *Argosy* for twenty-five dollars.

He had found El Dorado. He was able not only to sell children's stories to other newspapers and magazines, but also discovered he could write jokes for the humor magazines.

Late in life Sinclair tended to exaggerate a bit the age at which he began supporting himself by writing, claiming it had been thirteen, which stretches the truth, but by the time he was fifteen, the same age at which his grandfather had sailed from Norfolk to assist at Perry's "opening up" of Japan, he was supporting himself and contributing substantially to his parents' support. In addition to the jokes, he wrote and sold short pieces, either fiction or sketches from life based on what happened at his boardinghouse or on his vacations. While still a child, Upton was learning to see, to hear, to smell, touch, and taste, *as a writer*; that is, consciously to observe, to compare, to contrast, to imagine, and to record briefly and yet vividly.

By constantly practicing his craft he was becoming a remarkable storyteller—one who knew how to keep the story moving, to observe and recount enough detail to suspend disbelief and lend verisimilitude but not so much as to bore. Daily he acquired and preserved and polished all those elements of the storyteller's art that make the reader turn the page.

But it was as a joke factory that Upton became the family's chief support and his success led him to begin to reconsider his plans for a career. He had been offered an appointment to the Naval Academy at Annapolis. "This was regarded as my birth-right, but I declined it. . . . I wanted to be a lawyer; having come to the naïve conclusion that the law offered a way to combine an honorable living with devotion to books."

His joke production was organized on a twenty-four-hour, high efficiency, high production basis that prefigured in many respects his later literary mass production. "The quantity production of jokes is an odd industry. . . . Jokes are made up hind-end forwards. . . . you don't think of the joke, but of what it is to be about. There are tramp jokes, mother-in-law jokes, plumber jokes, Irishman jokes. . . . you decide to write tramp-jokes this morning; well, there are many things about tramps which are jokeable; they do not like to work, they do not like to bathe, they do not like bull-dogs. . . . You decide to write about tramps not liking to bathe . . . you think of all the words and phrases having to do with water, soap, tubs, streams, rain, etc., and of puns or quirks by which these words can be applied to tramps. . . . the jokes for which I was paid one dollar apiece . . . became an obsession. While other youths· were thinking about 'dates,' I was pondering the jokeableness of Scotchmen, Irishmen, Negroes, Jews. I would take my mother to church, and make up jokes on the phrases in the prayer-book and hymn-book. I kept my little note-book before me at meals, while walking, while dressing, and in college if the professor was a bore. I wrote out my jokes on slips of paper, with a number in the corner, and sent them in batches of ten to the different editors. . . . I had a book-keeping system, showing where each batch had been sent; jokes Number 321 to 330 had been sent to 'Life,' 'Judge,' and 'Puck,' and were now at the 'Evening Journal.' " Upton also sold ideas to cartoonists, quickly learning to do so only for cash.

With his same literary classmate as a partner, he wrote a novel that they took by hand to Street and Smith, publishers of pulp magazines. These were as widely read then as the comic books that replaced them became.

Novelists still in short pants being a novelty, they were received by editor Henry Harrison Lewis, who within a few years would be giving Upton all the work he could handle. He read, but did not accept this joint effort, suggesting, however, that the boys write another, and within a week they were back with the new one. "I have since learned that you must never do that. Make the editor think you are taking a lot of time, because that is one of his tests of excellence—despite the examples of Dumas and Balzac and Dickens and Dostoievski and other masters."

No matter how unimportant Sinclair's early efforts and his potboilers are now from a literary point of view, they do reveal what the young writer knew and, perhaps more interestingly, what he only thought he knew, a revelation suffered by all writers and talkers. He next worked alone on his own first full-length novel, *The Prairie Pirates*, which he would later confess bore a striking resemblance to *Treasure Island*.

He made enough money writing jokes by the winter of his seventeenth year to move away from his family to his own apartment near the Hudson on West Twenty-third Street. It was a top floor single hall bedroom that cost him a dollar and a quarter a week. He paid another three dollars a week for two boardinghouse meals a day and all his "other luxuries" cost another quarter a week. These included the laundering of his linen collars and cuffs, which latter he wore high up so that they would not soil so fast nor show so badly that they were soiled. He bought no clothes but wore the cast-offs of his hated Baltimore cousin, Howard Bland. He was thus able to live on four and a half dollars a week for two years, giving everything else he earned to his parents.

Upton was increasingly bumptious at college as he was increasingly bored, and early on he began those rites as traditional and mandatory for college students as are puberty rites for other young savages. He was delighted when his chemistry professor was angered by his sassing. But he was less pleased when his "debut as a revolutionary agitator," which amounted to writing a composition praising Robert E. Lee, failed to anger the college president, who had commanded a brigade at Gettysburg but agreed that Lee had been a great man.

It would be a mistake, however, to believe Upton's college days were miserable or bitter, no matter what he later wrote about them. Sweet-natured, curious, extraordinarily bright and energetic, he was remembered almost half a century later by one of his college tutors as "a diminutive Sub-freshman . . . who came to ask me to help you solve riddles, enigmas, etc. . . . Particularly do I recall your boyish exuberance and your gratitude. . . . Also your joy a week or so later when you came up to the desk to tell me you had won $2.00 on that particular puzzle." But again, as in his childhood, Upton was getting his education from what he was reading on his own rather than from what he was learning by rote at college.

In the first few weeks of each term, he read all his textbooks and after that composed verses in class and made sketches of the professors until he discovered that his poverty could be put to advantage. Allegedly to earn money, he obtained frequent leaves of absence which he spent reading night and day—Emerson's *Essays*, *Sartor Resartus*, a ten-volume life of Lincoln, whatever struck his fancy or was cheap enough to buy.

It was during his Christmas holiday in 1891, spent at his Uncle Bland's in Baltimore, that he discovered Shakespeare, not the tiresome "English" he was taught in school but all of Shakespeare's plays, which he read in two weeks. These were followed in the last few days of vacation by a set of Milton's works. Upton "lost his soul in that wonderland; he walked and thought no more like the men of earth." He had discovered the unacknowledged legislators and decided that the human race was to be saved by poetry. "I had made the acquaintance of Shelley, and conceived a passionate friendship for him. Then I became intimate with Hamlet, Prince of Denmark. . . . I too was a prince, in conflict with a sordid and malignant world; at least so I saw myself, and lived entirely in that fantasy, very snobbish, scornful, and superior. Any psychiatrist would have diagnosed me as an advanced case of delusion of grandeur, messianic complex, paranoia, narcissism, and so to the end of his list."

From this frenzied reading, combined with the strange, strong forces surging within the precocious and repressed young man, there arose a series of mystical experiences that Sinclair attributed to genius. "My mind was on fire with high poetry, I went out for a walk one night. I do not know my age at the time, but it was somewhere around eighteen or nineteen, a winter night, with hard crunching snow on the ground, and great bright lights in the sky; the tree branches black and naked, crackling now and then in the breeze; but between times silence, quite magical silence—and I walking in Druid Hill Park, mile on mile, lost to the world, drinking in beauty, marvelling at the mystery of life. Suddenly this thing came to me, startling and wonderful beyond any power of words to tell; the opening of gates in the soul, the pouring in of music, of light, of joy which was unlike anything else, and therefore not to be conveyed in metaphors. I stood riveted to one spot, and a trembling seized me, a dizziness, a happiness so intense that the distinction between pleasure and pain was lost.

"If I had been a religious person at this time, no doubt I would have had visions of saints and holy martyrs, and perhaps have developed stigmata on hands and feet. But I had no sort of superstition, so the ecstasy took a literary form. There was a campfire by a mountain road, to which came travellers, and hailed one another, and made high revelry there without alcohol. Yes, even Falstaff and Prince Hal were purified and refined, according to my teetotal sentiments! There came the melancholy Prince of Denmark, and Don Quixote—I must have been reading him at this time. Also Shelley—real persons mixed with imaginary ones, but all equal in this realm of fantasy. They held conversations, each in his own character, yet glorified, more so than in the books. I was a perfect picture of a madman, talking to myself, making incoherent exclamations. Yet I knew what I was doing, I knew what was happening, I knew that this was literature, and that if I could remember the tenth part of it and set it down on paper, it would be read.

"The strangest part about this ecstasy is the multifarious forms it assumes, the manifold states of consciousness it involves, all at one time. It is possible to be bowed with grief and transported with delight; it is possible to love and to hate, to be naive and calculating, to be hot and cold, timid and daring—all contradictions reconciled. But the most striking thing is the conviction which comes to you, that you are in the hands of a force outside yourself. Without trace of a preconception, and regarding the thing as objectively as you know how, the feeling is that something is taking hold of you, pushing you along, sweeping you away. To walk in a windstorm, and feel it beating upon you, is a sensation of the body no more definite and unmistakable than this windstorm of the spirit which has come to me perhaps a hundred times in my life. I search for a metaphor, and picture a child running, with an older and swifter person by his side, taking his hand and lifting him off the ground, so that his little leaps become great leaps, almost like flying.

"You may call this force your own subconscious mind, or God, or the Cosmic Consciousness, I care not what fancy name you give; the point is that it is there, and always there. If you ask whether it is intelligent, I can only say that you appear to be the intelligence, and 'it' appears to be the cause of intelligence in you. How anything unintelligent can be the cause of intelligence is a riddle I pass by. Life is built upon such antinomies.

"This experience came in unexpected places, and at unpredictable times. It was associated with music and poetry, but still more frequently with natural beauty. I remember winter nights in Central Park, New York, and tree-branches white with snow, magical in the moonlight; I remember springtime mornings in several places; a summer night in the Adirondacks, with moonlight strewn upon a lake; a summer twilight in the far wilds of Ontario, when I came over a ridge, and into a valley full of clover, incredibly sweet of scent. One has to go into the north in summer, to appreciate how deep and thick a field of red clover can grow, and what overpowering perfume it throws upon the air at twilight.

"This repeated experience made me into more of a solitary than ever. I wanted to be free to behave like a lunatic, and yet not have anybody think me one. A highly embarrassing moment, when I was walking down a lane, bordered with wild roses in June, and two little girls seated on a fence, unnoticed by me, suddenly broke into giggles at the strange sight of a man laughing and talking to himself! I became a haunter of mountain-tops and of deep forests, the only safe places.

"For a time it seemed to me that music was the only medium by which my emotions could be expressed. I longed to play some instrument, and began very humbly with a mandolin. But that was not enough, and presently I took the plunge, and paid seventy-five of my hard-earned dollars for a violin. . . ."

That the pubescent Sinclair's visions were so exclusively literary indicates clearly that his intellectual development was almost entirely the result of his ravenous reading.

"Was it really genius? That I cannot say. I only know it seemed like it, and I took it at its face value. I tell the story here as objectively as possible, and if the hero seems a young egotist, do not blame me, because that youth has been long since dead."

In a two-volume work that Upton considered a revolutionary explanation of love and sex, he later acknowledged: "These things came at the same time as another development . . . likewise portentous and unexpected. . . . There was a bodily change taking place in him . . . and with the strangest and most uncomfortable thrills. . . . He discovered new desires in himself, impulses that dominated him in a most disturbing way. . . . a girl of not very gentle breeding . . . [with whom he] spent the whole of one evening, sitting in a summer-house with an arm about her waist . . . then he passed the rest of the night wandering about . . . cursing himself, with tears of shame and vexation in his eyes.

"He was so ignorant about these matters that he did not even know if the changes that had taken place in him were normal . . . [but he] saw enough at the outset to make it clear that the time had come for him to gird up his loins. . . . he did not intend that the course of his life was to be decided by these cravings of the animal within him. . . . It seemed to him as if this craving came to a man in regular pulses; he could go for weeks, serene and happy . . . and then suddenly would come the restlessness, and he would go out into the night and wander about the streets for hours, impelled by a futile yearning for he knew not what—the hope of something clean in the midst of uncleanliness, of some adventure that would be not quite shameful to a poet's fancy. And then, after midnight, he would steal home, baffled and sick at heart, and wet his pillow with hot and bitter tears!

". . . On the one hand was slavery and degradation and disease; and on the other were all the heights of the human spirit. For if one saved and stored this mighty sex-energy, it became transmuted to the gold of intellectual and emotional power. . . . And this was no blind asceticism. . . . It was not a denial of love, but on the contrary a consecration of love. Some day . . . [he] would meet the woman he was to cleave to, and he would expect her to come to him a virgin; and he must honor her as much."

Temptations were all about Upton, sometimes where he least expected. On one occasion when he turned to intensive study to escape from sex and decided to learn about Renaissance art, he had to stop because "I found myself overwhelmed by this mass of nakedness; my senses reeled, and I had to quit."

Some thirty years later as he looked back at his youthful idealism, Upton may have been less certain of the rightness of the difficult path he had chosen, but he still was not displeased with the choice. "Along with extreme idealism and perhaps complementary to it, went a tormenting struggle with sexual desire. I never entered into sex relations with any woman until my marriage at the age of twenty-two; but I came close to it, and the effort to refrain was more than I would have been equal to, without the help of my clergyman friend. . . . there would begin a flirtation, with caresses and approaches to intimacy. But then would come another storm—of shame and fear; the memory of the vow . . . [to Moir, and] the idea of venereal disease. . . . I would shrink back and turn cold; two or three times, with my reformer's impulse, I told the girl about it, and the petting party turned into a moral discourse . . . [which] affords amusement to my 'emancipated' radical friends.

"There are dangers in 'Puritanism'; and there are compensations. My chastity was preserved at the cost of much effort, plus the limitation of my interests in certain fields. . . . What did I get in return for this? I got intensity and power of concentration; these elements in my make-up were the products of my efforts to resist the tempter. I have learned to work fourteen hours a day at study and creative effort, because it was only by being thus occupied that the craving for woman could be kept out of my soul. . . . Nowadays we hear a great deal about mental troubles caused by sex repression; it is the mood of the moment. We do not hear anything about the complexes which may be caused by sex indulgence. But my observation has been that those who permit themselves to follow every sexual impulse are quite as miserable as those who repress every impulse. . . . This problem of the happy mean in sex matters would require a volume for a proper discussion. As it happens, I have written that volume, 'The Book of Life.' "

After a close call with one girl, he discovered "something in his features that filled him with shuddering. . . . in his words . . . in the very tone of his voice . . . the sins of the fathers . . . anguish and remorse! These ecstasies of resolution that vanished like a cloud . . . the whole heritage of impotence. . . . he, too, was to struggle and agonize—and to finish with his foot in the trap!

"This idea was like a white-hot goad. . . . After such an experience there would be several months of toil and penance and of savage self-immolation. It was hard to punish a man who had so little; but . . .

[he] managed to find ways. . . . he would go without those kinds of food that he liked; and instead of going to bed at one o'clock he would read the New Testament in Greek."

Upton's mother had been an important influence in his boyhood. "The drinking of my father . . . caused me to follow my mother in everything, and so to have a great respect for women." But as Upton in his teens became the chief breadwinner of the family, his relationship with his mother changed, and for a time their roles were reversed—he was her comforter and teacher. When they were separated, he sought to cheer her out of her increasing depressions with affectionate letters of advice that reveal how his view of life was differing increasingly from hers: "Let me tell you, sweetness, that I would not take Uncle Bland's wealth if it were offered me today. I would not give up what spurs me to work & therefore keeps me happy. . . . I would not take Howard's wealth, bicycle & fine house & clothes. . . . I do not envy his easy going lazy gentleman of leisure habits. I have other ambitions. . . . I hope to get health, and fame, and knowledge & respect & love & happiness & Heaven . . . beside which wealth is child's play. . . ."

There are a good number, in the histories of the United States (and perhaps an even greater number in its fiction), of poor boys whose poverty inspired them successfully to become rich. Here, however, was a rarer bird, who, instead of grasping at capitalism's brass ring with greater fierceness, was already in his teens sincerely disdaining wealth. Without the steady and certain compass of a psychoanalyst's license, one cannot state with sureness the reasons Upton so early was heading toward Marx instead of money. But one may, before leaving Upton's boyhood and youth, speculate on what might have been some of the causes.

For a boy whose poverty is complete, who knows only poverty and has no experience outside of it, to be rich may promise a life as perfect as imagination can make it. But to a boy like Upton who has seen life among the rich, it is obviously not trouble-free; his rich relatives had petty problems that seemed to make them quite as unhappy as Upton's more serious problems made him.

Primarily, however, more than most boys, poor or rich, Upton had been shaped by books. He was filled with impossibly high standards of honor, continence, honesty, Christianity, and truthfulness. And as nothing sharpens a man's sight like envy, he could not fail to notice that his Baltimore relations loved money more than the Mosaic law, bought and bound books that they did not read, and were otherwise well below the standards set by Upton for himself and for the rest of humankind.

After his ecstasies, after his colloquies with Jesus, Shelley, and Hamlet, he came to see that wealth was not enough, that what he must have were those prizes and powers given only to saints and artists and heroes, those things that as a teen-ager he had already listed for his mother, "fame, and knowledge & respect & love & happiness & Heaven."

His lips had been touched by the coals. He had heard the call. Unlike the Danish prince, Sinclair did not reproach the spite that called him to put the times back in joint. He was certain that this was not his curse but his opportunity, his glory.

CHAPTER III

Author and Lover

A system could not well have been devised more studiously hostile to human happiness than marriage.   PERCY BYSSHE SHELLEY

IN HIS ADULT YEARS, Sinclair frequently boasted that before he had reached twenty-one he had published an output equal in volume to the works of Walter Scott. Although this is probably an exaggeration, it is unlikely that any other writer has had so much published at so early an age.

Graduating from the College of the City of New York in June of 1897, Upton did not wait for his commencement, but requested that his diploma be sent to him by mail. His college career had been thoroughly undistinguished, and he graduated in the middle of his class, winning a prize in differential calculus but nothing in literature, philosophy, or history. He fled to the upper St. Lawrence River, where, drifting alone in a skiff among the Thousand Islands, he indulged in an orgy of reading.

But, having decided to go to graduate school at Columbia to study literature and philosophy before becoming a lawyer, he came back to New York to find a source of income and called once again Henry Harrison Lewis, the Street and Smith editor, who provided Sinclair with a lavish meal ticket for the next three years. Lewis himself had been writing a story every other week about life at the United States Naval Academy at Annapolis for the *Army and Navy Weekly*, a five-cent pulp magazine. He offered Sinclair the job of writing a companion story of life at West Point on alternate weeks, and Upton was thrilled.

After three days of intensive note-taking at West Point, Upton wrote a twenty-five- or thirty-thousand-word manuscript about Mark Mallory, a plebe, under the pen name Lieutenant Frederick Garrison, U.S.A. So successful was he as a hack writer that in addition to writing a series of Mark Mallory stories, he took over from Lewis the adventures of Clif Faraday at Annapolis, writing under the name of Ensign Clarke Fitch, U.S.N. He was

33

writing a thirty-thousand-word novel a week and being paid forty dollars for each one, almost ten times what it cost him a week to live in his single room.

After February 15, 1898, when the *Maine* was blown up in Havana harbor, Upton's various heroes were mainly occupied in "killing Spaniards," at such a rate that he turned out eight thousand words every day including Sunday. To do this required two stenographers working full time, taking dictation for some three hours one afternoon and then transcribing it for the next day and a half. In the evening Upton revised manuscript and afterward, during a long walk, invented adventures for the next day's dictation. Every morning he taught himself to play the violin or attended classes at Columbia.

It is not possible to know precisely how much and what he wrote in this period. Years later he was himself unable to identify whether many of the works written under his various pseudonyms were in fact his, but during the eighteen-month period from June 1897 to November 1898—most of it coinciding with his full-time graduate study at Columbia University—Sinclair turned out magazine material totalling approximately 1,275,000 words, an impressive record for a young man barely out of his teens. And when one considers that for part of this time he was also writing a novelette of thirty thousand to forty thousand words, the output is staggering. It is this enormous capacity for work which characterizes Sinclair's entire career, the capacity which later led Sinclair Lewis to be astounded by his "ability to get so much done with only twenty-four hours a day to do it in!"

Not all of Upton's hack work was on contemporary subjects. There were sword and saddle epics set in the fifteenth century such as *In the Net of The Visconti*. Some critics later attributed whatever literary faults they found in Upton to the early forced march hack work. A similar schedule forced on the young Colette by Willy or for that matter forced on Balzac by himself had no such effect. While unrewarding literarily, this hack work gives insights into the author's personal life. What he left out was anything even remotely sexual. What he included was continuous unself-conscious glorification of honor, heroism, virtue, hard work, courage, respect for women, and a horror of wickedness in any form.

A man who pours out thousands of words a day, seven days a week, is undergoing something not entirely unlike the patient's part of psychoanalysis. Upton's words, therefore, serve as an interesting psychological barometer of those forces, however innocuously disguised, that struggled just below the surface of the boy-man who was finding it almost daily more difficult to concentrate exclusively on what he viewed as his high mission and to suppress what all his life he referred to as the wild beast that roared within him.

When Upton himself assessed the effects of his hack work on his later writing, he found both good and bad. It bred facility but habituated him to using exaggeration and cliché. He thought it significant that he could only do successful hack work as long as it amused him, and that once he had changed to serious writing he could never again turn out satisfactory potboilers even when he needed the money desperately.

Upton found writing potboilers more exciting than attending classes at Columbia, which he thought tedious, excepting those given by Edward MacDowell, the head of the music department. Nevertheless, he developed a system of learning there that worked well for him. He declared his intention to take a master's degree and paid a hundred and fifty dollars supposedly to pursue that intention. He was thereafter free to go on taking courses and dropping them at will at no further cost, and as his real purpose was the getting of an education rather than the getting of a degree, he resolutely refused to complete courses by taking an examination. Instead he fled to the country to read everything that interested him, returning every fall to begin a new set of courses and get the list of books required for them. So in four years he sampled more than forty courses.

Angry that he had spent thousands of hours looking up words in various foreign dictionaries but was still unable to read any foreign texts easily, Upton decided to learn the meaning of a word the first time he looked it up. Copying in his notebook every day a new group of words, he studied them while shaving, eating, walking, until they were fixed in his memory. And so devoting about a year to the literature of each language, including the reading and rereading of the Bible in each language as a kind of review, he taught himself German, French, and Italian.

German was his favorite tongue, the reading of all of Goethe giving him the same delight as going through his uncle's Shakespeare had earlier.

Always anxious to make his various personal efforts also serve as sources of income, when learning Italian he got permission from Gerlamo Rovetta to publish a translation of his *Mater Dolorosa*, but he failed to interest any American publisher.

He was shocked at French literature, both the classics of Molière, Daudet, Hugo, Flaubert, Balzac, Zola, "and enough of Maupassant and Gautier to be thankful that I had not come upon this kind of literature until I was to some extent mature, with a good hard shell of Puritanism to protect me against the black magic of the modern Babylon.

"Since then, such depraved literature has been poured in a flood over

America, and our bright young 'intellectuals' are thoroughly initiated; they have no shells of Puritanism, but try fancy liquors and drugs, and play with the esoteric forms of hetero and homo sexuality, and commit suicide in the most elegant continental style. Those who prefer to remain alive are set down as old fogies. At date of writing, I am one of them."

This priggish and xenophobic outburst was written not by the young student of French, but more than thirty years later by a man who had by then written what he believed to be a shocking manual on sex, *The Book of Life*, and *Oil!* a novel with enough explicity about sex to be banned in Boston. Presumably the French works remained "depraved" in his view because they were merely fiction, supposed attempts at the art of literature, whereas his works, including the novel, which was a fictionalized version of the Teapot Dome scandals, were frankly pedagogic and therefore *per se* not depraved.

As Upton studied literature and continued to write, he increasingly became convinced that what he wanted to express could not be expressed verbally, but only musically. And so he sought to flog himself into being a violinist in much the same way as he was making himself a linguist. Potboiling and Columbia limited his violin practice in winter, but in summer, when he went to the Adirondacks, he made up for it. After breakfast he set up his stand and his music in the forest and fiddled all morning until lunch, all afternoon until dinner, and there was still more practice in his room by oil lamp at night. "The wild things of the forest got used to this odd invasion. The squirrels would sit on the pine-tree branches and cock their heads, and chatter furiously when I made a false note. The partridges would feed on huckleberries all about me, apparently understanding clearly the difference between a fiddle-bow and a gun. Foxes took an interest, and raccoons and porcupines—and even humans.

"The guests from the cities arrived on an early morning train, and were driven to the hotel in a big four-horse stage. One morning one of the guests arrived and at breakfast narrated a curious experience. The stage had been toiling up a long hill, the horses walking, and alongside strode an old Italian woman with a couple of pails, on her way to a day of berry-picking. She was whistling cheerily, and the tune was the Tannhäuser march. The new arrival, impressed by this evidence of culture in the vicinity, inquired through the open window, 'Where did you learn that music?' The reply was, 'Dey is a crazy feller in de woods, he play it all day long for t'ree weeks.'"

At this same time Upton's Uncle Bland offered to train him for an important future with the United Fidelity and Guaranty Company. But the boy had too frequently dined with his uncle when the bonding company tycoon was opening his New York office. What Lincoln Steffens, Sinclair's fellow muckraker, would learn only by astute and careful investigation, Upton witnessed early in his family circle—the system which became known as "honest graft." In order to get the city's bonding business, his uncle had given Tammany chief Richard Croker a sizable block of stock, and lesser Tammany sachems and sagamores had received lesser blocks or jobs with the company: "it was no crime for a Tammany leader to become manager of a bonding company; and yet his profits would be many times as great as if he were to steal money from the city treasury.

"So there I was on the inside of America; watching our 'invisible government' at work. That pattern which my uncle gave me in youth served for the arranging of all the facts I later amassed. I have never found anything different, in any part of America; it is so that big business deals with government at every point where the two come into contact. Every government official in America knows it, and likewise every big business man knows it; talking in private, they joke about it, and in public they deny it with great indignation.

"The fact that the man from whom I learned this secret was one of the kindest and most generous persons I have ever known, ought to have made me merciful in my judgements. With the wisdom of later years, I know that business men who finance political parties and pull the strings of government cannot help what they do; they either have to run their business that way, or else give place to somebody who will run it no differently. The blame lies with the system. . . . But in those early days I did not understand any of this; I thought that graft was due to grafters, and I hated them with all my Puritanical fervor."

At about this same time, Upton had his own first experience in political action, one which combined puritanism with prurience, an admixture not without appeal in every age. A lawyer named William Travers Jerome, who was running for district attorney, had declared war on two of Tammany's chief supporters, the saloonkeepers and the whorehouse madams. His colorful speeches described excitingly rooms full of naked women for sale to any lustful man who had the money to buy downstairs a "brass check," which he could then take upstairs and exchange for whichever female body he thought most likely to satisfy the beast raging within him.

Upton not only helped raise funds for his candidate, but, along with other Columbia students enlisted in the cause, served as a poll watcher for the reform ticket. Upton had chosen as his battle station a ballot box in a strong Tammany district on the East Side, where he argued furiously with an old Tammany police magistrate. "I was probably never in greater danger in my life, for it was a common enough thing to knock an election watcher over the head. . . . What saved me was the fact that the returns coming in from the rest of the city convinced the Tammany heelers that they had lost the fight anyhow. . . ."

Early in 1900, Upton decided that the moment had come for him to take a major step. He found himself increasingly hostile toward both parents—his father because of the drunkenness, his mother because of her insensitivity to the world's ills and his concern about them. And he was disillusioned by the stupidity, hypocrisy, greed, and venality he saw all about him—at Columbia and in politics. He decided that he must himself begin at once to redeem mankind. As his means, he chose to write what was then anticipated in this country with widespread eagerness, the Great American Novel.

In April he took the train for Lake Massawippi in Quebec, just over the New York line, where he had rented for three months for twenty-five dollars a small log cabin called "Fairy Glen." Here Upton worked alone for three months and then moved to a nearby farmhouse in a sugar maple forest, where he wore a path several inches deep walking back and forth as he composed and rewrote, all in his head, putting nothing on paper until he was satisfied it was in near final form. Then he would write, sometimes for five or six hours without moving from his seat and for days without seeing another human being.

This was to be his method of writing all his life. "I never put pen to paper till I had whole pages by heart in my mind. I would walk up and down thinking it over and over and it would stay in my mind—whole scenes." It was true of his very best writing—the battle scene in *Manassas*, the wedding party in *The Jungle*.

In the Preface to this first novel, *Springtime and Harvest*, the twenty-two-year-old author wrote with almost hysterical self-pity of how "he lived entirely alone, doing a work so fearful that now, as he looks back upon it, it makes him tremble. . . . He burnt out his soul at his work. . . . he wrote sometimes sixteen hours a day, and he lived his life upon his knees before his vision. . . . When at last he had finished . . . [he knew it was] the highest thing of which his soul was capable."

Upton was not, however, entirely alone that summer, nor was his attention exclusively on his novel. In fact, possibly the summer's most important hours were spent with Meta Fuller, who, before the end of the year, would be his wife.

Meta's mother, Mary Eaton Fuller, always quick to point out that she was an F.F.V. (First Family of Virginia), and Upton's mother had been good friends since they first met some ten years earlier, when both lived, each with her husband and only child, at Colonel Weisiger's boardinghouse on West Nineteenth Street.

Meta was younger than Upton and once, when she was ten and he a very self-important thirteen, and she had sought to tease him away from reading his newspaper to join her games, he had irritably struck her with the paper, earning himself the title of "that horrid boy." But she had kept her eye on Upton, who "stood out from the other children, because he always seemed to be conspicuously alone. . . . When he wasn't reading a book . . . [he was] wide eyed and serious, conversing with some of the grown-ups who thought him a precocious youngster. . . . always carefully dressed in a blue serge suit with turned over collar and a flowing tie, his black ribbed stockings fitting neatly into buttoned shoes."

Mrs. Fuller and Mrs. Sinclair, when they both had the money to summer anywhere, often summered together at an inexpensive resort in Vermont or New Jersey. In June of 1900, the New York heat had driven them to Canada, near the farmhouse where Upton was, by painful parturition, bringing forth his novel. Meta, now about eighteen, had come along.

Years later, after three marriages and more scandals, Meta still looked beautiful even to people who disliked her, so at eighteen she must have been dazzling. She had long, thick black hair, dark skin, and dark eyes. She was full-lipped and full-bodied (newspaper reports during her adulteries not infrequently stated with the unembarrassed anti-Semitism of the day that she looked like a beautiful Jewess). Her tendency to flirt, even with her son, David, seems to have been constant, perhaps unconscious, automatic, and always disturbing.

Meta was an unhappy girl with vague immortal longings. She was certain she could be a poet, an actress, a dancer, an artist of some kind, if only her father would send her to Wellesley or Vassar. But William Marcy Fuller, a former newspaper writer and now Clerk of the Court of Special Sessions, said he couldn't afford it. Girls didn't need to go to college, and most girls would be well content to have as she did good clothes and plenty to eat. If she insisted on college, he said, she could go to normal school; and when told that normal school didn't teach inspiring subjects, he suggested that all the books on inspiring subjects were in the New York Public Library. She had only to bring them home and read them.

But Meta needed someone to tell her what she wanted to read. Hearing

Mrs. Sinclair's constantly expressed concern that her brilliant son was not eating while he wrote his novel, Meta offered to row down the lake and bring him nourishment, and Mrs. Sinclair was grateful.

So was Upton, though slow to show it, grateful not only to be spared the waste of time of preparing food, but even more grateful perhaps for an audience to hear and wholeheartedly admire his work as it progressed. He expressed his gratitude by agreeing to her request that he guide her education and never was there a more willing Galatea nor a sterner Pygmalion.

He started her with German, using his own crash program method, and studying the Bible. At great length Sinclair explained to her that his life must be as strict and dedicated as that of Saint Simeon Stylites. "I do not believe that there is any man more driven by the desire for life than I, and when I get at the essence of myself I do not believe I am a kind man. I have no patience with human hearts, their suffering and their weakness. There is only one thing that I value and that is my fidelity to my ideal."

Not too surprisingly, the more Upton warned Meta against himself, the more taken with him she became. And Upton's caveats that they must be only brother and sister, that the fiend whose lantern lights the mead were better mate than he, were continuous and ever more shrill as the net tightened.

When Meta returned to New York, Upton's cautionary letters followed. "Read Shelley's *Epipsychidion* in which he speaks of the peril of 'ceasing to love perfection and coming to love a woman . . .' . . . you have chased a man whose heart is filled with a sacred fire, the fire of a vision I did not seek. . . . the gift of genius . . . I desire a love of absolute purity and selflessness. I desire no other. . . . I may try to persuade myself that I love you more than anything else, but all the time, in the depths of me, I hear these words: 'You are a fool; you love power, and life, and achievement, and nothing else can ever satisfy you.'

"I have found myself wanting to sneak through my work . . . and enjoy myself. But you can't sneak with God, and that's all there is about it. . . . God made me for an artist and not for a lover!"

But artists who are writers do not get the immediate audience response granted performing artists, and Upton needed response. Not only the artist in him but the prophet needed to see results such as those he had witnessed when Meta was with him and he missed now that she had left. "Do you recall what Beethoven said—that he would like to take a woman he knew, marry her, and then break her heart, so that she might be able to sing? . . .

this is how I like to think of you. You are part of the raw material that I have to use. You were given me to master, and make of you what you ought to be. . . . Perhaps I am mad to say this, I do not love you, but I love the woman you are to be—the woman I will make you. I wonder if I am dreaming when I feel consumed with the wonder of this ideal of a woman's love, this utter and complete surrender of herself to her lover. . . . I give my life to you and I shall make of you a perfect woman—or else kill you."

The violence of Upton's passion is frightening, and although he chose to view it as poetically high-minded and noble, its basis was sexual. "I have enough heart's passion to satisfy every thirst that you feel. . . . I want you! I am drunk with the thought of *making* a woman to love." Despite his usual literary device of referring to himself as Thyrsis and to Meta as Corydon, the names of the two male shepherds in Milton's "L'Allegro," these letters make two facts clear—that he was wild with sexual desire and that he expected his marriage to be a master-slave relationship.

Meta doubtless was well aware of both, but carefully chose to play upon the first and mainly to ignore the second. "I bow in joy before your will, your certainty, your power," she wrote, and "I have no more to say, my precious one. Let it be even as you say; I am yours to do with as you will, and I shall adore you forever. You will take me and mold me to your will." But she could not limit herself entirely to what he so obviously wanted to read. Even she succumbed to occasional outbursts of anger at Upton's endless egoism and to other normal revelations that she was less than perfectly docile and submissive: "If you take me, I shall go mad—I shall love you like a tigress!" and "how impossible it will be to cease to love you, no matter what you do to me. I do not know *why* it is; I simply know it is, and perhaps someday I may teach *you* how to love. I do not imagine that you know how very well, at present—no Thyrsis, I don't."

On rare occasions, too, she was clear-eyed and prophetic. "I am in one of my cast-iron moods this morning—in a fighting mood, I do not care with whom or what. . . . you have often given me a dog's portion. I have been a slave, a cowering kitten before you, and you (unwittingly I know) have done much to destroy all my love by making me aware of what you call your higher self. Fortunately I *know* what your higher self is, quite as well as you do, if not a little better. . . . I have a right to life as well as you. . . . You say you are master—but it must be master of the right."

And so, before marriage, like everyone else, both Meta and Upton had seen clearly and at the same time had deluded themselves and one another. Each could say later, truly and of course uselessly, "But I warned you . . ."

and "But you promised. . . ." Upton's demand for "utter and complete surrender" had been answered with an abject bow, whereas in truth, Meta's reason for marrying was not to lose but rather to find herself. And Upton's promise "to satisfy every thirst that you feel" was only his penis talking, and it would too soon fall silent.

Upton worked feverishly to finish his novel. When in September that was in sight, he accepted the invitation of his old mentor, Moir, to come to Lake Placid where he reached the end of the book.

He returned to New York with the manuscript, absolutely convinced that he was finally free: free of the tyranny and tedium of school, free of the need to write the potboilers he had come to despise, free finally to free the world from injustice. But a force even stronger than his yearning for justice now controlled Upton's life—sex. As he would phrase it later, "Between Corydon and Thyrsis the determining factor, as in nine-tenths of marriages, was propinquity."

While the Macmillan Company was reading the manuscript, Upton and Meta were together all day and half the night reading Goethe and practicing Mozart sonatas for violin and piano. When his mother and Meta's parents suggested that it was improper in the city for Upton and Meta to spend every day together as they had in Canada, Upton told Meta that he did not propose to be subject to the wishes of others and that they must therefore marry immediately. Without telling anyone in advance, they were married on October 18, 1900, while downtown waiting for Upton's violin to be repaired.

The wedding was performed in the study of the Reverend Minot J. Savage of New York's Church of the Messiah, to whom Upton had come some years earlier after his disillusion with the dogma of Episcopalianism. Savage's Unitarianism taught that to labor is to pray, which perfectly suited Upton, and Savage himself was to support Upton financially and literarily in the years ahead.

The couple's wedding night was a rape. Upton's ignorance of sex was almost as total as it had been throughout his youth. He had prior to the wedding consulted a doctor on how to avoid having children, and the only birth control recommendation, presumably *coitus interruptus,* was so imperfectly explained or understood or followed that within five months Meta was pregnant.

Ignorance made Upton only more dogmatic and insistent on having his way, and so, Meta wrote later, "his love-making was fitful and precipitate and entirely futile. . . . At heart a puritan, with a decided strain of asceticism, it was difficult for him to enter into the role of lover. . . . [he] would come [to her] only when the sex urge was uncontrollable, apparently unconcerned with any mood or need of hers . . . [so that] she began to avoid such contacts as much as possible." He was, she added, "inclined to relegate sex to the limbo of unrestrained human emotions along with drunkenness, wife-beating, etc. In answer to some query . . . he would often say 'Oh that is just a sex impulse.' "

The example of Upton's father and his mother's horror of any form of "self-indulgence" were doubtless important in the writer's suspicion of and near contempt for sex needs. Significant too in Upton's attitude toward sex was his Southern idealization of the "good woman," further emphasized by his idealizing of his mother and contempt for his father. Any Oedipal feelings in a boy who so often slept alone with his mother were simply unthinkable. And, of course, no lady could really enjoy or want to enjoy anything as primitive as the sex act, despite what he would learn from reading about female sexuality and what his Socialist friends would tell him and indeed what he himself would write in *The Book of Life*.

But as important as these factors in Upton's attitude toward sex was his belief, so often and forcibly expressed to Meta before and all during their marriage, that writing was his first, last, and only mistress and that none of his strength could be wasted in any other area except when it became absolutely unavoidable.

Ironically, this attitude, which he hoped would strengthen his art, in fact substantially damaged it. Throughout his immense work, his ignorance of the real needs of women and of the enlarging and glorifying effects of sex is obvious, distracting, and one of the reasons that whatever else his writings are they are not great literature. Too important an element of the human condition is missing from his work. Because it was also missing from his life, this fighter against injustice was being brutally unjust to his wife and to himself.

CHAPTER IV

The Death of the Poet

There are no mute, inglorious Miltons, save in the hallucinations of poets. The one sound test of a Milton is that he function like a Milton.

H. L. MENCKEN

EARLY IN THE MARRIAGE, Upton's egoism and his inept sexual conduct began to make Meta's life miserable. Perhaps even more destructive to the marriage, however, was an entirely unforseen tragedy. The New York publishers to whom he submitted *Springtime and Harvest* not only found it less than the masterpiece its author thought it, they found it unpublishable. The shock to Sinclair would be difficult to exaggerate.

With a lack of modesty that typified him throughout his life, Sinclair sincerely believed he had written in *Springtime and Harvest* the novel Shelley would have written had the master chosen that form of expression. Unfortunately, however, it was only a typical, undistinguished, romantic novel of the period, no better than most published for consumption by Victorian ladies, and no worse, unless perhaps because of its sermonizing, rarely an improvement to novels or even biographies.

Helen Davis, its heroine, when first seen, is "clad in a dress of snowy white" and so beguiles nature itself that the wind steals "one strand of her golden hair" to play with, and the bobolink pauses in his song to make sure this paragon is watching him.

Upton's spokesman-hero, David Howard, has attained his eminent moral and artistic stature by enduring so much suffering he is crippled and ill. Not unlike the author's Meta, Helen tells David "you are never going to make this poor, restless creature happy until you have given her something stern to do, something that she may know she is doing just for your love and for nothing else, bearing some effort and pain to make you happy."

After Macmillan rejected the manuscript—which might, after all, have been no more than the isolated aberration of one publisher—others, including Scribner and Appleton, turned it down also. Upton, horrified and

44

hurt, decided to publish it himself. Earning some money by writing a potboiler and borrowing two hundred dollars from his Uncle Bland, Upton had a thousand, cheap, red-covered copies printed to sell for $1.50.

In the Preface he announced that he had learned "the stern lesson that publishers are not in business for the uplifting of souls" and that unlike them he disdained moneymaking. "He needs money, of course . . . to secure the right to do his proper work in peace. That will require very little, however; for the rest of his life's earning he has another purpose . . . a dream that some day he might build up a tremendous force for the spreading of light. He was not blind to the grotesqueness of his situation in founding a library with a single book, and in starving while he wrote that one; he will pardon anyone who smiles. This library is to exist for the purpose of increasing helpful reading among the people of our land; it is to contain the best books, and the best only. . . . 'Springtime and Harvest' may fail, and subsequent books may fail; but that library is quite certain to come. The writer is a man who gives all his time to his art, and some day or other, he will have money; it is by this use of it that he hopes to keep clean his artist's conscience."

The book did fail. Upton and Meta solicited every relative and acquaintance they could think of, but sold barely enough copies to repay Uncle Bland's loan. Upton learned, however a lesson about personal publicity from which he profited for the rest of his life. Two New York newspapers sent reporters to write human interest stories on the novelist and his young wife and these stories sold the only copies of the book bought by strangers.

As an indirect result of one of the many free review copies the couple could so ill afford to send out but had sent anyway, Funk and Wagnalls offered to bring out a new issue of the novel, with a new name, *King Midas*; a new name for the author, Upton Sinclair rather than Upton B. Sinclair, Jr.; and with the illustrations, blurbs, advertisements, and other promotion that Upton believed were all the book needed to achieve the popular success it deserved.

The author and his acolyte were so excited about this offer that they ceased their attempts by means of herb teas, exhaustive exercises, and repeated falls from the bed to the floor to abort their first child. In the summer of 1901 they took a train north for the Thousand Islands, where in a tent in the wild and lovely surroundings he liked best, Upton would produce another novel and Meta would improve her mind.

It was the one idyl of their life together. Optimistic about the recognition that was now shortly to be theirs from *King Midas*, and presumably not reminded of their sexual incompatibility because of Meta's condition, the couple were happier than they would ever be again. They raised two young birds, which nightly devoured any and all flies, mosquitoes, or spiders in their sleeping tent, and when they returned to New York at summer's end, it was with the surviving bird and high hopes for the completed new novel.

Prince Hagen is a novel about a Nietzschean Nibelung who pits his greed and his limitless underworld supply of gold against his counterparts on Wall Street and their women on Fifth Avenue. In it, as in *Springtime and Harvest*, Sinclair extols art, virtue, and kindness and contrasts their effects with the corrupting and brutalizing effects of the lust for money, power, and the trappings of high society. As in the earlier novel, there is not a word about Socialism. The transformation of the hearts of men and, therefore, of their society from greedy and consequently unhappy to loving and happy is still to come by means of music, literature, and beauty in all forms, rather than by means of economic or political action.

The reception of *Prince Hagen* by publishers was far worse even than that of *Springtime and Harvest*. Seventeen magazines and twenty-two publishing houses refused to have any part of it, and what made these rejections especially hurtful was that initially the couple's hopes had soared because Bliss Perry at the *Atlantic Monthly* was encouraging. But after weeks of suspense, Perry turned it down because, "We have a very conservative, fastidious, and sophisticated constituency" for whom the novel was inadequate.

There followed many painful episodes. Editors promised a quick reading and then took weeks or never read the manuscript at all. Sinclair never overcame the bitterness that built up in him over *Prince Hagen*. Thirty years later, when he had become one of the most successful writers in the world, he wrote vengefully in his autobiography about a Columbia professor who was fired over a breach of promise suit and about the poor man's subsequent suicide, when his chief sin had been promising and failing to have Dodd, Mead, the publishers, read *Prince Hagen*.

Upton's relations with book editors and a number of Columbia English professors who were their readers (though they preferred the title of "adviser") drove the young writer to near desperation and affected not only what he later wrote but also how he published. Ironically, the well-fed and well-clothed editors spoke to Sinclair of their doubts and hopes almost entirely in terms of sales and profits, whereas the threadbare and near-starving artist who could not support his family spoke instead in terms of art and of his messianic mission.

Sinclair's intense passion about this mission must have been off-putting. Even, or perhaps especially, a man who states that his message and art come not from his own merit or talent but rather from God's use of him as a mere instrument may instead of seeming modest appear to possess the ultimate vanity or at least to be unhinged and unreliable.

Sarcasm and Olympian contempt for this young idealist fill the reports of the English professors whose only claim to a place in history may be their error of judgment as to Sinclair's potential for success. Most, however, carefully hedged their adverse judgments with some expression, however jocular, of the possibility that this young man's passion might someday bring him to write a profitable book. Not having the young man's disdain for money, they did not want the small sums paid them as advisers cut off should Sinclair somehow succeed. Their tone, like the editors' cruelties, seems to indicate at least the possibility that some envied Sinclair's passion, if not his talent.

King Midas, which was to have been Upton's first triumph, was instead another failure, selling only some two thousand copies.

By 1926 Sinclair confided to Floyd Dell, "I wrote 'King Midas,' which I have never reread, but which I shudder to think about, because it must be an awful book, I mean sentimental and crude." And of *Prince Hagen* he wrote later, "The truth was that the story was not good enough; the writer was strong on emotions, but weak on facts." But when he wrote them, he believed the times out of joint and not his novels. If the system would not accept such noble works, it must be because it was in the control of ignoble men and so, partly as a result of this paranoia (which he never completely lost), Sinclair began working out in his mind a political system that had in fact been worked out already but of which he knew not, Socialism.

That winter of 1901–1902 was a terrible one. Sinclair's son, David, was born December 1, 1901. Meta's labor was a fourteen-hour ordeal. Upton remained by her side and would later write about it in great detail. As Upton's prospects became even more bleak, his father-in-law, who had been supplying the twenty-five dollars a month to his daughter that was the couple's only income, decided that a man who would not support his wife and child by doing normal work had no right to live with them. Meta and David went back to live with her parents, and Upton lived in a rented attic room and tried desperately to earn some money. Not only Meta's family but his own as well put on all the pressure possible for him to get a real job, do some real work, and give up this writing for which he was so obviously unfitted.

He wrote potboilers, but now even they didn't sell, the author seemingly having lost the knack on finding the higher call. He wrote jokes, essays, a blank verse narrative poem, sketches, book reviews, boys' stories, and humiliating, begging letters, pleading for any sort of help. He wrote publishers seeking work as a reader. He even wrote the New York Public Library suggesting they buy copies of *King Midas* for their branches. "I find myself just now driven from my work—perhaps forever—by the pressure of absolute starvation." And he asked how he might convince Andrew Carnegie to give a "scholarship for the young student of letters who aims to be a creator and not a scholar. . . . it is a matter of life and death to me, for I can't hold out much longer."

Perhaps the most heartbreaking letter is one to the poet Edwin Markham, because its overtones reveal that there are cracks of doubt in Upton's heretofore solid and passionate conviction that he was a poet consecrated by God to do His work. It was a desperate cry for help by a man who very shortly would have to give up what he believed his life's goal. "I have been living for the past year in the most extreme poverty and I am in debt; but my chief suffering, more than I can ever tell anyone, has been mental. My whole heart is centered upon the uttering of my spiritual conviction. . . . I want to *work*—to *work*. . . . I do not want wealth and I do not want fame. I live like a hermit and neither could affect me. I *want* to give every second of my time and of my thought, every ounce of my energy, to the worship of my God and to the uttering of the unspeakable message that I know he has given me. I have no other joy or care in the world but this; and I tell you my dear Mr. Markham before heaven I can not stand what I have stood much longer."

The spring of 1902 was a long nightmare. He was forbidden to see his wife and newborn child by his father-in-law, who had taken them in and supported them only on that basis—which deprivation may not have been for Upton an unmixed curse. His few publications were inconsequential articles in *The Independent*, which paid little and meant less, except as one, "A Review of Reviews," reveals the young man's increasing paranoia. In it he expressed outrage that his own publication of *Springtime and Harvest* had received few and mostly unfavorable reviews, whereas the same text, published more lavishly by a famous publisher with endorsements from Markham and Santayana received many times more, and these more favorable. That in fact his vanity publication had been reviewed at all was then and would be today remarkable.

In the summer, Meta went with her parents to the Catskills. Upton had earlier gone back alone and bitter to the same spot on Leek Island where a year before he had passed his brief idyl with Meta, while waiting for the world to acclaim its new poet. This year's adventures were symbolically as well as actually terrible. He nearly froze to death in an icy gale and set fire to the tent in his effort to stay warm. He almost starved when he ran out of food for several days because a storm made the channel uncrossable, and he attempted to eat a crow, the only game he could shoot, but found the flesh too vile.

Sinclair's stomach troubles started this summer, and so, first with treatments of pig pepsin, he began those experiments with foods and crank diets that he would continue the rest of his life.

As he waited for the cold weather to abate so that he might write rather than concentrating almost entirely on not freezing or starving, Sinclair, wrapped in blankets, read a new German book he had brought up from New York, *Also Sprach Zarathustra.* "The first night that I read it I kicked my heels together and laughed aloud in glee, like a child. *Oh,* it was so fine! And to find things like this already written!"

As had already been the case when he discovered Shelley, and was still to be when he would discover Socialism, this solipsistic savior was overjoyed to learn that the entire job of educating and redeeming mankind did not rest only on his shoulders, that some of the work had already been done.

Despite his misadventures, however, in a six-week period of work so intense that it was remarkable even for Sinclair, from late April to early June, he produced another novel, *The Journal of Arthur Stirling.*

On Monday, June 9, 1902, in *The New York Times,* the following death notice appeared:

> *STIRLING.*—By suicide in the Hudson River, poet and man of genius, in the 22nd year of his age, only son of Richard T. and Grace Stirling, deceased, of Chicago.
> Chicago papers please copy.

Interest in this suicide helped Sinclair sell his novel to Appleton, who continued Sinclair's hoax, publishing the novel in February of 1903 as the last words of the suicide. The book, while allegedly fiction, is more revealingly autobiographical than anything else Upton ever wrote. Although his autobiography covers a longer period, it does not expose the same depths of feeling. If the suicide of Arthur Stirling is fictional, the death of the poet so movingly described is real.

Arthur Stirling, "a tall, dark-haired boy . . . with a singularly beautiful face, and a strange wistful expression of the eyes," whose father was a drunk who died in a delirium, longs for excellence "as the lion longs for his food. . . .

"No one can understand this—no one who has not a demon in his soul. . . . I think only of the book . . . and my head on fire, and my hands tingling, until I sank down from sheer exhaustion—laughing and sobbing, and talking to God as if He were in the room. I never believed in God except at such times. . . .

"It is not merely the vision, the hour of exultation; that is but the setting of the task. Now you will take that ecstacy, and hold on to it . . . you will hold that flaming glory before your eyes, and you will hammer it into words . . . that leap the hilltops. . . . You will take them as they come, white-hot, in wild tumult, and you will forge them, and force them. . . . all that is the making of a poem. . . . you come down of sheer exhaustion; and you lie there, panting. . . . if it will not come you *make* it come, you lash yourself like a dumb beast—up, up, to the mountain-tops again."

Stirling cares passionately about music and he is not burdened with such modesty as would make him hesitate to compare his work to Beethoven's or even to suggest cuts in the master's music. He teaches himself to read five languages, has terrible doubts, and longs for love. "Am I a fool? I do not know—that is none of my business. It is my business to do my best.

"Oh men—oh my brothers—will you love me for this thing?"

He is a patriot and a believer in democracy, even though he knows the shortcomings of the people and is himself a snob. "Chiefest of all I think of my country! Passionately, I love this land of mine. If I tear my heart till it bleeds and pour out the tears of my spirit . . . it is for this land of Washington and Lincoln. There never was any land like it—there may never be any like it again; and Freedom watches from her mountains, trembling.

"—It is a song that it needs, a song and a singer; to shake the heart of every man in it, and make him burn and dare! . . . Is it to the heaping up of ugly cities, the packing of pork, and the gathering of gold? That is the thing that I toil for—to tear this land from the grasp of mean men and of merchants! . . . I understand by a tyrant a man whose happiness is the unhappiness of others. I read of the discoverers of Mexico, and how they found a pyramid of human skulls, raised as a monument; that has been to me, ever since, the type of tyranny. The forms of tyranny vary through the ages, but the principle is always the same; a tyrant is a man who is made great by the toil and sorrow of others."

"I wonder if anyone will even read this. . . . I suppose ten people will read gossip about the book for every one who reads the book."

Stirling knows intimately the numberless, small, bitter obscenities of poverty. "Shall I ever know what it is . . . to think of my work without the intrusion of these degrading pettinesses? . . . I plot and I plan all the day—I can not buy a newspaper without hesitating and debating. . . . when I think of the time that I lose . . . I walk miles when I am exhausted, to save a car-fare! . . . The boarding houses that I have lived in! . . . The landladies' faces—the assorted stenches—the dark hallways—the gabbling, quarreling, filthy, beer-carrying tenants . . . of those experiences I could make myself another Zola. . . . —Some day I shall put into a book all the rage and all the hate and all the infamy of these things."

For Stirling, religion offered no comfort, but instead the opposite. "My religion is my Art. I have no prayer but my work. Sometimes that is a glory, and . . . an agony . . . to have no inspiration outside of yourself. . . . To be the maker of a religion is to sweat blood in the nighttime. . . . God gave me a vision—it may not come again for a century, it can never come again—it is mine—*mine only*!"

But none of these makes life unbearable for Stirling. What finally defeats him, makes existence unendurable is: "*That my work should be judged by such men!*

" 'Exaggerated!' 'Hysterical!' And is there nothing hysterical in life then? And would you go through battle and pestilence with the same serenity that you sit there at your desk all day, you publisher?

"As if a man who is being torn to pieces would converse after the manner of Mr. Howells and Jane Austen!

" 'Tone it down!' . . . And tone down the Liebes-Tod—and tone down the Choral Symphony—and Epipsychidion—and King Lear! . . .

"I had never thought about the effect of The Captive [Stirling's epic poem] upon commonplace people. . . . And now these snuffy little men come peering at it!. . . . my appeal is to great minds and heroic hearts—to the ages that will come when I have gone."

And so Arthur Stirling killed himself.

And so Upton Sinclair killed his self, because for most of his life he had had no goal other than to be exactly the kind of poet Arthur Stirling was. Only by killing his *Doppelgänger* was he able to save his own life, that is, completely to change it.

Some time before his suicide, Stirling noted in his *Journal*, "Sinking down! Sinking down! To see yourself one of the losing creatures. . . ." Sinclair's father was a "losing creature," and rather than be one too, Upton would surely have killed himself. Instead, as he was able to see twenty years later, "time passed, and 'Arthur Stirling' ceased to be a poet, and became instead a muckraker."

CHAPTER V

The Poet Transformed—
Socialist and Historian

What distinguishes the chronically indignant rebel from the earnest revolutionary is that the former is capable of changing causes, the latter is not. The rebel turns his indignation now against this injustice, now against another; the revolutionary is a consistent hater who has invested all his powers of hatred in one object. The rebel always has a touch of the Quixotic; the revolutionary is a bureaucrat of Utopia. The rebel is an enthusiast; the revolutionary, a fanatic. Robespierre, Marx, Lenin were revolutionaries; Danton, Bakunin, Trotsky were rebels.　　　ARTHUR KOESTLER

UPTON'S CHANGE FROM POET to political activist was swift, but it was by degrees. His first step was to write a book about past history, after which he would turn to contemporary history, and only then would he try to affect history's future course by preaching in a variety of ways his newfound belief—Socialism. Before he could begin his book of history, however, he had first to write his worst novel and his best essay.

The catharsis of suicide had proven to be not enough for Sinclair. His accumulated bitterness required in addition a hideous murder, which he committed in his novel *A Captain of Industry*, written at the low point of his life, the winter of 1902–1903.

Even worse than the previous winter, this one found Upton still separated from his wife and child, living in a miserable Harlem lodging-house with his mother and ever more alcoholic father. So desperate was he, Upton would later allege, that he even tried gambling—penny ante poker—and found to his horror and terror that he had at last discovered his vice. Both in an effort to dramatize this period of his life and to sound a cautionary note for others similarly tempted, Upton later wrote that he had been powerless in the grip of a devastating emotion that combined a minimum of hope with a frenzy of greed and anxiety, and that he could not recall having won even once.

As a substitute for this form of self-destruction, Upton soon launched into a grotesquely vengeful, venomous attack on the rich, who had ignored Stirling in fiction and ignored Sinclair in fact.

"Robbie" van Rensselaer, the Captain of Industry, unknowingly takes as his mistress his own illegitimate daughter by an earlier and long forgotten affair, thereby adding to his long list of sins what the writer who had slept in the same bed with his mother may have considered the worst sin of all, incest. Robbie then makes some hundred million dollars in the stock market, gets drunk, takes his yacht to sea, and is drowned in a great storm. The degree to which Sinclair's out-of-control hatred ruined this short novel is obvious in the writing throughout, but nowhere more so than at the end.

"I share in Ruskin's distrust of the 'pathetic fallacy'; and I have no intention of implying that the waves had any sentiments whatever in connection with Robert van Rensselaer. It was purely an accident that they kept him in their grasp, and beat him against the cliff all day; that one by one they rushed up to seize him, and spent all their force in hurling him, in pounding him, until he had lost all semblance of a man. . . . there was no voice but the waves' voice, and all night long they called to each other on the beach, and tossed the body back and forth in the silver moonlight. When the morning broke it was swollen and purple, and it lay half hidden in the sand. . . . Was it not true that for twoscore years and more the earth had been searched for things rare and precious enough to help make up the body of Robert van Rensselaer? Think of the hogs-heads of rare wines that had been poured into it! Of the boxes of priceless cigars that had flavored it! Of the terrapin, and the venison, and the ducks—the strangely spiced sauces—the infinity of sweetmeats—the pink satin menus, full of elegant French names! Had not thousands of men labored daily to fetch and prepare these things, to serve them upon crystal and silver before that precious body—and to clothe it and to house it, and to smooth all its paths through the world? And now it lay at last upon the sand, to be devoured by a swarm of hungry crabs!"

No publisher would touch *The Captain of Industry* until Sinclair's worldwide success with *The Jungle* briefly created a demand for almost anything with his name on it. Even then, only the Socialist weekly newspaper, *Appeal to Reason*, would publish it, first as a serial and then in book form at the end of 1906.

Despite the often execrable writing, Sinclair demonstrated his great skill in describing, at the same time clearly, fully, and excitingly, a complicated business or industrial process.

Robert van Rensselaer's Wall Street bear raid prefigures Sinclair's extraordinary ability to simplify without distorting and to make not only interesting but thrilling to the layman, for example, various aspects of the coal or oil business. But although he would describe so well various business processes, he was much less effective in describing the motives and emotions of businessmen because he never really understood them. He was so burdened with ideas of honor and fair play that he was horrified at the everyday chicaneries of business. He never understood that they constitute an essential part of the fun of business. Nor did he have any inkling of the erotic aspects of moneymaking of which cruelty is not infrequently an element.

The most anguished and self-revealing essay Sinclair wrote was a defiant manifesto, "My Cause," that appeared in *The Independent* in May 1903. In this "war whoop," as he later called it, which was the very opposite of an admission of defeat, the defeated former poet announces to the world his new role. "I, Upton Sinclair, would-be singer and penniless rat . . . having now definitely and irrevocably consummated a victory . . . being in body very weak and in heart very weary, but in will yet infinitely determined, have sat myself down to compose this letter to the world."

What victory, if any, he had consummated is far from clear. It may have referred to the publication of *Arthur Stirling* three months earlier and its publicity stir, but in fact the novel rather than a victory proved to be yet another crushing defeat. It sold fewer than two thousand copies and paid its author not one cent of royalty. It seems more possible that Upton was being ironic and did not make it clear, a circumstance that repeated itself frequently throughout his long writing career. The only real victory he had accomplished was summoning the strength to go on writing, albeit in a new vein, despite his uninterrupted series of defeats.

In the essay he justifies his Arthur Stirling hoax and declares his intention to write *The American*, a trilogy of novels on the Civil War. Then he bravely declares his plan to establish the Sinclair Press and pleads for the establishment by rich men of an American University of Literature to subsidize young writers. Its purpose is to save them from "the brutalizing slavery of 'What the Public Wants' " and to enable them to produce what "God wants and what beauty and truth and righteousness want."

This failed poet, near starvation, ends on a note of almost hysterical defiance, "you may sneer . . . now, but you will live to blush for that sneer."

Three years later he wrote bitterly concerning this essay, "My error lay in supposing that it is literature that makes life, instead of life that makes literature."

Even twenty-nine years later, Sinclair could not read the essay without

pain. His passionate identification with struggling young poets remained so
fierce that in the years ahead he could continue to help even one he was well
aware had recently cuckolded him. And he always spent time he could not
afford to spare reading everything sent to him by aspiring writers and trying
to help all of those he felt had any bit of talent. He helped, among others,
Halldor K. Laxness when the future Icelandic Nobelist was unknown and
friendless in California.

As time went on, Sinclair revealed much less, and much less directly, the
psychological forces that moved him most and with more restraint came
better written and better selling books. But something was lost as well.

Floyd Dell, the novelist and editor, in criticizing the manuscript of
Sinclair's *American Outpost* thirty years later, found the autobiography too
controlled, too bland, too jocular, and Sinclair thereupon included much of
Dell's letter of criticism in the book. Dell compared the book unfavorably to
Sinclair's early manifesto. "I do not know how many other youths it affected
as it did me. . . . But that prose poem gave me the courage to face an ugly
and evil world. . . . It is no small thing to give strength to youth. Perhaps it
is the greatest thing that literature can do."

Dell pointed out that in "My Cause" and in *The Journal of Arthur
Stirling* Sinclair reveals himself as "a living, suffering bundle of conceit,
cruelty, selfishness and folly" and contrasted that with Sinclair's later wooden
heroes who "do not suffer enough nor sin at all. That is why your life is
more edifying . . . than your novels. . . .

"To put it in the simplest terms, all over the world there are young
people who wish sincerely to devote their lives to revolutionary betterment
of the world; and those same young people will probably fall in love with
the wrong people, and suffer like hell, and believe this and that mistaken
idea . . . and while Upton Sinclair cannot prevent that, nor tell them what
to do when it happens (or be believed when he tells them), he can do them
good by letting them know that he went through some of the same things.
Among these 'same things' I include asceticism—a commoner youthful sin
than you seem to think."

At twenty-four, aware that his life had so far been misdirected, Sinclair
was perhaps as desperately in need of a religion as he had been in his
unhappy childhood. He had followed after false gods, first in the
Episcopalian Church and then in the temples of the Muses of Poetry. Now
he needed a faith that would restore him and also redirect him into paths of
success and usefulness. And so he found Socialism.

By the time Upton heard of Socialism, the word had been in general use
throughout Europe for more than half a century to mean the doctrine, or

dozens of doctrines, which insisted that ownership and control of the means of production and exchange should belong to all citizens in common.

The words Socialist and Socialism had become common about 1830 in England in connection with the followers and teachings of Robert Owen and in France with those of Saint Simon and Fourier. Their ideas were soon felt in America by native writers and intellectuals, for example, when Brook Farm became Brook Farm Phalanx in 1846 because of Fourier's influence. One of the Frenchman's American disciples among possibly as many as two hundred thousand was the senior Henry James.

When Marx and Engels in 1848 drafted the *Communist Manifesto*, this narrowed definitions only somewhat and was the first step of modern "Scientific Socialism," the second being the organization in 1864 of Marx's International Working Men's Association (the first International). As Socialist parties were founded and grew in various countries of Europe, there came the need for an International Socialist Bureau, and one was founded in 1900, only a few years before Sinclair's discovery of Socialism.

Upton was not exceptional but typical of his countrymen in his ignorance of Socialism because, although a good many immigrants were Socialists, few native Americans knew much about it. Not until the hot Chicago summer of 1897 was the Socialist Democratic Party formed. In 1900 its nominee for President, Eugene Debs, got only one hundred thousand votes, but four years later he got four hundred thousand, a figure that the winner, Theodore Roosevelt, noted with concern.

Despite Upton's many years in high school, college, and graduate school, he had no idea of the existence of modern Socialism, which like venereal disease was simply not an acceptable topic for discussion. He was vaguely aware of Populism, as a sort of vulgar movement for the ignorant, and, of course, he was aware of various kinds of historical socialism, of Plato's *Republic* and More's *Utopia*. He had read and reread in half a dozen languages the socialism of the Hebrew prophets from Amos to Isaiah. But Upton always claimed that until he was at least twenty-two he was absolutely unaware that anyone other than himself had given thought to a struggle by America's working classes to free themselves from their enslavement under capitalism, and to the creating of a new and classless society controlled collectively by all the people in their own interest. Just as he had been delighted when he had learned that Shelley's and Nietzsche's works had prefigured his own role as the world's reformer-philosopher-poet, he would be overjoyed when he learned that Socialism had already done some of his work for him and that he was not alone.

Not untypical of Upton's education in political and social history was his point of view on the Haymarket martyrs and how he came by it. At the age of ten he had been taken to New York's Eden Musee, and among the waxwork tableaux in its chamber of horrors he had seen one of black-bearded, depraved scoundrels making bombs. As almost everyone did then and as some do still, he had thereafter lumped together all Socialists, anarchists, labor union activists, and other such malcontents into one vicious, degenerate, and foreign or traitorous group. Such people made bombs and free love in the back rooms of saloons, mocked and blasphemed against God Almighty, and wanted nothing so much as to destroy America.

Upton had not yet learned that reformers have always been accused of being wreckers of the Republic whether they were labor organizers, Socialists, or anti-war protesters. He was to become one of the proofs that, in fact, they have usually been its saviors. He, like they, helped it avoid the "terrible social convulsions . . . or the establishment of an absolute despotism" at least one of which if not both is inevitable, as Ignatius Donnelly pointed out at the 1892 Populist convention, if the hardships and injustices of too many citizens are not relieved.

Although Upton was revolted by and already writing against the country's Mammon worship, he said he was nevertheless "intellectually a perfect little snob and tory. I despised modern books without having read them, and I expected social evils to be remedied by cultured and well-mannered gentlemen who had been to college and acquired noble ideals." Upton may possibly have exaggerated both the obscurity of Socialism and his total ignorance of it, given his wide reading and all that was being published on the subject. But if he had been exposed to any modern Socialism it had not taken.

Then, in the fall of 1902, Upton met Leonard D. Abbott, at the *Literary Digest*, where he was already well on his way to becoming an editor. Although only five years in the United States from his native England and almost exactly Sinclair's age, Abbott proudly called himself a Socialist, gave Upton *Wilshire's Magazine* and some Socialist propaganda, and took him next door to meet John Spargo, then editor of a small Socialist monthly, who was two years younger and also from England, and who, like Sinclair, would later resign from the Socialist Party over World War I.

One of the Socialist pamphlets Upton read was written by George D. Herron, the Christian Socialist from Montezuma, Indiana, whose scandalous divorce and defrocking had brought him an aura of glamorous martyrdom among Socialists, and whose subsequent marriage to the daughter of one of his rich Socialist converts, Mrs. E. D. Rand, had given him funds to found the Rand School of Social Science in New York City and help other Socialist causes.

Upton wrote to Herron and was invited to a dinner where for the first time (but not the last) he learned that some Socialists lived in elegant apartments filled with expensive paintings and sculpture and wore evening dress to dinner. Here he met Gaylord Wilshire, another "millionaire Socialist," maker and loser of fortunes in Los Angeles real estate and worthless gold mines, editor and publisher of *Wilshire's Magazine*, founded only two years earlier. He and his wife, Mary, whom he married in 1904, were to be two of Upton's closest friends.

Herron, who, also like Sinclair and Spargo, would split with the Socialists over the World War, served during that war as a secret agent of Woodrow Wilson. He lived in Switzerland and negotiated confidentially for the President with the Kaiser's government, thus serving as an early model for Upton's last fictional hero, Lanny Budd. But more importantly now, he served as another of Upton's substitute fathers and, in fact, as his savior. After reading *The Journal of Arthur Stirling*, Herron agreed to subsidize the spiritually and financially exhausted Sinclair. For about two years, beginning in the spring of 1903, he provided the thirty dollars a month that enabled Upton and his family to live together again, while Upton wrote his Civil War novel, *Manassas*.

Grateful as he was for this financial support, Sinclair was and would remain quite as grateful to Herron for bringing him into the Socialist movement. This gave his life a new purpose and ended the terrible loneliness he had suffered since his teens when he had felt himself absolutely alone in the knowledge that class inequality and social injustice had to be eliminated, and that the responsibility for world reform was his. "It was like the falling down of prison walls about my mind; the most amazing discovery, after all these years—that I did not have to carry the whole burden of humanity's future upon my two frail shoulders! . . . The principal fact which the Socialists had to teach me, was the fact that they themselves existed."

But if that was the principal fact, it was hardly the only one. There was almost a century of Socialist literature to read and Upton devoured it much as he had earlier devoured German, French, Italian, and classical literature. And his new reading brought him revelations about the old, forcing him "to revise all his previous knowledge; he had to cast out tons of rubbish from the chambers of his mind, and start his thinking life all over again. Just as in the early days, he had exchanged miracles and folk tales for facts of natural science; so now he saw political institutions and social codes, literary and artistic canons, and ethical and philosophical systems, no longer as things valid and excellent . . . but simply . . . as fortifications in the class-war. . . . What a light it threw upon philosophy, for instance, to perceive it not as a search for truth, but as a search for justification upon the part of ruling classes, and for the basis of attack upon the part of subject-classes!"

He read Kropotkin's *Mutual Aid as a Factor in Evolution* and came to believe from it that the whole science of biology had been distorted to suit the purposes of the British ruling classes. He never acknowledged thereafter that even some part of man's aggressiveness and greed was instinctive and insisted that men would be near to angels if economic factors allowed it. This was typical of the Socialist canon, and one of the reasons it was ridiculed as patently impractical by both the capitalists on the right and Communists on the left.

Upton read Veblen's *The Theory of the Leisure Class*, published only a few years earlier in 1899, "in a continuous ebullition of glee." It enabled him also to tease Meta for being his "leisure-class wife," and when soon thereafter they came upon Hedda Gabler, he shuddered to observe that of all literature's heroines, this was her favorite. "Nor did he fail to observe the working of the thing in himself; the subtle and deeply-buried instinct which made him prefer to be wretched with a 'leisure-class wife' rather than to be contented with a plebeian one!"

Upton and Meta read Bellamy's *Looking Backward*, Blatchford's *Merrie England*, Kropotkin's *Appeal to the Young*, and another book about England that moved them even more, *The People of the Abyss* by Jack London, who was only two years older than Upton and whose childhood in San Francisco had been even worse than Upton's. London was already beginning to enjoy that enormous success that made him for a time America's most popular writer, and Upton "had visions of being the next to be caught up and transported to those far-off heights of popularity and power."

Upton and Meta were also becoming aware that women as a group were being oppressed just as labor was, and their cause the soon-to-be muckraker would shortly support very vigorously. Women were becoming a significant factor in the progressive movement, especially middle- and upper-class women who were reading, forming clubs to support various forms of culture, and who were just beginning to taste the sweetness of power—the power to change society, as well as the bitterness usually mandatory to the achieving of that power.

Meta read Charlotte Perkins Gilman's *Women and Economics*, which had appeared in 1898, and gave it to Upton, who went on from it to Bebel's

Women and Socialism and the works of Havelock Ellis. But although in principle Sinclair was second to no man in wanting justice as well as economic and sexual independence for women, and although he could speak and write tellingly about "marriage plus prostitution" and *psychopathia sexualis*, he was selfish, driven, egoistic, and almost as absolutely certain about sex as he was almost completely ignorant.

At this same moment when Upton began working toward his revolution, others initiated theirs. In 1907 Picasso produced *Les Demoiselles d'Avignon*, which insured that never again would man see himself as he had before. Gertrude Stein, whose *Three Lives* and *The Making of Americans* were being created at this moment, was making a revolution in writing. But they were trying to change the ways in which man perceives the world. Upton was trying to change the world.

With the help of Herron's loan and his promise of a monthly stipend which totaled finally about seven hundred dollars and was repaid many years later, Upton moved Meta and David to a patch of woods on a farm a few miles north of Princeton, New Jersey, both because the university there had the second largest Civil War collection after the Library of Congress and because Upton's experiences of the horrors that poverty inflicts on city dwellers had led him to the delusion that rural poverty was less terrible. Here he housed his family in a crude cabin and planned to feed and care for them for less than a dollar a day, which must also pay the farmer for the use of his land, the right to draw pails of water from his well, and the once a week use of a horse and buggy to go to town for supplies and to return one wagonload of books and take another to read.

Meta, after living apart from Upton for two years, had hoped Princeton would prove to be another idyl, like their summer on Leek Island. Instead, it was a nightmare.

For most of her waking hours she was alone with David in their miserable leaking cabin, which throughout the spring of 1903 and the following winter and spring was surrounded by a sea of mud six inches deep. While Upton, off in his tiny writing tent, worked hour after hour, oblivious of his wife and child, Meta tried to make some order in the welter of wet bedclothes, dirty diapers, groceries, stove, and pans set under the roof's many holes.

David had not learned to walk and the doctors had diagnosed undernourishment with a threat of rickets. They prescribed "intensive feeding" every few hours, boiled cereals with cream, raw beef pounded with a hammer and then slightly warmed, chicken that must be chopped bones and all into small pieces and then boiled for hours. Meta was resolved her child would be neither a cripple nor physically retarded, and that contrary to the doctors' predictions, he would walk before he was three. She would succeed in both resolves.

Obsessed with his new novel, Upton took his wife's efforts for granted and almost entirely ignored her needs, real and imaginary, as he did those of his parents. But worst of all for Meta was Upton's terror of having another child and his solution to the problem—absolute abstinence—to which solution not even he was able to stick perfectly.

"I adored him. . . . Whatever he said was so, *must* be true. When he said that sexual intercourse was justified only when one desired offspring, then forthwith I must learn to conquer my unsatisfied longings. . . . petting was debarred because he said it was silly and animalistic. Of course it was the fear of further offspring that made us go for months without intercourse."

In one of his wild and passionate letters, Upton had written to Meta that if he had to live the Reverend Moir's celibate life "I should be insane in a month." Knowing his need for sex and having always been worried that she was intellectually inadequate for him, she must now also have wondered if even in bed she was not also somehow unacceptable.

Abstinence did not make the heart grow fonder. One night Upton found Meta sitting up in bed, a pistol pointed at her temple, weeping miserably because she had been thus for hours, unable to summon the courage to pull the trigger.

Years later, Upton would admit his ignorance and cruelty. "She suffered from depression and melancholy. . . . Nowadays every disciple of Freud in Greenwich Village would know what to tell her. But this was the days before the invention of the Freudian demonology. Birth control, as explained by the family doctor, had failed, and could not be trusted; since another pregnancy would have meant the death of the young writer's hopes, there was no safety but in returning to the original idea of 'brother and sister.' Since caressing led to sexual impulse, and therefore to discontent, it was necessary that caressing should be confined to noble words and the reading aloud of Civil War literature. . . . This was, of course, a cruelty, and prepared the way for tragedy."

It was not, of course, before the days of Freud, whose seminal works appeared in 1899 and 1905. Indeed, Sinclair later claimed to have read Freud in German at this period, but he was and always remained basically antipathetic to Freud's canon that many of man's deepest desires are in opposition to the functioning of society. Sinclair believed that economic inequality was the primary source of society's ills and that once this inequality was corrected, society could and would function with little conflict. And despite Sinclair's genuine efforts to understand Freud's stress on sexuality, he never ceased to be offended by it.

Meta was, therefore, increasingly in need of that joking prescription for women in hysteria that Freud had learned under Charcot and had taken seriously: *"Penis erectus, usus normalis, quantum suficit."* And so she now began, at first timidly and tentatively but soon with boldness and abandon, seeking the sexual satisfaction denied her by her husband.

Neither sexual frustration nor even the substitution of the "noble words" of Socialism for demonstrations of affection, however, was the chief source of her discontent. Meta had believed that this marriage would bring her fulfillment in a variety of areas—that she would achieve through it first education and then understanding and, finally, expression in some form of the artistic instincts she was certain were imprisoned within her, instincts that were urgently, turbulently seeking release.

Even before her second marriage, her economic distress would disappear and she would have ample opportunity for fulfilling herself. But although she wrote prose and verse, year after year, no artistic talent ever revealed itself and her discontents continued.

That in the years of her marriage to Sinclair, however, she should have unrealistically attributed all of her many neuroses to the very real fact of his sexual ignorance and selfishness is quite as understandable as it is incorrect.

The results of their efforts at abstinence were pitiful for Upton too, whose desires were again as terrifying as before marriage and again magnified in the same proportion that they were repressed. Although he put on a stern unfeeling front at the time, nothing in his later writing is more poignant than his descriptions of their pathetic efforts at celibacy during that stupefying Princeton winter, aggravated by the necessity of piling what little bedding they had on a single cot "when night after night the thermometer went to ten or fifteen degrees below zero. . . . they were like two animals which crawl into the same hole to keep each other from freezing."

Upton flogged himself with all the old terrors of becoming like his father, "sexual intercourse became a self-indulgence, like the eating of candy, or the drinking of liquor." And when even this failed, he "waited each month in suspense and dread" to see if his weakness had been appropriately punished. "They were like people drawing lots for a death-sentence."

While *Manassas* is not very different in style from Sinclair's early romantic novels, unlike them it contains both some good history (of the decade in America that preceded the war) and some moving exposé (of the horrors of the South and its society built upon the obscenities of slavery), the two areas in which Sinclair would soon find his real calling.

Allan Montague, the book's hero, like its author and almost all its author's later fictional heroes, was an innocent, good-hearted idealist, painfully educated in the cold world of cruel realities—an American Candide. As Lanny Budd would later, Allan Montague, contrary to all laws of probability, met at first hand those of his contemporaries of historical interest whom Sinclair wished to sketch, including in this case Levi Coffin, Frederick Douglass, John Brown, Jefferson Davis, Lincoln, and William Seward.

Typically, the fathers of Upton's heroes are drunkards or weaklings or frequently dead. In Allan's case, his father is wounded and killed, and like the dime novel hero, Mark Mallory for example, must, like Sinclair himself, support his mother. When in 1927, in *Oil!* Upton departed from this pattern and created a strong, effective, loving father for his hero, Bunny, he produced his best novel other than *The Jungle.*

In *Manassas*, Sinclair appraised *Uncle Tom's Cabin*, published fifty years earlier. The appraisal is especially interesting coming from a man who would so shortly write *The Jungle*, which Jack London would characterize as "the *Uncle Tom's Cabin* of wage-slavery," and which would have a greater influence and wider sale than any other American novel excepting possibly Mrs. Stowe's (and would itself evoke much the same kind of criticism). " 'Uncle Tom's Cabin' was one of those books like 'Pilgrim's Progress' and 'Robinson Crusoe,' " Sinclair wrote, "which make their way in the world of literature from below, and are classics before the *literati* have discovered them. Even now it is the fashion to speak of it as having historical rather than literary interest . . . doubly strange in view of the recognition that the critics of its own day gave it; it was praised without stint by such widely different personages as Whittier and Heine, Lowell and Lord Palmerston, Macaulay and George Sand. In truth, its literary faults are evident enough, its skeleton sticks through its every joint; but he who can read a hundred pages of it, for the first or the twentieth time, with dry eyes, is not an enviable person. It was, when it appeared, and it has remained to this day, the most unquestionable piece of inspiration in American fiction; and probably nowhere in the literature of all the world is there a book more packed and charged with the agony and heartbreak of *woman*."

In *Manassas* a Socialist appears in a Sinclair novel for the first time, Sergeant Schlemmer, a German refugee, who introduces Allan to Socialism and to Wagner.

Upton finished *Manassas* in the spring of 1904 and it was published in August by Macmillan, again without the success its author always anticipated for each of his books. But although it sold fewer than two thousand copies, it led directly to Sinclair's greatest best seller, *The Jungle*.

At this time, Sinclair's writing was being affected not only by his readings on Socialism, but also by the realism that had been becoming more acceptable and important in the arts for some decades in America as in Europe. "Frank Norris had a great influence upon me because I read 'The Octopus' when I was young and knew very little about what was happening in America. He showed me a new world, and he also showed me that it could be put in a novel."

While he was researching and writing *Manassas*, Upton had also been reading modern American history in the Socialist newspapers and magazines that he had only recently discovered. Typically, he had no sooner started reading these than he also began sending them fiery pieces reflecting his own views on social justice. And poor as he was, he was far more concerned that his views be known than that they be paid for. He also began reading at this period the mass circulation magazines that were publishing the new journalism of exposure written by men and women who, like himself, were soon to be labeled "muckrakers."

Some magazine editors even before the Civil War had learned that virtuous campaigns against sin, dishonesty, and political corruption could be more than their own reward, that, in fact, they built circulation; and after the war, the point was repeatedly proven by *Harper's Weekly* in its attacks on the Tweed régime which, with the help of Thomas Nast's brilliant cartoons, tripled the magazine's circulation.

The new breed of newspaper publishers too, those who specialized in "yellow journalism," Scripps, Pulitzer, and Hearst, built enormous circulations on the "human interest story," sex, sin, the festivities and follies of the rich. This created, or at least intensified, among the common folk the demand for similar divertissements and didos (further increased later by movies and television), a demand that eventually reshaped America.

But most importantly it was the mass circulation magazines that shaped the era by revealing the sins of the corporations rather than those of the corporations' owners. *Munsey's*, *Everybody's*, *The Arena*, even the *Ladies' Home Journal*, *Collier's*, *Cosmopolitan*, and the *Saturday Evening Post*, each played a role, but it was *McClure's* that set the muckraking pattern with Ray Stannard Baker, Ida Tarbell, Lincoln Steffens, Samuel Hopkins Adams, and William Allen White. In an editorial in the January 1903 issue the magazine defined what muckraking at its best is all about—"The American Contempt of Law." Three different articles in that issue demonstrated three different facets of that same contempt. Ida Tarbell's chapter from *The History of the Standard Oil Company*, the editorial said, showed "our capitalists conspiring among themselves, deliberately, shrewdly, upon legal advice, to break the law so far as it restrained them, and to misuse it to restrain others who were in their way."

Ray Stannard Baker's article, "The Right to Work," the editorial went on, "shows labor, the ancient enemy of capital, and the chief complainant of the trusts' unlawful acts, itself committing and excusing crimes. And in [Steffens'] 'The Shame of Minneapolis' we see the administration of a city employing criminals to commit crimes for the profit of the elected officials, while the citizens . . . stood by complacent. . . .

"Capitalists, workingmen, politicians, citizens—all breaking the law or letting it be broken. Who is left to uphold it? The lawyers? . . . [who] advise corporations how they can get around the law. . . . the judges? . . . they restore to office and liberty men convicted on evidence overwhelmingly convincing to common sense. The churches? We know of one, an ancient and wealthy establishment [New York's Trinity], which had to be compelled by a . . . health officer to put its tenements in sanitary condition. The colleges? They do not understand.

"There is no one left; none but all of us. Capital . . . Labor. . . . These two are drawing together. . . . raising wages, and raising freight rates too. They make the public pay. We are all doing our worst and making the public pay. The public is the people. We forget that we all are the people; that while each of us in his group can shove off on the rest the bill of today, the debt is only postponed; the rest are passing it on back to us. We have to pay in the end, every one of us. And in the end the sum total of the debt will be our liberty."

The Appeal to Reason was America's most important Socialist newspaper, reporting weekly to its readers on social issues scrupulously ignored or distorted in the capitalist press. It had been founded in Kansas City in 1895 by Julius Augustus Wayland, who moved it to Girard, Kansas, two years later. Under Wayland and his editor, Fred D. Warren, the *Appeal* regularly published some three to seven hundred thousand copies and in special editions such as the Moyer-Haywood "Rescue Edition" the circulation could reach four million. The paper's subscribers, who paid fifty cents a year, were not the "plutes" it loved to denounce, who read a paper and threw it away, but poor people who passed around each issue to others, thereby giving it a much greater readership than its circulation figure indicated.

Wayland had been born in Versailles, Indiana, and Warren in Arcola, Illinois. In view of the long-cherished American tradition that Socialists are foreigners, it is ironic that Wayland, Warren, and their newspaper were products of Middle America, as indeed were Debs who (like Dreiser) was born in Terre Haute, Indiana; Clarence Darrow, in Kinsman, Ohio; William English Walling, in Louisville, Kentucky; "Big Bill" Haywood, in Salt Lake City; George Herron, in Montezuma, Indiana; Earl Browder, in Wichita, Kansas; Tom Mooney, in Chicago; and Norman Thomas, in Marion, Ohio.

In the summer of 1904 a strike against the meat-packers had been brutally broken and Fred Warren had published on the front page of the *Appeal*, Upton's ringing challenge to the defeated workers:

YOU HAVE LOST THE STRIKE!
And Now What Are You Going to Do About It?

When Sinclair sent him a copy of *Manassas*, Warren was enthusiastic about it, especially about the harrowing description of the hunted slave, and wrote asking whether the young novelist could do something similar about present-day wage slaves.

Upton was overjoyed. He answered that if as advance payment for the prepublication serial rights the *Appeal* would pay $500, that was all he would require for the year during which he would go to Chicago, research the stockyards, and write the novel. And Warren agreed.

CHAPTER VI

The Jungle, Part 1

There was never the least attention paid to what was cut up for sausage; there would come all the way back from Europe old sausage that had been rejected, and that was mouldy and white—it would be doused with borax and glycerine, and dumped into the hoppers, and made over again for home consumption. There would be meat that had tumbled out on the floor, in the dirt and sawdust, where the workers had tramped and spit uncounted billions of consumption germs. There would be meat stored in great piles and thousands of rats would race about on it. It was too dark in these storage places to see well, but a man could run his hand over these piles of meat and sweep off handfuls of the dried dung of rats. These rats were nuisances, and the packers would put poisoned bread out for them; they would die, and then rats, bread, and meat would go into the hoppers together. THE JUNGLE

THERE WERE FEWER PROBLEMS when each community had its own butchers. If one of these charged too much, put his thumb too often or too heavily on the scales, or sold tainted meat, his competitor got his business and as it required neither extraordinary talent nor much investment of capital for a man to become a butcher, there was usually no shortage of competitors. Butchers, like saloonkeepers, were rarely the least popular citizens in town, and although butchers were not at the same level in society's economic or educational pecking order as princes or priests, yet Shakespeare and Cardinal Wolsey were both sons of butchers.

More difficult problems came with the refrigerator car, patented in 1867 but developed commercially by Gustavus Franklin Swift by 1879, after which it was no longer necessary to ship meat on the hoof (with freight being paid on the whole animal) to be butchered locally. Instead it was possible to butcher meat in large quantities at one central point and then ship it, already dressed, to cities and towns far away, summer and winter. The local butchers became thereafter little more than retailers, increasingly dependent upon Armour, Swift, Cudahy, and Morris.

At the great central slaughterhouses in Chicago, the packers were able by acting in concert to drive down not only the prices paid to farmers and ranchers for their livestock, but the wages paid to the packers' employees as well. They were also able to stifle competition and create a beef trust by means similar to those Rockefeller had used to build Standard Oil, including railroad rebates. The refrigerator cars were owned by members of the beef trust and "loaned" to the railroads on the specific understanding that exorbitant freight charges would be levied against the packers outside the trust and rebated to its members.

In 1899, years before poet Sinclair would address himself to anything as vulgar as meat-packing, William Randolph Hearst had exposed the disgusting "embalmed beef" scandals and brought on the Senate investigation at which Theodore Roosevelt testified he would as soon eat his old hat as the canned goods shipped under government contract to the soldiers in Cuba. And still the putrid and poisonous condition of the meat, like the obscene conditions of the meat workers, caused no public outcry. In 1901 Hearst sent Ella Reeve Bloor, before she became famous as the Communists' "Mother Bloor," to report on the stockyards, and Hearst's exposures of the packers' brutalizing of their competitors led to fines and jail sentences in 1905, though the jail sentences were never served.

The packers were wiser about public relations than most businessmen of that era, arranging Potemkin village tours to carefully manicured parts of their plants and advertising their own virtues lavishly, which may not have been completely unrelated to favorable articles about them published in such magazines as *Success*, *Leslie's*, and *Cosmopolitan*. There were also, however, before Sinclair's first installment appeared in the *Appeal* on February 25, 1905, quite a number of muckraking exposés, ranging from A. M. Simons' 1899 *Packingtown* pamphlet to Charles Edward Russell's 1904 articles later published in book form as *The Greatest Trust in the World*.

The really germinal work not only for pure foods but against poisonous patent medicines, however, was begun decades earlier by Dr. Harvey Washington Wiley, Hoosier son of a clergyman and Abolitionist. Born in 1844, he briefly saw active duty in the war, then studied in Indiana, at Harvard, and finally in Germany where he seems to have first become interested in food analysis. For almost thirty years as chief of the bureau of chemistry of the United States Department of Agriculture (from 1883 to 1912), Wiley worked at investigating the adulteration of foodstuffs and later for the enforcement of the Pure Food and Drug Act of June 30, 1906, serving the cause of pure foods not only in America but all over the world.

In 1902 Wiley began showing, by means of his soon-to-be-famous "poison-squad" experiments on humans, the unhealthful effects of the dyes, boric acid, benzoic acid, and other preservatives used by unscrupulous businessmen and eaten unknowingly by the public in their foods. However, although it was Wiley and his associates who tirelessly did the basic scientific research that proved the necessity for the Pure Food and Drug Act, it would be the work of the muckrakers that finally got inspection and regulation enacted into law, despite the opposition of a venal and obdurate Senate.

Upton left for Chicago toward the end of 1904 and stayed some seven weeks to study the evils of the beef trust. Fellow Socialists and union men who knew him from his recent manifesto in the *Appeal* took him into their homes and all over the slaughterhouses, where he proved that he was a superb reporter.

So shabby were his own clothes that, by no more elaborate a disguise than the carrying of a dinner pail and armed with a few simple lies appropriate to the area in which he was investigating, he had no trouble going everywhere and noting everything.

He studied not only the stockyards and back of the yards, but to a lesser degree other aspects of the city of Chicago as well, from its great stores and banks to Jane Addams' Hull House, where he got into an argument with Miss Addams.

Quite by chance, Upton ran into Adolph Smith, the correspondent for an important British medical journal, *Lancet*, who had studied European slaughterhouses and could therefore confirm to neophyte Sinclair that such cruelty and filth were not only dangerously unsanitary but quite unnecessary as well.

It was also only a matter of happenstance that Sinclair's novel portrayed the miseries of immigrant working people. He had no special interest in them as immigrants, only as "wage-slaves." And yet, although other writers for years—women as well as men—wrote novels about America's mistreatment of its immigrants, neither native authors, such as Willa Cather with *O Pioneers* in 1913, nor immigrant authors, such as Mary Antin with *The Promised Land* in 1912, ever matched Sinclair's success, not even those who may have had greater artistry or experience.

Usually forgotten is the fact that Sinclair dedicated *The Jungle* "To the Workingmen of America" and that it was their brutalization rather than the filthy conditions in America's slaughterhouses that he sought to ameliorate.

Repeatedly after the publication and enormous success of the book, he would point out, "I aimed at the public's heart, and by accident I hit it in the stomach."

Once the material was assembled, Upton returned to Princeton and the "palatial quarters" of a sixty-acre farm he had bought for $2,600, with the help of a thousand dollars lent him by Dr. Savage. Although their living conditions were marginally improved on the farm, Upton and his family were still close to starvation. Despite the courageous, even defiant, face he put on in his articles, he was near despair, confiding in a begging letter to Owen Wister: "the life I am living almost drives me mad."

After finishing *Manassas*, he had fallen prey to that illusory desire often cherished by reformers—the yen to get back to Mother Earth and so never to be hungry again. But all his efforts to raise vegetables, fruits, and livestock met with equal disaster. His interest in farming was as secondary as his interest in Meta and David. His only real interest was in his new book, and on Christmas Day of 1904 he began writing the first chapter of *The Jungle*. He worked in the same eight- by ten-foot, tar-paper-roofed, one-windowed shed built by his own hands, which he had had moved to the new farm, and in which "stood a table, a chair, a home-made shelf for books, and a little round pot-bellied stove that burned coal—since the urgencies of inspiration were incompatible with keeping up a wood fire."

The Jungle is a tragic story of hopeful and hardworking immigrants, ground into waste by American industry—of the American Dream turned into a Kafkaesque nightmare. It opens with Upton's rejoicing description of the *veselija*, the wedding celebration, of the hero, black-haired, black-eyed Jurgis Rudkus of the mighty shoulders and giant hands and his less than sixteen-year-old, small for her age, fair and blue-eyed bride, Ona Lukoszaite. One Sunday afternoon in Chicago, Upton had by chance, "back of the yards," come upon just such a celebration in the rear of a saloon. He had watched it for hours, realizing these were to be the characters of his novel, had written and rewritten the scene in his head for two months, and he always maintained that when finally, for the first time, he committed it to paper back in Princeton, he had not changed a word.

In this scene, the best he ever wrote, Upton introduces all the major characters of his most tragic novel in an almost hysterically joyous Lithuanian celebration. There is, at least for these people, a lavish abundance of food. There is a prodigality of drink so exhilarating as to permit Upton to forgo, perhaps for the only time in his life, his usual cautionary sermon on the subject, though there is a brief mention of drink's ills. And there is frenetic, inspired music, that art dearest of all to Sinclair, music which began like the *veselija* itself at four in the afternoon and lasted until almost the same hour the next morning—the three-piece orchestra led by Tamoszius Kuszleika, who "taught himself to play the violin by practicing all night, after working all day on the 'killing beds.' " There is, in short, all the palpable, circumstantial detail—the texture and tone, scent and sound, the action—of the nineteenth-century novel at its best.

Yet even while describing the joyous *prestissimo* dancing, Upton points to some of the economic problems that inevitably make life "back of the yards" tragic.

During the three- or four-hour *acziavimas* which continues uninterrupted, the guests dance in a ring around the bride and one by one each man steps into the ring and dances with her. The moment he has finished, he is squared off by Ona's stepmother, Teta Elzbieta, who expects him to drop some money into her hat to defray the cost of the party and with luck to provide some extra, with which the newlyweds may begin their married life.

"Most fearful they are to contemplate, the expenses of this entertainment. They will certainly be over two hundred dollars, and may be three hundred; and three hundred dollars is more than the year's income of many a person in this room. There are able-bodied men here who work from early morning until late at night, in ice-cold cellars with a quarter of an inch of water on the floor—men who for six or seven months in the year never see the sunlight from Sunday afternoon till the next Sunday morning—and who cannot earn three hundred dollars in a year. There are little children here, scarce in their teens, who can hardly see the top of the work benches—whose parents have lied to get them their places—and who do not make the half of three hundred dollars a year, and perhaps not even the third of it. And then to spend such a sum, all in a single day of your life, at a wedding feast! (For obviously it is the same thing, whether you spend it at once for your own wedding, or in a long time, at the weddings of all your friends.)

"It is very imprudent, it is tragic—but, ah, it is so beautiful! Bit by bit these poor people have given up everything else; but to this they cling with all the power of their souls—they cannot give up the *veselija*! To do that would mean, not merely to be defeated, but to acknowledge defeat—and the difference between these two things is what keeps the world going. The *veselija* has come down to them from a far-off time, and the meaning of it was that one might dwell within the cave and gaze upon shadows, provided only that once in his lifetime he could break his chains, and feel his wings, and behold the sun; provided that once in his lifetime he might testify to the fact that life, with all its cares and its terrors, is no such great thing after all, but merely a bubble upon the surface of a river, a thing that one may toss about and play with as a juggler tosses his golden balls, a thing that one may quaff, like a goblet of rare red wine. Thus having known himself for the master of things, a man could go back to his toil and live upon the memory all his days."

His happy bride's faith in Jurgis is great, as great as his own faith in his ability to succeed by hard work in this new homeland. But their lives flow into Durham's slaughterhouse like the continuous stream of ten thousand cattle, the same number of hogs, and half as many sheep every day, "pressing on to their fate, all unsuspicious—a very river of death."

The horrors in the packing plants that Upton described in nauseating detail were almost endless. The hogs that arrived already dead of cholera and tubercular steers were processed and sold for human consumption as were "old and crippled and diseased cattle . . . which had been fed on 'whiskey malt,' the refuse of breweries, and had become what the men called 'steerly'—which means covered with boils. It was a nasty job killing these, for when you plunged your knife into them they would burst and splash foul-smelling stuff into your face; and when a man's sleeves were smeared with blood and his hands steeped in it, how was he ever to wipe his face, or to clear his eyes so that he could see."

Each worker in each part of the slaughterhouse had his "own peculiar diseases. And . . . bore the evidence of them about his own person—generally he had only to hold out his hand.

"Of . . . all those who used knives, you could scarcely find a person who had the use of his thumb; time and time again the base of it had been slashed, till it was a mere lump of flesh. . . . They would have no nails—they had worn them off pulling hides; their knuckles were so swollen that their fingers spread out like a fan. . . . There were the wool pluckers, whose hands went to pieces even sooner than the hands of the pickle men; for the pelts of the sheep had to be painted with acid to loosen the wool, and then the pluckers had to pull out this wool with their bare hands, till the acid had eaten off their fingers.

"Worst of any, however, were the fertilizer men, and those who served in the cooking rooms . . . in some of which there were open vats near the level of the floor, their peculiar trouble was that they fell into the vats; and when they were fished out, there was never enough of them left to be worth exhibiting—sometimes they would be overlooked for days, till all but the bones of them had gone out to the world as Durham's Pure Leaf Lard!"

There were of course no toilets, so human as well as rat excrement went into the sausage, along with the poisoned rats themselves. "There was not even a place where a man could wash his hands," is a phrase repeated in the book and although the euphemism, to wash one's hands, is not today used as commonly as it was in the first half of this century to mean urinate or defecate, Sinclair's meaning was understood even before photographs circulated all over the world substantiating his charge. It was such unsanitary details as these that moved Sinclair's readers far more than the obscenities perpetrated on the workers.

Ona is seduced by her boss, Conner, at the factory, who also insists she work at night in a brothel. She dies in childbirth at eighteen and her son, Antanas, drowns in a mudhole in the street while Jurgis is in jail for having attacked Conner.

Horror piled upon horror when merely listed or analyzed may seem as preposterous as Grand Guignol, but in the reading, *The Jungle*, at least until after the death of Ona and young Antanas, seems frighteningly real.

To get to that point, the nadir of Jurgis' fortunes, Upton had worked without stop for three months. "I wrote with tears and anguish, pouring into the pages all that pain which life had meant to me. Externally the story had to do with a family of stockyard workers, but internally it was the story of my own family. Did I wish to know how the poor suffered in winter time in Chicago? I had only to recall the previous winter in the cabin, when we had had only cotton blankets, and had put rugs on top of us . . . It was the same with hunger, with illness, with fear. 'Ona' was 'Corydon,' speaking Lithuanian, but otherwise unchanged. Our little boy was down with pneumonia that winter, and nearly died, and the grief of that went into the book."

Upton was better at transmuting his family's suffering into fiction and at describing his own anguish in writing than he was at making Meta feel his concern for her and David. Much of Sinclair's own suffering, not only recently in marriage but in his childhood as well, enabled him to feel and to express poignantly many of the pains and terrors of poverty. But his own experiences, searing though they had been, did not really compare to, and so had not prepared him for, the unspeakable obscenities of the slaughterhouse and the fertilizer plant, and most especially for the vicious inhumanities practiced on one another by the citizens of the Chicago slums.

After the death of his wife and son, Jurgis quits the slaughterhouses and works at an assortment of jobs, from strikebreaker to thief, giving Sinclair the opportunity to show in detail what he had learned as he did his research—the transfer of power from the rich men who own Chicago, through their agents, the politicians, to the police and their allies in the underworld. Sinclair has become a far more sophisticated observer and analyst of life in America than he was only a few years earlier when he was going to help Jerome reform New York. His new sympathy for the pickpocket, the whore, the election-day repeater, and even the saloonkeeper demonstrate an extraordinary and swift growth of the puritan's understanding. But what Sinclair could not understand or accept was the inhumanity of the poor toward one another, the thousands of grafts and cruelties they practiced on each other.

This reader of Shelley, even though he had read Zola (who would probably have ended *The Jungle* with the drowning of Antanas), was not prepared for the obvious hopelessness of the lives of his characters. Therefore, the young and clearly unacknowledged legislator of mankind found himself paralyzed; for the first time in his life he was unable to write and so incapable of finishing the book.

Jurgis' flight to the country solved nothing, just as Sinclair himself was learning that farm life was not the specific for life's ills he had thought it would be. In Upton's half-dime-novel days, any sort of *deus ex machina* would have done to end *The Jungle*—but no longer.

Worn out by writing and by the problems of his increasingly unsatisfactory life with Meta, Upton in the summer of 1905 stopped working on *The Jungle*.

Instead, he went to work virtually full time and with all his extraordinary intensity on an idea he had had some months earlier—the creation of an Intercollegiate Socialist Society. Still appalled that he could have gone through years of college and graduate school and not known about modern Socialism, he decided if "the professors refuse to teach the students about modern life, it was up to the students to teach themselves."

He wrote and sent out thousands of organizing letters and a call to such men as W. D. Howells, J. G. Phelps Stokes, Clarence Darrow, Jack London, Edwin Markham, Lincoln Steffens, and Thorstein Veblen, for permission to use their names. On September 12, 1905, at Peck's Restaurant on Fulton Street in New York, the society was formally organized with Jack London as president and Upton as first vice president. Although Debs was the one and only God of American Socialism, Jack London was its greatest hero, and his famous discourse "Revolution" set any Socialist crowd roaring with delight.

Shortly after the founding of the ISS, it held a mass meeting in New York at the Grand Central Palace at which London was to be the main speaker, but his train from Florida was late. Despite feelings of panic, Upton took over the meeting and successfully managed to hold the crowd together until London finally showed up. "I was prepared to give my hero the admiration of a slave. But we spent the next day together . . . and all that day the hero smoked cigarettes and drank. . . . he was the red-blood, and I the mollycoddle, and he must have his fun with me . . . [and so told tales] of incredible debauches; tales of opium and hashish . . . of whiskey bouts lasting for weeks!"

One who attended the first meeting of the ISS was a Wesleyan student named Harry Laidler. A few years later he was hired as its full-time secretary, running it for some sixty years, including those following 1921 when its name was changed to the less objectionable "League for Industrial Democracy," the Russian Revolution having made the word "Socialist" anathema to all right-thinking Americans. Among the students who at one time or another were in the society's various college chapters were Senator Paul Douglas, Walter P. Reuther, Selman A. Waksman (co-discoverer of streptomycin), Sidney Hook, Felix Cohen (advocate of American Indian rights), William L. Shirer, Ralph Bunche, and Walter Lippmann, "a very staid and proper young Jewish man at Harvard . . . [who] organized the chapter of the I.S.S. there . . . was its chairman . . . and ran it very efficiently. When he was graduated he gradually became a little more conservative."

Upton worked furiously for the success of the ISS and its triumph was his. Through it he met most of America's prominent Socialists and Socialist visitors from abroad, many of whom were somewhat taken aback by his enthusiasm, which sometimes bordered on the bumptious. Never one to underestimate the importance of his work, including the ISS, Upton introduced Florence Kelley at one of the society's dinners in New Haven as an example of how even nationally known persons were brought to Socialism by the society's activities. Mrs. Kelley, then a far better known writer than Upton, a translator of Engels, and leader of the National Child Labor Committee and National Consumers' League, suggested to Sinclair that she had been a Socialist before he was dry behind the ears.

Whatever may be the degree of importance of the ISS in American history, its importance to Sinclair was immense, because through its establishment and acceptance, he was able to convince himself that however hopeless the fate of his characters in *The Jungle* (and real people like them) appeared to be, someday by the educative and redemptive power of Socialism they would be saved. So he was enabled finally to return to work on *The Jungle*.

He himself was never satisfied with any of the endings he wrote for *The Jungle*, all of them being longer or shorter sermons on Socialism. He always offered a variety of excuses that the last third of the novel, Jurgis' life after he quits the stockyards, was not up to the first two thirds. Among other things he blamed Meta's illness and the lack of funds that precluded his returning to Chicago to do more research. But he was also able to laugh at what was a literary tragedy.

"I did the best I could—and those critics who didn't like the ending ought to have seen it as it was in manuscript! I ran wild at the end, attempting to solve all the problems of America; I put in the Moyer-Haywood case, everything I knew and thought my readers ought to know. I submitted these chapters to a test, and got a cruel verdict; the editor of the 'Appeal' came to visit me, and sat in my little living-room one evening to hear the story—and fell sound asleep!"

It is not given to many authors or reformers to record, let alone laugh about, such an experience.

CHAPTER VII

The Jungle, Part 2

Fifty years ago, few enterprises carried safety devices to protect workers' limbs and lives. Some protested that adoption of such devices would increase costs. Yet few firms today plead that they cannot "afford" to introduce safety devices. Is meaningfulness in work any less important?   DANIEL BELL

THE *Appeal's* ADVANCE OF FIVE HUNDRED DOLLARS for *The Jungle*, while not a vast sum, was more than half of everything Upton had earned on his four previous novels, and it was payment only for the serial rights—what he got for book rights was to be in addition. There was favorable critical notice about the novel almost as soon as its first installment was printed on February 25, 1905. And although these were in Socialist rather than literary circles, the perennially optimistic writer grew increasingly convinced that he had written a best seller. Knowing his subject was one of great public interest, he was certain *The Jungle* would have a large sale as a book if only he could convince a publisher.

In October 1904, two months after the publication of *Manassas* by Macmillan, Upton had written his editor there, George P. Brett, a memorandum that began: "The following is the outline of a purpose rather than the scenario of a story. The novel I plan would be intended to set forth the breaking of human hearts by a system which exploits the labor of men and women for profits. It would be—what none of my works have [sic] been so far—a definite attempt to write something popular. I have no idea of ceasing to do artistic work, but . . ."

Thus Upton started down the road he would thereafter follow, never turning away from things "popular" nor turning back to things more "artistic," such as, in his own view, his first four novels had been.

Brett had given Sinclair a five-hundred-dollar advance on the novel, but by spring in 1905 Upton was writing to explain that although he had expected by then to have finished the book, the "prolonged and desperate illness of my wife has held me up over two months . . . because I had to be

78

in N.Y.—most of the time on hospital duty for several weeks." Brett may have inferred from the letter that Sinclair's problems were more minor than in fact they were, because the young author spent a good part of the letter suggesting that Macmillan's advertising department use a more up to date photograph of himself and also that the publishers experiment with advertising in Socialist journals, hardly likely for so conservative a firm.

A month later he wrote asking for more money, explaining that the upkeep of the farm through the winter had proven more expensive than anticipated and that Meta's unspecified illness had cost more than the two hundred dollars the surgeons had originally estimated because she had suddenly required a second operation and that with nurse's and hospital bills his debts came to almost six hundred dollars. Neither Sinclair's assurance that his farm's crops in the fall would be worth about a thousand dollars, nor a quotation from his fellow muckraker, David Graham Phillips, characterizing Upton's novel as "the greatest ever written by an American . . . [and one that would] prove to be immortal" served to induce Brett to part with any more money.

Upton's problems were such that by June 10 he wrote Brett two letters on the same day stating plainly, "I understand your position, but . . . I need money now. . . . I have only 27 cents in my pocket. . . . Nevertheless I am going on writing this afternoon." The real degree of Sinclair's need, however, is made evident when for the first time he acceded to Brett's increasing pressure to expunge some parts of the book: "The subject of the publishability of certain parts of the ms. is open for debate."

Brett's readers had been and continued to be increasingly horrified by the brutal realism revealed in the *Appeal*'s installments of *The Jungle*. Professor G. R. Carpenter of Columbia predicted that although the tale was "told with great force, indeed with really terrific force at times . . . [and was] an extraordinary indictment, one that would be translated into several languages in all probability, & one that might actually have an effect on legislation . . . it is not a book that could have a wide circulation. It is not for the young. . . . it won't have a large sale; but it is a powerful tract, if Sinclair will be reasonable. . . . will pay a reasonable profit."

Another Macmillan reader wrote in regard to what was to be one of America's greatest best sellers, "I advise without hesitation and unreservedly against the publication of this book . . . [which] is gloom and horror unrelieved. . . . One feels that what is at the bottom of his fierceness is not nearly so much desire to help the poor as hatred of the rich. . . . As to possibilities of a large sale, I should think them not very good."

Sinclair had indicated he was willing to admit and try to correct faults in his work and to listen to reasonable suggestions that some of the horror be taken out. "I think that the incidents in the second half of my book move too swiftly and that its characters are insufficiently realized. The reasons for the fault were, first my exhaustion, and secondly my desire to keep the book from stretching to an unpublishable length, and thirdly, my comparative unfamiliarity with the rest of Chicago—except Packingtown, that is. I have this definite proposition to make, which is final, so far as I am concerned. I request you to publish the story this fall, cut off at the death of Ona; to consider this 100,000 words as 'The Jungle' of our contract; and to advance me a second $500 to complete a novel to be called 'The Story of Jurgis: A Sequel to "The Jungle".' If you will do this, I shall go away at once and take a much needed rest for a month or two, and I will then go out to Chicago and familiarize myself with the city's world of vice and crime, as I did with Packingtown. I will entirely rewrite the second half, making it a novel of say 125,000–140,000 words. I will elaborate the incidents and make the characters more definite. I will work the last chapters more carefully . . . making them less a matter of ideas and more of persons. . . . I will make other changes with a view to lightening up the story, and I think with the spoiled meat sensations that are in it and the enthusiastic comments which you will have from London, Phillips, Hunter, Merwin and others you can count upon making the book a success. . . .

"I have just recd this note from London: 'There has never been anything written like 'The Jungle.' I read it from week to week & am right up to date. I confess that I have envied you time & again for what you are doing. It is splendid & there's my hand on it!' "

It is unfortunate that Brett did not agree to Sinclair's proposal, for it might have resulted in two good novels instead of two thirds of one. But when he did not, Upton determined to bring *The Jungle* out in book form himself as it was. By that time, he was tired of Brett's pressure to take out the "blood and guts," and when he had sought advice from Lincoln Steffens on the problem, was unhappy with the older muckraker's answer, "It is useless to tell things that are incredible, even though they may be true."

After five other publishers had turned the novel down, Upton told the readers of the *Appeal* he had refused his publisher's demands to emasculate the book because "it would be [an] act of cowardice and unfaith to turn 'The Jungle' over to the profit-mongers without first giving my comrades a chance to say whether or not they were prepared to care for it." He went on to outline an offer which was but the first of many demonstrating his promotional genius. He warned the *Appeal*'s readers that he would wait only twenty days and then if enough orders had come in at a dollar and twenty cents, he would print exactly that number of copies, calling them the "Sustainer's Edition." On the same page appeared a plea by Jack London in the form of a command, virtually ordering all good Socialists to buy the book and saying "what 'Uncle Tom's Cabin' did for black slaves, 'The Jungle' has a large chance to do for the wage slaves of today."

Upton had written London begging for a five-hundred-word review and confiding that he had "taken the momentous decision. The book is to come into the world as a straight proletarian proposition with a low royalty for me & a price about ¢50 in quantities. . . . you will understand what this book means to me & what a grave decision it has been to trust it to the underground movement. . . . We have *got* to make this go. Among other things I shall die if it doesn't so if you ever want to see me!—"

The public response was not overwhelming. In the *Appeal*'s December 16 issue Sinclair announced that he had received 972 orders, but this was not enough, for he had planned to print an edition of two thousand five hundred at a cost of about eighteen hundred dollars, with about five hundred copies to be sent out free as review copies. Happily, however, Upton was also able to announce that "a publishing house of the highest standing" was willing to bring out the book on his terms, that is, he and they would use the same plates, they for the regular trade edition and he for his own Socialist edition (a pattern he would follow for many years). These high-standing publishers were in fact Doubleday, Page & Company, who were not only such "profit-mongers" as Upton held in contempt, but who also only a few years earlier had published Theodore Dreiser's *Sister Carrie* only to suppress it immediately at the insistence of the publisher's wife.

The Jungle was published about the end of February, but not before Walter H. Page had sent proofs of it to the managing editor of the Chicago *Tribune*, James Keeley, who sent back to Doubleday a long report contradicting Sinclair's allegations. When the author convinced his publishers to send out someone of their own choosing to investigate at first hand, the young lawyer chosen to do this met in Chicago a publicity agent of the packers who, unaware of the lawyer's purpose, confided that he had written the report Keeley had forwarded to Doubleday as the work of his own reporters. The young lawyer confirmed to Page that Sinclair's allegations were true.

Sinclair not infrequently had to defend the truth of his revelations about Packingtown. When the great meat-packer J. Ogden Armour himself chose indirectly to contradict *The Jungle* (without naming it or its author or addressing himself to specific charges) by means of an article in *The Saturday Evening Post*, Upton replied in *Everybody's Magazine*. Once again Upton had to prove his facts, this time to E. J. Ridgeway, editor of *Everybody's*, who was excited enough to stop the presses and replace an article of Charles E. Russell's with Upton's and to pay eight hundred dollars spot cash, but wanted proof first. Sinclair, always a hardworking reporter and often also a lucky one, had obtained an affidavit made by a former foreman of Armour's detailing how condemned carcasses instead of being destroyed were sold for meat in Chicago. When the company had offered the foreman five thousand dollars to retract his story, he accepted the money and then made another affidavit detailing the bribery. With these affidavits, along with numerous court records of guilty pleas by Armour to charges of selling adulterated meat in various states, Upton satisfied Ridgeway and his lawyers.

He confided delightedly to London: "I have got hold of a lot of red hot material about the Beef Trust. I stumbled onto a newspaper reporter in New York who during the Spanish War investigation had got into old Armour's office and stolen nearly 400 documents from his letter file. I have been looking them over and they make interesting reading. Here is one of them: a telegram from Washington. 'Pay Swift and Company $200,000 to keep out of Florida for one year." The acceptance and use of leaks or stolen papers has been characterized as wicked or at the very least as mere luck rather than investigative reporting by the victims of the exposures or the reporters to whom the material was not given. It hardly needs pointing out that more than luck is at work if one reporter consistently receives such material and others do not.

Almost incredible were the range, the intensity, the speed, and the duration of *The Jungle*'s influence. Sinclair seems to have hit the whole world in the stomach.

Dust-jacket puffs and advertising plugs by his fellow muckrakers and Socialists were, like funeral orations, not given on oath. But even they seem to show an unusual conviction. David Graham Phillips wrote Upton, "I should be afraid to trust myself to tell how it affects me. It is a great work. I have a feeling that you yourself will be dazed some day by the excitement about it. . . . I must restrain myself or you may misunderstand."

From Meta's heroine, feminist Charlotte Perkins Gilman, came word, "that book of yours is unforgettable. I should think the Beef Trust would buy it up at any price—or you, if they could."

Upton's hero, Eugene Debs, wrote, "It marks an epoch," which in fact it still does.

Only a few months after its publication in America, editions appeared in Britain and in seventeen translations—*The Jungle* was a world sensation. All over London advertisements proclaimed: "The amazing novel which has startled the world, & which forms the text of Mr. Winston Churchill's article in this week's issue of *T.P.O.*, has just been purchased for its readers by the weekly 'Dispatch'." *T.P.O.* was the new paper of the Irish journalist, nationalist, and sometime Member of Parliament, Thomas Power ("Tay Pay") O'Connor; and in it the young British aristocrat, never willingly far from publicity, wrote two long reviews. He noted that his original hope in reviewing the book had been to make it better known, and that in a matter of weeks this had become impossible, the book having become so famous as to have already "disturbed in the Old World and the New the digestions and perhaps the consciences of mankind."

Churchill attributed to Sinclair a plan that would not become apparent to anyone, including Upton himself, until the 1930s, "the destruction or bodily capture of the Democratic party and the installation in its place of a thorough and unshrinking Socialist organization."

Then follows perhaps the most interesting part of the two perceptive essays, coming as it does from the great parliamentary debater of the age. "Nothing can exceed the skill and determination with which the author has marshalled his arguments. He is one of those debaters who stand no nonsense from their facts. . . . [they are] drilled into order . . . and led to the assault. . . . One purpose and one purpose alone animates the mind of the commander, and inspires his army down to the humblest item which marches silently in the ranks—to make the great Beef Trust stink in the nostrils of the world, and so to contaminate the system upon which it has grown to strength."

One could hardly think of a famous British subject who was politically at a further remove from Churchill during all his life than George Bernard Shaw, who contemporaneously in 1905, in his Preface to *Major Barbara*, wrote, "Another contrast . . . between . . . splendor [and] the misery, squalor, and degradation of millions . . . is drawn at the same moment by a novelist, Mr. Upton Sinclair, who chips a corner of the veneering from the huge meat packing industries of Chicago, and shews it to us as a sample of what is going on all over the world underneath the top layer of prosperous plutocracy."

Shaw was not the only important playwright, nor was Britain before

World War I the only place and time, that *The Jungle* made itself felt. According to Martin Esslin: "Brecht's play 'Im Dickicht der Städte' (In the Jungle of the Cities) deals with Chicago, so does his 'St Joan of the Stockyards.' On 15 April 1920 Brecht wrote a review of Schiller's *Don Carlos* for the Augsburg newspaper *Volkseville*, of which he was dramatic critic, in which he compared Schiller's vision of freedom with the lot of workers in Chicago. . . . 'These days I have been reading in Sinclair's The Jungle the story of a worker who is being starved to death in the stockyards of Chicago. . . .' The review ends with praise for Schiller's play but adds, 'But occasionally also read Sinclair's novel The Jungle.' (Brecht Gesammelte Werke, Suhrkamp 1967, vol. VII, p. 9–10) . . . the evidence that Brecht knew Sinclair's book and was deeply influenced by it is conclusive."

Upton's novel was not received everywhere with praise. *The New York Times* devoted a long review to "A Dispassionate Examination of Upton Sinclair's Application of Zola's Methods to a Chicago Environment," which in the main addressed itself to the folly of Socialism and Socialists and doubted "that men and women need only to be emancipated from wage slavery and the barbarities of capitalism to become at once high-minded, virtuous, generous, forbearing, honest, enamored of the Ten Commandments, and eager to do unto others as they would that others should do unto them."

Writers being no more consistent than other mortals, their own statements as to what other writers influenced them often vary considerably and even contradict one another. Upton, for example, sometimes stated that in his writing of *The Jungle*, he had been influenced by Zola's *Germinal*, and at other times denied having ever read it.

It was not, however, the reaction of other artists nor of critics that so suddenly and swiftly metamorphosed Sinclair from a starving unknown to a world figure. It was the reaction of President Theodore Roosevelt.

Roosevelt was in a number of ways very like Sinclair. Both had been delicate boys who were later gifted with virtually inexhaustible energy and extraordinary talents for self-promotion and self-deception. As Sinclair was proud of what he considered his aristocratic Southern background, so Roosevelt was of his New York ancestors. They differed, however, in that Roosevelt was much more like most members of such elite power groups who attribute their privileged position to their innate merit and virtue and identify their own welfare with the state's. "There is something to be said," he wrote Sir Edward Grey, "for government by a great aristocracy which has furnished leaders to the nation in peace and war for generations."

Like Sinclair, however, Roosevelt expressed contempt for America's new aristocracy of money, made up of those parvenu "men very powerful in certain lines, and gifted with 'the money touch,' but with ideals which in their essence, are merely those of so many pawn brokers."

But if Roosevelt enjoyed "trust-busting" and excoriating "the malefactors of great wealth," at the same time he also admired America's industrial achievements. Finley Peter Dunne, too rarely thought of as one of the greatest of the muckrakers, best described Roosevelt's ambivalence: "Th' trusts, says he, are heejoous monsthers built up of th' enlightened intherprise iv th' men that have done so much to advance progress in our beloved country, he says. On wan hand I wud stamp thim undher fut; on th' other hand not so fast." Such ambivalence has been felt by many other Americans—from the first mild antitruster to the most recent lukewarm environmentalist—and encompasses both wanting to curb the ills resulting from the great corporations and at the same time wanting to enjoy the benefits the corporations provide.

Roosevelt tried earnestly if not always successfully to take a middle course, explaining to Boss Platt that he was "as resolutely against the improper corporate influence on the one hand as against demagogy and mob rule on the other."

About mid-January of 1906, review and publicity copies of *The Jungle* were sent out, and according to Mr. Dooley: "Th' hayro is a Lithuanian, or as ye might say, Pollacky, who left th' barb'rous land iv his birth an' come to this home iv opporchunity where ivrey man is th' equal iv ivry other man befure th' law if he isn't careful. . . .

"Annyhow, Tiddy was toying with a light breakfast an' idly turnin' over th' pages iv th' new book with both hands. Suddnnly he rose fr'm th' table, an' cryin': 'I'm pizened,' began throwin' sausages out iv th' window. . . . Since thin th' Prisidint, like th' rest iv us, has become a viggytaryan, an' th' diet has so changed his disposition that he is writin' a book called 'Supper in Silence,' . . . [and]Congress decided to abolish all th' days iv th' week except Friday."

Roosevelt had long been aware of Dr. Wiley's work and more importantly he quickly became aware of the voters' feelings which, as a result of many exposures but most especially of *The Jungle*, were reaching a crescendo. In the spring of 1906, Sinclair was invited to lunch at the White House where he listened to the President inveigh against various members of the Congress, and for the rest of his life Upton enjoyed mimicking Teddy. "I remember his words about Senator Hale of Maine, whom he called 'the

Senator from the Shipbuilding Trust'; you must recite the discourse with slow emphasis, showing your teeth, and hitting the table a separate thump at each accented syllable: 'The most in-nate-ly and es-sen-tial-ly mal-e-vo-lent scoun-drel that God Al-might-y-ev-er-put-on-earth!' "

Roosevelt was but confirming by his unfavorable comments on various senators much of David Graham Phillips' *The Treason of the Senate*, although it was this very work of Phillips' that so angered the President as to bring forth at the end of April the famous speech alluding to John Bunyan's man with a muck-rake. Said Roosevelt: "The men with the muck-rake are often indispensable to the well-being of Society, but only if they know when to stop raking the muck." Upton was learning that a President not infrequently speaks differently in private than in public and differently to different audiences.

When Roosevelt told Sinclair he was sending two men, Labor Commissioner Charles P. Neill and a social worker named James Bronson Reynolds, to investigate and report on conditions in the meat-packing industry, Sinclair was very concerned. He had learned from friends in the Chicago stockyards that the packers were working night and day to clean up or hide the worst abuses and was fearful that Roosevelt's investigators might be fooled by publicity men as Doubleday almost had been. Invited to go to Chicago for the investigation, he refused, but at his own expense sent two well-known Socialists, Ella Reeve Bloor and her husband, so that Roosevelt's commissioners might make contact with Chicago Socialists who would show them the truth.

Roosevelt's correspondence reveals what perspicacious students of American government have always known, that to be an effective President requires the bargaining tenacity of an Arab rug merchant as well as very considerable powers in extortion and blackmail by means, for example, of leak or threatened leak, and in bribery by means of pork barrel.

On March 12, 1906, clearly as a result of *The Jungle*, Roosevelt wrote Secretary of Agriculture James Wilson, "I wish you would carefully read through this letter [from Sinclair] yourself. It is evident that we do not want any merely perfunctory investigation at this time. The experiences that Moody has had in dealing with these beef trust people convinces me that there is very little that they will stop at. You know the wholesale newspaper bribery which they have undoubtedly indulged in. Now, I do not think that an ordinary investigation will reach anything. I would like a first-class man to be appointed to meet Sinclair, as he suggests; get the names of the witnesses, as he suggests; and then go to work in the industry, as he suggests. You must keep absolutely secret your choice of a man. Don't set about getting a man without consulting me. We cannot afford to have anything perfunctory done in this matter."

Three days later, the President wrote Sinclair: ". . . I have now read, if not all, yet a good deal of your book, and if you can come down here during the first week of April I shall be particularly glad to see you." He went on to explain carefully for the benefit of the younger man how uncomplimentary it was that Upton had been compared to Gorki, Zola, and Tolstoy: that Gorki's leadership would lead nowhere "save into a Serbonian bog," that "the net result of Zola's writing is evil," and that as for Tolstoy, his "*Kreutzer Sonata* could only have been written by a man of diseased moral nature. . . .

"In the end of your book various characters who preach socialism, almost all betray the pathetic belief that the individual capacity which is unable to raise itself even in the comparatively simple work of directing the individual how to earn his own livelihood, will, when it becomes the banded incapacity of all people, succeed in doing admirably a form of government work infinitely more complex, infinitely more difficult than any which the most intelligent and highly developed people has ever yet successfully tried. Personally I think that one of the chief early effects of such attempt to put socialism of the kind there preached into practice, would be the elimination by starvation, and the diseases, moral and physical, attendant upon starvation, of that same portion of the community on whose behalf socialism would be invoked. . . . there are doubtless communities where such self-raising is very hard for the time being; there are unquestionably men who are crippled by accident (as by being old and having large families dependent on them); there are many, many men who lack any intelligence or character and who therefore cannot thus raise themselves. But while I agree with you that energetic, and, as I believe, in the long run radical, action must be taken to do away with the effects of arrogant and selfish greed on the part of the capitalist, yet I am more than ever convinced that the real factor in the elevation of any man or any mass of men must be the development within his or their hearts and heads of the qualities which alone can make either the individual, the class or the nation permanently useful to themselves and to others."

Roosevelt added the postscript: "But all this has nothing to do with the fact that the specific evils you point out shall, if their existence be proved, and if I have power, be eradicated."

The sermon was not successful. Upton wrote a few days later to Jack

London, whom he credited for much of *The Jungle*'s success, "Oh, by the way, most important of all, Roosevelt has taken it up. I have had three letters from his majesty so far; the latest one a three-page discourse upon the futility of Socialism." In the same letter Upton displayed a delight at meeting the rich and socially prominent, which stayed with him always and would continually be pointed up by observers, Socialist and otherwise. He always explained it as a means of furthering his causes, or laughed at himself. "I met Mrs. Clarence Mackay at Hunter's last night. She has been distributing it [*The Jungle*] around among her friends; twenty-five copies altogether, and it was amusing to hear her tell some of the results. Also Doubleday told me that Mark Twain had told him he tried to read it and couldn't and that was the first time such a thing had ever happened to him in his life."

All the while Roosevelt was fighting for the Pure Food and Drug Act, Sinclair plagued him with letters, magazine articles, and newspaper interviews. Annoyed at this Socialist gadfly, he wrote Sinclair: "I have received your letter and also your telegram. From the latter you seemed a good deal more agitated than the facts warrant. . . . Let me repeat that both you and your correspondents must keep your heads if you expect to make your work of value. . . . Keep quiet, just as I shall keep quiet, and let the investigation go on. . . . [and, finally, in a handwritten second postscript] Your second telegram has just come; really, Mr. Sinclair, you *must* keep your head. It is absurd to become so nervous over such an article. Hundreds such appear about me all the time, with quite as little foundation."

Far from being awed by the President, the twenty-seven-year-old Upton by letter, wire, and in the press goaded Roosevelt, until finally the older man wrote: "you do not seem to feel bound to avoid making and repeating utterly reckless statements. . . . But my own duty is entirely different. I am bound to see that nothing but the truth appears; that this truth does in its entirety appear; and that it appears in such shape that practical results for good will follow. . . . Until these investigations are finished and until the results are in final form, I should most emphatically object to having them made public unless it should become necessary to make a preliminary and unfinished portion of them public in order to secure the passage of some measure substantially like the Beveridge amendment. . . . The vital matter is to remedy the evils with the least possible damage to innocent people. The premature publication that you request would doubtless cause great pecuniary loss not merely to the beef packers and to all those responsible for so much of the conditions as are bad, but also to scores of thousands of stock growers, ranchers, hired men, cowboys, farmers and farm hands all over this country, who have been guilty of no misconduct whatever. Some of the men thus hurt would be wealthy men. Most of them would be poor men. If it is necessary ultimately to hurt them in order that the reform shall be accomplished, then they must be hurt; but I shall certainly not hurt them needlessly nor wantonly. My object is to remedy the evils. The facts shall be made public in due time. . . . To 'give the people the facts,' as you put it, without pointing out how to better the conditions, would chiefly be of service to the apostles of sensationalism and would work little or no permanent betterment in the conditions. Now what I intend to bring about is just precisely this permanent betterment. . . ."

Seeing that letters to Sinclair were not effective, the President suggested to Frank Doubleday, "Tell Sinclair to go home and let me run the country for a while."

The President used as his chief agent in the Senate Indiana's Albert Jeremiah Beveridge, an old friend and ally who had already helped in the fight for railroad regulation and would later prove equally stalwart for the graduated income tax and legislation on child labor. Beveridge's bill cleared the Senate on May 25 as an amendment to the Agricultural Appropriations bill, but in the House of Representatives the walrus-mustached chairman of the House Committee on Agriculture, James W. Wadsworth, would not move.

On May 26, Roosevelt wrote Wadsworth warning him that the secret Neill-Reynolds report was "hideous" and that the outrageous conditions it described must be remedied at once. He confided that he was at first so indignant at the meat industry that he was going to send the whole report to the Congress, thereby making it public, but would not if Wadsworth would report out Beveridge's amendment. But his threat was plain. "I should not make the report public with the idea of damaging the packers. I should do it only if it were necessary in order to secure the remedy."

When the packers, who had been generous contributors to Roosevelt's campaigns, refused to believe his threat and had Wadsworth offer emasculating amendments to Beveridge's bill, Roosevelt sent the first part of the Neill-Reynolds report to the House with a message demanding passage. The effect of this government confirmation of Sinclair's worldwide best seller was a precipitous drop in American meat sales in Europe and the packers and their creatures in Congress crumbled after some further bargaining.

Roosevelt agreed to a few compromises, for example, that the government should pay the cost of inspections and, more unfortunately, that the date of inspection need not be put on canned products. But Roosevelt refused to compromise on civil service status for inspectors, the government's right to stop inspecting (that is, to stop approving) meat in plants that refused to act on its suggestions, and he killed the packers' plan to drown enforcement in a sea of litigation by appealing the legality or constitutionality of each unfavorable ruling.

It is hardly surprising that two such men as Roosevelt and Sinclair should each exaggerate his own role in the passage of the first enforceable national Pure Food and Drug Act and Meat Inspection Act while downgrading the other's.

Roosevelt, who would not even mention Sinclair or Wiley in his *Autobiography*, really feared that a revolutionary feeling was being built up by the muckrakers and the Socialist Party. He thought of Sinclair and the other muckrakers and even of Wiley as fanatics whose excessive demands did more harm than good, and who would have done little or no good at all without his moderating role as Solomon. So absent from Roosevelt's makeup were modesty and humility that Finley Peter Dunne had suggested he write a book called *Alone In Cubia*.

Just as the muckrakers were dependent on Roosevelt, or someone like him, to put their reforms at least partially into effect, so Roosevelt was dependent on the muckrakers to whip up enough feeling in the country to move a generally lethargic and venal Congress, and such dependence bred mutual anger.

Neither Sinclair nor Wiley was shy about taking credit, nor generous about giving any to the President. Roosevelt's contempt for fanatics was shared by theirs for cowards who did less than was possible. The bills as finally passed were, of course, less than ideal, but they provided a base upon which building is still going on, and in addition to eliminating some of the worst evils in the drug and food trades, the legislation extended the scope of federal administrative rule and enlarged the whole concept of a national duty and power to police and protect.

Upton Beall Sinclair and Priscilla Harden Sinclair, Upton's father and mother.

Upton in Baltimore about eight years old.

SAW IT IN TIME—FLY TIME.

Uncle Josh Green (in Bowery restaurant)—Look a
here, waiter; I just found this here fly in my soup.
Slopsy Muggs—Ah, dat's all right, boss. He didn'
have time to eat none of it.

Upton's writing career began when in
his teens he sold jokes, including this
one, to magazines and cartoonists.

∞

According to Upton, this photograph
was taken before *The Jungle* when he
was "too poor to get a haircut."

Meta Fuller Sinclair, Upton's first wife. (Courtesy David Sinclair)

Upton with his son, David, on the porch of the Princeton farm in 1905.

At Princeton during the writing of *The Jungle*.

At Princeton.

A postcard printed at the height of the scandal touched off by *The Jungle*.
The description reads: "What is said about the toilet facilities is best left
unprinted."

A world reformer and poet pauses to be photographed.

CHAPTER VIII

A Hard Act to Follow

I do not love the money. What I do love is the getting of it . . . . What other interest can you suggest to me? I do not read. I do not take part in politics. What can I do? PHILIP D. ARMOUR

"NOT SINCE BYRON AWOKE ONE MORNING to find himself famous," proclaimed the New York *Evening World*, "has there been such an example of worldwide celebrity won in a day by a book as has come to Upton Sinclair." H. G. Wells, before he set out for America in the spring of 1906, "was asked by a friend to look up a certain Upton Sinclair, a young writer of genius, who was starving in New York. Dutifully he promised, but arrived to find *The Jungle* the sensation of the year, and Sinclair not merely a wealthy man but the centre of the world's attention."

The young man who had so hated being ignored was not one to let such celebrity, once achieved, slip away. "I moved up to New York and opened an amateur publicity office in a couple of hotel rooms, with two secretaries working overtime. I gave interviews and wrote statements for the press until I was dizzy, and when I lay down to sleep at two o'clock in the morning, my brain would go on working. It seemed to me that the walls of the mighty fortress of greed were on the point of cracking; it needed only one push, and then another, and another."

In the years that followed, his enemies would admit his genius for self-promotion and attribute its incessant use to simple vanity. Upton would insist that because his Socialist ideas were forbidden subjects in the bourgeois press, the only way he could get publicity for them was to get publicity for himself.

Much written about him and Meta, in the daily press and especially in the Sunday supplements of the day was reportorial fiction, not infrequently put into the form of direct quotations from the young Socialist himself. A great many articles contained not only unintentional misinformation, but were assigned to reporters by their editors as blowup pieces. Upton was aware that publicity might harm as well as help. But despite his fervid protests against publicity he deemed unfair or inaccurate (which protests not infrequently got him and his causes even more publicity in the letters-to-the-editor columns), he operated all his life on Phineas Taylor Barnum's theory that any and all publicity is good publicity; that as he often put it in the phrase of the day, "every knock is a boost."

The sudden somebody of course made gaffes. He confessed in a letter to Jack London that fans complained when he autographed his books "The Author." He also sent London, whose fame he had so recently dreamed of and envied and would soon surpass, a letter he had received from Doubleday advising that on one day they had sold fifty-five hundred copies of *The Jungle.*

Upton reveled in the many evidences of his increasing fame: being asked by *Life* what good books he was reading; hearing from Herron "I find your books and your name everywhere here in England"; seeing himself parodied in the press; being asked by other prominent men such as Henry James to serve on honorary committees and to sign various protests, manifestos, and appeals; and even being asked to run for Congress on the Socialist ticket, which he did unsuccessfully a number of times. With the understanding that he would not have to devote any substantial time to running, he allowed the Socialists to nominate him in 1906 as their candidate for Congress for the Fourth District of New Jersey, and he polled only some 750 out of 24,000 votes.

But delightful as these badges of fame were, Upton's chief business was writing and the chief question was what to write now—how to top or even to equal *The Jungle.* For some time he continued to have intermittent illusions of returning to poetry. Asked by an interviewer if his next book would be modeled on the same lines, he answered firmly, " 'It will not. I am done with journalistic novel writing. I am a poet. My next story will be patterned after my ideals. Don't you think I have gone through enough to be entitled to this satisfaction?' "

But the truth was that Upton had at last found his real métier, as he explained in "What Life Means to Me," in *Cosmopolitan*: "to put the content of Shelley into the form of Zola . . . . The proletarian writer is a writer with a purpose; he thinks no more of 'art for art's sake' than a man on a sinking ship thinks of painting a beautiful picture in the cabin; he thinks of getting ashore—and then there will be time enough for art.

"And that is what life means to me. So far as I myself am concerned, the well-springs of joy and beauty have been dried up in me—the flowers no longer sing to me as they used to, nor the sunrise, nor the stars; I have become a soldier upon a hard campaign—I am thinking only of the enemy."

But before attacking the enemy with new books, Sinclair was determined finally to establish a satisfactory home in which to work. Money was no longer a problem, he had thirty thousand dollars in hand and as much more available as he cared to earn.

His back-to-nature, agricultural delusions had been forever dispelled by experience, and what he sought now was a cooperative establishment in which he and Meta would be spared most of the duties and problems relating to food, maintenance, and child care. Meta's increasing obsession with her own unhappiness had left to Upton more and more domestic responsibilities that kept him from his higher messianic duties. This would not be the first nor last time that a reformer tried to solve the world's problems by solving his own.

As a Socialist he had learned that having one's own home was only a foolish relic of bourgeois individualism, and he had also observed that in fact some of the very richest and most socially prominent people in America practiced, at least part time, cooperative living. They owned land in common and on it built or rented individual "cottages," but used a common living room, kitchen, and meeting rooms. They naturally used no revolutionary or radical language, their communal practice being called a "club."

After an article by Upton on his proposed utopia had brought together like-minded people, who formed committees and investigated various locations, the "colonists" bought a former boys' school, Helicon Hall, overlooking Englewood, New Jersey, with a view of the Hackensack Valley as far as the Ramapo Mountains.

Although all Upton's enemies and some of his friends always considered him a head-in-the-clouds visionary with no practical knowledge of everyday economics, he became, in fact, an extraordinarily able and imaginative money raiser. He was especially good at writing copy that effectively induced people to part with money, while at the same time he stayed within the Socialist rhetoric. In 1906 he had already begun the direct-by-mail promotion of his own books to his growing list of correspondents, friends, and customers. With the late 1906 flyer that announced an upcoming cheap edition of *The Jungle* as well as *The Industrial Republic*, he enclosed a prospectus of the Helicon Home Colony that stated: "If you would be interested in an investment, every dollar of which is secured by gilt-edged real estate, and which pays an income of eight percent, guaranteed by Comrade Sinclair personally, we will be glad to send you information concerning the Home Colony Company, which owns the property occupied by the Colony."

The colony had a diversified assortment of some forty adults—intellectuals, New Thoughtists, Socialists, Single-taxers, ranging from college professors to two Yale dropouts hired as janitors, one of whom, Sinclair Lewis, would thereafter be confused by much of the public with Upton Sinclair.

Lewis, as Upton himself had been earlier, was "thoroughly bored with years of sitting in classrooms sucking in secondhand wisdom." With his friend Allan Updegraff he spent a month at Helicon Hall where by his own account he was an unsatisfactory and underpaid general chore boy; where he fell in love with Upton's secretary, Edith Summers, who became his first fiancée but who married Updegraff; and "where else than at Helicon Hall could I have learned so many new things every minute; or of how little worth I am in manual labor, seen so many novel yet vital things and have met in intimacy and equality so many thoroughly worthwhile people?"

Helicon Hall was a cooperative colony rather than a Socialist one, but its members were nevertheless hypersensitive about the problem of paid servants that seemed inevitably to plague even the most egalitarian of utopian enterprises. Its members were perfectly willing, indeed anxious, to treat the cook, the laundress, and the chore boy as equals, so long as they themselves could avoid cooking, washing, and all onerous chores.

The colony had as members Columbia professors William Noyes and W. P. Montague, Edwin Björkman, the critic, and a stream of distinguished visitors ranging from John Dewey and William James to sculptor Jo Davidson. The latter brought with him the art critic Sadakichi Hartmann who was drunk and when refused a bed for the night and put out in the snow wrote a highly critical letter to the papers about the colony.

The press was full of stories about the founding and functioning of Helicon Hall. *The New York Times* in a large Sunday picture story poked rather gentle fun. "There is nothing of 'The Jungle' about cooperation as it will be practiced by Upton Sinclair's colony . . . filled with everything that the traditional ascetic [needs] . . . a huge swimming pool, a bowling alley, a theatre, a glass covered courtyard . . . wherein plays a fountain in the midst of tropical plants [including] . . . a gigantic rubber tree—the largest to be found north of Mexico."

Other stories concentrated on such controversial aspects of the colony as its women having the vote, evidences of prejudice against blacks and Jews, and especially, of course, on what virtually all American newspapers and their readers considered the *sine qua non* of Socialism, "free love."

"It was generally taken for granted," Sinclair wrote, "among the newspapermen of New York, that the purpose for which I had started this colony was to have plenty of mistresses handy. . . . I do not know of any assemblage of forty adult persons where a higher standard of sexual morals prevailed."

Such public protestations of sexual probity are not surprising from self-appointed reformers. What is surprising, however, is that Sinclair had an affair at Helicon Hall with Professor Noyes' wife, Anna; at least Meta in her diaries describes Upton's confession of the adultery in such detail as to make the affair seem real. Indeed, increasingly after the publication of *The Jungle*, both Meta and Upton had become disposed to "falling in love" and telling each other about it in great detail, in the firm belief that the other would understand. After his discovery of Socialism, Upton professed to believe that for women bourgeois marriage was a form of slavery and prostitution that would disappear as soon as women were legally and economically the equals of men. His emotions, however, were not always controlled by his intellect.

While Upton had been researching and writing *The Jungle*, Meta had been gravely ill and the sympathy and understanding of the hospital's young house doctor contrasted markedly with Upton's almost exclusive concentration on his novel. She told Upton she was in love with this man and of the peace she felt only when he visited her each night with his morphine needle. Sinclair wrote the doctor a letter that scared him off.

Her notebooks reveal: "By this time they had been married six years and she found that her girlish ardour for learning was beginning to wane. She found herself longing for something else . . . but when she made demands upon Thyrsis for this 'something else' . . . it irritated and annoyed him."

Upton's "spasmodic and desultory fits of love-making" left Meta with "unsatisfied longings for both . . . emotional and physical satisfaction." In the bitter later years, Upton would allege that Meta was dissolute and oversexed, and Meta would declare that he was underdeveloped and imply the possibility of suppressed homosexuality, but the truth more probably was that Meta, unfulfilled in many areas, sought solace in sex for all her various frustrations and that Upton was too selfish and too fearful of having another child. But his unwillingness to study and learn about sex when he took the time necessary to educate himself on so many other subjects must also have had deeper psychological reasons including both his attitudes toward his mother's goodness and toward his father's weakness.

Meta next tried and found temporary relief for her frustrations in Christian Science, which also infuriated Upton, because he said it was rank superstition, but possibly also because it gave Meta an authority to look to other than his. He bullied her into dropping it, and her pains and problems returned. Ironically, Sinclair's second wife would also seek and find comfort in Christian Science, and this time he would content himself with calling it "self-hypnosis," of which he approved. And Upton by his own account was later cured of a nearly fatal case of hiccoughs by a Christian Science practitioner.

But Meta was not alone in her dissatisfaction. Upton too found their sex life inadequate and made forays in search not only of sex but probably also of the kind of idolatry that Meta no longer displayed and that more often characterizes the beginning of an affair than a marriage of some years. Meta's first inkling that, like her, Upton was also subject to sexual temptation had come when she returned from New York to the farm in Princeton to discover that Margaret Mayo, the Broadway actress and wife of Upton's play broker, Edgar Selwyn, had been staying there. Upton had signed a contract to make *The Jungle* into a play and to list Miss Mayo as co-author. According to Meta: "He told Corydon that he and Mrs. X had become very well acquainted during their collaboration and that she had 'fallen in love' with him . . . . he wanted Corydon to know about it in minutest detail . . . . he even described the flimsy texture of her nightgown when she had sat upon the bed beside him. He had been horrified that he had allowed her to do so, when 'she had begged him for only a little happiness.' In much consternation at the excitement he admitted it had caused him, he urged her to leave him, which I believe she finally did, leaving him also inviolate."

One day at Helicon Hall, however, Upton simply asked Meta to come to his office, where she discovered when she arrived that he had also summoned Professor Noyes' wife. There he explained carefully that, just as in Edward Carpenter's *Love's Coming of Age*, which he had given Meta to study on the subject of "free love," he and Anna Noyes were "in love." Anna urged Meta not to worry, that it was not practicable for her and Upton to go off together and that she planned to advise her husband of the arrangement.

Later, when Upton and Meta were alone, he assured her this was in the nature of an experiment of which the outcome was as yet unpredictable and cautioned her to keep the affair secret because, "It wouldn't do to have the papers get hold of it."

Two weeks later he advised Meta that the experiment was over, and she confided to her diary that "she was truly glad and for awhile they came together as husband and wife." But with a timing clearly implying tit-for-tat, Meta's diary next reveals that although up to this time she had "never indulged in petting parties" she now did so with Armistead Collier, "but this was all." Her correspondence with Collier, however, suggests a far more intimate relationship.

Upton frequently wrote against the double standard and all forms of exploitation of women, which he equated with capitalism's exploitation of the laboring class. He subscribed not only to this good Socialist dogma, but also to the more poetic, indeed Shelleyan, views about women and marriage: that one should go, man or woman, married or single, wherever love led; that not love but only jealousy was an obscenity; that to the right-minded, love gave all rights and marriage took away none.

But his feelings as opposed to his resolutions and his rhetoric were not infrequently still closer to his early letters to Meta such as the one referring to Beethoven's breaking a woman's heart in order that she might sing. Upton could write of free love in marriage and could infrequently and briefly experiment with it himself, but he was basically monogamous and his only real wife was his work. It would be Meta who finally passionately practiced the free love Upton preached and it would horrify him.

A practicing, proselyting and imperfect feminist for most of his adult life, on those occasions when his reactions were sexist, he was usually able as he grew older, to recognize and confess it. "I am not able to think of anything that I dislike in women that I don't also dislike in men. I have been a feminist all my life, and I don't think I make any distinctions between my attitude toward women and that toward men. The first thought that came to me when I read your question was that I dislike women who argue persistently and in loud voices. I have known several such women, but then I have known men who do the same, and I find it equally unpleasant in the men. I dislike women who are prejudiced and unreasonable, and I dislike men of the same sort equally as much."

At Helicon Hall, Meta was not yet sure what she wanted, but increasingly she was becoming convinced that whatever it was, Upton could not supply it and if she was ever to be made into "a woman to love" as Upton had promised, she would have to do it herself with the help of a man or men other than he.

Helicon Hall may not have been a perfect Paradise for its forty adults, but it was delicious for its fourteen children, who frolicked in its woods, filled its indoor pools and rubber-tree jungle with imaginary wild beasts, and, uninhibited by parental restrictions, played "naked at night in the little theatre nursery, what bliss!"

The problems and blessings of utopia ended abruptly. Four and a half months after Helicon Hall had begun, a fire in the small hours of the morning entirely destroyed the colony. The only death was that of a visiting carpenter; no members of the colony or their children were seriously injured. Sinclair hinted to *The New York Times* that the fire had been set by the Steel Trust and stated that three weeks earlier a stick of dynamite had been found in the cellar.

Upton and Meta first moved in with the Gaylord Wilshires and then took a house at West Point Pleasant, New Jersey. Although Upton wept in print for his lost Paradise, he never started another.

Before Steffens' strikingly similar statement in 1919 to Bernard Baruch about the Soviet Union, Upton said repeatedly about his Helicon Hall experience, "I have lived in the future," and declared that all his later living conditions were drab and sordid by comparison. These statements would have been much more moving if they were not so transparently untrue. Nothing prevented Upton from starting a new Helicon Hall except the fact that he didn't want to. He had learned that the individual who leaves his own home to run a utopian colony does not lessen his problems but rather magnifies and multiplies them. He would live in a variety of other such colonies, at Fairhope, Alabama, and at Arden, Delaware, but as a visitor and not as the man in charge. His martyred tone in these statements is perhaps as offensive as their untruth, and happily both are rare in his writing.

Collecting from the insurance company and selling the land took some months, but apparently neither Sinclair nor any other stockholder of the Home Colony Company lost economically by the experiment.

What might have been another tragedy for Upton, but in fact was not, occurred on April 5, 1907, when his pathetic father died in New York. There is no mention of the date in the son's writings or correspondence.

Priscilla would survive, a lonely widow, another twenty-four years, seeing less and less of her famous but embarrassingly Socialist son, and hearing from him with decreasing regularity. For some years he sent her a monthly check ranging from twenty-five to one hundred dollars. But then even these stopped and she was supported entirely by her rich sister, Maria Bland.

Over the years, Upton would allege that his reason for not contributing to his mother's support was simple. "She has a millionaire sister who is well able to help her. The sister is cross with me for not doing it, but that seems to be the nature of most millionaires, so I don't worry about it." But the whole reason was not so simple. He would say that he was exasperated by his mother's dislike for his writing, his politics, his wives. But even this, in fact, was only a rationalization that derived from what was probably the primary cause. Like so many reformers, he cared for no one and for nothing other than his own mission, and he resented demands that implied this was self-centered—the more obviously it was, the more he was vexed.

But there were other important reasons too, such as those he confided to David when Priscilla died. "She was the best of mothers up to about the age (my age) of 16. Then I grew beyond her, & she wouldn't follow, or couldn't. If she'd let me alone, it could have been all right; but she still thought I was a child & stubbornly fought to direct my life & *mind*. So for 35 years I could not meet her without a controversy starting . . . .

". . . C's mother [his second mother-in-law] was always very kind to me, & sent me $50 a month for years. But my mother never was even polite to C—just blind jealousy, & the usual scolding . . . . my mother never had a gleam of interest in any of my ideals—never anything but holding me to & for herself."

Although after *The Jungle* Upton was often in debt, he was never again poor. He always had money enough to remain a free lance, almost in the medieval sense used by Walter Scott of fighting only for whom or what he chose and not employed permanently by a single master. That he sent no money to his mother and wrote her only when he needed her help to take care of David or to do him a favor indicates the strength of his repudiation of that extraordinarily close relationship with her he had as a child. The repudiation was also perhaps not unrelated to his fear to love and be loved—two of those difficult to control needs.

Meanwhile, tragedy was building for Meta. In the summer of 1907, following the fire, Meta by her own account "became pregnant which proved a source of worry to them both. It seemed to Corydon a terrible moment in which to conceive a child and subsequently the doctors felt she was in no condition to carry one . . . and three months later Corydon went to the hospital for another operation. After being there for two weeks they took a cottage at Point Pleasant. . . .

"They had been there but a few weeks when Corydon developed appendicitis." Meta nowhere made any mention of a miscarriage, and no child other than David was born to Meta during her marriage to Upton.

In his autobiography, Sinclair refers vaguely to a diagnosis of Meta's illness as menstrual and also to her appendicitis but makes absolutely no mention of her pregnancy or her first visit to the hospital and the operation that she mentioned but never described.

In fact, Meta had an almost fatal abortion, from which she suffered so terribly and remained in such critical condition that in mid-August Upton sent her and her mother and doctor to Dr. Kellogg's famous Battle Creek Sanitarium. Upton issued a statement to *The New York Times* about his wife's health, but the real purpose of the statement was to deny widely published stories that their marriage was troubled. He denied any trouble of any sort at any time and threatened court action against any papers that alleged to the contrary.

David stayed with Upton's secretary and a maid at Point Pleasant. The husband and father, typically, was undismayed by which of his two family responsibilities had the greater call upon his comforting presence—he fled "to the Adirondack wilderness to get away from the worry and strain of it all!" There he finished his novel *The Metropolis*, which was so bad that, despite Upton's notoriety, Doubleday would refuse to publish it and thus end the firm's relationship with Sinclair.

The triumph of *The Jungle* had been so great that Doubleday had contracted to publish all four of Upton's earlier unsuccessful novels. They would take over his plates and his unsold inventory, which he had bought from previous publishers. Doubleday also published in 1907 both *The Overman*, which he had written in 1901–02, and *The Industrial Republic*, most of which he had written at Helicon Hall.

The Industrial Republic, in which Upton prophesied that William Randolph Hearst would defeat Teddy Roosevelt for the Presidency in 1912 and would be followed within a year by a Socialist revolution, was a disaster. Because of the book's poor sales and also because Upton was embarrassed by its incorrect prophecies, it was one of the few books never reprinted by its author.

The Overman was equally unfortunate. Both proved that Sinclair's novels unless based on fact were usually bad. Because he lacked the imagination to invent fiction, his best novels, *The Jungle*, *Oil!* and *Boston*, were all solidly based on real people and events.

In *The Metropolis* Sinclair tried to expose the real life of the rich in the same way that he had exposed the life of the poor in *The Jungle*. His leading character, Allan Montague, son of the hero of *Manassas* and one of many innocents in Upton's fiction, is educated by his experiences in high society, experiences Upton himself learned about when he was taken up after *The Jungle* by New York's "smart set"—Mrs. Oliver Hazard Perry Belmont, Mrs. Clarence Mackay, and others less frightened of his radicalism than of boredom. The ladies taught Upton about life uptown on Fifth Avenue, while some of New York's best corporation lawyers, including Samuel Untermyer and James B. Dill, whom he met through Lincoln Steffens, amused themselves by teaching the charming revolutionary about Wall Street and life downtown. That politicians were often, if not usually, merely the creatures of rich businessmen was not, however, news to Upton.

Although Upton had told *Cosmopolitan*'s readers that his war against injustice no longer left him the time or inclination to enjoy the beauties of nature, it was untrue, and in *The Metropolis* he wrote one of the early American protests against the spoliation of nature by capitalist industry and its adjunct, outdoor advertising.

Sinclair later admitted *The Metropolis* was "a poor book," giving a variety of reasons—one cause, the apparently inescapable bedbugs, this time in the walls of the shack at Point Pleasant where he had begun writing the novel. However, in explaining why Doubleday turned the book down, he attributed it to the fact that they also published *World's Work*, a magazine that ran advertisements from the very banks and trust companies muckraked in the novel. This mild paranoia, if indeed it was paranoia at all, appears occasionally but usually jocularly in Sinclair's work. He complained, for example, that "the date selected by the Maker of History for the destruction of San Francisco by earthquake and fire" was the day before his answer to Armour appeared in *Everybody's*, thus providing "the capitalist news agencies . . . an excuse for not sending out any stories about the Condemned Meat Industry!" Similarly, soon after his novel *Oil!* was banned in Boston and Upton went there to capitalize on the publicity, Lindbergh returned from his solo flight to France and for some weeks "there was nothing in the American newspapers but the 'lone eagle' and the advertisements!"

On the other hand, Doubleday suppressed the book of Judge Ben Lindsey of the Denver Children's Court, which as "The Beast and the Jungle" had caused a sensation in *Everybody's*. Called the "Just Judge" by Steffens, Lindsey was one of Upton's best friends among his fellow muckrakers. Lindsey's long fight against privilege, prejudice, and corruption, and in behalf of juveniles and prostitutes resulted in his defamation as a sex pervert.

As Upton pointed out, Doubleday's was "the same trick they played upon Theodore Dreiser, but never upon Upton Sinclair, you can wager! If there should ever be another crop of 'muckrakers' in America, here is a tip they will find useful: put a clause into your contract to the effect that if at any time the publisher fails to keep the book and sell it to all who care to buy it, the author may have the rights to the use of the plates, and print and sell an edition of his own. That makes it impossible for the publishers to 'sell you out'; the would be buyer, when he reads that clause, will realize he is buying nothing."

Sinclair followed his own advice. During the busiest decades of his life

PCHS Media Center
Grant, Nebraska

he carried on an enormous business of publishing and marketing most of his own books. This took much of his time and energy and, for him, large amounts of capital, but it enabled him also to publish some of his most important books of exposure that were thought too hot to handle by commercial publishers.

His critics jeered that his keeping his own books in print long after there was any substantial demand for them constituted proof of Upton's vanity and doubtless it was that too. But also, and primarily, it enabled him to avoid suppression by what his friend Steffens had christened "The System," the suppression that Dreiser, Lindsey, and others suffered or altered their writings in order not to suffer.

The Metropolis appeared first in serial form in the *American Magazine*, which had been taken over in October 1906, when they left *McClure's*, by John S. Phillips, Ida Tarbell, Lincoln Steffens, Ray Stannard Baker, Finley Peter Dunne, and William Allen White. It was published in book form by Moffet, Yard and Company, from whom Upton, no longer shy about demanding money, had extracted an advance of five thousand dollars and a 20 percent royalty instead of the usual 10 percent graduating to 15. Even by his own account, however, the book sold only eighteen thousand copies, and so the royalty was meaningless and Upton had left behind yet another dissatisfied publisher.

Sinclair's next novel, *The Moneychangers*, was published September 19, 1908, by B. W. Dodge and Company and was dedicated to Jack London. It was another attempt to explain The System, specifically, as the cover announced, "How Wall Street manufactured the Panic of 1907." Upton had been told in great detail by the prominent attorney Edmond Kelly how the Panic of 1907 was begun by J. P. Morgan's forcing the failure of the Knickerbocker Trust Company. Upton signed a contract with the *American Magazine* to write a serial that might well have been the most important exposé of the period in terms of bringing about needed national legislation, but soon thereafter, John S. Phillips begged him to release the magazine from the contract, which Upton did. Historians now accept that the panic began as "a rich man's panic." At the time, however, virtually everyone except Sinclair was too afraid to blame it on Morgan and his cohorts, who in their turn blamed it on Roosevelt, the "mad messiah." This sufficiently frightened the President so that he shortly allowed Morgan's greatest creation, the United States Steel Corporation, to take over Tennessee Coal and Iron Company, thus suppressing competition by forcing the Southern steel mills to raise their prices to those of Pittsburgh.

In Upton's novel, Dan Waterman, a thinly disguised portrait of the elder Pierpont Morgan, is pictured as a wild boar, both in his business dealings and in his dealings with women. A steel magnate who sells the United States Navy faulty armor plate and ends his days building libraries is called Harrison, though transparently modeled on Carnegie; and when there is a major steel strike, Harrison leaves its cruel suppression to William Roberts, just as Carnegie had left the brutal breaking of the Homestead strike to Henry Clay Frick.

The hero of *The Moneychangers* is the same Allan Montague of *The Metropolis*. To him, wise, old Major Venable carefully explains the involuted business tricks of Waterman, just as Morgan's chicaneries had been carefully explained to Sinclair by Kelly, Dill, and Untermyer. Sinclair's skill in explaining complicated processes simply and interestingly continued to grow as he described how law courts upheld the rich and powerful and triggered the great panic itself. At the end of the book when the hero is asked what the remedy is, he replies, "to teach the people," but he plans to do so not by writing but by going into politics, as would the author a quarter of a century later.

Allan Montague is one of Sinclair's most cardboard heroes. Tempted neither by the sexual advances of Mrs. Winnie Duval (which are identical to those of Margaret Mayo as described by Upton to Meta) nor by the rewards of Wall Street (which had also been refused by Upton after *The Jungle*), he is, in fact, nothing but the author's surrogate. Upton had again planned a trilogy—*The Metropolis* and *The Moneychangers* were novels, but the third part, *The Machine*, was written as a play.

In 1913 Democratic Representative Arsene Pujo in the report of his committee and Louis D. Brandeis in *Other People's Money* would show that Morgan and a few fellow bankers controlled whatever they wanted in the country and would thereby help pave the way for the immediate enactment of the Federal Reserve Act, the Federal Trade Commission, and the Clayton Antitrust Act, as well as subsequent legislation to curb the power of The System. But in 1908 Sinclair was virtually alone in his criticism. Only the "yellow press" echoed Upton's charges, for example, the New York *American* of September 6, 1908:

U.S. NAVY ADMITS ROTTEN ARMOR
Carnegie Co.'s Profit, $700,000
ADMIRAL MASON SAYS OREGON
NOW CARRIED 400 TONS

Indiana, Massachusetts, New York and Others Also
Have Defective Plates
FACTS HIDDEN 15 YEARS
Revelations in Upton Sinclair's New Novel Are
Fully Verified

Washington, Sept. 5—Rear-Admiral W. P. Mason, Chief of the Bureau of Ordnance, in an interview to-day admitted that the battleship Oregon, once the pride of the United States Navy, has carried since the day she was built 400 tons of defective armor plate . . . .

The investigation made by the "American" was prompted by the assertion in Upton Sinclair's new book, "The Money-changers," that "there are ships in our navy covered with rotten armor plate that was sold to the Government for four or five times what it cost."

The next day Sinclair implied in a front-page story in the equally "yellow" New York *World* that the "Steel Crowd" had set fire to Helicon Hall to destroy his evidence of their frauds. He specifically named William E. Corey, the president of Morgan's United States Steel Corporation, as well as E. H. Harriman. This was the practice Sinclair would continue to follow—to attack the committing of evil by (or by the employees of) great public figures, men so prominent that some newspaper would be unable to resist printing the story. He took on the two most powerful men in America, Morgan and Rockefeller, at a time when even a Progressive President sometimes truckled to them. Not wanting anything in the giving (or the taking away) of such men, Upton was willing or perhaps even anxious to incur their enmity, and his attacks upon them did two kinds of good. First they exposed the particular evil and declared it unacceptable to a society so believing in social Darwinism that it accepted or at least condoned as unavoidable almost any evil committed in the name of free enterprise. Secondly, they gave a more accurate picture than most people had seen of the mythic hero of that America, the successful businessman.

But there was a darker side also to Upton's attacks. He was not always as careful as he might have been about the accuracy of some of his details, and he repeatedly pointed out that the important men he attacked would choose not to challenge any inaccuracies, at least not to contest them in a court of law, lest questioning there, under oath, might reveal other unknown sins they had committed.

Practically and legally, Sinclair was right. He was never successfully sued for libel or slander by anyone he attacked. But morally his position was unacceptable and claiming such an attack is in the public interest does not make it less unacceptable. The best way to avoid libel suits is not to "be sure that the criminal has committed worse crimes than the ones you reveal," but to seek scrupulously to avoid committing a libel.

Unfortunately, love for his own causes, hatred of sins or sinners or both, love of publicity for its own sake or for the purpose of selling more books, occasionally shoddy research, paranoia, and the excitement of the moment sometimes led Sinclair to public statements without substance. For example, in the September 7, 1908, article in *The World*, Upton's intimations that steelmen set the Helicon Hall fire were sensational but false, and that he later thought as much himself was indicated by his omission of this charge (without indicating the omission) when he quoted the article in *The Brass Check*, as well as its omission from his autobiography.

His anger also sometimes led him to *ad hominem* arguments, for example his attack in *The Brass Check* of "the sexual habits" of Adolph Ochs which were, of course, unrelated to the honesty or lack of it at *The New York Times*. It is especially ironic that Upton's attack follows pages of outrage at New York newspapers for printing scandal about George D. Herron.

But these were exceptional cases. Virtually everyone who knew Sinclair, then or later, dwelled on his loving nature. The great civil rights leader, Roger Baldwin, who knew Sinclair for sixty years, remembered especially: "against all evidence to the contrary, his optimism and hope. His expression was always sweet, slightly smiling with a good twinkle in his eye. There was always a certain boyishness about him. His voice was soft and I never heard him raise it in indignation or emphasis. Even when he spoke on the public platform there was this expression of smiling intimacy—he held the audience by his earnestness, without notes or gestures, just with his charm and wit."

Similarly, a visitor to Helicon Hall wrote long afterwards, "I have never forgotten his handsome, almost girlish face, his modest manner, his quiet voice; here, I felt, was an honest and dedicated man."

What made Sinclair seem sweet to those who met him was his quite genuine love for people, the same love that made him angry with the prevailing view of the day that people must inevitably be brutalized, that society was and should be a jungle in which only the fittest should survive. He was neither the first nor the only American writer to try to picture realistically the complex, often cruel, new industrial society America had become and to recognize with horror that to most Americans successful businessmen were more important and dramatic figures than even the cowboys and cavalrymen and ships' captains of earlier days.

In *The Octopus* in 1901 and *The Pit* in 1903, Frank Norris, who like Upton was much influenced by the naturalism of Zola, had portrayed the railroad as a giant sea monster squeezing the California wheat ranchers to death, and the Chicago wheat traders as wolves, only waiting for any sign of weakness to move in for the kill. In 1912, Dreiser, who had contemplated ending his life like Arthur Stirling because of the cruelty of a commercial publisher, would in *The Financier* picture life as no more than a lobster devouring a squid.

It was unacceptable to Upton that life in the country he loved should be no more than a death struggle on an ocean floor or in a forest or jungle. He was horrified at "The exclusive worship of the bitch-goddess success," which William James had diagnosed as America's national disease (a disease that Mark Twain at the same time condemned and embraced), and he seconded James' dictum that "The entire modern deification of survival *per se,* survival returning to itself, survival naked and abstract, with the denial of any substantive excellence in *what* survives, except the capacity for more survival still, is surely the strangest intellectual stopping-place ever proposed by one man to another."

Not only Darwin's, but the scientific insights of Copernicus, Newton, and Freud too have been misapplied by Procrustians. None more so, however, than was social Darwinism in America in the late nineteenth and the twentieth centuries. Darwin knew his theories were being corrupted to the most base and shabby use. He confided to Sir Charles Lyell: "I have received in a Manchester newspaper rather a good squib, showing that I have proved 'might is right,' and therefore that Napoleon is right, and every cheating tradesman is also right."

Such a cruel canon as social Darwinism, however, could not have become so almost integral to America were it not a secular confirmation of the Calvinist rock upon which the Republic was built. More than half a century later Richard Hofstadter observed that the very idea of a "welfare state . . . affronts the traditions of a great many men and women who were raised, if not upon the specific tenets of social Darwinism, at least upon the moral imperatives that it expresses . . . . And anyone who today imagines that he is altogether out of sympathy with that ethic should ask himself whether he has never, in contemplating the possibility of a nearly workless economic order, powered by atomic energy and managed by automation, had at least a moment of misgiving about the fate of man in a society bereft of the moral discipline of work."

Upton had, as he told *Cosmopolitan*'s readers, enlisted upon a long campaign. His fight for social justice would last longer than another half century and would be the chief occupation of his whole life, nothing else in that life being an even remotely close second. One must wonder, therefore, what were the real reasons for the fighting and the real feelings about fighting.

A dozen years later, Upton described at some length his feelings. "Now, when a man comes at me making a face like that, I have but one impulse in my soul—that is, to jump into a pair of seven-league boots, and turn and skedaddle as hard as I know how to the other side of the world and hide in a coal-bin. I am not joking; that is really the way I feel. There is nothing in the world I dread so much as a personal wrangle, and these fierce and haughty and powerful men throw me into a tremble of terror. The things I enjoy in this world are my books and my garden, and rather than go into a jury-room, and wrangle the fierce and haughty and powerful men, I would have my eye-teeth pulled out. But then I think, as I have thought many times in my life before, of the millions of pitiful wage-slaves who are exploited by these fierce and haughty and powerful men. I think of the millions of honest and true Americans who swallow the poison that is fed to them by our capitalist newspapers; and so I clench my hands and bite my lips together and turn on the fierce and haughty and powerful men with a yell of rage. Then a strange and startling, an almost incredible thing happens—the fierce and haughty and powerful men jump into *their* seven-league boots, and turn and skedaddle to the other side of the world and hide in a coal-bin!

"Why is this? Is it because I am an especially terrifying person, with an especially terrifying face? No; it is simply because, in these contests, I have always taken one precaution at the outset—I have made certain of having the truth on my side. I have cast in my lot with the truth; whereas these fierce and haughty and powerful men with whom I enter the lists of combat have made all their success out of falsehood, and fear truth as they fear nothing else on God's earth. . . .

"In the course of my twenty years career as an assailant of special privilege, I have attacked pretty nearly every important interest in America. The statements I have made, if false, would have been enough to deprive me of a thousand times all the property I ever owned, and to have sent me to prison for a thousand times a normal man's life. I have been called a liar on many occasions, needless to say; but never once in all these twenty years has one of my enemies ventured to bring me into a court of law, and to submit the issue between us to a jury of American citizens. Several times they have come near to doing it. I was told, by a lawyer who was present at the event, that there was a conference, lasting three days and a good part of three nights, between Mr. J. Ogden Armour and his lawyers, in which Mr. Armour insisted upon having me arrested for criminal libel, and his lawyers insisted that he could not 'stand the gaff.' Mr. William E. Corey threatened to sue me for libel; I am informed that young Mr. Rockefeller desired ardently to do it."

Part of this explanation is self-contradicting. It seems more likely that, to a man who has bragged over and over that his victims would not dare take him to court and whom experience has proven correct, fear of being taken from his books and garden and into a jury-room wrangle was only rhetorical.

But it is likely that fear of these men, fear of some or even a number of kinds, was an important part of what made Upton fight. Neither history nor everyday life wants for examples of men and women and perhaps especially children who are afraid of a fight and so fight to prove that they are not afraid of a fight.

But that the pale youth (as he almost invariably described himself and his heroes), who when he was lonely had prayed to Goethe and kept a photograph of the young poet in his pocket "to gaze at it as at a lover," felt "rage" as well as fear is clear throughout both his work and his correspondence. In fact, his desire to fight rich and powerful men, both the actual plutocrats of the day and the fictional ones he invented, was so strong that "lust" was his own word for the feeling. "Whenever Thyrsis met one of these men, whether in imagination or reality, he found himself with hands clenched, and every nerve of him a-tingle with the lust of combat."

Such a degree of rage and so long lasting a lust had not only many but doubtless some undiscoverable causes. It seems evident that one of these was a kind of resentment in which envy played a not insignificant role. Sinclair was but one of many who were or are or will be inclined to look at a person doing evil for his own benefit and say to himself, consciously or unconsciously, I too could do that, and with my intelligence and imagination and energy could do it better, but I will not allow myself to do it, so why in hell should you be allowed to?

The sociologist Svend Ranulf has suggested "that the disinterested tendency to inflict punishment is a distinctive characteristic of the lower middle class, that is, of a social class living under conditions which force its members to an extraordinarily high degree of self-restraint and subject them to much frustration of natural desires. If a psychological interpretation is to be put on this correlation of facts, it can hardly be to any other effect than that moral indignation is a kind of resentment caused by the repression of instincts."

Not his class but himself forced upon Sinclair "an extraordinarily high degree of self-restraint" and "much frustration of natural desires." Few persons frustrated of their natural desires do not in some form envy those who enjoy the satisfaction of those same natural desires.

To say that the good may on occasion envy the bad is to invite such criticism that one risks explaining it excessively and even out of proportion to the role of such envy in Upton's life. By envy, here, is meant hostility, enmity, ill-will, and mortification occasioned by the contemplation of superior advantages, *however come by,* possessed by another, and the longing, conscious or unconscious, for those advantages enjoyed by the other.

To say that envy is one of the stimuli toward justice is in no way to depreciate justice.

It cannot be without significance how few absolute monarchs have been virtuous in a Calvinist context, or that hagiography in no known time has been so popular as biographies of strumpets and scoundrels.

CHAPTER IX

Diet and Adultery

The psychology of adultery has been falsified by conventional morals, which assume, in monogamous countries, that attraction to one person cannot coexist with a serious affection for another. Everybody knows that this is untrue.

BERTRAND RUSSELL

IN OCTOBER 1908 Upton left Meta and David and began alone a trip of many months that signaled, despite numerous reconciliations, the end of his first marriage. It also convinced him that he wanted to leave the East and live in California permanently.

A year earlier, traveling across the country had seemed something to do not alone but with his family and indeed with other families. His newest idea had been just what the newspapers wanted, when he had told *The New York Times* that he planned a "Helicon Hall on the hoof, Utopians on a trek," a caravan of covered wagons that would tour for several years and would include maids and governesses and a stenographer. The colonists would be free from many problems that had perplexed them at Helicon Hall, "from plumbers and carpenters and steam heat and taxes. It will be a practical protest against landlords and also, needless to say, it will be fireproof . . . . We shall never trouble ourselves about what other people think of the women of our party, who will wear sensible costumes. That is one of the reasons why I am never happy in the city, because of starched shirts and collars. The last time I tried to wear a flannel shirt in New York, the hallboy of my mother's apartment house refused to let me in the elevator; and Jack London told me that one of the consequences of his protest against starched linen was that he had to knock down a Pullman car porter about once a month. I cannot knock down porters, so I prefer to live in a tent."

Instead of effecting the movable Helicon Hall, however, Upton and his family had sailed to Bermuda on December 18, 1907, after Meta's physical health had been sufficiently restored by her long stay in Battle Creek. In

Bermuda they lived for the next six months with another former colonist, Michael Williams, and his family. There Williams and Sinclair produced *Good Health and How We Won It*, a food faddist book based mainly on what they had learned at Kellogg's sanitarium. Williams wrote the book and Sinclair provided only the introduction and some editorial help, but it was published under both names, presumably to help its sales, which nevertheless were poor.

In Bermuda the children of both families played in a ruined mansion, supposedly the former home of a pirate chief. Upton met Mark Twain, played tennis regularly, wrote a play, and even went swimming in the nude to please Meta. But such occasional gestures and even his more frequent sexual demands were too late, and despite its pleasures, Bermuda was apparently not the place for a new Helicon Hall.

Sinclair and his family spent the summer of 1908 bickering in Lake Placid, while he completed *The Moneychangers*, and in the fall Upton installed Meta and David in an apartment in New York, where city life made her as happy as it made him unhappy. He turned West.

In Lawrence, Kansas, he visited with Harry Kemp, a student at the university who called himself "the box-car poet." Upton considered him the coming young poet of America and was eager to help, and Kemp would soon reciprocate the older man's kindnesses by cuckolding him. Kemp's gift for flattering members of both sexes who might be useful to him was at least as great as any gift he had for poetry. But for Upton, Kemp's greatest appeal lay in his complete lack of success combined with Upton's continuing view of himself as a poet manqué, which was stimulated by Kemp's confessions of admiration for Shelley, Jesus, and *Arthur Stirling*.

Kemp would continue to lick Upton's hand even after the Sinclairs' divorce, having all the characteristics of a dog, except loyalty. In fact, after the divorce, realizing that Upton could be of far more use to him than Meta, he dropped her and continued to flatter Upton outrageously until his own brief reputation became established. He then wrote a very thinly disguised autobiographical novel including his version of the adultery. When Kemp died on August 6, 1960, he was the best-known poet in Provincetown, Massachusetts.

In Denver, Upton met Judge Ben Lindsey and in Bishop, California, he met his friends Gaylord and Mary Wilshire and visited the Bishop's Creek gold mine. "The camp was run on a basis of comradeship, with high wages and plenty of Socialist propaganda," but it failed to produce gold in commercial quantities and the many good Socialists, whom Wilshire with

Upton's help had induced to invest their tiny savings, lost everything. "Socialists ought not to fool with money-making schemes in capitalist society," Upton wrote later, but he himself lost money doing just that, especially in producing his own plays and finally in producing an Eisenstein movie.

When he reached Carmel, Upton settled down for a while. He was "close to a nervous breakdown" and hoped that rest, escape from his domestic problems, plenty of tennis, and the company of his new friend, the poet George Sterling, would restore him. A year younger than Upton, Sterling was startlingly handsome, many remarking on his resemblance to Dante. Forced into the Roman Catholic Church by his disturbed father, Sterling left the church while still in college and lived as irreverent and sybaritic a life as he could until his suicide in 1926.

In 1892 Sterling met Ambrose Bierce, whose disciple he became and to whom he submitted every one of his poems until Bierce's mysterious disappearance in 1913. A poet of some notoriety but no reputation in his own day, Sterling was tremendously admired by Sinclair and returned the admiration despite Bierce's contempt for all Socialists in general and for Sinclair in particular.

Bierce's contempt for all reformers grew out of his own experience as a muckraker of considerable style. In 1896 he had been sent to Washington by Hearst to direct a fight against the Funding Bill, whose only real purpose was the enrichment of the Southern Pacific Railroad and Collis P. Huntington. "Mr. Huntington is not altogether bad," Bierce wrote. "Though severe, he is merciful. He tempers invective with falsehood. He says ugly things about the enemy, but he has the tenderness to be careful that they are mostly lies." But Bierce's exposure of wickedness and attempts at reform had only helped him along his way to misanthropy and despair, from which condition he loosed billingsgate on those who unlike him had failed to see the futility of advocating reform. "As to Sinclair . . . I would not believe him under oath on his death-bed . . . . The truth is, none of these howlers knows the difference between a million and a thousand nor between the truth and falsehood . . . . Upton Sinclair is the nastiest of the gang . . . . I would be a good deal of a SOCIALIST myself if they had not made the word (and the thing) stink."

Sinclair's reaction to this sort of vituperation was typical of him and so an important measure of his character. In his chapter on Bierce in *Mammonart*, he of course chided him as he did all writers who cared more for art than for social reform, but he paid admiring tribute to him as a Civil War hero and declared Bierce "was one of the most ethical men that ever lived . . . . He fought for his beliefs, and shrank from no sacrifice in their behalf. He was no man's man, but said what he thought . . . . He was the only one of those who fought through the war to tell the truth about it." Sinclair's quite extraordinary sense of fair play even made him quote in the chapter Bierce's wittiest and most telling lines attacking Sinclair's beloved theory of art.

Before starting West, Upton had written Sterling from Lake Placid asking if he might be acceptable to the group of artists at Carmel and assuring him that his notorious "spininess" was mostly a public pose but admitting he was "somewhat lacking in congenial vices." On arriving he stayed two days with the poet and then got the use of a bungalow belonging to a friend of Sterling's.

Despite the beauty of Carmel, the rain that precluded his getting exercise made Sinclair unhappy and by the end of the year he had moved to Palo Alto, where he stayed with another new friend, Mrs. Adele Munger, an independent and enthusiastic divorcée, who introduced Sinclair to the benefits of fasting. Her admiration was a solace to him for his relationship with Meta was growing even worse, as across the continent he showered her with dietary instructions for David and other unwanted long distance diagnoses and prescriptions.

Work was Upton's only real rest, and he was soon at work in a field that would always continue to tempt him, but in which he always failed, the drama.

The Millennium, a play he had written in Bermuda, had interested the producer David Belasco, with whom Upton corresponded at length. But Belasco complained of the same faults the critics almost always found with Upton—too much concern with ideas, too little with people and plot. The impresario promised to do his best to make the play a big hit if Upton would only add a story including a love interest.

Sinclair longed desperately for the money such a hit would bring him, but he was unwilling or unable to rewrite the play himself. He urged Belasco to change the play and produce it in absolutely any way he wanted, but the producer refused. How far Sinclair had come from the time when he saw himself as a poet whose words and style are important is repeatedly indicated by this increasing willingness to put his name on a work as author or even co-author (as he had already with Williams) when it was, in fact, written by another; as well as his willingness to accept ideas and changes from others in any of his own works so long as these did not change the message substantially, and sometimes even then. To say that he cared *more* about content than about style is not, however, to say he cared nothing for style. Many of his manuscripts show endless examples of rewriting for improved style, especially the better novels such as *Oil!* And to say that no serious poet would allow another to alter substantially the poet's own work one must ignore Eliot excising more than half of "The Waste Land" at Pound's behest.

In San Francisco a stock company at the Valencia Theatre produced Upton's dramatized version of his *Prince Hagen*. He also wrote three new, one-act, Socialist plays, which Stanford University refused to allow performed in its Assembly Hall. Thereupon, he invested several thousand dollars in "The Sinclair Players," which he hoped would be a successful touring company—successful both financially and as a method of converting non-readers to his religion.

The three one-act plays, all written to require only three actors and no scenery whatsoever were *The Second Story Man*, *John D*, and *The Reluctant Subscriber*. They were received enthusiastically by Upton's fellow Socialists in San Francisco and thereupon sank without a trace.

Upton's plays were quite as unsuccessful in published form as they were on the stage, but for him the theater was El Dorado. He always dreamed of making substantial money from plays or films that would also spread his gospel.

Far more moving and extraordinary than his plays were the letters Upton was writing to Meta. In some he urged her to come West. ". . . Things have come to a crisis with me . . . . For the last week I have found myself thinking with positive terror of going back to spend a winter in NY. I have a feeling that if I go for a while more as I have been, I shall go under altogether; & I came to think of it as an expedition into a country of cannibals. I was going back, of course, for gold; I was going to get away with a fortune [which would come from working with Belasco] but then I kept thinking suppose I *don't* get away? Suppose I collapse? And I asked myself, did I need to go—did I need the fortune? Even suppose the plays went by the board without me—I can earn enough by my novels to live in a rational way. It's only because I go to N.Y. that I need fortunes.

"You have known my cravings for a home. And here is the first place I have ever seen where it seemed to me we could be happy—all of us. I could have been happy in Bermuda—but here we can *all* be. And why not stay? . . . I dread that . . . journey back, as I dread a pilgrimage into hell. I think of the whole East as a plague-place . . . ."

Upton then wrote a long description of the beauty and simplicity of life at Carmel. The most telling letters, however, are those about diet. Upton continually experimented with different food fads, ranging from vegetarianism to a steak diet and was absolutely convinced initially that in each he had found the panacea for his frequent headaches and other ills, probably, in fact, caused by his terrible intensity and overwork. He insisted after Helicon Hall that David, whom his parents called "Bz," stick strictly to each of his miraculous diets. David and Meta always objected strenuously and if Meta insisted on eating things not on the diet, Upton did not want her to do so in front of him or the boy.

Arguments about diets between Meta and Upton were bitter and useless, and sixty years later David would still remember with an acute sense of injustice the whipping his father gave him for eating a tongue sandwich he had asked a Pullman porter to bring him because he was so desperately hungry.

Upton always offered each of his new dietary discoveries to his magazine readers with an enthusiasm undiminished by the last diet's failure to solve his problems. "I now know to be the greatest discovery of my life: the deadly nature of the cooking process, which destroys the health-giving properties of foods, incites to gluttony, and is the cause of 95 per cent of the diseases of the human race . . . . [I ate] whole-wheat cracker; but for this, I ate no cooked food for five months. I lived on nuts, ripe olives, salad vegetables, and a variety of 'the kindly fruits of the earth,' both fresh and dried . . . . We are descended from arboreal ancestors; and whoever saw a fire in a tree? We have the teeth of a nut and fruit eating animal; we have a stomach of that size, and a colon intended for all sorts of waste—fibers, seeds and skins."

After learning from Adele Munger about fasting, Upton of course wrote an enthusiastic book about it, *The Fasting Cure*, as well as a number of magazine articles. The book was dedicated "To Bernarr Macfadden, in cordial appreciation of his personality and teachings." In the hard-sell advertising technique of that day, "Before" and "After" pictures were used for everything from patent medicines to Charles Atlas' body building courses. The frontispiece of *The Fasting Cure* shows two pictures of Upton with a caption reading: "Mr. Sinclair's expression, as shown in the upper photograph, used to be called 'spiritual.' Systematic fasting has evolved the athletic figure pictured below."

When he was not fasting, Upton lived on what he jocularly called his "squirrel diet" of raw foods, but how serious he was he made plain in frenzied and pathetic letters to Meta that were often twelve or twenty-four pages long. "You will understand the fury of my letters when I tell you what

I've been doing . . . . I'd go through agonies of resolutions—sit down and *write* them out on paper—& then get up & go straight away & violate them . . . . at night—candy, nuts & stuff . . . . I made myself ill one night. *And I went right on!* . . . once I ate a lot of ice cream & cake, & again about half a pound of chocolates. Night before last a plate of taffy . . . . I can't tell you how ashamed & heartsick I am. Literally, I am a food *drunkard* . . . . It is simply the story of my poor degraded father all over again; & I have simply got to get down to a regular old fashioned wrestle with the devil . . . . I don't like to say I CAN'T be master of myself—suffice it to say the months & the years go by, & I AM NOT.

"Surely you would try to save me if it was whiskey that was killing me. And I tell you in deadly & most serious earnest that when it comes to sweet stuffs & cooked messes, I am a *drunkard*—a DRUNKARD . . . . I tell you this thing is serious . . . . Grotesque & ludicrous as it may all sound. It is more than my happiness, more than my health—it is my life that is at stake. It is my career, my art, all that I have to do . . . ."

Meta was not touched. She had seen him earn a fortune only to spend it on Helicon Hall. She had suffered for and with him and now wanted to enjoy life. Most importantly, experience had taught her he was not infallible and that this month's unbreakable canon would sooner or later be replaced by another. She had spent too many months cooking special diets for David as a baby to starve him now and considered Upton's dicta imperious and ignorant.

In addition she had ceased to want any sexual relationship with her husband and was finding comfort elsewhere.

And even if she were not too tired of his egoism to be tempted by his letters to come West, she would have been put off by seeing their photographs on the front page of the San Francisco *Examiner* with a story headlined "SINCLAIR SORRY HE IS MARRIED TO WIFE Thinks Nuptial Law of the Present Day is Relic of Barbarism. 'MARRIED WOMEN SLAVES!' "

At the same time as he was dictating to his wife what she could feed her child, he answered the *Examiner* reporter's question as to why he was prejudiced against marriage: "You might as well ask me why I am so prejudiced against slavery—or against thievery—or . . . murder. Marriage in this day is nothing but legalized—slavery; that's the most polite word to call it I fancy.

"The average married woman is bought just exactly as much as any horse or any dog is bought . . . . Marriage! Faugh! It really isn't a subject to be discussed at the table."

Despite his public protestations against marriage and despite the fact that he and Meta had discussed divorce quite as endlessly as their "falling in love" episodes and agreed that their divorce was only a matter of time, Upton periodically tried to salvage his marriage or at least became lonesome enough to want Meta's company. He was still in bad health despite his diet and fasts and was aware that for some time he had published nothing of any significance and had nothing important in work.

Meta agreed to meet him in Miami with David in April, so he took the train to Galveston and then a boat for Key West, where he arrived so ill he was put in a hospital for a week. Then, renting a cottage at Coconut Grove, Upton swam and rested and recovered enough to take his family to another rented beach cottage at Cutchogue, Long Island, where they spent the summer.

Here he wrote *Samuel the Seeker*, a novel about another Candide, Samuel Prescott, who at seventeen leaves the farm to seek after truth. He not only finds that the capitalists who employ him are corrupt, but when working as assistant sexton at St. Matthew's Church is further shocked to learn that clergymen are corrupted by their rich parishioners.

Like Jurgis, Samuel becomes a thief, a proper and logical progression for a truth seeker in capitalist society according to Sinclair, who quotes Herbert Spencer's "inability to catch prey shows a falling short of conduct from its ideal." Like Jurgis, he, too, finally finds truth in Socialism, and as the book ends he lies bloody and unconscious on the ground as his fellow Socialists are marched off to the station house bravely singing "The Red Flag."

> *Yours is the power of the club and jail, yours is the axe and fire,*
> *But ours is the hope of human hearts and the strength of the soul's desire!*

As a poet Sinclair was even less gifted than as a playwright, but could on occasion, as in this case, produce something stirring and occasionally also some acceptable topical jocular verse.

Gone now were the days of large advances from publishers. He had delivered too many books that sold poorly to too many different publishers. B. W. Dodge & Co. paid him only a six hundred dollar advance.

So wearied was Upton that he tried to solve all his economic problems by selling himself. He wrote Mary and Gay Wilshire: "My proposition is in brief that you buy ME." For a guaranteed fixed sum he would sell in perpetuity everything he would ever write from then on, including *Samuel* that he was just finishing, to be held in trust forever, not for the Wilshires' benefit but for the benefit of Socialism. ". . . never have I been able to write a single thing as I would have liked to write it, because of money . . . . Think of my having had to ruin the Jungle with an ending so pitifully inadequate, because we were actually without money for food . . . .

"For my mother, $500 a year while she lives. For Meta $1800 a year until she remarries, if she ever does. I want her to be able to live abroad if she wishes, and to spend $500 a year for instruction in music . . . . Freedom from money cares would never mean anything to me if Meta had to face them; and I think that what she has suffered for my sake entitles her to the chance to work out her own life problem in her own way. For David, $1,200 a year until he is thirty . . . . I want to make some sort of an artist out of my boy . . . and I don't think that any artist can complete his education till the age I have named . . . . For myself I want $2,500.

The Wilshires did not accept Upton's offer.

Between his moments of loneliness and doubt, Upton wanted desperately to be rid of his obligations to Meta and David so he could devote all his energy to his war. He prepared an article on divorce for *Wilshire's*, which Dell Munger warned prophetically that he should publish later but not now "because the law would not grant you a divorce if it became cognizant of a mutual agreement . . . . I am so glad to be years and years and years older than you are. It makes it possible to be such a good kind of friends."

Upton next took his family to Bernarr Macfadden's in Battle Creek where he hoped to regain his health. When Meta had stayed at Kellogg's alone she had met Alfred Kuttner, a rich, twenty-three-year-old, just graduated Harvard man, with whom she afterward carried on a constant correspondence and an intermittent affair. This second trip proved even more productive, and this time not only for Meta. She met Harry Kemp, who visited Upton at the spa for a few days. But Upton met Mary Craig Kimbrough, a young woman from the delta district of Mississippi, who was a patient at Kellogg's and would be his first mistress and his second wife. Perhaps the most attractive characteristic of Sinclair and surely the most unusual for a reformer was his active sense of humor. Almost half a century after Craig first saw him at Macfadden's giving a "health crank" lecture she recalled: "I doubt if I had ever laughed so much in my life, and I surely never expected to see my dignified mother wiping tears of laughter from her eyes."

Upton's relationship with Macfadden was to be long and profitable for both. The long haired health prophet charged him nothing, but got testimonials from the muckraker. He also bought many articles from Upton, not only for his magazine *Physical Culture*, but as his publishing enterprises grew, for *Liberty* as well.

At Battle Creek, Sinclair began a new scheme. Just as Helicon Hall, while alleged to have been started solely for the world's good, was, in fact, also started in order to solve some of Upton's own domestic problems, so his newest idea, the "Home Colony School" for boys, was started to rid himself of the problems of taking care of David. As usual he turned his experience (and in this case his need for boarders) to profit by writing a magazine article in which he explained his proposed cooperative school for boys from eight to ten to be run by Mrs. Munger. "We shall teach health as a religion . . . . and in our teaching we shall not forget sex health . . . base ball, swimming, skating and walking.

"Personally I care very little about book-learning for young children. I believe that they should develop their bodies and learn thru the hand and eye. I would have gardening and nature-study, the latter while wandering about in the woods and fields collecting. I would have the children learn to sing beautiful songs and hear poetry and stories read aloud."

He was so anxious to get the school started that he was writing Mrs. Munger daily, and once having got her to sell her house and plan to move East immediately, he flooded her with ideas and plans. The degree of his delight at the prospect of being freed from the problems of raising David is evident from his suggestion that the boarding school should run twelve months a year, to which Mrs. Munger objected strenuously, and when he proposed that she hire the same Mrs. Noyes whom he had known at Helicon Hall, the usually acquiescent Mrs. Munger asked somewhat sharply whether in fact she or he would run the school.

As suddenly as his plan had been begun, it ended, and Mrs. Munger good-naturedly set about unwinding her plans and getting a new place to live.

On a grander scale than his domestic problems were Upton's ideas about what he and many other Socialists saw as the worldwide war toward which capitalist statesmen were leading the nations, but which would be fought by each nation's poor men for no benefit to themselves. A short article in the *Saturday Evening Post* confidently proclaimed "Socialism's Triumph in 1913," but what he, in fact, feared by then was world war.

Because of *The Jungle* and also because he regularly sent carbon copies or galley proofs of everything he wrote as well as floods of letters to Socialist and other publishers, magazines, and newspapers all over the world, Upton was becoming, if he was not already, the best-known American Socialist.

Now he wrote "War: A Manifesto Against It," which was widely printed and reprinted from London to Melbourne. From Karl Kautsky in Berlin, however, he got a long letter explaining why ". . . I am not able to publish it and you will not find anybody in Germany—nor in Austria or Russia." Anyone who did, Kautsky explained carefully, would be arrested and imprisoned for some years for high treason, and though such a sacrifice would be worthwhile if there were some hope of success, here there was not and furthermore the manifesto "would mislead our own comrades, promise more to them than we could fulfill. Nobody, and not the most revolutionary amongst us Socialists in Germany thinks to oppose war by insurrection and general strike. We are too weak . . . . I hope, after a war, *after* the debacle of a government we may get strength enough."

Upton was so angered and insensitive that he planned to try to have Kautsky's letter published along with his answer, until Kautsky wrote begging him to abstain. The most important effect of this correspondence was its influence on Sinclair's later decision to break with Debs and the leading American Socialists and to support Woodrow Wilson's entry into World War I.

For the winter of 1909, Upton took his family and secretary to a single-tax colony on Mobile Bay at Fairhope, Alabama. Here, as in most such utopian colonies, all kinds of cranks were welcome and it was not mandatory to believe in Henry George's version of the *impôt unique* of the eighteenth-century Physiocrats—that all the land and its resources belong to everyone and all rents should therefore go to the government for everyone's welfare. Here Upton discovered Dr. Salisbury's diet of lightly cooked lean chopped beef, which he at once seized upon, dropping the uncooked food diet that only recently he had so fervidly described to Meta as the *sine qua non* of his existence.

Meta was visited in March at Fairhope by her young lover, Alfred, and in a quadrille of discussion by twos and by threes, they examined their "soul states." Upton was willing to share Meta with Alfred, but not to support her if she bore Alfred's child, which Meta found unreasonable of him. She was loath to lose Upton's support, but unwilling to sleep with him, a poetic justice lost on the muckraker. Alfred was charmed to consider intellectually any proposition—except marriage.

Meta, having again for the moment decided on divorce, went north to make arrangements, but would again back away from going through with it. Upton stayed at Fairhope and began his painfully autobiographical novel, *Love's Pilgrimage*, about the modern marriage of a couple who, when the time came for divorce, could proceed in a friendly fashion and remain friends. The dedication reads: "To those who throughout the world are fighting for the emancipation of woman I dedicate this woman's book."

A few of the sixteen chapter titles, all of which give clearly Upton's heartfelt view of marriage as a trap, are: The Victim, The Snare, The Bait Is Seized, The Torture—and finally, The Break for Freedom.

In the early part of the book he described his unhappy boyhood and his early contacts with Meta, writing that even then, "Thyrsis was domineering and imperious, and things must always be his way." There follow almost verbatim letters that passed between Meta and Upton during courtship. They picture poignantly first the terrible and prophetic doubts of an egoist whose only real love is his mission, drawn to marriage exclusively by his desire multiplied by his rigid celibacy and Corydon's provocatively innocent flirtation: ". . . I dare not marry you, I should be binding my life to ruin. . . . God made me for an *artist* not a lover! . . . You are a child, and you can not dream . . . of a great savage force of mine . . . —it cares for nothing in the world but the utterance of itself!"

Secondly, and more briefly, if no less poignantly, is drawn the young woman who longs to become somebody through marriage, who sees the man's egoism and dedication but deludes herself into thinking that she can change them. With his extraordinary sense of fairness and a perhaps equally extraordinary sense of his own inability to understand and express women's feelings, Sinclair urged Meta to write the most important passages about Corydon and told her he would "cheerfully agree not to change your manuscript except in such ways as to fit it into the story, and these changes will be simply suggestions." And the results were telling: "I shall be your wife. . . . And are you one of God's chosen ones? . . . Why do the moments blind you so, that you can speak to me as though I were a sawdust doll? . . . How do you expect God to value your soul, when you so lightly value mine? . . ."

In describing their poverty and Thyrsis' rejection by publishers, the story is moving. In describing Thyrsis' ignorance of and contempt for sex ("humiliating necessity"), it is horrifying.

Letters between Thyrsis and Corydon's lover are virtual duplicates of those that actually passed between Upton and Kuttner. The book ends with Thyrsis saying, "Let us redeem our great words from base uses. Let that no longer call itself Love, which knows that it is not free!"

In a graphic and for its day shocking description of Corydon in childbirth, Upton wrote what he fully expected would be suppressed. To gather ammunition for fighting the expected suppression, he sent advance copies to British and American authors and when their replies were not needed for a battle that never came, some were used for puffs. Jack London found it "the rawest, reddest meat that has been slammed at any American publisher in the last five decades. All I'm afraid of is that you won't find a publisher with guts enough to bring the book out."

On the other hand, Arnold Bennett thought Upton had dealt "with these matters in an admirably poetic, lofty, and honest spirit," and Havelock Ellis welcomed "the frank way in which you face these fundamental problems of life." Santayana, while defending Upton's freedom to write such a book, questioned its aesthetic and moral value, but even as severe a critic as Mencken, in answer to Dreiser's request that he add to Dreiser's list any important realistic novels, suggested *Love's Pilgrimage, The Jungle,* and *The Gilded Age.*

After being refused by a number of other New York publishers, the book was brought out by Mitchell Kennerly in March 1911 and sold very well until the scandal of Upton's divorce became front-page news for most newspapers. Thereafter, as Kennerly pointed out, there was little reason to pay $1.35 for what one could buy for two cents.

The public was right. For the next few years, Upton's life was much more interesting than anything he wrote.

Upton tried fiercely not to be possessive of Meta—to be the modern, liberated, utopian Socialist husband he wrote about who wanted his wife's happiness more than he wanted his own ego massaged. He urged Meta and Alfred to go off together camping. When they did, she wrote detailed letters and asked that they be read to David so that the elastic ménage would be no secret from him. It was, however, to be kept a secret from Alfred's mother, who "would be greatly shocked if she knew about me & our relationship and would probably disown him." Upton was even asked to supply "a minute description of Mrs. John Martin's place, as he has told his mother that was where he was going to visit."

Meta provided her husband with a running report of her adventures. When the lovers were awakened in the night by a grunting porcupine at the foot of "the bed," it was dispensed by "five bullets and a blow of the ax . . . . Alfred doesn't like lamming porcupines." In addition to the natural history, she described their fluctuating "soul states," and assured Upton "I will have an interesting time analyzing it all when we meet again, it will go well into the book."

Alfred had introduced Meta to psychoanalysis as well as to adultery, and for some time she was a patient of his analyst, Dr. A. A. Brill, to whom she once wrote "I sometimes feel as tho all the world were a lot of goblins bent on torturing me." But unlike Alfred, she never became enthusiastic about analysis, finding it more comfortable to discuss everything with Upton.

Usually Upton could accept their arrangement, even suggesting that all three of them move together to Germany. "There there would be no reason why we should get any divorce—at least at present, and no reason why he and I could not be friends . . . . We both play tennis! . . . suppose we were all to go to Germany— . . . And David and I could have the country which we need . . . and you and Alfred could have music and German and books."

But despite his principles, natural bourgeois jealousy sometimes exploded in him and he would want never to see her again, only to find himself lonely and miserable the moment she was gone. "I was like a man who sat in a furnace, and shrieked for an iceberg, and then after half an hour of the iceberg, was panting to get back to the furnace again . . . . [He proposes a reconciliation.] There is of course one proviso to all this: that the period of love affairs is past . . . . make up your mind as to whether the Alfred episode is to be put behind you; . . . in future whenever you have an *amour* that has to be prosecuted, you go away from me and don't come back till its over. I have had every bit of that sort of nightmare that I mean to have in my life."

More often, however, Upton's letters show a degree of unselfishness and broadmindedness almost unbelievable in the puritan reformer. "It is no use My Dearest, I give up. I cannot apply ethical codes to you or me—we have suffered too much. Of late as I have thought it over, I have come to feel that I have wrecked your health and ruined your happiness by insisting that Alfred marry you or leave you. And I cannot bear the burden of your suffering—I love you too much—so I surrender. I want you to go with him . . . ." He warned, however, that there was a limit to what he could stand and that for her and Alfred to have a child would be insanity.

Meta wrote Alfred "he brought himself to the willingness to share my love with you, but he cannot share the fatherhood—that apparently outrages some deep truth of him," but the matter was theoretical only, because in her relations with Upton, as with Alfred, "there have been too many words between us, and not enough action."

Upton did his best. "Dearest, has my gift come too late? Most gifts have come too late to you . . . . I have realized that all the torture you and I have been thru down here was because I have been unwilling to face the idea of your having both Alfred's love and mine; . . . Let us live a free life . . . . I do not discuss the question of its being too late, it is never too late, for the soul is without limits."

But it was too late.

CHAPTER X

Scandal and Flight

Women hate revolutions and revolutionists. They like men who are docile, and well-regarded at the bank, and never late at meals.   H. L. MENCKEN

AT WHAT PRECISE MOMENT Mary Craig Kimbrough decided she would have Upton Sinclair is not clear, but soon after meeting him in Battle Creek in 1909 she began her plan to appropriate him. She worked with cool and ingratiating guile and above all with an unhurried patience and calm that contrasted strikingly with Meta's chronic near-hysteria.

Like Meta's, Craig's soul had been full of undefined artistic intimations and vague immortal longings. All her life she dabbled in poetry and when she met Sinclair she was, she said, writing a biography of Winnie Davis, the unfortunate daughter of the president of the Confederacy. These literary leanings, so like Meta's own, helped her endear herself to Upton's unhappy wife, indeed to achieve in a very short time what was apparently her first goal, to become Meta's best friend. By twenty-six, an advanced age for a Southern belle still to be unmarried, she seems consciously or subconsciously to have determined that if she couldn't be an artist, she could eat one.

Born April 25, 1883, in Greenwood, Mississippi, Mary Craig was, according to her jejune and frequently unreliable autobiography, *Southern Belle*, the oldest child of "the richest planter in his part of the Mississippi Delta and [the "judge" who also] had handled the estate of Jefferson Davis. . . . This Southern belle came North to Yankeeland to a finishing school just across Fifth Avenue from one of the Vanderbilt palaces."

Part of a tiny white caste entirely removed from the starving, hookworm-infested, white "clayeaters" of the piney backwoods, "by the time I was born, things were about as they had been during the days of slavery." The rich whites spent all their time seeking pleasure, supported by blacks "not far in their minds from the jungles of Africa. . . . My father . . . [deplored] 'the natural defect in the blood of the Negro' which made him

125

shiftless . . . [but] he would not shoot them because he knew they would obey him and he needed their labor in the cotton fields."

In this world where gentlemen wore blue and white striped seersucker suits and her parents called each other "Mr. Kimbrough" and "Miss Mary Hunter," the bright little girl with long red-gold hair and big brown eyes watched and remembered. She was almost teachered to death by the piano teacher, voice teacher, elocution teacher, and dancing teacher; but it was from both Papa and Mama that she learned what were apparently the two equal essentials, ethics and etiquette, not by direct instruction but by observing an expression of distaste at the mention of anyone or anything improper.

Although "when she made out a grocery list, she wrote 'shugga' and when it was a laundry list she wrote 'pance,' . . . Mama was born a Southworth and . . . This consciousness of high origin produced in my darling mother a sense of ineffable superiority, lifting her and her brood above most temptations of the flesh and all weakness of the spirit."

It was not lost on the observant little girl that although her mother bore him ten children, she never loved her husband, despite the obvious fact that Allan McCaskell Kimbrough adored his wife and worked hard to earn enough money to indulge her desire for caviar and guava jelly, even while teasing her that these were not so much to her taste as proofs of her aristocracy. Along with her obsession with her own ancestors, Mary Southworth Kimbrough's chief interest was in the United Daughters of the Confederacy, in which she had earned an exalted status that further defined her worth and importance. Similarly, the chief joy to her of the Kimbrough's summer home in Gulfport, Ashton Hall, more than its giant, ancient liveoaks or its beautiful prospect of the Sound, was its proximity to Beauvoir, the Jefferson Davis home.

From this background, Craig grew into much the same kind of stern, demanding madonna as Priscilla Sinclair, a woman who could talk endlessly about family, duty, sacrifice, honor, discipline, and especially purity. That like Upton's mother she was a pure woman, a good woman, was not at all contradicted when she conceived a child by Sinclair (before he had divorced Meta) and while traveling with him as his mistress had an abortion in England with the help of Mary Wilshire.

Also meanwhile, unknowingly preparing for that future day when she would peremptorily argue politics with Walter Lippmann and philosophy with Albert Einstein, Mary Craig at thirteen matriculated at the Mississippi State College for Women and after three years was thought worthy to attend the Gardner School for Young Ladies, whose catalogue promised that at the school's receptions its young ladies would be presented to New York's millionaires.

Having grown to five feet seven inches, of self-confessed beauty, and having failed to capture or be captured by a New York millionaire, Mary Craig returned to Greenwood to practice how to flirt and otherwise handle men. "My grandmother gave me the recipe. . . . Flattery was the basic ingredient, the sugar; and a little mockery is the spice. Men like to feel that they are powerful—brave, capable, important. This isn't a wholly bad idea—they have to take care of a family later on, so why not let the poor dears feel as superior as they want to?—it makes them more willing slaves?"

In Greenwood, Mary Craig fell in love with and became engaged to one Calhoun Wilson, the only love of her life, but broke off with him irrevocably at her father's request, never asking why but assuming he must have proven himself unfit—whether by drunkenness, by excessive whoring in Memphis and New Orleans, or by some other unworthiness she never learned. But she never loved another man, a fact she did not hide from Upton. "I married Upton, because his splendid idealism gave me faith in something in the human spirit; faith in a purpose to live for." That she did not love Upton may indeed have been an attraction to a man who had learned he wanted a marriage of minimal emotional requirements.

Mary Craig came to New York ostensibly to sell her Winnie Davis manuscript and was soon introduced to both feminism and Socialism as well as to many of Upton's friends; the Wilshires, Jessica Finch of the Finch School, Sinclair Lewis, John Dewey, Emma Goldman, young Walter Lippmann, Miss Helen Stokes and her brother J. G. Phelps Stokes—both "millionaire Socialists" according to the newspapers, and to George Sterling who dropped to one knee, addressed her as "goddess," and said he was so agog over her beauty that he would write her a sonnet a day for a hundred days. He did, though apparently most if not all of the same sonnets had already served the same trick with other ladies whose beauty had had the same effect upon Sterling.

Although Craig carefully avoids mentioning Meta in describing this period in her meretricious autobiography, she worked at nothing harder than becoming Meta's confidante, even having her visit in Mississippi, allegedly to edit the Winnie Davis manuscript, which of course flattered Meta's literary pretensions delightfully.

In the spring of 1910 Upton had moved to the single-tax colony of Arden, at Edge Moor, Delaware, about twenty miles south of Philadelphia and close enough to New York for its members to attend to business in the city when necessary.

Even according to its founder, the conditions there were relatively primitive—no water in the houses and seas of mud in the spring; but such physical drawbacks were thought by Ardenites to be made up for many times over by the intellectual and socially concerned climate.

The colony had been started with money from Joseph Fels who had made a great fortune in Fels-Naphtha soap. Such more or less communal colonies have had a usually temporary attraction for many American writers from Nathaniel Hawthorne to Allen Ginsberg.

Upton had, since his days of suffering as an Arthur Stirling poet, dreamed of a millionaire or group of millionaires who would support talented young poets and enable them thereby to do their redeeming work. Recently as his chief candidate for the millionaire's role he had fixed his attention on Fels, and since Upton was himself no longer a poet, he had suggested Harry Kemp to be the beneficiary of Fels' largesse. "I know Harry intimately, and I can speak with authority. He is about 25, and a man without a vice. He has never known a woman, does not drink or smoke, and is without any petty unworthiness. This is the more remarkable, since he ran away from home at the age of 13, and has been all over the world as cabin-boy, sailor and tramp."

When Fels asked George Bernard Shaw about Upton's plan, the answer he got was not encouraging, but in spite of Shaw's letter, Fels did subsidize Kemp for six months for a total of $250, causing Kemp to write Upton, "Your friendship toward me is beyond any comprehension as yet—it is almost like the Love of God."

When Upton settled in Arden, he had a cabin built to his own specifications and also put up the big tent that had seen service since before his marriage, as well as a little tent for David alongside. He wanted a site as far as possible from everything else, with no neighbors, and reasonably near a bathing pond or brook, but settled on a piece of land next to Scott Nearing's cabin, which he also rented as his establishment grew to include his secretary, Ellen Barrows, and such visitors as Mary Craig Kimbrough and Harry Kemp.

He brought with him to Arden his by now almost automatic mode of attracting or creating publicity. He announced that a new civil war was at hand in which the people would gobble up the trusts and be free, with Teddy Roosevelt in Lincoln's role, Taft as Buchanan, Debs as Wendell Phillips, and La Follette as Sumner, and the newspapers ate it up. "Roosevelt and the insurgents don't any more mean to bring about the change they are going to bring about than did Lincoln and Seward intended, at first, to set the slaves free. They'll simply give the public what it wants. The socialists are educating the people to know what they do want."

This insistence upon the inevitability of a revolution that would lead to the New Jerusalem was not a publicity gimmick but an article of faith. As Upton's friend Margaret Sanger would later point out: "A religion without a name was spreading over the country. The converts were liberals, Socialists, anarchists, revolutionists of all shades. They were as fixed in their faith in the coming revolution as ever any Primitive Christian in the immediate establishment of the Kingdom of God. Some could even predict the exact date of its advent."

Upton benefited at Arden from the immense publicity value of being thrown in jail. Although theoretically there was unlimited free speech at Arden, even in utopia there are limits. An anarchist shoemaker, George Brown, who insisted on his right to talk at Arden's public meetings about any subject he chose, specifically in this case sex, shocked enough of the less than totally liberated ladies so that the executives swore out a warrant for his arrest for disturbing the peace, and Brown served five days on the rock pile at the state prison. This was the ultimate sin, to use the police of the capitalist oppressors against one's own, and Emma Goldman wrote Brown offering help in showing up "those fake reformers . . . I could just hug you for not paying the fine." But Brown arranged his own revenge.

Under a 1793 statute against profaning the sabbath, he had a group of Arden members including Upton arrested for playing tennis and baseball on Sunday, and when ten refused to pay their fines, they were sentenced to eighteen hours on the rock pile of New Castle County Workhouse. The newspapers had a field day, with Upton's enthusiastic cooperation; *The New York Times* devoted a series of articles culminating in a full-page story with six pictures of the criminals. Upton demanded the arrest and prosecution of Federal Judge George Gray and of the president of the Wilmington Country Club, and all other members of the judiciary and constabulary who played golf on Sunday.

Not to be outdone by *The Times*, *The World* in its stories reported that the prisoners had fasted during their imprisonment and that "All of the martyrs invaded an ice cream establishment after their release and ate more of that delicacy than had been sold at that place for months."

Seizing as he always did every possible opportunity to spread Socialist propaganda, Upton told the reporters, "My delight of getting out of jail would be much greater if I had not left 337 prisoners behind me. I would like to make my eighteen-hour experience a required course of every college student in America so that they might know something about the true causes of human degradation."

He also seized the opportunity to get a poem published, one he had written overnight in jail about his fellow prisoners, "The Menagerie." Except as part of a news story, it would not readily have found publication.

Newspapers all across America copied the stories in the New York press including those three weeks later announcing that Upton had won the tennis championship of Arden "in Sabbath play" but had not been rearrested.

Upton was not universally popular at Arden, his vanity about his career and his assumption of moral leadership causing both some amusement and some resentment. The children of the community were much given to mimicking the high voice in which he slowly dictated to his secretary in his open writing tent and his at least daily questions, "Any reporters to see me? Anybody looking for me?"

Scott Nearing sixty years later remembered too the little children beating their chests ostentatiously and shouting, "Sinclair! Sinclair!" And later, when he visited Upton in Pasadena, the old muckraker whom he hadn't seen for years met him at the door with no greeting, but instead with the question, "Have you seen the bust?" Without another word he led the confused Nearing to his office where placed opposite his desk so he could see it was a just finished bust of himself. But despite Upton's vanity, and even despite what Nearing viewed as his weak Socialist thinking, he remembered Upton as always vigorous and boyish and sweet.

Why Upton suddenly sued for divorce and in the most public fashion imaginable in August 1911 after so many years of indecision is not clear. His discovery of Meta's adulteries with her newest lover, Harry Kemp, may perhaps have been more offensive to him than those he had discussed so fully with her earlier. Possibly they seemed to constitute a personal betrayal by Kemp, whose purity he had vouched for and whose career he had forwarded. Or he may have resented their lying to him, assuring him that they were not having sexual relations when it was evident to everyone else at Arden, including Mary Craig, that they were.

As a good Socialist and Shelleyan he had tried mightily to understand and accept Meta's infidelities. But although Meta had been a slow starter, once begun she had progressed so rapidly and promiscuously that she had no time left for anything else—none for Upton and none for David. Upton was full of guilt about his mistreatment of her in the first years of their marriage and so was inclined to forgive her mistreatment of him, but it can scarcely have escaped his attention that in the eyes of many he appeared more a sap than a saint, which would not make his role as a teacher any easier.

Or it may have been because he finally saw in Mary Craig or in another brief relationship that he was not dependent on Meta for such love as he needed to receive. The winter before at a meeting of the Intercollegiate Socialist Society at Carnegie Hall, he had seen and on the moment fallen in love with Inez Milholland, a beautiful and rich young Vassar girl who had created a sensation in the New York press by joining the suffragette and Socialist movements. After the meeting they went to her hotel where, according to Upton, they sat in the lobby talking until the next morning and she warned him not to fall in love with her because she loved another. Nevertheless, as he confessed in his autobiography, "He fell in love—with such desperate and terrifying violence as he had never conceived possible in his hard-working sober life." But the beautiful Miss Milholland did not succumb to the muckraker's lovemaking either in person or by letter and the storm passed, never to come again.

One of the things that in the past had dissuaded Upton from pushing ahead on those occasions when he had wanted a divorce and Meta had not was the fear of causing a scandal that might disgrace or at least reflect unfavorably on Socialism. The importance of writers in that time before radio, movies, or television was enormous—their arrivals or departures by steamship let alone their marriages and divorces constituted exciting news. Theatrical and musical performers then had far smaller national audiences than writers, whose relative importance has now disappeared like the Chautauqua circuit on which they frequently earned more in lecture fees than from their writing.

Sinclair resented terribly those critics who condemned him as a chronic publicity seeker, alleging stoutly that he never sought publicity for himself, but only for his causes. Since most of his causes were ones that capitalist newspapers studiously ignored, it was necessary, Sinclair said, to have some personal element, shocking enough so that it could not be ignored, connected with the cause. Perhaps he had convinced himself that publicity on the archaic laws governing divorce would do more good than the scandal would do harm.

In any event, self-promotion has almost invariably been a part of the American success story. Whether it is an unknown starlet claiming to be pregnant by a matinee idol or a steel baron building libraries, the difference is one of degree rather than kind. Upton never matched, for example,

Artemus Ward who publicized his lecture on Mormons with tickets reading "Admit the Bearer and ONE Wife," or Mark Twain who promised that for those who came to hear him he would "devour a child in the presence of the audience, if some lady will kindly volunteer an infant for the occasion."

Whatever cause or combination of causes it was that convinced Sinclair he must move ahead on the divorce, and contrary to the accepted gentleman's code that the wife should be characterized as the injured party, it carried him through a long and terrible fight.

Meta had first gone up to New York where she stayed in her parents' empty apartment at 174 West 87th Street. She was almost immediately followed by Kemp. Upton then, with apparently no warning to anyone, announced to the press that his wife had left him to go on the stage and that he planned to sue her for divorce and name Harry Kemp as corespondent.

Meta was not displeased at first to find herself pursued by reporters and gave them just the kind of copy they wanted. She said she was attempting to solve for herself the sex problem, which was her own business, but that she understood the public curiosity because others with similar sex problems were anxious to learn from her experience. "Speaking for myself, now, I have the misfortune to have a very conservative husband. He is a conservative by instinct and a radical merely by choice. Mr. Sinclair is an essential monogamist, without having any of the qualities which an essential monogamist ought to possess."

In considerable detail she defined the qualities and obligations of a monogamist husband who expects his wife to follow his example of monogamy and pointed out her husband's inadequacies, most especially that his "intellectual work occupies his attention to the exclusion of the rest of his nature."

When reporters gleefully read excerpts of his wife's statement to him late that night, Upton replied: "I will make note of her suggestions of what the attributes of an 'essential monogamist' should be, for use in case I ever should remarry. But as Dr. Johnson says, a second marriage is a triumph of hope over experience."

The papers were so fascinated with the "free love Socialist-author" objecting to free love in his own family that they gave a $10,000 kidnapping ransom demand by the Mafia second place. Not only was Meta encouraged to contrast her "artistic Greek temperament with Mr. Sinclair's ascetic Hebraic temperament," but Harry Kemp too was asked for and delivered his views on life, art, sex, and marriage. Once all three addressed the press together at the Hotel Imperial, at which time Meta said she would not contest her husband's suit, but even the best begun divorces not infrequently turn bitter.

On his return from six weeks of hunting and fishing in the Hudson Bay region, Clerk of the Special Sessions William M. Fuller in an interview in *The World* characterized his son-in-law as "an unripe persimmon . . . an overweening egotist . . ." and stated Upton did not satisfy Meta. "He is too much the novelist and thinker and not enough the man."

When Meta implied she might fight the suit, Upton wrote her father an anguished and angry letter. "You have also told me that you considered that Meta was sexually insane. . . . Can you not realize what it meant to me to stand at the window of Nearing's house and watch Meta having sexual intercourse with Harry. . . . I crossed out what I started to write. I simply cannot tell you or anyone what I have suffered. . . . [But] I am in a position now where I either have to prove the truth, or be proven a scoundrel before the world; and I assure you I mean to put up a fight before I submit to that. . . . all I ask is that Meta will permit me to prove the truth at the trial—as little as I have to—and get a verdict and shut the thing up. . . . [If she will not] I shall certainly stop at nothing. I mean that I will write and give to the papers the full story of my life with Meta, and of her ten or twelve love affairs. . . . I shall file another suit at once, naming Jim Leathers on the evidence of her letters to me; and Alfred. . . . The point is, I don't want to have to use such evidence."

Meta's mother wrote Upton, "I have long since known the strained relations which have existed between you and Meta. I know that you loved her most unselfishly. I know that she loves you in her own peculiar way. I know all about Alfred Kuttner and deplore the situation. I sympathize with you, dear Upton, and shall always be your friend, for you are a dear, noble boy. I know you have done your best to make Meta happy."

There were endless stratagems and counter-stratagems, public protestations and private detectives, all those unfortunate things made necessary by the antagonists' psyches and by the requirements of the divorce laws of the state of New York, then much influenced by the Roman Catholic Church.

Finally, after all the depositions and recriminations and a hearing at which landladies from Sea Girt and Long Branch, New Jersey, testified under oath as to Meta and Kemp's adultery ("I told my husband they were too affectionate to be man and wife," said boardinghouse-keeper Mrs. Grace G. Schanz), the Supreme Court appointed a referee, William S. Kelley, who recommended to the court that the divorce be granted on November 29, and Upton believed his problems would be over by the year's end and he could flee to Europe. But on December 20 Supreme Court Justice Davis refused to sign the decree of divorce on the technicality that Referee Kelley had allowed Sinclair to give evidence against his wife instead of merely testifying that he was married and did not condone his wife's offenses. The case was sent back for rehearing and another referee again recommended a decree but was again turned down in February 1912, this time by Supreme Court Justice Newburger, in whose opinion Upton had contributed to his wife's conduct through his neglect to keep her out of temptation and that further his proofs were based too strongly on photographic evidence.

Upton was absolutely convinced even after the first refusal that the decision was not based on facts or law, but was politically motivated, and of course the second reversal only reinforced his convictions.

Meta and Kemp were now living quite openly together at West Point Pleasant, New Jersey, delightedly providing pictures and copy for the newspapers. "I don't give a damn about marriage, divorce, reports of courts or the findings of referees," she confided in the Christmas Eve issue of the New York *World*, ". . . I don't give a damn about anything except being left alone with Harry." And Harry, "long-haired and unshaven," fingered a shotgun to indicate the moment had come for the reporter to leave and relished the spotlight on his adultery, it having so long ignored his poetry. Sleeping with Meta and sympathizing by letter with Upton, he worked both sides of the street and watched for his chance.

Upton, again as desperate as he had been in the days before his literary success, was convinced that he appeared to the world as both a fool and a liar. Even before the second judge refused to grant the recommended divorce, he had decided to leave in February 1912 for Europe to establish residency in Holland. For months he had planned to go to Germany to live, but had postponed his departure in the hope of settling the divorce before leaving. In Holland the divorce laws required only one party to be a resident and required no proofs if the other party did not oppose the suit. Upton had learned about this from Frederik van Eeden, who served as Upton's surrogate father and most trusted adviser-critic after the decline of Reverend Moir's influence, and who was the really great attraction drawing him to Holland.

Born at Haarlem in 1866, Frederik Willem van Eeden had become a doctor of medicine at the University of Amsterdam in 1886. He made an important reputation as a psychologist, but gradually dropped the practice of psychology as his interest turned more and more to writing and to questions of social justice. He founded an unsuccessful communal colony he called Walden, successfully wrote poetry, essays, novels, and dramas, while at the same time becoming one of the major figures in European Socialism. He had long corresponded with Upton, criticized his manuscripts, and urged him to come meet the Socialist leaders of Europe, who were trying to reshape the world in much the same way that Upton was trying to reshape America.

Upton had already addressed himself to David's guardianship in case he should die, for the idea of leaving the boy in the hands of a woman he was now convinced was depraved horrified him, as did his increasing fear that he might never get free of her. He had chosen as David's guardian Mary Craig and wrote her detailing what he considered Meta's depravities in a long letter he thought she might need in the event Meta contested the guardianship. He described for page after page, Meta's determination to force him to support her during her various and sometimes simultaneous adulteries, as well as her almost total lack of interest in David. Even given the circumstances and the temptation to exaggerate, most of what he alleged was probably true, except his attribution of her problems to "an inherited taint," of which there is no evidence, and which especially ill became the son of a pathological drunkard.

Pulled between both parents and of primary concern to neither, the nine-year-old David suffered at this period emotional shocks and terrors that would mar his early adult life, until psychiatry and his own hard work later released him.

Nothing Upton was writing during this period required his staying in America and what little he was able to write seriously was not acceptable. He had completed *Love's Progress*, the sequel to *Love's Pilgrimage*, but both Kennerly and Moffatt Yard declined the manuscript and in fact it was never published. In the manuscript, using pseudonyms, Upton describes watching the coupling of Meta and Kemp and the continuing and undiminishing pain it caused him. When he also describes, passionately and graphically, his own adultery with Anna Noyes, however, there is no suggestion of its causing pain in any quarter.

Frustrated on every side, Upton, with his son in tow, left for Europe, where they spent February and March in England. He met his heroes Prince Kropotkin, Shaw, and others of the anarchist, Fabian, and Syndicalist circles, while he pretended to live in Holland at van Eeden's home establishing legal residency.

Upton's progress through Europe provided a balm of which his spirit was in sore need. He was hailed as an equal by the leading Socialists of Britain and the Continent and was happy to enter into the various local Socialist struggles and temporarily forget as much as he could his own country, chiefly because he remained convinced that the judicial rulings against his divorce represented an unjust punishment for his Socialist beliefs. He was not displeased to learn that he was now thought quite as prominent a figure in world Socialism as most of those upon whom he called.

In Florence he stayed with his hero and patron, George D. Herron, but the glories of Tuscany affected him otherwise than most first-time American tourists. What he saw "spoke of pain and enslavement, in America as in Italy. The grim castle of the Strozzi was an incarnation in stone of the Beef Trust. . . . crowds of olive-skinned starving children with sore eyes, peering out of doorways of tenements in the back streets of Florence, were simply 'Mulberry Row' in New York. Galleries full of multiplied madonnas and crucified martyrs spoke of Tammany Hall and its Catholic machine, with Catholic 'cops' twisting the arms of Socialist working girls on the picket-line . . . and Catholic judges . . . punishing Socialist muckrakers for being too decent to their erring wives."

Wherever he went, Italy, Switzerland, Germany, he visited as many publishers of Socialist books, newspapers, and magazines as he could, hopeful of finding multiple markets for his writings but frankly stating he was more interested in a larger audience than in a larger income. In the following years many whom he had visited printed quantities of the material with which Upton flooded them, making him the most read American writer outside of America.

In Berlin, Sinclair finally met Karl Kautsky, the official keeper of the Marx-Engels flame. Marx had died in 1883 when Upton was five and Engels in 1895, and since then Kautsky had been their chief prophet, although he would not long remain that. There was much upon which he and his American brother agreed, from production for use to the terrors of poverty. But it was immediately apparent to Sinclair that so long as the Kaiser and his Junker aristocracy held power in alliance with the rich manufacturers, Socialism had no more hope of success in the German Empire than in the Russian. Even to so severe a critic of American society as Upton, it was evident how much better off the workers in America were, at least in terms of the possibility of improving their lot.

But Upton's desire for *Kultur* for David, not entirely unprompted by a desire for more freedom for himself, led him to leave his son in boarding school in the Hartz mountains despite Germany's evil autocracy and the fact that nearby "were miles of potatoes and sugar beets, with Polish women working in gangs like Negro slaves." However, after a month or two, David's complaints to his father against the school's strictness and its glorification of the Kaiser won the boy a release and transfer for two years to a progressive English school at Highgate. David's stammer caused van Eeden to suggest "you ought to let him have some psychic treatment."

Upton tried unsuccessfully to get George Herron, among others, to take David, and finally in order to beat the submarine blockade, sent him back to America in the custody of the butler of millionaire Socialist Helen Phelps Stokes. No sooner home, he was sent off again to another boarding school, this time in North Carolina, "where we went around naked the best part of the year until it was too cold."

Upton's focus, before his trip, had been on bringing about Socialism's triumph in America, but meetings with his counterparts all over Europe gave him a greater interest in the worldwide aspects and possibilities of Socialism. Although there was no shortage of international Socialist committees, congresses, action groups, and other organizations, Sinclair, with that solipsism that seems essential to most reformers, felt the need for one he would be in charge of and so wrote prominent friends, new and old, asking them to join his international league.

Prince Piotr Alekseyevich Kropotkin, who had taken part in revolutionary activities in Czarist Russia before Upton was born, replied pleasantly from Brighton suggesting that the laborers themselves should found such a league if indeed there was any need for it and that the duty of intellectuals was "simply to help by all means their movement whenever they ask our support."

George Bernard Shaw replied: "Haven't you grown out of this baby stage of making world wide organizations?" and Romain Rolland also sent his regrets, explaining his belief that an artist must act as an individual and not as part of any group however noble its purpose.

If his International League was a failure, still Upton personally was a success. He met and formed friendships with Frank Harris, H. G. Wells, and especially Lord and Lady Russell. She insisted that Upton call her "Aunt Mollie," and because she was tired of seeing him so lonely, she also insisted that he convince Mary Craig to come to Europe.

From America he received during his tour news both of Meta and of Mary Craig. Much of it came from Harry Kemp, who wanted to regain Upton's friendship and wrote that he was finished with Meta who had left him first for a young Yale Forestry School graduate and then for others. Kemp also took the role of cupid or Pandarus between Mary Craig and Upton, encouraging each regarding the other, but neither really needed encouragement. Upton was writing regularly to his *himmlische Engel* as he had christened Craig, begging her to come to Europe, and although the Dutch divorce granting Upton custody of David would not be granted until the last half of 1912, Craig had apparently decided that this was her moment to move.

CHAPTER XI

The Triumph of Hope

Who are happy in marriage? Those with so little imagination that they cannot picture a better state and those so shrewd that they prefer quiet slavery to hopeless rebellion.   H. L. MENCKEN

PRECISELY WHY MARY CRAIG chose to marry Upton is no less difficult to assess than the decision to marry taken by anyone else. To her credit, she did not pretend she loved him as she had Calhoun. "He was still the little boy in need of a mother! He had outgrown his real mother, who did not understand him and disapproved of him so bitterly . . . [who] couldn't see why her son, who was born a gentleman, had to waste his talents on these 'low, ignorant foreigners.' "

Mary Craig's perceptive and frank younger sister, Dollie, who for years lived with the Sinclairs and served as Craig's confidante when the latter was too "nervous" to sleep and wanted to talk all night, thought "it was a tossup between Upton and George Sterling. . . . Sister had grieved·so that she was losing her beauty . . . and she didn't want just to sit there and be an old maid or marry someone in Mississippi. Upton opened up new avenues that she had known nothing about and were exciting to her."

One important reason for Craig's marriage was that it gave her life purpose. "I feel that my life has been worth while because I have rescued Upton from melancholia & perhaps death. And I know he is a great & high factor in the betterment of mankind."

Almost half a century later in a review of Craig's autobiography, which it characterized as "a truly romantic as well as a wonderfully goofy story," *Time* magazine pointed out other unconscious reasons why Craig may have married Upton and indeed why Upton may have become a Socialist. "She never seems to realize that the romanticism of early Socialism and that of the Old South were akin. However different the windmills they were tilting at, both Mary and Upton were American romantics. Besides, most social reformers are dedicated snobs (Upton himself, claiming kinship with the Duchess of Windsor, wrote a series of articles about her folks)."

Although at times there was considerable pretense that the two had not met in Europe and at other times that they had been secretly married in Holland, the truth was that they lived and traveled together there as man and wife when they were not. "We were supposed to be married, of course. The dark secret was kept; it was a terrible secret in those days. But I don't think it would frighten anybody now. We loved each other, and we wanted to be married, and we didn't see why two Catholic judges should be permitted to keep us apart."

Returning to America on the *Lusitania* in December 1912, she fell during a storm and thereafter ceaselessly complained of back trouble.

Her efforts to convince her father that a notorious divorced Socialist muckraker would make her a proper husband were entirely unsuccessful. But she had better luck with her mother, whose chief pride was her "royal descent" from Childeric I, fifth-century king of the Franks. When she learned from Upton's mother of his equally august genealogy and that both families had Charlemagne as a common ancestor, she agreed to attend the wedding, which took place suitably in Fredericksburg, Virginia, on April 21, 1913, at the home of her proper old maid cousins.

The newspapers made much of the marriage of this man, who had so often called marriage "nothing but legalized slavery," retelling the story of his cuckolding and divorce. When Craig's father was asked by a reporter in Mississippi if his daughter shared Sinclair's ideas on Socialism, feminism, and birth control, Kimbrough snapped, "My daughter does not share *any* of her husband's ideas!"

Shortly after the wedding, Upton signed a new will leaving everything to Mary Craig. With a quite extraordinary frequency, all during her marriage, Mary Craig had Upton write not only new wills, always making her sole beneficiary, but also various documents deeding to her all his interest in and income from both his past works and new works as they appeared. Although allegedly to repay her for loans, this practice in fact reflected her insecurity and her consequent need to dominate. Also, it had possibly not escaped her notice that in the divorce Meta had been given no money.

Sylvia, the novel published in 1913 and written the year before in Europe during Upton's *wanderjahre*, was based on those tales of her Southern upbringing that Mary Craig had told him, as was also its sequel, *Sylvia's Marriage*, published in 1914. Much in the two novels was invention, but much also was based on fact, so that years later Mary Craig would interrupt herself telling an anecdote and wonder aloud, "Did that really happen to me? Or is it one of the things we made up for 'Sylvia'?"

Both novels glorify women and point out those laws and traditions by means of which men have been able to exploit women. Sylvia Castleman herself is a flattering portrait of Mary Craig. "She was wise with a strange, uncanny wisdom, the wisdom of ages upon ages of womanhood—women who have been mothers and counselors and homekeepers, but above all, women who have been managers of men."

But Upton was also quite able to make fun of Sylvia: to point out that though she was sent off to college at thirteen, this was less imposing than it sounded because "it is easy to call yourself a 'college' in the South"; that for a Southern belle to look attractive is the *summum bonum;* and that to a provincial Southern girl "a foreigner was a strange, dark person who mixed up his consonants, and was under suspicion of being a fiddler or an opera-singer."

Upton would not, of course, have teased his beloved thus without her approval, and in what was perhaps a kind of tit-for-tat, he also makes fun of himself or at least of aspects and myths of Socialists. For example, Upton recognized that in society he and his fellow crusaders were no longer fearsome figures, in fact: "it was testimony to the headway we are making; that we are ceasing to be dangerous, and getting to be picturesque. In these days of strenuous social competition, when Mammas are almost at their wits' end for some new device, when it costs incredible sums to make no impression at all—here was offered a new and inexpensive way of being unique. There could be no question that men were getting to like serious women; the most amazing subjects were coming up at dinner-parties, and you might hear the best people speak disrespectfully of their own money."

Mitchell Kennerley, who had published without much success Upton's last three books, turned down *Sylvia,* as did John S. Phillips at *American Magazine* to whom Sinclair had offered it for serial publication. Although he too was a muckraker and believed in most of the same things that Upton did, Phillips was first an editor. "No, I don't want to publish your novel. I haven't read anything for an age that has so greatly disappointed me. Now, keep calm and don't back away. You have created one of the loveliest characters that I have come across in fiction for many a day. . . . But it offends to find her almost wantonly used . . . to illustrate our ideas of the current faults of life. By Heaven, it seems like a sacrilege. . . ."

Typically, Upton ignored Phillips' criticism, and when he sold the book to the John C. Winston Company, he quoted the editor of *American Magazine* on the front of the dust jacket only as having called Sylvia "the loveliest heroine in all fiction."

Along with women's rights, the subject of venereal disease had become obsessional with Upton. He was outraged that an innocent wife, such as Harriet Dabney in *Sylvia*, could be infected by her gross husband and as a result have her baby born blind. In magazine articles as well as in that novel and its sequel, he preached sexual hygiene to the degree then allowed and especially the need for sex education. He wrote so much on the subject of the need for birth control education that he regularly received letters asking for advice and help. Not anxious to go to jail for breaking the laws against disseminating such information, he answered with a form letter advising his correspondent to subscribe to the *Birth Control Review*.

With Bernarr Macfadden he had seen the opening American performance of a translation of *Les Avariés*, the then famous and scandalous play on syphilis by Eugene Brieux. Upton rewrote the play in the form of a novel that appeared first serially in Macfadden's magazine, *Physical Culture*, and then in book form as *Damaged Goods* in 1914.

In addition to *Physical Culture*, Macfadden, with an unerring vulgarity, was giving the public what it wanted and so building a magazine publishing empire that would include *True Romances, True Detective, Ghost Stories, Movie Mirror, Photoplay*, and *Liberty*.

While Upton was in Europe prior to his divorce, he had written at a hundred and fifty dollars each a monthly article for *Physical Culture*, ranging from food fad pieces to standard tourist's xenophobic sketches, "Paris and the Parisites," to advice on "Making Real Men of Our Boys." He also wrote short articles for Socialist journals in England as well as a melodramatic serial reminiscent of his dime novel days, but he was writing nothing really important and his income from writing was greatly reduced. "Alas, how are the mighty fallen! in price!!" he had written Craig, enclosing a letter from his American literary agent that reported how ten of the best large circulation magazines had declined Upton's serial offered at a thousand dollars and how only *The Coming Nation* had made an offer of one hundred dollars.

Upton and Craig spent the summer after their wedding traveling in Europe. Perhaps because it was their second honeymoon, Craig brought along Dollie and Upton brought David. Craig was resolved that Dollie should be independent and have her own career, such as she herself had wanted but missed. So she insisted the girl study dance with Dalcroze in England and stay on with the Wilshires when the honeymooners went back to America in the fall.

The Sinclairs had scarcely returned to America in October and settled in Arden, when a medical problem, whose nature neither ever revealed, required Craig to undergo an operation in New York City. Their continued secrecy about the operation points to another abortion, but in any event it was sufficiently serious for her to write her parents a long letter anticipating the possibility of her death. She suggested that if she died Upton might well marry Dollie, and that the main problem would be "helping to save U. [Upton] from Meta's child! The Meta in D. [David] I mean will make D. a problem always to poor Upton. And Upton is an easy prey & that poor little 11 yr old boy knows it well! . . . a child so like its selfish mother." Craig also implied that Dollie disliked David, whereas in fact she did not.

But Craig didn't die. Instead she and Upton went to Bermuda for the winter where he finished *Sylvia's Marriage* in a small white coral cottage surrounded by poinsettia, bougainvillea, and hibiscus. Every afternoon he played tennis at the Princess Hotel. All this was far more beneficial to his health than if he had accepted Arthur Brisbane's offer to go to Chicago and write only about prizefights for the Hearst press. Although he needed the money, Upton had declined this offer before leaving New York.

From Bermuda, Upton carried on his usual profuse correspondence at its usual furious rate, advising, criticizing, and correcting friend and foe alike. He argued by mail about prudery and propaganda with Max Eastman, whose literary editors at *The Masses* included Upton's friends John Reed and Floyd Dell and whose art editors included John Sloan, Arthur Young, Stuart Davis, and George Bellows. And his most successful controversy by mail was with Vincent Astor, the millionaire, with whom he argued about the lot of the American working man and the benefits of Socialism. This exchange of letters was widely reprinted in the papers and from it Sinclair learned that by attacking public figures in such a way as the daily press could not ignore he could get his ideas widely advertised in the capitalist newspapers.

In the spring of 1914, Upton and Mary Craig returned to New York. They took an apartment on Morningside Heights at 50 Cathedral Parkway, an address soon mentioned frequently in the New York press because from it Upton fought one of the fights of which he was always proudest.

In 1913 in Colorado, coal miners had gone out on strike, unwilling any longer to submit to dangerous and backbreaking working conditions from which they earned the right to live in the virtual slavery of company towns and company stores. Setting up a tent city, the miners of the Trinidad-Ludlow area and their families managed to survive for some months through the winter until gunmen paid by the Colorado Fuel and Iron Company set fire to the tents and fourteen women and children were burned or smothered to death.

When almost no word about the murders appeared in the capitalist press, Sinclair determined they must be publicized, and when John D. Rockefeller, Jr., who controlled the company, refused to see him, he organized a "mourning march" in front of Rockefeller's Standard Oil Building in New York at 26 Broadway. Peaceful picketing was uncommon in those days before the suffragists made it an everyday device, and so it was newsworthy, especially since the object of the picketing was to draw attention to John D. Rockefeller, Jr., "the murderer."

Sinclair proceeded with almost exaggerated good manners as he so frequently did when he was the most aroused, and as usual he committed almost everything to writing and sent copies to all members of the local press and the Socialist press all over the world.

On April 28, 1914, Sinclair wrote Rockefeller "a solemn warning. I intend this night to indict you upon a charge of murder before the people of this country. . . . But before I take this step, I wish to give you every opportunity of fair play."

Unlike Astor, Rockefeller ignored Upton, who made known his plans to indict him to sympathizers and of course to the press at a meeting in the Liberal Club at 35 Macdougal Street. "Mr. Sinclair is blue-eyed, fair-haired, and weighs perhaps 135 or 140 pounds [but] His eyes flashed . . . as he told of the terrible time he had to prevent his impulsive nature from running away with him and forcing him into an attempt to horsewhip Mr. Rockefeller."

In fact, as *The New York Times* report continued, Upton spent most of the time at the meeting stressing that the picketers must be peaceful and unresisting even if attacked themselves by police or street bullies. When Frederick Sumner Boyd, a leader in the Paterson silk strike, suggested there should be less talk of non-resistance and more talk of arms and ammunition, Upton suggested Boyd remove himself and have his own meeting. Boyd did so and was joined by Lincoln Steffens, one of many fellow muckrakers Upton had invited to help him.

Among those who chose not to join Upton in his fight with the formidable Rockefeller was Walter Lippmann, who only a few years earlier had been such a devoted Sinclair disciple in Harvard's Intercollegiate

Socialist Society. He wrote Upton that every man must decide what his own role was to be and then stick with that decision. He planned to be an analyst and critic, he explained, rather than an active participant, even though this might appear cowardly to some.

Upton was arrested for his entirely legal picketing, as he had expected to be, and by refusing to pay his fine, he got himself thrown in The Tombs. His arrest, trial, and jailing each gave him another opportunity to express in some slightly different form his story of how the revoltingly rich Rockefeller was brutalizing and murdering his slaves and their wives and children in Colorado. In jail, as always, he went on a hunger strike, a device Gandhi also used to keep public interest alive in the man and so in the issue.

Unlike Gandhi's undeviating devotion to nonviolence, Sinclair's attitude was occasionally ambivalent. "I have followed his [Gandhi's] work with the very greatest interest," he wrote ten years later, "and I shall watch with unprejudiced mind the outcome of the effort. . . . I am a person who has never used violence himself. . . . My present opinion is that people who have obtained the ballot should use it and solve their problems in that way. In the case of peoples who have not obtained the ballot, and who cannot control their states, I again find in my own mind a division of opinion, which is not logical, but purely a rough practical judgment. My own forefathers got their political freedom by violence; that is to say, they overthrew the British crown and made themselves a free Republic. Also by violence they put an end to the enslavement of the black race on this continent. . . . I fear it will sound very cynical, but I must confess that my feeling is about that expressed by an old labor leader of this country, who said to me: 'Never use violence, Upton—never use violence—not until you get enough of it.' In other words, if there is any chance of the people getting free by violence I should justify the use of it. At the same time, I recognize that a man like Gandhi may quite possibly put me to shame as an adviser to oppressed races. If it should turn out that the peoples, who, by their entirely helpless position are forced to employ non-violence, should teach us a higher ideal and a better way of life, why, I would be numbered among those who are willing to learn."

The newspaper reporters were aware that Upton was using them, but most could not fail to admire the thin little fellow with the high voice who was not afraid of the most powerful man in the country, a man their editors would be frightened to offend in the slightest. One such reporter would soon be famous as the very antithesis of Sinclair, the smartest of that smart set whose skepticism and *je m'en foutisme* followed the war. "Precious little reason for writing you," read a letter from George S. Kaufman, "except to express my admiration. . . . Back in 1913, it was I, then a reporter for the Tribune, who tied the mourning band around your arm before you picketed 26 Broadway. I was on that story for a year—made the jaunt to Tarrytown and was stoned out of town. . . ."

The national reports of Upton's jailing, along with a false report that Mary Craig too was in prison, so mortified her parents that Mrs. Kimbrough decided to come to New York and put a stop to this embarrassing conduct. Instead of desisting, however, Upton confided to his mother-in-law his upcoming plans in his fight with Rockefeller, and his passion convinced her to present a letter to President Wilson in Washington in behalf of the miners' families whose babies had been burned alive and to enlist the help of her kinsman, Mississippi Senator John Sharp Williams.

Meanwhile Upton, once released from The Tombs, carried the battle right to Rockefeller's home, the Pocantico Hills enclave near Tarrytown.

Forbidden his Constitutional right freely to speak in public, he warned a meeting of the Tarrytown governing body about "what would happen if they, the village authorities, continued in their course of Anarchy. . . . Gentlemen, I beg you to understand, I am making no threats. I am not a man of violence, I do not deal in violence, I would die before I would sanction violence. I can only tell you . . . what does happen when you deprive men of their rights, and shut them up to brood in secret over their wrongs."

His renewed notoriety brought him increasingly urgent invitations to lecture on the Chautauqua circuit, and he was also again appearing in what was then the most certain indicator of public interest, the topical jokes in the daily newspapers—the very sort he had once earned his living by writing.

THOSE MISLEADING HEADLINES

"Father," said the Deficient Child, "does Upton Sinclair run a fence?"

"No, Vladimir," returned the indulgent parent. "Why do you ask?"

"Because this paper says he had four pickets with him when he was arrested."

Although he tried to get every bit of publicity possible for himself and his causes, he never truckled to the papers and in fact was increasingly critical publicly of both the newspapers and their wire services and their suppression of news that might offend any element of the business community. When he was mistreated by the papers he fought back. Convinced that Hearst's *Evening Journal* had doublecrossed him, he wrote Arthur Brisbane that he would never give another news story to a Hearst paper. Brisbane replied in an urbane but ominous semi-apology that unfortunate as such a loss would be to Hearst, "not to have any mention in the Hearst publications" would be costly to Sinclair.

Upton brought an action for libel against the New York *Herald* for writing untruths about his conduct at Tarrytown and after many delays won two thousand five hundred dollars and an apology in an out-of-court settlement.

In later years, Sinclair did not underestimate the effect of his "Ludlow Massacre" campaign on the Rockefeller family. "There has been an enormous change in their attitude to the public since that time. John D., Jr., went out to his coal mines and danced with the miners' wives and made friends with the angry old Mother Jones; more important he made a deal to recognize the unions. . . . If you look at the record that his son, the present Nelson A. Rockefeller, is making as governor of New York State, you will see that our lessons were indeed learned by that family. . . . I know that our 'mourning parade' . . . changed the life course of the Rockefeller family; and this has set an example to others of our millionaire dynasties—including the Armours and the Fords."

Although none of the Rockefellers has felt a need to acknowledge publicly a debt to Sinclair, indirectly John D., Jr., did just that in his official biography by Raymond B. Fosdick. " 'The Colorado strike,' said Rockefeller, Jr., many years later, 'was one of the most important things that ever happened to the Rockefeller family.' What he meant, of course, was that it bred an awareness of the inequities and injustices of ignorant and outdated industrial practices. It dramatized for him . . . the responsibilities of management . . . [and brought him] a conception of what he called 'the kinship of humanity'—the common hazards, anxieties, and suffering that face all men alike."

It is almost impossible today to adequately appreciate how much courage was then necessary to stand up against Rockefeller or Morgan, because these men not only had an indirect political power through a President or a congressman but also a power as direct and immediate and sometimes as final as a policeman's club or a deputy sheriff's bullet. At this point in Sinclair's life he was, as he had been before and would be again, a rebuke to all who evade trying to improve man's state by that oldest of excuses, "What can one individual do against a whole system?" He knew that all that is ever done, of course, is what one individual dares to do and to inspire others to do.

CHAPTER XII

The Cry for Justice,
King Coal, and California

I never truckled; I never took off the hat to Fashion and held it out for pennies.
By God, I told them the truth. FRANK NORRIS

IN JUNE 1914, unable to stand New York City life any longer, Upton and
Mary Craig had rented a cottage at Croton-on-Hudson, an hour up the river.
Here the stone fences, the daisies, black-eyed Susans and wild pink roses, the
maples and oaks, and the apple orchards gave Upton the peace he never
found in cities and also provided Mary Craig with "Corot landscapes."

Nearby were "various members of the New Masses group . . . Max
Eastman, Floyd Dell, Robert Minor, Boardman Robinson. Each had a
cottage. We played tennis and when we were tired we sat around and solved
the problems of the world to our own satisfaction. Inez Milholland lived
nearby . . . [and a] sister of Isadora Duncan had a cottage and a group of
dancing children."

Lincoln Steffens was among the weekend guests. Pulled out of bed by
Upton for a long morning walk in the snow, Steffens complained to Mary
Craig that he had not even had his coffee—and thereafter she protected him
from her husband's health stunts. Despite Upton's warnings to her of dire
consequences, Mary Craig insisted upon drinking multiple cups of coffee
throughout the day.

Unlike Meta, she proved able, as she would for forty years, to put up
with Sinclair's changing food fetishes and especially with his single-minded
concentration on his causes. She fulfilled his need for a mother, watchdog,
and when necessary, sex partner. He provided her escape from bourgeois
Mississippi and was part of her purpose, her protest, and her education. She
had come a long way from the Delta. She not only listened to the liberal and
leftist intelligentsia expounding on art or politics or sex, but she held her
own, in conversation both verbal and physical. Once Sinclair Lewis was

seated next to her, and while talking, "he gently laid his hand on my knee and began to press it. . . . 'Is that [she asked] the way you make love in New York?' His hand was withdrawn and the conversation was not interrupted."

Upton spent his time working on an anthology of social protest, *The Cry for Justice*, with which he hoped to build up his resources, badly depleted by Bermuda, the long Rockefeller fight, and by the long absence of a real best seller.

In late 1913 and early the next year, *The Jungle* had been made into a silent film. Upton not only helped with the scenario, but also played the role of the street Socialist modeled on Debs. Upton had anticipated an enormous financial success that would enable him forever thereafter to forget money matters and to spend whatever he chose on his many crusades. But the film made little money and caused little stir, except in Chicago where officials were so foolish as to ban it and so give it publicity. But if it brought him no income, it brought him letters of the same kind as did his writing—letters that made his efforts seem worthwhile from people he thought were his most important audience, such as a tailor in Toluca, Illinois, who wrote: "About 350 people attended [a local screening] and if the picture man had it better advertised good many more would seen it. . . . Next time we will have twise as many to see it . . . caused a sausage and lard strike for weecks after. Good many trowed all their lard and sausage away. . . . It made Socialists of many, specely of the young people."

Upton took the film print over from the original producers circulating it himself in the following years to Socialist locals until the print was lost. He corresponded with Cecil B. De Mille, already billed as "Director General" of the Jesse L. Lasky Feature Play Company but still attending to such mundane matters as proposing to produce duplicate prints of *The Jungle* "at a cost (for one print) of five cents per foot . . . additional prints at four cents."

Upton refused to be discouraged by repeated failure to make big money in the movies. At one point he succeeded in interesting D. W. Griffith in a scenario based on Mary Craig's story of the sad life of Winnie Davis, but nothing came of it.

To get material for *The Cry for Justice*, Upton wrote authors and other public figures all over the world. Although a few refused him, most were delighted to have their own words sought after, including George Santayana, who wrote: "Your project is an admirable one, and I should be proud to think that some chance word of mine should ever come to figure in such a new gospel." But rather than suggest specific quotations, he advised: "It is always safer not to let a parent judge of the relative beauty of his children, for he may prefer his ugly ducklings, as most truly resembling himself."

As with most anthologies, Upton's choices were as revealing of the anthologist as of the subject. Marx was awarded four entries as was Shakespeare; Engels and Shelley, only two each; Mary Craig got one; and the anthologist himself got eight, one more than Isaiah.

In Jack London's Introduction (solicited by Upton only after Teddy Roosevelt and William Dean Howells had refused the honor), he predicted that "this humanist Holy Book" would stir and uplift its reader and make new converts, like the Bible, the Koran, and the Talmud. Upton, too, so hoped it would become the new gospel that refusals by authors or publishers to allow work to be reproduced moved him to a degree of vengefulness and paranoia unusual for him. He planned to use a bitter and skillful parody of Rudyard Kipling because the Englishman refused to permit his work to be included, but Louis Untermeyer warned him that "this purely personal attack, clever enough in itself, may detract from the dignity & large purpose of the work. . . . If it were I, I'd stifle my natural resentment—& forget about Kipling."

When Harper and Brothers refused Upton the right to quote some things from H. G. Wells, Mark Twain, Howells, and others, the muckraker attributed it to the fact that Harper's "has the misfortune to have an eight hundred thousand dollar mortgage reposing in the vaults of J. P. Morgan & Company . . . [and] the publishing-business of Harper & Bros. is managed to the minutest detail by this mortgage."

John Reed wrote, four months after publication: "Your anthology has made more radicals than anything I ever heard of," which delighted Sinclair, who hoped his anthology would prove to be an important part of a peaceful revolution in America. Despite accusations against him and even despite his own occasionally overly dire predictions, he was no Jacobin, but instead quintessentially American in his belief that reform in the United States must and would come not by bomb but by ballot.

The sales of the anthology, however, were disappointing and Upton blamed it on the book's high price of two dollars. It was his own works, especially among native-born Americans who were suspicious and afraid of the foreign ism, that proved to be effective. David Dubinsky, the garment workers' union leader who was himself an important participant in the events of the first half of the twentieth century, observed: "his writings had tremendous impact on working people because he wrote simply and concretely. He did not talk in generalities. . . . His greatest influence was among those socialists who were not from immigrant groups. He spoke to the native American in terms of his problems and situation. . . . He was . . . a great agitator. He did not spread the gospel by talking in abstractions. He always turned his attention to a specific evil and exposed it."

Despite the dogwood and other delights of Croton-on-Hudson, in the spring of 1915 Upton and Craig moved to Ashton Hall, the summer residence of the Kimbroughs, in Gulfport, Mississippi. She was delighted to "go home," and he looked forward to a peaceful period of concentrated writing, especially to writing a big new novel based on the Colorado coal war.

From there he still continued his fight against Rockefeller with an open letter to the millionaire. As would thereafter continue to be his practice, he sought as his cosigners not only dozens of the usual liberals—Brandeis, Debs, Darrow, Hillquit, and La Follette—but also as many prominent plutocrats as he could get, such as Mrs. O. H. P. Belmont and Theodore Roosevelt, and even Alfred Kuttner.

But he did not find peace in Mississippi. He was pursued there by Meta, who, although she had just been named as the other woman in a scandalous Atlanta divorce suit, came determined to get custody of David.

She seems to have been motivated not by a real desire to have the boy back, nor even by anger that Upton had reneged on his assurances given when he was seeking the divorce that she could see David whenever she wanted. Her efforts to see the boy had been, as they always would be, rare and sporadic, and apparently even these, more than on affection, were based on principle, as that word is used when "pride" or "self-justification" would be more accurate.

She was obsessed with the idea that her reputation had been destroyed by the divorce and its publicity and that Upton's had not, and she came to Mississippi to prove in court that she was fit to be a mother and that he was unfit to be a father. She was prepared to testify, unless Upton acquiesced, that he had set the Helicon Hall fire himself to collect the insurance.

She could not have been more ill-advised in her tactics and her choice of battleground, or more mistaken in her appraisal of Upton, whose concern for his good name was hardly less pronounced than hers and had possibly been his main reason for seeking a divorce in the first place.

Judge Kimbrough gathered together his family, his tribal allies, and all those bound to him by affection, fear, or simple suspicion of the outsider, and Meta soon realized her case was quite hopeless. She agreed to accept the right to visit David, wherever he was, just once a year for two weeks, and Upton also insisted upon and got an adjudication by the court as to his fitness as a parent and the legality of his guardianship so that these matters were settled finally and would never again be subject to Meta's recurrent needs for self-justification.

Although David's life with his mother unquestionably would have been extremely difficult, his treatment by his father and stepmother was usually shabby and traumatic. Mary Craig could not stand to have this reminder of Meta around. She always insisted, contrary to the records, that David was a poor and lazy scholar who needed the discipline of boarding school or, at least, other children in the home. When she and Upton left Mississippi, she prevailed on her husband to leave David behind to live with his young step-relations who, he found, were "little monsters and I spent half my time fighting them off."

The help that Craig brought to her husband included now not only her family's occasional support, but also what came to be called "putting clothes on Mary Burke", help with his writing. Mary Burke was the heroine of his novel *King Coal* and as Craig pointed out, so concerned had Upton been with the political and social aspects of his novel and so little with its characters, that Mary must be naked, for Upton had never even bothered to put clothes on her, let alone describe her psychologically.

The genesis of *King Coal* had been Sinclair's trip to Colorado in the spring of 1914 after his release from The Tombs. He had gone seeking facts to help him in his fight against Rockefeller. But a year later, after completing *The Cry for Justice*, Upton began shaping what he had seen into a novel.

Throughout his relationship with Sinclair during the writing of *King Coal*, George P. Brett, the Macmillan editor who had refused to publish *The Jungle*, worried that the author would write not a novel but a political tract. Despite Upton's repeated requests for a contract and some money in advance, Brett refused until he should have an acceptable and complete manuscript in hand. Again and again he urged, "bear in mind that it is a *novel* you are writing and not a work of history or controversy," and knowing Upton's need for an audience, he added: "As a novel it will reach a thousand readers, where as an historical narrative it would reach one."

Upton, however, was far more concerned with historical and technical accuracy than with the story, sending his manuscript for corrections to various members of the United Mine Workers of America, founded only a few years earlier.

The result was that, to Upton's horror, Brett refused to publish the manuscript.

Seeing how depressed her husband was by the rejection, Craig wrote secretly to Brett. "Because your criticism of the book is exactly the same as my own . . . I write you clandestinely. . . . The emotional and physical fatigue from which he suffers at the conclusion of a novel, and which makes him protest against re-writing, is passing with each day. . . . Please do not reply directly to me. . . . Simply tell him whether or not you would be interested to see him re-write the story. . . ."

Brett did suggest rewriting and Upton worked at it all summer, writing in August to Jack London, "my poor wife is a nervous wreck because she insists on fussing with me over my female psychology. She insists I can't portray women—& I have no doubt you'd agree with her."

When the rewriting was finally done and the arguments about it with Craig ended at last, Upton wrote van Eeden, "today I finished the book and feel like I have lost a baby; or, as we say, coughed up an alligator."

Brett finally accepted *King Coal,* which Upton dedicated "TO MARY CRAIG KIMBROUGH To whose persistence in the perilous task of tearing her husband's manuscript to pieces, the reader is indebted for the absence of most of the faults from this book." The editor did not accept, however, Upton's suggestion that Rockefeller be sent a prepublication copy and his criticism or even his refusal to criticize it be used as publicity for the book.

Badly in need of money, Upton hoped to increase sales of the book by getting a famous and popular author to write a Preface for it. Several appeals to Shaw were useless, though he promised to visit the Sinclairs if he ever came to America. John Galsworthy also refused, and Anatole France seems simply to have ignored the request.

The hero of the novel is another Candide-like rich young man, Hal Warner, who, inspired by the muckrakers, leaves college, his friends, and his fiancée to work as Joe Smith in a coal mine, and learn about the real life of American workers. Hardly an original idea, it had been best used in American literature in 1901 by Isaac Kahn Friedman in *By Bread Alone.*

Whether, despite its rewriting, the novel was still too propagandistic or whether by the time of its publication in September 1917 interest in the coal miners had been replaced by interest in the daily more terrible war in Europe, the book did not sell well, and the sequel to it that Upton wrote, *The Coal War,* was never published.

Late in 1915, the Sinclairs decided to leave Mississippi for California. Upton had wanted to live there for years because he would always be warm and would be able to play tennis all year round. They first tried Coronado, where they both contracted whooping cough and suffered from the winter winds off the Pacific.

In the spring of 1916 they moved to Pasadena and for most of the next forty-five years were delighted with southern California. Mary Craig, who unlike her husband believed in putting away money, gradually bought the lots abutting theirs and from time to time bought a vacant house and had it moved to their property and joined to their house. So the Sinclair home, a rainbow of different colors and styles, grew as Upton needed more and more space for his papers and Mary Craig for her relatives, some of whom came to visit and others to live.

From the moment she married Upton until her death forty-eight years later Mary Craig enjoyed poor health but she was nevertheless hyperactive with her houses, gardens, real estate activities, and her family's problems. ". . . you make me smile," wrote George Sterling to Upton, "when you write of Craig never resting. The only way to get her to do that is to put morphine in her milk."

Although he never wanted to be rich himself, Upton had no objection to having rich friends and, in fact, in southern California he had a considerable number of them who from time to time proved useful. These included Luther Burbank, the "plant wizard," Charlie Chaplin, an oil heiress named Aline Barnsdale, Bobby Scripps, the son of the founder of the Scripps-Howard newspaper chain, King C. Gillette, the razor millionaire, and, most especially, Mrs. Kate Crane-Gartz, the heiress to the great Crane plumbing fortune.

Upton, because he was a good Socialist, and Mary Craig, because she considered herself at least the social equal and more likely the superior of these people, were especially careful not to appear obsequious or at all impressed by their friends' wealth. That they, like most people, *were* impressed by the cost of things is perhaps best demonstrated by Mary Craig's self-contradicting statement in her autobiography almost half a century after the event that "Upton was not impressed" by the very expensive lunch that Frank Harris bought him at London's Savoy Hotel, along with Upton's own even later recollection of the same event in his autobiography.

King Gillette had written a book, *The People's Corporation,* on how to abolish poverty and war. He wanted Upton's help in revising it and having it brought out by a commercial publisher. The muckraker was not enthusiastic, even though Gillette, when he first came to see him, had sent in a crisp new hundred dollar bill along with his calling card. But Mary Craig convinced him that for five hundred dollars a month he should help this man who was horrified by the word "Socialism" but whose recommendation that all the country's basic enterprises be turned over to a giant "People's Corporation" was in fact the same socialism as Gaylord Wilshire's "Let the nations own the trusts."

For some months Upton worked two mornings a week with Gillette, but when it became evident that the millionaire was really paying mainly for the pleasure of repeating his ideas over and over to the famous writer, Upton called a halt. He turned Gillette over to Horace Liveright, who published Gillette's book in 1924 when the razor king agreed to provide twenty-five thousand dollars to advertise it, but the book had no sale.

Among the people who came to California for the mild winters were Henry Ford and his wife, whom Upton met and then introduced to King Gillette in the vain hope that if a notorious Socialist could not liberalize Ford's views, perhaps another millionaire might. Gillette was equally unsuccessful.

But what was demanding and getting most of Upton's attention was the war, and it was to Woodrow Wilson that he sent his most urgent advice, for he believed that in order to proceed with the redemption of America one had first to end the threat of Germany.

CHAPTER XIII

World War I

When great changes occur in history, when great principles are involved, as a rule the majority are wrong.   EUGENE V. DEBS

THE WORLD WAR signaled the end of the Socialist Party in America as the potentially significant political threat to the two major parties that Teddy Roosevelt had considered it, except in a few local elections. Socialists, whose love for one another and for the party had withstood cruel tests, were divided by the war as families had been earlier divided by the Civil War.

The party's official position was against the war, which would be as always, they said, fought by the many against their own interest and exclusively for the benefit of the plutocratic few. The saintly Debs would be sent to the federal penitentiary for maintaining this position, and many other Socialist leaders who held to it would be thought at best cowards, at worst pro-German.

But many prominent Socialists voiced the opposite view. Charles Edward Russell, whom Hillquit had sought to nominate for the Presidency in 1912, came out against the Central Powers and for the Allies in December 1915. William English Walling, J. G. Phelps Stokes, John Spargo, and W. J. Ghent, among others, would resign from the Socialist Party over the war issue.

Already on September 20, 1915, Upton had expressed his feelings in a letter to the Committee of the Anti-Enlistment League. "I know that you are brave and unselfish people, making sacrifices for a great principle . . . but I cannot join you. . . . I believe in the present effort which the allies are making to suppress German militarism. . . . I would approve of America going to their assistance. I would enlist to that end, if ever there be a situation where I believe I could do more with my hands than I could with my pen. . . . I doubt if there is anyone in America who hates militarism and all the trappings and symbols of militarism more deeply and instinctively than I do . . . [but] I believe it is a work of civilization the allies are doing. . . .

"You will see from this that I am not a consistent non-resister; only a person requiring a tremendous lot to make him fight. Belgium did not quite provide enough; neither did the Lusitania; but all the lies and knavery since have done so. . . . this attitude on my part will continue until the last German soldier has been driven back from the soil of France, Belgium and Russia. Then I should favor peace, and oppose war."

Sinclair's love for Debs did not lesson because they disagreed and he supported Debs all during the years he was in prison, writing frequent letters and sending books to him, and being one of those who worked hardest with both Presidents Wilson and Harding to get Debs the Presidential pardon that came finally at Christmas 1921.

Although there was often much bitterness in the Socialist Party between those who held strongly differing views, Upton stayed friends with all who would stay friends with him. In fact, when America entered the war and Mike Gold and others left the country to avoid serving in the military, Upton regularly sent them money.

In his letter of resignation sent to the members of the Pasadena Local of the party, Sinclair said he intended to go on working for Socialism and might seek readmission after the war. He stressed that he had not "gone over bag and baggage to the capitalist system" and that there was "work of enormous importance to be done by the forces of radicalism in the present crisis. We have to compel a clear statement of peace terms by the Allies and to see that those terms contain no trace of the imperialist programs of the aristocracies of England, Italy, and France."

Three and a half years later, Sinclair would see and admit the error of his ways and apply for readmission. "Today, confronting the ruins of my beautiful hopes," he would point out that he had not given uncritical support to all war policies but had protested strongly against the espionage laws, the invasion of Siberia, the secret treaties of the Allies, and Wilson's unwillingness to demand from them a *quid pro quo*. The degree of his anger and disillusion would be evident in his contemptuous descriptions of Wilson's cabinet members: "A convict slave-driver from the South [Burleson] . . . A ruffian disguised as a Quaker [Palmer] . . . A bland foolish old ignoramus [Daniels] . . . A little military martinet [Baker]." But for the moment he was in the grip of that patriotism instilled in him in his youth.

Even though he rejoined the party after the war, he would again resign from it in the 1930's, so it could be said of him as Winston Churchill said of himself, he "not only ratted, but re-ratted."

Upton had considerably changed his position that inspired Socialists could prevent war, about which Lenin had written in the spring of 1915 explaining at length his reasons for declaring that: "Sinclair is an emotional Socialist without theoretical grounding."

For a man who was so often characterized as naïve by his critics, Upton's letters and telegrams to President Wilson reveal an able sense of diplomatic bargaining and also, occasionally, a shrewd sense of prophecy. In a wire sent February 3, 1917, he urged the President to offer the American fleet to keep open the sea lanes to England, but warned him first to "obtain agreement by allied nations that all territory taken from central powers shall be neutralized and made forever independent under international guarantees."

Increasingly, Wilson was permitting his fatuous Postmaster General, Albert Sidney Burleson, to censor any dissent or criticism aimed at government actions or policies, such as Max Eastman's *The Masses*. Upton wrote, and released publicly, an impassioned letter to the President emphasizing the futility of "helping to win democracy abroad, [while] we are losing it at home." He suggested that if the government felt a magazine was incorrect in its facts, it should insist the magazine print a short reply giving the correct facts and only if the magazine refused this should it be barred from the mails.

"It is hard to draw the line, Mr. President," Sinclair continued, "as to the amount of ignorance permitted to a government official, but Mr. Burleson is assuredly on the wrong side of any line that could be drawn by any one." It seems very unlikely that when he insulted Burleson Upton had yet decided that within a few months he would start his own magazine.

Wilson instructed his secretary, Tumulty, "to write Mr. Sinclair a letter saying how much I appreciate the frankness and sincerity and also the generous personal kindness of his letter and . . . that his suggestion interests me very much and I shall certainly consider the feasibility of acting upon it." It will perhaps not astonish students of such matters that Wilson then forwarded the suggestion to Burleson asking his opinion of it.

Before sending his suggestion that the government take equal space in journals rather than suppressing them, Upton had written a number of his comrades for their opinion of this idea, asking for answers by wire. Max Eastman of *The Masses* found it acceptable, as did Abraham Cahan of *The Jewish Daily Forward*. Frank Harris did also, but added: "The government will not consider it. Hatred of opposition in government is like love of drink in a man, it grows continually."

The New York Call, however, as contemptuous of the idea as of the idea's defected author, replied it "would repudiate most thoroughly any suggestion of compromise of its constitutional rights. . . . The Socialists of America can be relied upon to fight their own cause without any outside assistance."

When Upton later suggested to Wilson that political prisoners who on religious or humanitarian grounds expressed opposition to the war be put on a farm colony, the President forwarded it to Attorney General Thomas Watt Gregory, who, like his fellow Texan Burleson, did not agree with Sinclair's suggestion.

Nor can it have endeared Upton to the Administration when he began a petition to obtain pardons for more than a thousand antiwar prisoners after the Armistice had been signed and was so impertinent as to point out that in the land of the free and the home of the brave, Eugene V. Debs and sometime cigar worker sometime millionaire Socialist Rose Pastor Stokes had been sentenced to twenty years in jail whereas the government of the autocratic Kaiser had sentenced Karl Liebknecht, the anti-militarist Socialist, to only four years.

Fellow muckrakers as well fell out with Upton on occasion. Charles Edward Russell had become so ardent a warrior that he abused Sinclair for writing about a "Clean Peace" and the furtherance of social justice after the war declaring: ". . . it is utterly fatuous now to be discussing terms of peace. We are confronted with the destruction of democracy . . . and there is nothing else worth talking or thinking about and for my part . . . I think you might be in better business."

Although Sinclair's main concern was winning the war and establishing an enduring and socially just peace, he did not forget his other causes such as women's rights and birth control. Margaret Sanger had written him proudly when she was indicted for her articles on birth control and sex, "I 'specially requested the inspectors to wait a few weeks (until the July and August publications of other articles) so I could give them something really to indict me on."

She, like others, had learned from Sinclair that arrests and trials were one way to get the unmentionable widely mentioned. But a year and a half later she was writing him, "My trial has been again postponed. . . . it is the trick of the authorities to try to kill the great interest upon the subject of Birth Control as well as to exhaust me physically, spiritually and financially." She urged Upton to write Federal Judge Dayton demanding a speedy trial or a quashing of the indictment.

Events in Russia were of passionate concern to Upton, who hoped to see them turned to the benefit of the Allies as well as of the Russian people. Along with Charles Edward Russell, Walling, Ghent, Stokes, and others, he had on April 19, 1917, urged on Kerensky all the reasons that a separate peace between Russia and Germany would be disastrous to the international Socialist movement and harmful to Russia herself, sending copies to Wells, Kropotkin, and Zangwill in Britain.

Another suggestion Upton offered Kerensky was that the Czar and his family be sent to America for permanent safekeeping. "Catalina Island, off Los Angeles, could be made into an island for kings and used as a refuge for rulers abdicating or dethroned after this war. The islands have a salubrious climate and are populated by sheep, the proper subjects for autocracy."

Upton was hopeful that, especially after the Russian experience, there would come a Socialist revolt in Germany if not before the war ended then after. He also predicted quite correctly that the Russians would cease fighting unless the Allies forswore any territorial gains and promised the internationalization of Alsace, Armenia, and Palestine, and he warned that Russia's leaving the war would prolong it and cost American lives.

By September 10, 1917, in a letter to Max Eastman, he predicted that: "Assuming the Russians do as they are doing now, falling back step by step but not collapsing completely, I believe that the German line will crack early next summer. I think I know this, in the same way that I would have known in the fall of 1864 that the Confederate line would crack in the spring of 1865, assuming that Grant kept on his hammering. I spent two years studying the Civil War, for my novel 'Manassas'; I studied it from the inside, through the documents of the time, and so I know how it feels to live through a long war, a war of attrition. . . . [but] if Russia were to be put out completely, which is of course a possibility, the war might last over to 1919; but the end in German collapse would be inevitable."

Upton predicted in the same letter to Eastman, who thought America's proper policy was only coastal defense, that if Germany were not defeated: "With ten years more of Prussian preparing, the aeroplane would be able to cross the ocean and destroy cities at leisure—because our easy going democratic government with our innate humane pacifism would have been asleep while such preparations were being made."

Morris Hillquit and others thought it outrageous that anyone expect the Russians to do more than "work out their own salvation without unsolicited outside advice or interference." But Upton warned prophetically, if not too accurately, that the Germans were "sending hundreds of social-revolutionists into Russia . . . [with] millions to spend upon their propaganda both openly and secretly" and that he saw a peril not merely to Russian Socialists, but to the whole world.

As early as 1915 Sinclair had also warned against peace terms "so humiliating as to leave a permanent sense of wrong," and on October 6, 1918, he was again writing Wilson, urging no "punishment" and international guarantees of independence or international government for dozens of the world's trouble spots as the best guarantees for peace.

To some, however, Upton's leaving the Socialist Party, commending Wilson, and urging Kerensky not to make peace, proved only that he was anti-German. One of these, an Austrian named Otto Fleischman, told the muckraker, "If you want war, I'll give you all the war you want," and threatened to kill him, causing Sinclair to write to Shaw about "the entertaining time we are having just now with an anarchist lunatic who is at large and who is trying to get a shot at me, because of my supporting the war. We have to keep all the curtains in the house drawn and steal out the back way, as if we were in the Indian country. I am wearing out all the pockets of my clothes carrying deadly weapons. I hope to be able to report that the news of my death is greatly exaggerated." However jocular his tone, Upton applied for and received permission to carry a concealed revolver, and Mary Craig worried.

With so much to say, the muckraker decided that the best way to say it was to start his own magazine, *Upton Sinclair's*, whose first issue would appear in April 1918. It would suffer many of the same problems of Post Office Department harassment that Upton had complained to President Wilson about in behalf of Max Eastman's *The Masses*.

Hoping to build a subscriber list quickly, he asked for the membership lists of the Young People's Socialist League, the Nationalist Party, and other Socialist and liberal groups that he had founded or helped for many years. He was shocked at the number of evasions and outright refusals he received and grieved at the number of people who viewed him simply as a turncoat jingo. One old Socialist wrote: "I do not care to be personally associated with you in any way. You are a renegade from the Socialist Movement, a deserter in the face of the enemy, deserting at a crucial time in the battle when if ever in the history of the movement we needed the support of all our troops. You go in, in my mind, with Judas Iscariot and Benedict Arnold."

Except on the very rarest occasions, Upton's good manners prevailed, and often his sense of humor as well, in the face of such attacks. Throughout his public life, he received great numbers of hate and crank letters, and others arguing against his positions. Many such he published in his magazine, well aware that they livened up his too tendentious pages and that answering his answerers permitted him to repeat his arguments. "I grant every man," he wrote later, "the right to disagree with me—the more the merrier, it is all advertising."

Many of his regular correspondent critics were the most important writers, politicians, editors, and teachers of the day. Thanking Upton for the first issue, Mencken wrote: "There is excellent stuff in it. . . . What we need in this country, beyond everything else, is absolutely free discussion. At the moment, of course, it doesn't exist. You will be barred from the mails if you are not very careful."

There was an encouraging letter from H. G. Wells that included his own cartoon of a hydrocephalic Lenin. Gertrude Atherton and Count Ilya Tolstoy sent congratulations and also Maxwell Anderson, who gave Sinclair permission to print one of his poems. But perhaps more meaningful were letters from unknowns. "I think it is the greates [magazine] ever written on worlds peas. . . . Your views on religion are exactly my views. . . . herewith a dollar bill for a years supscribtion."

Among Sinclair's most interesting correspondence of the period, some of it reproduced in his magazine, was that with John Reed, who in so few months would be dead and buried in the Kremlin before he had reached thirty-three. Reed came from a rich family in Portland, Oregon, and his activities at Harvard as a member of the *Lampoon* and the Hasty Pudding Club scarcely prophesied the intense reformer he became under the influence of the muckrakers, especially of Lincoln Steffens and Ida Tarbell. He had quickly become far more radical than his exemplars, his writing in *The Masses* having been the main cause of its indictment for sedition.

Upton, saddened by Kerensky's overthrow and the Russians' separate peace with Germany, nevertheless hoped the Russian Revolution would succeed and that he might soon see where the truth lay concerning the emerging Bolshevik government, as between Reed's euphoria and Gorki's despair. He worried too that a great Socialist hero such as Peter Kropotkin was thrown in jail by the Bolsheviks and continued to wonder how Reed, like so many of his other radical friends, could doubt the necessity of defeating the Germans. "American capitalism is predatory," Upton wrote Reed, "and American politics are corrupt: The same thing is true in England and the same in France; but in all these three countries the dominating fact is that whenever the people get ready to change that government, they can change it. The same thing was not true of Germany, and until it was made true in Germany, there could be no free political democracy anywhere else in the world—to say nothing of any free social democracy. My revolutionary friends who will not recognize this fact seem to me like a bunch of musicians sitting down to play a symphony concert in a forest where there is a man-eating tiger loose. For my part, much as I enjoy symphony concerts, I want to put my fiddle away in its case and get a rifle and go out and settle with the tiger."

Although Sinclair would be accused by his enemies of being a Communist, he never was—not at the first moment of their victory nor any time later. He withheld his criticisms of the Communists, hoping against hope they might in fact someday develop a Socialist state in Russia, but as he went on to explain in this letter, he was against the Communists and against their methods for other countries where he hoped for Socialist revolution.

With simplistic brutality, Reed dismissed Gorki as a sick old man and Kropotkin as "suspected with pretty good reason of plotting with the English against the Soviets. . . . You are simply a theoretician, Upton. . . . Bolshevism is not for intellectuals; it is for the people. . . . To you, Upton, there is only one tiger in the forest. To me there is a whole flock of tigers—the tiger who eats me and the tigers who eat other people. These tigers are fighting, and whichever side wins, I get eaten just the same. Under those circumstances it is a bit heartless to imagine any of us, at any time, playing symphony concerts. I have been around a bit, like you, in Colorado, Bayonne, Lawrence, and on the battlefields of Europe. I have yet to see the world's working-class playing symphony-concerts—but I hope to see them, sitting on the carcasses of those tigers."

Sinclair corresponded too with Reed's wife, who replied when he asked how she wanted to be addressed: "I am and was—Louise Bryant— . . . Yes, I'm really *Mrs.* Reed. One has to do that, you know, in order to get passports and be comfortable. Besides a marriage certificate never seemed of sufficient importance to us to make a fuss about—one way or the other."

When she wrote that Upton had hurt Jack's feelings, the muckraker sent him an apology. Highly sensitive to insult to himself, real or imagined, as such egocentric people often are, Sinclair was not infrequently insensitive to how his words might hurt others, but once made aware of it, he usually hastened to explain and apologize.

As its masthead declared, *Upton Sinclair's* was firmly dedicated to such serious matters as "A Clean Peace and the Internation." But it also had a lighter side. Mary Craig's sonnets did little to lighten the tone, but some of her uncomplimentary opinions of her husband, which he chose to print, were good fun. "Upton Sinclair presumes to review a book [by Arnold

Bennett] about a woman. He knows as much about women as—well . . . .
Upton knows nothing whatever about human nature, except that he is
determined it shall be changed."

As his friends had predicted, the magazine was uneconomic and
although he offered his books at large discounts as premiums he could not
get enough subscriptions. After four months he found that for every dollar
he took in he paid out two dollars and forty cents despite the fact that he and
Craig and one secretary did most of the work other than printing, and
neither he nor his wife took any salary. His rate of loss diminished slowly,
but in the first eight months his expenses exceeded his receipts by almost
three thousand dollars.

He had saved no money the year before. His income tax for 1917 had
been eight dollars and sixty-five cents, which he had paid with a check that
bounced.

In the winter of 1918–19, he negotiated a deal with Emanuel
Haldeman-Julius whereby the Kansas publisher absorbed *Upton Sinclair's*,
giving Upton's subscribers *The New Appeal* for the balance of their
subscriptions. Upton was guaranteed four columns of the *Appeal*, to be called
"Upton Sinclair's," and here, for fifty dollars a week, he would write on
whatever subjects he chose to an audience many times larger than the ten
thousand readers he had gotten for his own magazine.

In addition he sold Haldeman-Julius the serial rights to two new books
he had managed to complete while publishing his magazine, *The Profits of
Religion* and *Jimmie Higgins*.

CHAPTER XIV

The Profits of Religion
and Jimmie Higgins

We ought to get rich if we can by honorable and Christian methods and those are the only methods that sweep us quickly toward the goal of riches.
RUSSELL H. CONWELL, *Acres of Diamonds*, a lecture the Baptist minister had delivered over six thousand times and that had made him rich

THE WAR HAD SIGNALED the death of muckraking. The reason, some said, was that the muckrakers had strained their readers' attention span; people were sick of hearing what was wrong—especially now that there was a war on—and wanted to hear what was right and noble and worth fighting for. And after the war even more, they wanted good times, liberation both economic and moral.

As far as Sinclair was concerned, however, his own call to muckraking would never die. He was just beginning what he called his "Dead Hand" series of books, each describing the strangling effect of a different institution on American liberties. *The Profits of Religion, The Brass Check, The Goose-Step, The Goslings, Mammonart,* and *Money Writes!*—taken all together, these had perhaps as important a muckraking influence in the history of America as even *The Jungle.* But the muckraking movement itself in the mass circulation magazines was either dead or dying fast, and as Upton would explain in detail in *The Brass Check,* one of the two best books in the Dead Hand series, the chief causes of death were not natural. The movement was murdered.

Whether a murder victim has any complicity in his own death has been argued vehemently in a variety of cases and times. But in this case the answer was clearly affirmative. As the muckraking magazines became big and rich, they also became dependent on large amounts of advertising and bank credit, and so became subject to economic pressure from the business community.

Means other than the withholding of credit and advertising were also tried. There were efforts, none successful, to build up magazines of similar style and format but sympathetic to business. There was an attempt to buy out already successful magazines and thereupon change the magazines' focus of attention. Butterick Company's purchase for three million dollars of E. J. Ridgeway's *Everybody's* was a prime example of this tactic.

Another method included pressure brought by the major magazine distributor, the American News Company, which merely by announcing it would no longer follow the industry practice of accepting the return of unsold copies could frighten newsstands out of handling a magazine. And there was an unsuccessful attempt by the Taft Administration to raise from one cent to four or five the postage rate on magazines.

But it was bare, brutal bullying by bankers, as in the cases of *Collier's* and *Hampton's*, that cured or killed most effectively and that Sinclair explained and excoriated in *The Brass Check*.

Collier's, much in debt to the banks, was ordered by them to cease the publication of muckraking articles, did so, and flourished thereafter as a journal of entertainment and escape. *Hampton's*, on the other hand, was destroyed by the bankers after Ben Hampton refused the order of Charles S. Mellon to kill an exposé of the New York, New Haven & Hartford's monopoly that was strangling New England.

To Finley Peter Dunne, however, who was perhaps less paranoid than most reformers and whose Mr. Dooley had earlier commented to his friend Hinnissy on the decreasing pleasure of reading magazines, it was clear that boredom as well as bankers played a role in ending this phase of muckraking "But now whin I pick me fav'rite magazine off th' flure, what do I find? Ivrything has gone wrong. Th' wurruld is little better than a convict's camp. . . . All th' pomes be th' lady authoresses that used to begin 'Oh moon, how fair!' now begin 'Oh Ogden Armour, how awful!' . . . Graft ivrywhere. 'Graft in th' Insurance Comp'nies,' 'Graft in Congress,' 'Graft be an Old Grafter,' 'Graft in Its Relations to th' Higher Life,' be Dock Eliot; 'Th' Homeeric Legend an' Graft; Its Causes an' Effects; Are They The Same? Yes an' No,' be Norman Slapgood.

"An' so it goes, Hinnissy, till I'm that blue, discouraged, an' broken-hearted I cud go to the edge iv th' wurruld and jump off. It's a wicked, wicked horrible place, an' this here counthry is about the toughest spot in it. I don't thrust anny man anny more. . . . it's slowly killin' me, Hinnissy—or it wud if I thought about it."

The chief effect of the muckraking magazines, however, had not been the passage of new laws but rather the changing of Americans' thinking.

Never again would business and businessmen and their practices be accepted absolutely and unquestioningly as proper and inevitable. The urge for reform would wax and wane, would be temporarily replaced by Mencken's scorn or by concentration on hedonistic freedom in the roaring twenties or the terrible scramble for mere survival in the thirties.

But it would be reborn with a vengeance as "consumerism" in the sixties and seventies, and in the intervening decades it was kept alive by Sinclair and others in books rather than magazines.

The first such book in Upton's series of exposés and attacks on the American institutions that he believed corrupted by capitalism—the church, the press, the schools, the arts—was *The Profits of Religion, An Essay in Economic Interpretation.* If no one is more religious than a whore gone honest, so conversely no one could be more anti-religious or at least anti-church than a fallen true believer, a bishop manqué, like Sinclair. His contumacy, his exaggeration and lack of balance in failing to distinguish sufficiently between real religion and religiosity, between genuine faith and hypocrisy, seriously damaged the usefulness of this well-researched book for which there was a great need in America.

In an "Offertory," Sinclair states plainly: "This book is a study of Supernaturalism from a new point of view—as a Source of Income and a Shield to Privilege." And he frankly admitted that the basis of the book was his own childhood disillusion with the Episcopal Church he had loved and now viewed only as the "Church of Good Society."

"So little by little I saw my beautiful church for what it was and is: a great capitalist interest, and integral and essential part of a gigantic predatory system. I saw that its ethical and cultural and artistic features, however sincerely they might be meant by individual clergymen, were nothing but a bait, a device to lure the poor into the trap of submission to their exploiters . . . until the venerable institution which had once seemed dignified and noble became to me a sepulchre of corruption.

". . . All day Saturday I ran about with the little street rowdies, I stole potatoes and roasted them in vacant lots, I threw mud from the roofs of apartment houses; but on Saturday night I went into a tub and was lathered and scrubbed, and on Sunday I came forth in a newly brushed suit . . . and a pair of tight gloves which made me impotent for mischief. . . . And all churchmembers go through this same performance; the oldest and most venerable of them steal potatoes and throw mud all week—and then take a hot bath of repentance and put on the clean clothing of piety. In this same way their ministers of religion are occupied to scrub and clean and dress up their disreputable Founder—to turn him from a proletarian rebel into a stained-glass-window divinity."

Sinclair gave to American readers, who were for the most part unquestioning Victorian believers, dozens of examples not only of religion's basis in human fear and ignorance, but also examples of priestly greed among the Babylonians, Assyrians, Hebrews, Parsees, Buddhists, Aztecs, Tibetans, and, of course, Christians. He pointed out how religion had repeatedly justified both slavery and the subjugation of women as inferiors and gave examples of "the damning record of the church's opposition to every advance in every field of science," such as the Scotch clergy's denouncing the use of chloroform in obstetrics because it sought "to avoid one part of the primeval curse on women."

Although Sinclair never doubted the splendor of his own ecstasy and revelation, he had little use for "readers of the entrails of beasts and interpreters of the flight of birds . . . burning bushes and stone tablets on mountain-tops." He was outraged by these men and women who arrogated all knowledge and right to interpret such divine revelations, differentiating themselves from lesser castes by wearing special costumes. Even more outrageous to one who trusted the use of the mind as much as he mistrusted the senses was the skillful use by priesthoods of both the arts—architecture, sculpture, painting, music, poetry, and dance—and also such physical appeals as candles, incense, bells, and gongs.

Upton had at one point intended to call the book *The Dead Hand*, and later, *The Bootstrap-lifters*, because he thought organized religion was as useful in overcoming life's ills as trying to lift one's self by one's bootstraps. He said the priests of all religions, including "the Baptist Bootstrap-lifters, whose preachers practice total immersion in Standard Oil," belonged to the "Wholesale Pickpockets' Association." And he attacked every religion as "the natural ally of every form of oppression and exploitation," but his most bitter attacks were upon Catholicism, which, with that curious snobbery so unbecoming a Socialist, he called the "Church of the Servant Girls." Writing about the Knights of Columbus he demonstrated a prurience that frequently attaches to prejudice, particularly to puritan prejudice, which tends to make the reader discount any accompanying accurate charges and good reportage. "It is these societies which, in every city and town in America, are pushing and plotting to get Catholics upon library boards, so that the public may not have a chance to read scientific books; to get Catholics into the public schools and on school-boards, so that children may not hear about Galileo, Bruno, and Ferrer; to have Catholics in control of police and on magistrates benches, so that priests who are caught in brothels may not be exposed or punished."

But the Jews, those "International Shylocks," and each of the various Protestant denominations, "the Church of the Slavers, the Church of the Merchants, and the Church of the Quacks," also get a full share of criticism, much of it accurate, along with some ill-conceived conjecture and occasionally some bad research. In a careless effort to confute Genesis—for example, Upton wrote, "The distribution of fossils proves that land animals originated before sea-animals"—he was guilty of poor research or of using theories he must have known to be false.

Sinclair had great fun with many of the loonier sects of his day and among those he attacked as crackpot religions were Christian Science. "Just as Billy Sunday is the price we pay for failing to educate our base-ball players, so Mary Baker Glover Patterson Eddy is the price we pay for failing to educate our farmer's daughters."

"What all this means," Upton wrote, "is that we have a continent, with a hundred million half-educated people, materially prosperous, but spiritually starving; so any man who possesses personality, who looks in any way strange and impressive, or has hunted up old books in a library, and can pronounce mysterious words in a thrilling voice—such a man can find followers. Anybody can do it with any doctrine, from anywhere, Persia or Patagonia, Pekin or Pompei. I would be willing to wager that if I cared to come out and announce that I had had a visit from God last night, and to devote such literary and emotional power as I possess to communicating a new revelation, I could have a temple, a university, and a million dollars within five years at the outside. And if at the end of five years I were to announce that I had played a joke on the world, some one of my followers would convince the faithful that I had been an agent of God without knowing it, and that the leadership had now been turned over to him."

"I care not," he wrote, "how sincere, how passionately proletarian a religious prophet may be, that is the fate which sooner or later befalls him in a competitive society—to be the founder of an organization of fools, conducted by knaves, for the benefit of wolves. That fate befell Buddha and Jesus, it befell Ignatius Loyola and Francis of Assisi, John Fox and John Calvin and John Wesley." And yet, despite his own warning, Upton ended his book preaching his new religion of Social Revolution. He printed quotations from Emma Goldman, Alexander Berkman, Bill Haywood, and Eugene Debs, and then confided to the reader that the quotations were really from the Apostles and saints, which proved they were Socialists. He then rewrote the twenty-third chapter of Matthew, turning Jesus' words into modern Socialist doctrine without much difficulty.

Finally, Sinclair predicted not the end of the churches, but their reformation, and addressing himself to young radicals, men and women, he warned against impatience, against rejecting everything old merely because it was old and embracing everything new merely for newness' sake. Not only slogans and enthusiasm and fervor would be needed but also wisdom and work. Not so simplistic as his enemies pretended, he pointed out that neither the reformation of the churches nor even the acceptance of Socialism would "remove the necessity for struggle for individual virtue" and he predicted several times in the book that psychoanalysis would play an important role in the search for virtue.

One sometime radical upon whom *Profits* had an influence was Sinclair Lewis, who wrote Upton praising it and later told him he reread the book before beginning his own *Elmer Gantry.*

Eugene Debs wrote: "Let me congratulate you especially upon your courage in unmasking hypocrites in high places and telling the naked truth about the superstitions, frauds and false pretenses which masquerade in the name of religion"; and from London came an unexpected letter of praise and proselyting from A. Conan Doyle, warning, "don't run down spiritualism. It is the one solid patch in the whole quagmire of religion. Of course there are frauds & quacks, tho that has been exaggerated."

Profits, along with his other books, had an important influence on both ministers and their flocks, according to Walter G. Muelder, Dean of the School of Theology at Boston University. "Proponents of the social gospel movement in Protestantism read his novels eagerly, while on the theological side they were being fed and illuminated by the writings of Walter Rauschenbusch. Upton Sinclair probed into the very basis of the American economic system and by depicting crisis situations in various dimensions of the economic order taught thousands of religious leaders to be concretely aware of social evils concerning which they and their congregations had been too complacent. The more militantly oriented wing of the social gospel movement was particularly attracted to Upton Sinclair."

For the rest of Sinclair's life, this book would be quoted by his enemies to prove him an atheist, but he was now no more an atheist than in the terrible December of 1901 when he had written Edwin Markham: "I want to give every second of my time and of my thought, every ounce of my energy, to the worship of my God and to the uttering of the unspeakable message that I know he has given me."

In later books as well, Sinclair's criticisms of religious groups, sometimes straightforward and sometimes jocular, were such as to guarantee their offending and angering many people and thereby causing future problems for the author. "At Bethany, West Virginia, is a college of the religious body who [sic] call themselves the 'Disciples of Christ', or 'Christians'—to distinguish themselves from Baptists and Methodists and Presbyterians and other kinds of heathen."

Sinclair published *The Profits of Religion* himself, the first of more than fifty titles he would personally publish and distribute over the next three decades. The publishing venture began well. *Profits* sold briskly considering that all its sales except a very few in Socialist bookstores were by mail. In a note to the fifth edition in 1926, Upton proudly announced that it represented a sale of more than sixty thousand copies, not counting a dozen translations. Its good sales were a happy surprise, for contrary to his usual conviction that each prospective work would be a best seller, he had thought it would not sell but that he must write it anyway.

He had hoped to make money from a farcical movie, *The Hypnotist*, for which he had written a scenario and sent it to Charlie Chaplin, whom he had just met and whom he would bring to Socialism. But nothing came of it.

Toward the end of 1918, Upton completed another novel, *Jimmie Higgins*. The name Jimmie Higgins had been invented by Ben Hanford, a Socialist Party candidate for the Vice Presidency, to symbolize the members who cheerfully and loyally do the dog work—ringing doorbells, addressing envelopes, running errands—all the tedious, unrecognized chores that are quite as necessary as, but much less glamorous than, the speechmaking and the going to jail.

Upton's Jimmie Higgins could hardly have been more humble, even to taking as his wife a girl from a brothel. But, like Allan Montague earlier and Lanny Budd later, fate miraculously puts him in the path of the great and famous—in Jimmie's case that of the king of England. Nothing, however, can save this novel because, although its action takes the hero from America, to the battlefields of Europe, to death in Siberia, it is in fact no novel at all but rather a vehicle for propaganda for all of Sinclair's many causes. Half a century before industrial pollution would arrest the attention of most Americans except for a few cranks, Sinclair lamented in *Jimmie Higgins* that "when there is a town every ten miles or so along a stream, with factories pouring various kinds of chemicals into it, the job becomes too much for the restoring forces of Mother Nature."

Upton hoped that the novel would sell enough copies and earn enough money so that he could then take the time necessary to research his next muckraking book. But he had some difficulty selling the novel at all. With no false modesty, he offered it to President Wilson, suggesting that it be "used by the Government as a piece of propaganda for your ideals," and pointing out that it could be distributed to war workers at less than ten cents per copy.

George P. Brett of the Macmillan Company refused the novel because "I find in this book the fault which I consider the most grievous one that can happen to a story, i.e., that the book is written not from the standpoint of the story, as it should be, but because of the propaganda and other material with which the book is, in my opinion, overloaded."

Upton sold the book finally to Horace Liveright and it was published by Boni and Liveright at the end of May 1919. When the Armistice came, November 11, Upton moved Jimmie's death from the Western Front to a jail in Archangel. One of the many all over the world who hailed the Bolshevik Revolution as a dawning of a great day of freedom for Russia's millions, Sinclair was outraged at America's military intervention in a Russian matter—an intervention entirely unknown to or soon to be forgotten by most Americans. So bitter was the anti-Bolshevik feeling after the war that Upton, fearing the book might be suppressed, offered to alter the Boni and Liveright version, while leaving unchanged the simultaneous publication he was doing under his own name, but no alteration proved necessary.

Although not a best seller, the novel sold well. Even though it was neither one of his good novels nor one of his great muckraking books of exposé, it nevertheless had its influence. The reason was that reading all of Sinclair's work, each new example as it appeared, books and articles, good and bad, was an essential of their education for thousands of Americans. "When I was 14 or 15 years old the novels of Upton Sinclair were sold on indescribable sort of paper [sic] and in tiny print for about 25 or 30 cents," writes Saul Bellow, "and I read any number of them—The Jungle, Boston, Jimmie Higgins, 100% American—and then other things like The Goose Step, The Brass Check, etc. These books made a great impression on me, and an older brother who disapproved burnt them all in the alley to save me from radical influences. I must say that although I admired Sinclair and felt indebted to him I seemed to understand even in adolescence that he was ,something of a crank—one of the grand American cranks who enriched our lives. I came to think of him together with people like William Jennings Bryan or Henry Ford or Vachel Lindsay—you can see that this was not at all an ideological line up."

And according to Studs Terkel: "He was a strong influence on my life. I remember as a kid, seated in the neighborhood library, reading 'Cry for Justice'—his anthology of writings of rebels down through the ages & of course 'Oil' and 'The Flivver King' and 'Boston.' And, I guess it was he who coined the phrase *Jimmie Higgins* for all the anonymous, non-celebrated labor people who did all the rough chores—the heroic 'nobodies.' "

CHAPTER XV

The Brass Check

What the proprietorship of these papers is aiming at is power, and power without responsibility—the prerogative of the harlot throughout the ages.

STANLEY BALDWIN

TO AND FROM THE SINCLAIRS' HOUSE at 1407 Sunset Avenue in 1919 and in the years that followed there flowed rivers of correspondence, often dozens of letters a day, requests for books from comrades in prison; requests for help, advice, and money from around the world; threats and thanks; letters from cranks; and the one kind of request that he never refused, that he read and comment upon hundreds of manuscripts sent him by aspiring poets and writers. Upton answered them all, patiently, logically, endlessly.

From every continent came constant requests for the right to translate and print his works in dozens of languages, and that he subscribe to manifestos, committees, brotherhoods, proclamations, and petitions, all of which he carefully read and carefully answered.

He worked to get Debs released from jail ("when this wrong is finally righted, as it certainly will be," Debs wrote, "you will be entitled to a larger measure of credit [for it] than any other") and to release Mary Craig from her recurring terror of poverty by regularly assigning and reassigning to her all title to his works.

He was supplying every issue of the *Appeal* with a full page, for which he received three hundred dollars a month from Emanuel Haldeman-Julius, who not only printed many of Upton's books in his Little Blue Book series, but also printed many serially in his magazine.

Much of Upton's correspondence of course concerned his publishing business, and with his genius for sales promotion, he made use of all of the methods of his day, such as printing at the end of each book advertisements for his other books. But he also devised new schemes to advertise there, including one that amounted to an Upton Sinclair book club, which he proposed in an ad in the back of *100%* in 1920 some six years before the founding of the Book-of-the-Month Club. Each "Sinclair Subscriber" was to agree to take at least one copy each of three or four books to be published every year, of which one or two would be new and the rest old titles reprinted. The cost of these was to be a dollar twenty each in hardcover, sixty cents in paper. He further anticipated the modern high-pressure book club by sending his list of subscribers a circular letter advising them that they must write him if they did not want automatically to be sent his new book.

In order to stimulate sales of *The Goose-Step* among the young he would offer in the *Haldeman-Julius Weekly* a prize for the best review of the book by a college or high school student, the prize being—a set of the books of Upton Sinclair.

Although he usually reserved such promotional schemes for his own books, sometimes he dreamed up schemes for his friends as well. He had helped Ruth Le Prade publish *Debs and the Poets*, a collection of tributes to Debs meant to raise money in the prisoner's behalf, and he then convinced Warden Zerbst to agree to let Debs autograph five hundred copies while he was still in jail.

Throughout 1919, Upton was working feverishly on the most telling of all his books in the Dead Hand series, *The Brass Check*, his exposé of the American press.

Sinclair had unconsciously been researching and storing away evidence for this book since his boyhood experience of helping to elect reform candidate William Travers Jerome, who had during his campaign so provocatively described the exchange of the brass check for a woman's body in the brothels of New York, but had done nothing about closing the brothels once he was elected. An important part of Upton's education had been working for and selling to newspapers, seeing what they would publish and what they would not and about whom, until he had from his own experience "learned the grim lesson that there is more than one kind of prostitution which may be symbolized by the BRASS CHECK."

Although Upton complained excessively in *The Brass Check* about all the wrongs done him by the press down to and including the minuscule and the imaginary, he did admit that he was and always had been a natural and tempting target. "I had been a sort of 'guy'; a young poet—very young—who believed that he had 'genius,' and kept making a noise about it. So I was pigeon-holed with long-haired violinists from abroad, and painters with fancy-colored vests, and woman suffragists with short hair, and religious prophets in purple robes. All such things are lumped together by newspapers which are good-naturedly tolerant of their fellow fakers. The public likes to be amused, and 'genius' is one of the things that amuse it: such is the attitude of a world which understands that money is the one thing in life really worth while, the making of money the one object of grown-up and serious minded men."

Some of these examples are peevish and petty, taken singly, but taken all together they proved clearly Upton's definition: "Not hyperbolically and contemptuously, but literally and with scientific precision, we define Journalism in America as the business and practice of presenting the news of the day in the interest of economic privilege."

The retired Wall Street lawyer Samuel Untermyer warned, "Upton, you can't possibly publish that book. It contains a score of criminal libels and a thousand civil suits."

Sinclair's friends and admirers wrote concerned letters expressing their fear for the muckraker's life. "No doubt your name has been prominently displayed in the 'son of a bitch' list heretofore, but it is quite certain that now you have published 'The Brass Check' you have been placed at the head of the '*god damned* son of a bitch' list. . . . I think you had better quadruple the amount of your life-insurance, because any man who has the ghastly temerity to write such a pitiless expose will have to sleep thereafter with one eye constantly open. I wouldn't wager two cents that you will live another year."

His friends also expressed admiration for his courage, and not the least attractive part of his courage was his effort to separate his friends and associates from the risks he gladly assumed himself. He wrote Liveright: "I want to put out this book without any advance notices, and to get a large number into circulation quickly. The reason for this is that there is a libel suit on every page. . . . If you would want to make any sort of arrangement with me, I would like to consult some good lawyer and work out an arrangement whereby I could own the plates and the book and be the publisher, and you simply be a distributing agent, so that any legal proceedings would have to lie against me."

When Liveright and all the other trade publishers Upton approached were afraid to touch the book, he published it himself and surprisingly found he had a best seller on his hands.

Unable to buy paper for a reprint, he was convinced that "the interests" were putting pressure on the paper suppliers not to sell to him. Finally by means of a loan from Untermyer and by buying incognito, he obtained a carload of lightweight brown "Kraft" wrapping paper and by August 1920 had published eight printings totaling one hundred and forty-four thousand copies.

He did not copyright *The Brass Check*. "I would have been perfectly willing for anybody to reprint it," he wrote a friend, but since the possibilities of libel suits almost guaranteed that no one but its author would publish it, his gesture was perhaps less generous than it first appears or than Tolstoy's refusal to copyright.

Robert Benchley was but one of many reviewers who regretted Upton's ranting about trivial wrongs he had suffered, but he pointed out that "ranting or not there are serious charges here. . . . The normal reader will easily be able to distinguish where the author's unfortunate persecution complex ends and where the real meat of his disclosures begins."

The book is filled with examples of news suppression. "In New York City one of the Gimbel brothers, owners of a Philadelphia department store, was arrested, charged with sodomy, and he cut his throat. Not a single newspaper in Philadelphia gave this news! This was in the days before Gimbel Brothers had a store in New York, therefore it occurred to the 'New York Evening Journal' that here was an opportunity to build up circulation in a new field. Large quantities of the paper were shipped to Philadelphia, and the police of Philadelphia stopped the newsboys on the streets and took away the papers and the Philadelphia papers said nothing about it!"

A good Socialist, Sinclair did not believe that regulation of the capitalist press was feasible because "to talk of regulating capital is to talk of moralizing a tiger; I would say that to expect justice and truth-telling of a capitalist newspaper is to expect asceticism at a cannibal feast."

Blaming capitalism exclusively for the evils of the press brought the author much ridicule. Walter Lippmann criticized his old hero's analysis. He was outraged that Sinclair's indignation, so evident when capitalist newspapers were unfair to radicals, was completely absent when Socialist newspapers were equally unfair to employers. Lippmann scoffed at Sinclair's grandiloquent allegation that American reporters prostitute "the fair body of truth . . . and betray the virgin hopes of mankind into the loathsome brothel of Big Business."

Lippmann expressed doubt whether a body of known truth existed or any set of well-founded hopes, are prostituted by a conscious conspiracy of rich newspaper owners, but suggested that if such a theory were correct then inevitably a certain conclusion followed. "It is that the fair body of truth would be inviolate in a press not in any way connected with Big Business. . . . There is such a press. Strange to say, in proposing a remedy Mr. Sinclair does not advise his readers to subscribe to the nearest radical newspaper. Why not? If the troubles of American journalism go back to the Brass Check of Big Business why does not the remedy lie in reading the papers that do not in any remote way accept the Brass Check? . . .

"He cannot convince anybody, not even himself, that the anti-capitalist press is the remedy for the capitalist press. He ignores [the existing radical press, and the obvious logic that] if you are going to blame 'capitalism' for the faults of the press, you are compelled to prove that those faults do not exist except where capitalism controls."

Many American crusaders, from Upton to Senator Joseph McCarthy and before and since, regardless of their particular crusade, have suffered in varying degrees from moral absolutism, a tendency to believe in simplistic solutions, and from paranoia. In much the same way that impossible standards set by Upton in his personal life (admittedly exacerbated by ignorance and egoism) had helped ruin his first marriage, so his sometime refusal to recognize the inescapable imperfections in all humans, newspaper owners, editors, reporters, and readers alike, made his goals in *The Brass Check* too perfectionist. His demonologic view on occasion led him to attribute solely to capitalism, as others did and do to the Communists, the Catholics, or an international Jewish conspiracy, some problems that are at least as firmly based in the human condition itself as in any politico-economic system.

Upton offered two temporary solutions for the problem of the prostituted press, while awaiting the ultimate solution of all problems—the triumph of Socialism. First, a reporters' union and, second, *The National News*, a national newspaper to be devoted to the truth, and nothing but the truth, which devotion would be guaranteed by an executive board of such luminaries as William C. Bullitt, Max Eastman, Mrs. J. Borden Harriman, Charlotte Perkins Gilman, Amos Pinchot, Lincoln Steffens, Ida Tarbell, Oswald Garrison Villard, and Rabbi Stephen F. Wise.

Sinclair hoped not only to suggest but actually to found such a national newspaper and corresponded about it with Scott Nearing, Robert La Follette, Louise Bryant, and many others. When the losses to be anticipated from the founding of a new paper were, according to Nearing, too great, Upton worked out detailed arrangements with Louis Kopelin and Emanuel Haldeman-Julius to buy the *Appeal* for $200,000 and remake it into the ideal newspaper. But nothing came of it.

Sinclair's proselyting for a reporters' union had better results. He would live to see such a union built and would be honored late in his life by it.

In *The Brass Check*, he also fiercely attacked the Associated Press for censoring the news for the benefit of capitalism rather than reporting accurately. And over the years, the AP would first become more careful in its censorship and then finally cease it.

Mencken wrote Sinclair congratulating him on *The Brass Check* but disagreeing with his proposed cures. "The newspapers fill you with indignation. They fill me with agreeable amusement for they convince me that, as a capitalist (small but tight) I am quite safe. . . . Your case against the newspapers is perfect, but your remedy makes me weep." In fact, Mencken explained, there was no remedy. "The longer I live the more I am convinced that the common people are doomed to be diddled forever. You are fighting a vain fight. But you must be having a lot of fun."

However, in his review of the book in *The Smart Set*, Mencken was far less gentle, revealing his own misanthropy in the same degree as he brilliantly exposed and exaggerated Upton's Pollyannaism. "Upton Sinclair's long anticipated philippic against the reptile press . . . winds up with a remedy that is simple, clear, bold and idiotic. . . . [He is] the incurable romantic, wholesale believer in the obviously not so. The man delights me constantly. His faith in the wisdom of the incurably imbecile, the virtue of the congenitally dishonest, the lofty idealism of the incorrigibly sordid is genuinely affecting. I know of no one in all this vast paradise of credulity who gives a steadier and more heroic credit to the intrinsically preposterous. . . .

"What ails the newspapers of the United States primarily—and what ails Dr. Sinclair's scheme of reform quite as plainly—is the fact that their gigantic commercial development compels them to appeal to larger and larger masses of undifferentiated men, and that the truth is a commodity that the masses of undifferentiated men cannot be induced to buy. The causes thereof lie deep down in the psychology of the Homo boobus. . . . the primary evilness is not in the trade or the traders but in the customers."

Even some fellow muckrakers, liberals, and Socialists were critical of *The Brass Check*, on literary as well as political grounds, most especially those who felt Upton's paranoia and egoism had marred a much needed exposé. Heywood Broun complained that he was tired of Sinclair's partisans asking why he hadn't reviewed the book when he had reviewed or commented on it four times already. "Some of our readers we feel sure, believe that on the morning The Brass Check was published every newspaper reviewer was summoned to the telephone and told, 'This is J. P. Morgan speaking and John D. Rockefeller is here with me. If any of you fellows so much as mention Upton Sinclair's The Brass Check we'll break you. Do you understand that?—break you!'

Broun's readers must have enjoyed the implication that the iron fist of Morgan was as unlikely to fall on a reviewer of Sinclair's work as the sky itself was to fall on Chicken Little. But, in fact, the danger was quite real. Morgan had already brutally destroyed *Hampton's.* Then, as now, exposing the chicaneries of private citizens was both more dangerous and more difficult than exposing those of public officials, and Upton was always more tempted by the difficult road.

The physical danger to Upton was more than imaginary, for those were the days when Attorney General A. Mitchell Palmer and his local business leader imitators all over America sent bully boys to raid and burn union halls and local Socialist headquarters and beat up or tar-and-feather the "Reds" they found. "I have been looking to see you killed right off the bat," wrote Governor George Hunt of Arizona, and from Europe, George Herron declared, "Your courage is enough to stagger the archangels," while Romain Rolland observed, "It requires bold courage to dare, when one is alone, to attack the monster, the new Minotaur, to which the entire world renders tribute: The Press."

When a student named Sidney Hook at New York University was so ill-advised as to object when his journalism professor, James Melvin Lee, attacked *The Brass Check,* he was beaten up and then threatened with suspension from the university. "McCarthyism was child's play, at most a nuisance, compared with those post World War I years."

Sinclair's courage displayed itself in his ability to joke with his readers about what might happen if his home were raided and his papers stolen: "I shiver, contemplating the day when they raid my office, and publish all the queer manuscripts that arrive in my day's mail! Manuscripts of health-cures, manuscripts of bible-prophecies, manuscripts of plans to abolish money, to communicate with Mars, to exterminate the vermin in the Los Angeles County Jail!" But, in fact, Craig and Upton lived "in hourly expectation of some kind of raid."

Sinclair kept *The Brass Check* and a number of pamphlets connected with it in print in spite of threats and endless money problems. These problems resulted from the book's great popular success, from Upton's having reprinted too many on the "Kraft" paper, and from such slow payments by bookstores both Socialist and capitalist that the Sinclairs had to mortgage their house to pay the printer. The author wrote to a reporter: "You ask what book influenced my life the most. The answer is the book to which I gave the most thought, which is probably 'The Brass Check.' "

The book also influenced an extraordinarily wide variety of American writers and editors including F. Scott Fitzgerald, Kurt Vonnegut, Jr., Erwin S. Canham, Edward Weeks, and George Seldes.

In October 1920, eight months after publishing *The Brass Check*, Sinclair published a brutal new novel he said he had written in six weeks, *100%: The Story of a Patriot*. It is about Peter Gudge, a police spy, agent provocateur, petty lecher, and professional perjurer. It also describes the atrocities committed by businessmen and by agents of federal, state, and local governments against labor unions, working men and women, intellectuals, and any others who could, however remotely, be connected with "the Red menace."

The problems in America after World War I, when the troops returned, controls ended, and prices skyrocketed, were blamed by the war-rich, white-collar middle class on radicals and foreigners and especially on organized labor and its strikes that involved some four million laborers in 1919 alone. The abuses against which the strikers complained were real: the twelve-hour day, the seven-day week, starvation wages paid for dangerous work. But nevertheless it was with the strike-busters, with those who promised "law and order," and with those who baited the Red, Negro, Jew, and radical that the majority of Americans identified, and the baiters rather than their victims were rewarded.

Peter Gudge in *100%* was frighteningly like Harry Orchard of the Moyer-Haywood trial. In fact, Upton in the Appendix points out in some detail what in his novel was based on real people and actual events or institutions—on Tom Mooney, A. C. Felts of the Baldwin-Felts Detective Agency, the new Bureau of Investigation of the Justice Department that would become the FBI, and the Centralia case. Frank Harris wrote Sinclair objecting to the "accumulation of horrors. . . . The scene of beating and mutilation in the wood, the twisting of the women's breasts is simply appalling. . . . I was sickened with the bestial cruelty."

But as Upton also pointed out in the Appendix, quoting an IWW pamphlet, it was a time in America when a majority of its citizens at least tacitly condoned "bestial cruelty" to save their property, when "Michael Hoey was beaten to death in San Diego. Samuel Chinn was so brutally beaten in the county jail at Spokane, Washington, that he died from the injuries. . . . Two [I.W.W.] members were dragged to death behind an automobile at Ketchikan, Alaska. . . . The shock and cruel whipping which they gave one little Italian woman caused her to give premature birth to a child."

But America was in no mood to face up to its cruelties and injustices. It wanted to ignore them and silence the radicals like Sinclair who exposed them and offered cures. Exactly five months before the publication of *100%*,

Warren Gamaliel Harding had expressed the mood of his countrymen: "America's present need is not heroics, but healing; not nostrums, but normalcy; not revolution but restoration; not agitation, but adjustment; not surgery, but serenity; not the dramatic, but the dispassionate; not experiment, but equipoise; not submergence in internationality, but sustainment in triumphant nationality. . . . The world needs to be reminded that all human ills are not curable by legislation, and that quantity of statutory enactment and excess of government offer no substitute for quality of citizenship."

CHAPTER XVI

Mundus Vult Decipi

"There's no use trying," she said: "one can't believe impossible things."
*"I daresay you haven't had much practice," said the Queen. "When I
was your age, I always did it for half-an-hour a day. Why, sometimes I've
believed as many as six impossible things before breakfast."*

LEWIS CARROLL

IN THE FALL OF 1920 Upton began *The Book of Life*, the purpose of which
was no less than "to tell you how to live, how to find health and happiness
and success, how to work and how to play, how to eat and how to sleep, how
to love and to marry and to care for your children, how to deal with your
fellow men in business and politics and social life, how to act and what to
think, what religion to believe, what art to enjoy, what books to read. A
large order, as the boys phrase it!"

Sinclair confessed what was obvious from such an undertaking, that he
was an optimist burning up with faith that he had the necessary knowledge
and that his fellow men wanted it and would profit from it. So extraordinary
was the range of instruction he offered that it filled two volumes. The first,
The Book of Life: Mind and Body, gave its readers information on
spiritualism, on Freud, on fasting, and such assorted health tips as the
"bowels should move freely two or three times every day." It recommended
the four-hour workday and advised its readers: "In the disintegration of the
atom we have a source of power which, when we have learned to use it, will
multiply perhaps millions of times the powers we are now able to use on this
earth."

Before *The Book of Life* appeared in book form, it ran serially in the
Appeal, but it did not fulfill Upton's hopes either critically or financially.
Because George Brett of Macmillan, who had published the first volume,
refused Volume II, *The Book of Life: Love and Society*, Upton published it
himself in 1922. In it he discussed the liberation of women both
economically and sexually. There are his usual few examples of puritan

prurience and racism, but he made a strong case for the millions of women who "marry and live their whole lives without ever knowing what passionate gratification is."

He preached the sermon whose validity he had learned at first hand: "to explain that the emotions of women are more slow to be aroused than those of men, and that husbands failing to realize this, often do not gratify their wives. . . . that if the desire of a woman in marriage is roused, and then left ungratified, the result is nervous strain, and in the long run it may be nervous breakdown. . . . Great numbers of people believe that women are naturally less passionate than men . . . but the normal woman is every bit as passionate as a man . . . [and] she will remain so all through life. . . . I say to married couples that they should devote themselves to making and preserving passionate gratification in love; because this is the bright jewel in the crown of marriage, and if lovers solve this problem, they will find other problems comparatively simple."

Sinclair had apparently solved this problem in his own ménage, for he specifically went on to contradict Robert Blatchford's dictum that marriage cannot be all honeymoon, asserting that he has proven in his second marriage that the honeymoon could continue indefinitely. He also repeated his favorite idea from Blatchford's *Merrie England*, that capitalist competition is comparable to a dozen men who go out to catch a horse but instead spend all their time preventing one another from catching it.

A number of authors wrote Sinclair about the book. From England, H. G. Wells confided that Upton had beaten him to the draw: "I should have been at that in a year or so. I may do it still in spite of you. Why do you always think of things first? I am older than you."

A literary critic wrote Upton at length detailing the sexual misfortunes of his marriage. And there were moving letters from persons unknown to Sinclair: "I am a young woman of 22 newly married and as we are poor I am very anxious to learn how to prevent conception," confessed one.

Anxious as the muckraker was to be of service, he had to draw the line at giving birth control information by mail for which he could have been fined and jailed. He was, however, sending advice on sex to his son David, now a student at the University of Wisconsin at Madison, who had complained of his father's lack of interest. David had been briefly allowed during his high school years to live with his father and stepmother. But Craig had found having the boy around so unbearable that Upton had insisted David go to a college away from California, even though he was making no contribution toward the tuition, insisting that the boy must earn his own way. Faced with the usual temptations at college, David had written to his father about them.

"This newspaper clipping," Upton replied, "made me think of you saying that you knew a lady (or a woman) you thought was fast & that might be exciting. I have met a number of fast ladies & watched a number of men try that variety of excitement, & it does not pay in the long run. I have yet to learn of a woman who was 'fast' in sex matters who was not treacherous in other ways, or who could be counted on to play fair in anything: & there is an infinite variety of mix-ups and troubles always very evident after it's over, but never possible to foresee. Here is this fellow in the papers—he thought he was having a cheap & harmless flirtation with a manicure lady & presently he was invited to pay for the rent, & to have his father blackmailed; and now he's in the loathsome Arbuckle mess, which would ruin him for life, if he had any need of reputation (which he may not have, being a movie actor.) [sic] If I can find a letter I got from Wilshire last week [I'll enclose it] about Meta & the fellow Raoul, who met a fast lady & lost his wife! And there was poor Harry Kemp—he said I made him the 'goat' but it wasn't so; he just came and 'butted in' & made a goat of himself.

"You see no woman lives in a world by herself; she has relatives & friends, a whole world of complications. Maybe she has a husband who wants to get rid of her, or whom she wants to get rid of. Maybe she has a father or brothers who shoot a fellow's head off or tar & feather him. Maybe she gets into trouble, & blames the last man, tho he mayn't be to blame. Maybe she has a notion to stop being fast, & fall really in love, & then if the man wants to quit she goes & drowns herself. A year or two ago there was a college boy who got accused of murder under just such circumstances, & of course his career was ruined. And if a woman stands alone—even then there are complications, her own heart, or perhaps her own greed, her lack of heart. It's something every father has to warn his son about—there are thousands of women who live by blackmailing inexperienced boys; and of course they know all arts, & all the roles to play. It may seem funny to you since you have nothing—but please bear in mind that I am supposed to be a man of wealth, & I can especially ill afford to stand any publicity of that sort. Even if I did not think a good deal about your happiness, I have a right to warn you about this sort of thing for the sake of your own. [sic] Let me tell you—All the imagination of all the novelists in the world could not portray the possibilities of insanity & hysteria in the souls of sexually parasitic females. One came recently from Chicago to be my secretary—enraptured admirer of my work, pretty, frail little woman, I had an uncomfortable feeling that she was going to fall down in the midst of dictation & kiss my shoe tops. So of course I was doubly careful to be rigidly correct at every moment. She got into a fuss with every other girl in the office & I had to fire her—& then you should have seen the little wildcat! She spends her time denouncing me & Craig all over Pasadena, & every week or so she walks by the house & flaunts her skirts at us, & writes us saucy notes. Perfectly crazy, of course. But now & then I think, suppose I'd been the kind of man that falls for feminine arts, and had ever given a hint of anything sexual to that crazy little bundle of egotism & vanity & jealousy—what a hell of a mess I'd have been in!

"Take it from me, there is no woman who really cares for a temporary sex union. They always want permanence & they try to get it by hook or by crook. They may think they don't want it, but they find they are wrong & change their minds. Or, if they pretend to be satisfied, it's because they expect to be paid for it.

"There is no possibility of happiness in sex life—under our present social system, at any rate,—except to find a decent girl who will be true to you & to whom it's worth being true; a girl who has sense, and can understand what marriage means, & make an honest effort to make a success of it. There is only one thing now that I am concerned about for you—you have learned to take care of yourself, & you have a sound mind in a sound body; I want to see that you don't fall into the trap of sex & get yourself tied up in one of those endless & horrible tangles, of which I have seen so many. It is all so delightful at the beginning, often innocent & harmless, & always, as you say, 'exciting.' And then at the end, it's like a big drink of poison that you have to go on drinking for the rest of your life. You have met some decent girls, & know what they are; so make up your mind to the necessary self-discipline, & wait till you can get one in the honest & enduring way! With love, Father.

"C has mislaid the letter from Wilshire. He told of having met the former Mrs. Raoul, of Atlanta, & what she told him of Meta's carrying on in her home."

After two years at college, David, who was suffering from unrequited love again, wrote his father, who urged him to find another nice girl and not to turn to "dance hall tarts." When David found his father's sex advice inadequate and wrote him so, Upton replied: "I am humbled by yr writing me that I might give you help in sex matters if I were not a puritan. I am not that, & the word has no meaning applied to me—except as the person applying wants to excuse the degrading of love. . . . you will not be able to get me to change my opinion that 'sex' without love is a degradation of all the best there is in us."

Although most of Upton's letters to David were dictated and typed, the ones on sex were hand written including one of five closely written pages in which he urged his son to marry. "Celibacy means torment, & there is no way to escape it. You can put down the sex craving for a time, but it comes back again & again, and it will take these low & vulgar forms, if it does not find the normal expression in love." And a few days later: "I believe in early marriage" and in some detail explained why patience is necessary to satisfy a wife sexually.

Upton was far more generous with advice than with funds. Not only had his son to work for any money he needed, but also, unbeknown to David, his father had written yet another will, again leaving everything to Mary Craig. It contained the pathetic excuse: "My son will understand that the little property which I possess has been mainly the gift of others, who wished me to keep my books in circulation, and that I therefore do not regard it as mine in a personal sense. . . ."

Upton left entirely to Mary Craig's "judgement the decision as to any financial aid of which he [David] may through illness or accident stand in need." That this almost grotesque caricature of a wicked stepmother, who had kept David exiled from his father during most of her marriage, would find any financial need of David's compelling was about as likely as that she carry out his other wish: "I entrust to her of continuing my life-work, of keeping my books available at the lowest possible prices." Much of her time was spent arguing fiercely and not unreasonably with Upton that if the public would not buy enough of his books for him at least to break even, then the publishing of them related to ego rather than need.

The will specified that even if Mary Craig died before Upton, David would get only his father's library—everything else to go to the American Fund for Social Service of New York City to be used for "keeping my books in circulation as cheaply as possible."

Upton's correspondence of the period is full of evidence of the unprofitability of his book publishing business, and yet he even tried to enter other aspects of publishing. When Haldeman-Julius, who unlike Upton was no longer willing to promote Socialism or anything else unless it yielded a profit, killed the no longer profitable *Appeal*, Sinclair was "seized by an overwhelming impulse to take up the paper. . . . What I have in mind is a paper similar to the 'Appeal,' except that it will contain no patent medicine advertisements and no sex lures . . . will serve the movement instead of exploiting it. . . . I propose to give a year of my time, without compensation, and also to give five thousand dollars' worth of my books, which I will sell at the meetings in order to raise funds for the organizing expenses."

Just as his correspondence was both with the world famous and the unknown, so were his financial affairs. Admirers from all over lent him small sums when he pointed out his need in his circular letters, and then as they too became hard-pressed, they would write asking for repayment.

Similarly, when he was seeking detailed information on any subject, correspondents from as diverse institutions as Harvard Law School and Tipton High School in Tipton, Indiana, would volunteer it. After any exposé of his appeared, unsolicited examples confirming or contradicting his conclusions arrived endlessly. Or an admirer who could not induce his public library to buy a Sinclair book would send the alleged reason to the author, who might then get publicity out of it with a letter to the editor of the local paper.

Often the mail from abroad was even greater than from American correspondents. A Socialist deputy from Rome reported on translations and "the *patriotic* movement of the *fasci*, which has brought about the destruction by fire of our buildings and meeting halls all through Italy." Bertrand Russell wrote, "I am an admirer of your books, and have got into trouble with various Americans by quoting them as an authority on American conditions. . . . be so kind as to send me . . . '100%,' 'The Brass Check,' 'The Profits of Religion,' for which I enclose $1.80."

In the Soviet Union American visitors even in the Tartar Republic of Kazan were asked "clamorously for news not of Warren G. Harding, but of Upton Sinclair." Russian readers were pleased both by the muckraker's frequently expressed enthusiasm for their Bolshevik Revolution and by his moving denunciations of capitalism's injustices. His works, which under the Czar had been known in Russia to only a few revolutionaries, were in the decades after 1918 printed in the Soviet Union in enormous editions.

Gorki wrote about *100%* and *Jimmie Higgins*: "You are writing better and better every time and I congratulate you with it from all my heart!" He followed the compliments with a request for an article for his new literary review.

Louise Bryant reported that Nadejda Constantinova Krupskaya, Lenin's wife, also liked *Jimmie Higgins*. " 'It is a good book,' she said, 'it gives me a very definite idea of what an ordinary American Socialist is like. It is sad also and disillusioning and therefore instructive. I would like to know about Sinclair. Is he a Communist? And has he written other books?'

"I told her briefly what I know of Sinclair. She was interested and said she would like to read the 'Jungle' and the 'Brass Check.' I said: 'I'm sure he would send you autographed copies of them all if he knew you were interested.'

"Krupskaya was pleased but unconvinced. 'Really,' she said: 'why should he? He has probably never heard of me.' There was something very charming about her naïveté."

Sinclair was delighted when Krupskaya did write to him. He was frequently in correspondence with various Russians about the publication in the Soviet Union of his books and articles as well as about motion pictures. He sent information on how movies were made. Until his last copy of the film version of *The Jungle* was lost, he offered to give the Russians prints of it at cost. And he got Mary Pickford, Douglas Fairbanks, Charlie Chaplin, and his other glamorous Hollywood friends to sponsor the showing of Russian films or benefits for Soviet causes. "The moving pictures furnish the principal intellectual food of the workers at the present time, and the supplying of this food is entirely in the hands of the capitalist class, and the food supplied is poisoned. . . . At present you may use all my books without compensation to me: some day in the future, if Russia succeeds in winning out against the attacks of the capitalist world, and if the Russian workers have money, they may pay me some of it, and I will use it to make a picture for the American workers."

Crude and doubtful changes were increasingly being made by the Russians in their translations of Upton's books. In addition to making freely whatever ideological improvements they wanted, his editors in the U.S.S.R. criticized Upton's liberal Socialist and other non-Communist connections. The muckraker answered softly, always finally permitting whatever editing the Russians wanted but repeatedly explaining the position that he refused to change. "I am willing for you to make the necessary changes if you see fit, but I should think you would be willing to let my works speak for themselves. You could not expect an American author to see eye to eye with you on every subject; people in different parts of the world naturally have different points of view. Would it not be better for you to put in a preface, in which you set forth your point of view, and the difference between your point of view and mine? I am not voicing my sentiments, but those of the character. Even though you think the reactionary regime will never come back, you must be aware of the fact that many of the reactionaries do expect to come back, and it would be perfectly natural for them to make this boasting prophecy."

As Erasmus had been labeled a coward by both sides when he tried to make peace between his Lutheran and Catholic brothers, so more and more in the years ahead Sinclair would be attacked by those both to his right and his left. But he would remain always "completely *sui generis:* a faddist, a Puritan, and a socialist," preferring to be scorned by both sides rather than to choose the lesser of two evils when, in fact, he thought there was yet another, better way.

The little radical magazines in America had historically been produced by a variety of writers and artists holding a rainbow of views from liberal to anarchical. They attacked not only the "plutes" but also other of the various leftist fragments whose views differed fractionally from their own. They also, in the main, were or tried to be first of all artists and only secondarily propagandists.

But as the Communists increased in strength, they wanted neither criticism nor competition and insisted that art, if given any role at all, was not only secondary to practical politics but its servant. *The Liberator* was taken over in 1922 by Robert Minor and Joseph Freeman for the Communists and, thereafter, those whose main concern was art drifted away from the magazine.

Upton, however, for many years not only refused to have any enemies on the left but also refused not to take advantage of any journal, of the left or right, to expound his views: "I always advise the workers to keep their guns trained upon the enemy; and in portraying the movement I try to understand the point of view of all the different groups, and to reconcile them when it is possible."

He continued writing for and stayed friends with Robert Minor, for example, pointing out that "Mainly I used to kick [to *The Liberator*] at the superfluity of unlovely nude ladies; and I am glad to note that these ladies have for the most part betaken themselves to other quarters."

Although there was much that separated Upton from the Communists, they did agree that there was not time for nudes—at least the Communists felt the sex and art problems should not be addressed until Communism had won its power struggle. So Minor corresponded regularly with Sinclair on such serious, unerotic subjects as a coalition government of Socialists and Communists in Saxony and Thuringia, anxious to keep Sinclair's enormous prestige associated with the Communists and his name appearing in *The Liberator*.

In 1923, Upton tried unsuccessfully to interest Mike Gold in joining him to start a new radical literary magazine, but although the younger man was interested in the idea, he was afraid that Sinclair, who sometimes mistook himself for a public movement, would dominate the undertaking. Gold believed there was a real chance "to make a bright, artistic, brilliant magazine that would captivate the imagination of the younger generation and rally them around something real—not the sterile mockeries and jibing at the boobs that Mencken has taught them."

But he was frankly afraid also of Upton's well-known puritanism. "It is like being asked by a pure young girl in marriage when one is a battered old roué with five or six affairs on hand. . . . I can't be as pure, fervent and puritanical as yourself, Upton, and I would not want to be. The mass of humanity, stupid or intellectual, is fond of any kind of fun, sensuality, relaxation, sport and frivolity, and I am one of them."

Sinclair's reassurances to Gold only confirmed the latter's fears. He wrote Gold that he was "mistaken in understanding the matter as being a proposition of working under me. . . . What you say about [my wanting] a personal organ, etc., has nothing to do with the case. . . . I have definitely decided that I can do more for the world by writing books, and I would not take the responsibility of another magazine, and I did not have that in mind when I wrote you." But he went on to demonstrate prejudices that chilled Gold: "a good deal of the space of the 'Masses' was taken up with pictures of naked ladies, dancing in woodland groves and taking sun-baths on beaches . . . [and] At one time during the Negro period of the 'Liberator's' career we were treated to ecstatic descriptions of the joys of rolling about on couches with naked brown flesh. . . . I believe in true and honest love, and to fight for its rights in a radical paper would be all right, of course, but I do not believe in degeneracy, and I don't think the younger generation needs any help from me in its effort to revert to savagery."

Gold and others, unable to stomach *The Liberator* once it was taken over by the Communists, did get their new magazine in 1925 when the same Garland Fund that had refused to subsidize Upton's personal publishing business decided to underwrite *The New Masses*. The fund had been set up by young Charles Garland who on graduating from Harvard and coming into his patrimony decided to use it in the furtherance of radical causes. Upton would be a contributor to *The New Masses*.

So much of Upton's time was taken up by an endless flow of visitors that he tried repeatedly to hide behind a post office box number and an unlisted telephone number, but without much success. "Back in 1923," Luis Muñoz Marín remembered, "in passing through Los Angeles, I spent about an hour and a half riding with him in trolley cars and discussing the possibility of translating some of his books into Spanish. . . . As I began my political career as a Socialist in Puerto Rico, I can say I was profoundly moved and influenced [by him and impressed] by his kindliness and generosity."

In contrast to his treatment of his own family, Sinclair was very generous to some members of his wife's family, whose misfortunes added to his financial obligations. His delicious sister-in-law, Dollie, with her invalid husband, Robert Irwin, and young daughter, Shel, lived for many years next door to the Sinclairs in a house also owned by Upton and Craig. Dollie helped Upton bear the burden of Mary Craig's ever-increasing hypochondria.

A brother of Mary Craig's, Hunter Kimbrough, for years lived with the Sinclairs. Hunter had apparently enjoyed little success in a series of schools, followed by a less than spectacularly successful career in business as a young man. Thereafter, his chief source of support, according to his sister Dollie, was his brother-in-law. Upton tried periodically, without much luck, to find Hunter employment and ironically, a job he arranged for Hunter was one of the contributing causes to a major disaster of Sinclair's own life.

The muckraker continued to see to it that his name appeared regularly in the press by giving out suitably provocative statements, such as suggesting amnesty for conscientious objectors to the first world war; declaring that wives should be paid suitably for their work as home managers and mothers; and by regularly allowing his name put in nomination for public office on the Socialist ticket and running well ahead of other Socialist candidates.

There were a few kinds of publicity, however, that even Upton did not want. When Horace Liveright sent him the manuscript of Harry Kemp's forthcoming book, *Tramping on Life*, the cuckold objected at great length but with little result that it presented him unfairly and made him look a fool. Kemp's book was soon forgotten. But nothing made Upton appear so foolish as his own credulity when combined with his stubborn determination.

No other single example of his credulity brought on him more ridicule than his sponsorship of Dr. Albert Abrams and none, in retrospect, seems more avoidable. Both his error and his refusal to admit it, therefore, are revealing.

In June of 1921, a friend whom Abrams was treating for syphilis, wrote to Sinclair praising the doctor so extravagantly that in September Upton went to San Francisco to see Abrams' work. Abrams demonstrated for him his miraculous machine, the "oscilloclast," that he claimed infallibly diagnosed electrically any and all diseases from blood samples, either fresh or sent by mail. Upton also watched Abrams train both homeopathic and medical doctors from all over America in the use of this machine. After their training these doctors were allowed to lease or buy one of the oscilloclasts and some of them when they went home discovered, *mirabile dictu* that the machine had curative as well as diagnostic powers.

Van Eeden wrote in October suggesting "quackery," but Upton refused to heed his warning and by the following April was planning a book on the miraculous doctor and had written to *The Journal of the American Medical Association* defending Abrams. The *Journal* printed Upton's letter and expressed shock that Upton took at face value the testimony of men who leased Abrams' machine, pointing out "that these disciples of Abrams, who are enjoying incomes from $1000 to $2000 a week, should speak favorably of the Abrams method was inevitable!"

The hypochondriacal Mary Craig, usually suspicious of Upton's causes, was on this occasion equally taken in by Abrams, as was Theodore Dreiser, but Dreiser wisely refused to be quoted. David Sinclair, however, was not fooled. He wrote, but kept secret from his father, a song to the tune of "Yes, We Have No Bananas" making fun of the quack.

The New York Times of August 19, 1924, stated: "The Abrams claims were impaired recently by the sudden death [Jan. 13, 1924] of Dr. Abrams in his sixty-second year from pneumonia caused by overwork with his machine which was put forward as a sure cure of pneumonia and all other diseases. . . . [According to the *Scientific American*'s report] 'His death came on the eve of his scheduled appearance as the star witness in the trial of Dr. Mary Lecoque, an E.R.A. practitioner, at Jonesboro, Ark., charged with using the mails to defraud. The prosecution charged that Dr. Lecoque had diagnosed the blood of a chicken as that of a human. . . . [Abrams] left an estate valued at from $2,000,000 to $5,000,000.' "

Despite such evidence and despite the endless ridicule, Sinclair refused to repudiate Abrams.

That so devout a meliorist as Sinclair should fall for so palpable a fraud is hardly startling. Throughout his life he contained the contradiction of a suspicious investigator sometimes made credulous by the intensity of his desire to see man's lot improved. And to a considerable degree, Sinclair would automatically be favorably disposed toward anyone who was, like Abrams, opposed by the American Medical Association.

Voters often vote *against* a candidate rather than *for* his opponent and tend to study and excoriate their *bête noire* and ignore his opponent. Similarly, to Sinclair, what he viewed as the errors and outrages of the AMA were more visible than Abrams' chicanery.

Mencken understood the phenomenon and wrote about it enthusiastically, making fun of his old friend. "When the history of the late years in America is written, I suspect that their grandest, gaudiest gifts to *Kultur* will be found in the incomparable twins: the right-thinker and the forward-looker. No other nation can match them, at any weight. The right-thinker is privy to all God's wishes, and even whims; the forward-looker is the heir to all His promises to the righteous. The former is never wrong; the latter is never despairing. . . . I give you Upton Sinclair and Nicholas Murray Butler as examples. Butler is an absolute masterpiece of correct thought; in his whole life, so far as human records show, he has not cherished a single fancy that might not have been voiced by a Fifth Avenue rector or spread upon the editorial page of the New York *Times*. But he has no vision, alas, alas! All the revolutionary inventions for lifting up humanity leave him cold. He is against them all, from the initiative and referendum to birth control, and from Fletcherism to osteopathy. Now turn to Sinclair. He believes in every one of them, however daring and fantoddish; he grasps and gobbles all the new ones the instant they are announced. But the man simply cannot think right. He is wrong on politics, on economics, and on theology. He glories in and is intensely vain of his wrongness. . . . it takes long practice and a considerable natural gift to get down the beliefs of Sinclair. I remember with great joy the magazine that he used to issue during the war. . . . he advocated . . . sex hygiene . . . the Montessori method, paper bag cookery, war gardens . . . chiropractic, Esperanto, fasting . . . deep breathing, the Little Theatre movement . . . *vers libre,* mental telepathy, the abolition of grade crossings . . . and the twilight sleep. . . .

"I have a wide acquaintance among such sad, mad, glad folks, and know some of them very well. It is my belief that the majority of them are absolutely honest—that they believe as fully in their baroque gospels as I believe in the dishonesty of politicians—that their myriad and amazing faiths sit upon them as heavily as the fear of hell sits upon a Methodist deacon who has degraded the vestry-room to carnal uses. . . . Call them the tender-minded, as the late William James used to do, and you have pretty well described them. They are, on the one hand, pathologically sensitive to the sorrows of the world, and on the other hand, pathologically susceptible to the eloquence of quacks. . . . the forward-looking heart simply refuses to harbor the concept of the incurable [which explains] . . . the protean appetite of the true forward-looker—this virtuosity in credulity. . . .

"What is to be done for him? . . . Answer: nothing. He was born that way, as men are born with hare lips or bad livers. . . . He must suffer vicariously for the carnal ease of the rest of us. He must die daily that we may live in peace, corrupt and contented . . . [and be shaken down by numberless societies] for protecting poor working-girls against Jews and Italians, for putting Bibles into bedrooms of week-end hotels . . . for making street-car conductors more polite, for training deaconesses, for preventing cruelty to mules and Tom-cats."

Sinclair was aware that he was out of step with Mencken and the period's other sophisticates. In 1921, in *The Beautiful and the Damned,* F. Scott Fitzgerald defined the *summum bonum* as "the final polish of the shoe, the ultimate dab of the clothes brush," and, in 1925, he published the definitive novel of the twenties, *The Great Gatsby*. In 1922 Sinclair's novel attacking the same superficialities of the period as *Gatsby* was published. Entitled *They Call Me Carpenter: A Tale of the Second Coming*, it could hardly have been more heavy-handed or more deservedly forgotten, with such chief characters as Abey Tschnicczklefritszch, a movie producer with a burlesque hall Jewish accent, and Mary Magna, a great movie star who is redeemed from her wicked ways and brought to salvation by The Carpenter before He is lynched by the American Legionnaires of Mobland.

Instead of shocking people as its author had hoped, and perhaps because of its manifest vulgarity, *Carpenter* was seized upon by a medium usually closed to Upton, *Hearst's International Magazine*, where its success opened another market to its author. Hearst's editor, Norman Hapgood, paid twenty-five hundred dollars for only the American serial rights. It is ironic that a work of such consummate lack of artistry, which Upton had tossed off in five weeks, should earn so much money and reach such a wide audience, when others on which he had labored long to make them great works of art or thorough works of exposure had less success and less exposure. Nor was this the only such experience he had.

In the summer of 1923, Upton began a weekly column in Hearst's *New York American*. With sensational headlines, cartoons, and photographs, he revealed to Hearst's readers that "Plutocracy Rules American Colleges," "U.S. Colleges Under Control of Morgan Gold," "Banker 'Grand Dukes' Control Snobbish Princeton," and "Secret Societies Rule Yale, 'Democracy' Gone." It is impossible to say with any degree of certainty whether William Randolph Hearst sponsored these attacks because of his own expulsion from Harvard or because he had neither in college nor later been himself a really full-fledged member of society's top drawer, or simply because he was a good enough psychologist and newspaperman to know that millions of Americans although called to lowly stations in life were therefore all the more curious about the arcana of Yale's secret societies and Harvard's final clubs. But Upton's columns, based on his upcoming muckraking book,

The Goose-Step, were sufficiently pleasing to Hearst or his readers or both that they were followed by another series of Sinclair columns on subjects ranging from "Getting the Big Hogs' Feet Out of the National Trough," the perils of secret diplomacy, and the liberation of women, to the "Desperate Struggle for the World's Oil," Gandhi and the "World's Most Colossal Experiment in Political Idealism," "Modern Psychology . . . by Which Miracles Are Wrought," and "Now, as in the Days of Thoreau, Massachusetts Has Its Greatest Soul [Vanzetti] in Jail."

Many of Upton's friends, who were in some cases perhaps not entirely free from envy, criticized the muckraker whenever he took Hearst's money, and to them Upton explained quickly and clearly his attitude both toward Hearst's money and Hearst's enormous readership. He published his work, he said, wherever he could reach the widest audience on the theory that it spoke for itself, and he spent whatever money he earned in this way on furthering his causes. He admitted that he had on occasion censored his own message in order to get it into a mass magazine, on the basis that half a loaf of his truth for those readers was better than none.

In addition to writing for the sensational press, Upton continued to reach its readers by colorful direct action. In 1923, he was kidnapped by the Los Angeles police.

Transport workers of the IWW were on strike in San Pedro and were being brutally repressed by the police at the command of the Los Angeles Merchants' and Manufacturers' Association. Sinclair went to San Pedro on May 15, 1923, where he had carefully prearranged to address a mass meeting of strikers and their families to be held on private property with the owner's written permission. No sooner had Sinclair begun reading the First Amendment of the Constitution to the crowd than he was arrested.

The police drove him around for hours, taking him from one station house to another but refusing to book him anywhere. Mary Craig, wild with terror, was unable to get a writ to free him. In a time and town notorious for the killing of prisoners "resisting arrest" or "attempting to escape," her fears, for once, were not unreasonable.

Sinclair was held incommunicado overnight and until late the next afternoon. The plan of the Los Angeles police chief, Louis D. Oaks, was to bring him into court moments before it closed at five. He would then immediately have the judge appoint defense lawyers, commit Upton to jail without bail, and then hide him again. Luckily, one of Oaks' own subordinates secretly telephoned the plan to Mary Craig who had attorneys with a writ in court when Upton was brought in.

The episode was the making of the southern California branch of the

American Civil Liberties Union, which Sinclair had recently founded and of which he would for many years be the chief support. Its repercussions were national and international. Liberal and Socialist organs and capitalist newspapers as well expressed outrage. Typical was a Hartford *Times* editorial: "Granted that the chief of police was right in assuming that a speech by Upton Sinclair would ruin the Los Angeles climate . . . There is nothing to indicate that the Constitution and the preamble thereof are to be read only at Fourth of July meetings, convocations of the Ku Klux Klan . . . and teas for Women Patriots. There is nothing in that preamble to indicate that the blessings of liberty were suspended during dock strikes or that they do not apply to socialist novelists. . . . it only requires a few instances of this sort of stupid oppression to prove to the satisfaction of many people of a certain unfortunate type of mind the truth of all the unkind things that Mr. Sinclair has been saying about the United States of America."

Bertrand Russell wrote asking, "Is it true you have got into trouble with the authorities because they take the same view of the Declaration of Independence as George III took? If so, you have my warmest sympathy and good wishes."

As a direct result of his arrest, Upton wrote a play, *Singing Jailbirds*. He corresponded about it first with former IWW prisoners and then with members of the Provincetown Playhouse group, including Kenneth Macgowan, John dos Passos, Em Jo Basshe, and Eugene O'Neill. "The play is fine stuff," O'Neill wrote, "strong and true—and I've been deeply moved by it."

When Upton published the play himself, *The New York Times* critic declared it "a drama that is intense in the extreme and undeniably an application of Expressionist methods. . . . the play may be read for its vivid qualities as drama alone. Expressionism is as yet an experiment in the American theatre and it will be both instructive and interesting to note how it develops from the introductory attempts of Eugene O'Neill, Elmer Rice, John Lawson and Mr. Sinclair. The last named should not stop at 'Singing Jailbirds' but should continue, for the form appears to be one that he can handle with success, although one never can tell until an actual stage production is made."

Four years later, Basshe directed a production of *Jailbirds* that opened December 4, 1928, at the New Playrights Theatre in New York, financed with the help of Upton's own money as well as that of some of his rich friends. As though confirming Upton's belief that often the Fates were against him, his daughter-in-law wrote him after the opening: "I am enclosing the reviews. Unfortunately, Mr. Ziegfeld chose last night for the debut of 'Whoopee,' and captured the leading critics."

The reviews in both the capitalist and the Movement press were generally favorable. In early January the play was moved to the larger Grove Street Theatre, in hopes of increasing income, but it continued to lose money and closed in early February.

The play, like Upton's continuous correspondence with convicts, wardens, prison chaplains, and his endless propagandizing for prison reform is significant chiefly as another proof of his passionate identification with prisoners, perhaps best expressed by Debs' declaration in *Labor and Freedom*: "While there is a lower class I am in it. While there is a criminal class I am of it. While there is a soul in prison I am not free."

CHAPTER XVII

The Goose-Step,
The Goslings, the Jews

*Education is an admirable thing, but it is well to remember from time to time
that nothing that is worth knowing can be taught.* OSCAR WILDE

EARLY IN 1922 Sinclair had begun his study of the educational institutions of
America. He wrote letters to teachers and administrators all over the country
soliciting information for a book he then planned to call *Footbinding* or *The
Footbinders*, after the crippling Chinese custom. Only a tiny fraction of these
were willing to reply in writing, so he set out on a cross-country trip to get
answers orally. In both cases, anonymity was usually demanded and received.
He was gone from the beginning of April to the end of June and went from
Spokane, to Chicago, to Madison, Wisconsin, to New York, to Boston, to
Baltimore, and to Washington, D.C.

Mary Craig believed herself too ill to accompany Upton, so he wrote her
frequently about his lectures, his tennis games, and about her unkept
promises to hire a maid and go on a milk diet. From Baltimore he wrote:
"Funny to get back where you were a little boy: all the streets where I
played. Everything looks so small—like a toy city. . . . Mencken here
[Blands' house] to dinner . . . a clever chap, but I guess I'm easy to bore.
He's written a chapter in his new book, so he says, 'abusing me.' I'm the
man who has 'believed more things than any other man in America.' You'd
agree with him!"

While in Boston, Upton visited Bartolomeo Vanzetti in Charlestown
Prison, who thereafter occasionally wrote to the author. "Dear Comrade
Sinclair:—

"I will never forget your visit, nor what your golden pen—that so many
good battles valiantly fought in behalf of the truth and of the freedom—had
wrote in my defence.

"What you have said about my innocence is but the truth.

"I understand and appreciate the reasons by which you were adviced to exalt me far above my little merit. If there is a little of goodness in me—I am glad of it—but really I do not deserve your praisers (as they are)

"I think that there are some prisoners within these very four walls wich exile me from society, which are much better than I.

"I have finished a short novel which will soon be published—at least—so I was told; and I will send a copy to you. Please, do not believe that I am conceited—I know my littleness—Humble I wrote for the humble who must conquire the world to peace and freedom; and I try to make plaine humble but ignored truths.

"Yours with great heart."

Of all the different elements of the American promise, none perhaps inspired more hope than the idea of free, public, and universal education. It was a canon of the American religion that education for all would bring to all the good life, meaningful liberty, and not only the pursuit but also the capture of happiness.

America was trying to do what had never anywhere been done before—to educate *everyone.* In 1860 there had been only one hundred public high schools, but by 1900 there were six thousand, and some sort of law making school attendance compulsory existed in thirty-one states and territories, although these laws did not require attendance through high school and were not enforced uniformly nor excessively.

From 1870 to 1910 the average number of years that young Americans attended school rose from four to six; the number of pupils enrolled rose from 6,800,000 to 17,800,000; and total expenditures on education rose from $63,000,000 to $214,000,000 and from $1.64 to $4.64 per capita.

That the commitment to education was not total, however, was made evident by the fact that in 1900 the average annual teacher's salary was only $325, below that for unskilled labor. Education's relative unimportance in the real economic world as opposed to the ideal world of Fourth of July rhetoric was further evidenced by the fact that it was left to women, who at the turn of the century comprised some 70 percent of public school teachers. Even most women regarded teaching not as a profession but rather as an unfortunate, temporary expedient hopefully soon to be ended by marriage— with the result that more than half the teachers were under twenty-five and almost a fourth under twenty-one.

Upton returned from his cross-country tour with two passionate

PCHS Media Center
Grant, Nebraska

convictions. The first was that educating so many millions inevitably offered frequently irresistible opportunities for dishonest financial gain and that such opportunities must be ended or at least made far more difficult. The second and most important was that the kind of education determined the kind of citizen—that if American society was to move in the different direction he hoped for, its members would have to receive a very different education.

When the superabundance of material made it clear that one book could not contain all he wanted to say on education in America, Sinclair decided on two, *The Goose-Step* on the subject of college and university level education and *The Goslings* on the earlier levels.

As with virtually all his books, Sinclair's *Goose-Step* is in large measure autobiographical. It suggests ideas and remedies for what he viewed as unacceptable ills—remedies that to most Americans at the time seemed almost insane. During a period when the most brutal competition in education as in business was accepted, indeed glorified, as an essential of Social Darwinism, Sinclair began his book wondering whether it was proper that "the great purpose of life was these 'marks.' If you got good ones, your teacher smiled at you, your parents praised you at home, you had a sense of triumph over other little boys who were stupid. You enjoyed this triumph, because no one ever suggested to you that it was cruel to laugh at your weaker fellows. In fact, the system appeared to be designed to bring out your superiority, and to increase the humiliation of the others."

Sinclair complained that when he was there in 1901, Columbia had been "a hollow shell, a body without a soul, a mass of brick and stone held together by red tape." For half a century his complaints continued to be ignored, until the rioting Columbia students of the 1960's repeated them verbatim in their revolutionary newspapers. He was outraged that after fighting a World War to defeat the German regimented ideal of *Kultur*, there prevailed in America's universities the totalitarian educational philosophy that Johann Gottlieb Fichte advocated: "To compel men to a state of right, to put them under the yoke of right by force, is not only the right but the sacred duty of every man who has the knowledge and the power. . . . He is the master, armed with compulsion and appointed by God."

Sinclair put the blame for all the ills of American education on the same "interlocking directorates" whose existence in business had been exposed before the Pujo Committee in 1913; and the muckraker quoted from an article in *Harper's Weekly* by Louis D. Brandeis explaining the expression: " 'Mr. J. P. Morgan (or a partner), a director of the New York, New Haven and Hartford Railroad, causes that company to sell to J. P. Morgan and

Company an issue of bonds. J. P. Morgan and Company borrow the money with which to pay for those bonds from the Guaranty Trust Company, of which Mr. Morgan (or a partner) is a director. J. P. Morgan and Company sell the bonds to the Penn Mutual Life Insurance Company, of which Mr. Morgan (or a partner) is a director. The New Haven spends the proceeds of the rails in purchasing electrical supplies from the General Electric Company, of which Mr. Morgan (or a partner) is a director. The General Electric Company sells the supplies to the Western Union Telegraph Company, a subsidiary of the American Telephone and Telegraph Company, and in both Mr. Morgan (or a partner) is director. The Telegraph Company has a special wire contract with the Reading, in which Mr. Morgan (or a partner) is a director. . . .'

"But Mr. Brandeis stops his story too soon"; Sinclair continued, "he ought to show us some of the wider ramifications of these directorates. He ought to picture Mr. Morgan (or a partner) falling ill, and being treated in St. Luke's Hospital, in which Mr. Morgan (or a partner) is a trustee, and by a physician who is also a trustee, and who was educated in the College of Physicians and Surgeons, of which Mr. Morgan (or a partner) is a trustee. He ought to picture Mr. Morgan dying, and being buried from Trinity Church, in which several of his partners are vestrymen, and having his funeral oration preached by a bishop who is a stockholder in his bank, and reported in newspapers whose bonds repose in his vaults. Mr. Brandeis might say about all these persons and institutions just what he says about the Steel Corporation and the General Electric Company and the Western Union Telegraph Company and the Baldwin Locomotive Works—they all patronize one another and they all deposit their funds with J. P. Morgan and Company.

"Men die, but the plutocracy is immortal; and it is necessary that fresh generations should be trained to its service. Therefore the interlocking directorate has need of an educational system, and has provided it complete. There is a great university, of which Mr. Morgan was all his active life a trustee, also his son-in-law and one or two of his attorneys and several of his bankers. The president of this university is a director in one of Mr. Morgan's life insurance companies, and is interlocked with Mr. Morgan's bishop, and Mr. Morgan's physician, and Mr. Morgan's newspaper. . . ."

If for the phrase "interlocking directorate" one substitutes in Sinclair's book the more current expression "the Establishment," it immediately becomes obvious that the changes of the last half century have not been extravagant. Although today "the Establishment" includes many more members, not only money men but also military men and politicians as well as some token artists, blacks, and even women—there are only more hands and one hand still washes the other.

He had the impertinence more than half a century ago to be outraged that Columbia University owned securities in enterprises made profitable by the exploitation of human beings. He named such corporations as Standard Oil and Bethlehem Steel and specified their industrial obscenities. Nor did he limit his charges to Columbia, but also pointed out Harvard's interest in having the State Department and the United States Marines interfere in the affairs of Central and South American governments whose securities the university owned along with those of the infamous United Fruit Company.

He even went so far as to suggest that slums in the neighborhood of a great university might be worthy of notice and concern. He used as an example Princeton, under the shadow of whose multimillion dollar buildings were tenements so foul that the infant mortality rate in 1916 in the town of Princeton was more than 50 percent higher than in New York City.

Sinclair had other wild ideas in 1922—that it was perhaps not in the natural and immutable order of things that "not one woman" sat on Harvard's Board of Overseers; that teachers had no tenure or union or any real job security. He wondered if sex education might be as important as Latin and further: "I have ventured to suggest student representation on boards controlling our colleges."

Much less than in other of his muckraking books did exaggeration and paranoia lead him to foolish conclusions that brought ridicule on him and made it easier to avoid his valid charges. He could not resist, however, becoming overexcited at the honorary degree racket, pointing out that Herbert Hoover had twenty-four whereas Brandeis, La Follette, Borah, Darrow, and Steffens had not one to divide among them. His outrage at the "mutual back scratching" of university presidents in awarding one another honorary degrees was hardly appropriate for a writer who almost automatically signed manifestos and wrote favorable reviews, puffs, and plugs for books by his fellow Socialists and liberals and expected them to do the same for him. In reply to a request for a letter of support from the liberal lawyer Arthur Garfield Hays, for example, Sinclair answered that he knew nothing about the subject, but that "if you will have your secretary write on the enclosed sheet of paper the letter which you think I ought to write, I will be pleased to sign it. How is that for a vote of confidence!"

In those days before "ethnicity" had become fashionable, he suggested: "If I were a cultured Jew in America, I know what I should do. I should not flatter the race conceit of Anglo-Saxon colleges; I should make it my task to persuade wealthy Jews to establish an endowment and gather a faculty of Jewish scientists and scholars—there are enough of them to make the most wonderful faculty in the world. And then I should open the doors of this university to seekers of knowledge of all races—save that I should bar students who had anti-Semitic prejudice!"

Some of his Jewish friends were horrified, some thought it a joke, when he wrote, "I should like to outline a model faculty, after the fashion of our all-star baseball teams," and asked for additions to his own list which included Albert Einstein, Charles P. Steinmetz, Henri Bergson, Sigmund Freud, Walter Lippmann, Harold Laski, Louis D. Brandeis, Felix Frankfurter, Leon Trotsky, Mustapha Kemal "(half Jewish)," Marcel Proust, Maurice Ravel, Max Reinhardt, Jacob Epstein, Leon Bakst, and Leo Stein.

There are also a few of the usual imprecations against students who "go to hell with canned jazz and boot-leg whiskey and 'petting parties.' " But mainly he exposed accurately and at length and recommended specific remedies for the ills of college education. "How can dull men, absorbed in dull routine, hold the attention of large groups of wide awake youngsters? The answer is that they do not, and that is the failure of our colleges. . . . No wonder that Bertrand Russell remarked that 'Education has been one of the chief obstacles to the development of the intelligence.' "

Sinclair never ceased voicing his contempt for the pedants he had known at Columbia. Not long before his death he told an interviewer: "I started a course . . . with William Peterfield Trent. He was a kind and friendly gentleman, but he was conventional, he was academic, he was rather dry, and he hurt my feelings terribly by saying: 'It's curious. I once came upon a grammatical error in Shelley's poetry. I've forgotten where it is, and sooner or later I'm going to go through it and try to find it.' To me, that was the most offensive remark about literature I had ever heard. Shelley was one of my gods . . . A man who could go through Shelley's poetry to look for a grammatical error—I decided I didn't want to go on with that course any more."

Like Veblen a few years earlier in *The Higher Learning in America,* Upton ridiculed the college athlete, bought and paid for by alumni and kept at college regardless of illiteracy or such breaches of the rules of conduct as would have resulted in instant expulsion for a mere scholar.

The professional graduate schools just like the colleges, Sinclair pointed out, taught only selfishness and an attitude of the public be damned: "the students learn what the real world is—a place of class distinctions based upon property—what William James calls 'the worship of the bitch-goddess Success.' "

Hardly an admirer of either of the Jameses or of Harvard, Upton in his horror of the assembly line, uniform products of the American university factories nevertheless also quoted "William James, once of Harvard: 'Our undisciplinables are our proudest product.' "

For once, most of the critical response and the sales of his book exceeded even Upton's perennially optimistic estimate. Mencken's review in the May *Smart Set* confirmed Upton's views. "The doctrine . . . that the American colleges and universities, with precious few exceptions, are run by stock-jobbers and manned by intellectual prostitutes . . . will certainly give no fillip of surprise to steady readers of my critical compositions."

Upton had directed his printer, Conkey, to print sixteen thousand copies, nine thousand cloth and seven thousand paper-bound, and having promised Mary Craig that he would either make a profit or cease publishing his own books, he priced the books two dollars and a dollar as opposed to a dollar for cloth and fifty cents for paper as in the cases of *Brass Check* and *Profits of Religion.*

Goose-Step sold well and brought its author the usual flood of correspondence. Often in replies to letters, Upton made some of his important ideas clearer than he had in his book. "Nearly everybody who reads my books gets the idea that I think that people act from definite conscious financial selfishness, but I don't mean that at all. I merely mean that their ideals and manners and customs and morals are all growths out of the soil of their class interests."

Upton was aware that where large sums of money were involved, for buying land, constructing school buildings, for the purchase of books, and equipment, simple dishonesty frequently appeared. But in his view, the book publishers who paid bribes and the school employees who received them were both performing functions inevitable under the capitalist system.

Upton wrote *Goose-Step* in the hope that it would influence American education and educators. "I think *Goose-Step* had some effect," wrote Robert M. Hutchins, a half a century later. "It made at least some universities nervous, for a while, about the selection of trustees, but not very many, or very much, or very long."

A broad range of educators, however, view Sinclair's effect on the country as rather more significant and enduring. Some of these include John W. Gardner ("an example of the kind of critic every healthy society needs"); Herbert Marcuse; S. I. Hayakawa, McGeorge Bundy ("a historical and literary figure of real importance"); and Wilbur J. Cohen, dean of the University of Michigan School of Education and former secretary of the Department of Health, Education, and Welfare.

In higher education, as in every other area in which Upton fought, America has not yet achieved that level of justice for which one may reasonably hope. Freedom of political activity is too often a rhetorical aim rather than a reality, and if college teachers can no longer be fired out of hand for their social views, these views may still count against them, especially when they seek reappointment, tenure, or transfer to another college.

Teachers' right to express freely their socal views still tends to diminish rapidly as one descends from the few exceptional universities to the rest and to high school and grade school levels. But thanks to Sinclair's propaganda and that of others, there has been improvement since his time, and the situation is far better in America than in most countries. Both trade unions and such organizations as the American Association of University Professors have given teachers some of the power Sinclair preached they must get. But when, since *Goose-Step,* the problems of excessive trustee domination and of administration insensitivity to faculty and student needs were dealt with at all, it was insufficient to avoid the confrontations of the sixties, which have since accelerated the process. It would, however, be a sanguine prophet indeed who predicted that American education had been freed forever from the "red scare" in some form or other.

Early in 1924, Upton himself published *The Goslings,* written from the material about American grade schools and high schools that had proven too much to include in *Goose-Step.* Horace Liveright had written a long letter explaining why Boni & Liveright would not bring it out. "I must admit that the fact that I have a text book department and have on the advisory council of this text book department several people whom you are lambasting in *The Goslings* does make some personal difference to me. . . . I simply don't feel, as I've said before, that I want to complicate my personal relations too much. If this be treason, cowardice, or whatever you care to call it—make the most of it."

There is in *The Goslings* a sharper focus on both petty and large scale graft, from colored crayons and calendars to what real estate is chosen for "the placing of magnificent new high schools [in Los Angeles] which the city is building for the children of the rich, and which determine the population and the price of real estate for whole districts. It goes without saying that these schools are put where the active speculators want them;

three such schools are now going up in districts where there is practically no population at present. Meanwhile the old, unsanitary fire-traps in the slums are left overcrowded and without repairs. They have passed a regulation districting the city, and compelling the children to attend school in their own district. The children of the poor may not travel and attend the schools of the rich!"

As with *Goose-Step*, Upton relied extensively on favorably disposed experts in the field for information, correction of mistakes, and even rewriting, a practice he would continue with future books. "Feel free to chop up this chapter," he wrote a Philadelphia high school teacher, "in any way you like; but the best thing to do would be to dictate me a nice long letter, giving me all the details, supplementing my material, and also referring to the new incidents. And then I will do the work of linking them into shape."

The Goslings is somewhat less outraged and intense than *Goose-Step*. Upton had fun, for example, with the Portland, Oregon, druggist who during World War I successfully routed Goethe from the high school curriculum. The muckraker also laughed at his patriotic fellow Pasadenans who ousted Jung from the public library although "this great authority happens to be a Swiss, but he has a German name, and moreover, he was rumored 'obscene.' "

For millions of Americans the movies were the chief source of education and, as Sinclair was well aware, Will Hays, ostensibly the censor of America's movies, was in fact only the creature of the big studio heads. It was they who paid his then unbelievably enormous salary of one hundred and fifty thousand dollars a year, and Hays knew that quite as important as protecting the public from excessive sex, his job (and the job of various local censors across the country) was to prohibit any labor or Socialist ideas or propaganda from finding their way onto the screen. As well known as these facts were within the industry, Sinclair's blunt statement of them in *The Goslings* did not endear him to either the studio heads or to Hays, himself.

Upton's old maid puritanism did again lead him into a few foolish accusations. Against the snobbish Eastern prep schools, for example, he charged there existed "a general prevalence of smoking and wine drinking, and practice of self-abuse so general that many of the boys were mentally helpless. . . ."

But chiefly *The Goslings* urged teachers to organize and get power; to realize that "they too are workers, and that, far from being superior to the proletariat, they are actually less paid and less respected than carpenters and masons and machinists, who are organized and able to protect themselves in the wage market. I am not for a moment overlooking the fact that educators are idealists and social ministrants; [Upton ended his book,] but I assert that they are also members of the intellectual proletariat, having nothing but their brain power to sell, and I appeal to them to realize their status, and to act upon the realities and not the fairy tales of the capitalist world. The educator is a worker, a useful worker, and the educator's place is by the side of all his brothers of that class. 'Workers of the world unite. You have nothing to lose but your chains; you have a world to gain.' "

In his *Baltimore Sun* review of *The Goslings,* Mencken chided Upton for his foolish "assumption that it is the aim of the public school to fan the intelligence . . . and to produce large numbers of alert and curious youths of both sexes. . . . the state maintains its control of elementary education, not primarily to reduce illiteracy and turn the eyes of the plain people toward the stars, but to make sure that they are not taught anything that is subversive. Public education is thus a police measure. The goal it moves toward is perfect standardization, perfect discipline, perfect imbecility. Mr. Sinclair denounces it bitterly because it is succeeding. He is a romantic fellow, and life is constantly shocking him. But he has written an extremely instructive and amusing book."

For proof that in grade schools and high schools many of the ills Upton denounced and Mencken thought inevitable still exist, one need look no farther than the three-year, three-hundred-thousand-dollar Carnegie Corporation report of 1970. "The tragedy is that the great majority of students do not rebel; they accept the stultifying rules, the lack of privacy, the authoritarianism, the abuse of power—indeed, virtually every aspect of school life—as The Way Things Are. . . . what grim, joyless places most American schools are, how oppressive and petty are the rules by which they are governed, how intellectually sterile and esthetically barren."

The Goslings did not sell as well as *Goose-Step.* Upton was anxious to begin work on *Mammonart,* the fourth exposé of his Dead Hand series and the one he was certain would be his *magnum opus.* To earn a lot of money quickly, he agreed to a lecture tour. He even proposed debating Nicholas Murray Butler on education and Clarence Darrow on "Is Life Worth Living?" with Darrow taking the negative as he always did. But neither of these debates took place.

Lectures also gave him the opportunity to sell books and especially in a few titles, his inventory was much larger than the rate of sale justified even by Upton's own lenient standards. As he confessed in his May 1924 promotional newsletter to his twelve-thousand-name mailing list, "we have some 20,000 books lying idle in a warehouse," and he offered ten copies of *100%* bound in cloth for two dollars or paper-bound for one dollar. In this same newsletter he also tested the market for his newest idea of how to solve his publishing problems forever.

He had tried to sell himself before to the Wilshires. Now he tried again, but this time to the American Fund for Public Service, or as it was more commonly called, the Garland Fund.

For years Upton had watched Emanuel Haldeman-Julius selling millions of Little Blue Books at five cents each and had seen the Kansas entrepreneur grow richer and richer by publishing fewer and fewer radical political books and more and more trash. Sinclair, therefore, decided that the way to reach a much wider audience was to republish thirty of his titles in some eighty pocket-size paper volumes to sell for a nickel each or packed all together in a cardboard box as "The Two-Foot Shelf of Upton Sinclair" for four dollars. To accomplish the large volume savings on which his estimates were based, he planned to make new smaller plates and print some five thousand sets or four hundred thousand volumes, plus an inventory of another four hundred thousand volumes to be sold singly.

The necessary investment he carefully estimated at twenty-five thousand dollars. He applied to the Garland Fund for this sum on behalf of a proposed Sinclair Foundation, which was to be run by five independent trustees. In his detailed proposal he agreed for his part to turn over to the foundation all his inventory, his customer list, his book rights on all he had written to date or would ever write in the future, and to manage the foundation as long as he lived for three hundred dollars a month.

Those who view Upton as an economic naïf would do well to study this proposal which states, for example: "It is agreed that this sum shall be interpreted to mean the purchasing power of $300 a month at the present value of the dollar. If there should be a general increase or decrease in prices, the trustees shall increase or decrease in the same proportion the amount of compensation allowed to Upton Sinclair or to Mary Craig Sinclair [who was to take over and run the foundation at the same three hundred dollars in the event of Upton's death]." Upton also kept for himself the serial and the dramatic rights to his writings. Doubtless Craig had carefully studied this document and its wisdom in economic terms is doubtless also attributable to her.

Sinclair believed passionately that the enterprise would from its inception be profitable. He pointed out that in the past twenty years he had sold almost four hundred thousand copies of his works in expensive editions and grossed some three hundred thousand dollars. But he stressed that Haldeman-Julius, by selling some thirty million Little Blue Books a year, had proven how much greater the market would be for really cheap editions. Once his own books were printed and selling, he confessed, he would come back to the fund for another thirty thousand dollars to issue in the same five-cent format "a library called 'The People's Classics,' or some such title, to consist of one hundred volumes containing the greatest works of a radical tendency from all the literatures of the world. . . . I can sell at least one or two million of the books of Upton Sinclair every year, and I believe that with a library of Socialist classics the whole radical movement can be supplied with the best ammunition in the cheapest form. That is the goal toward which I am aiming, one step at a time."

Upton was sure he had never been so close to achieving the dream he had long cherished, the dream of having a whole library of his work permanently in print at prices everyone could afford. The Garland Fund was run by old associates and friends—Scott Nearing, Harry F. Ward, Roger Baldwin, William Z. Foster, Sidney Hillman, Robert Morss Lovett, Mary E. McDowell, and Norman Thomas. And Upton believed, too, that it was he who had inspired young Charles Garland to establish the fund in the first place.

So when Roger Baldwin wrote that the board was unwilling to subsidize the publication of any one author's work, however valuable it might be, Sinclair was horrified. To be within reach of what he believed to be his whole life's purpose and to be deprived of it by men he now considered worse than incompetent was unacceptable. Resolved that all his planning should not be wasted, he proceeded to try every way he could imagine to raise the money himself—from soliciting capitalist businessmen to begging from those in the Soviet Union who had for so many years promised to pay him for the many thousands of copies of his books and plays they had published.

But all his efforts failed, and for many more years he himself continued to bear the burden of his publishing business.

During this period, Upton had constant and increasing family problems, with his in-laws, with Craig's hypochondria and terror of poverty, and with his much neglected son who suddenly wrote he was considering becoming a Communist. Upton sent a long hand-written reply. "I think it would be a great blunder & it would distress me very much. . . . I very emphatically think the C way is the wrong way—for this country. (I am not discussing any other country.) We have the ballot widely enough distributed to make it possible to get what we want by convincing the majority. That is what we shd do—& I think the Cs have helped to make the job harder. I think the program of violence is a tragic blunder for the USA; & that the C program is one of violence is something which you ought to know if you don't. The rest is just camouflage; and I prefer to say what I mean. To choose a program which you *can't* avow is a thing much to be avoided. If you do avow it, then it's jail—and while I'm willing to go to jail when necessary, I think it's great folly to go when you don't have to; or to choose a course which makes it necessary either to go to jail or to lie. If I didn't think the C program a blunder, I'd have joined them long ago. The fact that some of my best friends belong doesn't matter—I don't necessarily let politics interfere with friendship. . . .

"What I want you to do at the present stage of yr life is to get yrself a technical training, so you will know how to do something important when the workers need you. You can be a thousand times more useful to them that way. You can be more useful to them if you get a profession—consider for example the career of Steinmetz & the prestige he brought to the movement. If you go in for wild talk at this stage of yr life, you'll not be able to get that training, & you'll be simply a hanger-on in the movement, comparatively of no influence or use. That is not cowardice but simply common sense. . . .

"I appreciate the idealism which makes you think of it. If we were in the position of Old Russia with no other possible way, & martyrs called for, I'd say go. But we have another, & in the long run both cheaper & quieter way—& I want you to give yr time to educating both yrself & the workers. Meet a few Socialists & you'll find them not such old fogies after all!"

Upton's position on Communism remained unchanged until after World War II. He defended the rights of Communists at home and refused to criticize them abroad long after Stalin's crimes became known. But he never joined them. Because he defended them, he was frequently labeled Communist and attacked by their enemies, and because he refused to join the Communists, they too attacked him with increasing bitterness.

David's welfare was not the only reason Sinclair sought to dissuade him from becoming a Communist. He did not want the bother of a notorious son nor the embarrassment of having to explain publicly why he had been unable to keep even his own son in the Socialist camp. A better measure of his concern for David was his repeated refusal to see him.

As an undergraduate at Wisconsin, David was attracted to women, but psychiatric difficulties contributed to by his troubled childhood combined with the puritan training he had received from his father exacerbated the natural problems of inexperience. Letters from his mother alleging interest in his welfare but in fact more concerned with her own self-justification further confused him.

When he graduated, David had additional genuine problems he needed to discuss with his father. It was now essential that he settle on a career and he was terribly torn between his desire to be a musician and wanting also to be a scientist. He became so desperate to see his father after the years of exile imposed by his stepmother that he swallowed his pride and begged for an audience.

Upton answered with a long letter forbidding him to come because Mary Craig was "close to a complete nervous breakdown, she has been at death's door more than once . . . is at the cancer age, and has fits of terror about it—she spent literally weeks of agony, sleepless nights and hysterical days. . . . Craig is having 'change of life.' " Mary Craig had suffered from all these and other symptoms since almost immediately after her marriage and nothing so aggravated them as Upton's demonstrating the least affection for or even interest in his son.

The hypocrisy of his father's lengthy explanations that Craig's health must not be endangered by a house guest was made bitterly clear to him when Dollie and her family and Hunter Kimbrough lived as Upton's guests where David was forbidden the briefest visit. Even so practiced an egotist as Upton could not fail to see how grotesque his position was, and he went on to express the feeble hope "that you may understand a seemingly unnatural attitude on the part of your father."

When David's own needs proved so great that contrary to a lifetime of obedience he hitchhiked all the way to California, Upton refused to let him stay in the same city, much less come to the house at 1555 Sunset Avenue. He was put on the first train out of town.

Many years before, in *Love's Pilgrimage*, Upton had briefly considered what priority, if any, the child of an artist might have, writing about himself: "He had made a martyr of the child he loved, he had sacrificed it to what he called his art; and how had he dared to do it? . . . Himself, no doubt, he might scourge and drive and wreck; but this child—what were the child's rights? He would try to weigh them against the claims of posterity." Or of ambition and vanity, selfishness and cowardice. The claims, of course, should not have been mutually exclusive in Sinclair's mind. But they had been, and so the son of a bad father had become himself a bad father.

Much of the blame was Craig's. She was just the kind of wife Upton wanted, but for this she demanded her price. She took care of and so relieved him of all domestic details. She provided quick and uncomplicated sexual satisfaction as needed. She was a fierce and effective guardian dragon at the gate—keeping away visitors whom Upton would not have refused and who would therefore have taken him from his work. Her extreme reluctance, as she lost her looks, to accept social invitations that the more gregarious Upton would doubtless have accepted, also served to keep him at the grindstone, for which he was grateful.

She usually stopped him from spending all his money, and more, on the Movement, and so protected him from many economic difficulties that would otherwise have plagued him, and she spent no money at all on herself for frivolities.

Indeed, her demands for herself were minimal. She was as satisfied as he with meals that took less than ten minutes to prepare, eat, and clean up. And her demands for sex could likewise be disposed of with dispatch. Her more time-consuming claims for Upton's attention to her health problems, in fact, served a useful purpose for him. He accepted that he was henpecked, quoting Craig in *Mammonart*: "In our family the men have a traditional saying: 'It's all right to be henpecked, but be sure you get the right hen!'" Craig's demands and show of dominance were not unlike those of Priscilla Sinclair when Upton was a boy. They were taken by him as proofs of her concern and love. Perhaps even more important for the egoist, his acceptance of her limited dominance and his acquiescence to her claims gave him whatever proofs he needed that he was a loving person. And, unlike Priscilla, Craig kept her demands and criticism within limits acceptable, indeed useful, to Upton.

To some degree, too, his feelings of guilt about the unfair position of women in society were assuaged by his relationship with Craig. He revealed these feelings in a passage he wrote about his relationship with Meta, whose demands were excessive and unbearable rather than comforting like Craig's: "a man has to be ashamed of advantages given to him by nature and society, and so to put himself chivalrously under the feet of a woman—raising her, an image of perfection, upon a pedestal of his own self-reproach."

Craig's sometimes maternal but acid criticism of Upton's work also provided proof that she loved him and his work. And the *quid pro quo* she required for all this—David's absence—did not seem to Upton an excessive price.

Upton had inherited from his father and his early background an automatic and unconscious anti-Semitism and racism, which, along with anti-intellectualism, resentment of "the effete East," and Anglophobia, has formed the traditional American demonology. Upton's Progressive and Socialist beliefs were to a degree influenced by the lower-class expression of anti-Semitism repeatedly found in Populism. But he was especially heir to an upper-class anti-Semitism that often accompanies such strident claims to aristocracy as his mother's, as well as to the Christian parochialism and racism of the Episcopal hymnal.

In his autobiography, Upton insisted on more than one occasion and at some length that neither in his youth nor later was he ever in the slightest anti-Semitic. ". . . When I was sounded out for a 'frat' I actually didn't know what it was, and could make nothing of the high-sounding attempts at explanation. If the haughty upperclass man with the correct clothes and the Anglo-Saxon features had said to me in plain words, 'We want to keep ourselves apart from the kikes and wops who make up the greater part of our student-body,' I would have told him that some of the kikes and wops interested me, whereas he did not.

"About two thirds of the members of my class were Jews. I had never known any Jews before this, but here were so many that one took them as a matter of course. I am not sure if I realized they were Jews; I seldom realize it now about the people I meet. The Jews have lived in Central Europe for so long, and have been so mixed with the population, that the border-line is hard to draw. In my case, as a socialist writer, half my friends and half my readers have been Jews. I sum up my impression of them in the verses about the little girl who had a little curl right in the middle of her forehead, and when she was good she was very, very good, and when she was bad she was horrid."

Upton's claim that he seldom realized when people were Jewish is repeatedly proven untrue by his published work as well as his correspondence. When he was aware that anyone about whom he wrote or spoke was Jewish, Upton almost invariably pointed it out, even when it was obvious from the name and whether or not it was important in the context. For example, in the same autobiography, he had felt it was mandatory to point out that a classmate was "a Jewish boy" whose short story was accepted by a monthly magazine "published by a Hebrew orphan home," when neither fact was relevant to the fact that the episode inspired Upton's first commercial literary effort.

When the autobiography appeared, Upton expressed dismay when this former classmate wrote him: "In my autobiography will be this: In my class was a short-panted Christian lad named Upton Beall Sinclair. He was blatantly Christian; fearfully Jew and Catholic conscious; lasciviously chaste; he was a hot-biscuit addict and showed early signs of disturbed metabolism."

Upton was no more anti-Semitic than were most non-Jews in his America, and far less so than many. The most obvious statement of his anti-Semitism was in a brief article he wrote for a labor group in Vienna. He ascribed to Jews a superior commercial ability, the ability to create great religions such as Christianity and Socialism, and a powerful sex instinct which when combined with their business ability enabled Jews to produce films that stimulated sensuality and thereby corrupted youth. "In olden times, Jewish traders sold Christian girls into concubinage and into prostitution, and even today they display the same activity in the same field in southern California, where I live."

When various Jews objected that Sinclair's premise was anti-Semitic or at least promoted anti-Semitism, his replies further revealed his prejudice and insensitivity. "I think that the Jewish race has a remedy at hand; . . . They can reprobate and ostracize these persons [such as the Schuberts and Laskys of Broadway and Hollywood] and they can make it plain that the decent Jewish people are as much in revolt against commercialized sensuality as are the American people. . . . I think we need a Jewish prophet right now. . . . We Americans have a great many intelligent and noble-minded members of our race, who have risen above our national vices of bragging and bunkum, and I understand that likewise there are a great many members of the Jewish race who do not make millions out of selling depravity to our children."

The projection of one's own sexual fantasies (whether aberrant or normal but deemed to be wicked because of one's own puritanism) onto objects of one's prejudice (Jews, blacks, Latins, *et alia*) has long served multiple purposes. Many delude themselves that their indulgence in racial prejudice is acceptable by disguising it as condemnation of sexual excess or irregularity, and conversely, some are enabled to enjoy sexual fantasies they would otherwise consider unacceptable by attaching these to some other group. This latter game need not even require ethnic overtones and is the everyday work of censors and book burners from grand champions such as Godfrey Lowell Cabot to one's friendly local movie or library book censor, whose superior strength or education enables her or him to read about or view things sexual that would be irreparably corrupting and dangerous to weaker vessels.

Some kind of sense of superiority is essential to the optimal practice of

Comstockery, and rare is the reformer who does not, unconsciously at least, view him or herself as better than some lesser breed. The fact that Sinclair's disavowals of anti-Semitism were so regularly accompanied by at least an admonitory sentence or two concerning the excessive sensuality and prurience of his good friends and good customers, the Jews, derived from the prejudice learned from the pathetic Southern aristocrats of his youth and especially from his failed drummer father. It may also evidence an otherwise usually well-sublimated or suppressed prurience of his own.

Although most of the muckrakers ignored all aspects of racism in America, a few understood and wrote about prejudice against blacks or Jews. Steffens nailed a mezuzah to his office door and Hutchins Hapgood's *The Spirit of the Ghetto* displayed an understanding no less extraordinary for a gentile in 1902 than at any other time.

There were writers of the period other than Upton, of course, who were anti-Semitic, Dreiser for example. But unlike Upton, who was unable to recognize it, Dreiser once he saw it in himself fought against it. Dreiser had also revealed his feelings in an essay in *The American Spectator* where he stated that "the world's quarrel with the Jew is not that he is inferior, but that he is superior," and he proposed that the Jews establish their own nation. When Hutchins Hapgood wrote him criticizing the essay, Dreiser's answer revealed his prejudice against Jewish movie executives, not like Sinclair because of their sensuality, but because: "If you listen to Jews discuss Jews, you will find that they are money-minded, very pagan, very sharp in practice."

Upton, like the Russians for the last half century, was never able to take Lenin's position: "The Jewish bourgeoisie are our enemies, not as Jews but as bourgeoisie. The Jewish worker is our brother."

Upton at twenty-nine with the poet he so admired, George Sterling, in Carmel, California.

Upton at Arden in 1911 with the poet Harry Kemp.

∞

With his second wife, Mary Craig Kimbrough Sinclair, in Bermuda.

Mary Craig in hand-me-down clothes from a wealthy patron.

∞

Upton enjoying the only diversion from work he allowed himself, in a tournament at Long Beach in 1917.

One of Upton's favorite portraits, inscribed: "To Horace Liveright friend to authors."

Upton tried to have himself arrested after his 1927 novel, *Oil!* had been banned in Boston by selling copies on the street.

In the summer of 1928, Sinclair's picture appeared on the cover of a magazine in the Soviet Union.

The Torch!

Cartoon in the anniversary issue of *New Masses* by Upton's friend Art Young, who designed covers for some of his books.

Upton's Christmas gift to his mother in 1929 was this inscribed photograph.

Left to right, Upton, Mary Hunter Kimbrough (his mother-in-law), Dollie Irwin (his sister-in-law), Ostoja (his resident medium), and Shel (Dollie's daughter), circa 1930.

Early enthusiasts of flying. From left, Upton, Ostoja, Dollie, and the pilot. Circa 1928.

Dr. Albert Abrams, Charlie Chaplin, and Upton, circa 1930.

CLASS OF SERVICE		SIGNS
This is a full-rate Telegram or Cablegram unless its deferred character is indicated by a suitable sign above or preceding the address.	**WESTERN UNION** NEWCOMB CARLTON, PRESIDENT J. C. WILLEVER, FIRST VICE-PRESIDENT	DL = Day Letter NM = Night Message NL = Night Letter LCO = Deferred Cable CLT = Cable Letter WLT = Week-End Letter

The filing time as shown in the date line on full-rate telegrams and day letters, and the time of receipt at destination as shown on all messages, is STANDARD TIME.

Received at   1931 NOV 21 AM 11 35

SA155 VIA RCA=CD MOSCOU 118 21 2030

UNITED STATES OF AMERIKA UPTON SINCLAIR STATION A=
PASADENA (CALIF)=

LETTER RECEIVED STOP BODY OF SURVEILLANCE ACCUSES DANASHEVSKY
OF SABOTAGE STOP MATERIALS WE HAVE IT SEEMS TO ME DONT SPEAK
IN FAVOUR OF DANASHEWSKY STOP IF YOU INSIST I CAN SOLICITE
BEFORE THE HIGHPOWERED BODY FOR THE AMNESTY STOP EISENSTEIN
LOOSE HIS COMRADES CONFIDENCE IN SOVIET UNION STOP HE IS
THOUGHT TO BE DESERTER WHO BROKE OFF WITH HIS OWN COUNTRY
STOP AM AFRAID THE PEOPLE HERE WOULD HAVE NO INTEREST IN
HIM SOON STOP AM VERY SORRY BUT ALL ASSERT IT IS THE FACT
STOP WISH YOU TO BE WELL AND TO FULFILL YOUR PLAN OF COMING
TO SEE US STOP MY REGARDS STOP 2783 21/11 31=
STALIN.   (regards)

The cable from Stalin that presaged the end of the Eisenstein affair.

Sergei Eisenstein, on the right, displaying his Rabelaisian tendencies which so shocked Sinclair.

CHAPTER XVIII

Mammonart, Money Writes!, World Correspondent

Puritanism can only ask "Is it righteous?," "Is it edifying?," "Is it worthy?," even when the appropriate questions are "Is it pretty?," "How does it taste?," "What makes it go?"

NAOMI BLIVEN

IT MUST HAVE BEEN an essential of Sinclair's sanity, or perhaps of his very life, to believe that his own failure as a poet was not due to a lack of artistry but rather to the state of society. Therefore, none of his other books seem to have been more necessary for him to write than *Mammonart* and *Money Writes!* None are so burdened with his worst fatuities. But he published both although he knew, even without the repeated warnings of his friends, that these books would call down upon him the scorn of enemies, friends, and critics.

From at least the moment in *Arthur Stirling* when Sinclair realized, consciously or unconsciously, that he had failed as an artist, he had rejected as a primary concern any idea of art for its own sake. A year later in 1904, his "Our Bourgeois Literature" in *Collier's* magazine prefigured *Mammonart*, and even at the very height of the success of *The Jungle*, as well as in all the years that followed, it was rarely far from his thoughts that "Some day I hope to write a series of essays upon 'the economic interpretation of literature.' "

So when *Mammonart* was published in 1925, he declared his purposes boldly at the beginning of the book. He would disprove the degenerate and elitist lie of art for art's sake and prove that all art is and must be propaganda.

The psychology of the artist and his art are inevitably determined by the economic forces of his time, Sinclair declared, and so established artists of any period are in sympathy with its ruling classes. Homer, by Sinclair's assessment, was little more than an Establishment flack who advocated the sovereignty of a king rather than that of all the people "just as our members of good society preach 'law and order' to the lower classes." Balzac was "the most perfect type of predatory artist." Even a former Sinclair hero was not safe because: "When Keats writes 'A thing of beauty is a joy forever,' it is perfectly plain that he is making propaganda—and false propaganda, since standards of beauty are matters of fashion, varying with every social change." And the muckraker's long list of reactionary literary villains include, among others, Aeschylus, Sophocles, Aristophanes, Shakespeare, and Corneille.

In Sinclair's proletarian Pantheon are found Euripides, Dante, Cervantes, Milton, Molière, Swift, Tolstoy, and, of course, Shelley, whose "beauty of spirit and sublimity of faith, [are] not exceeded by the utterances of Jesus" and who had "the finest mind the English race has produced."

Perhaps nowhere in all of Sinclair's work is he more tiresome than when writing about Coleridge's *Kubla Khan*. "Moreover, . . . almost every image in this poem turns out on examination to be a lie. There is no such place as Xanadu; . . . There never was a river Alph. . . . There are no 'caverns measureless to man'; . . . while as for the 'Abyssinian maid,' she would have her teeth blackened and would stink of rancid palm oil."

Happily Sinclair had become too knowledgeable a writer not to contradict frequently his own basically untenable criteria, for example, by recognizing and admitting what he had denied vigorously in his youth—that Harriet Beecher Stowe and Edward Bellamy were failures as artists because "their impulse to teach and to preach ran away with their inspiration." And, he confessed, "I know all about that, having done it." Acknowledging a fault, however, is not renouncing it, and Sinclair not only admitted but was too often proud that his purpose and his method were the opposite of what Beckett later said about Joyce, "he is not writing about something, he is writing something."

Sinclair could not, of course, resist digressing from his main subject to proselyte for another of his many causes. In his chapters on Ibsen and Strindberg, for example, he made his usual arguments for sex hygiene and equal rights for women.

The book contains examples of stacking the cards by selective use of evidence. When Sinclair disapproved of an artist, Raphael for example, he dwelled on the artist's mistress, but when he approved, as with Michelangelo, he overlooked even sodomy and syphilis. And when he makes a dogmatic Socialist interpretation of a non-Socialist, indeed nonpolitical, work of art, he blithely quotes from Shaw's *The Quintessence of Ibsenism*, "The existence of a discoverable and perfectly definite thesis in a poet's work by no means depends on the completeness of his own intellectual consciousness of it."

Nor is this book any more free than earlier ones from the kind of traditional, American, Know-Nothing, anti-intellectualism Sinclair had learned from his father, which had been accentuated by the critical rejection of Upton's pre-muckraking romantic works. It prompted not only comment on "the effete East," but also the ostentatious Philistinism that boasts *The Importance of Being Earnest* "put me to sleep," *The Brothers Karamazov* is unfinishable, and *War and Peace* is incomprehensible.

Some of Upton's friends outdid the critics in chiding him about *Mammonart*. He had sent George Sterling parts of the book as he completed them. "By all means let me see the complete MS. When I see a friend about to make a world-ass of himself, I feel that I should do what I can to lessen the infliction. I never wilfully try to hurt you, but you are so colossal an egoist that one has to hit hard to make you even 'sit up and take notice.' " and from France, Frank Harris wrote about Upton's criticism of Shakespeare, "it is some of the worst I've ever read."

Edmund Wilson in a perceptive and generous review of *Mammonart* declared that Sinclair had a real appreciation of literature and taste in books, but allowed them to be misled by his prejudices when he failed to see that art for art's sake is as essential to the achievement of greatness in literature as mathematics for mathematics' sake is for the discoveries of a Gauss or an Einstein.

In his mailing to his customer list, Upton included brutal criticism such as that from the New York *World*: "He contradicts himself, he misquotes history. . . . he is . . . as humorless as a barn door," perhaps on the theory that with his constituency, a pan from a capitalist source was in fact a boost; and others that made fun of the muckraker: "Having just returned from the office of J. P. Morgan with a certified check for one hundred thousand dollars and explicit directions as to the method of saving the Republic, I fall upon Upton Sinclair's *Mammonart* and denounce it. . . ."

In *Mammonart* Upton had hoped to cover his subject up to the moment of his book's publication. But the material was too vast, so in 1927 in *Money Writes! A Study of American Literature*, Upton did for his contemporaries what he had done for Homer, Shakespeare, and others in *Mammonart*—he proved to his own satisfaction that most of them had been bought. "I am not going to make in this book the mistake which I made in 'Mammonart' of covering too much ground," Sinclair wrote Mike Gold as he began. His "thesis that most modern writers have sold themselves for limousines" was evident from the preliminary title *Honeypots.* "Incidentally, of course, it will discuss the darlings of our present day intellectuals, whose test of greatness is that they are muddled and don't know where they are going or how." But if he was angry at the "intellectuals" who had rejected him, he had hopes of better luck with their successors. "I am going to try to make it a book that the young intellectuals will have to read and take note of."

Again, the reaction of the friends to whom he sent the manuscript was similar to the reaction of many readers of the finished book—varying degrees of outrage. "I beg you not to . . . set yourself down—this time with no come-back—as a reckless slinger of hysterical foolishness, in the minds of all the people who are interested in literature, by that silly passage—a variant of the idiotic one you wrote about a book of mine, in which you accuse [James Branch] Cabell [in *Jurgen*] of being the cause of venereal infection in thousands of young men and women." These were strong words from Floyd Dell who had just written an admiring biography of the muckraker. "I will simply say," he continued, "that it is a God-damned lie, and a libel, and that as a writer I resent it, and charge you with gratifying your infantile phobias and hysterias on the subject of sex in reckless and silly and scandalous falsehood."

No one registered greater exception to *Money Writes!* than Upton's former Helicon Hall janitor, Sinclair Lewis, whom it drove first almost to tears and then to fury. "I would advise you to withdraw it from the market, and to pray for humor and, still more, for accuracy. . . . [and after listing Upton's errors concludes] I did not want to say these unpleasant things, but you have written to me, asking my opinion, and I give it to you, flat. If you would get over two ideas—first that any one who criticizes you is an evil and capitalist-controlled spy, and second that you have only to spend a few weeks on any subject to become a master of it—you might yet regain your now totally lost position as the leader of American socialistic journalism. I could make this letter rather long. I could point out that the two times you quote me in 'Goose Step' you quote me with such inaccuracy that I sound in your book like a liar. But I think I have said enough. You will, of course, regard this only as the wrath of a millionaire best-seller, and go on being the only authority on all known subjects— . . . My God, Upton, go and pray for forgiveness, honesty, and humility!"

Mammonart and *Money Writes!* served their author as a means of settling some old scores with writers both living and dead that he envied, and with critics as well. He had confided with relish to Mencken that in "dealing with our living artists I am going to tear the hides off a great many of them," and in an article on *Money Writes!* more self-revealing than perhaps he was aware, he confessed "the fundamental fact of human nature, that we get more pleasure out of contemplating the faults of other persons than we do out of contemplating our own faults."

But the even more fundamental cause for writing the books was Upton's anger not against individual artists but against capitalism; his conviction that capitalist society ground down artists as much or more than other citizens; and his unshakable faith that not until Socialism had finally freed all men to achieve their greatest potential could the artists achieve theirs.

His belief that "the essence of art was unselfishness" is as incapable of proof as Mencken's dictum that "The essence of a self-reliant and autonomous culture is an unshakeable egoism." But these books would always be cited to prove that their author was no artist himself, for as Oscar Wilde had pointed out, "No artist desires to prove anything. Even things that are true can be proved." And to many they served as proof that Sinclair was in fact anti-art, because "There are two ways of disliking art. . . . One is to dislike it. The other is to like it rationally."

But Sinclair would live to see this Wildean view increasingly questioned by those more taken with the idea of *artiste engagé.*

The volume of Upton's published writing was enormous, but it did not approach that of his correspondence, written to virtually every spot in the world where mail was delivered and to an astounding assortment of young and old of both sexes. A reporter interviewing him glanced at a batch of at least a hundred letters including some from Iceland, New Zealand, Mongolia, the Dutch East Indies, and various parts of Africa. "I noticed one from an unknown people called the Shans. Who were they, I inquired. Alas, he knew not; had never heard of them. A paragraph in an encyclopedia reveals the Shans to be a tribe of some 3,000 natives of far off Asia."

Like most meliorists, Upton comforted himself that if he and his contemporaries could not achieve all they hoped for in their own lifetimes, the young could in theirs. Therefore, much of his correspondence was with students all over the world. His interest in them was as great as his interest in poets and prisoners, and one whose satisfactions were perhaps greater. He subscribed to their newspapers; mailed them his books and pamphlets; and urged them to learn all they could about the social problems uniformly ignored in the college curricula by reprinting and debating his *Goose-Step* and by reading radical books and bringing in radical lecturers at their own expense and despite all opposition.

When a Berkeley student was threatened with expulsion for expressing opposition to California's criminal syndicalism law, Upton wrote: "Well, courage to you. I will do what I can to call attention to your fight; and I promise you this one thing: if you are expelled for publishing this editorial and questionnaire, and the answers, I will print the material in a pamphlet, and mail a copy to every student publication in the civilized world. If the University of California wants to be famous for bigotry, this will be its chance."

In answer to a list of questions from Reed College in Portland, Oregon, that sought to establish the causes of radicalism in men before the age of twenty-five, Upton suggested among various others that a "man will become a radical because he is resentful of injustice against himself. Thus jealousy is a strong factor in the making of radicals, and this makes them hard to organize, and causes them to spend a great deal of energy in factional disputes." Obviously Sinclair is using "jealousy" when in fact he means "envy," and obviously, too, his own envy of his Baltimore relatives is not forgotten decades later.

To a young Chinese student at Stanford who asked for an expression on the Chinese revolution, Sinclair wired, "Young China awakening & taking charge of its own country offers the most inspiring example of this hour. It is a cruel shame that the American people are blind to the meaning of these great events."

A CCNY student wrote that the Social Problems Club had organized resolutions and protest meetings against the compulsory course in military science, but all in vain. Upton sent back words of encouragement and told of his own difficulties in founding such a group in his senior year of college.

In Sinclair's long career there was nothing of which he was more proud than having founded the Intercollegiate Socialist Society. He wrote on its twentieth anniversary: "the way to be happy and successful in this life is to identify yourself with some great cause, which has a future. Of course, you must be careful and wise in picking your cause. You won't get much happiness if you set out to prove that the earth is flat or that Jonah swallowed the whale. But if you tie up your faith with the working class of the world and gamble upon the certainty that sooner or later they will abolish our system of organized greed, then as you grow older you will see things beginning to come your way, and you will have many great satisfactions."

For more than thirty years, beginning in 1918, and totaling by 1951 more than three hundred letters, Upton's most amusing correspondence was with Mencken, whom he chided for his skepticism, while his fellow Baltimorean made fun of Upton's panaceas, which varied from eating sand by the tablespoon as a specific for constipation to ESP. "The trouble with you amateur doctors," Mencken declared, "is that you begin to prescribe before you know what ails the patient. I believe you kill many poor Christians thereby, for which may God have all the glory!"

In Upton's letters to Mencken, he only rarely tried to be funny. Once, after Mencken had humorously compared him to Aristotle, Sinclair wrote he would not rest until he had been compared to another great man, "until I find somebody who proclaims me the intellectual equal of Henry Lewis [sic] Mencken."

But more often, Upton lectured Mencken on his studied and unshakable ignorance of the muckraker's favorite subjects—Socialism, fasting, and the benefits of prohibition.

When Mencken wrote he was coming to California, wanted to hear Aimee Semple McPherson preach, and wondered, "Is her arm worth pinching?" Upton urged him to stay with him and Craig and promised, "I have never laid eyes on Aimee, but we will call if you promise to behave yourself."

"My very best thanks for your invitation. I'd accept at once," replied Mencken, "if it were not for fear that my bawdy habits might disgrace you and perhaps even get me into jail." Although he was not arrested while in Los Angeles, he might well have been when with some drunken companions Mencken went to a Hollywood brothel in Tom Mix's white Rolls-Royce, where Mencken repeatedly played *The Battle Hymn of the Republic* on the piano until one of the ladies of the house who had been promised a hundred dollars if she could bed him applied her most persuasive arts—whereupon Mencken merely switched to *Lead Kindly Light*, not even removing his hat.

He did attend one of the Baptist high priestess' services, wiring a friend, "Was baptized by Aimee last Tuesday night you can have no idea of the peace that it has brought to my soul. I can now eat five Bismarck herring without the slightest acidosis."

In *The Profits of Religion*, Upton had expressed his horror of, and seriously attacked the repeated enrichment of, such enthusiastic evangelical types by ignorant Americans with bad consciences. But now he was able to treat the subject more lightly, as in some dogged doggerel, "An Evangelist Drowns," which made fun of Aimee's alleged kidnapping some weeks earlier. It appeared in the *New Republic*, opposite Allen Tate's review of T. S.

Eliot's *Poems: 1909–1925*. That in the same issue were pieces by John Dewey, Edmund Wilson, and Lewis Mumford indicates the level at which Upton was considered by his contemporaries.

Sinclair's letters could be angry, as when he wrote the Pasadena Tennis Club complaining that the rule against allowing singles to be played when members were waiting for a court was not being enforced. And he complained sharply whenever a capitalist newspaper referred to him as a "Communist writer" and even more sharply whenever any real or imagined disparagement of himself or his work appeared in a friendly journal. When a reviewer in the *Nation* suggested that Ida Tarbell's research was frequently superior to Sinclair's, Upton wrote the editor that his former fellow muckracker "will take her place as the lady Judas of America." In addition to his anger at the invidious comparison, Sinclair was outraged at what he and his fellow radicals viewed as Tarbell's sycophantic biography of Elbert H. Gary, the steelman.

Usually, however, Upton's letters were good natured and sometimes even whimsical. Petitioning the Pasadena Board of City Directors against requiring him to take down a cement retaining wall, he ended his formal letter: "and I therefore respectfully petition the Board of Directors . . . to vacate this five foot strip . . . thus granting to my wall that feeling of security and permanence which all good cement walls should possess."

In many of his letters Upton was trying to be helpful, whether advising Charlie Chaplin that he had discovered a Negro who looked like Chaplin's identical twin; giving Sergei Eisenstein, the famous Russian movie director of *Potemkin*, a confidential appraisal of Douglas Fairbanks; sending Bertolt Brecht requested information on the Chicago Corn Exchange; or explaining to the American Association for Advancement of Atheism how his views differed from theirs. "I understand an atheist to be a person who asserts that there is no God. I am sorry that I cannot lay claim to such difficult knowledge. It seems to me that an atheist is just as dogmatic as a Christian. I suppose I am what is called an agnostic, since I do not know.

"Of course, if you mean by God the ancient Hebrew tribal deity, I am quite sure that no such God as that exists, and the same thing applies to the Christian Trinity, and if that is what you mean by being an atheist, then I am one. But I feel quite sure that there must be a creative energy animating and directing the universe, and I suspect that it knows more than I do and has purposes which I am not entirely able to understand. I think that it is possible to have such an idea without surrendering one's mind to any of the superstitions, whether theological or moral, which are found in the old tribal religions. I am very much opposed to teaching these superstitions, especially to children, and I consider them a great barrier to human progress and welfare."

In addition to letters from all kinds of religious cranks, Upton heard regularly from unknown correspondents anxious to advise him or learn from him, about everything from "black magic for sex purposes" to the threat of "cannibal gypsies."

Beginning in 1925, Sinclair had a long and intense correspondence with various liberals who had become increasingly concerned about the brutal treatment of political prisoners in the Soviet Union. Upton consistently refused to use any influence he may have had with the Russians, repeatedly taking the position, in replying to his friends' many pleas, that any criticism of the Soviet Union by its friends would be seized upon by the capitalist press. "I am greatly shocked to discover that conditions of such prisoners in Russia are about the same as the conditions of political prisoners in the state of California," but "I consider preservation of Soviet Russia [the] most important single task in the world today."

Sinclair's natural enemies on the right and also some liberal friends such as Roger Baldwin believed his reluctance to criticize the Soviet Union was directly related to a fear that he would never be paid anything by the Russians, despite the enormous sale of his books there, if he criticized their regime, however justifiably and however mildly. As a matter of fact, Sinclair had just received his first payment ever from the Soviets, two thousand five hundred dollars cabled from Moscow. But if one were searching for some sort of venality—although it is remotely possible that a threat to the continued publication of his books might lead to his vanity corrupting his judgment—it is ridiculous to believe that Sinclair could be bought by money on a matter of principle.

He explained to Sir Arthur Conan Doyle: "I think you cover the facts pretty well when you compare the Soviet leaders to Robespierre; . . . My attitude to the Russian revolution is very much like that of Thomas Paine's toward the French revolution. I oppose the terror. Nevertheless I cannot blind myself to the fact that the revolutionary forces have a great bulk of the right on their side, and are bringing a new stage of civilization into birth."

Upton usually had more ideas for letters, articles, and books than time to write them. But he almost invariably took the time to admit and write about his errors; proposing, for example, to write for *The Nation* two thousand words on his mistaken World War I position of a decade earlier. Such a willingness is rarely exhibited by anyone and almost never by reformers.

Much of the immense correspondence concerned his work. Before its author had reached fifty, *The Jungle* had already become a classic and Bennett Cerf was writing regularly for permission to include it in his Modern Library series despite other existing editions.

Sinclair had publishers and literary agents and translators from Canton to Sidney to Durban to Budapest, whom he had to write regularly.

And all the while he was also endlessly producing dozens of short and long articles, verses, book reviews, and letters to the editor. These appeared in the *American Mercury, New Republic, Nation, New Leader, Labor World, Haldeman-Julius Monthly, Physical Culture, Hearst's International, Daily Worker, Modern Quarterly, Screenland, New Masses, Saturday Review, Bookman,* among hundreds of others. In addition he regularly produced special articles for foreign journals. And he constantly submitted many copies of most of his works to dozens of different publishers in much the same way as he had his jokes in his youth; trying now, however, to place them with more than a single buyer, providing the markets were noncompetitive. So the same article might appear in a small liberal American magazine, in a Serbian or Lithuanian or any of the dozens of foreign-language newspapers then published in this country, in a Japanese magazine, and a Bombay newspaper virtually simultaneously.

The members of the ACLU and indeed all liberal and labor groups, for their part, tended to treat Upton as their trained bear, expecting him to perform whenever they needed him to fill a hall and raise some money. If he was absorbed in a new novel or too exhausted and refused, they wrote him outraged letters: "the prevailing sentiment was that you owed it to the [Socialist] party and to Debs' memory to speak on that occasion. . . . We recognize that the writing of your novel is extremely important but we do not believe that making this one speech will seriously interfere."

Despite Craig's protests against the endless instances of "this one speech," Upton acquiesced. "The Comrades have no means of knowing how tired I am just now and what a struggle it is to save my time for the finishing of my book. However, I wrote Comrade Anderson that I would come in and speak at the meeting for fifteen minutes."

In February 1926 he allowed the Socialists to nominate him as their candidate for governor of California although he did not plan to wage an active campaign because he was hard at work on his major novel, *Oil!* However, he wrote a platform advocating public ownership of utilities and calling for the repeal of the state's criminal syndicalism laws, which were used to imprison men and women for no more than expressing liberal opinions.

From Italy, Lincoln Steffens wrote suggesting that although most

Russian and European Socialists were no nearer Socialism than most Christians were near Christianity, nevertheless he thought Upton would make a good governor and so "I enclose a small cheque for the campaign. It is money made in Wall Street so keep it mum."

A year earlier Upton had engaged in a prolonged public controversy with Governor F. W. Richardson over the jailing of Charlotte A. Whitney under the criminal syndicalism laws. He made clear that the governor had given the Communists a much needed martyr and many times more publicity than they could ever have received without his help. "I point out to you that under this law Abraham Lincoln could be arrested for reading his first inaugural address; because in that address he stated that: 'This country, with its institutions, belongs to the people who inhabit it. Whenever they shall grow weary of the existing government, they can exercise their constitutional right of amending it, or their revolutionary right to dismember or overthrow it.' Can you deny, Governor, that this is precisely the kind of declaration which is explicitly punishable by fourteen years imprisonment under the California criminal syndicalism law? Or consider what would happen to Thomas Jefferson, third president of the United States, when he wrote that 'The tree of liberty must be refreshed from time to time with the blood of patriots and tyrants. It is its natural manure.' "

He sent this exchange of letters to *The Nation*, urging their readers to write the governor because "This is a State of boosters and we care a great deal about outside opinion, because we think of every person as a potential buyer of our particular parcels of real estate."

As Upton received more and more publicity in California as the champion of social justice, the possibility of his changing from a symbolic to a serious candidate for governor grew and with it grew his horror of unfavorable publicity. When Frank Harris sent him an unsolicited copy of his scandalous *My Life and Loves*, the Post Office threatened to charge him publicly with the crime of importing a book "of an extremely obscene nature." In an uncharacteristic display of bad temper, Upton wrote a series of pettish letters to Harris and the Post Office. He attacked his old friend and disclaimed "the vilest book I have ever seen." Years later, having regained some balance, Sinclair described Harris as "the strongest combination of genius and devil I ever encountered. . . . He was a blackmailer and a scandaler, and he was the most divine talker I ever listened to."

Harris had gently given his views on Sinclair: ". . . there's a Puritanism in him that I can't stomach and that, I believe, injures all his work. . . . So few are called to great work. Why will not Sinclair put his hand to the plow and give us the masterpiece we expect from him."

Based on the rate of sale for the previous month, Upton had on April 15, 1925, a nine-year supply of copies of *Arthur Stirling* in cloth, a thirteen-year supply in paper, with comparable excessive inventories of *Brass Check*, *Metropolis*, *Manassas*, and *Jimmie Higgins*. Of *Samuel the Seeker* there was a supply sufficient for twenty-five to seventy-five years, and of a volume of Mary Craig's sonnets that her husband had thought it mandatory to publish, there were enough to last for eternity. The world's dilatoriness in buying what it so badly needed would have discouraged a less certain savior.

But not Upton, who made yet another effort to be rid personally of the financial burden of his publishing enterprise, without ceasing to publish. He corresponded at great length during 1925 with Dr. James P. Warbasse, president of the Co-operative League of the United States, hoping to turn his business into a co-op. His hope was not realized, but Sinclair's study of cooperatives later led to another book, *Co-op*, which like his *Letters to Judd* and *Flivver King* was intended painlessly to educate his fellow Americans in economic alternatives to laissez-faire capitalism.

Craig, perpetually enjoying ill health, had all her teeth pulled, literally speaking. This treatment was chosen after many others had been considered and rejected, including an operation by Steinach in Vienna and suggestions that she go to Harvard or the Mayo Clinic for examination. She occasionally leaned toward Christian Science, as had Meta, but this time Upton wisely chose to find it acceptable.

His old secretary, Clement Wood, wrote Craig: "You'll get well, if you want to. Psychoanalysis by a non-strict Freudian, a Jung or Adler or Kempf follower especially, might aid you: or a vacation from Upton—I don't care how wholly devoted he is; . . . As to Jesus, I never met him: and, like Mayor Hylan in the Hearst papers, I think his reputation is overestimated."

Whether to kill two birds or as an inducement to Craig, when she had all her teeth out, Upton also had had six of his pulled, with the result that "my cheeks are swelled as if I had a hickory nut in each one, and Craig laughs every time she sees me, and I laugh every time I see her so we are a gay family."

Typically, however, he recovered quickly, whereas Craig complained endlessly about badly fitting false teeth that she refused to wear because she was terrified they were giving her cancer, which increased, if possible, her unwillingness to see people because she felt she looked grotesque. Upton fruitlessly spent time and energy looking for new dentists and refusing to pay old ones.

Her bad health, both real and imaginary, increased steadily throughout her marriage, but failed to stop her from keeping compulsively busy. She canned by the hundreds jars of figs and apricots from her Pasadena house orchard. She worked furiously to convince all her neighbors to sign an agreement undertaking never to sell their property to Japanese or to Mexicans or, most especially, to the Negroes who, as Upton wrote to Albert Rhys Williams: have "moved so near here that it has killed every chance of her getting anything out of her real estate."

Nor did it stop her from doing what she obviously enjoyed most, raising hell with whomever was at hand, her husband, his secretaries, or her sister Dollie. She had begged Dollie and her invalid husband and child to come live near her, keep her company while Upton was writing, and help her to survive menopause, flu, an inflamed appendicitis scar, and a numberless variety of imaginary cancers. But once they came to California, she periodically felt the necessity to prove her authority over them. She made them give their little daughter's dog away after they arrived, and when Dollie complained to Upton about it, Craig forbade her sister ever to speak to him again on any subject whatsoever without first getting her permission. Craig sometimes worried about, but more often reveled in, the fact that "my temper is too bad & I *like* to get boiling mad when I'm mad!"

Real events only peripheral to Craig's fears, when in fact they were related to them at all, regularly confirmed and exacerbated them. For example, her terrors of finding herself poverty-stricken increased as her father, like so many Mississippi planters in the thirties, was becoming bankrupt, although he suffered no change in his style of life and was allowed by his creditors to live in his home until his death. Craig resolutely refused to be reassured by the obvious fact, closer to home, that unlike his capitalist father-in-law, Upton was doing very well financially. His net earned income for 1931, after deducting very substantial expenses for tax purposes, was $21,381.64, an enormous sum in the midst of the Depression, especially for an allegedly naïve Socialist.

Convinced that an even greater isolation than they had already achieved would be beneficial both to Craig's health and to Upton's work, the couple had moved in 1926 to the tiny weekend house they owned at Alamitos Bay in Long Beach, where they lived for several years and from which Upton ran his publishing business. The Pasadena house had been rented to a boys' school. But the move only marginally reduced Craig's complaints or even as Upton noted, "the stream of people coming to my home who have become a part of her 'complex'. . . . Among my callers have been one dangerous maniac, and at least half a dozen potentially dangerous maniacs. Also a vast variety of nuts and bores, and it is a sad problem in an author's life, and a worse one in his wife's."

For even at Long Beach there was a constant flow of visitors, ranging from the future Nobel laureate but then unknown Icelandic poet Halldór Laxness to Craig's mother, who arrived "absolutely determined that Craig should be converted to the Mississippi brand of religion."

Sinclair had more time for his work than most people because he had virtually no social life after he and Craig moved to Long Beach. "For many years now, nobody has had a meal in our home," he apologized to a friend. "This is because of my wife's ill health and extreme nervousness, and it applies to our best friends as well as to strangers. We have no servant. We live in a very small and crowded place. I get my own meals and my wife is unwilling for anybody else to see how I get them. So you see, if you had had a meal you might not have enjoyed it!" But regardless of where the Sinclairs moved, the curious and the cranks and the converted Socialists determined to see their saint found them and rang their doorbell day and night. Because Craig would keep no servants, their only protection was not to answer the doorbell, which further increased their reputation as hermits and eccentrics.

After some two years in Long Beach, Upton was eager to move back to Pasadena where he had his books and records and room to work. Even when they were traveling together, he and Craig each required a separate bedroom because they did much of their work in bed and slept at different hours. "Craig has been trying desperately to get up the nerve to go home, but then she backs out. She is like a squirrel in a treadmill," Sinclair confided to Dollie, "but don't tell her I said so. . . . I have tried to get the squirrel out of the treadmill, but I get my fingers bitten."

However, since she was well enough to make a trip to Mississippi to visit her sick mother, she was well enough for them to move back to Pasadena at the end of 1929.

CHAPTER XIV

Dell's Biography and *Oil!*

There are few less exhilarating books than the biographies of men of letters, and of artists generally; and this arises from the pictures of comparative defeat which, in almost every instance, such books contain. ALEXANDER SMITH

ALTHOUGH SINCLAIR was only forty-seven years old, he suggested to Floyd Dell, whose New York writing and editing career was growing, that because of allegedly persistent demands for it from Russia, Germany, and Norway, the younger man might write his biography. Upton said he thought Horace Liveright would publish it in America and that for one-third of the money it brought in from abroad, he himself would handle all foreign rights. Dell immediately responded favorably but wondered, "there are things in this universe upon which we are not quite in agreement. Are you willing to take your chances?"

Revealing at least partially why he had picked Dell, Sinclair replied: "When I had to differ with you concerning your books, you stood the racket like the fine soul that you are, and I will have to display equal courage. I have entire confidence in your love of truth. If you get any facts wrong I will point out the error. If it is a difference of opinion and interpretation, all I will ask is that you will quote my opinion clearly in one or two sentences, and then fire away as hard as you please, and the reader can judge between us."

There followed long queries from Dell. Upton answered all of them and sent copies of whatever Dell requested. Occasionally in defending himself against a charge of Dell's, Upton unconsciously confirmed it. "You were brought up in a Puritan environment and so you idealize the cavalier attitude. I was brought up in a cavalier environment and so I swing to the other extreme. . . . You say that I have always been opposed to the play aspects of life. The fact was this: being a precocious child, overdeveloped mentally, I was always encouraged to every kind of play. As a boy I did every kind of playing that boys can do. I played tennis in Central Park, football and baseball on vacant lots, and was nabbed by the police in great style. . . .

"At the present time, when my wife is so ill and I have to stay at home nearly all the time, I play [the violin] an hour or two every day—always sight reading, and I get as much excitement out of struggling through a Mozart sonata as some people get out of a horse race. I get as much fun out of a tennis tournament as any of the young fellows. I have also been devoted to the theatre having never missed seeing a good play except because of poverty.

"Theoretically I am opposed to play under the following circumstances; first, when it is cruel and involves wanton suffering to either human beings or animals. I have always enjoyed hunting and fishing, but the game or fish were always eaten; second, when the play is destructive to health, and that is the basis of my objections to the kind of play which involves alcohol. . . . I think that jazz dances are awkward and ugly, being imitations of savage sex dances. Of course as time goes on, if they survive, they will be idealized."

True to their prearrangement, Dell included some of Upton's differences of opinion as footnotes in the book. Upton, however, had some doubts about this procedure when he read the final manuscript and wrote Dell that they seemed out of place: "My comments as you have quoted them strike me as impertinences, like a man getting up and butting in on a meeting where he has no business to speak. . . . I have done so much defending of myself in the newspapers, and I have an idea it is something the public is tired of." He left the final decision to Dell, who chose to print Upton's comments.

Upton, for his part, did not try to suppress Dell's criticisms. He even supplied him with very unfavorable comments that Dell had earlier made to him in letters, for example that Upton's descriptions of sex "do not inform the reader who needs information—they excite his lascivious envy, which masquerades as moral indignation."

While this correspondence was going on, Upton was writing *Oil!* which contained passages on the sexual activities of its characters not only more explicit and casual than anything he had written before, but, along with its references to contraception, sufficient to cause the book to be banned in Boston. It seems probable that Dell's comments during this period were a significant influence in Sinclair's new departure in this area.

The muckraker, who had so often in the past interpreted criticism as attack, refused to be angered by Dell's charges, sometimes beginning a letter "My Dearest Floyd." Correspondingly, Floyd sometimes tempered his criticism. "The fact is, Upton, you're a curious mixture, hard to define, very hard not to do injustice to . . . a Utopian in a great hurry. . . .

". . . You must therefore permit me to regard you as a neurotic in certain respects, and to deplore that fact. . . . I ought to say that to all the other things I admire you for, I must add the way you've taken, as evidenced by your marginal comments, some of the things I've written about you in my book!"

It is possible that Dell was attributing to Sinclair his own ideas, ideas with which no puritan could have agreed. But both authors agreed at least on the importance of the sale of their books, and Sinclair vigorously and successfully promoted the sale of Dell's biography to his own list of customers. He also continued to seek Dell's candid criticism on almost everything he wrote. No one else, excepting only Craig, was regularly so forthright, even brutal, in criticizing not only Sinclair's writings but also his life as was Dell in his letters. Here he more than made up for his excessively flattering biography and repeatedly gave insights which, to Sinclair's credit, never outraged their subject.

Upton was, however, sufficiently at odds with enough in Dell's book that it helped move him five years later, in 1932, to publish his first autobiography, *American Outpost.* These memoirs, which he sent to Dell in manuscript, would provoke further criticism from Dell regarding Upton's writings on sex.

At the end of Dell's very brief biography, *Upton Sinclair*, he maintains, "it is as one of the leaders of a significant American literary movement that he has here been studied . . . one of the great pioneers in the fictional discovery and exploitation of modern America." In fact, however, the book's subtitle, *A Study in Social Protest*, better defines its content.

"Modern industrial America is a new portent in an old world; and the world has looked to American literature for realistic description and intellectual interpretation of it—and has found these things chiefly and best in the writings of Upton Sinclair." Admitting that other American writers were better psychologists, Dell nevertheless ranked Sinclair with Cooper, Twain, and Whitman as an interpreter of his epoch of American life. "The Voltairean tradition of the literary man as a fighter against wrong, a champion of the oppressed, still survives in Europe . . . [where] they do not regard it as an unliterary eccentricity, but as a kind of heroism appropriate to a profession which has not abandoned its pretensions to courage."

As he ended his Freudian and sympathetic biography, Dell quoted Upton's letter to Los Angeles Police Chief Oaks. "I am not a giant physically; I shrink from pain and filth and vermin and foul air, like any other man of refinement; also, I freely admit that when I see a line of a hundred policemen with drawn revolvers flung across a street to keep anyone from coming on to private property to hear my feeble voice, I am somewhat disturbed in my nerves. But I have a conscience and a religious faith, and I know that our liberties were not won without suffering, and may be lost again through our cowardice."

Dell's book was reviewed by Walter Lippmann, who had joined Sinclair's Intercollegiate Socialist Society at Harvard, and who, like Sinclair, spent his life attempting to move his country in what he believed the proper directions. As Lippmann's view of America differed substantially from Sinclair's, so the columnist's view of Sinclair differed from Sinclair's own view of himself.

He questioned Dell's contention that Sinclair changed from a poet to a realistic writer, pointing out that "psycho-analysis is a game at which any number of amateurs can play, and so I herewith state that I am prepared to show . . . Sinclair never did become the realist Mr. Dell thinks he is.

"What I quarrel with is Mr. Dell's theory that . . . Sinclair had been transformed from a person with a morbid distaste for actuality into the greatest American reporter of actuality. . . . If you look at the record set down by Mr. Dell you find that when Thyrsis ceased to rebel against women the tempter he immediately went into violent rebellion against Mammon the tempter. He shifted from one object of rebellion to another, . . . The child has been father to the man. The lonely young poet, afraid of his own instincts, afraid of money, afraid of women, afraid to make friends, did not become clear-eyed and perceiving when he was converted to socialism. He simply used the socialist philosophy to barricade himself more elaborately against the world whose contamination he dreaded.

"But to say that he has discovered the fictional possibilities of modern America is quite a different thing from saying that he has discovered America. . . ."

"What Upton Sinclair has really tried all his life to discover is not America but the Messianic Kingdom. He is an apocalyptic socialist. . . . But the vision itself is a dream which recurs again and again throughout history as the religion of small minorities who cannot endure the life of their times. This religion never conquers the world until it renounces its own essence, becomes worldly, and ceases to demand that which it once held to be all important. But though it never conquers the world, it often produces saints and heroes who, by the contagion of their ardor for righteousness, manage to stir men somewhat out of their lethargy, and to set their eyes on distant goals.

"In the present manifestation of this faith Upton Sinclair undoubtedly has a considerable place. He is one of its saints, and he is a hero."

When Sinclair's *Oil!* was published in 1927, many events in the Teapot

Dome scandals were still fresh in the public's mind. Many others had not yet taken place; Albert B. Fall had not yet been convicted of taking bribes nor Harry F. Sinclair sent to jail for contempt of the Senate. Ironically, in that drama of business control of government, some real life characters displayed a far greater mixture of both sensitivity and insensitivity, good and evil, than had many of Upton's earlier black or white creations.

Although, for example, Woodrow Wilson in 1915 had set aside the Teapot Dome near Casper, Wyoming, as a Navy Department oil reserve, the former Princeton professor had curtly and consistently refused to free Debs from his long and unjust imprisonment. On the other hand, President Harding pardoned Debs on Christmas Day 1921 but handed over the Teapot Dome and Elk Hills, California, oil reserves to his Secretary of the Interior, Fall, who in turn secretly leased them to Harry F. Sinclair and Edward L. Doheny without competitive bidding, in return for bribes of $308,000 and a herd of cattle.

What moved Sinclair to write *Oil!* however, was not the scandals so much as his own experience when two lots in Long Beach that Craig had acquired in the course of her real estate dealings brought the Sinclairs into the frenzy of the Signal Hill oil boom: "And there sat a novelist, watching, listening, and storing away material."

In his novel, Sinclair showed how the great oil companies operated— how corruption of government officials by bribery, from county courthouse to White House was as essential to that industry as suction or pressure is to a pump. He would live long enough to see that in contrast to the oil companies' extraordinary technological changes, bribes arranged and paid in the general stores of the smallest Louisiana parishes or the most exclusive Washington, D.C., clubs provide the industry's one constant.

In the twenties, however, Teapot Dome seemed to Sinclair the ultimate corruption of capitalist government in America. Although no one's laurels are safe forever, Harding had for the moment won first place as a President owned by business. For a man like Sinclair, who loved his country and knew its history, it was a sad day.

But Upton was not discouraged. Even more remarkably, he was not so angered that he whipped out merely another jeremiad in the form of a novel. *Oil!* would be his first novel in five years, and he was firmly resolved it should be a real novel rather than merely a transcription of contemporary events interlarded with propaganda, like his unfortunate *King Coal.*

Perhaps to help keep himself from his habitual literary sins, he wrote letters assuring his correspondents that he had "taken the trouble to invent sufficient story to carry my ideas" and "there is no propaganda in it, at least not so far!" These claims are mainly true, and as a result, *Oil!* is one of Sinclair's three best novels, the others being *The Jungle* and *Boston*.

On the opening page, Upton made clear that *Oil!* was not a *roman à clef*. "Shuffle the cards, and deal a new round of poker hands: they differ in every way from the previous round, and yet it is the same pack of cards, and the same game, with the same spirit, the players grim-faced and silent, surrounded by a haze of tobacco-smoke.

"So with this novel, a picture of civilization in Southern California, as the writer has observed it during eleven years' residence. The picture is the truth, and the great mass of detail actually exists. But the cards have been shuffled; names, places, dates, details of character, episodes—everything has been dealt over again . . . [so that] the reader who spends his time seeking to identify oil magnates and moving picture stars will be wasting time, and perhaps doing injustice to some individual, who may happen to have shot off his toe to collect accident insurance, but may not happen to be keeping a mistress or to have bribed a cabinet official."

In teamster Jim Ross who had made himself into J. Arnold Ross the oil magnate, Upton created one of the most interesting and believable of his hundreds of characters. Ross is not Sinclair's usual priapic capitalist cartoon. Instead he is the kind of strong, disciplined, courageous, loving father Upton wanted but never had and is referred to as "Dad" throughout the novel.

Bunny, Ross' son, is a more typical Sinclair character, the innocent hero, "a pretty boy . . . with wavy brown hair, tumbled by the wind" and "with sensitive red lips like a girl's." Also, like many Sinclair heroes, Bunny is the product of a broken home. His mother tries to use Bunny to influence her former husband, just as Meta periodically tried to use David. Similarly, Paul Watkins, the young Socialist whom Bunny takes as his hero, becomes so disillusioned with capitalist America that he joins the Communists, just as David Sinclair had considered doing.

In *Oil!*, as in so many of Sinclair's books, much of the best writing is found in his descriptions of business experiences, ranging from the putting out of an oil well fire to how a fundamentalist, faith-healing preacher fleeces his flock. Sinclair's memory for details is also evident here as throughout his books. Analogizing from what he had once seen thirty years earlier, for example: "As the Indians in the Hudson Bay country kill a moose in the winter-time, and move to the moose, so Dad started an oil-well, and moved to the well."

But Sinclair also writes effectively in *Oil!* about human relationships, especially the one between Bunny and his father.

Upton had come a long way since the days when the saloonkeeper and the whoremaster were his villains. In *Oil!* he skillfully makes plain that bribing the local Republican county boss is mandatory if Dad wants to be in the oil business and that even after he has become one of the richest men in the state, Dad is not free. He is, in fact, less independent of the bankers than one of his tool dressers or roughnecks or cathead men.

An equally extraordinary change in Upton is made evident by his inclusion and treatment of Bunny's sexual relations with his high school classmate Eunice Hoyt and later with the movie star Vee Tracy. Recognizing that sex existed and putting it in the novel, however, did not mean that Upton really understood the role of sex any more than he understood the sovereign role of exposition of character in the novel.

"I am not satisfied," Floyd Dell wrote him, "with your treatment of the love relationships in the book, because they lack the interaction of personality— . . . You do not present the relations of Bunny and Dad as the relations of a young Socialist with a middle-aged capitalist—but as essentially the relations of a father and son. It seems thus *quite* true. These two people have personalities which exist prior to and independently of their opinions, and these two personalities are seen having an effect upon each other. That I miss in the love affairs. They are sex on the one hand bringing them together, and ideas on the other hand pulling them apart. But neither of the two girls whom Bunny is supposed to be in love with ever seems to mean anything to him as a personality—nor he anything to them. . . . it is impossible for me to think of Bunny as so hard-boiled: after all, a girl is something besides her sexuality and her ideas and her class. . . . It is usually (I should think invariably) a fact, that in intimate sexual relations with a girl, a man learns something of her personality that was hidden from him in a merely friendly relationship. . . . I don't feel that I could know Dad any better if I had known him all my life. But I am sure that if I had 'slept' with Eunice or Vee, I would know something about them, of real importance to your story, that you have not even wondered about! Why, asked Luther, should the devil have all the good times? And why, I ask, should you let novelists who are not capable of a general idea, who know nothing about what makes the world go round, beat you at this personality game?"

In fact, Dell was mistaken about his friend. Upton was "hard-boiled" and "limited in that way." The muckraker was aware that his own sex urge was strong and must be satisfied and be put out of the way. He continued to view it as a necessary evil, a distraction from his work, and a necessary but unfortunate waste of energy, rather than as any glorification of his or his partner's life. And so, not surprisingly in his work also, he considered sex only unavoidable. It had to be recognized, and it helped to sell books; but it did not reveal character significantly nor play an important role in the plot. In *Money Writes!* published after *Oil!*, Sinclair wrote that the "use of the arts in the glorification of depravity is covered by a formula: it is 'What the Public Wants.' " But increasingly from *Oil!* through the Lanny Budd novels, Upton gave the public the sex it wanted.

In fact, the time soon came when Craig and Dollie would read the manuscript of *The Wet Parade* and protest that there was too much sex in it.

The "personality" that Dell and others begged him to be more concerned with was still unimportant to Upton. Programs not people, ideas not individuals were what interested him. He told his tale well, but he did not draw most characters in depth. In his answer to Dell, however, he promised to reform, but any such promise was quite as meaningless as his father's many promises to stop drinking. "The trouble was, Floyd, the darn thing ran away with me. . . . Next time I won't plan so much, & will have more time for personality."

How little time Upton had, or how little he took, was revealed in another letter to Dell: "I wrote the words 'The End', to 'Oil!', at eleven o'clock this morning and at one o'clock came your chapters of the biography. Now I have the problem of which I should do first, revise my own chapters or read yours."

However superficial Upton's passages in *Oil!* about sex were, they nevertheless were about to have an important effect on the author's life and future.

It was ironic that Horace Brisbin Liveright should be the publisher who turned down *Oil!* Upton's first modern novel. He could hardly have been more different from Sinclair—being a devoted womanizer, gambler, and high liver. A Jew in what had long been in America a Christian gentlemen's business, he was most importantly the avant-garde publisher of Pound, Cummings, O'Neill, and Eliot. So that he should refuse to publish Sinclair as had so many other publishers was perhaps less surprising than that he had ever published the muckraker's work. In any event, the incidence of sex in the book could not have been a contributing cause.

Albert and Charles Boni, who published *Oil!* did not consider it first class but believed that, sooner or later, Sinclair would produce another best seller. They had only a few years earlier broken with Liveright and formed their own publishing firm, and they frankly wanted to make money. According to Albert Boni: "I wrote a number of well-known writers, some of whom I had known at Boni & Liveright, proposing that they allow my brother and me to publish their next work. Sinclair replied quickly, sending his manuscript of *Oil!*"

Born in New York in 1892, Albert Boni at the age of twelve had been converted to Socialism by reading Robert Blatchford and at sixteen had joined the party. Among his many bright ideas were the Washington Square Players (which developed into the Theatre Guild), the Modern Library, and the Microprint-Readex system. Soon after Upton associated himself with the new publishers, Charles Boni broke with his brother, founded his own publishing firm, which failed, and shortly thereafter died of cancer.

On May 27, 1927, the Bonis wired Upton that *Oil!* had been banned in Boston. They suggested he issue a statement saying he would go to Boston and sell a copy of the book himself.

Upton leaped at the opportunity for publicity. He issued bulletins, sent wires, wrote letters, and hired a Boston lawyer before leaving for Boston, where he promised also to bring his son to prove the falsity of Municipal Court Judge John Duff's statement that *Oil!* contained passages "manifestly tending to corrupt the morals of youth." High school and college "petting parties" at which participants "went all the way" had been witnessed by his son, Upton explained, and they were rapidly becoming the rule rather than the exception.

Once in Boston, he obtained a "Peddler's and Hawkers' Certificate" and a "Special Permit to . . . use a portion of the public streets for the purpose of advertising . . . with sign on hat and coat."

He failed to convince the authorities to let him take the place of the book clerk, John Gritz, who for selling a copy of *Oil!* was found guilty and fined one hundred dollars. Sinclair also failed in his attempt to get himself arrested for selling a copy of his banned book to a policeman. When he revealed that the copy of *Oil!* he had sold to the officer was in fact a copy of the Bible inside a cover of his book in order to draw attention to the fact that on a number of his offending pages he was quoting from the Songs of Solomon, the charges against him were dropped.

But he was a delight to the reporters who covered his performances and reported them fully. To satisfy those who wanted to see a political conspiracy in the banning, he declared that the reason for the suppression of *Oil!* was its description of how the oil interests bought the Republican Convention that nominated Harding. "Unlike Samuel Hopkins Adams's 'Revelry,' Mr. Sinclair mentions Harding's name in connection with the oil scandals."

For those who preferred comedy, he printed a few copies of what he called a "Fig Leaf Edition" of *Oil!* in which the offending pages were censored out by a large black leaf silhouette. A picture of Sinclair with sandwich boards in the shape of two fig leaves hawking this edition was reproduced in papers all over the world and helped the book become an international best seller.

Upton hoped, in vain as it turned out, for a real court trial of the obscenity issue and so wrote to authors and public figures for their opinions. John Masefield, Havelock Ellis, Lewis Mumford, and Norman Thomas were among those who wrote defending the book.

Some addressed themselves to more than merely the obscenity charge. "I read it with keen interest, and consider it a splendid novel of fact," wrote D. H. Lawrence. "It is absurd for anyone to call it indecent. . . .

"And why should they put a ban on it? The real hero is 'Dad'— J. Arnold Ross—and the thrill of the book is the way he becomes an oil magnate: the old American thrill of a lone hand and a huge success. The book won't make Bolshevists: whoever reads it will want to be like 'Dad,' not like Paul or Bunny. And so long as people want to be like J. Arnold Ross, what danger is there? Anyhow he's more of a man than any of the other characters.

"But the novel seems to me a splendid big picture of actual life: What more do they want?"

Edith Wharton was less flattering. "I received your novel 'Oil' a few months ago, and read it (from the point of view of your skill as a novelist) with great enjoyment and admiration.

"It seems to me an excellent story until the moment, all too soon, when it becomes a political pamphlet. I make this criticism without regard to the views which you teach, and which are detestable to me. Had you written in favour of those in which I believe, my judgment would have been exactly the same. . . .

"Having said this, I hasten to add that the charge of obscenity is absurd, and I am glad to join in protesting against it, from the moment that it is clearly understood that my protest applies to that charge only."

It is understandable that book banning reached such a peak in "the roaring twenties." Historically in America, pietism often increases inversely with faith. In the disillusion that followed the World War, religious faith suffered and hypocritical observance of religious forms increased. Americans who with increasing ease winked at their own wickedness were outraged by wicked foreigners in their midst and by the working classes, who had not only to be protected from reading "dirty" books but even more seriously from trade union agitators who were leading them away from the Calvinist ideal of hard work.

An age of relaxation and innocence was ending, its permanent demise assured by the rise of great totalitarian states with the power to end the world if they believed their existence was threatened. But Upton remained religious, innocent, and hopeful. If by naïve is meant ignorant of the evils and chicaneries of this world, he was not naïve. But he was an innocent, as a saint even when covered with obscenities remains innocent. And he retained the childlike optimism of the innocent.

Such innocence and optimism seem so almost unimaginable today that it is perhaps necessary to point out Upton was not some singular simpleton. Virginia Woolf is a writer whose literary product could scarcely be more different from Upton's and is much more appreciated today than his. But her view too of the sweetness and promise of Socialism was much the same—"a tremendously enlarged version of the feeling I can remember as a child as Christmas approached."

CHAPTER XX

Boston

"I could never believe that Providence had sent a few men into the world, ready booted and spurred to ride, and millions ready saddled and bridled to be ridden."   RICHARD RUMBOLD, on the scaffold

IN ONE of his typical, harmless self-dramatizations, Upton claimed he had decided to write his novel, *Boston*, at precisely nine thirty (Pacific Coast Time), the evening of August 22, 1927, when a friend had telephoned the news of the execution of Sacco and Vanzetti. In fact he had decided earlier: "I am no longer interested in making a fuss about 'Oil!' in Boston. The situation there is too tense and serious for that kind of joking. What I want to do is to go very quietly and gather the material for a big novel, and take a couple of years to write it. I will call it by the name 'Boston,' and make it a by-word to the rest of the civilized world."

Sinclair's animus against Boston, conscious and unconscious, had abided within him for many years. Although different individual events stirred it more or less, it stemmed from the fact that he was an outlander—one who had never been accepted by Boston as had his fellow author William Dean Howells.

New England in general and Massachusetts most particularly viewed themselves (increasingly as their economic and political power dwindled) as the birthplace in America not only of literature but also of moral reform and reformers from the days of the Mathers through those of the Abolitionists. But for Sinclair there had been no "apostolic succession . . . [no] laying on the hands" as had been vouchsafed Howells by the heirs of Emerson and Thoreau. Such notice as Sinclair had received adjudged him neither a first-class writer nor even a first-class moralist, but only an opportunistic journalist, and Sinclair smarted at the slights of the self-styled Athenians. He still resented Bliss Perry's rejection of his *Prince Hagen* manuscript and Boston's refusal of help to finance him when he had wanted so desperately to write his Civil War trilogy.

Both before and after their execution, the Italian anarchists inspired widespread and passionate interest among artists. Edna St. Vincent Millay (now married to Eugen Boissevain, the widower of Upton's unrequited love, Inez Milholland) wrote the more moving than immortal *Justice Denied in Massachusetts*. Plays on the subject ranged from Maxwell Anderson's *Gods of the Lightning* (banned in Boston) and *Winterset* to James Thurber's *The Male Animal* in 1940. It was not a writer, however, who dealt most effectively with the subject. It was instead the painter and printmaker Ben Shahn.

Not since the conviction of John Brown had a court's decision about a previously unknown individual so stirred Americans on both sides of the issue. All during the months of trial and appeal, Upton had acted individually and in concert with others, trying first to obtain justice for the men and finally just trying to save their lives. It would be difficult to exaggerate the intensity of his feelings or the degree of his outrage. "SV execution most shocking crime that has been committed in American history since assassination of Abraham Lincoln," and he predicted, "It will empoison our public life for a generation. To the workers of the whole world it is a warning to get organized and check the bloodlust of capitalism."

So intense was Sinclair's bitterness after the execution that he dismissed entirely his plan to take several years to write his Sacco-Vanzetti novel; instead, after his research in Boston, he wrote and revised it at a furious rate. "I can't recollect ever being so tired of writing," he confided to Mike Gold. "I have written a two volume novel in nine months." He decided *Boston* would be published on the first anniversary of the execution, August 27, 1928, but even at his feverish pace he could not make it, nor his second self-imposed deadline, September 20, 1928, his fiftieth birthday.

Sinclair financed the research trip to Boston by lectures, for which he was usually paid more than two hundred dollars each, because, as he advised his lecture agent, "people who come to hear me, come expecting to be shocked, but I am careful not to shock them any more than they expect."

His research there was impressively thorough and evenhanded. But even more exhaustive was his research by mail. He wrote hundreds of letters to dozens of correspondents. "I would like to know these details, for the reason that I am now writing of Vanzetti's arrest and the Plymouth trial: first, any physical details about the Plymouth jail and how one saw visitors there, at what hour, and did the visitors have to talk to the prisoner through a wire screen, or would they sit together in a room, as was the case in Charlestown? What did Vanzetti wear in the Plymouth jail? About how long did the Plymouth trial take? . . ."

To make his career-long device of mixing real and fictional characters in the same novel work, Sinclair had to make certain, for example, that no one in Boston bore in fact the names of his fictional creations. And so he had one of his many on the scene helpers check all his fictional names against those in the Boston city directory. Different helpers frequently gave Sinclair conflicting interpretations of the same event, and he had either to select which parts of which versions to use, or he might give his own characters such conflicting stories as made the story seem more real. He usually avoided errors by sending parts of his manuscript to those who had given him the facts in those parts, requesting that any errors be corrected.

If as a reporter, Sinclair had himself carefully covered the ground he wrote about in Boston, Plymouth, Dedham, in the governor's mansion, the cordage factory, the slum, it would still have been difficult enough to reconstruct all the many complicated events in the many different locales. But to do it by long distance with so many helpers, and to do it so well, seems almost unbelievable.

He had sold the prepublication serial rights to Seward Collins for four thousand five hundred dollars. As these episodes appeared in *The Bookman*, Upton wrote dozens of friends, including the authors John Dos Passos and Mike Gold; Robert Morss Lovett, an editor of the *New Republic*; and E. A. Filene, the millionaire Boston merchant, urging them to read the parts monthly and send him corrections and ideas for the book.

From Floyd Dell and James Fuchs, another friend from whom Upton frequently sought advice, he requested and insisted on paying for long and detailed criticisms of style as well as content. Dell's letters, sometimes dozens of pages long, were not infrequently brutal. "I don't agree with your idea," Upton answered one, "but I have respect enough for your judgement to do it for you, since you feel so strenuously about it."

A discovery revealed by his research might have stopped Sinclair from writing the book at all. Like everyone else on the left, he was certain of the anarchists' innocence, but he soon found it was not a certainty. When he stated the uncertainty and refused to write a hagiography, he brought down on himself some of the worst attacks he ever suffered, from Communists, anarchists, and others on the left. Bob Minor called him "a hired liar, a coward and a traitor," but Upton replied calmly: "The plain truth is this, that when I began to have doubts it seemed to me that I could not possibly write the book. The only reason I went on was because I realized that it would be cowardly to turn back, and anyhow, it would do no good, because I had advertised that I was going to write the book, and people would not fail to guess the reason."

To another critic Sinclair admitted: "All these matters are terribly complicated. . . . my problem was the hardest I have ever faced in my life. . . . It is my belief that if I had taken an entirely naïve attitude toward the Sacco-Vanzetti defense, and represented the defense as all white and the prosecution as all black, I would have done very little good to the case, because too many people know the truth, and it is bound to come out sooner or later. The only thing I would accomplish would be to destroy entirely my own reputation as a trustworthy writer. I have never hesitated about my own reputation where it was in a good cause. But I really could not see any sense in making myself foolish to no purpose."

Repeatedly he explained his position. "When I went East . . . gradually I became convinced . . . that Sacco and Vanzetti had at least known about the holdup . . . that the Italian radicals believe that Sacco was guilty and Vanzetti knew it.

"I left Boston feeling that I did not really know, and that I could write my book on the basis of certainty that they did not have a fair trial. But in Denver I met Fred Moore [the first defense lawyer], and he told me how he had framed the witnesses . . . and he gave me permission to tell everything as it really happened, provided I would make it plain that it is the universal custom in big criminal trials. . . . Moore is absolutely certain that Sacco was guilty. He is not certain about Vanzetti, but thinks he was. I do not think so. I think that Vanzetti might have saved himself, but he went to his death rather than tell about Sacco.

". . . I am asking you to consider it absolutely confidential . . . because there really is a possibility that some anarchist might think it his duty to keep me from finishing the book, and I do want to finish it!"

It was pointed out to Sinclair that if Fred Moore, who had been dismissed as defense counsel, betrayed to the muckraker the confidentiality of his relationship with his former clients, he was obviously less than perfectly reliable. But even after the lawyer refused to discuss the case any further or to read or comment on the book, Upton chose to continue to believe Moore because, as he wrote his publishers, he had separate corroborating evidence. "I know positively that a considerable part of the Sacco-Vanzetti defense was made of perjured testimony. I first discovered it from the record. I then got admissions from witnesses (in strict confidence, of course)."

At a later date, when the most furious emotions had somewhat calmed, another writer of the left then well on his way toward the right, Max Eastman, would come to much the same conclusions Upton had expressed while still in the eye of the storm. But the world continued to believe the men innocent, and they have never satisfactorily been proven otherwise.

Not only Sinclair but other muckrakers too repeatedly demonstrated restraint, refusing to lie in behalf of men and causes they supported—contrary to Theodore Roosevelt's allegations and contrary to the practice of the capitalist press. For example, in reporting on the earlier Moyer-Haywood trial, the muckrakers and most especially Christopher Power Connally for *Collier's* zealously sought the truth from both sides in the belief that the truth would set free not only anyone falsely accused but all Americans. For this they were much abused by many miners and Socialists who saw the whole affair as a major battle in the class war and wanted Haywood and the others saved at any cost and regardless of any possible guilt. But this factual and objective reporting was far more effective.

Sinclair's outrage at the injustice done the Italians and its significance for the country continued for many years and took many forms. He suggested an annual reenactment of the trial in Boston or that he would help create a "pageant play . . . and there is no reason why a play like this could not become a New England tradition similar to the Passion Play at Oberammergau." He expected the author and actors would be arrested and so continue to publicize around the world the tale of the martyred anarchists.

When Fremont Older suggested Upton write a novel about Tom Mooney, the labor agitator, the muckraker's answer reflected his earlier experience. "I have thought many times about a novel on the Mooney case. The trouble is this: While Mooney didn't commit the crime for which he is in prison, he did some other things which are an essential part of the story, and I doubt if he would be willing for me to write frankly about those things. Perhaps it would hurt more than it would help his cause while he is still in prison. On the other hand, you can see that for me to write a book about his case without mentioning those things would be foolish as well as dishonest."

In his novel, Upton portrayed Boston as capitalist America at its ultimate. "It was feudalism in frock coats." Not devoid of snobbery himself, he understood it as some Socialists did not. "The [Irish] politicians and police might laugh at the blue-bloods, but they respected and feared them, because of very real powers they still held; not merely finance, utilities and the choicest real estate, but solidarity, knowledge, culture—the latter a far-off, mysterious thing, but awe-inspiring, like the power of a voodoo magician. . . . The lower orders, having captured the city, were afraid of their captives, and dared not make use of their power; they stood, fierce-eyed barbarians, at the doors of the temples, and watched the priests, clad in frock coats and high hats. . . . In the end the barbarians capitulated, and sent their sons to study at the temples, and become as much like the conquered caste as they could!"

But Sinclair himself was not taken in by the lords, temporal or spiritual. When his "runaway grandmother," the fictional heroine Cornelia Thornwall, goes to plead with the nonfictional William Cardinal O'Connell "to say a word for mercy to Sacco and Vanzetti; . . . he was cautious and preferred to talk about Japanese art and Buddhist philosophy." From top to bottom, in every one of its capitalist institutions, Sinclair saw and described the "badda sistema," as Vanzetti, who appears under his own name, calls it.

Sinclair had always written in favor of moderation and against violence in accomplishing the revolution for social justice in America. But in *Boston*, more and more of his characters preached the doctrine that was being preached at Upton by his friends who had become disillusioned with Socialism and moved left to Communism. Even his heroine when she reads to Vanzetti from the first issue of the *Liberator*, published nearly a century earlier, says: "William Lloyd Garrison—learn it, Bart, a good name to quote in this part of the world. . . . 'I will be as harsh as truth, and as uncompromising as justice. On this subject I do not wish to think, or speak, or write with moderation. No! No! Tell a man whose house is on fire to give a moderate alarm; tell him to moderately rescue his wife from the hands of a ravisher . . .'"

Upton contrasted in *Boston* the effectiveness of two kinds of suffragists, "the respectable ones who made dignified speeches and circulated petitions and got an inch in the newspapers once a month; and the militants, who set themselves the goal of a front-page story twice a day, and made it most of the time."

When Cornelia, arguing against Vanzetti's position that "never men get free wit'out fight," points out that Negro slaves didn't fight, her niece breaks in, "Other people had to fight for them; and if they aren't really free yet, maybe that is the reason, because they haven't done their own fighting."

To Cornelia, who is reluctant to believe that her gentle Bart could use violence, Pierre Leon, the fictional French Communist editor, explains: " 'all militant anarchists believe in bombs. Not all make them—any more than all Christians sell their goods and give to the poor. It is too uncomfortable and dangerous. But the faith calls for it, . . . and when some young enthusiast comes along and wants to practice, the preachers can't very well say no. And when the boys get into trouble, then of course the movement has to rally and defend them.'

" 'And that, of course, includes telling the world they are innocent?' . . .

" 'Naturally. It goes without saying that anybody who will fight will try to deceive the enemy. What you have got to get clear is the central doctrine of anarchism, that property used for exploitation is theft. That makes capitalist society a gigantic bandit-raid, a wholesale killing; any killing you have to do to abolish it, or to cripple it, always is a small matter in comparison. . . . [Capitalist society] intends to take our lives by the tens of millions; and we are denied the right to save ourselves—because . . . the effort means killing a few capitalists and kings and judges and police spies. . . . You can see that, to an anarchist, such an idea is childish.'

" 'Or to a communist . . .'

" '. . . Between the anarchist and the communist is a question of technique. I once heard an American labor leader put it effectively: "Never use violence—until you have enough of it!" ' "

In *Boston*, as throughout his work, Sinclair scoffed at capitalist society's hypocrisies about "law and order." His naïve character Samuel the Seeker had been shocked to find that the church could not punish its dishonest members because they owned the church. But in *Oil!* Sinclair had shown that nothing at all was sacred from use by the rich and powerful, even Army, Navy, and Secret Service intelligence files being at the service of businessmen. "How could the rich, . . . be so blind? How could they overlook the consequences of teaching the workers such contempt for law?" he asked in *Boston*.

What made *Boston* one of Sinclair's three best novels, despite its extraordinary two-volume length, was his relatively minimal preaching and his ability to invest this more than twice-told tale with suspense. And because it is a more effective novel it is more effective propaganda.

The leaders of the American establishment at the time were able neither to anticipate nor even to understand the intensity of the worldwide interest in the two anarchists. That was because they had ceased to believe in the American dream. But millions throughout the world still believed and so did Sinclair.

Most reviewers recognized that Sinclair had written a novel that was in fact a novel. Journals of his own political persuasion, such as *The Nation*, were lyrical. "What Fielding was to the eighteenth century and Dickens to the nineteenth, Sinclair is to our own. The overwhelming knowledge and passionate expression of specific wrongs are more stirring, more interesting, and also more taxing than the cynical censure of Fielding and the sentimental lamentations of Dickens. Where Mr. Sinclair does not deliberately intrude his woe-conscious philosophy and his political propaganda into the action of his story, he achieves narrative that by the standards of both art and life is as great as any work of his masters."

And even the chronically unfriendly *New York Times* declared *Boston* "deserves praise as a literary achievement. . . . it is wrought into a narrative on the heroic scale with form and coherence . . . full of sharp observation and savage characterization . . . [and demonstrates] a craftsmanship in the technique of the novel that the author has seldom displayed before. . . ."

Individuals too who had been critical in the past expressed a newfound admiration. Paul H. Douglas, who had angrily protested Sinclair's misuse of his statistics in *Letters to Judd* wrote him that he had "been perfectly captured by the book. . . . Since we have . . . had several controversies in the past I am all the more anxious to tell you of my hearty admiration . . . [and] also congratulate you upon fifty years of such useful service to the downtrodden of this country."

Lewis Mumford, whose comments on Sinclair often approached the contemptuous, wrote the muckraker: "It is not merely your own finest achievement: it is nothing less than an epic document, and it will last as long as the memory of Sacco & Vanzetti themselves. Your imaginative history of *the* American Tragedy must supplant every other work, for it has the finality of truth and art."

A. Conan Doyle wrote in connection with *Boston,* "I look upon Sinclair as one of the greatest novelists in the world, the Zola of America. . . .", just as in France *Oil!* was declared one of mankind's masterpieces. It was understandable, therefore, that having repeatedly been so extravagantly praised from so many quarters as one of the planet's great artists, Upton on occasion thus viewed himself and expected proofs and patents and prizes confirming his prominence.

Just after the publication of *Boston,* Robert Herrick, the professor-novelist, had written about his friend Sinclair to Robert Morss Lovett, who was serving on the Pulitzer Prize Committee. Herrick declared that if Lovett could not compel the prize to be given to Sinclair's novel, Lovett ought in self-respect to resign from the committee and state publicly why.

Upton confided to Lovett that unlike Sinclair Lewis who had refused the Pulitzer Prize for *Arrowsmith,* he would accept it, using the money to present a thousand copies of his novel to colleges and public libraries.

Shortly thereafter, the chairman of the 1928 Pulitzer Prize Committee declared that only the "socialistic tendencies" and "special pleading" of *Boston* had kept it from winning and although his publisher, Charles Boni, wired that this presented far better opportunities for publicity than actually winning the award, Upton was hurt and angry.

Felix Frankfurter wrote, "I should think you would be one of the last persons to attach any importance to Pulitzer prizes," but, like Boni, the Harvard law professor underestimated Sinclair's terrible need for recognition and praise.

In one of his printed letters sent en masse to all his direct mail customers, friends, and acquaintances, Sinclair pointed out that the book selected by the committee, *Victim and Victor*, was far more tendentious than *Boston*, that its special pleading was merely for a religious or clerical cause rather than for Socialism. Embarrassed by the whole public squabble, Columbia University ignored the committee's recommendation and awarded the prize to Julia Peterkin's *Scarlet Sister Mary*, and Upton urged his readers to send him contributions so he could distribute copies of *Boston* as he had planned to do with the prize money. Many did.

Many others as disparate as Leslie Fiedler, Theodore White, and Norman Mailer in America, and Arthur Koestler and Frederic Morton in Europe, read the novel and decades later testified to its great effect on them. If a similar influence was exerted by the prizewinning novel, the evidence is undisclosed.

For Sinclair the episode was another in an endless list of slights and injustices dealt by capitalism to its tireless exposer and enemy.

During the publication of *Boston*, he carried on by letter and telegram a protracted fight with the Bonis, objecting to their "absolutely intolerable treatment" and culminating with his "request that our relationships may be terminated." Sinclair took his work and himself seriously and would not suffer the publisher's typical shabby and careless treatment. Although this was in part a matter of temperament, it was also a practical matter. When he was not sent on time the dozens of sets of proofs he had been promised, for example, it meant that he in turn could not send them on time to magazine, newspaper, and book publishers all over the world who were also publishing the work and to whom he had given his promise of timely delivery.

The Bonis, however, promised to reform. They were for the moment unwilling to lose a best-selling author, especially one so anxious to have his books sell that he contributed toward their advertising much of his royalties. By the end of 1928, Charles Boni was encouraging Upton's idea of writing an autobiography and urging that he leave out explicit political argument and remember "that the propaganda is implicit in your life."

Worn out by *Boston*, Sinclair also tried to reduce his immense foreign correspondence by asking his British agent to handle all his foreign rights. But he was temperamentally unable to turn over decisions about his work to others. And he was willing to spend time, when a book didn't sell, arranging to give it free to a Movement publisher—something one could hardly expect an agent to do whose income came from a percentage of sales. He was also constantly sending advice to his foreign publishers on how to get publicity for his books, including his standard effort to get himself sued for libel by some prominent person. "I will agree to stand half the legal costs of any libel suit [brought by Kipling]," he wrote his British publisher, ". . . try to fix something that is just libelous enough for a nominal award—if you can do that!"

Much of his time went to correspondence with and work for the dozens of groups, committees, and little magazines, of which he was a member or contributor. "I have grave doubts about the propriety of letting my name be used on the letterheads of organizations in which I am not able to take an active part," he would write occasionally in a usually vain effort to extricate himself from an old obligation or avoid a new one. In the National Council for Protection of Foreign Born Workers, the International Labor Defense, the Debs Memorial Radio Fund, and many other groups of the same kind, Sinclair served with the same names again and again—Elizabeth Gurley Flynn, Clarence Darrow, William Z. Foster, Robert Morss Lovett, Norman Thomas, Earl Browder, W. E. B. Du Bois, Sidney Hillman, A. Phillip Randolph, Morris Hillquit, Abraham Cahan, Elizabeth Gilman, Louis Budenz, Max Eastman. Just as he knew he might soon be calling on them for help, so he dared not refuse their calls to him. So, also, when from abroad Henri Barbusse, Maxim Gorki, Bertrand Russell, and Romain Rolland asked him to serve on the *Comité de Direction* of a new publication or league or relief association, along with Madame Sun Yat-sen, Reinhold Niebuhr, or Darius Milhaud, it was hard to say no.

Upton was aware that so many committees had a funny side too: "I will be pleased to join the committee . . . for Heinrich Heine, but the great poet will laugh at us from the elysian vales where he waits, because he will think we are a little too late. He would rather have had something to eat while he was alive."

But no matter how worthy an organization might be, if it had ever acted against the interests of social justice, as Upton believed the Red Cross had during the Russian Revolution, he would refuse to help and urge others to refuse likewise.

Despite his resolutions to reduce the large number of his commitments, he in fact continually added to the list. He continued to be especially vulnerable to the pleas of prisoners. These ranged from melon pickers trying to organize a union in California's Imperial Valley to his own translators abroad who were regularly imprisoned for radicalism.

Hundreds of men and women, each with a different cause of his or her own—to stop "the looting of the Nez Perces" or the brutalizing of "thousands of women and little white American children" in the South—wrote to Sinclair asking that he give money, give his name, or write a book exposing the evil. If he failed to give as much effort to each cause as his correspondent wanted, he was often denounced.

Just the new and unexpected requests in each day's mail would have been enough to occupy an ordinary man full time. Leonard Abbott, who had first introduced Upton to Socialism, wrote asking for help finding a job. An Omaha reader wrote: "I'm only a poor school girl, sir, with a feminine weakness for chiffon hosiery. I am entering the University of Chicago the first of October. I want your books very close to me all year, to help me keep in mind the things I really want from life."

A man wrote asking whether sexual relations with a woman when she was menstruating were to be avoided, quoting various authorities who said it was. "All I can say," Upton replied, "is that I have not found from experience there [sic] statements to be justified."

The distinguished architect Richard J. Neutra wrote asking for help in promoting housing appropriate to the needs of workers.

Worshipful letters from admirers all over the world were frequent and often touching. From Prague, as the threat of Hitler became daily clearer, a reader wrote asking for a photograph. "I intend to have it put in a frame and hang it over my bed in order to remember, at the beginning and the end of each day, that there is somebody in the world, who is not afraid to work openly for justice of all the peoples . . ."

Trotsky wrote from exile in Turkey about arranging the translation into Turkish of all Sinclair's works.

Norman Thomas advised, "There is, I know, a strong sentiment for you as [the Socialist Party candidate for] Vice President. I have heard no other name mentioned so often. . . ."

He told an interviewer about a few recent correspondents. "Some one wants me to market his invention—an engine operated by static electricity. Another considers it my duty to help him launch what he calls 'a new kind of marriage camp.' Just what a marriage camp is, I don't know. A third has a medicine which will cure all ills.

"The questions they ask! When should a baby be weaned? What is the best way to reduce? . . . Is it true that such-and-such a chemical will harmlessly turn blond hair red?

"There arrive at least three letters a week asking me to expose something. The 'something' varies from hotel restaurants to detectives, from insane asylums to the evils of the tipping custom."

"Does anyone ever threaten to kill you?"

"Not very often. Perhaps once or twice a year."

The letters from Mencken kept arriving regularly. On rare occasions they were mellow. "I hope your increasing age is subduing you and throwing your thoughts in the direction of higher things. In a few years now, both of us will be in the crematory. Let us cultivate our souls while the going is good." But usually they were the opposite. "As always, you are right—save in matters of politics, sociology, religion, finance, economics, literature, and the exact sciences."

Some of Sinclair's own letters were obvious attempts to get publicity. He released to the press, for example, a letter refusing an invitation to meet Count Hermann Keyserling because, despite Prohibition, the German demanded his hosts provide champagne. And he was well aware that his correspondence with a Soviet worker living in the provinces was pleasing to the Russians and likely to find its way to a Moscow newspaper. Often multiple copies of his letters and telegrams were sent to what he called his "publicity list," a constantly updated list of wire services, publications, and individuals both in America and abroad.

When Heywood Broun declared in *Life* that Sinclair was living on nuts and lettuce, Sinclair wrote begging Broun to advise his readers that "I used to live on nuts; now the nuts live on me."

Broun was, like Upton, a Socialist and so wrote often on the same subjects as the muckraker, but usually with more humor. When his editor, Ralph Pulitzer, accused Broun of expressing his opinion on the Sacco-Vanzetti trial "with the utmost extravagance," Broun replied, "I spoke only to the limit of my belief and passion. This may be extravagance, but I see no wisdom in saving up indignation for a rainy day. It was already raining."

Writing as he often did dozens of letters a day, Upton was constantly revealing both his worst and best qualities. When *The Nation* listed him as one of America's best authors, Upton thanked its editor, Oswald Garrison Villard, but protested that Hemingway had also been listed. "I really think the literary opinions of The Nation ought to have some trace of harmony with its political opinions."

When Mike Gold finally seemed ready to write the book he had talked about for years, which would turn out to be *Jews Without Money*, Upton wrote: "If you want to go to Europe and really write that book, I will take a chance to the extent of $50 a month for ten months."

He finally even gave his son, David, eight hundred dollars to pay for graduate work in physics at Columbia, the boy having given up his hopes of a musical career. Earlier, when after graduating from college David was devoting himself to studying voice and piano full time, Upton had suggested that as a means of earning money he sell Gaylord Wilshire's newest promotion, the "Ianaco." Apparently nothing more than a large coil of copper wire, this "magnetic belt" was supposed to cure almost as many ills as Dr. Abrams' machine. Upton tried it on his own rheumatic shoulder "with no result as I can see." He nevertheless hoped David could sell it profitably, taking the position that whether or not the beneficial results allegedly obtained from the machine by others was merely autosuggestion he could not tell. "Of course the doctors are bitterly opposed to it," he explained to David as a possible proof of its efficacy.

On September 3, 1928, David married Bettina Mikol, who was usually called Betty. She was also at Columbia, where she worked as an editor of the *Political Science Quarterly.* Upton promised one hundred and twenty-five dollars a month through the following January. After that, David would again be on his own as he had been all through college and after, except for a gift of fifty dollars each Christmas and a hundred on his graduation.

The November 1928 issue of *The New Masses* had celebrated Sinclair's fiftieth birthday with his picture on the cover and various tributes inside. One, by Mike Gold, was made of extracts from his diary. "October 3—Upton invited me to join his friends on a visit to San Quentin. We talked to Tom Mooney. . . . Then we drove south, and had lunch in a meadow. Upton Sinclair ate a whole apricot pie. 'I never eat pie,' he said briskly, 'it is really poison, but today I shall have an orgy.'

"Sinclair is a surprise to all who first meet him. One expects to meet a solemn bearded Tolstoy, but finds instead a brisk American youth. . . . He has bright twinkly eyes; they are paternal, naïve, the eyes of a cheerful country doctor, or of a daring theological student. . . . When he decides that he needs relaxation, he carefully plans for his fun in the blithe spirit of Henry Ford planning a new carburetor. . . . But he really is charming. He believes everything everyone tells him. He is incapable of imagining baseness in other people. He beams hopefully on the world, like a child the night before Christmas. It is not sentimentality; it is the poetry of William Blake. But he tempts you continually to fool him; you want to sell him some gold-brick or other, just to teach him a lesson. . . .

"Along with his naïveté goes shrewdness and strength. Upton is the perfect incarnation of the small town American. . . . The sophisticated critics don't understand him, because they don't understand America.

"But he has a touch of the fanatic. This is what makes him different from the millions of other Main Streeters. The critics think he is a Puritan, and therefore a man like William Jennings Bryan. But he is a Puritan, and therefore a man like Robespierre, or Thoreau, or Percy Shelley. It is this extremism which makes him hate pie for decades, then suddenly gulp a whole apricot pie in a Californian meadow. It also keeps him a lonely, stubborn Socialist writer for thirty years in a hostile land.

"He is hard to explain. At times he irritates you; he seems so self-centered, so unaware of others, so completely an ego. Many people have this impression of him. It is a false impression. He is only as egotistic as the rest of us. But he has not learned what every ward heeler knows; how to drape the social lies around one's naked ego."

In a letter to Gold about the article, Upton suggested, ". . . I don't think you are quite scientific when you say that I believe what everybody tells me. . . .

"My personal attitude is this. I do not deny that the Revolution may come in this country by violent means but I am not going to advocate that it should come that way and I think it is a great practical blunder and a great waste of moral force to commit or promote the first act of violence. I think it better tactics to let the enemy begin as Lincoln did in the struggle with the slave power. I can suggest a number of constitutional methods by which the workers might get control of industry. And it seems to me the part of wisdom to advocate those methods and try and apply them. I think we could afford to pay an enormous price for the big industries of this country and still have all the workers better off than if we should attempt to seize the industries with all the confusion and waste that would result. I look at Italy and see the frightful results of premature action by an unarmed proletariat and think it a lot better to wait a while and use such freedom as we have, freedom of propaganda to educate the workers and form them into great solid unions thoroughly instructed and aware of what they want. I am aware that that seems an old-foggyish idea to many impatient young comrades, but it is the way I feel and anyone who finds my books worth while and who really wants to understand my ideas on politics can read my pamphlet called 'Letters to Judd.' Since the price is only 15¢ I hope that your readers will forgive me this amount of boosting of my own sales.

"Yours for Socialism as fast as possible, but no faster."

CHAPTER XXI

American Outpost, Mental Radio, and Three Novels

Biography is the only true history   THOMAS CARLYLE

PARTLY IT WAS REACHING his fiftieth birthday that gave Sinclair the desire for a summing up. But mostly it was because he was exhausted and wanted to write a book that required, comparatively speaking, no research. "I had a right to be tired . . . after 'Boston,'" he wrote Floyd Dell. "I would have liked to take a trip . . . but the state of Craig's health made it necessary for me to settle down at home . . . and I decided that I would write a book of reminiscences in a semi-playful and non-propaganda vein. . . . It is, of course, the easiest kind of writing, and to do a thousand words a day of it is a mild and harmless entertainment for a middle aged horse, which has got accustomed to the treadmill."

He succeeded in keeping the book lighthearted and jocular with the result that his son and daughter-in-law thought it "conceited and cheap" and Floyd Dell, who usually criticized Upton for being too heavy-handed and tendentious, now criticized him for a lack of seriousness and also for a lack of Freudian analysis. But it was the pitiable objections of his mother to the book that moved Upton to postpone its publication. "I have decided to put off the reminiscences indefinitely because the early part makes my mother very unhappy, and she is suffering from an incurable disease caused by an injury to the spine."

He had begun it at the end of 1928 and was finished by March 1929, but he waited more than three years, until after his mother's death, to publish it because she was so horrified by his unvarnished revelations of her snobbery, her husband's alcoholism, and most of all his own vulgar concern for the lower classes.

Sinclair had himself declared that a biography must reveal "the facts about the dead man's intimate life, his domestic tragedies, his diseases. . . .

When we are dead we no longer have any right to privacy whatever. Just as our bodies should go to science to afford what knowledge they can, so our souls should be offered for autopsy. The blunders we have made and the price we have paid for them should serve the purpose of saving others from making the same blunders and paying the same price. If there is anything in our writing of any importance to posterity, then critics and students of our work are entitled to every detail of our personality and experience, in order to be able to understand and interpret our work.

"And all this of course is 'scandal.' It cannot be anything but scandal. Stop a moment and consider some of the great biographies of the world, those of men we feel we really know. There is Cellini; there is Rousseau; there is Samuel Johnson; there is Benjamin Franklin. . . . [If one] cut out all the scandal, how much of the priceless biographies would there be left?"

In *American Outpost,* for which one of his many alternate titles had been *The New Frontier,* Sinclair avoided the very intimacy and "scandal" he had declared were requisite for a great biography. He would perhaps have given as his reasons, first, that the subject was not dead nor were others who would have been identified, and second, that these intimacies had already been revealed elsewhere in his work, if disguised at all then only slightly. But their absence lessened the book's interest, although it was favorably reviewed and, as always, lavishly praised by his friends in their letters.

From Duke University's Department of Parapsychology, Professor J. B. Rhine wrote: "Your mind reminds me of a colossal refinery. . . . I would like to peek in at you when you are running full blast. I should expect high tension whirrings, white heat, and charged atmosphere."

John Chamberlain, reviewing *American Outpost* for *The New York Times,* was critical of Upton's excessive fervor in behalf of his various causes, but having registered his demurrers, commented favorably on the "very mellow quality to 'American Outpost,' and humor is its outstanding characteristic."

In his *Farewell to Reform,* published the same year as *American Outpost,* Chamberlain called Sinclair the "most effective pamphleteer of the Progressive movement. . . . *The Jungle,* it can be said categorically, stands with *The Call of the Wild* and *The House of Mirth* as one of the three really respectable American novels not written by Henry James between 1901 and the publication of *Jennie Gerhardt* in 1911."

For thirty years, Upton had been aware of the literature about experiments in telepathy, clairvoyance, and other psychic phenomena. At Columbia he had studied with James Hyslop, a psychic researcher. Minot Savage, the minister who had married Upton and Meta, had experienced conversations with a ghost. Sinclair's foster-father, Frederik van Eeden, believed telepathic messages were to be heeded, and Bernard M. L. Ernst, Upton's New York attorney, was a serious amateur of matters psychic.

Throughout the twenties, what had been a minor interest grew. Upton read increasingly about hypnosis, psychiatry, telekinesis, and spiritualism. Eager not to be taken in by frauds, he corresponded with Harry Houdini, the famous magician, on the tricks of the trade.

Alone at Long Beach when Upton made his trips to Boston, Craig, in the hope of curing her multiple problems, had intensified her own psychic research, reading in Henri Bergson, William James, William McDougall, Jean Martin Charcot, Pierre Janet, and dozens of others. There too she had begun writing a record of her dreams and making telepathic experiments. She took herself and her work dreadfully seriously, often working on her notes until two in the morning.

More and more throughout his work, Upton had his characters show interest and belief in such phenomena. Mrs. Winnie discussed spiritualism with Allan in *The Metropolis* in 1908, and Dad in *Oil!* in 1927 finally married a spiritualist, Mrs. Alyse Olivier. By the time Upton wrote the Lanny Budd series in the 1940's, psychic phenomena had become one of his chief crusades. Therefore Lanny, skeptical in so many matters, nevertheless believes in the Polish medium Madame Zyszynski and her control, who is an Iroquois Indian.

For several years the Sinclairs kept their own private medium, Count Roman Ostoja, whose allegations of nobility Upton sought unsuccessfully to confirm by correspondence with the Embassy of Poland in Washington, D.C. Handsome, dark-eyed, slim and muscular, he was, Upton wrote *The New Republic*, "practically a member of our family . . . [able to perform wonders of] telepathy . . . to induce anesthesia in portions of his own body and to stick pins through these portions at will. . . . Ostoja possesses the ability to induce in himself a cataleptic trance, in which his body becomes completely rigid, and can be placed between two chairs on the heels and head, and a hundred and fifty pound rock can be broken with sledge hammers. The rock placed over his abdomen. I have myself stood upon his body and I have a moving picture film of the breaking of the rock, which was witnessed by physicians known to me. . . .

"In my home in the presence of fourteen of my friends, while in a trance and tightly held by both knees and ankles, Ostoja caused a thirty-four pound table to rise four feet in the air and move slowly eight feet to one side. There was sufficient light in the room so that I could see Ostoja and the table and be certain that he was slumped down in a chair, breathing evenly in a trance. I am positive that there was no apparatus in my home and no confederate among the group of physicians, scientists, and writers whom I had invited, and every one present was convinced that the thing was super-normal. I know of course what a mass of fraud there is in this matter and that the scientific world will never accept anything that is done even in semi-darkness, but Ostoja assures me that in a sufficient time he can train a medium and give this medium suggestions so that he will produce the phenomena in light so that a moving picture film can be taken of it. He claims to have produced such phenomena in Poland, and I for one would like very much to see the experiment tried."

To guard against fakery at his seances, Upton took serious and elaborate precautions. In the case of the flying table, for example, Ostoja was held on either side by two ladies whom the muckraker trusted, one of these being Dollie. "Let me introduce you to my sister-in-law; one of these modern young ladies who are 'hard-boiled' on purpose and by conviction, knowing what they want in the world and going after it. At the age of seventeen she was singing for suffrage at Sylvia Pankhurst's street meetings in London, and she smuggled in to the National Gallery a hammer which was used to smash a priceless painting. Now she plays golf, or drives a car a couple of hundred miles a day. She fastens onto Ostoja's right wrist, having assured me privately that not all the devils in hell will get that wrist loose until the lights are turned on again. Also, she puts Ostoja's right leg under the chair and winds her own leg around it, and locks her toes in the rung of the chair. Mrs. M. [Mason] does the same on the other side; she is the same kind of lady as Dolly, even huskier in build, and unless I greatly misread human faces, she is going into this thing in a mood of sneering incredulity, determined that Ostoja is not going to fool her as he had fooled the other doctors' wives of her acquaintance."

The seances at the Sinclairs' were conducted not only by Ostoja but by others as well, including the most famous medium of that time, Arthur Ford. To these seances Upton invited his best-known friends such as Charlie Chaplin and Theodore Dreiser, urging them not to be polite but rather to be skeptical and to tell him any tricks they saw or even suspected. Dreiser, with some help from alcoholic spirits, slept throughout one seance and so was a less than ideal witness as to what really took place.

The two most respected American specialists in what would later come to be called the field of parapsychology were Dr. Walker Franklin Prince of the Boston Society for Psychical Research and Professor William McDougall who had headed the Department of Psychology first at Oxford, then at

Harvard, and finally at Duke. Upton submitted all his evidence to these two experts and after McDougall's death, to his successor at Duke, J. B. Rhine, whose ESP research became well known.

Prince eventually conducted experiments in Boston with Ostoja and declared him a fraud, whereupon Sinclair dropped the Pole. But he did not therefore drop spiritualism.

Sinclair also corresponded with people abroad who shared his interest, especially Arthur Conan Doyle, who wrote: "Your wife must, if I may say so, be a very beautiful character. I, also, am blessed with a mediumistic wife, but her powers run in other world channels rather than telepathy. I wish your wife would explore those higher regions and bring conviction to you. . . . Believe me, in the whole quagmire of religion, this is the only sound subject. It is provable and it satisfies the reason. These two things can be said of no other cult."

Upton collected Craig's telepathic experiments into a book that he finally called *Mental Radio* and asked Bertrand Russell to write an introduction to it. But Russell, despite the many liberal causes they had fought for together, replied "it is quite impossible for me to express any opinion on the subject of telepathy. My feeling is that there is nothing in it, but I do not know enough to support this opinion, and I am most unwilling to spend time upon what I believe to be humbug."

Charles Boni too was wary of the subject of Sinclair's new book. "I am too much bothered about what effect its publication will have on your reputation. . . . After all, a life time work is behind your present reputation, and you should not risk that reputation too lightly." When Upton insisted, the Bonis published the book, but it was the last book of his they published.

After Russell turned him down, Upton asked McDougall for an introduction and the professor agreed. In it he wrote that Upton "has with characteristic courage entered a new field, one in which reputations are more easily lost than made. . . . Even if the results of such research should in the end prove wholly negative that would be a result of no small importance; . . . Mrs. Sinclair would seem to be one of the rare persons who have telepathic power in a marked degree and perhaps other supernormal powers. The experiments in telepathy, as reported in the pages of this book, were so remarkably successful as to rank among the very best hitherto reported. . . . we can reject them . . . only by assuming that Mr. and Mrs. Sinclair either are grossly stupid, incompetent and careless persons or have deliberately entered upon a conspiracy to deceive the public in a most heartless and reprehensible fashion."

Before endorsing the Sinclairs' book, McDougall had visited the couple at Long Beach and insisted that Craig submit to some of his tests. These she passed impressively. Upton, with his not infrequently exaggerated sense of his own importance in history, wrote many years later in his *Autobiography*: "The outcome was that McDougall said he was satisfied, and would go to Duke and set up the new department. He did so, with results that all the world knows."

Sinclair did not need Charles Boni, McDougall, nor any of his other friends to warn him that he had little to gain and much to lose by publishing a book on this subject. He knew the field abounded with charlatans and that even the few serious scientists who would touch the data were inclined to put off the public by stressing how little they knew or were likely soon to learn. But it was precisely because he had a reputation as a truth teller and his statement would therefore have some weight that he felt he had to make it. The threat of ridicule and of mild martyrdom were also doubtless tempting, but not decisive.

Sinclair allowed parts of *Mental Radio* to be published in the pulp magazine *Ghost Stories*, even though, as he wrote McDougall, it was "apparently patronized by spiritualists and seekers of ghostly thrills. It doesn't worry me, because I have always taken the position that my work may be published anywhere that I can get readers. The only thing I care about is that they publish what I write as I write it, and this the magazine has done. My wife, however, is afraid that you may be troubled, because your introduction was quoted in such a publication. It may bring you a few letters from cranks. It will be certain to bring me some, but I am used to it since all kinds of cranks accept me as a brother."

Upton was not shy about sending copies of this book to prominent figures, hoping to receive in return comments useful for promoting it. He sent one to Thomas A. Edison, and when the American saint did not reply, wrote him a second letter, but it was all in vain, as was his writing to Sigmund Freud.

On the other hand, Albert Einstein thanked Sinclair for the "highly worthy book" and expressed his willingness to write an Introduction for the German edition.

A few months later, Upton wrote Einstein: "I have just read that you are coming to Pasadena, . . . if you want a quiet garden to come to and be let alone in, we will provide it. You had better bring your fiddle along, and we will play duets if you don't mind my being out of tune occasionally." The duets of the discoverer of relativity and the author of *The Jungle* were less than historic—in fact, they were hardly bearable to a listener.

Of all the many honors that came to Sinclair in the course of a long life, none meant more, he said, than the inscription Einstein wrote on a photograph he gave the writer in 1933 that hung always thereafter by Sinclair's desk.

> To whom does the dirtiest pot not matter?
> Who knocks the world on its hollow tooth?
> Who suspects the now and swears by tomorrow?
> Who never troubles about 'undignified'?
> Sinclair is the valiant man.
> If anyone, then I can attest it.

Sinclair tried repeatedly over the years to get his friend to take a public position on matters Sinclair felt strongly about. But Einstein, who in Germany had allowed his name to be used however Upton wanted, now sometimes refused to take part in local political matters.

From prison, Gandhi wrote Sinclair about *Mental Radio*, and in later years among the literate Indians yearning for freedom from colonial status, who gave Sinclair a large readership, was its future Prime Minister, Indira Gandhi. "Mr. Sinclair's thinking reflected the social conscience of the times and his later books seemed to be part of current history rather than fiction. I enjoyed his books and hardly missed any of them. He was an effective writer, indignant at exploitation and not afraid of expressing his emotion."

At the time there were only a very few articles that took seriously Upton and Mary Craig's experiments. But forty years later when the subject itself had finally achieved some respectability, the dignified journal *American Psychologist* reproduced Mary Craig's crude drawings of objects whose images she had received telepathically and commented on the book: "Because Upton Sinclair and his wife were laymen, you will have to pay particular attention to their competence and motivation. On the other hand, one important feature of Sinclair's book is that you do not have to be a scientist to understand it. Even though you may not have studied statistics and psychology, you can read the book yourself and make up your mind as to its value on the basis of common sense. When you do, I think you will arrive at the same conclusion that many scientists have reached by entirely different kinds of experiments. I think you will decide that extrasensory perception is a reality regardless of the skepticism of the psychological profession."

The Sinclairs' experiments no longer seem so odd as they once did. Rhine has sought to prove more elaborately and beyond a statistical doubt the existence not only of ESP (humans communicating with each other telepathically) but also of PK (psychokinesis, the influences exerted by the human mind on inanimate objects). With Heisenberg's Uncertainty Principle, black holes and white holes in the universe, and the backward flow of time, there has come recognition that many kinds of reality exist. Arthur Koestler, who has repeatedly expressed his debt to Sinclair, has described psychic and other phenomena and postulated possibilities that might have shocked even Sinclair.

The third easy-to-write book Sinclair allowed himself following the ordeal of *Boston* was *Mountain City*, a novel he wrote in two months. After devoting six weeks in Denver in the summer of 1929 to another libel suit, Craig and Upton had returned first to Long Beach and then to Pasadena, where in mid-July he began working on it.

He had brought an action for libel against the *Rocky Mountain News*, which in its book review of Dell's biography had taken the opportunity to characterize Sinclair in detail as a publicity-seeking fraud and scoundrel. Asking for two hundred thousand dollars because the paper had gone "beyond the customary [bounds] of journalistic untruth," Upton had been on the stand for six hours a day for three days, but he had lost.

It is possible that his wife insisted Sinclair write the book because she had been so much more outraged than he by their treatment and their defeat that she had wanted to continue the fight. "She was so furious for a few days it was hard to get her to give up. She wanted to . . . appeal the case, but I persuaded her that the apricots were ripe at home."

Mountain City is a typical, straightforward nineteenth-century novel, also partly a *roman à clef*. According to Sinclair, the character T. J. Goodson, publisher of the *Mountain City Mail*, is a reproduction of Fred Bonfils, the Denver publisher, and Goodson is, of course, a translation of Bonfils. As Sinclair advertised on the book's cover, it is "the story of Success in America," of how its hero, Jed Rusher, began life miserably as an abused child who, "while he crawled about in the muck of the sugar-beet fields, wielding a heavy 'topping-knife,' . . . dreamed of ease and power . . . rose in the world, elbowed his way into a rich man's home, and married a child of privilege, and made fifty millions before he was thirty. . . . It is also the story of Lulu Belle Macy, who was watched by a fond Mamma and an Episcopal governess, and when she was fourteen thought it would be nice to have a 'live dollie' to play with. Since her Mamma wouldn't tell her how to get it, she asked the nice Mr. Rusher."

When David and his wife expressed their disgust that the book was so insignificant, the author replied gently, arguing that although a writer ought to make all his books his best books, it was not possible at the moment because "I have to be a good part of the time a sort of head nurse in a sanitarium. . . . and it seems to me a useful social service to expose the present developments in Wall Street to a few people. I might write a pamphlet about it, but nobody would read the pamphlet, and if I get them all as worked up over the matter as I have you I will have given the Socialists a boost—or maybe it will be the Communists."

To his daughter-in-law he had written: "What you write is very much like the literary opinions I have had all my life about my attempts at novels. It might all have been taken from an article by Van Wyck Brooks . . . reviewing 'King Coal,' 'Jimmie Higgins,' and '100%,' . . . he couldn't find language to say how unreal and cheap they were. Yet, they have all given pleasure to millions of people all over the world, and I hope, also, they have brought them a little instruction incidentally.

"Love to you both, and go on scolding me, because I always learn something from it even though I may seem to be rejecting everything you say."

Many critics found fault with this work, but one whose judgments on twentieth-century writing may have more weight for a longer time than most was more complimentary. "Have just read yr/ Mountain City with considerable enjoyment," Ezra Pound wrote from Rapallo. "Doubt if it will quench any young hopeful's avarice, tho might make it harder for any particular freshman to get away with it as easily. You'll have all of 'em trying it.

"I believe you are at yr/ best when you are LEAST trying to put over any partic. idea. I don't consider the purely literary attitude a dilletantism. If you get the thing written down as it is, it does its own talking, and has more effect than any labled preaching. . . ."

Upton replied, "You are a very jolly fellow, and I wish we might get together some day and have a real good argument. . . . Of course I am glad to hear that you found 'Mountain City' interesting. Most of our highbrow critics have just jumped all over it."

Pound and Sinclair had corresponded regularly and would continue to do so far more amiably than the more extreme partisans of either writer might imagine possible. "I shd. be delighted to have your volumes. I have long admired your cannonade," Pound wrote. "There are I suppose several minor points on which we, let us hope amiably and with mutual tolerance, disagree, but I take we are both firing in the same general direction."

When Sinclair sent Pound autographed copies of *Mammonart* and *Money*

Writes! with the confession that he was waiting "with some trepidation to see how much they annoy you," Pound suggested amiably that they might turn any differences to their mutual profit. "Do you think an open argument wd. serve any useful purpose? . . . If we do it, who publishes the damn thing? I shd. think yr. distribution was about umpthundred times as efficient as mine."

Despite periodic protestations that he was tired and needed a holiday, Sinclair never took one. "We had a quiet Christmas," he wrote his mother on December 26, 1929. "I played tennis in the morning, and started a new novel in the afternoon, and in the evening I wasted a couple of hours seeing the Marx brothers in the movies. It is pleasant to know that this is one set of public favorites I will never have to see again."

Sinclair did not keep Christmas, and he offended his daughter-in-law by returning the silver pencil and shawl she and David had given him and Craig for Christmas. And not only did he ignore holidays, but so also did his secretaries, unless they put on his letters the date they were written rather than the date they were transcribed.

Regularly asked for Christmas statements, he as regularly delivered himself of short Socialist sermons: "You ask me for a Christmas greeting. I am one of those unusual Christians who think every day ought to be Christmas. That is to say, the spirit of love and service which we celebrate on that day ought to apply to all our lives."

Although Priscilla Sinclair was dying, her son ignored her appeals for money. In refusing her requests, and alleging poverty, Upton went so far as to lie. In answer to her query, he wrote that he did not know where "they" had got the money for the New York production of his play *Singing Jailbirds*, although he himself had supplied some of it and raised much of the rest. Only a few months before her death, when he was pouring thousands of dollars into the production of an Eisenstein film, he wrote her: "we have to go without a lot of things. Your doctor will have to wait, as so many other people are doing." He only grudgingly wrote her now and then. He believed that the only news he had to write was either Greek to her or repugnant, since it mainly concerned not respectable people but the poor and many of these were foreigners with foreign ideas.

David wrote regularly, chiding his father for not coming east to visit the dying woman, but Upton replied softly. "If there were any concrete thing that I could do I would consider the matter more urgent, but when it is merely a matter of making Mother 'happy,' I have to be what you call hard-hearted, and remember my previous efforts in this direction. I have never been able to make her happy, because she has always wanted all of everything, and I have never been able to give enough. You must understand that this situation is not new to me, because the doctor wrote me about it a couple of years ago, and the last time I was in New York I tried to do what I could to make mother 'Happy,' and only realized once more that it could not be done."

Priscilla Sinclair died October 19, 1931, without having seen her son again. The same day Sinclair wrote David, "I hope you will not fall a victim to the graft of funeral directors and undertakers." Almost all the long letter was addressed to money matters, especially the author's wish that the manuscript of *The Jungle* might be found in her apartment at 332 West 85th Street, because, he said, a book dealer had told him it was worth twenty-five thousand dollars.

Upton was the sole heir of Priscilla Sinclair's five-hundred-dollar estate. When Howard Bland, the cousin he had hated and envied since childhood, spurned the hundred dollars Upton sent him for cremation and burial expenses, it was used by David to apply on his grandmother's long overdue doctor's bill. David wrote his father that the terrible bitterness between his grandmother and her rich sister reminded him very much of the beginning of *Boston.*

Craig's mother had died in Mississippi on March 23, 1930. A few days before, Craig had returned to Pasadena, having refused to stay with her to the end.

Roman Holiday, the novel begun on Christmas Day, was finished in less than two and a half months and was brought out by Upton's new publishers, Farrar & Rinehart, who were also Floyd Dell's publishers. Very different from the brothers Boni were Stanley Rinehart and John Farrar who stressed "beyond anything, we want you to come to look on us as your publishers, and feel you can work closely and frankly with us on your whole future writing program. . . . Won't you write your own contract?"

Sinclair received from Edgar Lee Masters and more surprisingly from Yale's William Lyon Phelps complimentary letters on the new novel, which analogized the Roman and American plutocracies. But it was an unimportant work, except, as any work may be individually important, it exerted a great influence on the social thinking of the young Howard Fast.

In his next novel, *The Wet Parade,* Sinclair attacked his ancient enemy, alcohol. What apparently had moved Sinclair finally to write the prohibition novel he had so long considered but always put off had been a poll by

Literary Digest suggesting that the sentiment in the country might lead to the repeal of the Eighteenth Amendment. So strong were Upton's own feelings about Prohibition that they blinded him to the facts and led him to write, "Prohibition will never be rescinded in America. The majority of our people are overwhelmingly for it. He even gave up his resolution not to lecture or debate. He tried to arrange a filmed debate, with an actor declaiming his "dry" arguments against such a prominent "wet" as Mencken, Sinclair Lewis, Clarence Darrow, Fiorello La Guardia, William Randolph Hearst, or Al Smith. But nothing came of his efforts.

He had no illusions about its literary merit. "When I finish my very bad prohibition novel, I hope to write a very good one about Russia." His time was so taken up that to write the novel at all he had to do it beginning at five or six in the morning and he had Craig "putting clothes on the outside of my women and psychology on the inside."

Craig also saw to it, as usual, that "all royalties & other income" were assigned to her.

"Mr. Sinclair undertakes a feat unprecedented in swell letters:" marveled Mencken in his review of *Wet Parade*, "he makes a Prohibition agent his hero." The skeptical editor was as little admiring of Sinclair's style as of the hero's calling. "His cunning as a literary artist does not diminish. His dialogue is highly polished. ' "Please, please, Papa!" cries Maggie May to her wine-cursed father, Mr. Roger Chilcote. "Do not drink any more!" "Oh, little girl, little girl," he replies, "what can Papa do? I cannot give it up! It is a fiend that has got me!" ' "

Sinclair enjoyed and needed Mencken's abuse. "One of the reasons the Methodist Church published this play [made from *Wet Parade*]," Upton wrote Mencken, "was because I showed them there was a possibility that you might poke fun at it. Please do not fail me." Earlier he had begged "do not ever restrain your impulse to ridicule me. That is the way my reputation has been made. Do anything but ignore me. . . ."

His usually flattering friend Fulton Oursler wrote, "For God's sake, throw it in the fire."

Ironically, not only did *Wet Parade* sell better than many novels with which Sinclair had taken far more time, but also it was his only novel made into a major sound film. It was bought for twenty thousand dollars by Irving Thalberg for Metro-Goldwyn-Mayer, then Hollywood's most prestigious motion picture studio. The world premier of the film was at Grauman's Chinese Theatre, March 17, 1932, and it starred Myrna Loy, Robert Montgomery, Jimmy Durante, Walter Huston, and Lewis Stone.

Upton felt that his message had been excessively muted, but at least he recognized his story, as opposed to his earlier experience with *The Moneychangers*, which was changed from an exposé of J. P. Morgan to a tale of the Chinatown dope traffic. Seizing or inventing publicity opportunities that would increase interest in the film or help sell the novel, he urged Sid Grauman to set up a table in the lobby of his theater and sell the book; he helped promote a debate on Prohibition between Aimee Semple McPherson and Walter Huston; and, as on all his anti-alcohol books, he solicited support from all the various temperance forces, in this case getting a plug from Billy Sunday, whom he had reviled in *The Profits of Religion*.

Although movie critics generally praised the actors, especially Walter Huston and Lewis Stone as the drunkards, they ignored or made fun of Upton's cautionary tale.

For decades Sinclair had wanted a stage or film success, because it would give him money for his causes and because he felt that was the only way he could reach a new large audience who did not read his books. But years of rejection had convinced him that his reputation as a radical and his concern with the working-class point of view probably excluded him from Hollywood's golden trough. "This is something which has been explicitly stated to me over and over again in the course of the past twenty-five years by the recognized leaders and masters of capitalist drama and screen. Not less than a hundred times in my life I have been approached by these great ones with a proposition to do some work for them—always on condition that I would 'leave out the socialism.' Not less than two score times they have gone so far as to sign contracts with me, and either they have broken the contracts when they got the Socialism, or they have set to work to undo my efforts, thus forcing me to break with them."

Like many scorned applicants, he occasionally pretended not to want what he ceaselessly sought after unsuccessfully. "I refuse to do movie writing because it inevitably becomes trash, owing to the need of rewriting to suit the ideas of a dozen persons who have their finger in every picture." This was hardly convincing from a man who allowed his work to be rewritten by his wife, his friends, and even, on occasion, unknown correspondents. Hollywood was obviously willing to buy from Sinclair when he produced what they wanted, since they paid twenty thousand dollars for *The Wet Parade*. Furthermore, not only did Upton not "refuse" to do movie writing, he actively solicited such work all his life. As Craig wrote Dollie: "Upton went to dinner last night at the Edgar Selwyns' to meet Zukor of Paramount. Arch Selwyn is trying to get him a job, but the studios are still afraid of

Upton's political activities—afraid he'll go back to crusading and scare the wits out of them again, so Selwyn is having him meet one after another of the big ones at dinner, so they can hear Upton say he's had his fill of politics."

That Hollywood would not hire the muckraker was disproved when in 1932 he was offered and accepted ten thousand dollars merely to evolve a plot and a set of characters at conferences with Irving Thalberg. The studio's trust in the avowed Socialist was made evident by the clause in his contract that stated specifically that payment was contingent not on acceptance of his work but instead would be made immediately on Sinclair's statement that he had no more to say on the subject. And he was paid, although nothing resulted from his eleven-page outline of a film Thalberg had called *The Star-Spangled Banner* and Sinclair had rechristened *The Gold-Spangled Banner.*

Sinclair not only gave M-G-M his unlisted phone number, which he usually guarded so fiercely, but he bought a most un-Socialist mansion in Beverly Hills. Fearful that his friends and readers would think he had "gone Hollywood," he explained apologetically that the Pasadena place was a burden for Craig to keep up because it had become so dilapidated, that he now needed to be nearer Hollywood, and that it was a bargain. "We have profited by the misfortunes of the world to the extent of getting it for about one third of what it cost," he wrote his daughter-in-law—a capitalist statement par excellence. But to David he confessed: "I suppose I am going to be in for some teasing over having moved into such a fashionable place as Beverly Hills, but I will try and live it down. . . . Evidently fashionable life is not meant to agree with me, because it was on a polished hardwood staircase landing that I slipped and hurt my head. However, I am all right again, and have learned to walk more discreetly."

But inevitably the large and elaborate house was a continuing source of sometimes amused, but more often acid, comment. The Los Angeles *Times* sarcastically made fun of a Socialist who required a "palatial residence . . . next door to the luxurious residence of E. L. Cord, automobile and aviation magnate."

Considering the occasional evidences of snobbery displayed by Craig and Upton, it is possible that the fine house represented a patent of the recognition they both yearned for so fiercely. In Upton's case, his vigorous campaign to get a Nobel prize, after he had been cheated out of the Pulitzer prize, was evidence of his continuing hunger for recognition.

He recognized that inevitably most prizes are given to conformists, however tedious, and not to nonconformists, however exciting. Only a few years before an instructive contretemps had taken place in Paris. When it was proposed that nonconformity had become so acceptable to judges of art that there was no longer any need to continue the Salon des Indépendents, one critic offered twenty-five reasons the Salon should be continued—these being the names of twenty-five winners of the French government's Prix de Rome. All, except Rouault, were orthodox ciphers. The same critic then listed twenty-five artists who had exhibited at the Salon des Indépendents who could not conceivably have won the Prix de Rome, including Braque, Cézanne, Daumier, Degas, Gauguin, Matisse, Picasso, Toulouse-Lautrec, and van Gogh.

Similarly, the list of France's great writers not invited to join the maximum of forty "Immortals" who constitute the Académie includes Balzac, Flaubert, Gide, Mallarmé, and Sartre.

Sinclair in *Mammonart* and in scores of letters, articles, and essays had repeatedly made the same point—but he nevertheless lusted after prizes at least as much as anyone else.

Sinclair Lewis in his speech accepting the Nobel prize in 1930 had expressed the same concern, in connection with the American Academy of Arts and Letters. The list he recited of those whom the Academy had not taken in included Dreiser, Mencken, Willa Cather, Eugene O'Neill and Ernest Hemingway (who would win Nobel prizes in 1936 and 1954 respectively), and "Upton Sinclair, of whom you must say, whether you admire or detest his aggressive socialism, that he is internationally better known than any other American artist whosoever, be he novelist, poet, painter, sculptor, musician, architect."

Lewis' speech was a very model of magnanimity in mentioning other American writers whom he admired and who, like himself, had sinned against their fatherland by criticizing it. "Dreiser more than any other man . . . has cleared the trail from Victorian and Howellsian timidity and gentility in American fiction to honesty and boldness and passion. . . . Mr. Eugene O'Neill, who has done nothing much in American drama save to transform it utterly, in ten or twelve years, from a false world of neat and competent trickery to a world of splendor and fear and greatness. . . . Mr. Upton Sinclair, being a Socialist, sins against the perfectness of American capitalistic mass production; . . . [just as] Mr. Ernest Hemingway . . . uses language which should be unknown to a gentleman."

Upton too could be modest and generous in regard to other writers as when he offered his ideas to Lewis on a novel about labor because "I know that you would reach a larger audience than I could." But he felt himself as deserving of the Nobel prize as Lewis; he *wanted* it; and he went after it.

He was quite as organized and energetic in this as in any other of his enterprises. Of course he did not want it too obvious that he was pushing himself, so the front man became his "friend," Ernest S. Greene, in fact, his former secretary. Paid by Sinclair, Greene conducted the Nobel prize campaign from New York City, which helped it appear independent of its real guiding hand.

Greene became the secretary of a committee that solicited support in behalf of Upton's candidacy. Each member of the committee had been asked by Sinclair to serve and included John Dewey, Paul H. Douglas, Albert Einstein, Robert Herrick, Harold J. Laski, Robert Morss Lovett, Edwin Markham, William McDougall, and Bertrand Russell.

Among the seven hundred and seventy more or less distinguished signatories rounded up from some fifty-five countries by Sinclair and Greene were George Bernard Shaw, Sir Arthur Pinero, Siegfried Sassoon, and Romain Rolland. Among the many solicited whose signatures were not forthcoming were Sigmund Freud, H. G. Wells, Jane Addams, and M. K. Gandhi.

Enemies of Sinclair and friends of other candidates attacked the muckraker's qualifications and his active seeking of the prize. And even Mencken protested: "I can't imagine Sinclair himself conniving at the campaign. Certainly a man who hates capitalism as ardently as he does, and has so vast a special contempt for munitions magnates, could not conceivably be imagined accepting the money of a dynamite manufacturer.

"I assume that he has not heard of the petitions and memorials that are now being passed round. I look for him to denounce them with Christian indignation the moment they are brought to his attention. Like all the rest of us, he has his faults, but I don't think that a sniveling and prehensile hypocrisy is one of them."

But, if he was serious, Mencken failed, as had others, to understand Sinclair's hunger. In fact, during this campaign, Upton was so concerned with his reputation that when the University of Chicago Library queried him as to his authorship of a particular title, he answered, "When I was a youth I wrote a lot of very trashy dime novels, and this may or may not be one of them. I could not tell unless I read it, and I am not sure I could say even then. I am extremely reluctant to have this stuff listed under my name, and you would do me a great favor if you would inform me how it came to be listed. Somebody has done me a very poor service."

But all the efforts availed nothing.

When Sinclair Lewis won the prize, his former wife had wired congratulations and immediately petitioned for more alimony. Perhaps Upton's failure had saved him from contact with Meta, which so horrified him. But until his death, almost four decades later, he continued to long for the prize, and although four additional Americans won it in that period, he was not one of them. He also continued to imply that George Bernard Shaw and others, whom in fact he had solicited, had tried on their own to get him the prize.

These same needs for recognition were slowly changing Upton's role as a politician. For years he had *pro forma* allowed his name to be used as the nominee of the Socialist Party. He had no expectation of being elected and he wasted virtually no time campaigning. His candidacy got his name and occasionally, even a few of his ideas, into the papers, but he made few speeches and simply sent forth written propaganda when he thought it appropriate.

In the summer and fall of 1930, as the Great Depression was beginning and unemployment and misery increasing, he was the Socialist Party's candidate for governor of California. He stated his positions in letters addressed to various groups, which were often circulated by them. He wrote the California Teachers Association that he favored their receiving tenure, an adequate retirement salary, their political rights as citizens, and their rights to organize a union. As governor, he said he would also want enacted state income and inheritance taxes, and especially a tax that would absorb the entire unearned increment on land.

Chided by his fellow Socialists for not running harder, he reminded them: "You said you would not ask me to do any more than speak at one mass meeting in Los Angeles, and now you must not ask for more and you must not hope for it because if you do you will be dissatisfied and irritated with me, and that will not be fair. Every evening for the next eight or nine months I expect to spend my time from eight to eleven wandering about quiet streets in Pasadena, living in my mind with the characters of this novel [The Wet Parade]. I expect to go to bed with my mind full of these characters, and wake up with nothing else on my mind, and spend the morning hours putting them on paper. In the afternoons I expect to read and rest and work a little in the garden. That is to be my life, and the reason for it, as I have explained to you many times before, is that I know I can accomplish a hundred times as much for Socialism that way as I can by travelling about making speeches. I have explained this to you many, many times and it is now up to you to explain it to the comrades throughout the state, so that they will understand my point of view and not think that I am lacking in interest in the work they are doing."

He allowed the party to borrow money from him and to pay it back. And when the unexpected occurred, as often happens in political races, he took advantage of it. The California secretary of state certified Upton as the Republican rather than the Socialist candidate, which amused everyone except the Republicans, and allowed Upton to get a lot of mileage out of the mistake.

When he was defeated he was proud of the reaction in the capitalist press: "A surprising result was the relatively large vote cast for Upton Sinclair, Socialist candidate for Governor. It is indicated that his total will run not less than 50,000, which is about five times the Socialist registration." The signs were already beginning that as the Depression deepened, non-Socialists by the hundreds of thousands would soon be willing to vote for Sinclair. And he kept his name before the voters. The moment the election results were clear, he wired the victor, James Rolph, congratulating him and urging a pardon for Tom Mooney. In the months that followed he lost no opportunity to criticize "police brutality" or any other political injustice in California that came to his attention.

In the spring of 1931, Heywood Broun wrote from New York that he and Norman Thomas wondered if they could convince Upton to head the Socialist ticket in the next national election.

Upton was delighted to be thought of as a Presidential candidate. He thanked the newspaperman but confided that he hoped to go to Russia and write a novel: "the man who runs next year ought to be prepared to go on with the job. It is a career and may easily end in the White House, and certainly ought not to be undertaken by a man who would be all the time looking over his shoulder thinking of the books he was failing to write. I have the belief that things are going to change fast in this country when they start, and I do not think of myself as a practical man and an administrator." As a postscript, Upton added "Perhaps you do not know that I talked this matter out with Norman [Thomas] when I was in New York in 1927. He urged me then to consider taking the nomination, and I told him what I have told you. But in spite of that I let myself be nominated for governor—and then I took a new vow."

Sinclair's hunches in the past had sometimes been wrong, but his belief in upcoming fast change was right. It would begin to quicken with Roosevelt's election in 1932 and Upton's own race for governor of California in 1934 would also be a significant factor in accelerating change all over the country. Much of what Sinclair had so long preached was about to be put into practice.

Convinced that any publicity for himself was publicity for his ideas, Upton continued to make use of his talent for self-promotion. A series of daily front-page articles on the "famous radical" ran in Los Angeles' sensational *The Record* with many pictures, including one of Upton in a bathing suit, standing beside the tiny backyard swimming pool he had dug himself. That competing front-page stories offered "Hubby Divorces Film Actress," "Crazed Lover Shoots Lover," and " 'Bears' Beat Down Stocks," only proved that the mild Upton had lost none of his ability to charm and surprise reporters: ". . . a slight man with graying hair, glasses, and a smile. . . . This is a flaming radical? This is the world-famous 'muckracker' and exposer of the shames of his nation? . . . Why he looks like a self-pleased member of the chamber of commerce . . . a college professor of economics, or maybe a minister of some small flock. . . . About the rather thin face with its high curved nose, long upper lip, . . . the stamp of the intellectual life. . . . The emphasis on things of the mind and spirit, rather than on the grosser satisfactions of the flesh . . . is stamped on the outer shell of him." Overworked and underpaid reporters could write as feelingly about the day Upton prophesied when all would enjoy four hours of work, four hours of study, eight hours of play, and eight hours of sleep, as they could about the sexual shenanigans of such movie magnates as Howard Pantages. Delighted to find a reputed puritan who was "pro-play," they quoted his theories at length. "Our civilization has destroyed play. . . . We regard the desire to play . . . as a form of vice. . . . We allow children to play after school hours, on Saturdays; but for grown-up, serious-minded men and women to play would be almost as disreputable as for them to get drunk. What could be more pitiful than the spectacle of tens of thousands of men crowding into our ball parks . . . to watch other men play for them. Imagine . . . a crowd of people gathering in a restaurant or theatre to watch other people eat for them. . . ."

Most working reporters, and also, surprisingly, a number of editors, whose public views were far different from Sinclair's, were extraordinarily fond of him. No other newspaper in America was as unfriendly to him and all his ideas as the Los Angeles *Times*, yet its editor, Harry Carr, burst out, "Upton, why in hell do I like you, anyhow?" to which the muckraker replied, "Some time when you and I get off in the desert together, where nobody else can possibly hear us, I will tell you why I like you and why you like me!"

His correspondence continued at its usual flow of several dozen letters a day. He sold the list of his correspondents to magazines to be solicited for subscriptions and was paid in free advertising space, which he sometimes tried to sell for cash to others.

The smallest waste of money, whether his own or not, elicited a letter from Sinclair. If a clipping bureau sent him copies of the same syndicated story about himself from several different newspapers, he threatened to fire them unless in the future they would carefully send and charge for only one, and he wrote the International Bureau of Revolutionary Literature in Moscow, "you should certainly have a registered code name, as it wastes a lot of your money, and also of your correspondent's, to cable a long address such as your name and box number." Even with readers who lent him money when he asked for help, he carefully made certain they got no more discount on buying his books than they had been offered in his solicitation.

He regularly practiced as well as preached what would come to be called consumerism. When his New York publisher sent him a package via airmail that came by surface transportation, he was outraged and wrote Rinehart: "It amounts to $3, and I wish you would write a letter to the post office about it and let me know the results, because if they refuse to refund the money, I will write a nice warm letter to the Nation and the New Republic. I have had this happen before. . . ."

He reported to the Interstate Commerce Commission in Washington, D.C., what he considered to be a sharp practice of the Railway Express Company. And when any newspaper, magazine, or book publisher tried to take advantage of him, he was quick to report them to the Authors' League, and if that failed, to pay his own New York attorney to continue the fight. He believed that if more American citizens reported abuses and asserted their rights to city hall, to their state capital, or to Washington there would be fewer abuses.

He wrote letters supporting most individual attacks on social injustice brought to his attention. He wired Governor Gifford Pinchot of Pennsylvania about a milk fund for underfed children of striking and unemployed miners in his state, and along with Dreiser and Dos Passos he was one of the sponsors of an art sale in which works of Alexander Archipenko, Thomas Hart Benton, Charles Burchfield, José Clemente Orozco, Alfred Stieglitz, and William Zorach were sold "to voice the need for adequate relief for the unemployed."

When individuals at home or abroad wrote him attacking the feminist movement or any aspect of it, he answered them fully and sometimes surprisingly sharply. "Your protest against Margaret Sanger's appeal to save women and children from the evils of this man-made world must have taken a good deal of courage; you being a man and not a woman." And: "I am grateful to you for your kindness in seeking to educate me, but I think I ought to explain to you that you are dealing with a hopeless case. I was one of the few men who marched in the first woman suffrage parade in New York more than twenty years ago, and I am an ardent feminist. My office is run by two ladies who seem to enjoy it, and we get along very nicely."

In some areas, however, such as censorship, he was a far from wholehearted supporter of the principles of freedom, refusing on occasion to protest book banning because "a reformer like me has to see some reason for being in a book before he can rush to defend it." In a reply to the National Council on Freedom from Censorship, he expressed fear lest children be left free to buy "pornographic postcards" and asked: "Do you deny that there is in New York at present 'commercial pornography' in plays? Do you deny that there is in Hollywood 'commercial pornography' in moving pictures? And will you trust to the sense of decency of these industries?"

He constantly dreamed up new projects and worked fiercely on them. For the twenty-fifth anniversary of *The Jungle* he tried, and failed, to raise the money to publish an expensive edition illustrated by Diego Rivera, the Mexican Communist artist. He tried to raise over a million dollars to organize a National Educational Radio station because he recognized it was a way to reach millions who would never read his books, and in fact presented an opportunity "equal to the possibilities of human culture." He predicted it would be the most important thing he had ever done, but he could not raise the funds.

Occasionally he even faced reality in regard to the real demand for one of his own books. He wrote his printer that since there was "no call" for the cloth edition of *Letters to Judd,* his tedious primer on Socialism, a copy was to be mailed with the compliments of the author to all five hundred and fifty college libraries listed in the World Almanac and then to every city library until the inventory was reduced to fifty copies.

Upton was usually not amused when he was confused with Sinclair Lewis. But when Harry F. Sinclair's photograph was used to illustrate a newspaper story about Upton, the writer was outraged, especially as it was not the first time this had happened. Upton forthwith sent dozens of sets of publicity photographs of himself to newspapers, magazines, and his many book publishers all over the world. He urged each publisher to supply a picture to every news agency in his country.

He was regularly encouraged by letters from the most ordinary people, who formed his natural following: "a common laborer, a mucker," wondering if he should try to go to a university; a bookstore owner "ready to give up my business, if there is a place where I can be of any use in the cause"; an almost illiterate oilfield worker seeking advice on how to promote Socialism in Texas; and "a girl, 23 years old, 5 foot 3 inches, large grey eyes, light brown hair" who lent *Boston* to a friend. "He is married. Now, his wife is threatening a divorce suit and planning to name me co-respondent on the charge that I lent her husband 'smutty' books to read. Can you beat it?"

He sent his books to any penitentiary libraries that would accept them, and he was not displeased when one of his correspondents at San Quentin wrote that the prisoners preferred his books to those of Zane Grey or Max Brand.

Sinclair believed strongly that a writer's popularity outside his native land was the surest possible omen of the immortality of his work. He repeated and elaborated this theme in books, articles, and letters throughout his life. It was, therefore, with glee that he regularly reported to the recipients of his newsletter his latest information on this score. ". . . I decided to compile a bibliography. The first edition is dated August, 1930, and I will send it free with any order provided you ask for it. It is a 36-page pamphlet, giving particulars as to 525 separate titles, in 34 different countries. The total sales in Russia alone exceed two million copies."

William Allen White, ten years older than Upton, wrote him in an autumnal tone: "I read everything you write with interest and delight. . . . We have seen great changes in the world . . . I hate to leave the show in the midst of the second act, but maybe there is a purgatorial lobby just outside the play-room, down where we can linger and listen to the show. If there is, you and I will sit on a cloud for a decade or two and talk things over." Neither muckraker was in fact about to leave the show. Although he would not reach ninety as would Upton, the Kansas editor lived until 1944. Indeed, with the exception of the murdered David Graham Phillips, most of the great muckrakers lived long lives. Finley Peter Dunne and Lincoln Steffens died in 1936, Ida Tarbell in 1944, Ray Stannard Baker in 1946, and Samuel Hopkins Adams in 1958. Only Upton, however, continued to observe and comment upon the scene until 1968.

In 1931, Steffens published his *Autobiography* and Upton wrote him: "I am enraptured with it. It is exactly what I hoped you would do, and it is exactly right. Tell your publishers that if it will be of any use to them, they may quote me as saying that if a more interesting book has ever been published in America, I would not know where to look for it."

The critics of the early thirties, however, were writing about the famous muckrakers: "Mr. Sinclair still has the divine gift of righteous indignation, but most of the others have sunk into respectable desuetude."

Steffens in his turn was soon trying to help Upton with constructive comments on Upton's biography of William Fox, the movie producer, who had recently lost most of his immense fortune in a prolonged and vicious battle with Wall Street bankers and other movie producers. Steffens wrote that the book would benefit if Fox "told more of the crooked things he did. . . . it would be a far better story even for his own uses. . . . Make him come clean, as we crooks say. . . . you appear . . . too much as a special pleader . . . making a case for him."

David Sinclair was horrified that his father "could write a biography of a business man from so nearly Ida Tarbell's point of view!!!" This was the ultimate insult, because radicals denounced Tarbell's biographies of Judge Gary and Owen D. Young as a lickspittle's acts of betrayal to the cause of muckraking.

Historian W. E. Woodward, to whom Upton had also sent the manuscript of *Upton Sinclair Presents William Fox,* sent back a very lengthy, page-by-page analysis, full of corrections, and the repeated warning that the businessman had got himself beaten in a sordid business war and now was merely using the leading Socialist of America to justify himself.

In his answering letter, Upton pleaded: "Don't you think that the public will make some allowance for the price I have to pay in order to get this story and pass it on? What I mean is, if I had taken the attitude which you take, and ask me to take, I would never have had the story in the beginning, and I am afraid if I insisted upon taking it now, the book would never be published. Is it not obvious that Fox would have no motive in telling the story if it were to present him as no particle better than those whom he was fighting." There is no doubt that Upton mistakenly attributed some of his own liberal views to Fox and also accepted or at least published many self-serving pieties of Fox's that were contradicted by the producer's whole life. Less clear, however, is the order of importance of various causes for Upton's deception or self-deception and his apparently ambiguous feelings toward Fox.

What Upton was not revealing to Woodward or Steffens or anyone else was that Fox had approached him with an offer of twenty-five thousand dollars to write the book and had paid twenty thousand of it in 1932.

In fact, Fox had commissioned the book not merely as Woodward suggested to justify himself, but for a more devious reason of which Upton was unaware. Fox naïvely believed that his business enemies would be so horrified by the threat of their wicked deeds being revealed that he would be able to extort from them, in return for his suppression of his own book, some of the properties they had taken from him. For this reason, he repeatedly refused to give Upton final permission to publish the book, but the moment Upton learned from Floyd Dell what Fox was up to, he published the book immediately without Fox's permission.

Not only because it was good publicity and because he never understated his own courage, but also because he genuinely feared the book might be suppressed, Sinclair urged in his newsletter that his customers buy the biography at once. "Do your part, and quickly, because I have never tackled enemies so powerful as in this case." And to Judge Henry Neil he wrote: "In order to prevent the possibility of suppression, I am distributing an edition of 10,000 copies all over the country. . . . I am taking the liberty of sending ten copies in your care. Perhaps you will know of some bookseller who would like to take these off your hands, anyhow do what you can to place them. If they are a trouble to you I will arrange to take them off your hands."

That Upton resented Woodward's comments is shown by the weak excuse for refusing to review Woodward's next book, *Money for Tomorrow*. He wrote the historian's wife: "I didn't think it would help the book for me to say what I thought—that Socialists ought not to seek to patch up the ramshackle and collapsing old system. Bill's remedy might do it, and still might do it if Roosevelt would apply it. But I do not want to see him apply it. I want to see his party destroyed." In only a few months, Sinclair would join Roosevelt's party and seek Roosevelt's endorsement, so either when he wrote Helen Woodward or when he joined the Democrats he was deceiving himself.

The likelihood is that his resentment was part of the guilt he felt about taking Fox's money or he would not have kept the fee secret for so many years and then, when he revealed it in his *Autobiography*, have stressed that the decision to accept it was Craig's. The main reason Upton made the deal with Fox was that the Sinclairs needed money desperately, for they had become involved in movie-making themselves—in what became known as the disastrous Eisenstein affair.

CHAPTER XXII

Que Viva Mexico!

It is worse than a crime; it is a blunder.   JOSEPH FOUCHÉ

DESPITE UPTON'S REPEATED PROTESTATIONS that he went into the Eisenstein affair only to help a Socialist fellow artist who had been mistreated in America, there is ample evidence that he in fact thought he was finally going to do what he had longed to do for years—make a killing in the movies.

Sergei Mikhailovich Eisenstein was brought to Hollywood in 1930 by Paramount Studios. Since the triumph of his film *Potemkin* in 1925, the Russian had been generally considered to be one of the world's few genuine cinematic geniuses. Otherwise it would have been unthinkable for an American studio to hire a Bolshevik director.

Eager to come to America to study the new techniques of motion pictures with sound, Eisenstein had some years before his arrival written America's most famous Socialist for information about Douglas Fairbanks. Upton had replied frankly and had also suggested some of his own works for Eisenstein scenarios, and although the Russian had diplomatically expressed interest, nothing had come of it.

At Paramount, Eisenstein discussed without success a number of different story ideas, and he wrote a scenario based on *An American Tragedy*. Part of his inability to satisfy the studio may perhaps be inferred from the Russian's horror at a studio writer's summary of Dreiser's novel: "Oh, that is the story about the guy who got hot nuts, screwed a girl and drowned her."

But Paramount had been put off after Eisenstein came, mainly by right-wing attacks on him as a "Jew-Communist." Only four months after his arrival in Hollywood, the studio publicly announced the termination of his contract on October 23, 1930.

When Eisenstein told Charlie Chaplin he wanted to make a film in Mexico, Chaplin suggested he discuss it with Sinclair, whom the director approached through mutual friends. Had Upton been less driven toward making a success in the movies, he might have asked himself why Chaplin, who was also a Socialist and was far better equipped than Sinclair both economically and in experience, had not himself seized the opportunity. But instead he immediately began a campaign of telegrams and letters to senators and others in Washington, D.C., to keep the suddenly unemployed and undesirable director from being deported. Simultaneously, Sinclair mounted another campaign to raise the capital needed for Eisenstein to work in Mexico.

Although Sinclair was always optimistic about his projects, in no other enterprise did he as repeatedly assure those from whom he solicited money that they would "make two or three hundred percent profit." Even more significantly, Craig, who was chronically skeptical about her husband's optimism, this time shared it, so wholeheartedly in fact that most uncharacteristically she would put much of her sacrosanct separate property into his undertaking. She would even borrow money by mortgaging her beloved real estate.

Indeed, the contracts drawn in November and December 1930 were not between Sinclair and Eisenstein, but between Craig and the Russian director. Under these, Eisenstein agreed to go to Mexico "for a period of from three to four months" to produce a movie that "will be non-political, and worthy of his reputation and genius." Craig was to put "not less than Twenty-Five Thousand Dollars [clearly an invitation to misunderstanding]" for the film, which "will be the property of Mrs. Sinclair." Eisenstein was to receive 10 percent of the income from the film after Craig had been repaid and Craig's "world rights" did not include the Soviet Union, which was given free of charge the right to show the film within its borders.

In addition to Eisenstein's assistant director, G. V. ("Grisha") Alexandrov, and the cameraman, Edouard Tissé, it was then arranged that Craig's brother, Hunter Kimbrough, would also go to Mexico—a decision that would play its part in the disaster. Kimbrough, according to his sister, Dollie, had never earned much of a living and also had a drinking problem.

Upton and Craig claimed that Kimbrough had given up a good job selling securities to go to Mexico, but this was untrue. Kimbrough had no end of letters of recommendation but no significant earnings. Perhaps never before had he held any comparable authority or disposed of so much money, or would he again, and sadly these apparently brought out the worst of his prejudices. He would soon write his brother-in-law that Eisenstein, "like a negro" could not be controlled by kind words but only by rough talk and rough treatment.

When Eisenstein later complained that "*most* of the time in lesser or greater degree Hunter is *drunk*," both Upton and Craig pretended that such conduct by this Southern gentleman was unimaginable. But both knew otherwise. Upton had in fact warned his brother-in-law at the very beginning of the project: "There is one embarrassing matter that I have to mention to you. Craig asked me to get you to promise, before you left, that you would not drink anything while in Mexico."

Once in Mexico, Eisenstein was even more fascinated by the land, its peoples, and its past than he had anticipated. He traveled all over, including Yucatan, shooting endlessly everything that interested him from pre-Columbian ruins to traditional and modern fiestas. Months later it would seem scandalous to Upton, who had always been horrified if he discovered a few cents wasted, this shooting of almost a quarter of a million feet of film for a picture that would finally run some nine thousand feet. To Eisenstein, who had shot slightly more feet in making *Potemkin*, it was unimportant.

It seems evident that at least part of the reason Eisenstein prolonged his stay in Mexico was his pleasure at working without ideological constraints. But he of course protested violently Edmund Wilson's allegation that he was working in full liberty for the first time in his life. "This is a mean insult to all of us, who work creatively in the Soviet Union, and who consider it the greatest ambition to do things our country need . . ." But his actions were perhaps more instructive than his words.

Although more than one scenario was written, not only for the Mexican government, which was suspicious of possible attacks on the state or the church, but also for the Sinclairs' investors, there was in fact no fixed "story line." Eisenstein had a plan, or at least a number of ideas, but like all his films, this one would really be defined only in the cutting room.

As weeks passed into months and endless letters and telegrams from Mexico called for more film and more money, it became evident that the original estimates of how much time and capital would be necessary had been meaningless. Sinclair found that virtually all his time was being spent raising more and more money and addressing himself to the other myriad details of a film producer—from how to get the whole party out of a Mexican jail and answering the various objections of Mexican customs agents and Mexican censors to finding and sending Eisenstein books, including D. H. Lawrence's *The Plumed Serpent*. Sinclair had no experience as a producer and, in Eisenstein's opinion, made important mistakes by his premature efforts to get publicity and in discussing various distribution possibilities for the film.

Sinclair was increasingly irked at not having time to write books, to direct his campaign to get for himself the Nobel prize, to make his perennially postponed trip to the Soviet Union, or even to have a much-needed hernia operation.

Kimbrough warned that Eisenstein seemed to want to stay in Mexico forever and was "some kind of pervert." In the years that followed, it was to Eisenstein's alleged homosexuality that Sinclair repeatedly ascribed much of the disaster and which he used to justify his own conduct. However, Marie Seton, Eisenstein's biographer, maintained that virtually all his sex drives were sublimated into his artistic work, leaving him sexually passive, possibly androgynous, but definitely not the active homosexual Sinclair charged.

Long before the almost invariably optimistic Upton, Craig began to have serious doubts about the enterprise, and her wrath as she began to realize the very real perils was commensurate with her terror. But Upton continued sanguine despite Eisenstein's complaints that Hunter "was put in jail in Merida for public indecency in a bordell, after a wild adventure with throwing whores in the swimming pool," and other problems of the "Kimbrough question." Suddenly, however, a cable from Joseph Stalin in October 1931, responding to a letter from Upton on another subject, confirmed what Craig had suspected for some time, that Eisenstein was out of favor at home and possibly defecting. Eisenstein's activities increasingly had seemed to her to indicate he had no intention of completing the Mexican project and returning to the Soviet Union. Instead, she believed, he would drag out matters until another foreign project came along. And, indeed, instead of returning home as his government repeatedly ordered, he sought other work outside the Soviet Union, in India and in Japan.

Upton nevertheless wrote a long letter to Stalin defending Eisenstein, and he continued for some time to hope for the best. He tried to raise the additional money Eisenstein endlessly demanded, fearful that otherwise, as the Russian continually threatened, there would be no picture at all and that the more than fifty thousand dollars already invested would be lost entirely.

Craig had now lost any hope of a profit and worked only to minimize the losses. Angrily, repeatedly, she demanded that the filmmakers and all their film be brought back forthwith to Hollywood. Hunter's youthful delusions of grandeur had led him to write about making future pictures with Eisenstein in Louisiana and again in Mexico. Craig sharply cabled her brother: "STOP BEING DUPED."

Once the Sinclairs had finally stopped the shooting in Mexico, however, their troubles had not ended but instead actually intensified. No longer willing to trust Eisenstein, they still needed him to transform miles of film into a marketable movie.

But the returning party was stopped by immigration officials at Laredo, Texas, in February 1932, and only Hunter was allowed to reenter the United States. Eisenstein and his two associates were kept waiting in Laredo for weeks. Then finally they were given a thirty-day transit visa to go to New York and thence to Russia, but were not allowed to go to Hollywood to cut the film or, indeed, to do any work in America.

Sinclair carried on a series of Machiavellian negotiations with Eisenstein and his group, with Soviet authorities both in America and in Moscow, as well as with his own investors, the press, and others. Peter Bogdanov of Amtorg, the Soviet trading company in New York, and other Soviet representatives, plotted with Sinclair to get the reluctant Eisenstein safely back to Russia. One device of Sinclair's was to assure the director that he would be allowed to cut his film in Moscow rather than Hollywood.

The fact that Sinclair explained to the Russians the usefulness of a "Moviola" in cutting films may be taken as evidence of his real intention to have Eisenstein cut the film. But, of course, it may also be characterized as only a method of giving that impression when in fact he had no such intention.

More convincing proof that Upton really wanted to give Eisenstein every possible benefit of the doubt and every possible opportunity to express his poetic genius had been evident when he gave Craig the highly valuable *Wet Parade* "and all it might bring in, in exchange for her rights to the [Mexican] picture. So I have the final say about the matter. My wife will abide by this agreement, but she feels free to say what she thinks, and this of course is every woman's privilege."

Sinclair knew that if Eisenstein cut the film himself, the best artistic results would be achieved. But he was plagued with terrible doubts about letting Eisenstein have a print of the film in Russia. He was acutely aware that even if Eisenstein cut and returned an edited movie from the print: "The question then becomes what to do with the waste? We cannot leave it in the hands of Eisenstein, because any portion of it can be 'duped'—that is to say a negative can be made from it and bootleg pictures could be put on the market not merely in Russia, but all over the world. We cannot trust Eisenstein in this matter, and so we shall have to make absolutely certain that every foot of waste is destroyed." Upton even contemplated sending David to Moscow along with the print to make certain that every frame of scrap film was burned.

Probably Upton's greatest hope, however, and certainly Craig's, was that Soyuzkino, the Soviet state movie monopoly, through Amkino, their American company, might buy the film for Eisenstein to finish in Russia. In that case the Sinclairs would get their own and their fellow investors' money back with some profit and be rid of their nightmare, and the responsibility for producing an artistic film would be where Upton felt it belonged.

But the likelihood that the Russians would buy the film was never great. They only wanted their wandering genius back, because "Russia does not want the outside world to think her artists are deserters." Sinclair seems never to have been ashamed of his part in convincing Eisenstein to return to the Soviet Union, nor was he, as he had hoped to be, rewarded for it. "The Russian Government got their great artist back and avoided having him turn into a White, as Rachmaninov and Chaliapin have done. They owe this solely to our efforts, and we thought they would be ready to do the fair thing about the picture."

Upton's idea that the Russians would in business "do the fair thing" was not only naïve but also ran directly opposite to his experience with them both with his writing and with earlier negotiations regarding the Eisenstein film. At one point, when Eisenstein was still in Mexico, Amkino had made a firm contract to supply twenty-five thousand dollars toward completing the production and then simply reneged on the contract. Rather than sue or even threaten to sue, Upton had done nothing, which again demonstrated his reluctance to do anything that might publicly embarrass any part of the Movement. This reluctance had always played an extraordinary role in his adult life. It had been one of the reasons he hesitated so long to sue Meta for divorce.

Another example of it was on the horizon. Very shortly, Upton would be subjected to the most venomous attacks he had yet endured. These would come from political and artistic partisans of Eisenstein and equally from the Communists. Although Upton believed that he could completely confound these attacks, which embarrassed him painfully, by releasing the text of Stalin's cable and so prove that he was in the good graces of the Kremlin and that Eisenstein, not he, was there regarded as the villain of the episode, for years he resolutely refused to do so. He thought that would be washing the Soviet Union's dirty linen in public and would provide the capitalist press with the opportunity to exploit Russia's inability to keep its great genius at home and satisfied.

In his complicated dealings, Upton may have used Eisenstein, but the Russians unquestionably were using Upton by pretending they might buy the film. Could they have got it at no cost, they would of course have taken it and then decided what, if anything, they would do with it. But with the Stalinist Boris Shumyatsky, Eisenstein's implacable enemy, in charge of the Soviet film industry since 1930, nothing beneficial to Eisenstein's interests was likely to happen regardless of promises or strategic moves. All unaware of this, Upton continued to hope for the best.

As so often happens, however, something unrelated to the real issues triggered the tragic denouement. A practical joke with which Eisenstein intended to embarrass Sinclair so shocked and horrified the puritan as to accomplish what all Craig's worst bitchery had failed to achieve. It permanently hardened Sinclair's heart toward this Russian Arthur Stirling.

Into the top of a trunk full of things he was sending to Sinclair, Eisenstein slipped a group of his own obscene drawings, where the United States Customs inspectors were certain to see them and cause trouble, because "it was the vilest stuff they had ever seen—and they see a lot." One of these colored drawings was shown to Sinclair, a pornographic Golgotha. In it, the penis of the Son of God was sufficiently elongated to reach and enter the mouth of one of the thieves crucified at His side.

Sinclair had complained too of "the fact that E. spent a lot of his time and our film in shooting pictures of animals copulating and of human beings in degrading positions." Unlike the unquestionably pornographic drawings, however, the photographs were by any reasonable standard neither pornographic nor erotic. They show Eisenstein and his companions with phallus-shaped gourds either held to the front of their own trousers or laughingly pointed toward the rumps of Mexican burros and other photographs including some of a bare breasted Indian girl.

During the time the group was in Mexico, Craig had once railed nonstop at Upton for three days and three nights, until he had to be taken to the hospital with an attack of hiccups from which he nearly died; but he had refused to do as Craig demanded and take the film away from Eisenstein. Indeed, his patience and generosity toward the often unreliable and difficult Russian were exemplary.

But once he had finally decided against Eisenstein's finishing the film, he was adamant. Sinclair ordered his lawyer to insist that the print, which was at the Amkino offices in New York, be returned to him in California. He had decided to sell the film in America to a studio, or, if necessary, to have the film cut and then sell it.

When the print reached California, he discovered that contrary to Amkino's repeated assurances several hundred feet of film had been removed during the time it was stored with Amkino. Nevertheless, Upton, making one last effort to sell the film to the Soviet Union, sent Stalin a long cable to which he got no reply.

During part of Upton's long ordeal, David Sinclair and his wife had in 1931 visited Russia, where bad food and the bedbugs Upton so abhorred gave them a more realistic view of the dictatorship of the proletariat than Upton had. They learned too that chauvinism and xenophobia were at least as strong there as in capitalist states. "At best we eat only one square meal a day and we're both getting quite thin," Betty wrote. "Every morning I wake up with new bed-bug or flea bites. You can exit only from the front of the [street] car, & that means ploughing through a mass of unwashed (there's a soap shortage) & smelly humans."

A few weeks later she advised her father-in-law: "I slept on a divan in another room the first night we came to this apartment & got all flea-bitten, so I prefer the floor. . . . don't make Craig come. . . . I personally don't think she could stand the dirt & lack of proper nourishment. And the excitement and nervous tension is terrific. . . . I am still not hardened to the sight of women with infants in their arms, sitting on the filthy street begging. . . . Russia has taught me that I am a doubting bourgeois."

She was shocked to be told "We may make use of Sinclair, but we must be very careful in dealing with him." The Russians pretended surprise when she chided them for the unauthorized use of Sinclair's name, protesting: "If we sign his name without asking it shows that we trust him."

David's reports, too, surprised his father. "The authorities don't care at all what happens to Eisenstein. His ideology is wrong. . . . He should be filming the new life in Uzbekistan instead of the old life in Mexico. The . . . Russians . . . think that the U.S.S.R. is the only place where anything of importance is happening except maybe China or Germany. Anyhow your emphasis that the money [promised but long overdue book royalties] was for Eisenstein was all wrong. You should have said you wanted to buy a house or take a trip around the world or something for you. They are giving the money, if & *when* they give it, to you and for no other reason. If Eisenstein counted at all, he could have gotten money for himself. . . . They are just afraid of making you sore. . . ."

With most foreign authors, the Russians did not even pretend they would send payment for pirated works. But with Sinclair they regularly promised payment and very rarely sent any.

As soon as negotiations ceased with Amkino and it was clear that the film would be finished by someone in America and not by Eisenstein in

Russia, Sinclair was subjected to countless vituperative attacks that would continue for decades. Many came from American Communists, understandably frustrated by their own powerlessness and therefore delighted to turn upon this lily-livered Socialist that animus they felt against the powerful capitalists but dared not fully reveal.

Communists all over the world echoed this animus against the man Lenin had so correctly called an emotional Socialist, whose rembourgeoisement (if indeed he had ever been anything but a bourgeois) had wrecked the work of a great and loyal Communist artist. Sinclair's regularly repeated concern for the money invested by his capitalist associates and by his wife and himself was cited as proof that he merely disguised himself as a sometime Socialist.

There could, in fact, scarcely have been a more consistently committed Socialist—but yet there was also something at once half amusing and half moving about Sinclair's pride in playing by certain bourgeois ground rules. For many years he had corresponded with the great Wall Street banker and philanthropist Otto Kahn, who was the largest outside investor in the Eisenstein film. Upton was so immensely pleased that this Kuhn, Loeb partner approved his business ethics that he never lost any opportunity to quote Kahn's words: "I am telling all my friends that if I had money to invest and wanted it handled carefully and reported on fully I would invest it with Mr. Upton Sinclair the Socialist."

Upton was generous in praising the great capitalist for making a contribution to a young German who had solicited Upton's help and for ordering some of his books: "I want to express . . . my appreciation for your open-mindedness . . . You are certainly setting a standard in willingness to give all sides a hearing, and I for one want to tell you that it is appreciated."

In the Eisenstein affair, the most pettish and censorious outbursts came from shrill and occasionally epicene worshipers of Eisenstein, some obviously psychotic.

His chief antagonist, Seymour Stern, excoriated Sinclair for daring to think that anyone other than Eisenstein could cut the film, but Stern had nevertheless offered himself as a candidate for cutting the film instead of Eisenstein and had been refused. Stern was a sometime assistant to the head of Universal Studios, but it was as editor of *Experimental Cinema* that he could express his idolatry for Eisenstein.

But much of the fault for the fury of his attackers lay with Sinclair himself. His unwillingness or inability to get rid of Kimbrough was bad enough, but he might at least have admitted the problem was one he could not solve. Instead, he simply stated to Eisenstein, "I have known Hunter since he was sixteen. I have never seen him drunk, nor can I find anyone else who knows him, who has seen him drunk. This aspect of the matter is settled, and I ask you not to refer to it again." Sinclair would have been the first to condemn in anyone else this nepotism compounded by pretense and to call it by its real name, hypocrisy. (Whatever the degree of Hunter's then drinking problem, it was one he was later to overcome.)

Craig was also tormented by her fears about Hunter's problem and after the Mexican misadventure had ended, even more than Upton, she remembered, acknowledged, and resented her brother's drunkenness. She once forbade her husband to recommend him to Harry Hopkins for a job. "She does not doubt your honest intention to refrain from drinking," Sinclair wrote Kimbrough, "but she has no assurance as to your ability to do it. She is not satisfied with any promise to abstain from hard liquor, because she has been told by friends of yours that beer makes a fool of you. She has been told by several members of the family that . . . you . . . were drinking to extremes in Mississippi."

Sinclair's reluctance to admit his brother-in-law's failings during or after the Eisenstein affair had many causes. One was that he had repeatedly assured so many of the film's investors that Kimbrough "is as dependable as any man I have ever known." It is always difficult to admit an error, but Upton had admitted others. In this case, however, it would have amounted to admitting to the world and especially to himself that one of the causes for the tragedy lay not with Eisenstein but with himself.

Because of Sinclair's seeming hypocrisy about Kimbrough, Eisenstein presumably considered the writer a fool or a liar or more likely both, and in any event one who did not deserve to be dealt with straightforwardly, being himself dissimulating. Whether Eisenstein might have acted any better had he been less provoked is impossible to know, but he can scarcely be blamed if he chose to make the crime fit the punishment.

When none of the major studios whose interest Upton had tried hard to stimulate nor any of the individual groups that had expressed interest could be induced to help finish and market the film, he turned the job over to an independent producer, Sol Lesser, and offered him only a minimum number of suggestions.

In allowing Lesser to cut Eisenstein's film, Upton was unwittingly proving the validity of Craig's warning to Hunter given at the very beginning of the enterprise: "There must be something more . . . in

Eisenstein's picture or it'll be a flop. That something must be the indescribable *spirit* of *art*—which is a thing not done to order like a mechanical operation." Craig's sense of what art is and is not was better than Upton's. For him the message was all, and letting others edit Eisenstein's work seemed neither shocking nor even dangerous.

It is easy to visualize Craig as the termagant. It is more difficult to picture her as Upton's helpful, understanding, and complementary wife—but she was that too. In the same letter to Hunter, she wrote: "The artist must have the right mood & state of mind for this spirit to develope [sic] in. Help him [Eisenstein] now in every way you can, even if you have to do the difficult but brave moral thing called 'humility.' It is said that this is the most difficult moral act ('humility')." Lacking though she was in many of the virtues she preached, Craig did usually practice this one of putting her husband's writing ahead of everything else.

Lesser was a successful but highly commercial Hollywood producer, who cut the film into a movie that was an all-around failure.

Eisenstein had planned his film to be an anthology of some six episodes symbolic of Mexico. Lesser took one of these episodes and turned it into a melodrama of rape, revenge, and cruel punishment—preceding it with pieces from the other footage made into a palimpsest montage of Mexico throughout the ages. Although originally it was to have been called *Que Viva Mexico!* it was finally released as *Thunder Over Mexico*.

As it became evident that there would be no substantial return on the film Lesser had put together, the Sinclairs were increasingly anxious to sell bits and pieces of it as stock shots, for example, when Walter Wanger Productions wrote: "We have been looking for a beautiful sunrise and have been advised that you can supply same."

All told, however, the investors got back less than half of their money. Most of the film finally came into the collection of the Library of Congress.

In considering both the financial and the artistic disasters, it is significant that none of Sinclair's attackers ever raised a dollar to take over the film from him and save it despite Sinclair's repeated suggestions that they do so.

As with all things that might have been, one may attribute to the Mexican film, had it been completed by Eisenstein himself, a perfection impossible for anything actually completed by the hand of man. But that an important work of art was forever lost there can be no doubt.

The blame for this tragedy, as with most, is impossible to place exactly, and "the truth is, as usual, somewhere betwixt and between; but much more in Sinclair's favour than in Eisenstein's," according to the *Times Literary Supplement.*

As usual, there was not one exclusive villain and there was more than enough blame to share among each of the participants in the tragedy—Eisenstein, Hunter Kimbrough, the Sinclairs, and their shrill attackers.

The most important effect of the tragedy on Craig was that it established the Communists once and for all at the very top of her hierarchy of villains—a conviction that over the years would ripen into real paranoia. Upton wrote David that Craig "is in a white fury with the Communists, and the gangster tactics they have been trying on us in the effort to get the picture away from me. . . . [she's threatened] she'd go to Miss & never return, so I just had to give up."

Increasingly throughout the thirties as the Stalinist obscenities were partially revealed and as it became obvious that the dictatorship of the proletariat stubbornly refused to wither away, Upton's determination not publicly to criticize the Soviet Union was frequently challenged. But again and again he defended and excused.

When Communists in America brutalized Upton's Socialist brothers, he chided them privately. But in public he would not criticize Communists or the Soviet Union. His basic position he stated in various forms, over and over again. "I do not think it matters what particular label one wears in the movement, as the movement is much bigger than all the little parties and sects."

It is impossible to give its appropriate comparative weight to each of the many various elements in Upton's life from his childhood lessons in patriotism to his firsthand experiences with Communists that determined why he never became a Communist. But much is revealed throughout his writings. Reminiscing in his seventies, he wrote: "Somewhere about 1909 a group of young rebels among the Greenwich Villagers started a magazine called *The Masses.* Sometimes when they were in the mood of bitterness because the workers would not take their advice and vote the Socialist ticket, they would make a pun by shifting the space between the two words and would talk about *Them Asses.*

"Most of these young people were very 'radical' in mood. They were ardent, impatient, and prone to become embittered. As I look back upon this period I am struck by the fact that during a year I spent in England, I met great numbers of Socialists, and cannot think of a single one who afterwards went over to the Communists. But in the case of *The Masses* crowd nearly all went over, and some of those who became reddest of all afterwards reacted to the other extreme. The Englishmen, you see, had been trained and taught over a long period of years, and no matter how Red they became they remained Englishmen. The Americans, on the other hand, were undisciplined, and determined to have their own way at once. This was true of the rebel workers, and even more true of the sons and daughters of the well-to-do."

Although Upton refused publicly to criticize the Communists, he now avoided seeing them in private. "What finished me with the Communists," he wrote his daughter-in-law, "was the Eisenstein affair. Now I never see one if I can help it."

The loss of money through the Eisenstein affair was not so important to Upton as it was to Craig. That it kept him from his planned trip to Russia was more important. In October 1930 he had written European publishers, agents, translators, and friends expressing his yearning to go to Russia the following spring and summer, his desire to lecture on the way, and his plan to collect in Russia material for a novel he had longed to do for many years about the role young Americans such as John Reed had played in helping the Soviet Union.

When *The New Masses* had earlier printed a request for John Reed material, Upton had sent copies of his and Reed's first world war controversy. "I am not proud of it," he wrote, "because Reed was right and I was wrong, and if you quote it please say so." A man usually this unafraid to admit and publish when he was wrong, had he seen with his own eyes in Russia what he chose to rationalize or ignore when it was reported to him by others, would probably have changed his point of view and admitted his error again. For Upton had a genuine horror of violence—a horror as great as that he felt for injustice. Had he seen in the thirties that violence and the threat of violence was what kept peace in the Soviet Union, he would probably not have waited so long to denounce it.

The Russians had sent Sinclair a compilation of his works published in the Soviet Union from 1921 to 1929. It revealed that more than a million copies of one hundred and twelve titles had been printed, which did not lessen his desire to go. But the Eisenstein contretemps kept him in America through 1933, and by then Sinclair had become involved in what was the most extraordinary and uncharacteristic fight of his life, a serious campaign to become governor of California.

CHAPTER XXIII

EPIC

It is difficult to . . . believe the story of that vast hippodrome, that hectic, whirling dizzy three-ring circus with the NRA in one ring, the AAA in another, the Relief Act in another, with General Johnson, Henry Wallace and Harry Hopkins popping whips, while all around under the vast tent a whole drove of clowns and dervishes, the Henry Morgenthaus and Huey Longs and Dr. Townsends and Upton Sinclairs and a host of crackpots of every variety—leaped and danced and tumbled about shouting in a great harlequinade of government, until the tent came tumbling down upon the heads of the cheering audience and the prancing buffoons. I do not exaggerate, I assure you.   JOHN T. FLYNN

WHAT WAS TRUE OF AMERICA IN 1933 seemed even more true of California—unemployment, starvation, fear, creating despair with old leaders and a desperate yearning for new ones and turning citizen against citizen.

Thousands upon thousands of the nation's dispossessed had migrated west on the premise that "at least it was better not to have to worry about freezing as one starved to death." But once arrived, even good weather could not make the squalor, misery, and terror of their lives appreciably more acceptable than what they had left behind.

Farmers and ranchers in California before the Depression had traditionally exploited foreign migratory workers—Mexicans, Filipinos, Chinese, and Japanese—playing one group off against the other. But by the end of 1934, white native Americans made up half of those competing for the ten-to-fifteen-cents-an-hour "stoop labor" field wages. Less willing to be bullied than the long brutalized foreigners, these Americans by the thousands went on strikes, which were answered by the outraged employers with an ever escalating violence not only condoned but actually encouraged by the California press. American men, many of them highly skilled, brought up in the tradition of hard work and rugged individualism, who had never before been out of work but who were now unable to find any but the meanest employment, were reading in the papers that they were Communists and layabouts.

Nor were matters any better in the cities, where for years the work force had already been swelled by young men and women convinced that anything was better than life on the farm. Food prices in Los Angeles were often ridiculously low: lettuce a penny a head, bread a nickel a loaf, steak eight cents a pound. But even these prices were too high when one person in four in the city was on relief, receiving an average of four dollars and a half a month.

San Francisco politicians such as George Creel pretended that only "southern California was the world's closest approach to bedlam and babel." But now even civilized San Francisco was racing toward that terror of every great city—the General Strike. Tension mounted from the strike declaration of the International Longshoremen's Union on May 9, 1934, through "bloody Thursday" two months later. Once Governor Frank Merriam ordered out the National Guard, it soon became clear that for the San Francisco Industrial Association no price in violence, bloodshed, and death was too high to pay to keep labor in its place. The General Strike was voted July 16, but collapsed in four days.

It was appropriately in southern California, however, that Sinclair's candidacy for governor started first and flourished best. All over America were crazy cults, zany religions, political and religious medicine men, the few rich with ducal delusions and fear in their bellies, the many poor with nothing in their bellies, the resentful middle classes, worn out oldsters, impatient youngsters—but southern California was America to at least the third power. From fiction perhaps even better than from fact can the anger and despair of many southern Californians be felt, for as Nathanael West pointed out in *The Day of the Locust:* "The sun is a joke. Oranges can't titillate their jaded palates. Nothing can ever be violent enough to make taut their slack minds and bodies. They have been cheated and betrayed. They have slaved and saved for nothing."

In an interview in 1931 in Los Angeles, Bertrand Russell said the city had achieved "the ultimate segregation of the unfit," which was confirmed at quite the opposite end of the political spectrum by Westbrook Pegler's diagnosis that the whole area should "be declared incompetent and placed in charge of a guardian."

But the sickness was not only local. The whole country was undergoing a nervous breakdown, an identity crisis from which it would emerge radically changed, never again to return completely to its comfortable and simple faith in the gods of the marketplace.

Over the years Sinclair had slowly and for a long time quite unconsciously been becoming convinced that Socialism was and would remain for an overwhelming majority of Americans a foreign word for a foreign ideology. Therefore, if he wanted to see Socialism in America, which he did as much as ever, it would have to be brought about under another name. As Craig explained: "They do not want the old names and phrases of the two radical parties, these being unsuitable for more reasons than one. For example, we have no industrial working-class in this country any more. . . . We now have an America in which all classes are in trouble. It is, therefore, to America as a whole that we should appeal. The large middle-class is now ruined and many of them cannot hope for their lost property to be restored to them under Capitalism. So they can be organized—our radical theory about them notwithstanding. We *are* different from Russia and Europe. Marx did not know our psychology.

"Do you want to be one of a committee to call on the Captains of Industry for a bloodless and classless revolution? . . . This is Young America, asking Papa to sign the checks and join the gang. Long-haired 'foreigners' and Russian Communists and German Socialists can't tell us how to run our country. We are going to SHOW THEM!"

Sinclair wrote a book called *Letters to Perry*, and when Craig objected that the title was too colorless, Upton wrote John Farrar: "Any title that you all agree upon will be satisfactory to me, but do not put the word 'Socialist' or any word of that sort on to the title, as that will scare away the very people I want to reach. They will find out it is Socialist before they get through."

Always against revolution by violence for America, Sinclair was getting closer in his views to those of his fellow muckraker Finley Peter Dunne's Mr. Dooley: 'Th' noise ye hear is not th' first gun iv a rivolution. It's on'y th' people iv the United States batin' a carpet."

The book was published as *The Way Out: What Lies Ahead for America* and was addressed to business and professional men, white-collar as well as blue-collar workers, to whom Upton explained that laissez-faire capitalism was as disastrous for them as for anyone else, that only Socialism could bring the nation out of this Depression and keep it out of future ones.

Upton's increasing and largely unconscious sense of alienation from the left had a number of different causes. Just as Freud's theories were metamorphosed from a quasi-science into a quasi-religion with dogma, heretics, saints, devils, and endless arguments approximating that about the standing room on the head of a pin, so Socialism had developed doctrinal squabbles, apostates, anathemas, and the inevitable power struggles that are never the result of personal ambition or pique but always of moral principle.

Upton's feelings toward the Communists who attacked him and his fellow Socialists did not approach Craig's, but he was tired of the schisms and dissensions, tired of losing and seeing most Socialist candidates lose, and, even worse than losing, being ignored by both major parties.

At just the moment when Upton "had come to feel that both doctrine and vocabulary cut Socialism off from American life," he was urged by a rich Santa Monica capitalist to run in the Democratic primary for the nomination for governor. So ready was Upton that less than twenty-four hours later on September 1, 1933, he had quietly changed his registration from Socialist to Democrat.

His apostasy, picked up by the newspapers and broadcast around the world, horrified his until then fellow Socialists. No one was more appalled by the seeming sellout than his son who telegraphed: "GLAD LEND YOU SEVEN HUNDRED OUR ENTIRE SAVINGS CAN RAISE ANY ADDITIONAL NEEDED BOTH ALMOST COLLAPSING GRIEF INSANE OPPORTUNISM IS IT POSSIBLE YOU HAVE LOST ALL INTEGRITY AS MAN AND SOCIALIST STOP LEADERS HERE THUNDERSTRUCK NO OVERWHELMING CIRCUMSTANCES CAN JUSTIFY RENEGATION PLEASE RECONSIDER."

Sinclair did need money and for that reason he had undertaken some assignments and sought still more that he would otherwise have refused. He had sunk Fox's secret twenty-five thousand dollars into Eisenstein's film and the Beverly Hills house, and now he needed more money to pay the printer and to advertise the Fox book. The New York opening and promotion of *Thunder Over Mexico* was calling him east and creating still more expenses.

He even offered to edit, promote, and write a preface for a "cancer cure" book for five thousand dollars. "I cannot endorse your cancer cure, because I do not know anything about it, but . . . I can endorse your fight for medical freedom. . . ."

But it was not his need for money that had led him to change parties. It was his conviction that only from within one of America's two major political parties could the changes he believed essential for the country be effected. "It is a magnificent idea," he wrote David. "Whether it'll ever be any more I cannot tell—but I hope not!! I'd sure hate to be a gov. But I think I can reach the Dems of the whole nation." And again the next day he wrote David, "this seemed to be a good chance to educate the Democrats right now. As you know, I have never been much of a party man—I am more interested in spreading the ideas, and this seemed to be an especially good opportunity for that. I hope you and Betty won't be too much disappointed."

Norman Thomas wrote Upton: "Words are symbols. You alone, or you with the help of a certain number of California voters, cannot make the word Democratic a symbol for Socialism. That word with its capital D is a symbol for the party which bitterly discriminates not only against Negroes but white workers in the South, for the party of Tammany Hall in New York, and Hague in New Jersey." Always kind, Thomas later wrote Sinclair "how very keenly I feel your loss," but predicted Sinclair would fail and would "regret this error in judgement almost as much as you regretted your support of Wilson in the 'war to end war.' "

Thomas was well advised to be frightened by what he called Upton's "sublime naïveté," for its example was soon to be followed by men unlikely to be accused of being *naifs*, David Dubinsky, president of the International Ladies' Garment Workers Union, and Emil Rieve, president of the Hosiery Workers, who in May 1936 would resign from the Socialist Party to support Roosevelt.

Upton both symbolized and typified what had been happening to the Socialist Party in America since World War I and the death of Debs in 1926. As the left wing of the Democratic Party increasingly appropriated parts of the Socialist program, and as many of the most dedicated and bravest radicals left to join the Communist Party, the organization disintegrated until the United States finally became the only industrialized country in the world without a significant Socialist Party.

To thousands of Socialists all around the world, Sinclair had suddenly changed from a heroic figure into Browning's Lost Leader, and many wrote him letters of outrage or sadness or bewilderment. But in addition to these, Sinclair received letters of encouragement—from Steffens, from Dos Passos, and from Ezra Pound who from Italy diagnosed Upton as "not a monomaniac; but a polymaniac."

But Sinclair heeded neither encouragement nor criticism. He had the bit in his teeth and he plunged into the 1934 Democratic primary with an energy that surprised even those who knew him well.

For a practicing politician with a professional organization, let alone for a tyro like Upton, winning the Democratic nomination for governor would have been a difficult and doubtful prize in this one-party state that had had no Democratic administration since 1899 and where the Republican registration usually exceeded the Democratic by three to one. There were, however, signs of change. According to the Los Angeles *Times*, the city in 1933 and 1934 lost eighty-two thousand Republican and gained one hundred and twenty-six thousand Democratic registrants—the Republicans being outnumbered for the first time in forty years.

There were eight other candidates running against Upton. His main opponent was George Creel, Woodrow Wilson's former propaganda chief. Creel had the backing of William Gibbs McAdoo, the Georgian who had made his fortune in New York, served as Wilson's treasury secretary and son-in-law, defended Doheny in the Teapot Dome scandal, and was now the new Ku Klux Klan-supported United States senator from California.

Upton's EPIC program (End Poverty in California) was based on twelve principles explained in his *I, Governor of California and How I Ended Poverty: A True Story of the Future*, a pamphlet that he published himself and that sold in the hundreds of thousands.

1. God created the natural wealth of the earth for the use of all men, not of the few.
2. God created men to seek their own welfare, not those of their masters.
3. Private ownership of tools, a basic of freedom when tools are simple, becomes a basis of enslavement when tools become complex.
4. Autocracy in industry cannot exist alongside democracy in government.
5. When some men live without working, other men are working without living.
6. The existence of luxury in the presence of poverty and destitution is contrary to good morals and sound public policy.
7. The present depression is one of abundance, not of scarcity.
8. The cause of the trouble is that a small class has the wealth, while the rest has the debts.
9. It is contrary to common sense that men should starve because they have raised too much food.
10. The destruction of food or other wealth, or the limitation of production is economic insanity.
11. The remedy is to give the workers access to the means of production, and let them produce for themselves, not for others.
12. This change can be brought about by action of a majority of the people, and that is the American Way.

These generalities were not new, nor was Sinclair the first politician to demand an end to poverty. The "Great Engineer," Herbert Hoover, had assured his countrymen in his Inaugural Address in 1928 that "Our first objective must be to provide security from poverty and want." But grain prices were at the lowest point in three hundred years and yet the poor could not buy bread. The public increasingly doubted those who promised that prosperity was just around the corner, particularly rich men like John J. Raskob who two months before the Wall Street crash had assured readers of the *Ladies' Home Journal*: "I am firm in my belief that anyone not only can be rich, but ought to be rich. [If only one would invest fifteen dollars a month in good stocks.]"

The twenties, a decade of unreasoning and ebullient optimism, had now been followed by a general feeling of suspicious and pervasive pessimism. And yet, just as, less than a decade later, the personal example and courage of Winston Churchill would infect his beleaguered people, so Franklin Roosevelt's example and his assertion "that the only thing we have to fear is fear itself" encouraged Americans, including thirteen million unemployed, that this new leader would not repeat old platitudes but instead would, however timidly at first, try new cures for old ills.

In California, Upton was obviously a political amateur, but hundreds of thousands of people preferred his courage and the possibilities however remote of his innovations to the platitudes of those who offered only more of the same. Sinclair spelled out his program not only in generalities but also with specifics of how he would combine idle land, idle factories, and idle people into model land colonies and factories that in local self-governing communities would achieve his long held goal of production for use instead of production for profit. He would repeal the sales tax. He would recommend a graduated income tax, beginning with annual incomes of five thousand dollars and taxing at 50 percent all incomes over fifty thousand dollars a year. As he would exempt entirely from his income tax incomes below five thousand dollars, so he would exempt from ad valorem taxes homes and farms worth less than three thousand dollars, but great landholdings would be taxed greatly and he proposed large increases in the inheritance tax.

Like other candidates in other times, his strength of conviction and his natural candor in fact drove him to be too specific when generalities would not only have quite satisfied the voters but would also not have frightened some of them and would have provided his opponents with less to misquote, misinterpret, and tear apart.

In a state that had never wanted for messianic programs, however, Sinclair's was sufficiently impressive that voters gave him in August 1934 more primary votes than all his Democratic opponents combined.

Across America, similar shamans were springing up who achieved a more than local congregation—an understandable phenomenon in a country whose traditional priests, clerical and capitalist, had failed. Like Sinclair, Huey Pierce Long, United States senator from Louisiana; Reverend Charles E. Coughlin, the rabble-rousing Detroit priest; and Dr. Francis E. Townsend, the perennial California candidate of the aged, provided a kind of salvationist leadership along with their promises of practical panaceas. The fundamentalist, revivalist religious nature of Upton's campaign would be fascinating to reporters who later came from the east in large numbers to cover it and appraise his audiences. "Thus under another influence," *Collier's* told its readers, "they would have greeted Aimee Semple McPherson Hutton as she wafted whitely across her platform in Angelus Temple a few miles away. Or the Reverend Billy Sunday as he bounded to his pulpit croaking his homely anathema upon forty-seven devils. Or Gypsy Smith scratching his whiskers with a holy thumbnail. . . . Anyway, you are pretty well convinced by now that this mob is just about as radical as the horde that followed Cromwell. Or Luther. Or stumbled after Peter the Hermit. If you expected to hear La Marseillaise or the International sung, you'll have to be satisfied with Onward, Christian Soldier and The Son of God Goes Forth to War."

And the *Christian Century* reported that: "moral passion, deep sensitivity and a consuming concern for cleansing the world from its social sins cannot be denied. That he is an egotist is clear. Sentences begin with 'I,' but it is an egotism so simple and direct as to be disarming and winning. He is Sir Galahad, and he knows it, and he knows where the Holy Grail will be found."

Upton even wrote a "Political Prayer" during the campaign, and although partly it was for the purpose of contradicting his opponents' repeated charges that he was an atheist, it was also to appeal to the obvious needs of these voters, many newly arrived from Iowa and Oklahoma and Alabama and missing the comfort and community of their little churches as much as they missed their ruined homes.

This Isaiah in pince-nez understood their yearning for Jerusalem the Golden, because in his own way he felt it himself; and for the same reason they trusted this stranger despite the fact that all the newspapers reviled him as anti-Christ and Communist.

What had been regarded at first by many as a joke, and by the candidate

PCHS Media Center
Grant, Nebraska

himself as no more than an educational exercise, had, when Sinclair won the nomination, become a very serious matter. The conservatives who had jibed that EPIC stood for Empty Promises in California stopped joking and started hating quite as fiercely as the Communists, who in the August *New Masses* labeled the turncoat Socialist a "Fascist." *The Nation* was one of the few journals that rejoiced: "We do give profound thanks that one man has had the courage to stand up and announce his candidacy without consulting a boss, or a newspaper proprietor, or any financier or capitalist, and has gained the first round." While in London, Harold Laski suggested: "The real implication of this most remarkable of his many remarkable experiences is that the labor forces of America should learn the lesson of it. The time is ripe in America."

The new Democratic candidate, to the embarrassment of some of the party's national leaders, announced he would go east to visit Franklin Roosevelt at Hyde Park.

Upton had with his usual lack of shyness asked Eleanor Roosevelt in October 1933 for an invitation to the White House, and on receiving one, he and Craig had taken tea with her there. Then early in 1934 he had sent her his EPIC program with a letter hinting at his hopes for her endorsement.

Her reply, carefully headed *"Private—not for publication"* was typically kind: "I have read your book and I have given it to my husband to read. Some of the things which you advocate I am heartily in favor of, others I do not think are entirely practical, but then what is impractical today is sometimes practical tomorrow. I do not feel, however, that I am sufficiently in accord with your entire idea to make any public statement at present."

For the record at least, Eleanor was already doing what her husband would later advise regarding Sinclair: "1) Say nothing and 2) Do nothing."

The President had publicly declared his hands-off policy in all the midterm elections of 1934. This was intended to save him from association with any failures, from charges of bossism, and from involvement in intraparty feuds, but it also prevented his support of men he hoped very much would win, such as Senator Key Pittman of Nevada and Senator Robert La Follette of Wisconsin.

According to Rexford G. Tugwell, a member of Roosevelt's Brain Trust, the President knew that the demagogic game of men like Huey Long and Father Coughlin was "to propagate impossible goals and to condemn Franklin . . . for not having done enough. . . . The most interesting figure among all of them, and the only one about whom Franklin had curiosity, was Upton Sinclair, who . . . was himself not of the Long-Coughlin breed.

. . . Franklin at least took pains to see that he should be kept friendly."

In addition to his curiosity, however, and despite the fact that to many around the President Sinclair's candidacy was at best a bad joke, in Roosevelt's usually correct, politician's view "it looks as though Sinclair will win if he stages an orderly, common sense campaign but will be beaten if he makes a fool of himself."

Making abundantly clear, both to the candidate by telegram and to the public in the newspapers, that their meeting was to be "non-political," the President had invited Sinclair to Hyde Park and less than a week later Sinclair arrived for a meeting that had been scheduled for an hour and lasted for two. From it, he emerged "in manifest elation, stripped off his coat to sit down and talk with the correspondents.

" 'I think I had the most interesting two hours talk I ever had,' he began rapidly, without waiting for questions. 'I talked with one of the kindest and most genial and frank and open-minded and lovable men I ever met. He talked for two hours, and that was his fault and not mine.

" 'I did not intend to stay but an hour. He told me to tell you that.

" 'We folks out in California speculate as to what he is doing and how much he knows about it. I am very happy to tell the people of California that he knows . . .

" 'The President said he had only one grudge against me,' Mr. Sinclair went on. 'That was that when he was young his mother read "The Jungle" aloud to him at the breakfast table. I asked him, "And it spoiled your lamb chops?" and he said, "Yes." ' "

Sinclair always insisted thereafter that Roosevelt had said his mother read *The Jungle* to him when he was young and it tells much about both men that the President could have told such an anecdote and that Sinclair could believe it. In fact, it is almost as inconceivable that Sara Delano Roosevelt read her son the book as that Sinclair could have invented the story. The President, a notoriously charming flatterer when he wanted to be, must have said something that Sinclair at least heard as being what he repeated to the reporters immediately afterward. It would have been a typical Roosevelt tale, but almost certainly untrue, both because Sara Roosevelt did not read that kind of book—let alone read it aloud and at meals—and, more obviously, except as one chooses to ignore the obvious, when *The Jungle* was published Roosevelt was no longer "young" but was a married student at Columbia Law School and so presumably not often read aloud to by his mother at mealtime. What exactly happened is unknowable—perhaps Roosevelt had confused Sinclair's book with Kipling's, which his mother well might have read to him in his childhood.

Whether or not Franklin Roosevelt had in fact had a dining room experience similar to that ascribed by Mr. Dooley to Theodore Roosevelt a quarter century earlier was far less important to the upcoming elections than what he had said he would or would not do to help Upton's candidacy. Sinclair insisted that the President had positively assured him that before Election Day he would make a speech endorsing production for use. At this point in his Presidency, Roosevelt was still trying to get along with or at least not completely alienate big business. On the same day he met with Upton he had also met with the president of the New York, New Haven & Hartford Railroad and Joseph P. Kennedy of the Securities and Exchange Commission. It is extremely unlikely that Roosevelt had given Upton such a commitment, but not at all unlikely that Upton absolutely believed he had, that "like so many others in the excitement of the presidential audience, Sinclair construed affability as assent. Or he may have transferred a Rooseveltian speculation from the future conditional to the future."

On other occasions, Upton also mistook Eleanor Roosevelt's goodwill and good manners for complete and wholehearted support only to find when he sought an unqualified endorsement from her she quickly retreated from his overeager embrace.

"I've been taken into the family," Upton happily advised reporters some days later in his room at New York's Hotel Algonquin, adding that Postmaster-General James Aloysius Farley had told him "Just call me Jim," and "Mr. Morgenthau said to me: 'Whatever you need, just ask for it.' "

In Washington, D.C., Sinclair called on Harold Ickes, Harry Hopkins, Jesse Jones, Henry Wallace, and Supreme Court Justice Louis Brandeis. On this same trip he saw Father Coughlin in Detroit and, as with Roosevelt, came away with the false impression that Coughlin would endorse him prior to Election Day.

In California, meanwhile, a ten-million-dollar campaign of slander and vilification was building to a crescendo. It set a pattern often imitated but never again equaled in the Golden State. Not until almost forty years later, and then only on a national level, guided by southern Californians, would there be another campaign of such ferality, venality, and obscene extravagance as that mounted against Sinclair.

The leader of the forces against Sinclair was Louis B. Mayer of Metro-Goldwyn-Mayer. He made up in bullying brutality what he lacked in fairness of face, form, or sense of justice, and he represented all the other movie magnates. They were fearful of losing their immense fortunes, as men often are who know that these were made not by talent or hard work but by an extraordinary good fortune that could disappear quite as uncontrollably as it arrived. Having made money, Mayer in the classic pattern of the parvenu, was now seeking social stature, chiefly as a money raiser for the Republican Party. But even more than ambition, it was terror that moved him and other movie sachems. As Billy Wilder, recently arrived from Austria, noted, Sinclair "scared the hell out of the community. They all thought him to be a most dangerous Bolshevik beast."

Throughout the movie industry, simple extortion was thought to be the most efficient way to raise vast sums for the defeat of Sinclair and the reelection of Governor Frank Merriam. At first every employee at M-G-M earning over one hundred dollars a week was expected to contribute a day's pay. But soon not only stars and the highest paid employees but also "Stenographers, technicians, writers, and all other employees [were tapped]. . . . few studios were not involved in the drive. . . . Many employees were given blank checks made out to Louis B. Mayer. . . . [an anonymous and indignant scenario writer stated] 'At our studio the head man asked for the donations and the implication was obvious. . . .' "

Only a handful of movie people had the resources—spiritual or economic—to stand up and oppose the studios, among them Charlie Chaplin, Dorothy Parker, Nunnally Johnson, Jean Harlow, James Cagney, and Morrie Ryskind, who, with Gene Fowler, organized a writers' committee for Sinclair. A court action was begun in an effort to stop the coercion, but EPIC had too much to do and too little time or money.

One of the most foolish threats made by movie executives was that the studios would close and move to Florida if Sinclair were elected. "That's the biggest 'piece of bunk' in this entire election," Upton told delighted audiences. "They couldn't move out if they wanted to. It would cost them too much. Their investment here is too great. Besides, think of what those big Florida mosquitoes would do to some of our film sirens. Why, one bite on the nose could bring a $50,000 production loss." And he added, he just might "put the state into making pictures. . . . I'll ask Charlie Chaplin to run that part of the show."

But at the nadir of the Depression with one out of seven people in Los Angeles County on relief, it was difficult to laugh even at the most preposterous threats and it was in playing to the voters' economic fears that the studios did their most outrageous and effective job. Fake newsreels were made and distributed free to California theaters in which well-dressed, nice-looking people spoke favorably of Merriam and criminal-looking types with Russian accents expressed their hopes for Sinclair's victory. The most frightening film showed trainloads of hobos on their way to California to partake of the largesse Sinclair would provide with the taxpayers' money and to compete for the already too few jobs.

Although this was widely said to be the work of Mayer, after the election, Irving Thalberg, the supposed gentle intellectual, admitted: "I made those shorts. Nothing is unfair in politics. We could sit down here and figure dirty things all night, and every one of them would be all right in a political campaign. . . . I used to be a boy orator for the Socialist party on the East Side in New York. Do you think Tammany ever gave me a chance to be heard?"

Other industries besides the movies worked feverishly and spent lavishly in the hope of defeating the pariah. The oil companies, the railroads, and the public utilities, all of whom had raped the state's citizenry for years were generous and fervid in the face of this threat.

But it was the California newspapers who most effectively savaged Sinclair.

That same William Randolph Hearst whom Upton had predicted at the beginning of the century would be elected President and lead his countrymen to a New Jerusalem came back to California to join the "Stop Sinclair" campaign. Originally he had pronounced Sinclair "a perfectly well-meaning man but a wholly impractical theorist" and chided the American people for "traipsing after every irresponsible adventurer with a penny whistle to play and a seductive song to sing"—a charge proven untrue by at least the number of times Hearst himself had been refused public office by the electorate.

But when Hearst saw that Sinclair was in fact favored to win the election, the "well-meaning" description vanished. Hearst's Los Angeles *Herald-Express* regularly attacked the "Communist" and along with a number of other California newspapers printed a picture of a hobo mob arriving by freight train to take over the state. The "hobos" were soon recognized as actors in Warner Brothers' *Wild Boys of the Road*, but the fake stills like the fake newsreels helped convince many Californians that however little they had, they would lose even that if Sinclair were elected.

Don Belding, later a partner of Foote, Cone & Belding but then West Coast manager of Lord & Thomas, admitted: "We hired the scum of the streets to carry placards through the cities 'Vote for Upton Sinclair,' and speculated that if the campaign had lasted a little longer the whole thing might have backfired and Sinclair been elected."

Joseph Knowland's Oakland *Tribune*, George T. Cameron's San Francisco *Chronicle*, and every newspaper in California opposed the author of *The Brass Check*, but none with the malevolent virulence of Harry Chandler's Los Angeles *Times*. After Upton had exposed the fake movies and stills of the hoboes, he began joking with his audiences that Chandler himself had come to Los Angeles as a bum on a freight train and hadn't amounted to much until he married the boss' daughter at *The Times*. Turning in the direction of the Times Building, Upton would cup his hands to his mouth and shout, "Come on, Harry! Give the *other* bums a chance!" and the audience roared. But Chandler was not amused.

Hiram Johnson, senator from California from 1917 to 1945, once said of Chandler's father-in-law, "In San Francisco . . . with all the criminals who have disgraced us we have never had anything so degraded, so disreputable, and so vile as Harrison Gray Otis. . . . He sits in senile dementia, with gangrened heart and rotting brain . . . chattering in impotent rage against decency and morality. . . ." If in little else, Chandler was at least his father-in-law's equal in spewing vitriol, and in this campaign he set an example followed first throughout California and later across the country.

What was mounted against the muckraker by an alliance of all who feared him was "the first all-out public relations *Blitzkrieg* in American politics." Much of the most effective propaganda was the work of two press agents, Clem Whitaker and Leone Baxter, who wisely lost no time trying to "sell" the Republican candidate but instead concentrated on vilifying Sinclair. "We had one objective," Baxter confessed later, "to keep him from becoming Governor. But because he was a good·man, we were sorry we had to do it that way."

"That way" consisted of secluding themselves for three days with Upton's writings and putting together a collection of accurate quotations, misquotations, partial quotations, outright inventions, and lies. They devised a plan of attack that would serve to convince a wide variety of voters that Upton was a monster and the only possible course was to "Hold your nose and vote for Merriam."

According to Whitaker: "It was one we hated to handle. Sinclair was an old friend of the Whitaker family. It's always difficult to fight against a man you like personally . . . Upton was beaten . . . because he had written books."

Upton had predicted precisely this kind of attack. "Of course I am vulnerable as candidate, because I have written so much, and not always temperately. They are going to take passages out of 'Love's Pilgrimage' and call it 'free love'; passages out of 'The Profits of Religion' and hurt the feelings of the various religious sects. Their main effort will be to pin the Red label upon us."

Millions of pamphlets appeared issued by organizations real and imaginary. A "Veterans' Non-Partisan League" asked: "Is Upton Sinclair for Americanism or Communism?" and answered its own question by listing among Sinclair's "associates" William Z. Foster who had run for President in 1932 on the Communist Party ticket and "Paxton Hibben, deceased, whose ashes now rest in Russia where they were buried by Communists."

Another leaflet, "Out of His Own Mouth Shall He Be Judged," gave quotations proving the candidate was for sexual promiscuity, especially among the young, against marriage, and against all religions as well as all their ministers. Since he was confused with Sinclair Lewis, he was burdened not only with his own sins but with *Elmer Gantry* and the sin of standing up in church and defying God to stop his watch.

Law and order would disappear, Upton's detractors warned—the San Francisco General Strike "was but a minute sample of what California may expect with Sinclair in Sacramento."

EPIC phones were tapped; EPIC mail was stolen; and Upton warned: "Of course thousands of persons have my letterheads and signature. These can easily be reproduced; so do not be surprised if, in the last days of the campaign, you see facsimile letters, or photographs of letters, in which I call for the overthrow of our Government, or for the abolition of the Christian religion, or the nationalization of our virgins, or the cutting up of babies for soup-meat."

There were reports and warnings, some responsible and some paranoid, that "proofs" of a direct link with Moscow would be planted in an EPIC headquarters or that the Republicans were giving huge sums of money to Townsendites to help defeat Sinclair. Tom Mooney warned Sinclair that he might "become the victim of some Agent Provocature's [sic] rash and murderous deed at the last minute when you will not have time to explain that your enemies did it and made it appear that it is done by your supporters. . . . The very people who framed me are the ones who perpetrated the crime they accused me of. Look at . . . the Reichstag Fire two days before the election in Germany; Hitler's gang did it and accused the communists of it."

In order to defeat Sinclair, money had been raised not only in California but from Texas oilmen as well, and many non-politicians were spending it. "How much money was poured into the campaign never will be known with exactness. Only a fraction of it passed through the hands of the Republican

Campaign Committee. Most of it was spent directly by the financial and industrial interests which sprang openly into the fight. One California official has fixed $10,000,000 as a conservative estimate of the total amount spent to re-elect Governor Merriam. It could hardly have been less."

In the face of this extravagant campaign against him, Upton's own campaign was run along the lines of a church social, a covered-dish dinner, or a graduating class picnic. But its obvious effectiveness, the snowballing strength of these political tyros, had the political pros worried, unable to appraise the situation.

So many employers had threatened to fire any employee working for EPIC and to reduce staff or close shop if Sinclair were elected governor that although the unemployed were willing to admit being for Sinclair, no one with a job could afford to. Even to out-of-town reporters, who might in fact turn out to be management spies, almost everyone with a job said he or she would vote for Merriam, and yet the EPIC rallies were crowded with people who were obviously not unemployed.

The EPIC organization grew spontaneously, haphazardly, and without any significant funds from the central headquarters, but it grew tremendously nevertheless until by November 6 there were almost two thousand EPIC clubs all over the state. Nearly half a million people had voted for Sinclair in the primary and an extraordinary number of these felt a personal need to work for their candidate. The EPIC clubs really were clubs of like-minded people, most of whom had not known each other previously. There was a family atmosphere in many of these clubs. Workers helped one another in private matters as well as working for their candidate. With feelings perhaps not unlike the early Christians, they conspired to sneak notices into their church bulletins, congratulating one another on each little victory and consoling each other for the many defeats. And many formed friendships in these clubs that lasted for years after the election.

These amateurs each did whatever he or she could do to spread the faith. They sold Upton's books and pamphlets, an EPIC newspaper, campaign buttons, song sheets, cakes and cookies, old clothes, and junk. They organized barbecues, banquets, auctions, sewing bees, dances, and even rodeos, anything to attract voters and raise funds to attract more voters.

Nothing so astounded the reporters from the East as seeing people pay admission to a political rally when most politicians had to spend huge sums on advertising and entertainment and refreshments to attract a crowd. Anyone who could not afford to pay a quarter or a dime to attend was of course admitted free of charge, but as the primary campaign ended, more than ten thousand supporters in San Francisco flocked to hear Sinclair at the Civic Auditorium, paying twenty-five cents a head downstairs, ten cents in the balcony and many gave again when the hat was passed.

That such a collection was often taken up at these meetings after most of the audience had already paid to get in especially frightened and infuriated EPIC's opponents, because it demonstrated the vitality of the movement.

The EPIC campaign financed itself entirely on the money collected by the stalwarts of the EPIC clubs, many of whom were recent converts from other True Beliefs and would soon move on again. They had been Rosicrucians or Utopians and would later become Technocrats or Bahais or adherents to some pseudo-Oriental cult. Many had come from small towns out of state to what they dreamed would be their New Jerusalem. When they hadn't found it, they determined to create it in the great metropolis in a desperate effort to find their own lost consequence, and so became twentieth-century Petrists or Thomistes, following after now one archimandrite, now another, and not infrequently several simultaneously.

Because of this obvious need of religious exaltation in Sinclair's crowds, his opponents induced Aimee Semple McPherson and others of the cloth in October 1934 to stage a mighty pageant in Los Angeles's Shrine Auditorium. Upton was exposed as "the red devil" who was leading his forces of evil to the long prophesied Armageddon where the American Constitution along with the sanctity of marriage and motherhood would be destroyed unless Californians forthwith got with God and Frank Merriam. Reading aloud from *The Profits of Religion,* a clergyman at the pageant revealed Sinclair's alliance with Lucifer—although what was read aloud was in fact Upton's rewrite of the words of Jesus.

But the bulk of Upton's supporters were ordinary citizens seeking a better way than they had witnessed nationally under Harding, Coolidge, and Hoover, and in California for the last forty years under relentlessly Republican governors.

Although they could not vote, students were enthusiastic workers for EPIC, playing such a large role as would not be duplicated again in America for decades. They knew his published views about education and compulsory military training and were grateful to him for reaffirming them. The alliance of intellectuals and youth greatly encouraged Sinclair who wrote his daughter-in-law: "The movement is going like wild fire. I talked to the graduate students of the University of Southern California at luncheon yesterday and the place was so packed that they had to put a loud speaker outside on the campus. More than one dozen professors volunteered active campaign work."

American messiahs from Billy Sunday through Billy Graham have found whooping and howling, wiggling and waving, to be indispensables of successful salvationism. But Upton would have none of it. "He of all is the least bombastic, the least bunkfull, the most independent and thoughtful," *Collier's* told its readers. "He is much less feverish than his competitors. Unlike the conventional aspirant he has not chased after the masses; rather the masses have flocked after him. On the professional political tongue his speeches would be rabble-rousers, the bellowing of the demagogue. But he doesn't bellow. He is noticeably devoid of platform mannerisms of posturing, of studied declamatory arts. There is nothing at all new in anything he says. It is merely the world-old-gospel of the underdog, streamlined and air-conditioned. And yet as he speaks in his slow, precise, unaffected voice these thousands hang tensely upon every syllable as if every word and every thought were new and fresh as tomorrow morning's dew. A normal child could understand what he is saying. This lack of surface fire in the man fascinates you. Here's a prophet, follow him or not."

The New York Times too commented on "the appeal of the Sinclair stump manner. A quiet, slight figure, with a pleasant smile constantly on his lips, suggesting inner certainty rather than humor or political winsomeness, Mr. Sinclair avoids emotional appeals and the stage tricks of fighting virility. In an even, bland voice, almost a monotone, with all the intimacy of an informal lecture on the better society in some one's front parlor, he talks at once plainly and brilliantly. With uncanny definiteness and concreteness he creates out of things which have not happened yet but are about to happen, a California as real as—if manifestly more agreeable than—the daily tangle of Los Angeles traffic."

Except for the *EPIC News* or when he spoke on the radio, whose station owners required that he submit the text of his speech in advance, Sinclair never wrote out his speeches nor even made notes. He was, after all, only repeating what he had believed with all his heart for many years.

The content of his speeches, as well as his style, affected his audiences. He was effective because he was so obviously expressing his convictions. In the same simple language in which he had written about them for years, he now spoke about his views on economics, politics, and justice. He talked sense to the people and so he could assert: "Whatever else may happen, it is a fact that we have made the people of California talk and think about the realities of this depression."

Upton was one of the first of many who transformed from a crackpot idea to a part of conventional wisdom the premise that society is best served when most people have enough income to buy what society has determined to produce.

All over the state, to large groups and small, he explained the various details of his program. He was never more delighted than when Republican or Communist hecklers appeared. He would invite them up on the platform and then demolish their arguments to the delight of his audiences, who loved the demonstration of fair play as much as they loved the fight.

The Communists were running their own candidate for governor and attacking Sinclair not only locally and nationally but even in the Soviet Union. Earl Browder later said that the EPIC campaign was what convinced him to go to Moscow in the spring of 1936. His purpose was to reverse the Comintern order that the American Communist Party actively support Franklin Roosevelt for reelection. Browder felt certain that the direct support of the Communists would cost the President more votes than it got him. He was able to persuade the Comintern, he said, that by running their own Presidential candidate, the Communists would indirectly help Roosevelt by partially clearing him of the curse of Communist support.

In Sinclair's case, he had the worst of both worlds—he had been called a Communist too long. Even when the Communists attacked him and ran a candidate against him, these could no more undo the damage than his denying the lie and repeatedly insisting "we should see every destitute man and woman in the State of California made independent and secure by democratic and strictly American methods."

One of Upton's campaign practices was especially impressive to voters who had been made increasingly skeptical of politicians by the earlier exposures of Sinclair, Steffens, and the other muckrakers. He revealed the individual bribes offered EPIC in the form of campaign contributions. These ranged from fifteen thousand dollars each from insurance companies desirous of part of the state's business to fifty thousand dollars from the rock-sand-and-gravel interests to "anything within reason" from the gamblers. Individual state offices were sought for different prices—Upton was offered fifteen thousand dollars for the post of Fish and Game Commissioner.

Whatever may have been his real feelings when he began the race and despite what he would later occasionally allege to the contrary, as the campaign heightened in intensity, Sinclair wanted to become governor. His happy and optimistic letters to Craig from all over the state revealed his joy in the enthusiasm of his immense flock and of his devoted disciples. The crusade was also a holiday on which dishes of normally forbidden ice cream often replaced the usual sensible meals. "I cannot tell you how unreal the world of books seems to me now," he wrote Floyd Dell. "I doubt if I ever write any more books! Of course I may find that I am mistaken on November 6, but that is the way it looks at the moment."

It looked so not only to Upton, but also to the gamblers in Los Angeles' Spring Street, who in the weeks after he won the nomination were quoting odds of seven to five that the muckraker would win the election. Terrified by the gamblers, who replaced the soothsayers, sibyls, priests, and prophets of an earlier time, Upton's enemies redoubled their efforts. A suit to disqualify twenty-five thousand Los Angeles voters for allegedly fraudulent registration was defeated by Sinclair's forces, but the threats of fines and even jail sentences nevertheless successfully frightened many of his supporters away from the polls.

The campaign was raising issues of such wide interest, and had begun as such a David and Goliath match, that reporters from all over the country were sent to California and in journals all over the world pundits tried to interpret the local significance of Sinclair's battle. Never before or since has there been such out-of-state-press interest in a governor's race. *The New York Times* alone had half a dozen by-line writers doing articles as well as anonymous reporters.

A series of short articles in *Time* culminated in a cover story. "What will happen in California on Nov. 6 is an enormous question mark placed at the end of a tense and terrible political campaign. . . . Not only will California then choose a new Governor but all the rest of the country will be supplied with a gauge to measure the size and significance of the New Radicalism. . . . No politician since William Jennings Bryan has so horrified and outraged the Vested Interests. . . . They hate him as a muckraker. They hate him as a Socialist. They hate him as an I.W.W. sympathizer. They hate him as a 'free-love' cultist. They hate him as a Single Taxer. They hate him as an atheist. . . .

"He has a face that looks like Henry Ford gone slightly fey, a pleasing voice, a wide smile and immense persuasiveness on the rostrum. . . . Prime epithet used against Upton Sinclair is that he is 'an agent of Moscow.' Fact is, Upton Sinclair is as American as pumpkin pie.

"To be a national sensation once more is felicity's zenith for Upton Sinclair, a fact which neither his enemies nor his friends have properly assayed. He is not a crackpot, but he is inordinately vain. He has not made a livelihood of scandal-mongering; he has written because he was hurt. He is not an atheist; he is disgusted by commercialized religion. He is not a 'free-love' cultist; he is an ascetic. His soft manners, his kindly eye, his

intense, humorless and uncritical idealism, his obsession with the struggle of
Labor and Capital for the fruits of Industry mark him for the archetype of
old-fashioned Socialist. Yet the Socialists have out-grown him and Grade A
radicals believe that if EPIC is given a trial, its failure will set U.S. radicalism
back 50 years."

Time published Sinclair's irate answering letter which ended: "You also
write of my 'inordinate vanity.' That is a matter of opinion: you have yours
and I have mine. My opinion is that you live in a world so depraved that the
conceptions of sincerity, integrity, and self-sacrifice are wholly lacking from
your mentality." Below the letter appeared only: "Time's opinion is that its
world would be duller without Upton Sinclair.—Ed."

The magazine's treatment of US had, in fact, been relatively fair and
even admiring.

Many weekly and monthly national magazines responded to their
readers' interest, including *Esquire*, who asked Theodore Dreiser to do an
article on the candidate. "I would like to write the thing about Upton
Sinclair very much," Dreiser replied, "because I know his books and I know
that he was twenty years ahead of the rest of the critics of America who are
now so loud in their condemnations. His foresight, in my judgment, is only
to be matched by their vociferous hindsight."

The article that Sinclair believed most influenced the campaign appeared
in *Literary Digest.* It revealed that the magazine's poll showed Merriam
would get 62 percent of the vote and Upton only 25 percent. Research by
EPIC workers proved that 75 percent of the ballots had been sent to
registered Republicans and that some two hundred ballots had been passed
out by one Los Angeles employer to his employees. It is probable that
ineptitude, rather than guile, was the cause of the magazine's incorrect
prediction as would also be true in its terminal error regarding the
Presidential race in 1936.

However, as Upton pointed out: "The error did us irreparable harm. It
encouraged our enemies, it weakened our friends, and it shifted the betting
odds; in short, it started a chain reaction of unfavorable events. Many people
were waiting to know which band wagon to climb onto, and now they knew.
Some of these people occupied important positions. I have good reason to
believe that it was the *Literary Digest* Poll which started the bad news out of
Washington."

But although the out-of-state press delighted in reporting on Sinclair's
efforts to "take the wild beast of greed by the beard," the California papers,
except for articles devoted to calumniating him, covered his activities and

speeches in a great cloud of silence. To reach the California electorate Upton had only radio, which he could ill afford, and his own weekly tabloid the *EPIC News.* The paper's circulation grew from twenty thousand a week to almost two million in its last two issues before the election, a figure Harry Chandler himself might have envied.

The opposition's chief scare tactics were economic. Sinclair's joking remark to Harry Hopkins that "when he was elected half the unemployed of the United States would rush to California" was characterized as a serious prediction already in the process of coming true. The State Registrar of Motor Vehicles announced that the flood of unemployed to California had "reached a daily average of about 100 persons, or about half the proportions of the famous gold rush of 1849."

When critics called Upton's writing humorless, he regularly pointed out examples of his written attempts at humor that were taken seriously to his disadvantage. In terms of harming him, no other was as bad as this jest to Hopkins.

Not only the California papers, of which local citizens could be justifiably suspicious, but also the *Wall Street Journal, Time,* and other out-of-state journals, which tended to lend credibility to local tales, published reports of an enormous flight of investment capital from California and of real estate contracts being written with a clause making them invalid in the event Sinclair was elected. According to *The New York Times,* in the last weeks before election day "a sense of Armageddon hangs in the bland California air."

As Sinclair's position weakened, the Bank of America's A. P. Giannini and others who could not stomach Merriam and saw that some change was mandatory tried to convince Sinclair to withdraw in favor of the Progressive candidate, Raymond Haight. Sinclair suggested instead that Haight pull out and endorse him.

Preparations for departure from Sinclair's ship and even outright ratting were soon evident as it daily became clearer that the one thing necessary to guarantee Sinclair's victory, Roosevelt's endorsement (promised or not), was in fact not forthcoming. Word came that neither Harry Hopkins nor even Secretary Harold Ickes, who was already going to San Francisco on other business, would speak in support of Sinclair, despite the *EPIC News* announcement that they would. Postmaster-General Farley repudiated his earlier letter supporting Sinclair's candidacy. It was, he now discovered, a mistake, a form letter with a rubber stamp signature, sent by an incompetent secretary. Senator McAdoo revealed that speeches for Democratic candidates in Arizona and Utah would preclude his reaching California before election day and George Creel, whom Upton had beaten in the primary, now repudiated his party's candidate.

Republican newspapers, usually not the most reliable reporters of Roosevelt's actions let alone his motives, apprised their readers that the President was secretly repudiating Upton, or at least "Withholding Aid From Sinclair as Strategy To 'Save Face' . . . [so] That California Rejection of Radical Should Not Reflect on Democrats Nationally."

The unkindest cut, however, was an at least tacit secret alliance made by Comptroller of the Currency J. F. T. O'Connor with Governor Merriam. If Merriam won, he would admit it was only with Democratic help and no defeat for the New Deal, and in return Roosevelt would not endorse Sinclair. O'Connor was not Roosevelt's agent, but many interpreted his visit to Merriam as an unofficial laying on of hands for the governor and a repudiation of Sinclair.

The New York Times reported two to one odds quoted in California against Sinclair, who would be defeated, the paper now predicted, by two hundred thousand votes. His campaign " . . . is more than a political crusade, . . . in the opinion of these more sober Californians. Its roots are in religion—the 'old-time religion'—and its goal is peace and happiness this side of the river. . . . Had Mr. Sinclair stopped with the enunciation of his principles, the belief here is that he could not have been stopped or even checked in his march to the Governor's chair.

"But he went into method and there his anti-capitalistic, anti-profit proposals flared out to scare this community out of its boots.

"It is the view now that Mr. Sinclair's defeat would but add impetus to his crusade."

Sinclair lost the election. But he received 879,537 votes to Merriam's 1,138,620 and Haight's 302,519, and these figures were not hard to interpret. Merriam had received less than a majority of the votes and had there not been a Progressive candidate, Upton would probably have been governor. Had the President not withheld his endorsement, Sinclair, even with Haight in the race, would probably have been swept into office in the country-wide affirmation of Roosevelt that propelled Democrats by the dozens into governors' mansions and both Houses of Congress—including Harry S. Truman who was introduced to the Senate.

Nor were these results lost locally or nationally on observers who wanted to recognize rather than ignore their significance—that things had to happen in America if the Fascism or Communism engulfing the rest of the world were to be avoided here. To A. P. Giannini and right up to President Roosevelt, for example, the results indicated that the moment for Social Security legislation had arrived. No less able than Disraeli at stealing the Whigs' clothes when they were bathing, Roosevelt joyfully appropriated from the left and even from the right whatever programs and policies he wanted.

In less than a year, Roosevelt sent to the Congress a tax message designed to redistribute radically wealth and power in America by the same means Sinclair had proposed in his EPIC plan—increased inheritance taxes, a gift tax, and graduated corporate and individual income taxes. It is, of course, impossible to determine with any accuracy the comparative degrees to which similar influences acted on Roosevelt to bring him increasingly throughout the balance of his Presidency closer to Sinclair's views. Frankfurter played a role, as did Roosevelt's growing anger at the essential selfishness of most businessmen.

Sinclair's ideas, large and small, expressed during the campaign affected men in Roosevelt's administrations as well as many important citizens who themselves influenced Roosevelt and his successors. Upton had issued a White Paper, "Music, Dramatic and Allied Arts under EPIC," on state support for artists and the arts that anticipated and influenced Roosevelt's Federal Art Project.

Thurman Arnold headed the Antitrust Division of the Department of Justice and to many was the chief symbol of FDR's determination that America's citizens rather than its corporations should be the country's main concern. He wrote Upton "your book 'The Jungle,' which I read years ago in college, had as much influence on me as any book I can think of."

One measure of the degree of Sinclair's influence in 1934 was a poll the *Literary Digest* took of two hundred and forty American newspapers asking who were the outstanding persons in the world for that year. Sinclair was preceded by only three: Roosevelt, Hitler, and Mussolini.

Increasingly, since the days of Roosevelt's "Brain Trust," among those who surround and advise American Presidents, replacing the royal almoners and jesters of earlier societies, are prominent economists of the moment. Sinclair throughout his career influenced the social point of view of economists, both at first hand and at second and third, whether they agreed with him or not. As he influenced such men as John Kenneth Galbraith, Paul A. Samuelson, Henry Hazlitt, and John W. Gardner, he influenced the country.

"He clearly contributed to the dissatisfaction of many regarding the effects of the system," wrote Milton Friedman, Goldwater's economic adviser, "and helped lay the groundwork for the development of a philosophical attitude among intellectuals favorable to government intervention. . . . In retrospect, it seems to me that the shift of opinion towards greater and greater governmental control of economic activity is a shift that threatens personal freedom as well as the welfare of the masses. It was far more difficult to see in prospect."

The chairman of President Kennedy's Council of Economic Advisers, Walter W. Heller, diagnosed that on himself "there was undoubtedly a significant indirect impact. . . . I vividly remember the impact that some of the revelations in *The Jungle* and *Oil!* had on me. The effect was to reinforce, through his vivid and pointed writing and sense of outrage, the determination I already had to concentrate on the policy of applied aspects of economics in a career combining university work, public education, and public service."

In California, the EPIC campaign proved to be one of the most successful experiments in mass education ever performed. As Arthur Schlesinger, Jr., observed, "Sinclair got licked all right. But the manner of his licking reshaped California politics for a generation. The Republican success marked a new advance in the art of public relations, in which advertising men now believed they could sell or destroy political candidates as they sold one brand of soap and defamed its competitor. Humdingery and dynamite dominated California politics from then on. In another twenty years, the techniques of manipulation employed so crudely in 1934 would spread east, achieve a new refinement, and begin to dominate the politics of the nation. . . . rich businessmen had corrupted the democratic process. The success of this effort led some to wonder whether democracy and the business system were compatible. California's susceptibility to Communism in the next years dated in part from the trauma of the Sinclair defeat."

But good resulted from the campaign too. The California Legislature had been so terrified in 1934 by the prospect of Sinclair's victory that it had placed most state positions under Civil Service.

A number of EPIC candidates went on to successful political careers, including Culbert Olson, who was elected governor four years later, and Sheridan Downey, Sinclair's running mate, who went to the United States Senate from California in 1938. It was Downey's decision not to run for reelection to the Senate that resulted in the fight between Helen Gahagan Douglas and Richard M. Nixon.

"The EPIC campaign thus left behind a ferment of local radicalism not unlike that stirred by Floyd Olson and the La Follettes—a new popular militancy, fairly loyal to Roosevelt and the Democratic party but constituting a leftward pressure on the New Deal."

Once reelected governor, Merriam embraced a number of Sinclair's proposals, including a state income tax, with the result that the San Francisco *Argonaut*, which had during the campaign attacked Sinclair and puffed Merriam now asked: "Would Sinclair have done worse in the gubernatorial chair than the man that defeated him? It may well be doubted. He might even have done better for he had an atom or two of genius in his composition while all one can discern in Merriam is cobwebs from an empty skull."

Twenty-four years later, as Sinclair was reaching his eightieth birthday, a Los Angeles reporter asked him how would California be different if he had won in 1934. "We did win. We gave California and all the other States an exciting awareness of what democracy really is. F.D.R. was listening to us. And a young District Attorney in Alameda County was listening. A fellow by the name of Earl Warren."

Sinclair's reaction to his defeat was typical. In a few weeks he whipped out a new book, *I, Candidate for Governor—and How I Got Licked.*

Upton Sinclair, about to address a crowd on July 1, 1934, at Inglewood during his EPIC campaign for the governorship of California.

Working in the garden of his Beverly Hills mansion during the campaign.

Broadcasting by radio a campaign speech from his home.

The *Sacramento Bee*, like all California newspapers, repeated endlessly in editorials, cartoons, and news stories that if Sinclair was elected governor, the poor of the whole country would descend on the state to enjoy the welfare programs he proposed.

An example of the "funny money" designed to discredit Sinclair's campaign promises and distributed widely by his opponents.

The UAW sent out publicity stills explaining its use of Sinclair's novel *The Flivver King* in the effort to unionize Ford Motor Company.

Mary Craig Sinclair.

Governor and Mrs. Nelson Rockefeller with Upton and his third wife, May (seated).

Upton Sinclair on his eighty-
ninth birthday.

At eighty-nine at the White House with President Lyndon Johnson on December 15, 1967, for the signing of a new bill designed to protect against abuses in meat-packing that still existed sixty-one years after *The Jungle*. (Wide World)

CHAPTER XXIV

"Enlisted for the War"

The rights and interests of the laboring man will be protected and cared for—not by the labor agitators, but by the Christian gentlemen to whom God has given control of the property rights of the country. GEORGE F. BAER

ON THE DAY AFTER HIS DEFEAT Sinclair smilingly told reporters, "We are just starting. This election has been only a skirmish and our people are enlisted for the war." In fact, however, he would henceforth fight the war not as a politician, but as a writer. The EPIC movement continued only for a short time because as he withdrew more and more from it to escape the inevitable squabbles and intrigues, the movement had no acceptable leader.

Craig and his friends maintained that they were relieved that he was not governor. "As I read that this cup had passed from you," Albert Einstein wrote, "I rejoiced even though it had not gone exactly according to your wish."

Upton was later informed by a fellow writer, whom he believed, that a California businessman had written his will, obtained a revolver, and made firm plans to shoot the EPIC candidate at a radio station on election night had he won the governorship. The reclusive Craig's relief at Sinclair's defeat was hysterically joyful, and Upton too maintained thereafter: "It was a relief to me to have coughed up that EPIC alligator."

Upton's next book, *How I Got Licked,* was first serialized in papers all over the country, including many of the California papers that had taken part in the dirty tricks the book described. But the author was not bitter and had not lost his sense of humor. He wrote the book's publishers two days after the election: "An important feature of it will be the cartoons, many of which are good and clever—in spite of being against us."

He was, however, at least as angry as he had always been to see the proper functioning of democracy perverted by the rich. "What beat us was money, then more money, and still more money. . . . see what money can do in America and what it is prepared to do when its power is threatened."

Sinclair was happy to be able to turn his full attention once again to his usual work. During the hectic year of his candidacy he had had to turn over much of his correspondence to others. But even so, hundreds of matters of especially keen concern to him he had handled himself. He had kept trying to salvage something from the Eisenstein disaster; he had sent his circular letters to his customer list and had continued to sell the list to others; he had helped unknown writers; and he was one of the very few who bothered in September 1933 to attend the funeral of Horace Liveright. In addition, no one but he could make the many decisions required by his widespread publication overseas.

From the beginning of Sinclair's own success to the very end of his life, in nothing was he more consistent than in his efforts to help other writers. In 1939, reviewing *Grapes of Wrath,* he wrote: "I have come to the age when I know I won't be writing forever. I remember reading how Elijah put his mantle on the shoulders of Elisha. John Steinbeck can have my old mantle if he has any use for it."

He came out of the campaign for the governorship so deeply in debt that it took his day and night effort for the next several years to get even again—six books in 1935 and 1936 alone, in addition to countless shorter works. Like Balzac, Sinclair was almost always working feverishly to pay off his debts; but the former's were incurred in the gratification of pleasures of the flesh, while Upton's resulted from the gratification of the no less burning desires of the salvationist.

The quickest way for Upton to make money was by debating and lecturing. On two tours in 1935 he traveled by automobile more than twenty thousand miles with Craig and Duchess, their German shepherd, and earned more than seven thousand dollars. He also debated from California to New York with opponents as disparate as Norman Thomas and Congressman Hamilton Fish, who was being mentioned as a possible Republican candidate for the Presidency. Upton was an effective debater and his Republican opponent in the campaign for governor had wisely ignored repeated challenges to debate. In addition, Upton wrote magazine articles about his experiences lecturing, making fun of himself and the "white-haired ladies and church deacons [who] come to enjoy the cool breezes from the lake and at the same time have their minds entertained by high class vaudeville [at Chautauqua]. . . . Strolling on the shady walks you hear the ladies debating—shall they take in the Sinclair-Fish show, or shall they play bridge this afternoon, and wait for the Swiss yodelers and the Belgian bell-ringers in the evening."

During the lectures he had candy butchers selling his books, and, in fact, his efforts to earn money in a variety of different ways from the same work occasionally caused complaints. "We have no objection to Mr. Sinclair selling books, but we don't want that to be made the main feature of the meeting. Report has reached us that in Butte, Montana, Mr. Sinclair spent much of his time reading from his books and would stop his speech occasionally to let the agents pass through the audience to sell them. This caused a very unfavorable reaction and was anything but pleasing to the sponsors."

Despite his past experiences, he continued to try to make money writing for the theater and the movies. His play *Depression Island* was refused production and his proposal for a movie "musical comedy kidding the Townsend Plan" understandably got nowhere. Another movie idea "of having Cervantes also appear as Don Quixote, or . . . dissolve back and forth between reality and fiction" was less impossible but proved to be equally unacceptable.

So anxious was Sinclair to reduce his debts that, trading on his fame, he contracted for fifteen hundred dollars to make a week of "personal appearances" at Hollywood's Pantages Theatre to increase audiences at a poorly attended film.

His financial problems were further aggravated as the flow of funds from his millionaire friends diminished. Upton and Craig both found increasingly that their association with Mrs. Gartz, the Crane plumbing fixture heiress, was so trying that they preferred not to cash the checks she sent them and, therefore, felt free to refuse to see her.

Mary Craig's poor health, paranoia, and self-pity had increased during the campaign, and after her father's death in January 1935, although it would seem difficult to believe they could, got worse. A letter she had written after she and Upton had taken tea at the White House with Eleanor Roosevelt was as revealing of its author as it was incorrect about its subject: "Everyone who knows them [the Roosevelts] says she is the boss, & that he just does what she says."

For as Craig's fears increased, so did her need to be boss. She demanded and received from Upton, for example, written promises to refrain from any political activity.

Typical of Upton's submission to the demands of Craig's increasing paranoia was their experience with Irving Stone. Because Sinclair had liked Stone's biography of Jack London, he offered Stone his own papers and submitted to interviews by him in preparation for a new biography. Fearful that Stone might be a Communist or EPIC spy, Craig insisted on the right to eavesdrop on the biographer's interviews and Sinclair agreed, but when Stone learned this, he immediately dropped the project.

Unwilling to wear her false teeth and unwilling to be seen without them, Craig stayed at home while Upton went "to the movies 2 or 3 nights a week alone" and to "intellectual" dinner parties at Charlie Chaplin's, where he met visiting fellow celebrities such as Aldous and Maria Huxley.

Craig usually forbade visits at home by outsiders which precluded the courtesy calls considered *de rigueur* when one reigning liberal monarch visited the territory of another.

She allowed Upton to write Einstein and J. B. Rhine asking for help in getting David a better job as a physicist which was proving difficult to find because "his father is 'poison.' " But when David wrote that he was getting a divorce, Upton refused any financial help because, he explained, he needed every penny to keep his books and pamphlets in print, and despite the fact that David had not asked for money.

The help David got from Meta consisted of a long tirade blaming the young man's sex problems and her own on Upton. From 1940 through 1944, David was in psychoanalysis, successfully dealing with his sexual and other problems related to childhood influences and the obvious indifference to his needs displayed by both his parents. Upton and Craig, both outspoken in their opposition to psychoanalysis, were also offended by the criticism of their treatment of David that his need for analysis implied.

A number of Sinclair's letters responding to David's written criticisms were brutal, for example, a cruel and self-serving reply to David's complaint that Sinclair had not given his own son the liberal advice on sex matters that Lanny Budd's father offered Lanny. "I tell you plainly that I do not care to take any more of it. I have done my best, and the circumstances which have caused your unhappiness throughout your life were wholly beyond my power. I shall be willing and glad to return to a basis of affection with you, but only on the terms set forth in this letter. You do not need to reply unless you care to, . . ."

Two months later he wrote David: "Here is the letter. Destroy it. I had no desire to 'lay down terms,' except one, that my letters to you are not for publication without my consent."

Some of David's letters criticizing his father are missing from the Sinclair files at the Lilly Library. That they existed at one time is proven by Sinclair's answers to at least some of their charges, of which there are copies in the library and of which David has the originals. If these were destroyed or sent back to David by his father, it is a not insignificant action by a man who saved every scrap of paper for posterity.

From time to time, Upton wrote apologetically and even affectionately to his son. "I have . . . only sorrow that I was so ill equipped to be a father. The story of social reformers who failed in their human duties is an ancient one, & that seems to suggest that there is a basic cause for it. So try to forgive me." And: "I love you. I am sorry you are not happy. I am sorry, also, for the many blunders of my life. I am trying to learn & do better."

But when in January 1944 David's work took him to California, Upton refused to see him, after which there was no communication between them for three and a half years. Then, under the happy influence of his second wife, Jean Weidman, whom he had married on April 1, 1944, David resumed corresponding with his father.

Again and again, Craig demanded and received assignments from Upton granting her a half interest in everything he had ever written, and new wills that were no different from the old ones since they all left her everything. These assignments were meaningless, because they gave her only what was already hers by right under California law.

In 1942 the couple left the Pasadena house to which they had returned when they sold the Beverly Hills mansion after the EPIC campaign. They moved to 464 North Myrtle Avenue in Monrovia, and Upton justified such an expenditure by explaining that the Pasadena house had "become the haunt of moths, rats, and black widow spiders." From the two-story, Italian-style villa in Monrovia at the edge of the Sierra Madre mountains, "we can see the Pacific ocean, some 20 or 30 miles away. That is, we could see it when the air was clear, but since the war began Los Angeles has become an industrial district, as smoky as London."

In fact, however, the Monrovia house's chief attraction was that it was a fireproof steel and concrete structure where presumably Upton's papers of thirty-five years would be safe. For Craig was becoming more and more obsessed with fears for the safety not only of the papers, but also for Upton and herself.

The Russians, Craig was convinced, were committed to destroy her and her husband. "Watch out for spies. They don't just report secrets. They find out your family skeletons (if any) & your bank acct. Then they get to work to drag you or needle you into their camp."

Soon even the steel and concrete house at Monrovia was not safe enough and after World War II the couple bought a trailer and moved constantly from small town to small town in southern California, but: "They find us, even in auto-camps where we never use U's name. . . . I'm still investigating 'caves' . . . in North Dakota . . . but this should be secret. New Zealand is probably the best place."

A combination of Craig's worsening health and Upton's working difficulties, inevitable when writing and researching while in full flight from Communist assassins, drove the couple back to Monrovia. Their life there was almost completely reclusive, Upton writing old friends "I have not made an appointment to see anybody during the present year." His cloistered existence was entirely devoted to writing. "Every morning from 9 to 12 I sit in the garden unless it's raining, and type Lanny. After lunch I revise and read what I need for the next day, and in the evening I walk in the garden for an hour or two and think up the next batch. I average four or five typed pages a day and finish the writing of a book in seven or eight months, the rest of the year goes to revision, checking, proofreading etc, and reading . . . for the next vol."

The books Sinclair turned out under the post-EPIC financial pressure were unfortunate. In 1935, *How I Got Licked* was followed by *We, People of America,* "A Four-Year Plan to make over America. To capture the Democratic primaries and use an old party for a new job." This work was so inconsequential that Upton had to write *The Nation, New Republic,* and *Christian Century* and urge them to review it because even they found it unworthy of comment.

His four books in 1936 were almost as bad. *What God Means to Me* was a rehash of his religious views prompted partly by the election campaign charges that Upton was an atheist. When Alfred Kazin in *The New York Times* declared it was "without consistency or substance," Upton wrote he would appeal the verdict to the court of posterity, but the likelihood of a reversal is minimal. The book got Upton a letter from a man in Missouri to whom God had spoken and perhaps more importantly at that moment three thousand dollars from the *Woman's Home Companion* for the serial rights.

A novel called *Co-op* brought admiring letters from Dreiser and John Dewey but deservedly disappeared.

In his first and only book for children, *The Gnomobile,* Upton advocated conservation, but it was an undistinguished book, later to be made by Disney into an undistinguished film.

In *Wally for Queen,* Upton demonstrated only that he had not lost his skill at extracting a maximum of publicity from a minimum of substance—the fact that the mother of the suddenly prominent Mrs. Wallis Warfield Simpson was his cousin. He briefly planned to go to Washington, D.C., and do research there with the help of another cousin, Mrs. Simpson's aunt, "and then write a full length novel portraying the adventures of a young radical bureaucrat in the New Deal."

But instead he wrote two books published in 1937, an impassioned but third-rate novel on the Spanish Civil War, and more important, *The Flivver King,* a novel whose chief character was Henry Ford.

In 1919, while walking with Ford in the Pasadena hills, Upton had tried to convert him to Socialism and when he failed, he had brought King Gillette together with Ford for the same purpose. The razor millionaire had failed too.

Sinclair was more successful with Walter Reuther of the United Automobile Workers and with his brother, Victor, who later wrote: "Upton Sinclair . . . helped found our union . . . helped shape my conscience before I even knew I had a conscience . . . [by] his books, the central treasure of our family library.

"Then in the middle thirties, when the workers in the auto industry began to organize, it was Upton Sinclair who fulfilled every image I had of him by writing the best single organizational document ever written, *The Flivver King.* . . . I suppose, it does not rank with *War and Peace* and *Moby Dick* as among the greatest novels ever written; but I saw Ford workers reading this book aloud to their families, and I heard them say with great satisfaction, 'That's what I meant!' At last someone had come along who expressed for them what they deeply felt should be said.

"There was a time when you could not walk into a union hall in Michigan without seeing the green covers of *The Flivver King* sticking out of the back pocket of a union man. In practically every case, the man had read the book. Now he was carrying it around to refer to in an argument, to prove his point, to reassure him, to be a companion."

Rather than publishing *The Flivver King* to sell in the usual way, Upton had made a deal with the United Automobile Workers to print two hundred thousand paperback copies for them to sell to their members. Although he had been one of the muckrakers who exposed the false advertising practices of the capitalists, he suggested to the UAW officials that they advertise the pamphlet at twenty-five cents a copy so it would seem to be a bargain when it was sold for a dime.

Because he chose this unorthodox way to distribute *The Flivver King,* his only significant book of the seventeen published between the 1934 EPIC campaign and 1940 was not widely reviewed, although Edmund Wilson thought it "very good" and Dos Passos wrote that it "seems to me to be one of your very best pieces and one of the few important things written recently in America."

Years later, Allan Nevins, a biographer of Ford, would write Sinclair: "It is too bad that Ford did not include you in those famous camping trips with Edison, Firestone, and John Burroughs; you would have done him far more good than they did."

In his *Autobiography* and elsewhere, Sinclair stated that Ford would have closed his plants rather than allow them to be unionized but that Mrs. Ford's threat to leave her husband if he did had stopped the millionaire. Sinclair admitted it pleased him to believe that Mrs. Ford's position was a result of her having listened carefully and wordlessly in 1919 to his lectures to her husband.

After *Flivver King*, Upton's next book, *Our Lady*, was so bad that after thirty-nine publishers had refused it, he finally had to resort to an obscure publisher in Emaus, Pennsylvania. His lack of judgment about his own works was confirmed a quarter of a century later when he confessed about *Our Lady*, "I think I love that best of all my books." Especially with regard to his poorest work, he loved to point out how distinguished critics came to precisely opposite views.

Although no longer a practicing politician, Upton tried to influence Franklin Roosevelt's policies by sending the President advice both directly and through Mrs. Roosevelt. He also used such other devices as threatening to run against him in 1936 as a favorite son candidate and to form or support a third party if Roosevelt's programs were not sufficiently liberal.

After the beginning of World War II, however, all Sinclair's letters to both Roosevelts expressed only encouragement and support.

His change of role from active political candidate to occasional political critic did not, however, remove Sinclair as a target. Mencken in a scathing analysis of "The New Deal Mentality" in May 1936 wrote: "My belief is that there are other jitney messiahs among us who, if they had the same power, would use it much more imperiously—for example, the sunkist Utopian, Upton Sinclair. . . . Sinclair is essentially an early Christian demonologist, and sees the Republic as a den swarming with devils. . . . I do not name any of these devils, for they change from time to time as Sinclair proceeds from one revelation to another. But you may be sure that if he is ever thrust into the eminence he dreams of beneath his California upas tree, and finds himself with the power of a Hopkins or a Genghis Khan in his hands, he will fall upon his current abominations with a kind of ferocity that will make that of Hitler and Mussolini look puerile."

In the next two issues of his *American Mercury,* Mencken published letters of Upton's countering the charges against him, but Sinclair's earnestness was at first view no match for Mencken's wit. "I think that is rather atrocious of you, and I am writing to tell you that you ought to be ashamed of yourself. You can search the record of my entire life, including everything I have ever written, and you will not be able to find one sentence to justify it. I have made freedom of discussion the basis of all my preaching. I have stood on Jefferson's fine sentence which I frequently quote, that 'truth has nothing to fear from error where reason is left free to combat it.' "

In addition to his salvationism, what made Upton vulnerable to criticism was his resolute and continuing refusal to speak out against the obscene Soviet trials. As Mencken wrote him: "You protest, and with justice, every time Hitler jails an opponent; but you forget that Stalin and company have jailed and murdered a thousand times as many. It seems to me, and indeed the evidence is plain, that compared to the Moscow brigands and assassins, Hitler is hardly more than a common Ku Kluxer and Mussolini almost a philanthropist.

"If you will denounce the orgy of sadistic fury that has gone on in Russia in terms at least as violent as those you have applied to your political opponents for years past, then I'll be glad to print your denunciation, and to hail you with joy as a convert to fair play."

Fellow Socialists, friends, and disciples were also saddened by Sinclair's position. James T. Farrell, who acknowledged he was Sinclair's literary heir, urged him not to "take my remarks as impertinence," when he wrote: "I am deeply disappointed to find your voice absent from the protest against the trials."

Sidney Hook wrote: "It was thru your writings that I became a socialist in my high-school days, even before I had read Marx," and "you have always been a symbol in my memories of a fighting faith in truth and justice. The people who framed Vanzetti and Mooney were 'pikers' compared to those who staged the Moscow trials."

Dos Passos warned: "I have come to think, especially since my trip to Spain, that civil liberties must be protected at every stage. . . . In Spain I am sure that the introduction of G.P.U. methods by the Communists did as much harm as their tank men, pilots and experienced military men did good. The trouble with an all powerful secret police in the hands of fanatics, or of anybody, is that once it gets started there's no stopping it until it has corrupted the whole body politic. I'm afraid that that's what's happening in Russia."

But despite all these and other warnings, Sinclair refused to criticize the Soviet Union. "The capitalist-Fascist war against the Soviet Union seems to me as certain as anything in human affairs can be. . . . I can only repeat that in my view the Soviet Union is today a city under siege, and its people enjoy only such liberties as are possible under those circumstances."

Upton's refusal to see the truth had several causes including a naïve ignorance of the limits of heroism. "I cannot recall," he wrote Hook, "in the years I have given to studying public questions a psychological absurdity greater than the belief that several score trained revolutionists could be induced by any method whatsoever to go into court and admit actions which they had not committed. Those old Bolsheviks had got used to imprisonment and torture under the Czar and nobody ever made them confess. Stalin could have done no worse, and my belief is that he might have torn them to pieces inch by inch and they would never have said yes if the truth had been no." The Southern myths of invincible heroism and honor taught him in his youth blinded him to the realities of twentieth-century brainwashing and torture.

Upton was, as Arthur Miller wrote of Manuel Cortes, "only as naïve as his millions of contemporaries around the world in that generation, the last European generation to believe in the virtue of the masses and their inevitable triumph." It was the same naïveté that made Upton write: "I think that in a society based upon Production For Use and cooperation, Anti Semitism would be forgotten in less than a generation. I think that the case of Russia proves it."

It was perhaps not too surprising that Upton found it difficult to believe ill of a country in which he was a greater cultural hero than at home and whose leader he addressed frequently and casually as an equal. He believed his messages to Stalin were more likely to reach their destination than those he sent to Roosevelt, and he was no more shy than he had ever been about sending advice to world figures he felt stood in need of it, from Gorki to Gandhi.

In 1938, Upton was negotiating to write a regular column for *Pravda* and to write jointly with a Soviet author a Russian novel he had tentatively titled *Red Gold*.

During this period he continued to make plain that he was not and never had been a Communist, but that he considered himself a more knowledgeable Marxist than most Communists. He often quoted Marx's 1872 statement in Amsterdam: "Of course I must not be supposed to imply that the means to this end [the revolution] will everywhere be the same. We know that special regard must be paid to the institutions, customs and traditions of various lands, and we do not deny that there are certain countries, such as the United States and England, in which the workers may hope to secure their ends by peaceful means." And then he would explain: "All my differences with so-called Marxists come from the fact that I read these words of Marx many years ago and paid attention to them, while the so-called Marxists do not even know they were spoken."

With the advent of the second world war and the Hitler-Stalin alliance, Upton's old position became untenable. At first he merely pointed out that Stalin "has achieved a masterpiece of diplomacy in getting his two deadliest enemies to fighting, while he sits on the sidelines and waits."

But by the end of 1939 he confessed to the editor of the Socialist *Call* that the invasion of Finland by the Soviet Union was the most painful public event of his lifetime. Because the Soviet Union stood in great danger of attack by Germany with the backing of Britain and France they had chosen a course which he thought made such an attack far more likely. If this should come to pass, he predicted, America would almost certainly get into the mess and be in for a period of terrible reaction, ruled by Dies, Garner, Hearst, Hoover, Coughlin, and Ford. "I am afraid that we have a dark night ahead of us," he concluded. "If anybody can find any satisfaction in the fact that some of my hopes have been blasted, I grant him that privilege."

But Upton still refused even then to attack the Soviet Union. "I feel about like the fellow whose best girl deserts him. I am much disappointed but I am not going to fight with her."

He was at least partially able to reconcile his viewpoint by means of his early instilled and lifelong felt American patriotism. "I admit that if I had learned most of my Socialism from Marx, Lenin, and Stalin, I would hasten to 'reconsider.' But I learned a good part of mine from Robert Owen, Albert Brisbane, Horace Greeley, Wendell Phillips, Edward Bellamy, Lester Ward, Thorstein Veblen—quite a list of Americans who have dealt with American problems in American terms, and to whom liberty has been just as important as equality, or justice, or whatever name we give to our economic demands. I have never called myself a Marxian; I have in that respect followed the example of Marx, who said he wasn't one. So I have not so much to learn as some others. . . . But the fact that the Soviet Union has failed to build Socialism is no reason why we in America should fail. What we have to do is teach our citizens the meaning of the Socialist formula: 'the social ownership and democratic administration of the instruments and means of production.' It does us no good to have the government control industry unless we, the people, can control the government. And in order to do that we must preserve freedom of discussion as the brightest jewel in our crown. . . . Come and learn the American way!"

When the Germans attacked their Russian allies Upton was pleased that he had refused to attack the Soviet Union. Throughout the war he repeatedly expressed the hope that America's alliance with the Soviet Union, the most gratifying development in modern history, would continue after the war until both countries had achieved what he believed was their common democratic goal.

Only a few years later, however, as the cold war was heating up on both sides, Upton was being regularly assailed by the Soviet Union and answering in kind. Moscow's *Literary Gazette* in words that would have been funny were they not tragic, branded him in 1948 "a money-grubbing careerist, Wall Street lackey." His writings, along with those of Shaw, were banned in the Soviet Zone of Germany, and *The Daily Worker* declared him a lying Fascist propagandist.

Sinclair for his part in the same Los Angeles *Times* that had so often lied about him was declaring "Russia is a slave state," and to the encouragement of Mrs. Roosevelt, he now criticized the Soviet Union over the Voice of America.

In 1938, on his sixtieth birthday, Upton wrote seventeen letters, somewhat fewer than usual. His printed form letter to his mailing list began: "Today is my sixtieth birthday, and my New York publishers, Farrar and Rinehart, are publishing my sixtieth book, a novel called 'Little Steel.' " The letter also updated his bibliography to "772 titles in 47 languages and 39 countries."

A few days earlier he had told a *New York Times* reporter, who noted, as had so many others, the muckraker's almost continuous smile and the intensity of his blue-gray eyes: "if I were asked to name the one definite thing I have accomplished in my public career I believe it would be that I got an exercise courtyard in the State prison of Delaware." But despite Sinclair's pose of modesty, the reporter was aware that: "He has seen reforms for which he battled become accepted elements in American life. His failures he does not regard as lost causes; he prefers to call them delayed victories."

Two important things differentiated this Sinclair from the one who some four decades earlier had discovered Socialism and so did not have to invent it. First, he no longer believed that Socialism could bring forth a New Jerusalem overnight. He confessed to the reporter: "A man who is sensible and knows the world can't expect to change it in a lifetime." And second, having in more than fifty books addressed himself to a wide variety of reforms for his own country, Sinclair was now turning his attention to the whole world and its salvation.

The reasons for this were doubtless many and interdependent. There were no longer any American problems of significance to him on which he had not already said all he had to say. Many of his reforms had been adopted and those that had not would not be until the world situation improved. But another reason was temperamental, for as he wrote an EPIC associate who chided him for ignoring California politics, "All my life I have offended and hurt people because of the fact that I have moved on from one job to another job."

Just as the threat of German imperialism a quarter century earlier had led him to put defeat of the Kaiser ahead of Socialist goals as Debs saw them, so now he wrote a friend: "I hope you won't be too shocked if I tell you that I am praying for war. I want to see it come before Spain is wrecked, and I do not believe that Fascism can ever be put down except after a war. I do not expect barbarism after it, but social revolution, and I think it will be wiser and not repeat the blunders which the Russians had to make."

This represented a considerable change from his view three years earlier that "America should keep out of all wars of whatsoever character, and stay at home and put its own economic and social affairs in order."

And once his prayer had been answered and war came, Upton's attention became fixed. "My thoughts are entirely on Europe. . . . I think that our destinies are being decided there. . . . If we can wipe Nazism and Fascism from the world, then I think we will have a good chance to improve America."

Upton's change of interest, long gestated, burst forth in late 1938. "I got a big idea. It kept me busy all day and most of the night—the biggest story I have ever written. The scenes are to be laid all over Europe during the past twenty-five years. It was perfectly marvelous the way the thing just unfolded itself like one ocean wave rolling in after another. . . . This novel has been knocking at the gate of my mind for several years, but I would not let it in, because it seemed impossibly big and some of the episodes were so terrible, but apparently the story has gone on writing itself in my subconscious mind all the time."

So excited was he with his new project that he wrote about it to a number of his friends, among them Einstein and his boyhood chum, who had become an art dealer, Martin Birnbaum, whose help he already knew he would need. Birnbaum's help became so important that Upton paid for it according to what percentage of each book was based on information supplied by him.

Lanny Budd, Upton's new hero, is partially based on a number of men Upton knew—Birnbaum, Cornelius Vanderbilt, Jr., and such rich young idealists as J. G. Phelps Stokes and William English Walling. Vanderbilt served on occasion as an agent for Franklin Roosevelt and was a valuable if less than accurate source for Upton. Lanny is also, despite his enjoyment of the fleshpots of the world, very like his author, whose final subject became no less than a history of the western world in the twentieth century.

Upton's modern Scarlet Pimpernel, born with the twentieth century, meets regularly with many of its most important real figures, from George Bernard Shaw in Lanny's childhood to Lincoln Steffens and William Bullitt at the Versailles Peace Treaty conferences. Lanny is the illegitimate son of a great munitions manufacturer and a world famous beauty. He becomes an art dealer and a secret agent of President Franklin Roosevelt, and in these roles meets with Hitler, Stalin, and Mao, along with dozens of such lesser lights as Goering, Pétain, and Einstein.

Although Lanny's education serves also as the reader's, he is not the innocent so typical of Sinclair's earlier novels. He is ruthless in his business of buying art, adventurous if not promiscuous sexually, and he drinks spirits. He is, unlike his predecessors among Upton's heroes, Allan Montague and Bunny, the very opposite of Candide. In fact, a *New York Times* reviewer declared: "The character of Lanny Budd is surely one of the more fabulous creations of our time. Possessing the insouciance of d'Artagnan, the penetration of Sherlock Holmes, the sartorial elegance of Beau Brummel, the gymnastic skill of the late Douglas Fairbanks, the ubiquity of Superman . . . the sociological profundity of Herbert Spencer . . . [and] the sexual prowess of a Casanova."

Isadora Duncan's proposal that Lanny copulate with her is rejected, but he is so frequently married and bedded that Craig and Dollie feared such concupiscence might put off the middle-class women who were America's important book buyers and book club members. But Upton now imitated both those writers he formerly condemned who pandered by "giving the public what it wants" and the licentious Broadway and Hollywood Jews who, he had said, commercialized sex. In his letters to the major Hollywood studios, he stressed the "love story" between Lanny's mother and a boyhood chum of Lanny's, now a German spy eighteen years her junior.

Upton initially had thought he would need only two or three volumes to tell his tale, but it finally required eleven: *World's End, Between Two*

Worlds, Dragon's Teeth, Wide Is the Gate, Presidential Agent, Dragon Harvest, A World to Win, Presidential Mission, One Clear Call, Oh Shepherd Speak! and *The Return of Lanny Budd,* giving Sinclair in his sixties and seventies a second literary career.

The immensely profitable series was published entirely by Viking after John Farrar, who had published so many unprofitable books of Upton's, misjudged the salability of *World's End.* The editor, who became one of Upton's few close friends, was Ben W. Huebsch.

Determined that each of the thousands of details be historically correct, Upton wrote "a thousand letters to persons who were eye witnesses of this or that scene, or who had access to inside information." These helpers included Eleanor Roosevelt, President Truman, J. Edgar Hoover, and Albert Einstein. And Sinclair also received and sometimes made use of unsolicited suggestions, ranging from Earl Browder's on Roosevelt's preparations for Teheran and Yalta to an unknown schoolgirl's on the joys of flute playing.

The first novel in the series was selected by the Literary Guild, some of the others by other book clubs, and all were important best sellers, bringing Upton such an enormous popularity as he had not experienced since *The Jungle.*

Sinclair was still his own most blatant and shameless promoter. During the war he sought unsuccessfully, through Vice President Henry Wallace and Coordinator of Inter-American Affairs Nelson A. Rockefeller, to have the Lanny Budd books widely circulated in South America as pro-American propaganda. Similarly, after the war, he deviled President Truman and General Douglas MacArthur because he believed, quite incorrectly, that there was a prohibition against the publication of the series in Japan.

With his Lanny Budd series, Sinclair realized some of the public honors for which he had so long yearned and fought in vain. For his third Lanny Budd novel, *Dragon's Teeth,* published in 1942, he was awarded in 1943 the Pulitzer prize in fiction, and the same year he was elected to the National Institute of Arts and Letters. One of the Pulitzer prize jury members, John Chamberlain, declared in *The New York Times:* "When all the arguments have been marshaled against 'Dragon's Teeth,' however, it remains true that Sinclair has done something fairly remarkable. . . . almost alone among our novelists, he has realized that contemporary history, as it comes through to us every day in the headlines, has become so overpowering that many individuals can have no significant emotional life apart from it."

However, there were and there continued to be many critics who condemned as ridiculous *per se* any such mixture of history and fiction. An automatic contempt that declares worthless any recounting of history in the form of a novel and that declares it the more so when the novel is a best seller is quite as foolish as had been Upton's contempt in his *Mammonart* days for "graces and refinements" when what the world needed was social revolution. For as Van Wyck Brooks had pointed out: "It was the 'graces and refinements' in the characters of the novels of Dumas, of all writers in the world, let Mr. Sinclair remember, that aroused in Maxim Gorky his first revolutionary feeling."

If some critics scoffed, some observers did not. From England, Shaw wrote: "I have regarded you, not as a novelist, but as a historian; for it is my considered opinion, unshaken at 85, that records of fact are not history. They are only annals, which cannot become historical until the artist-poet-philosopher rescues them from the unintelligible chaos of their actual occurrence and arranges them in works of art. . . . When people ask me what has happened in my long lifetime I do not refer them to the newspaper files and to the authorities, but to your novels. They object that the people in your books never existed; that their deeds were never done and their sayings never uttered. I assure them that they were, except that Upton Sinclair individualized and expressed them better than they could have done, and arranged their experiences, which as they actually occurred were as unintelligible as pied type, in significant and intelligible order."

More than what the critics wrote or what his admirers wrote, however, Upton cared most about the effect his books had on individual readers and through their lives on the lives of others. One reader, Mrs. Lyndon B. Johnson, said she "gained a more vivid recollection of foreign affairs (the rise of fascism and the American involvement in the Second World War) through the adventures of Lanny Budd, than she did through reading the newspapers at that time!"

Hugh Sidey, who as Time-Life's Washington analyst in the years following Sinclair's death was widely read, recalled that: "The Lanny Budd series as I remember it now were the first serious books I read discussing the political-social problems of this age. . . . I must have been about 12 or 13, I guess, but I pursued them all after that first taste. . . . they presented to me in interesting and seemingly authentic fashion, a picture of the world beyond Greenfield, Iowa. . . . Sinclair's books gave me the first suggestions of the forces of wealth, intellectualism, even sex and their interplay."

It was appropriate that the eleven Lanny Budd novels should serve to educate so great a variety and number of Americans. They did the same for their author. During their appearance, a new edition of *The Jungle* was brought out and reviewers found that despite its horror it gave also "a sense of nostalgia . . . for the days when socialism was a warm and generous philosophy that attracted many of the young. . . . You had only to convince people of the evils of the capitalistic system and capitalism would disappear." In his Introduction to this new edition, Upton confessed, "Man-made calamities have taught the author of *The Jungle* that he had placed far too high an estimate upon the intelligence of the human race, and its moral qualities."

But if Sinclair had achieved a more realistic sense of human limitation, he had nevertheless not despaired. He was still willing, as he had always been, to confess his own limitations and to laugh at himself.

It was fortunate that he could, and that he could stand being laughed at. When so inveterate a reformer of American society changed his scene and his style as well, many critics found irresistible the temptation to scoff at the adventures of the ubiquitous Lanny as "a Rollo book on an international scale, or *Tom Swift and His Electric Historoscope*"; although even this scoffer admitted, "He also makes his whole 859-page canvas as shamelessly ingratiating as a barroom nude."

"The style is as corny as ever," declared Perry Miller, a Harvard historian, in his *New York Times* review. "It is easy to make fun of the books. . . . It can be childish, and yet it is a version of modern history, and it is more coherent than most. It is much more on the beam than are several professional historians. And this seems to be because Lanny incarnates the dogged sanity of old-fashioned, grass-roots socialism, which can remain level headed and clear eyed in the midst of hatreds, dogmas, stupidities and violence, sustained by the knowledge of what could, were we up to it, save us. . . . Every time I am ready to call the books silly, and to sign off, I am struck with admiration for the monumental simplicity of the conception, and, sighing like Lanny over the muddle of the world, I eagerly await my annual installment."

Another *New York Times* critic wrote: "Mr. Sinclair has grown, one would say, during the past few years. He has mastered his earlier tendency to put the idea and the symbol first and the character last. He has produced some real people, and one or two notable ones. . . . The artist in Sinclair gets the better of the old crusader. He is ready to admit that human life is too complicated to fit into a formula. . . . Mr. Sinclair emerges as the successful painter of an epoch, as a first-class mingler of fiction with historic fact."

And an American novelist that none of the critics failed to take seriously, Theodore Dreiser, wrote:

"As I look back over Upton Sinclair's period in the world I am struck by the fact that, had people read his books twenty years ago, America would not be in the dire condition it is now, struggling for breath under the massive posterior of the corporations. Sinclair was that rare manifestation, a thoroughly honest writer . . . showing up the Fuhrers of American business for what they are."

There is some hope that the reading of history helps mankind, and not the least, helps the young. It demonstrates that even great change is not the end of the world but only of a stage; that *angst* and riot and idealism and despair have existed before and may easily be less significant than they first appear to be. If the methodology of such quasi-historians as Sinclair is unacceptable to academic historians, it is nevertheless true that such quasi-history reaches millions not otherwise reachable; and it is difficult to argue that such history does not, like academic history, help in understanding the past and dealing with the future.

CHAPTER XXV

Sinclair and the Critics

Reviewers, with some rare exceptions, are a most stupid and malignant race.
As a bankrupt thief turns thief-taker in despair, so an unsuccessful author
turns critic.   PERCY BYSSHE SHELLEY

MOST OF AMERICA'S LITERARY CRITICS were not complimentary of Sinclair's work. Typical of their view are comments by Van Wyck Brooks or Howard Mumford Jones. Brooks, in *The Confident Years*, had little literary use for the whole school: "So while none of the books of the muckraking circle,—nor all of them together,—could be weighed with one of Willa Cather's novels, they represented nevertheless a mood that focused the minds of writers as the cause of abolition had focused them sixty years before."

Brooks acknowledged that *The Jungle* was the most notable work of the muckraking movement and judged it comparable to *Uncle Tom's Cabin* in its effects. But he declared that although Sinclair was "hypercompassionate," he had small interest in human nature, small feeling for character or tolerance of it, and therefore his characters, as a rule, were puppets whose function it was to express the author's ideas.

The critic speculated that it had been Upton's grinding out the early nickel novels that "perhaps gave him the fatal facility and established the commonplace style that he scarcely ever transcended as a serious writer."

Brooks, however, qualified his criticism. "But while one was obliged to quarrel with Sinclair as a novelist, one could regard him quite differently from another point of view, as a publicist who used fiction for an ulterior purpose, no doubt, but used it, now and again, with great effect. He was obviously something on a large scale that literature had to include, though he did not fit into the usual categories and a versatile author, moreover . . . an intellectual descendant of Jefferson, Voltaire and Thomas Paine." And even while damning a Sinclair character as "a figure of pure melodrama" or, in the case of Lanny Budd, as "shapeless and boneless as a shadow," Brooks admitted, "one followed him, nevertheless, wherever he went on his travels, and followed him with zest, because of the writer's extraordinary gift for the story-telling that most novelists ignore and that appeals so strongly to our common human nature."

In his correspondence with Lewis Mumford, Brooks expressed surprise at letters by Albert Einstein and C.G.Jung, which Upton had sent him, that praised some of the writer's poorest work.

Mumford replied: "The problem you raise in connection with Upton Sinclair's work is one of the hardest in all literature to solve; . . . he has a decent, but commonplace mind. . . . the very commonplaceness of expression makes him more readily understood by a European like Einstein or Jung, he has a way of drawing out from such people more favorable responses than his books deserve: indeed, he extracts praise in the way a broken down actor, known to everybody in his palmy days, extracts dollars from people who once knew him at least by reputation. His subject matter is indeed of the greatest importance and I honor him for sticking so resolutely to his guns over such a long period, but his method of treatment does not do justice to the substance and therefore doesn't work any profound changes in the reader. This is of course at the opposite end of the scale from having nothing to say and saying it exquisitely; but in the end is it not equally barren?"

Sinclair wrote hundreds of letters to critics, both about their criticism of his own work and about their criticism of the work of others. These letters were occasionally pettish or obvious attempts to get publicity. But usually they were balanced and reasonable and, especially when they dealt with the work of other writers, generous. He wrote Brooks a very long and humble letter in response to the critic's appraisal. "I got the book originally out of curiosity to see what you said about me—a human weakness. . . . You may be surprised to know how completely I agree, not merely with all your literary judgements but also with your basic attitudes. . . .

"I have tried to think carefully and dispassionately about your judgments on my own writing. That, of course, is difficult to do. You are right in many of these judgments; I know I have been much too fluent and that my early having to earn a living by grinding out pulp fiction had something to do with it. Also, it is true that as a rule I am more interested in ideas than in personalities."

In reply to "that extraordinarily interesting letter," Brooks wrote, "It really won me completely, so I knew that my account of you was all wrong somehow. . . . All I can say now is that I shall rewrite what I have written and that the result will be quite different.

"Now you say that you agree with what I say of other writers, and may I say that what I wrote about you was the only part that left me with a very uncomfortable feeling. You would not gather that I regard you as a great human being, for I do, and as it happens, I have a deep feeling of friendship with you because of your 'basic attitudes,' as you describe them. And all the more at present [1953] because the literary tide has turned so completely away from all that we have in common.

"Where you say that 'institutions are higher products of evolution than individuals,' the natural answer would have to be: 'But novels are about individuals,' and when you say in *American Outpost*: 'I was impatient of every form of human vanity and stupidity' the natural answer again would be 'Yes, but the business of the novelist is not to be impatient with them but to be *interested* in them.' And I think that's right and that great things result from this function of fiction, which you don't achieve at all, *even while* I perceive that if I can't 'put down' your Lanny Budd there must be some great virtue in it that is not in the usual fiction. . . . I only do want to say again that I'm glad you are alive and that in a time of great talents with small hearts it makes me very happy to think of your big one."

Brooks' promise was not an idle one. He rewrote his appraisal of Upton in *The Confident Years*, using phrases from Upton's letter. "I added two more pages about you, so at least it's better—but not right yet.

"You are a very difficult person to be right about."

Brooks was always very anxious not to hurt Sinclair's feelings and to be fair with the writer whom he had met in England at the Gaylord Wilshires' at the beginning of the century. His many letters to Sinclair are all friendly and admiring, "you are one of the great figures of our time," and Sinclair was so pleased with Brooks' final appraisal, expressed on a visit to the Sinclairs in California, that it forms the end of Craig's autobiography, *Southern Belle.*

In a charmingly modest and self-revealing letter to Brooks, Sinclair once confessed: "There is a phrase which came to me in the night—that some novelists I know collect their material with a microscope, and I collect mine with a telescope."

Unlike Brooks, Howard Mumford Jones had no qualms at all about hurting Sinclair's feelings nor about whether he was right. In the *Atlantic Monthly* Jones declared Upton's distinguishing trait was "a sub-literary belligerence," but the Harvard English professor's own belligerence became increasingly evident as he equated Lanny Budd with Superman, Dick Tracy, Captain Nemo, and Phineas Fogg.

To Sinclair's favorite argument that he must be a great writer because he had been translated into so many foreign languages, Jones' answers were even more brutal than Lewis Mumford's, but as the professor's review continued, his outrage seemed to lessen. Reluctantly he admitted "Mr. Sinclair's prose has a certain low order of competence," and in the next paragraph he called *The Jungle* "a minor masterpiece." Warming gradually, Mr. Jones continued to praise Upton with fainter damns and limited commendation. "His expository writing is sometimes admirable, never more so than when he is explaining a mechanical process like the sinking of an oil well. In that case the necessity of following the process step by step confines his didacticism and his loquacity. His insight into society is sometimes shrewd, and his prophecies are occasionally correct. Above all, his courage is the admirable courage that Mr. Granville Hicks rightly celebrated in *The Great Tradition* and that President Conant of Harvard called for in his celebrated article, 'Wanted: American Radicals.' It is the courage of American individualism, which has nothing to do with the socialism of Mr. Sinclair's dream.

"But," the review concluded: "what Mr. Sinclair does not understand is that persons who do not like his 'radicalism' would still oppose his ideas, even if he wrote with the pen of Burke or Milton; and that competent literary judges, however 'radical,' would still have patiently to declare that most of his prose is essentially vulgar prose—that is, prose that does not lift into the perfection of literature, however righteous the intent of its maker may be."

In his reply in the *Atlantic*, Sinclair suggested that some writers must be "vulgar," that is, "popular"; that "somebody has to write for the masses and not just the Harvard professors." Throughout his career he repeatedly made clear why he had opted for simplicity and explicity: "I have tried to make my meaning plain, so that the humblest can understand me."

However, Upton's work received from time to time glowing critiques. Especially when these critiques were read selectively he was able to convince himself of what he needed to believe—that if he were not another Milton, still he possessed the talent to be a great artist if his primary duty as a propagandist ever left him the time. He could read in the *Literary History of the United States*, for example: "[In *Manassas*] the unsparing battle scenes come alive with a sense of reality equal to those in Crane's *The Red Badge of Courage*. . . . Little in Zola or Dostoevski surpasses the nightmarish strength . . ." of the scenes where the penniless Jurgis is befriended by a young drunk, or where he haggles with a reluctant midwife, while his helpless Ona lies dying in childbirth."

Among the few who, like Carl Van Doren, praised Sinclair was the American critic who was probably the most influential of all, Edmund Wilson. Like almost everyone else, Wilson could not accept Upton's too inflexible puritanism and contrasted it unfavorably with Steffens' tolerance and skepticism. ". . . Sinclair's innocence, egoism, priggishness, sometimes irritate us. Yet he ends by inspiring us with respect. A fundamental earnestness and sweetness take the curse off his attitude of moral superiority; a devotion to values beyond his own interests outweighs his egoism. After all, he had kept faith with himself, put through what he had undertaken. True, Mrs. Sinclair had to suffer; but then Upton himself was taking every possible loss, including that of losing his wife.

"As we read this story of Sinclair's early adventures, we remember the stink of the mucker publicity with which, after the appearance of 'The Jungle,' the newspapers went on to exploit Sinclair's colony at Helicon Hall and the break-up of his second marriage,* and we find it strangely moving to read today the human story behind it. In the world of those newspapers of the early nineteen-hundreds, there was at any rate one man who had the courage to run counter to all their assumptions and give the lie to all their legends. . . . Practically alone among the American writers of his generation, he put to the American public the fundamental questions raised by capitalism in such a way that they could not escape them.

"There was something in Upton Sinclair of the innocent Shelleyan radicalism which assumes that if people were only given a chance they would be as pure and gentle as oneself and something of the Rousseauesque Puritan radicalism which draws strength from its own maladjustment for the condemnation of a social system."

As America's first critic, Wilson felt no need to be condescending to Sinclair's Lanny Budd series, much less to the whole field of historical fiction. He was secure enough to acknowledge its usefulness: "One of the characteristic forms of our period has been the novel of contemporary history, based on a socialist analysis of society." Among its practitioners he singled out André Malraux, Ignazio Silone, John Dos Passos, Jules Romains, and "the Old Archetype, Upton Sinclair, to whom the whole school owes much—including even the fiction and theatre of the Soviet Union itself in its more serious Marxist phase."

As Wilson acknowledged, Sinclair's early career was not without its

---

* Wilson mistakenly took the scandalous breakup with Meta to be Sinclair's second, for which both he and the *New Republic* president, Bruce Bliven, apologized.

influence on the critic, and Wilson's feelings were sometimes indistinguisha-
ble from Sinclair's, for example in *The Shores of Light* on the 1929 crash and
its aftermath. Almost until Sinclair's death, Wilson wrote him encouraging
and complimentary letters, and when Wilson died, his *New Yorker* memorial
could equally well have served to memorialize Sinclair: "For a writer, the
rarest privilege is not merely to describe his country and time but to help
shape them. Wilson was among the fortunate handful of writers who have
succeeded in doing this, with books that are like bold deeds and that will live
a long time after him, keeping him with us against our need."

Sinclair's contention that what he said was more important than how he
said it was part of what his critics considered old-fashioned about him. His
view was one that frequently falls out of fashion, but just as frequently
returns—Jean-Paul Sartre is only the most obvious among those sharing that
view. And as Joyce Carol Oates, one of the finest stylists writing today,
wonders, "what use is art if it doesn't help people live better? . . . I want to
move toward a more articulate moral position, not just dramatizing
nightmarish problems but trying to show possible ways of transcending
them."

Many of Sinclair's critics, both in his lifetime and since, have explained
that his work was inartistic and would have no enduring interest because it
was polemical. The notion that a polemical work cannot be art nor have
enduring interest is as arbitrary and foolish as Sinclair's view in *Mammonart*
that no work that fails to be polemical can be art. If polemics are *per se*
excluded from literature, then so is much of Tolstoy, Swift, Voltaire, and
Dostoevski.

Although Upton seized upon almost every critical review of his work as
an opportunity to write an answering letter that might be published, in truth
he seems to have cared much less about what the critics said than one might
have expected in one so hypersensitive. He thought of the book critics of the
capitalist press as poor kept creatures, typified by the literary editor of the
New York *Evening Telegram* who in 1903 had found "tiresome and
amateurish" the poetry he attributed to the author of *Arthur Stirling* but
which in fact was written by John Keats.

Rather than with critics, Upton's concern was to influence voters and
other writers who would in turn influence voters. He therefore took
astonishing amounts of time to review and comment on, in person and by
mail, the work of younger men, such as Edward Dahlberg. The lives of
American writers as disparate as S. N. Behrman and Budd Schulberg were
influenced by Sinclair, as well as those of countless European writers who

read him in translation. To a testimonial dinner honoring Sinclair a few years before his death, where Eleanor Roosevelt, Walter Reuther, and other warriors in the fight for social justice paid tribute to the muckraker, Arthur Koestler wrote: "Perhaps a writer is judged by posterity not so much by the actual text of his work as by the size of the hole that would be left in the fabric of history had he never lived. Other authors in our age outshone Sinclair in artistic quality, subtlety of characterization, and so on, but I can think of no contemporary writer whose non-existence would leave such a gaping hole in the face of the twentieth century than Upton Sinclair's."

After Upton's unexpected second career with Lanny Budd, a second serious critical appraisal of his works appeared. For example, in Malcolm Cowley's *After the Genteel Tradition*, Robert Cantwell wrote: "This pale and soft-voiced ascetic has been involved, ever since he began to write, in knock-down and drag-out conflicts of such ferocity and ruthlessness they might well demoralize a dozen hardened captains of industry. . . . Few American public figures, . . . have jumped so nimbly from so many frying pans into so many fires, and none has ever managed to keep so sunny and buoyant while the flames were leaping around him.

". . . He is the first important American novelist to see in the struggle between capital and labor the driving force of modern industry; he has hammered away for a lifetime at the cruelties and injustices of exploitation as well as at the grossness and insensitivity of life among the exploiters, and his books, with all their unevenness and vacillations, have a simple literal honesty about them that makes the work of most of his contemporaries seem evasive and affected. He has done more than any other American novelist toward breaking the path for a full and realistic treatment of working-class life in fiction—the battles he had been engaged in, the enemies he has attracted and the silence and persecution with which his books have been met being his personal cost for that pioneering work. In his concern with the moral aspects of exploitation, his strong religious feeling, his indifference to Marxian theory, his reformism and his hope for a peaceful solution of the class struggle, he has been the outstanding literary representative of the Second International, in the way that a writer of the type of André Malraux—intense, defiant, scornful—promises now to become the voice in fiction of the hard-pressed and violent life of the Third."

Critics and historians as well stressed Sinclair's sweetness and romanticism and contrasted it to the more usual thundering threats and dour interdictions of Old Testament and Roundhead reformers. Alfred Kazin predicted: "he will remain a touching and curious symbol of a certain old-fashioned idealism and quaint personal romanticism that have vanished from American writing forever. Something more than a 'mere' writer and something less than a serious novelist, he must always seem one of the original missionaries of the modern spirit in America, one of the last ties we have with that halcyon day when Marxists still sounded like Methodists and a leading Socialist like Eugene V. Debs believed in 'the spirit of love.' . . .

". . . Sinclair was one of the great social historians of the modern era . . . one of the great contemporary reporters, a profound educative force. He was a hero in Europe, and one of the forces leading to the modern spirit in America . . . almost glory enough."

Reviewing the first Lanny Budd novel, Granville Hicks predicted: "Because his behavior has been in so many ways contrary to the accepted standard for serious men of letters, and because his faults are always so conspicuous and never the fashionable ones, Mr. Sinclair has been either dismissed or patronized by the majority of critics and literary historians. Yet I am willing to wager that his chances of survival are as good as those of any living American author."

Three years later, Hicks in a long essay, "The Survival of Upton Sinclair," further elaborated his views: "[Sinclair] still does not exist for the serious critics, especially the younger ones—those nourished on the seven types of ambiguity. . . . The truth is that Sinclair has always had the ability to withdraw himself from the struggle and to write with an astonishing degree of objectivity. He has not always exercised that gift. . . . Yet, what he has done, he has done well, and it is time to stop depreciating him in comparison with those who are to be praised only for their aims and not for their achievements. If Tolstoys came by the dozens, we could afford to smile at Upton Sinclair, but the actual state of contemporary literature scarcely warrants condescension . . . It may be true, as some critics say, that in the future only social historians will be interested in his work; but even that is a larger claim on posterity than most of his contemporaries will be able to make, and in any case the debt our generation owes him is enormous."

CHAPTER XXVI

What Can One Man Do?

Si monumentum requiris, circumspice. (If you would see his monument, look around.)   CHRISTOPHER WREN's epitaph in St. Paul's Cathedral

TO CELEBRATE SINCLAIR'S reaching the age of eighty in September 1958, the League for Industrial Democracy, which he had founded more than half a century earlier, sponsored a banquet in his honor. The extraordinary compass of the tributes that flowed in was perhaps the greatest tribute of all. Not surprisingly, there were messages from politicians ranging from such old-timers as Norman Thomas to a young United States senator, Richard L. Neuberger, and including ex-President Harry S. Truman who wrote: "He has been a burr under the saddle of people who cannot appreciate what workingmen have to contend with."

Old friends like Helen Keller and grateful labor leaders sent encomiums. "Upton Sinclair's writings may have created more social idealists, economic reformers and effective labor leaders than any other individual influence of the last two generations," wired the president of the electrical workers' union. "Those generations and the generations to come must be eternally indebted to him."

And a chorus of literary figures praised the man and his work. "Most of all," wrote Louis Untermeyer, "I congratulate you on your unwavering courage. It takes a special kind of hardihood and a particularly tough integrity to remain true to one's youthful vision these disillusioned days. What you have done is important enough. What you have stood for—and still stand for—makes the performance the important thing that it has become, and perhaps surpasses it."

Fellow authors, journalists, and radicals sent praise, John Dos Passos writing, "I wish I could see a few young men like him growing up in the new generation," and former opponent Sidney Hook stating, "Upton Sinclair's life is an illustration of what one man can do, of how an individual can become a movement without founding a cult, and above all an illustration of man unafraid."

And there were the tributes from abroad—from present or former prime ministers of Great Britain, France, Norway, Holland, Austria, New Zealand, and India.

It has long been recognized, however, that eulogists are not under oath and that their praises may often be profitably contrasted with the judgments of historians who are presumably more concerned with accuracy and with how their own judgments will in turn be judged by future historians. Whether or not Sinclair's place in American literature will finally be deemed to have been significant, the importance of his role in his country's history seems secure. It is virtually impossible to find a history of America at the college or secondary school level in which his contributions are not described and usually there is more than one reference to his achievements as well as quotations from his works. Nor has he been entirely without influence on historians themselves such as Perry Miller and Arthur Schlesinger, Jr.

In college and secondary school textbooks on American literature, however, Sinclair and his work are mentioned only about half as often, but there seems to be an as yet mild revival in this area. *The Jungle* in a new paperback edition is increasingly appearing on lists of required reading as students demand more "relevance," confirming, for the moment, Sinclair's own conviction, that all great literature must perforce be great propaganda Many who presently cry loudest for "relevance" seem, in fact, to have confused it with "topicality." But it is not impossible that when this current mania for topicality has passed, some of Sinclair's best novels, *The Jungle, Oil!* and *Boston* especially, will continue to be read precisely because they are relevant—that is, realistic novels of very considerable skill, of great feeling, and of rather more importance literarily than is presently acknowledged, that direct our attention not merely to the present and the local but also to the timeless and the universal.

In the last years of Sinclair's life, his activities were curtailed not so much because of age but principally because he had to spend most of his time acting as Craig's nurse. He himself was remarkably fit. Despite his crank food ideas or because of them or possibly unrelated to them, the sickly boy had grown into a superbly healthy man. At almost eighty he passed the California test for his driver's license renewal, after which he continued to drive badly and too fast.

His wordy and exaggerated expressions of love for Craig in her last years surpassed only slightly those that throughout their almost fifty years of marriage had been so hyperbolic as to raise the question why he protested so much. In some measure, at least, it may have begun as a way of convincing himself that he could love someone other than himself. But over the many years, a variety of needs, including interdependence, had developed into love. He was grateful to her for her admirable service as his resident skeptic, literary critic, physical and economic guardian, and for her acceptance that not she but his various crusades were his first loves.

Increasingly too, just as his writing powers were finally beginning to ebb, she satisfied his lifelong need for duty, discipline, and sacrifice. In the last ten years before her death, she required more and more of his time. In addition to her paranoia that kept them moving from town to town in southern California, she found the smog in the Los Angeles area so unbearable that in 1951 they moved to Buckeye, Arizona. But a series of heart attacks made it necessary for Craig to stay closer to her doctors, so in 1954 they moved back to California and thereafter virtually all Sinclair's time was spent caring for her.

Upton had always saved every scrap of his writing and correspondence, and Craig was zealous in protecting the collection against weather, vermin, and her husband's willingness to send bits and pieces to anyone who needed convincing on any point. But as the collection grew to an enormous size, the burden of keeping it grew too and both Sinclairs, as the evidences of their own mortality increased, wanted a safe and permanent home for it.

Leslie E. Bliss of the Henry E. Huntington Library inspected the papers at length and wanted to buy them for Upton's asking price of $10,000 a year for five years. But despite his urging, his trustees refused to make the purchase. Upton alleged this was because ex-President Herbert Hoover was their chairman.

For some ten years, beginning in the late 1940's Upton dealt with dozens of university librarians in his efforts to sell the collection, including the shrewd former buyer of rare books for Charles Scribner, David A. Randall, at Indiana University's Lilly Library, who advised his superiors that Upton's price was very reasonable and he would, were he still in trade, not hesitate to pay it and confidently expect to make a handsome profit on the materials.

In 1957 the collection was purchased by Indiana and thereafter Upton, until his death, worked to add to it.

During the forties, to take Craig's mind from her real and imagined problems, he began writing what eventually appeared in the form of her autobiography, *Southern Belle.* She protested: "Upton is really putting his heart & soul into . . . a romantic story of 'Craig'! I didn't start it. I don't want to be the heroine he thinks I am . . . the 'lovely, noble, brilliant lady' he considers me to be."

Although she at first refused to allow him to publish, finally she agreed to have it appear as her own work in 1957. Afraid that because so much of the manuscript was in Upton's handwriting it would reveal who the real author was, she wrote Randall that she had been too ill to write herself and so she had dictated the book to her husband, but that "None of it was written by Upton."

But whether Upton wrote the book and she rewrote it or vice versa became unimportant, because she insisted upon adding to his outrageous flattery so many of her own pretensions and inventions, couched in such an unfelicitous style, that it was in fact her book.

After Craig's death Upton spent thousands of dollars sending free copies of the book to any library anywhere that would accept the gift.

Upton's energy and his published work slowly lessened, but his vast correspondence continued. Proud parents wrote him about the accomplishments of sons named Upton or Lanny, and from around the world in various forms there came thank yous to "my teacher and my great friend! You were my university." Ex-EPIC workers advised him of their conversions to new doctrines; unknown authors sent him their works, which he usually read; and candidates for graduate degrees asked for help with dissertations based on his life and work. Despite the longing for immortality that had not left him since he had admitted it as a boy to his mother, Upton was able still to joke about himself with these graduate students as he always had: "what did the reading of all my books do to your mind? I hope they didn't do any permanent damage."

In his life there was no shortage of those ironies that touch most lives. After hoping in vain since his youth for an unexpected legacy to help him carry on his work for reform, at sixty-eight Upton suddenly found himself the beneficiary of a two hundred-dollar insurance policy that his father had assigned in 1893 to a saloonkeeper. And when the puritan's *A Personal Jesus: An Essay in Biography* was refused by all of the many publishers to whom he had submitted it and he ran an advertisement in the *New Republic* seeking a publisher, he received an admiring letter offering help from Errol Flynn, Hollywood's reigning rakehell of the 1950's. Strangely enough too, it was about this book and another, equally uninspired, that Upton had a thoughtful correspondence with the psychologist C. G. Jung.

It was ironic also that Upton's reputation had so changed within his own lifetime from that of a revolutionary free lover to a symbol of rectitude that one of the songs in a Broadway musical comedy had the line: "My life will be selfless and pure like Upton Sinclair. . . ."

His name had made it to Broadway but his own plays did not, despite his dogged refusal to stop writing them. A retelling of the Faust legend in terms of the atomic bomb and a retelling of *Pamela* earned him kind letters from playwright friends but no commercial production.

Albert Camus who had successfully written and directed stage adaptions of Faulkner's *Requiem for a Nun* and Dostoevski's *The Possessed* praised *Cicero*, a play Upton tossed off in his eighties. They corresponded about a Paris production of it which never came off although it was presented off-Broadway. The praise from Camus, however, meant much to one who in *The Jungle* had shown how well he understood the myth of Sisyphus.

Throughout the 1950's and much of the 1960's, Upton bestowed his unsolicited blessings and advice on public figures of whose conduct he approved and chastised those he believed to be in error, whether he knew them or not—just as he had Teddy Roosevelt, Wilson, Harding, Stalin, and F.D.R. He asked Marshal Tito for the release of a political prisoner, and to the Democratic Presidential candidate Adlai Stevenson, he first offered to make a national broadcast supporting him and later wrote comforting him in his defeat and offering advice for the future.

When he published a collection of the letters sent to him over a lifetime, he heard from many of the correspondents, including Ezra Pound and his old friend Margaret Sanger, who wrote: "Dear dear Upton—So you like me 'are there'—We are tough ones you & I. . . . Yes Upton the 'world do move,' if we push hard enough and care to have it move."

The purpose of much of Sinclair's correspondence continued to be self-promotion, as when he offered his books free of charge to President Nasser of Egypt for translation into Arabic and when he hoped in vain that he might publicize favorable comments by Caroline Kennedy on his *Gnomobile.*

Upton's great desire for personal publicity led him to doing inconsequential and even foolish things such as writing pettish or silly letters to the editor or submitting questions to quiz programs: "You used my question about a mole on Abraham Lincoln's cheek. That is the first time I ever knew you to fail to give credit to the sender of a question." But whereas these had once been lost in the great flood of his meaningful publications, in his last years they stood out as somewhat sad reminders of the little boy whose need for attention had been so terrible and was still not satisfied.

Age was finally reducing not only the amount of his work but the degree of his contentiousness and contumacy. Where once he had sought libel suits he now carefully avoided them, and he was now reluctant to give his name to protests.

He was finally outspoken, however, in criticizing Communists, domestic and foreign, and had given up any hope for the Socialists. As he wrote Norman Thomas: "The American people will take Socialism, but they won't take the label. . . . I certainly proved it in the case of EPIC. Running on the Socialist ticket I got 60,000 votes, and running on the slogan to 'End Poverty in California' I got 879,000. I think we simply have to recognize the fact that our enemies have succeeded in spreading the Big Lie. There is no use attacking it by a front attack, it is much better to out-flank them."

Although Sinclair's own muckraking efforts perforce diminished, he never stopped encouraging and publicizing the work of younger men, just as he had that of Sinclair Lewis and John Steinbeck. With that bountiful ingenuousness that blessed his whole life, he wrote Vance Packard: "Let's be friends! . . . Your book makes me recall the thrill when I came on Veblen. A strange silent man—he sat & listened for an evening while I talked with another prof at Stanford." Typically, Sinclair had unsolicited sent Packard's publisher two plugs on his book, *The Waste Makers*.

The mellowing Sinclair wrote David: "how impressed I am by having a son whose work [on aerosols] is found worthy of publication by the Atomic Energy Commission." And after hearing from Meta's third husband, John Anthony Stone, Upton carried on a correspondence with him: *"Be assured that I have no hard feelings toward Meta."* But Upton could still not bring himself to write directly to Meta, even after she wrote him that the *Autobiography* he sent had "cleared up a dark corner of my mind." To Stone's letter that "she seems to have an obsession that you are out to 'destroy' her," Sinclair replied: "I am sorry indeed that Meta thinks I wish to 'destroy' her. I beg you to assure her that I have no trace of bitterness in my heart. I rarely think of her & when I do, it is with sympathy. I know that I was not a proper husband for her. . . . I have nothing but kindly memories of her."

Less than six months after Craig's death on April 26, 1961, the eighty-three-year-old Upton married Mary Elizabeth Willis, a seventy-nine-year-old, widowed great-grandmother, after a one-month courtship. In those months, he had been miserable alone, confiding to a friend that he had tried sex with a secretary and found it unsatisfactory.

He told a *Newsweek* reporter covering the wedding: "The last thing my [late] wife said to me was: 'Don't marry a floozy.' Well, I don't know exactly what a floozy is but I'm sure I'm marrying one of the finest women in the world."

Two years later he was asked by a television reporter: "You mean to say that a man at eighty or eighty-two can have the same physical feeling about a lady as he did sixty years prior to that?" Sinclair replied, "I mean he can have a lot more if it's the right lady." Until her death after six years of marriage, Sinclair slept in the same bed as his third wife and seems to have found her "the right lady."

He now had more time both for social life and for travel. With May, as she called herself, he made lecture tours of college campuses from Whittier, California, to Milwaukee to Buffalo; from the University of Texas to Indiana University to his own alma maters, CCNY and Columbia. At Indiana, where he visited the Lilly Library, some forty-four hundred attended his lecture and he was also enormously successful at Berkeley and Stanford where he had so long been *persona non grata.*

He was delighted to discover that the young felt strongly about the same problems that had always concerned him—social injustice, business immorality, and improving the educational system—and that there was reviving interest in feminism, food fads, and mental telepathy. He was equally delighted that in his eighties he could attract audiences of thousands of these young people and hold them spellbound, when his old enemies, the college professors, so often had trouble keeping their attention.

When Sinclair was eighty-five, a leader of the Students for a Democratic Society wrote him: "indebted as I am to your founding efforts fifty-nine years ago, for in the historical sense what you did then has become my political home now."

He was treated as a celebrity on these tours. He appeared as a guest on national and local television and radio shows, and he met such other celebrities as the former United States Supreme Court Justice Arthur Goldberg, who told Sinclair he had "done more for labor than any other man in the United States."

Other trips with his new wife were made to receive those public honors he still coveted. The United Automobile Workers honored him and Eleanor Roosevelt with their Social Justice Award and the New York Newspaper Guild gave him their Page One Award for "books that have advanced public enlightenment."

In the summer of 1966 the Sinclairs moved from California to an apartment in Rockville, Maryland, where she could be closer to her married daughter in Washington, D.C., and he closer to David and his wife who were living at Martinsville, New Jersey.

Shortly before his eighty-eighth birthday, Sinclair and May lunched at the White House with Mrs. Lyndon Johnson. At eighty-nine, he returned to the White House to watch President Johnson sign the Wholesome Meat Act of 1967, designed to plug some of the loopholes in the 1906 law for whose passage *The Jungle* had been chiefly responsible.

Lyndon Johnson was scarcely less obsessed with getting good personal publicity than Sinclair himself. He had, therefore, also brought to that White House signing consumer advocate Ralph Nader, who like Upton and perhaps like most men did not overestimate the achievements of others as compared to his own. "I sort of felt," Nader said later of the encounter with Sinclair, "that two historic consumer ages were meeting. . . . Maybe this time, I thought, the work will have some effect."

Despite Nader's probably unconscious minimizing, the work of the earlier time, of course, had not only "some effect" but an enormous one. In fact, it is impossible to imagine Ralph Nader as anything more than just another unknown and unsuccessful crank had not Sinclair and the many other muckrakers been fighting the fight for the previous sixty years. It was they who had created, organized, and led the public demand that had brought about both the laws and the agencies to enforce those laws to protect citizens. The point of view of most Americans in the days of Jurgis Rudkus had been one of more or less patient acceptance. It was the muckrakers, and chief among them Sinclair, who had transformed the climate in America into an ever-increasing demand by the public for social justice and consumer protection as a matter of right.

Evidences of this changed climate abound, most significantly perhaps, in the fact that an increasing number of American corporations present some sort of social accounting not only in their advertising to the public but also in their annual reports to stockholders. Even the obscene behavior of such a corporation as International Telephone and Telegraph indicates the change in public point of view, because the corporation seeks to hide or lies about its many activities that were usual and acceptable during the first third of Sinclair's life.

Similarly, the regular reporting in newspapers and on television of business abuses is also a tribute to the muckrakers' effectiveness, because before their efforts, such matters were scrupulously avoided in the press.

Corporations are not in serious danger of overemphasizing social responsibilities at the expense of profits and there is a continuing pattern of business atrocities. In the field of Sinclair's most famous fight, spoiled, adulterated, and misrepresented foods, there are also still almost daily proofs that the fight, far from being over, is as endless as human greed. But that variants of these abuses continue is not surprising. What is perhaps surprising and gratifying is the recent increased interest both in what has come to be called consumerism and in a balanced ecology. Of course, some businessmen still collude to fix prices and avoid competition and some still bribe politicians. Some citizens are still too rich and overpaid and others too poor and underpaid. Nor is it any longer only those who have always had the greatest power or money who are cheating, but also many laborers now cheat the public with shoddy work, protected by the powerful unions and unemployment benefits Sinclair fought for. Indeed, big and corrupt unions have now joined big and corrupt businesses as appropriate and everyday targets for the latest generation of muckrakers.

The triumph of that technology which Sinclair believed should improve the human condition has intensified and complicated the problem of who will control that technology and how—a problem he insisted could be handled by "industrial democracy," which has yet to be tried.

All this merely proves that a generally higher standard of living does not by and of itself produce Eden, but thanks to Sinclair and others, many of whom were inspired by him, the rules of the game are somewhat stricter.

Uncle Tom's Cabin, The Jungle, and *Grapes of Wrath* are the three most effective muckraking novels in America's history to date. But the future should see comparable works, indeed America seems likely, unless dictatorship prevents it, to witness even more muckraking than in the past. There are now more media, there is a wider audience, and there are also more subjects, for nothing is sacred any more and therefore nothing is above criticism. That the muckrakers of today and of the future owe a debt to Sinclair and to others influenced by him is indisputable. As the Washington *Post* reported: "What Drew Pearson writes in the newspapers and Ralph Nader writes in the magazines, what James Ridgeway writes in *The New Republic* and I. F. Stone in his newsletter is directly traceable to the muckraking tradition of American journalism. It is a tradition built upon outrage, and an almost Talmudic interpretation of ethics. The classic practitioners of the art were Lincoln Steffens, Jacob Riis and Upton Sinclair . . . the most famous of the three. . . . When today the public is informed about the financial machinations of Senator Dodd by Pearson, or American automobiles by Nader, or the universities by Ridgeway, or the military-industrial complex by Stone, it ought to understand that it owes a debt to the Sinclairs, the Steffenses, and the Riises. They were the men who pioneered the art form, who saw injustice and tried to right it, who believed absolutely in the wonderful cleansing properties of the embarrassing fact, bluntly disclosed."

Sinclair had lived so long and done so much that in the 1950's and 1960's it was as though he were seeing the movie again. Books of his published as early as 1904 and 1906 were being reprinted and reviewed by a whole new generation. Some of these new critics pointed out that the New Deal and subsequent prosperity had stolen his thunder, to which he replied mildly: "Someone has remarked that 'the business of people with ideas is to have them stolen,' and I was happy to be robbed by two presidents, Theodore and Franklin D. Roosevelt."

Although some found Sinclair's ideas old-hat, others judged them to be unfortunately more relevant than ever and now not only on an American but a worldwide scale. The critic Harvey Swados wrote: "*The Jungle* must renew its hold on the imaginations of an entirely new generation of readers.

". . . We are entering a new time. We sense uneasily that we do not have it made, that with . . . prosperity have come new and staggering problems, and that there is a vast suffering world beyond our national boundaries, struggling in a variety of ways to accumulate capital and thus to move, as we have moved, up into the twentieth century. We sense, too, that throughout this world, no matter how the capital is accumulated . . . it is being done at a stupendous cost in human suffering. There is a close parallel between the payment in hunger, blood, and agony of the peoples of the underdeveloped world and that extracted from the immigrant builders of the American empire.

"It is a parallel that we will neglect only at our own peril; it is one that should fill us with humility and compassion for all who must strain like beasts of the field to bring the world to the next epoch; it is one that *The Jungle* will help to sustain in the forefront of our consciousness, which is where it belongs. To the extent that it fulfills this function, this book now begins a new and vital existence as a force in the spiritual and social lives of a new and, it is to be hoped, a responsible generation of readers."

For a man who had been in turn ignored, ridiculed, and maligned, it was sweet now on occasion to see himself apotheosized. "Upton Sinclair is of the American type most brilliantly exemplified by Jefferson, the two Roosevelts and possibly, Kennedy—he was a traitor to his class," declared Gerald W. Johnson, "a propagandist miles above Thomas Paine and Henry George, and not far below Aquinas, Erasmus and Voltaire. Propagandists are kittle cattle; critics and historians have never known how to classify them. Zola couldn't write, but he wrecked a social order. Socrates never wrote at all, but he wrecked a world. Upton Sinclair . . . has shaped the thinking of millions who never heard of any other American writer."

But if he was a hero to some, Sinclair was both aware and proud of the fact that to others, especially many revolutionaries, he was at best a figure of fun—mild, peaceful, and (the ultimate insult) bourgeois. Those of his contemporaries who most fiercely affected the Bolshevik or anarchist styles of rhetoric, of dress, and of action were the most scornful of him, although in terms of effecting changes in America, none of them could approach him. Similarly, such necktied and jacketed bourgeois types as Ralph Nader and John Gardner would effect substantive changes in society after Sinclair, whereas the Samson syndrome actions of Mark Rudd or Rap Brown would prove counterproductive.

An old-timer may serve a number of purposes for new young heroes and heroines. First he can be railed against like parents for obtuseness, insensitivity, and generally for having allowed the times to get so out of joint. Later, an old campaigner like Sinclair, who no less than the average suffered from human vanities and oddities, provides excellent instances not only of successes but also of how *not* to do it. And perhaps finally, as today's and tomorrow's heroes grow older, having fought the good fight without having plucked out all the world's ills, root and branch, he may become a source of comfort and hope, a motivating example, at least to those to whom a knowledge of history gives hope and a sense of proportion.

After the death of his third wife on December 18, 1967, Sinclair moved to a nursing home near Bound Brook, New Jersey, to be close to David and his wife, Jean, and they took him wherever the opportunity to serve his causes called him, even if that was only the local high school. Almost until the moment of his death, he remained healthy and insistent on working as hard as his diminishing energies allowed. A New York editor found him "exuberant, still optimistic," and a Bridgewater-Raritan High School student remarked to him shortly before his death, "You're cool, Mr. Sinclair."

He died peacefully on November 25, 1968. A few years earlier he had written: "The English Queen Mary, who failed to hold the French port of Calais, said that when she died, the word 'Calais' would be found written on her heart. I don't know whether anyone will care to examine my heart, but if they do they will find two words there—'Social Justice.' "

Notes, Acknowledgments, and
Bibliographical Information

In these notes I have included the sources of most facts in the text. In many instances I have also provided additional information—sometimes from Sinclair's own pen, sometimes from other sources. By these two practices, which account for the great length of these notes, I have tried to keep the text itself short enough for the ordinary reader of biography, while at the same time providing more information and background, as well as sources for still further information, for those who may desire such. All letters quoted from, excepting those to Leon Harris, are in the Lilly Library collections at Bloomington, Indiana, unless otherwise noted.

Another reason for so many notes is that this biography contains more direct quotations than most. Many of these would by another biographer have been paraphrased or otherwise included in his own narrative. I chose the other course because, for me, the actual words of contemporary participants and witnesses more than make up in interest what they may lack in literary felicity and because such direct quotations give a biography the kind of immediacy and life that dialogue gives a novel.

No page numbers are given for quotations from the Stone mss., the collection of Meta Fuller Sinclair Keene Stone (also at Lilly), because there are a number of almost identical versions of her novel-autobiography, some unpaginated and undifferentiable by any method save line by line comparison.

Almost all of Sinclair's papers from before March 16, 1907, were destroyed in the Helicon Hall fire of that date, except for a few in his mother's scrapbooks and some correspondence after 1900. Therefore, all the events and quotations of his childhood and youth in this book, unless otherwise referenced in these notes, are from his autobiography, *American Outpost* (1932), or its slightly rewritten version, *The Autobiography of Upton Sinclair* (1962).

I am indebted to David and Jean Sinclair for their help.

Mrs. Dollie Kimbrough Kling has also been generous, helpful, perceptive, and candid.

Another debt, one too great to define, is to Alden Whitman, and like every other student of Upton Sinclair, I am forever beholden to Professor Ronald Gottesman for his massive and brilliant articles, interviews, speeches, and other work on Sinclair, as well as for his help and suggestions on this book and his unfailing kindness.

Others whose assistance I most gratefully acknowledge include: Edward Allatt, Franklin Balch, John Randolph Bland, Earl Browder, Mrs. Floyd Dell, Cyndi Flores, William Foley, John E. George, Sarah Jane Horton, Justin Kaplan, Lester Keene, Harry T. Levin, Lorna Smith, John A. Stone, and many others whose help is made evident in the notes.

Although some forty-seven libraries supplied information for this book, it is from the Lilly Library at Indiana University—David Randall and his generous and accommodating associates—that most of the manuscript material on Sinclair comes.

Sources quoted from or mentioned in the text are cited in these notes and all titles as well as their authors mentioned in either the text or these notes are listed in the index. Therefore, there is no bibliography. But I would like to mention here the authors of some of the many books which were useful to me, were influential in Sinclair's life, or are essential to an understanding of this era. They fall into four groups: 1) Sinclair's most obvious fellow muckrakers such as Samuel Hopkins Adams, Ray Stannard Baker, Edward Bok, Finley Peter Dunne, Benjamin Flower, Burton J. Hendrick, Robert Hunter, Thomas W. Lawson, Benjamin B. Lindsey, Samuel Merwin, Gustavus Myers, David Graham Phillips, Jacob Riis, and Brand Whitlock; 2) other of Sinclair's contemporaries such as Jane Addams, John Peter Altgeld, Louis D. Brandeis, Clarence Darrow, William DuBois, Samuel Gompers, Charlotte Perkins Gilman, George D. Herron, Jack London, Bernarr A. Macfadden, John Reed, Bertrand Russell, George Bernard Shaw, and H. G. Wells; 3) authors of the standard seminal works of Socialism, Anarchism, and reform such as M. A. Bakunin, August Bebel, Edward Bellamy, Alexander Berkman, Robert Blatchford, Eugene Debs, Henry George, William James Ghent, William Godwin, Karl Kautsky, Peter A. Kropotkin, Henry Demarest Lloyd, Ernest Poole, John Spargo, Norman Thomas, Leo Tolstoy, Leon Trotsky, and William English Walling; 4) those historians to whom I am most manifestly indebted, particularly Frank Freidel, as well as Oscar Handlin, Daniel J. Boorstin,

Henry Steele Commager, Richard Hofstadter, and Samuel Eliot Morison.

The abbreviations used in these notes are as follows:

AK—Alfred Kuttner
AO—American Outpost
AUTO —The Autobiography of Upton Sinclair
B—Boston
DL—Day Letter
Dollie Mabel Kimbrough, who became Mrs. Robert Irwin and
    subsequently Mrs. John Kling
DS—David Sinclair
EH-J—Emanuel Haldeman-Julius
ER—Eleanor Roosevelt
FDB—Upton Sinclair: A Study in Social Protest, Floyd Dell
FDR—Franklin Roosevelt
FvE—Frederick van Eeden
GBS—George Bernard Shaw
GG—*Sergei Eisenstein and Upton Sinclair: The Making and Unmaking of
    Que Viva Mexico!* Geduld & Gottesman
HK—Hunter Kimbrough
HLM—Henry L. Mencken
HST—Harry S. Truman
JH—Jimmie Higgins
KM—King Midas
L, Ls—Letter, Letters
LH—Leon Harris, in order to avoid any possibly ambiguous references
    to "the author"
LP—Love's Pilgrimage
Mam—Mammonart
MCS—Mary Craig Kimbrough Sinclair
Meta—Meta Fuller Sinclair Keene Stone
MLIL—My Lifetime in Letters
MR—Mental Radio
MW—Money Writes!
NA—The Nation
NL—Night Letter
NM—The New Masses
NR—The New Republic

NYHT—New York Herald Tribune

NYPL—New York Public Library

NYT—New York Times

100%—100%: The Story of a Patriot

SB—Southern Belle

SM—Sylvia's Marriage

SRL—Saturday Review of Literature

TBC—The Brass Check

TBOL—The Book of Life

TG—The Goslings

TG-S—The Goose-Step

TJ—The Jungle

TJOAS—The Journal of Arthur Stirling

TPOR—The Profits of Religion

TR—Theodore Roosevelt

US—Upton Sinclair

USPWF—Upton Sinclair Presents William Fox

WWI—World War I

WWII—World War II

INTRODUCTION

Page 1   "All biography . . . is concerned": L. Edel, *Literary Biography*, London, 1957, 2–7./ a better writer: L, Granville Hicks to LH, Jan. 31, 1971: "he did have greater gifts than he is usually given credit for."

Page 3   "he was one": L, Sevareid to LH, Nov. 12, 1970./ "Sinclair's *Jungle*": L, Menninger to LH, Feb. 2, 1971./ "He did influence me": L, McNamara to LH, Aug. 10, 1970. Other businessmen so influenced include: Ls, John J. McCloy to LH, Sept. 14, 1970: "His writings certainly opened up some points of view which up to that time I had not been exposed to"; Robert B. Anderson LH, Mar. 31, 1971; W. Averell Harriman to LH, July 23, 1970./ "Sinclair influenced my family": L, Ginsberg to LH, Aug. 14, 1970./ "Sinclair was much in my mind": L, Moynihan to LH, July 11, 1970./ "Upton Sinclair had no particular": L, Mailer to LH, Aug. 4, 1970./ Writers as unlikely as: L, Hart to US, Oct. 30, 1959: "It may or may not surprise you to know that you are an old hero of mine. I grew up on 'The Jungle' and 'The Brass Check' and all the others." L, Kaufman to US, Nov. 15, no year, see Chapter XI of this book./ journalists with audiences: L, Cronkite to LH,

Aug. 20, 1970; also, L, Shirer to US, Aug. 6, 1958: "You were an inspiration to me in my college days back in the Coolidge era when it was so difficult for a young American to get at the truth. That inspiration has continued to this day." Other journalists influenced by US include John Fischer, L, to LH, Oct. 8, 1970, and Theodore H. White, L, to LH, Oct. 13, 1970: "He was one of the men like Lincoln Steffens whose writings touched every adolescent of the 1920's and 1930's. *The Jungle* had an enormous impact on me and so too did his book on the Sacco-Vanzetti trial."/ Politicians: L, Hubert H. Humphrey to LH, July 30, 1970: "As a young man I . . . recall that his views of economic reform and his reaction against the injustices of unregulated economic competition impressed upon me the need for a new direction for U.S. leadership." Also, Ls, Birch Bayh to LH, Apr. 8, 1971; Paul H. Douglas to LH, July 16 and 27, 1970./ political activists, blacks as well as whites: Ls, Ralph J. Bunche to LH, Nov. 19, 1970; A. Philip Randolph to LH, Sept. 30, 1970; Stokely Carmichael to LH, Oct. 10, 1970./ "I expect like others": L, Galbraith to LH, July 10, 1970. Some of our most prominent economists assert US's influence on them, including (see notes for Chapter XXIII of this book) Paul A. Samuelson, Henry Hazlitt, John W. Gardner, Milton Friedman, and Walter W. Heller, among others.

Page 4   "I have sensed": L, Ramsey Clark to LH, Dec. 23, 1970./ Brecht was clearly influenced: L, Martin Esslin to LH, July 28, 1970; Chapter VII of this book; and Esslin's *Brecht, the Man and His Work*, Garden City, 1961, 51 and 109. See also, L, Eric Bentley to LH, Feb. 10, 1972. Also, L, US to Elisabeth Hauptmann, June 3, 1926. Other European writers influenced by US include Arthur Koestler, L, Koestler to LH, July 6, 1970; André Malraux, L, Malraux to US, n.d., but probably 1937; Pierre van Paassen, L, van Paassen to US, June 6, 1946; Frederic Morton, interview with LH; Stefan Lorant, L, Lorant to LH, Feb. 14, 1971./ from Eisenstein to Solzhenitsyn: For Eisenstein's experiences with US see Chapter XXII of this book. Also, references to US, Solzhenitsyn, *The First Circle*, NY, 1968, 297, 380, and 555. For Lenin on US, see Chapter XII of this book. "I remember that I read": L, Marcuse to LH, Nov. 4, 1970./ first inspired Chaplin's interest: Chaplin, *My Autobiography*, NY, 1964, 350./ more than 250,000 letters: Gottesman, "Upton Sinclair and The Sinclair Archives." *Manuscripts*, Vol. XVII, No. 4, Fall 1965, 11–20./ *"Je n'impose rien"*: *Eminent Victorians*, London, 1967, 22. On the preceding page Strachey wrote what every biographer risks having thrown in his face if he quotes it: "It is perhaps as difficult to write a good life as to live one."/ "Writing biography": André Maurois, *NYT Magazine*, Dec. 22, 1953.

Page 5   "biography is essentially": H. Nicolson, *The Development of English Biography*, London, 1927, 64.

I. CHILDHOOD

All the quotations in this chapter not identified below are from *AO*: 4, 24, 140–141, 12–13, 4–5, 29, 41–43, 27, 27–28, 26–27, 20–21, 40, 22, 36–38, 24–25, 3–4.

Page 7   "Men always hate most": *Prejudices*, Ser. IV, NY, 1924, 130./ "We never had but one room": But US's real feeling about bedbugs is better expressed, for example, in *TJ*, when Jurgis spends money his starving family needs for food on some product to kill the maddening pests and the product proves useless, 80./ boardinghouse on Biddle Street: L, US to William Cunningham, May 18, 1939. Also, L, US to Ray W. Sullivan, July 25, 1934./ Mark Twain blamed the Civil War: In US's own novel of the Civil War, *Manassas*, 19, he wrote: "To be sure they had an English governess and they read Sir Walter Scott and dreamed of chivalry." US even interrupted his novel to retell the tale of his grandfather and David Farragut, 314. Like most of US's books, *Manassas* contains ample evidence of his love for and faith in the United States, 317./ Sinclair naval officers: See Columbia Oral History interview by Gottesman, p. 4 of transcript. Although US repeatedly alleged indifference to his ancestry, he included in both his autobiographies a summary of a long genealogical and historical manuscript, *The Fighting Sinclairs,* written by Albert Mordell with financial help (L, Mordell to US, Jan. 8, 1930) from the by-then famous US, as well as with his perhaps less than candid prediction that Mordell's work would likely be published, which it never was. US's strong encouragement of Mordell clearly contradicts his professed boredom, and, in fact, he was immensely proud of those naval officer ancestors. The Sinclairs who were US's relations and ancestors pronounced their name with the accent on the first syllable.

Page 8   "It was the Highway of Lost Men": *LP*, 3–4./ "three boys sleeping in one bed": *Mam*, 260.

Page 9   When Thomas Wolfe was accused: A. Turnbull, *Thomas Wolfe*, NY, 1967, 10./ Upton's tight-lipped, stern-faced mother: L, Floyd Dell to US (n.d., but written after 1920): "I went to see your mother the other day, and I really liked her very much: a nice hardheaded, conventional old reactionary. . . . She is the very antithesis of you. If the world were made up exclusively of people like her, there would be no progress; if it were made up exclusively of people like you, it would prematurely explode! . . . I think it very amusing that you should be her son."/ When Upton was about ten: There are a number of conflicting dates in US's autobiographies, letters, and articles concerning when he and his parents moved from Baltimore to New York, but they range only from "eight or nine," *AO*, 22, to "about ten years old," L, US to Floyd Dell, June 7, 1926./ houses on Maryland Avenue: L, US to William Cunningham, May 18, 1939. His grandfather Harden died when US was eleven and thereafter the boy stayed with the Blands when he was in Baltimore./ "I do not know why": *Auto.*, 12. Also, "My Cause," *Independent*, May 14, 1903, 1122: "The deepest fact of my nature . . . is a fiery savage hatred of wealth."

Page 10 "I will spend my money": L, US to his mother, from Baltimore, June 18, 1892./ "to explain the appearance": All his adult life, US would be especially alert to the same syndrome in others. In explaining the career of Jonathan Swift, he wrote, *Mam*, 142: "his fate in life was to be brought up a 'poor relation' and to eat the bitter bread of dependence." And of Heine, *ibid.,* 209:

"Another element was the shame of the 'poor relation'; he had a rich uncle, a millionaire banker in the bourgeois city of Hamburg. . . ."

Page 11   "Charlie Chaplin used to": L, US to Aline Law, Mar. 30, 1946./ He devoured books: see *LP*, 11–12./ "I was an extraordinarily devout": *TPOR*, 92.

Page 12   "Nevertheless, on Easter-Even": the confirmation card is among US's papers.

Page 14   "He worshipped General Lee": *LP*, 7./ Both kinds of repugnance: See J. Bensman and A. Vidich, *The New American Society*, Chicago, 1971, 40./ "His nursery had been haunted": *LP*, 7–8./ "visited various Springs" and "I could write a regular": L, US to Dell, July 19, 1926.

Page 15   an insensitivity common to most of the muckrakers: Ray Stannard Baker, Oswald Garrison Villard, and William English Walling excepted. See, H. Shapiro, "The Muckrakers and Negroes," *Phylon*, XXI, 1970, 76–88. On the one hand, US could describe "a racing meet, and an orgy with negro women in a stable" as one of the "Depravities in Capitalist Society," on "Upton Sinclair's Page," *Appeal to Reason*, May 7, 1921; and on the other hand, on those infrequent occasions when he considered the black as an individual, as in *Manassas*, US could write very movingly about him./ Walter Lippmann would later: *Drift and Mastery*, NY, 1914, 4–5./ Arthur Sinclair and . . . David Farragut: *FDB*, 17–18; also, *AO*, 7./ "In the most deeply significant": *TPOR*, 281./ "duty held him": *LP*, 9.

II. YOUTH AND ECSTASY

All the quotations in this chapter not identified below are from *AO*: 42–43, 39–40, 44–45, 31–35, 35, 48–50, and 57–58, 57, 58, 32–34 and 24, 64, 75–78, 74, 65–66, 64–65, 10–11.

Page 20   "The impulse to create": *Prejudices*, Ser. V, NY, 1926, 189./ "how you were saved": L, Dell to US, March 8, 1927./ "(I suspect he was a fairy!)": *ibid./* his ignorance of homosexuality: when interviewed by LH, Harold J. Salemson stated that as a young Socialist journalist just returned from Europe, he went to Pasadena in 1931 to interview his hero, who was by then the most read American author in Europe, and US asked him: "You being from Paris, can you tell me what female homosexuals do to each other? I can imagine what males do, but not females." Salemson stated that he was so shocked by the older writer's naïveté that he did not answer.

Page 21   sublimated homosexual: US was quoted as using those words in notes taken by Irving Stone in late 1938 or early 1939, for the latter's planned but never written biography of US. Stone-LH interview./ "I taught them": *TPOR*, 92–93./ Thomas Paine's *Age of Reason* . . . Moir was not at all shocked: *LP*, 17–18, and *AO*, 43–45.

Page 22   rather his political visions: Had Shelley really been faced with the choice between whether to be a poet or a politician, his choice might have been surprising if he meant what he wrote T. L. Peacock, Jan. 24, 1819: "I consider poetry very subordinate to moral and political science, and if I were well, certainly I would aspire to the latter." See also, G. Santayana, "Shelley: or the Poetic Value of Revolutionary Principles," *Winds of Doctrine*, NY,

1926, 159. K. Cameron, *The Young Shelley*, NY, 1950, suggests that because Percy was brought up by his mother, his father being away in London, "he was ill-adjusted to normal group relationships . . . [which] not only produced a sense of isolation and retaliation, it also laid the psychological basis for that hatred of tyranny. . . ." Also like US, Shelley was a writer when still in his teens; romantic, occult, mysterious Gothic tales and poems of terror were for him what the pulp novels were for US. But earlier on than US, he became a political radical resolved to devote his life to the service of humanity./ "The same means": *Queen Mab Notes*. See also Shelley's *The Necessity of Atheism* and *A Refutation of Deism*./ views on business, on marriage, on politics, and even on diet: In *Queen Mab Notes* see: "Commerce, beneath whose poison-breathing shade"; "There is no real wealth but the labor of man"; "disguising dead flesh . . . of its bloody juices and raw horror." See also Shelley's *The Masque of Anarchy, A Vindication of Natural Diet*, and *On the Vegetable System of Diet*. To say that US was strongly influenced politically by Shelley is also to say he was influenced by those who had molded Shelley's views, Paine, Godwin, Condorcet, Halbach, and Volney.

Page 23   "A brighter dawn awaits": *Queen Mab*.

Page 24   sold it to *Argosy*: "Tommy Junior the Second," July 1895, 357–362./ claiming it had been thirteen: see the opening sentence of the Preface to *Auto*./ by the time he was fifteen: L, US to Dell, June 7, 1926. "I began to write jokes and sketches at the age of fourteen or fifteen, and from that time on to take care of myself, and later of my mother, that is from about sixteen on." It is perhaps not insignificant that he wrote "of my mother" when, in fact, it was both parents he was supporting./ had sailed from Norfolk: On Nov. 24, 1852, also noted in his obituary was the fact that he was the last survivor of that cruise.

Page 25   He made enough money: L, US to Dell, Dec. 2, 1926.

Page 26   "a diminutive Sub-freshman": L, Sept. 28, 1941./ first few weeks of each term: *LP*, 16–17; also, *AO*, 67./ Christmas holiday in 1891: According to *FDB*, 33–34, US's reading all of Shakespeare and Milton took place in the summer of his thirteenth year, but US states it was during a Christmas holiday./ "lost his soul": *LP*, 19.

Page 27   "around eighteen or nineteen": FDB, 42, puts US's first ecstasy when the boy was sixteen.

Page 28   US's college friend Martin Birnbaum, who decades later served as his chief adviser on the Lanny Budd series, gave US violin lessons. L, US to Frank Harris, Sept. 10, 1917: "I set out at 17 to try to learn the *violin* and I practiced ten hours a day practically every day for two or three years. I mean that literally; 8 to 12, 2 to 6 and 8 to 10."

Page 29   "These things came": *LP*, 21–30.

Page 30   "something in his features": *LP*, 35–36, and see also 11.

Page 31   "Let me tell you": L, n.d., but noted in US's later hand, "Date, 1894 or 5."/ nothing sharpens a man's sight: see T. Fuller's *Gnomelogia*, No. 3674.

III. AUTHOR AND LOVER

Page 33   "A system could not": *Queen Mab Notes.*

Page 34   unable to identify: Gottesman, "The Upton Sinclair Dime Novels," *Dime Novel Round-Up*, Mar. 15, 1964, 20–23./ during the eighteen month . . . do it in!": *ibid.*/ "1,275,000 words": *FDB*, 47 (F. Dell, *Upton Sinclair: A Study in Social Protest*, Long Beach, 1927), gives much higher estimates, "56,000 words a week . . . more than two million words a year."

Page 35   "and enough of Maupassant": *AO*, 88–89.

Page 36   "The wild things": *ibid.*, 78–80.

Page 37   "it was no crime": *ibid.*, 90–91.

Page 38   "I was probably never": *ibid.*, 92–94./ "I never put pen": L, US to Frank Harris, Sept. 10, 1917.

Page 39   Meta was younger than Upton: according to DS's birth certificate, Meta was born Feb. 7, 1880. In her writing she states that she was three years younger than US. Her L to Phyllis (Collier), Mar. 5, 1953, states she is seventy-six, or some four years younger than US./ "that horrid boy" and "stood out from": Meta Fuller Sinclair (later Keene and still later Stone) wrote several outlines and sample chapters for a book that was to be called variously *Corydon and Thyrsis*, *Love's Pilgrimage*, and *An Autobiographical Novel*. There were different versions and corrections beginning prior to her divorce from US in 1912 and continuing through 1942. The manuscripts, never published, contain verbatim many letters between Meta and US, Meta and her lovers, and between the lovers and US. The manuscripts describe a period from Meta's first childhood meetings with US through the divorce. In these so-called "Stone manuscripts" at the Lilly Library are parts of Meta's correspondence until almost the date of her death, Sept. 3, 1964. All direct quotes of Meta not otherwise identified, as well as much of what she thinks and does in this book, come from these Stone mss./ still looked beautiful: A first cousin half a century later recalled that she thought her older relative "the most glamourous adult I knew. She was quick-witted, amusing, loving and lazy. Today one would say that she dressed 'mod' and always 'did her own thing' . . . hopelessly spoiled, an only child, very beautiful . . . I would call her a Mediterranean type . . . with a prominent nose, slightly slanted eyes, and a generous mouth . . . a striking individual with great magnetism. Sexy, if you like." Ls, Darley Fuller Gordon to LH, Aug. 3 and 19, 1970./ tendency to flirt: In an interview with LH, DS recalled, "I was somewhat afraid of her, partly because of my conditioning by my father's thinking—he was afraid of her. And I remember one time I visited her in her apartment in 1925 and I got this frightening feeling that she was trying to make love to me, not literally, you know, spiritually, metaphorically speaking, she sort of sidled up to me. She was sort of coy . . . the only way I can describe it is that she was sort of trying to seduce me, you know, not physically, of course, but that was the source of my fright . . . some kind of subconscious reaction."/ vague immortal longings: In interviews with both of Meta's sons, LH found that they believed her chief reason for marrying US was to help her realize her artistic potential and to increase her education.

Page 40   "I do not believe": Stone mss. Many of the love letters quoted in the Stone
           mss. are also quoted in US's *LP* and although they are substantially the same,
           the differences are edifying./ "Read Shelley's *Epipsychidion*" and "Do you
           recall what Beethoven said": *ibid.*

Page 41   "I have enough heart's passion": *LP*, 110./ two male shepherds in Milton's
           L'Allegro: who, according to Vergil's *Seventh Bucolic*, were "both in the
           flower of youth, both Arcadians and peers of pastoral song." In 1924 André
           Gide would use "Corydon" as the title to his essay defending homosexual-
           ity./ "I bow in joy": *LP*, 117./ "I have no more to say": Stone mss./ "If you
           take me," "how impossible it will be," and "I am in one of my cast-iron
           moods": *LP*, 117–123.

Page 42   "Between Corydon and Thyrsis": *AO*, 108./ "his love-making was fitful":
           Stone mss.

IV. THE DEATH OF THE POET

           All the quotations in this chapter not identified below are from *TJOAS*: 121,
           vii, 81, 4–6, 7, and 10, 30, 26–27, 18–19, 27.

Page 44   "There are no mute": *Prejudices*, Ser. III, NY, 1922, 89./ "clad in a dress" and
           "one strand of her golden hair": *KM*, 14./ "you are never going to": *ibid.*,
           304.

Page 46   "We have a very conservative": *AO*, 116–117. Also, L., US to Perry Miller,
           Dec. 31, 1951./ a Columbia professor: Harry Thurston Peck, *AO*, 85, and
           117–118.

Page 47   "I wrote 'King Midas' ": L, US to Dell, June 7, 1926./ "The truth was": *AO*,
           117.

Page 48   "I find myself just now": L, Dec. 12 (no year), NYPL mss./ "I have been
           living": L, US to Edwin Markham, Dec. 7 (no year)./ "A Review of
           Reviews": *Independent*, Feb. 6, 1902.

Page 52   "time passed and 'Arthur Stirling' ceased": Postscript to the Third Edition of
           TJOAS, Nov. 1923. That he was Arthur Stirling, US made plain in his
           books, his letters, his conversation. In a "Postscript" to the book dated Aug.
           16, 1906, he wrote: "No truer book than *The Journal of Arthur Stirling* has
           ever been written; it is the book of all my boyhood's hopes and dreams and it
           is as dear to me as the memory of a dead child."

V. THE POET TRANSFORMED—SOCIALIST AND HISTORIAN

           All the quotations in this chapter not identified below are from *LP*: 535–536,
           537, 539, 556, 116–117, 470–474.

Page 53   "What distinguishes the chronically indignant": *Arrow in the Blue*, NY,
           1952–1954, 54.

Page 54   "I share in Ruskin's distrust": *A Captain of Industry*, 58–59./ No publisher
           . . . until: another unsuccessful short novel not published until after *TJ*
           became an international best seller was *The Overman*, written in 1901–02 and

only published by Doubleday, Page & Company in September 1907. It was a
failure both literarily and economically./ often execrable writing: although
US as the years passed became less emotional about his early novels and even
became critical of them, in the case of *A Captain of Industry*, which he called
the "most ferocious of my stories," he instead developed delusions that it was
a prophetic and revolutionary work of some importance. Because of its
furious anti-capitalist rhetoric, this novel was and still is much printed and
quoted from in the Soviet Union./ "I Upton Sinclair, would-be singer":
Independent, May 14, 1903, 1121–1126./ "My error lay": *Postscript, TJOAS*,
Aug. 16, 1906.

Page 56   "I do not know how": *AO*, 126–128.

Page 58   "intellectually a perfect little snob": *ibid.*, 142.

Page 59   agreed to subsidize . . . Sinclair: in gratitude, US dedicated *Prince Hagen*,
published June 6, 1903, by Colonial Press, to Herron, quoted liberally from
Herron in *The Cry for Justice*./ "It was like the falling down": *AO*, 143./ "to
revise all": *LP*, 535–536.

Page 60   "in a continuous ebullition" and "Nor did he": *ibid.*, 537–539. Joyful
ebullience is not usually the most evident characteristic of the reformer, but
it was of US who remembered when he first read Shaw's *Man and Superman*
lying in a hammock "kicking my heels in the air with delight," *AO*, 151. His
boyish joyfulness was the single most frequently reported characteristic by
those who spoke or wrote to LH about US, including Roger Baldwin, Earl
Browder, Scott Nearing, Carey McWilliams, Halldor Laxness, and Ronald
Gottesman, among others. Witness after witness testifies, as did Louis
Untermeyer, L, to LH, July 7, 1970: "I was struck by his combination of
knowledge and naïveté."/ "had visions of being": *LP*, 556.

Page 62   "I adored him": L, Meta to DS, Jan. 19, 1940. US's letters and writings
amply confirm his efforts to enforce celibacy./ "I should be insane": *LP*,
116–117./ "She suffered from depression": *AO*, 135./ whose seminal works:
The Interpretation of Dreams, 1899, and *Three Essays on the Theory of Sexuality*,
1905./ claimed to have read Freud: *TBOL* I, 71./ basically antipathetic to
Freud: "Both my (second) wife and I have found ourselves becoming more
and more repelled by the whole thing [psychoanalysis], mainly from
watching its effects on people. In the 35 years we have known about it, we
have never known it to help anybody." L, US to Melville Kress, Aug. 11,
1944.

Page 63   chief source of her discontent: DS believes his mother was so shallow,
spoiled, and incurably neurotic that, quite regardless of his father's admitted
faults, the causes of her unhappiness were within herself and based on an
unconquerable egoism greater even than her husband's./ "when night after
night," "sexual intercourse became," "waited each month," and "They were
like people": *LP*, 470–474.

Page 64   " 'Uncle Tom's Cabin' was": *Manassas*, 57–58. The criticism of Mrs. Stowe's
book that US quotes and his answer to the criticism are almost precisely
identical to the later criticisms of *TJ* and his answers to those criticisms./
again without the success: Because *Manassas* was unsuccessful, US never

began the two other Civil War novels, *Gettysburg* and *Appomattox*, that were to have completed his trilogy.

Page 65   "Frank Norris had": L, US to Willard E. Martin, Jr., Nov. 19, 1930. Also, L, US to Frank Harris, Sept. 10, 1917. *The Octopus* was published in 1901./ new journalism of exposure: See L. Filler, *The Muckrakers*, Chicago, 1968, A. and L. Weinberg, *The Muckrakers*, NY, 1961, and C. Regier, *The Era of the Muckrakers*, Chapel Hill, 1932. Also, A. M. Schlesinger, *The American as Reformer*, Harvard, 1950./ even before the Civil War: for example, *Frank Leslie's Illustrated Newspaper* in its campaign against the selling of milk from diseased cattle in New York.

Page 66   *The Appeal to Reason*: After Wayland's death in 1912, the *Appeal* was bought from his son in 1919 by Louis Kopelin and Emanuel Haldeman-Julius. It underwent a number of name changes; see notes for Chapter V of this book.

Page 67   strike against the meat-packers: See E. Pook, "The Meat Strike," *Independent*, July 18, 1904, 179–184, and Filler, *op. cit.*, 157–170./ "YOU HAVE LOST THE STRIKE": *Appeal to Reason*, Sept. 17, 1904, 1.

VI. *THE JUNGLE*, PART 1

All the quotations in this chapter not identified below are from *TJ*: NAL Signet edition, NY, 1960: 136, 18, 37, 104, 136, 148–154, 188–190, 209, 249–250.

Page 68   the refrigerator car: *Harper's Weekly*, Oct. 21, 1882, 663.

Page 69   refrigerator cars were owned: despite their contributions to Republican Party campaign coffers, on Dec. 15, 1905, in Kansas City, Armour, Swift, Cudahy, and Morris were charged by a federal grand jury with having received illegal freight rebates, *NYT*, Dec. 16, 1905./ favorable articles: see Filler, *op. cit.*, 157–158./ born in 1844: Wiley died June 30, 1930, twenty-four years to the day after the passage of the Pure Food and Drug Act.

Page 70   toward the end of 1904: US gave several different dates: See *Appeal to Reason*, Nov. 17, 1906; *AO*, 154; L, US to Pvt. John M. Mickelson, Nov. 23, 1942; and "Introduction" to a new edition of *TJ*, Viking, 1946./ argument with Miss Addams: See L, US to Addams, May 29, 1905, Swarthmore College Peace Collection, Jane Addams Papers./ sixty-acre farm: See L, William M. Dwyer to US, Aug. 4, 1964, and *AO*, 157.

Page 71   "the life I am living": Oct. 10, 1904./ "stood a table": *AO*, 157–158./ One Sunday afternoon: *ibid.*, 156, and L, US to Frank Harris, Sept. 10, 1917.

Page 74   "I wrote with tears": *AO*, 158.

Page 75   "the professors refused to teach": *ibid.*, 159./ such men as: L, US to Edwin Markham, Dec. 12, 1904, from Wagner College collection./ London as president: R. O'Conner, *Jack London*, Boston, 1964, 241; and *AO*, 159–161.

Page 76   "I was prepared": *Mam*, 364./ "a very staid and proper": US-Gottesman interview, 66–68./ Florence Kelley: E. Bloor, *We Are Many*, NY, 1940, 79./ its importance to Sinclair: and first pointed out by Gottesman in his dissertation.

Page 77   "I did the best": *AO*, 161./ Moyer-Haywood case: Charles Moyer, president of the Western Federation of Miners, and "Big Bill" Haywood, a founder of the IWW, were acquitted of planning the murder of Idaho's ex-governor, Frank Steunenberg. The man who "confessed" the murder (and was convicted) and testified for the prosecution at the famous trial in May 1907 was Harry Orchard, a squalid labor spy and provocateur.

VII. *THE JUNGLE*, PART 2

All the quotations in this chapter not identified below are from E. Morison, *Letters of Theodore Roosevelt*, Cambridge, 1952: 176, 178–180, 208–209, 287–289, 289.

Page 78   "Fifty years ago": "Work, Alienation, and Social Control," *Dissent*, Summer 1959./ "The following is": NYPL mss./ "prolonged and desperate illness": L, US to Brett, Apr. 30, 1905, NYPL mss.

Page 79   a month later: L, US to Brett, May 31, 1905, NYPL mss./ a second operation: see Chapter XIII of this book./ David Graham Phillips: A biography of US cannot address itself to the achievements of his many fellow muckrakers. But mention must be made of Phillips' "The Treason of the Senate," which began to appear in *Cosmopolitan* in March of 1906, a year after *TJ* had begun serially in the *Appeal*, and which revealed the horrifying truth about the Senate as no one had ever dared to before and perhaps at a degree of risk to its author taken by no other muckraker./ June 10, he wrote Brett: NYPL mss./ C. R. Carpenter: memorandum, June 14, 1905, NYPL mss./ Another Macmillan reader: R. D. Townsend, memorandum, Sept. 18, 1905, NYPL mss.

Page 80   "I think that": L, US to Brett, Sept. 13, 1905, NYPL mss / "with a view to lightening": it is possible the word is not "lightening" but "tightening."/ "Hunter, Merwin and others": Hunter was Robert Hunter, a "millionaire Socialist," brother-in-law of Graham Phelps Stokes and author of the germinal book, *Poverty*. Merwin was Samuel Merwin, a romantic novelist who turned muckraker and as editor of *Success* changed it into an important magazine of exposé./ "It is useless": *AO*, 162./ After five other publishers: *ibid.*, 162./ "it would be an act": *Appeal*, Nov. 18, 1905.

Page 81   "taken the momentous decision": L, US to London, Sept. 28, 1905, Huntington Library mss./ Doubleday, Page & Company: L, US to Brett, Dec. 8, 1905. Also, L, US to Brett, Dec. 12, 1905, NYPL mss./ had to defend the truth: see, for example, "Is Chicago's Meat Clean?" *Collier's*, Apr. 22, 1905, 13–14, or "Is 'The Jungle' True?" *Independent*, May 17, 1906, 1129–1133.

Page 82   Upton replied in *Everybody's*: "The Condemned Meat Industry: A Reply to J. Ogden Armour," May 1906, 608–616./ stop the presses: L, US to Jack London (signed by secretary's initial signature, A.M.P.), Mar. 19, 1906, Huntington Library./ "I have got hold": L, Mar. 7, 1906, Huntington Library./ "I should be afraid": quoted *AO*, 159./ "or you, if they could": what may have been an attempt by the packers to bribe US is described in *AO*, 168–169.

Page 83   "this week's issue to T.P.O.": Vol. 1, No. 1, week ending June 16, 1906, 25–26, and Vol. 1, No. 2, June 23, 1906, 65–66. US considered Churchill so unimportant that he made no mention of this review as late as *AO*, in 1932, but thirty years later in his *Auto.*, he quoted Churchill at some length, 121–122.

Page 84   "Brecht's Play": L, Esslin to LH, July 28, 1970./ "A Dispassionate Examination": Mar. 3, 1906, 123./ influenced by Zola's *Germinal*: See, Ls, US to Marc Bernard, Oct. 9, 1952; US to Arnold Biella, Jan. 2, 1955; and US's book review, *NYT*, Aug. 9, 1953./ reaction of President Theodore Roosevelt: both Isaac Marcosson, *Adventures in Interviewing*, London, 1920, who handled publicity for Doubleday, and US himself, *AO*, 166, had sent copies of *TJ* to the President./ "There is something to be said": L, Nov. 15, 1913.

Page 85   "men very powerful": *ibid.*/ Boss Platt: Thomas C. Platt, who supported TR as Republican nominee for governor of New York when the Rough Rider returned a hero from Cuba./ "th' Hayro is a Lithuanian": "Mr. Dooley on the Food We Eat," F. P. Dunne, *Collier's*, June 23, 1906, 15–16./ lunch at the White House: *AO*, 166–168. The luncheon was after Phillips' "The Treason of the Senate" had begun to appear in *Cosmopolitan* in Mar. 1906./ "I remember his words": *AO*, 167.

Page 86   "The men with the muck-rake": The speech in this particular form was delivered at Washington, D.C., Apr. 14, 1906, at the laying of the cornerstone of the Office Building of the House of Representatives. *The Outlook*, Vol. LXXXII, Jan.–Apr. 1906, Apr. 21, 1906, 883–887. The exact occasion on which TR first used the term "muckraker" is in some dispute, and he seems to have tested it privately on a number of occasions, the earliest perhaps being March 17, according to J. Bishop, *Theodore Roosevelt and His Times*, NY, 1920.

Page 88   "Oh, by the way,": L, US to London (signed by secretary, A.M.P.), Mar. 19, 1906, Huntington Library.

Page 90   Roosevelt . . . really feared: see TR's Ls to Charles F. Gettemy, Feb. 1, 1905; and to William H. Taft, Mar. 15, 1906./ thought of Sinclair . . . other muckrakers: see L, TR to Owen Wister, Apr. 27, 1906./ Neither Sinclair nor Wiley: See L, Wiley to US, Jan. 15, 1930./ taking credit: US's, Wiley's, and even TR's self-serving recollections are models of modesty when compared to *The Memoirs of a Publisher*, NY, 1972, F. N. Doubleday's ridiculous self-eulogy.

VIII. A HARD ACT TO FOLLOW

Quotations in this chapter not identified in these notes, as well as ideas or scenes from *AO* for which there are no notes, appear in *AO* on pages 170, 170, 182, 188, 191–192, 190–196, 166, 207.

Page 91   "I do not love": quoted in Williams, Current, and Freidel, *A History of the United States (Since 1865)*, NY, 1965, 110./ "was asked by a friend": *Works of H. G. Wells*, 135.

Page 92   fans complained: L, US to London, Mar. 7, 1906, Huntington Library./

received from Doubleday: L, Byrne Hackett to US, June 6, 1906, Huntington Library. Across it US wrote: "We have met the enemy & they are ours!"/ being asked by *Life*: *Life*, Mar. 7, 1907./ "I find your books": L, Herron to US, Aug. 10, 1908./ Henry James: L, James to US, Mar. 5, 1908./ run for Congress: *NYT*, Oct. 5, 1906./ " 'It will not,' ": *Human Life, The Magazine About People*, Sept. 1906, 5, 6, and 8./ in *Cosmopolitan*: Oct. 1906, 591–595.

Page 93   Meta's increasing obsession: L, US to Wilshires, June 28, 1909, quoted in H. Quint, *The Forging of American Socialism*, Columbia, 1953: "Then came the Jungle, and I made a lot of money, and I might have rested. But because Meta was almost out of her mind, and I did not know what to do with David, I started Helicon Hall."/ After an article: "A Home Colony," *Independent*, June 14, 1906, 1401–1408.

Page 94   Sinclair Lewis: In their correspondence with one another and in their works, both men frequently acknowledged the confusion./ "thoroughly bored": quoted in M. Schorer, *Sinclair Lewis*, NY, 1961, 110–122./ by his own account . . . and "where else": "Two Yale Men in Utopia," NY *Sun*, Dec. 16, 1906. Lewis and Updegraff left Helicon Hall Dec. 2, 1906./ Edith Summers: See *NYT Book Review*, Mar. 11, 1973, 48; also, L. Summers to US, June 29, 1929./ The press was full: See, NY *Sun*, July 1906, and *NYT*, July 8 and Nov. 12, 1906./ "There is nothing": *NYT*, Oct. 7, 1906./ Jews: L, US to Eugene B. Williams, May 20, 1932, "There was no objection to Jews and there were two or three Jews in the colony."

Page 95   She told Upton: Stone mss./ "spasmodic and desultory fits" and "unsatisfied longings": *ibid.*

Page 96   signed a contract: Oct. 1, 1906./ "He told Corydon that he and Mrs. X": Stone mss. Meta refers to Miss Mayo only as "Mrs. X."/ "which I believe": Even though Meta believed no adultery had been consummated with Mayo, when US later sued her for divorce on grounds of adultery; she threatened to allege that he too had been guilty and before she had been, with Miss Mayo as well as with Anna Noyes.

Pages 96–
97   One day at Helicon Hall . . . but this was all": Stone mss.

Page 97   Upton frequently wrote: *LP*, 650, 662–663; *TJ*, 327 328, 336./ referring to Beethoven's breaking: *LP*, 110./ "I am not able": L, US to Judith Chase Churchill, June 21, 1944./ "naked at night": L, Oct. 28, 1932./ Four and a half months: Helicon Hall opened on Nov. 1, 1906. The fire began at three or four in the morning, Mar. 16, 1907, *NYT*, Mar. 17, 1907.

Page 98   Collecting from the insurance company: memoranda to the stockholders from US, Mar. 22, July 19, Aug. 13, 1907, and later./ April 5, 1907: Baltimore *Sun*, April 7, 1907, 1./ another twenty-four years: Baltimore *Sun*, Oct. 20, 1931./ "She has a millionaire sister": L, US to A. R. Williams, Aug. 31, 1925.

Page 99   "She was the best": n.d., marked "1931, D.S.," in the collection of DS and used with his kind permission./ "became pregnant": Stone mss./ In his autobiography: *AO*, 190–191, mentions only one hospital visit, although US's L to Brett (quoted Chapter VII of this book) mentions two operations (as she wrote of "another operation") while carefully failing to define them. In a L to DS, Jan. 1, 1931, US confided "Meta had to have an abortion." Collection of DS./ in mid-August: *NYT*, Nov. 6 and 7, 1907.

Page 100   Doubleday had contracted to: L., July 3, 1906, and later Ls./ *The Overman*: See notes for Chapter V of this book./ met through Lincoln Steffens: Gottesman interview, 33.

Page 101   "put a clause": some variant of this is now standard in most book publishers' contracts, but only because US and others fought for it.

Page 102   Edmond Kelly: *TBC*, 80–85, 260./ "a rich man's panic": F. Freidel, *America in the Twentieth Century*, NY, 1971, 78–79./ law courts upheld: *Moneychangers*, 79./ panic itself: *ibid.*, 143–151. Here again his characters and so his readers were "in at the making of history"; as Morgan-Waterman explains, the panic is useful to curb the President, 148./ "to teach the people": *ibid.*, 181.

Page 104   He was never successfully sued for libel: US was sued unsuccessfully for libel by Mrs. Rosika Schwimmer, the originator of Ford's Peace Ship, for statements about her made by Fox in *USPWF*. See *Auto.*, 139, 258. Also the bringing of a $1,000,000 libel suit caused US to apologize publicly in a Negro newspaper, the St. Louis *Argus*, No. 41, Jan. 25, 1935, 7.

Page 105   "be sure that the criminal": *Auto.*, 139./ quoted the article: *TBC*, 85./ "sexual habits": *ibid.*, 118–119. More than twenty-five years later in the midst of his work on Lanny Budd he took time out to write pettishly, L, to J. R. Cominsky, Oct. 2, 1946: "My attention was caught by your reference to the 'personal habits' of Ochs. You left out one—his treatment of young women who came into his office. If you are curious on the subject, see page 118 of 'The Brass Check.'"/ "against all evidence": Baldwin in Ls to and conversation with LH from June through Sept. 1970. Carey McWilliams in an interview with LH stressed about US that "unlike many successful men he was very approachable, very pleasant. . . . he was charming personally, with a very soft voice—much pleasanter to meet in person than through his writings."/ "I have never forgotten": W. and A. Durant, *Interpretations of Life*, NY, 1970, 47–48.

Page 106   re Dreiser and US: See F. Matthiessen, *Theodore Dreiser*, NY, 1951, 83, 130–131./ "welfare state": *Social Darwinism in American Thought*, Boston, 1955, 3–12 and 85.

Page 107   "Now when a man": *TBC*, 266–270. The man in question was H. R. Galt, managing editor of the St. Paul *Pioneer Press* and the St. Paul *Dispatch*, who was threatening a libel suit he, in fact, never brought.

Page 108   had prayed to Goethe: *LP*, 41. See *ibid.*, 333, "beautiful, pale and sensitive—a haunted boy."/ "to gaze at it as at a lover": *ibid.*/ "Whenever Thyrsis met one": *ibid.*, 347–348./ "that the disinterested tendency": *Moral Indignation and Middle Class Psychology*, NY, 1970, 198, 199–204.

IX. DIET AND ADULTERY

Page 110   "The psychology of adultery": *Marriage and Morals.*/ told *The New York Times*: *NYT*, Nov. 27, 1907, datelined Battle Creek, Mich., Nov. 26.

Page 111   swimming in the nude: Stone mss./ "The camp was run": *AO*, 208–209.

Page 112   "Socialists ought not": *ibid./* "close to a nervous breakdown": *ibid.,* 204./ his new friend: according to Sterling's diary at Bancroft Library, University of California, they met Oct. 31, 1908./ "As to Sinclair": L, Bierce to Sterling, Jan. 9, 1909, NYPL Berg Collection.

Page 113   Upton had written Sterling: Sept. 10, 1908./ moved to Palo Alto: L, David Belasco to US, Jan. 6, 1909./ Belasco complained: L, Belasco to US, Nov. 28, 1908.

Page 114   Stanford University refused: NY *Sun*, Jan. 27, 1909./ sank without a trace: On Jan. 15, 1912, Mitchell Kennerley published *Plays of Protest*, four of US's plays: *Prince Hagen, The Second Story Man, The Machine,* and *The Naturewoman. The Machine* was written in lieu of the third of US's planned trilogy of novels that began with *The Metropolis* and *The Moneychangers*. Even FvE wrote, L, Dec. 31, 1909, that the play "ends like a candle burning out." And for *The Naturewoman,* even US's fellow Socialist George Bernard Shaw could not find a word of praise (though US nevertheless printed Shaw's critique in his Preface to *Plays of Protest*)./ "Things have come": L, US to Meta, n.d., but clearly winter of 1908–09, Stone mss.

Page 115   "I now know": "A New Helicon Hall," *Independent*, Sept. 9, 1909, 580–583./ "You will understand": n.d., Stone mss.

Page 116   imperious and ignorant: L, US to Meta, Feb. 15, 1908. Also see, L, Meta to DS, Jan. 30, 1939: "It is very difficult to be an efficient mother unless one is a happy wife. And so unfortunately you suffered as a consequence. Even when Upton was in California about 1906–7 he wanted to dictate to me by mail how your life should be managed especially with regard to eating. In one of his letters he said in effect 'if you persist in feeding David beefsteak and potatoes and cornbread, etc. I shall simply have to wash my hands of both of you'. Believe it or not this was written in deepest concern about our welfare, what he considered our welfare. Don't you see what he was unconsciously doing? He was setting himself up as God. He thought he was always right. His egotism became an obsession. And when during the latter years I opposed him on the grounds of love and sex, both of us could not be right, and so I had to be in the wrong and take the consequences, which I did to my utter un-doing and alas in a measure to yours also. His only explanation to himself and others as to the cause of our smash-up was that I had a perverted sex instinct, or rather that I was oversexed. In the light of subsequent data I found myself to be normal as regards my sex impulses and him to be sub-normal. So, of course, *you* had to be brought up on the idea that your mother was little better than a harlot and therefore sex had to be presented to you as a bugaboo."/ San Francisco *Examiner*: Jan. 30, 1909. US claimed the quotes were inaccurate.

Page 117   "inability to catch prey": *Samuel the Seeker*, 147./ "Yours is the power": "The Red Flag," *The Socialist*, Melbourne, Australia, Aug. 20, 1909, 3, and *Appeal*, Sept. 3, 1909./ six hundred dollar advance: Contract of Jan. 8, 1910./ "My proposition is": L, June 28, 1909.

Page 118   Wilshires did not accept: the Wilshires' letter is not to be found apparently because US sent it to Meta. "You see from the enclosed, that Gay doesn't want to buy any authors," L, July 2, 1909, Stone mss./ "because the law": L, July 7, 1909./ Alfred Kuttner: Born July 3, 1886; graduated from Harvard 1909; died, still unmarried, Dec. 1, 1942./ "health crank" and "I doubt if I": *SB*, 62–63.

Page 119 "We shall teach": *Independent*, Sept. 9, 1909, 580–583./ asked somewhat sharply: L, Munger to US, Aug. 15, 1909./ *Saturday Evening Post*: May 8, 1909.

Page 120 "War: A Manifesto Against It": *Wilshire's*, Sept. 1909, 7./ from Karl Kautsky: Sept. 25, 1909./ until Kautsky wrote: Nov. 1, 1909.

Page 121 "Thyrsis was domineering": *LP*, 12./ "I dare not marry": *ibid.*, 126–127./ Sinclair urged Meta: L, US to Meta, Mar. 7, 1911, and L, Edith Barrows to Meta, Aug. 23, 1932, Stone mss./ "cheerfully agree": L, US to Meta, Apr. 11, 1911./ "I shall be your wife": *LP*, 130–132./ "humiliating necessity": *ibid.*, 205./ for its day shocking: these "seven thousand words of horrifying prose" (*Auto.*, 84) had been written in the winter of 1901 when DS was born.

Page 122 "rawest, reddest meat": L, London to US, Feb. 10, 1910./ "with these matters": L, Bennett to US, Mar. 30, 1911./ "the frank way": L, Ellis to US, Apr. 4, 1911./ Santayana: See *MLIL*, 100./ Mencken, in answer: Dreiser *Letters*, Philadelphia, 1959, 185./ other New York publishers: L, US to FvE, Apr. 4, 1911./ little reason to pay: *AO*, 246, US mistakenly remembered the price as $1.50./ "who would be greatly shocked": L, Meta to US, n.d. [1909], Stone mss./ "the bed" and "five bullets": L, Meta to US, Aug. 4, [1909?], Stone mss./ "I will have": *ibid.*, the book in question is *LP*.

Page 123 "I sometimes feel": L, Meta to Brill, n.d., Stone mss./ "There there would be": L, US to Meta, n.d., but probably July 2, 1909, Stone mss. Many of US's most personal letters throughout his life were dictated to various secretaries, male and female, and often not even read and signed but sent off with a typed signature, like this one, with his nickname "Mubs."/ "I was like": L, US to Meta, n.d., but probably early 1910, Stone mss./ "It is no use": L, n.d., Stone mss./ "he brought himself" and "there have been too many words": L, Meta to AK, May 24, 1910.

X. SCANDAL AND FLIGHT

Page 125 "Women hate revolutions": *Prejudices*, Ser. IV, 252./ "the richest planter": *SB*, vii./ "by the time" and "not far in their minds": *ibid.*, 1–3.

Page 126 "when she made out": *ibid.*, 16, 13./ conceived a child: from interviews by LH with Mrs. John Kling, MCS's youngest sister, "Dollie," who went to Europe with US and MCS in 1913, and stayed with Mary and Gaylord Wilshire in England for some time after her sister and US had returned to America. Mary Wilshire confided to Dollie all the details of the abortion, an undertaking then of almost unimaginable gravity. Dollie insists US and MCS were secretly married at the time of the abortion but US stated in his Columbia Oral History interview, 183, that the secret marriage had been only a pretense.

Page 127   "grandmother gave me": *SB*, 98./ "I married Upton, because": L, MCS to "Cranie" Gartz, n.d./ a sonnet a day: these *Sonnets to Craig* were published by US's publishing company some years later in what was a gracious tribute to both his wife and to the poet./ visit in Mississippi: L, Meta to AK, Mar. 29, 1911.

Page 128   according to its founder: L, Frank Stephens to US, Mar. 6, 1910./ "I know Harry intimately": L, US to Fels, Jan. 3, n.d., but sent from Fairhope and therefore 1910./ the answer he got: L, GBS to Fels, July 8, 1910, Historical Society of Pennsylvania./ "Your friendship toward me": L, Kemp to US, Feb. 11, 1910./ "Roosevelt and the insurgents": Philadelphia *North American*, July 10, 1910.

Page 129   "A religion without a name": *Margaret Sanger, An Autobiography*, NY, 1938, 69./ Emma Goldman wrote: quoted NY *World*, Aug. 1, 1911./ Newcastle County Workhouse: US is fourth in the list of ten prisoners on the receipt of Aug. 1, 1911./ newspapers had a field day: *NYT*, Aug. 2, 3, 6, 1911; NY *World*, Aug. 1, 2, 3; NY *Tribune*, Aug. 3.

Page 130   children mimicking: George N. Caylor and Scott Nearing in interviews with LH./ "the bust": US sat for visiting Swedish sculptor Carl Eldh in May 1926; L, US to R. Wagner, May 21, 1926; also, *Auto.*, 305. The bust is in the Lilly Library./ weak Socialist thinking: "Like [Norman] Thomas and the *Forwards* [Jewish Socialist newspaper] crowd, Upton believed in the bourgeois idea that civil liberties and Socialism were one ball of wax." Nearing, same interview. See also, Nearing, *The Conscience of a Radical*, Harborside, 1965.

Page 131   "He fell in love": *AO*, 237–239./ or by letter: Inez Milholland told US that she had destroyed all of his letters, *ibid.*/ "devour a child": J. Kaplan, *Mr. Clemens and Mark Twain*, NY, 1966, 29.

Page 132   Whatever cause: US wrote Frank Harris, Sept. 10, 1917: "I married an innocent girl and spent eleven years watching her turn by slow stages into a nymphomaniac. At least, that was her mother's description, and it comes nearer than anything I know. When I got through, she was living with three men at once, and I found it out all at once—all three I mean, and I went crazy."/ announced to the press: all NY papers, Aug. 24 and 25, 1911./ "Speaking for myself" and "intellectual work occupies" and "I will make note": NY *Sun*, Aug. 28, 1911.

Page 133   "an unripe persimmon": Sept. 6, 1911./ "You have also": Sept. 11 [no year, but clearly 1911]./ "I have long since known": typed extract presumably from L, Mrs. Fuller to US, n.d.

Page 134   to leave in February: L, FvE to US, Sept. 13, 1911.

Page 135   wrote her detailing: Dec. 15, 1911./ *Love's Progress*: L, US to Meta, Oct. 23 [1911]. Mss. of *Love's Progress* is at Lilly Library./ pretended to live in Holland: "My dear Lodger," FvE wrote facetiously, Mar. 22, 1912, to US in England.

Page 136   "spoke of pain and enslavement": *AO*, 247./ "were miles of potatoes": *ibid.*, 248.

Page 137   English school at Highgate: Interview, DS by LH./ "you ought to let": L,

FvE to US, Apr. 25, 1913./ George Herron among others: L, Herron to US, Sept. 3, 1912./ "where we went around naked": Interview, DS by LH./ "simply to help by all means": L, Kropotkin to US, May 28, 1912./ "Haven't you grown": Apr. 23, 1912./ Romain Rolland: L, Sept. 30, 1912./ from Harry Kemp: see Ls, Kemp to US, Feb. (n.d.), Mar. 30, 1912 and others of n.d. and Ls, Kemp to MCS, Apr. 12, 13, 15, 26, 30, May 8, June 22, 1912, and others of n.d.

Page 138   last half of 1912: In May 1912, US wrote FvE, "Jolles [US's lawyer] writes I get the divorce May 24th next . . ." Eeden mss., University of Amsterdam. It was granted sometime between that date and December. L, Aunt Mollie [Lady Russell] to US, June 3, 1912: "I rejoice with my whole heart at your news."

XI. THE TRIUMPH OF HOPE

Page 139   "Who are happy": *Prejudices*, Ser. III, 245./ "He was still the little boy": *SB*, 118–127./ "It was a tossup": Dollie-LH interview, 3, 13./ "I feel that my life": L, MCS to "Mamma & Papa," Nov. 17, 1913, Collection of Mrs. John Kling./ "A truly romantic": Nov. 18, 1957, 118–122.

Page 140   "We were supposed": Gottesman interview, 183./ on the Lusitania: L, US to McDougall, Feb. 3, 1931, and *AO*, 260./ "royal descent": In the Lilly Library a genealogy styled "The Royal Descent of the Southworths" purports to show MCS was descended from Childeric I, fifth-century King of the Franks (through the presumably unmarried St. Arnolf, seventh-century Bishop of Metz). Also carefully preserved there is a genealogy of the Sinclairs, alleging US's descent from Charlemagne and assorted other kings of France, Scotland, Hungary, and Naples, as well as endless numbers of nobles of rank both great and small and some mere aristocrats./ "My daughter does": *AO*, 266./ Signed a new will: dated June 11, 1913, and witnessed by Priscilla Sinclair and Elsie S. Pratt.

Page 141   "Did that really happen": *AO*, 252./ "She was wise" and "it is easy": *Sylvia*, 15, 24./ "a foreigner was": *SM*, 47./ "it was testimony": *ibid.*, 68–69./ "No, I don't want": L, Phillips to US, Jan. 31, 1913.

Page 142   John C. Winston Company: this Philadelphia publisher, also in 1913, brought out US's *Damaged Goods* and the next year *SM*, as well as *The Cry for Justice* in 1915. These all had only fair sales and thereafter Winston, too, dropped US./ *Birth Control Review*: L, US to Dear Friend, July 21, 1925./ With Bernarr Macfadden: L, US to GBS, Apr. 23, 1913./ "Alas, how are the mighty fallen!": L, n.d., but spring of 1912, and enclosed L, from Paget Literary Agency, Apr. 11, 1912.

Page 143   to write her parents: Nov. 17, 1913, Collection of Mrs. John Kling./ in fact she did not: Dollie-LH interview, 16: ". . . my sister caused Upton to repudiate David. . . . It bothered me, her attitude toward David. . . . You see, I *loved* David."/ Arthur Brisbane's offer: L, Brisbane to US, Dec. 1, 1913./ He argued . . . with Max Eastman: L, Eastman to US, Mar. 28, 1914.

Page 144   Paterson silk strike: In an earlier display of direct action, US in 1912 had joined the IWW's "Big Bill" Haywood, future Communists Elizabeth Gurley Flynn and John Reed, and anarchist Carlo Tresca in the celebrated strike of the silkworkers in Paterson, New Jersey.

Page 145   He wrote Upton: L, May 6, 1914./ "I have followed his [Gandhi's] work": L, US to Rene Fulop-Miller, Mar. 24, 1923. US sent all his books to Gandhi, who wrote him Nov. 30, 1930, from Yeravda Central Prison: "I read your *Mammonart* with absorbing interest and *Mental Radio* with curiosity. The former has given me much to think, the latter did not interest me. . . . I will now avail myself of your kind offer and ask you to send me your other volumes. . . ." Louis Fischer, Gandhi's biographer, wrote US, L, July 13, 1942, from Gwalior, India: "I spent a week with Gandhi in his village. He asked me about two Americans and you were one of them."/ "Precious little reason": Nov. 15, no year indicated.

Page 146   "what would happen if they": L, US to citizens of Tarrytown, July 1914./ to lecture on the Chautauqua circuit: L, Alfred L. Flude, general manager of the Chautauqua Managers Assn., to US, June 2, 1914./ THOSE MISLEADING HEADLINES: NY *Call*, May 6, 1914.

Page 147   he wrote Arthur Brisbane: Jan. 1, 1914./ brought an action for libel: *TBC*, 188–189, *Auto.*, 202. Although on occasion US gave the sum as $3,000, in Alden Whitman's interview of Melville Cane, the partner of US's attorney, Cane stated the figure was $2,500 of which the attorneys got one-half./ "There has been an enormous change": *Auto.*, 202, 327–328./ " 'The Colorado strike,' ": R. Fosdick, *John D. Rockefeller, Jr.*, NY, 1956, 167. See also L, US to Nat Wartels, July 22, 1957. On Aug. 22, 1959, US wrote Rockefeller: "I will merely say—which I think is a Christian action—that your public career since that episode has earned our sincere regards." Until his death in 1960, John D. Rockefeller, Jr., never answered any Ls of US. In 1916 in a L commenting on US's proposed book, *King Coal*, he wrote, "I should not expect anything from his pen to do me justice" (quotation but no copy of the L supplied in L, Steven V. David, Rockefeller Family and Associates, to LH, Aug. 17, 1970).

Despite US's efforts (see L, US to J. D. Rockefeller III, May 5, 1966), Rockefeller's sons also refused to see or answer his Ls. To attempt to assess the degree of influence of a single factor on someone, even or perhaps especially one's self, is iffy work at best. But page after page in Fosdick's book testifies to the effect of the Colorado affair on Rockefeller and especially of his appearances before the Commission on Industrial Relations, which investigated the Colorado horrors. See L, Frank P. Walsh, chairman of the commission, to US, June 30, 1915.

XII. *THE CRY FOR JUSTICE, KING COAL*, AND CALIFORNIA

Page 149   "I never truckled": *The Responsibilities of a Novelist*, NY, 1903./ "Corot landscapes": L, MCS to "Dear Auntie," Oct. 15, 1914./ "various members of the New Masses": US, "The Masses," *Institute of Social Studies Bulletin*, Fall 1952, 74, 80–81.

Page 150 "he gently laid his hand": *SB*, 69. Also Schorer, *op. cit.*, 185./ played the role: L, US to FvE, Apr. 23, 1914./ "About 350 people": L, Jan. 18, 1915. See also, Gottesman dissertation and GG, 17./ "at a cost (for one print)": L, De Mille to US, Mar. 8, 1917./ He interested D. W. Griffith: L, Mary H. O'Conner to US, Mar. 19, 1917./ "Your project is": Aug. 27, 1914.

Page 151 "this purely personal attack": L, Jan. 15, 1915./ "has the misfortune": *TBC*, 260–262. In later editions Harper's allowed the quotations and the change was footnoted by US./ "Your anthology has made": L, Jan. 23, 1916./ "his writings had tremendous impact": L, Dubinsky to LH, July 2, 1970.

Page 152 an open letter: printed circular dated May 25, 1915./ she had just been named: "Ex-Soul-Mate of Sinclair in New Triangle," NY *Tribune*, June 30, 1915./ reneged on his assurances: L, US to Meta, Oct. 1, 1911.

Page 153 contrary to the records: Beginning with his "Terminal Report" from the Home School in Highgate in 1913 through college and graduate school, DS's record is exemplary./ "little monsters": DS-LH interview./ "putting clothes on Mary Burke": *SB*, 197–198./ United Mine Workers: Ls, John R. Lawson to US, Oct. 19, 1915; and E. L. Doyle to US, Dec. 2, 1915./ founded only a few years earlier: Jan. 25, 1890./ Brett refused to publish: L, May 9, 1916.

Page 154 "Because your criticism": May 1, 1916./ "my poor wife": Aug. 29, 1916, Huntington Library./ "today I finished": Oct. 29, 1916./ appeals to Shaw: L, GBS to US, May 3, 1917./ John Galsworthy: L, Galsworthy to US, Apr. 15, 1917./ Anatole France: see L, US to editor, *L'Humanité*, Mar. 2, 1917.

Page 155 ". . . you make me smile": L, Dec. 17, 1917./ "Upton was not impressed": *SB*, 144; also, *Auto.*, 181–182.

XIII. WORLD WAR I

Page 157 "When great changes": *Speech*, at trial at Cleveland, Ohio, Sept. 12, 1918./ Upton regularly sent: told to LH by US's then secretary, who later became Mrs. Floyd Dell./ letter of resignation: quoted in *NYT*, July 17 and 18, 1917, also Chicago *Tribune*, July 22, 1917./ "Today confronting the ruins": L, US to the Membership of Local Pasadena of the Socialist Party, July 2, 1920.

Page 159 "Sinclair is an emotional Socialist": "English Pacifism and Dislike of Theory," first published in *Pravda*, No. 167, July 27, 1924. See Lenin, "The Imperialist War," *Collected Works*, Vol. XVIII, International Publishers, NY, 1930, 165–167. Also published in a somewhat different translation in *International Press Correspondence*, Vol. 4, No. 60, Aug. 21, 1924, 630–631./ wire sent February 3, 1917: at the Lilly Library is a copy on White House stationery. On Mar. 23, 1917, US along with Walling, Ghent, and Charles Edward Russell condemned the anti-war resolution adopted by the Socialist National Executive Committee. See A. Link, *Woodrow Wilson and the Progressive Era*, NY, 1954, 274./ "helping to win democracy abroad": Oct. 22, 1917./ "to write Mr. Sinclair": quoted in R. S. Baker, *Woodrow Wilson*, Vol. 7, Garden City, 1927–1939 (Apr. 6, 1917–Feb. 28, 1918), 318–319./ written a number of his comrades: form letter, Oct. 19, 1917./ Max Eastman . . . Abraham Cahan . . . Frank Harris . . . *The New York Call*: a typewritten transcription of their replies is in the Lilly Library.

Page 160   political prisoners . . . be put on a farm colony: Circular letter, July 9, 1918, and "Capitalist vs. Socialist Peace," *Upton Sinclair's*, I, Sept. 1918, 3–5, as well as "An Appeal to President Wilson," 5, in the same issue. Also, L, US to United States federal attorney, New York City, May 3, 1918./ sentenced Karl Liebknecht: See *NYT*, Nov. 19, 1918./ ". . . it is utterly fatuous": L, Russell to US, Mar. 25, 1918./ "I 'specially requested": L, Sept. 23, 1914, quoted in *MLIL*, 148–149./ "My trial has been": Feb. 18, 1916.

Page 161   "Catalina Island": *NYT*, Apr. 26, 1917. US would make the same suggestion during World War II in regard to enemy leaders./ Socialist revolt in Germany: L, US to Walling, May 16, 1917./ "work out their own salvation": quoted in the *NYT*, May 9, 1917./ "sending hundreds of social-revolutionists": *ibid.*, May 25, 1917.

Page 162   "so humiliating": "What Terms of Peace Shall Close Them?" *Clarion*, London, May 7, 1915./ "If you want war": Deposition of Frank Bohn, State of California, County of Tulare, May 22, 1917./ "the entertaining time": L, May 19, 1917./ permission to carry a concealed revolver: NY *Tribune*, May 19, 1917./ Post Office Department harassment: *Auto.*, 218–219./ "I do not care": L, Feb. 19, 1918.

Page 163   "I grant every man": *AO*, 199./ "There is excellent stuff in it": L, HLM to US, Feb. 26, 1918. See also HLM, *Newspaper Days, 1899–1906*, NY, 1941, and *A Book of Prefaces*, NY, 1917./ Gertrude Atherton: L, Feb. 25, 1918./ Count Illya Tolstoy: L, Mar. 4, 1918./ Maxwell Anderson: L, June 21, 1918./ "I think it is the greatest": L, Charles Boeckman to US, May 3, 1918./ worried too that . . . Peter Kropotkin: L, to Reed printed in *Upton Sinclair's*, Dec. 1918, 3–4./ "American Capitalism is predatory": *ibid.*, 4, L, Oct. 22, 1918. The reason US used the past tense, in a letter of Oct. 22, 1918, is that he had later corrected it for printing in *Upton Sinclair's* after the armistice.

Page 164   a Communist, he never was: L, US to Dr. Albert Shiels, Apr. 18, 1919: "I am a Socialist, and I am pleading with our propertied classes to display a little wisdom and self-sacrifice, so that the rest of the world may not be driven into Bolshevism." And, L, US to W. J. Ghent, May 10, 1919: "I would not be willing to defend Bolshevism, because I am not a Bolshevik. I did not advocate Bolshevism for Russia and I certainly do not advocate it for America. . . ."/ dismissed Gorki: L, Reed to US, June 19, 1918./ "suspected with pretty good reason": L, Reed to US, Nov. 6, 1918./ "I am and was—Louise Bryant": L, Bryant to US, Mar. 9, 1918./ when she wrote: L, Bryant to US, Dec. 1, 1918; see also US to Reed, May 14, 1919./ "Upton Sinclair presumes": *Upton Sinclair's*, Oct. 1918, 16.

Page 165   for every dollar he took in: report dated May 1, 1918./ his expenses: L, US to Rudolph Spreckels, Oct. 24, 1918./ a check that bounced: US may not have been insolvent but only absent-minded, for as a note from the Internal Revenue of May 10, 1918, pointed out, the check was written on a Commercial Trust Bank account that US had closed./ negotiated a deal: L, EH-J to US, Dec. 22, 1918. *The New Appeal* was the old *Appeal to Reason*, and during the four years US wrote for it the name changed from *The New Appeal*, Feb 8 to Feb. 22, 1919, to *The Appeal to Reason*, Mar. 1, 1919, to Nov. 4, 1922, and after Nov. 11, 1922, to *The Haldeman-Julius Weekly*.

XIV. *THE PROFITS OF RELIGION* AND *JIMMIE HIGGINS*

All quotations in this chapter not identified below are from *TPOR:* 94–98, 55, 22–23, 14–15, 17, 124, 58, 271, 257–260, 253–254, 275, 297.

Page 167   "But now whin I pick": See Hofstadter, Aaron, Miller, *The American Republic*, Englewood Cliffs, 1959, 368–369. See also, H. U. Faulkner, *The Quest for Social Justice, 1878–1914*, NY, 1931.

Page 171   predicted several times: 302, 309./ One sometime radical: frequently in their correspondence US expressed concern for Lewis' radicalism and the younger man reassured him. L, Lewis to US, June 16, 1922. See Schorer, *op. cit.*, 333–334. Lewis was deceiving US (and himself) about still being a radical. Although he still visited Debs and Mrs. Debs (L, to US, Aug. 19, 1922) and still said he would write a "labor Novel" (Shorer, *op. cit.*, 532–533), the truth was he was a novelist not a propagandist and especially not a public demonstrator (telegram, Lewis to US, Sept. 20, 1916)./ Sinclair Lewis who wrote Upton: quoted in Schorer, *op. cit.*, 219./ reread *Profits*: L, Lewis to US, May 14, 1926. "I am at length starting the novel on preachers which I have planned for years and I have just reread *The Profits of Religion* with vast pleasure." US's reply, May 21, 1926./ "Let me congratulate": Oct. 28, 1918./ "don't run down spiritualism": July 25, 1918./ "Proponents of the social gospel": L, Muelder to LH, Feb. 25, 1971.

Page 172   "At Bethany": *TG-S*, 354./ first of more: excepting, of course, his first novel./ a happy surprise: L, US to Frank Harris, Sept. 5, 1917./ a farcical movie, *The Hypnotist*: L, US to Chaplin, Aug. 18, 1918./ "when there is a town": *JH*, 11; see also *TBOL*, II, 165.

Page 173   "used by the governments": L, US to Wilson, Sept. 18, 1918./ "I find in this book": L, Brett to US, Oct. 30, 1918./ might be suppressed: US wrote EH-J, who was publishing the book serially, that "to avoid any trouble with the authorities," he should destroy the ms. after Chapter XVII and use the revised version, Mar. 19, 1919./ "When I was 14 or 15": L, Bellow to LH, Oct. 8, 1970. Bellow clearly has reference to the Haldeman-Julius Little Blue Books, from which several generations of Americans learned about a number of forbidden subjects from Socialism to sex./ "He was a strong influence": L, Terkel to LH, 1970. Clement Wood wrote US, June 19, 1919, suggesting that in the next edition of *JH* he give Ben Hanford credit for the name, Jimmie Higgins, which he did not do in the novel but eventually did in his *Auto.*, 220.

XV. *THE BRASS CHECK*

Quotations in this chapter not identified in these notes, as well as ideas or scenes from *TBC* for which there are no notes, appear in that book on pages 15–16, 27, 118–119, 222, 221, 224, 349, 381.

Page 175   "What the proprietorship": borrowed from Rudyard Kipling, quoted by K. Middlemas and J. Barnes, *Baldwin, A Biography*, NY, 1970, 599–600; also quoted in H. Macmillan, *Winds of Change*, NY, 1966, 238./ "when this wrong": L, Debs to US, May 4, 1919./ Emanuel Haldeman-Julius: Ls, EH-J to US, July 28, 1918, and Feb. 4 and 11, 1919./ an Upton Sinclair book club: *100%*, 355.

Page 176   a circular letter: Sept. 10, 1922./ in the *Haldeman-Julius Weekly*: Mar. 24, 1923, 6./ convinced Warden Zerbst: L, US to Zerbst, Oct. 7, 1920, also, L, Debs to US, [Oct. 1920].

Page 177   "Upton, you can't": quoted in *Auto.*, 223./ "No doubt your name": L, Alanson Sessions to US, Feb. 10, 1920. Perhaps still the best article on "s.o.b. lists" is Maxwell Anderson's "The Blue Pencil." *NR*, Dec. 14, 1918. See also, *TBC*, 250–254./ "I want to put": June 2, 1919./ "I would have been": L, to Ruth Le Prade, Oct. 20, 1920.

Page 178   "ranting or not": Robert Benchley, "Books and Other Things," NY *World*, Sept. 8, 1920. Also, L, US to Benchley, Sept. 8, 1920./ Walter Lippmann criticized: *Public Opinion*, NY, 1921, 209./ "It is that": *ibid.*, 212–213.

Page 179   *The National News*: Pasadena, Dec. 1, 1919, pamphlet of 12 pages by US. See also, "Strangling the News," *New Justice*, May 1, 1919, 3–6. Also, "Building an Honest Newspaper," *NA*, Feb. 7, 1920, 168–170./ losses to be anticipated: L, Nearing to US, May 8, 1920./ buy the *Appeal*: see Agreement dated May 18, 1920.

Page 180   "The newspapers fill you": L, Feb. 23, 1920: "I by no means argue that the capitalistic case is good. On the contrary, it is infinitely unsound. Capitalism in America is much worse than even you make it out to be, just as journalism is much worse (as I shall say in my Smart Set review) [of *TBC*]."/ "The longer I live": L, HLM to US, Jan. 28, 1920. HLM had been persecuted for his pro-German views during the war, and one reason these two men, so diametrically opposed on so many issues, nevertheless admired each other was that each recognized in the other a courageous fighter for the right to dissent./ "Upton Sinclair's long anticipated": April 1920, 138–144./ Even some fellow muckrakers, liberals, and Socialists: Ls, Steffens to US, Oct. 18, 1920; Frank Harris to US, Mar. 31, 1920; Roger Baldwin to US, Sept. 28, 1920. Other liberals were critical in retrospect, L, Bruce Bliven to Alden Whitman, Nov. 26, 1972: "His view of society was much too simplistic; for instance, *The Brass Check* is far too black and white." See also, Ls, Bliven to LH, June 30 and July 18, 1970, and Ls, Bliven to Horace Lorimer, June 24 and 29, 1921, Historical Society of Pennsylvania. "Some of our readers": NY *Tribune*, "Books," Aug. 27, 1920.

Page 181   Then as now: See Edward Jay Epstein. "Offshore Reporting," *The New Yorker*, Jan. 22, 1972, 89–99. Epstein points out that since 1917 nearly three times as many Pulitzer Prizes have been awarded for exposing political corruption as for reporting on business community activities./ "I have been looking": L, George W. F. Hunt, the first governor of Arizona, to US, Feb. 15, 1920./ "Your courage is enough": L, Herron to US, Mar. 8, 1920./ "It requires bold courage": L, Rolland to US, Oct. 6, 1919./ "McCarthyism was child's play": L, Hook to LH, July 25, 1970./ "I shiver" and "in hourly expectation": L, US to Mrs. Warbasse, Feb. 27, 1920./ a number of pamphlets: *Press-titution*, *The Associated Press and Labor*, and *The Crimes of the* [N.Y.] *'Times'*. The *NYT* refused even to accept US's paid advertisement for *TBC* accompanied by a certified check, L, US to Advertising Department, *NYT*, Mar. 7, 1921, Louis Wiley Papers, Rush Rhees Library, University of Rochester./ endless money problems: Ls, US to W. B. Conkey Co., Dec. 11, 1920, Apr. 21, 1921./ F. Scott Fitzgerald: L, "John Grier Hibben" (Fitzgerald) to "Bunny" (Edmund Wilson) postmarked Jan. 24, 1922, quoted in A. Turnbull, *Letters of F. Scott Fitzgerald*, NY, 1963, 329./ And L, to Maxwell Perkins, *circa*. Mar. 5, 1922, *ibid.*, 154–155./ Kurt Vonnegut, Jr.: L, to LH, July 22, 1971. "Upton Sinclair first got to me when I was fourteen or so. I remember spending a Great Depression summer in a cottage on a lake near Culver, Indiana. There were five books in the cottage, and I read them all. I do not have a good memory, but I can name those five books. Four were detective novels. The fifth was *The Brass Check*, by Upton Sinclair. With no encouragement or discouragement from the relatives around me, I became a socialist. It was so easy. I'm still one. . . . Muckraking is still meat and drink to me. I'm not sure why. It makes me feel as though I were at an awfully good stag movie.

"Sinclair Lewis became a hero of mine when I was twenty or so, and I was enchanted to learn that he had once stoked Upton Sinclair's furnace.

"I read several of the Lanny Budd novels, and I noted that Sinclair wasn't much of an artist, but that didn't bother me. I continued to be fond of my idea of the man. I never met him."/ Erwin D. Canham: L. to LH, Oct. 8, 1970. "His books on the press and on religion interested me very considerably. . . . I think in retrospect I was impressed with the vigor of his strong, reformative, muckraking position, but I was not fully persuaded."/ Edward Weeks: L, to LH, May 6, 1971. "Upton Sinclair became a legend to me as an undergraduate after a walk I took on a spring Sunday with Geoffrey Parsons who was then the managing editor of the New York *Tribune*. As we footed it along Singing Beach at Manchester, he asked me what I had been reading and when I told him of my academic assignments he remarked, 'Well, there are two books you ought to look at and they will be quite a change—THE BRASS CHECK by Upton Sinclair, and Frank Harris' 'Life of Oscar Wilde.' THE BRASS CHECK, with which as an over-serious editor of the Harvard *Advocate* I did not wholly agree, led me back to THE JUNGLE, and when I read of Sinclair thereafter I ranked him in the same category with Lincoln Steffens."/ George Seldes: L, to LH, June 23, 1970. "I always maintained that since he had never had any newspaper experiences he made many serious errors in The Brass Check—nevertheless, it was the book which changed my whole journalistic career." See also, L, US to Seldes, Sept. 4, 1935./ Four other journalists who acknowledge they were affected by US's example rather than by any one work or group of works are: (1) I. F. Stone, who, when asked if he had been influenced by any of the original muckrakers replied: "Yes, Upton Sinclair. Much of his writing, but especially *The Brass Check*," quoted by Judson Grenier, "Upton Sinclair and the Press: The Brass Check Reconsidered," *Journalism Quarterly*, Autumn 1972, 427; (2) Arthur

Krock, L, to LH, Aug. 13, 1970: ". . . I of course recognize him as an important figure in life and literature and the motive power of reforms in the American system"; (3) Ramond Gram Swing, L, to US, Nov. 24, 1941: ". . . your undaunted, pioneering spirit has long been an inspiration to me"; and (4) Elmer Davis, L, to US, Oct. 23, 1943: "And I am much encouraged by the example you have set in riding the waves without ever letting them capsize you."/ Even a phobically reactionary journalist like Westbrook Pegler in a critical and bad tempered L to US, Dec. 29, 1941, admitted: "It is very kind of you to send me your new book and I shall read it immediately. I first met you in the pages of the Chicago *American* when I was a kid and they printed *The Jungle* serially. It made a great impression on me."

Page 182   written in six weeks: L, US to Frank Harris, Nov. 11, 1920./ "law and order": *100%*, 92 and 164. See also "talk about law and order," *JH*, 37./ "accumulation of horrors": L, Harris to US, Oct. 31, 1920.

Page 183   "America's present need": May 14, 1920. *100%* was published by US, Oct. 15, 1920.

XVI. MUNDUS VULT DECIPI

All the quotations in this chapter not identified below as well as ideas from *TBOL* for which there are no notes, appear in *TBOL*, I, viii: 10–11, 81–90, 61–73, 169–181, 185–186, 163, 54, 3–14, 36–45, 79–82, 15–35, 46–78, 27, 62, 59, 76–78, 56, 161.

Page 184   "There's no use trying": *Alice Through the Looking Glass*, Ch. 5.

Page 185   "I should have": L, Aug. 5, 1921. A quarter century later (US's answer is dated Apr. 8, 1947), James Jones, at twenty-five, wrote US, n.d., "I forgot about studying your BOOK OF LIFE, until after I had broken my first fast improperly and got for my trouble a packed bowel."/ a literary critic wrote: June 30, 1922./ "I am a young woman": L, Feb. 25, 1922.

Page 186   "This newspaper clipping": Sept. 27 [no year, but probably 1921, the year of the Fatty Arbuckle scandal], Collection of DS.

Page 187   "With love, Father": DS had complained in L to US, n.d., that "you used to be 'Papa,' " but US's signature remained "Father."/ "I am humbled": Mar. 24, 1923. Collection of DS.

Page 188   "Celibacy means torment": Sept. 23, 1923./ "I believe in": Oct. 17, 1923./ yet another will: holographic will dated Apr. 16, 1923./ evidence of the unprofitability: L, MCS to Ames, Feb. 4, 1921; L, US to W. B. Conkey Co., Apr. 29, 1921; Deed, To Whom It May Concern, May 3, 1921; and *passim*./ "seized by an overwhelming impulse": L, US to Roger Baldwin, Nov. 16, 1922.

Page 189   not induce his public library: L, George F. Bowerman, librarian of the Public Library, Washington, D.C., to S. C. Evans, gives as his reason for not buying *TBOL*, #2 of the form letter, "Books inferior in literary merit, of low moral tone, or poorly printed, etc."/ "the *patriotic* movement": L, Arthur Carsti to US, May 9, 1921./ "I am an admirer": Nov. 19, 1922./ "clamorously for news": M. Eastman, *Love and Revolution*, NY, 1964, 359./ "You are writing better": L, Mar. 16, 1923./ " 'It is a good book.' ": "The First Woman of Russia," *Liberator*, Nov. 1921.

Page 190   about motion pictures: Ls, Malkin to US, Nov. 1, 1922; US to Malkin, Dec. 6, 1922; US to Dr. J. W. Hartman, Apr. 10, 1923; Rose Karsner to US, Nov. 19, 1923, and *passim. JH* was made into a film in the U.S.S.R., but US never saw it./ "The moving pictures furnish": L, US to Nikolai Lebedev, May 4, 1923./ "I am willing": L, US to Joel V. Shoobin, May 15, 1923, in answer to Shoobin's L to US, Apr. 17, 1923, q.v.

Page 191   "completely *sui generis*": D. Aaron, *Writers on the Left*, NY, 1965, 46. See also Aaron, *Men of Good Hope*, Oxford, 1951./ "I always advise": L, US to Joel V. Shoobin, May 15, 1923./ continued writing for: *LIBERATOR*, July 1923, May 1924. See also, L, Minor to US, Oct. 31, 1923./ "Mainly I used to kick": L, US to Robert Minor, June 14, 1923.

Page 192   mistook himself for a public movement: US could be infuriatingly egoist one moment and the next genuinely modest, attributing his success to good fortune. Typically in the Gottesman interview, 74: "There are any number of propagandists and idealists of great sincerity who haven't had the judgment or the good luck to stumble on sound ideas, and they waste their time trying to accomplish all kinds of fantastic things. I think I had the good luck."/ "to make a bright, artistic": Gold's letters to US are not dated but most are in response to US's which are. Others can be dated by their content./ "mistaken in understanding": Mar. 23, 1923./ "Back in 1923": L, to LH, Aug. 20, 1970. Another Latin American political figure influenced by US was Juan Bosch, see J. Martin, *Overtaken by Events*, NY, 1966, 407.

Page 193   Upton tried periodically: L, US to EH-J, Mar. 14, 1923./ wives should be paid: NY *American*, Oct. 9, 1923./ Dollie, with her husband . . . chief source of support: Dollie—LH interviews and correspondence./ his name put in nomination: *NYT*, July 22 and Nov. 10, 1922: and Mar. 20 and Apr. 26, 1923./ *Tramping on Life*: NY, 1922./ the cuckold objected: L, US to Liveright, June 6, 1922./ a friend . . . wrote: Ls, June 8 and Aug. 17, 1921.

Page 194   Van Eeden wrote: L, Oct. 3, 1921./ planning a book: Ls, US to doctors, Apr. 18, 1922./ The *Journal*: April 29, 1922./ Theodore Dreiser: L, Dreiser to US, Dec. 23, 1921./ David Sinclair: L, DS to LH, Oct. 15, 1973, with words of the song attached.

Page 195   "When the history": *Prejudices*, Ser. III, 213–231.

Page 196   Norman Hapgood paid: L, Hapgood to US, Mar. 1, 1922./ tossed off in five weeks: L, US to EH-J, Feb. 27, 1922.

Pages 196– New York *American*: "Plutocracy," June 17, 1923; "U.S. Colleges," June
197   19, 1923; "Banker," June 21, 1923; "Secret Societies," June 22, 1923; "Getting the Big Hogs," Aug. 12, 1923; perils of secret diplomacy, Nov. 25, 1923; liberation of women, Sept. 30, 1923; "Desperate Struggle," Dec. 23, 1923; "World's Most Colossal," Dec. 30, 1923; "Modern Psychology," Dec. 16, 1923; "Now, as in the Days," Sept. 16, 1923.

Page 197   explained quickly and clearly: L, US to *NA*, Mar. 30, 1923./ he was arrested: *NYT*, May 17, 1923, also June 16, 1923.

Notes

Page 198 Liberal and Socialist organs: NY *Call,* May 17, 1923; *NA,* June 6, 1923./ "Granted that the chief": May 18, 1923. See also Cincinnati *Post,* May 23, 1923; Johnstown, Pa., *Daily Democrat,* May 17, 1923; and the Baltimore *Sun,* May 24, 1923./ "Is it true": L, June 2, 1923./ As a direct result: *Singing Jailbirds,* "Postscript," 87. Also, *Auto.,* 228–232./ Dos Passos: Dos Passos had been especially anxious that the New Playwrights Theatre do the play if it were rewritten, writing US, Apr. 24, 1927: "Would you mind if I undertook that?" See also, Ls, Dos Passos to US, May 1, 1927; US to Dos Passos, May 3, 1927; and also T. Ludington, *The Fourteenth Chronicle,* Boston, 1973./ "The play is fine stuff": L, O'Neill to US, Aug. 22, 1924. About US's earlier play, *Hell,* O'Neill had written him on Mar. 26, 1923: "It would be extremely interesting to attempt it," but no production resulted. On Aug. 12, 1923, he wrote US: "I'm sure glad you're a 'fan.' It's reciprocated, believe me! I've been one of yours ever since way back in 'Jungle' days, and I think I've read everything of yours—except 'The Goose-Step'—since then."/ "a drama that is intense": Oct. 5, 1924, 2./ "I am enclosing": Dec. 5, 1928.

Page 199 Upton's continuous correspondence: Ls, San Quentin 45445 James McCann to US, Feb. 1, 1929; Chaplain S. B. Hannah to US, n.d., and *passim.* Also, see *TG-S,* 476–477.

XVII. *THE GOOSE-STEP, THE GOSLINGS,* THE JEWS

All the quotations in this chapter not identified below, as well as ideas from *TG-S* for which there are no notes, are from *TG-S:* 2, 15, 18, 19, 20, 21, 21, 24–25, 65–66, 115–116, 89, 49, 470–471, 366–368, 362, 145, 398–399, 379, 378.

Page 200 "Education is an admirable": *The Critic as Artist./* Only a tiny fraction: *TG-S,* 403–407. Also L, Arthur M. Schlesinger to US, Aug. 27, 1922, from the University of Iowa./ "Funny to get back": L, June 13, 1922./ visited Bartolomeo Vanzetti: L, Vanzetti to US, May 30, 1922./ "Dear Comrade Sinclair": L, Oct. 4, 1923, from Massachusetts State Prison. The novel of Vanzetti seems never to have been published.

Page 201 to educate *everyone: everyone,* of course, did not include blacks, Mexicans, or Indians.

Page 204 "if you will": Jan. 23, 1927.

Page 205 "I should like to outline": L, US to Joel E. Spingarn, Sept. 23, 1922./ "I started a course": Gottesman interview, 153./ *The Higher Learning in America,* NY, 1918. Also J. Dorfman, *Thorstein Veblen, His America.* NY, 1966./ "The doctrine": May 1923, 141–144.

Page 206 "nearly everybody": L, US to Professor James Harvey Robinson, Apr. 18, 1923./ Robert M. Hutchins: L, to LH, Sept. 28, 1970./ John W. Gardner: L, to LH, Oct. 5, 1970./ Herbert Marcuse: L, to LH, Nov. 4, 1970./ S. I. Hayakawa: L, Hayakawa to US, Mar. 31, 1942./ McGeorge Bundy: L, to LH, Sept. 2, 1970.

Page 207 Wilbur J. Cohen: L, to LH, Dec. 7, 1970: "in about 1931–32, I read all of Upton Sinclair's writings up to that time. . . . When I came to Washington as Assistant Secretary, I found myself in 1962 involved in handling the complex and protracted negotiations on the Kefauver drug bill. The importance of protecting the consumer remained with me from *The Jungle* and was a significant driving force in helping to retain my ability to continue to work for some constructive legislation against overwhelming opposition. Upton Sinclair had a great deal to do in sustaining my lifelong interest in consumer protection and in defending the public interest. . . . Upton Sinclair might be viewed as a teacher and a teacher's influence never stops—it goes on into eternity."

Also, L, Cohen to LH, Dec. 28, 1970: "I have never studied his [EPIC] plan but I am astounded to realize that my proposal to abolish poverty in the U.S. [see *Congressional Record, Proceedings and Debates of the 91st Congress, First Session*, Vol. 115, No. 201, Dec. 5, 1969. "A Program to Abolish Poverty"] must have unconsciously drawn from him or the same sources he drew from. Who can tell how ideas are disseminated or how they influence others?"/ "I must admit": Oct. 17, 1923./ petty and large scale graft: *TG*, 40–44./ "the placing of magnificent": *ibid.*, 42.

Page 208 "Feel free": L, US to H. E. Wildes, Oct. 9, 1923./ "This great authority": *TG*, 139./ "a general prevalence": *ibid.*, 365./ "they too are workers": *ibid.*, 444.

Page 209 Baltimore *Sun* review: Feb. 23, 1924. In his *American Mercury* review, Apr. 1924, 504–5, HLM continued in the same vein./ "The tragedy is": *NYT*, Sept. 20, 1970. Also C. Silberman, *Crisis in the Classroom*, NY, 1970; J. Kozol, *Death at an Early Age*, Boston, 1962; and C. Jencks, *Inequality*, NY, 1972./ lecture tour: L, US to J. B. Salutsky, Aug. 25, 1924./ opportunity to sell books: L, US to Symon Gould, Sept. 20, 1924./ his inventory: for most of US's publishing years there are regular inventories and rates of sale in the Lilly Library.

Page 210 reach a much wider audience: *Proposition to the American Fund for Public Service*. Also telegram W. B. Conkey Co. to US, Apr. 18, 1924.

Page 211 Roger Baldwin wrote: May 8, 1924./ worse than incompetent: L, US to Berkman, May 8, 1924./ soliciting capitalist businessmen: L, US to Charles E. Carpenter, June 2, 1924./ those in the Soviet Union: Ls, US to Albert Rhys Williams, June 30, 1924; and to Comrade Lunacharsky, June 30, 1924./ "I think it would": Feb. 4, 1924.

Page 213 "close to a complete nervous breakdown": June 1, 1925./ David's own needs: DS interviews with LH./ "He had made a martyr": 610–611.

Page 214 uncomplicated sexual satisfaction . . . her demands for sex: MCS assured Dollie that sexual needs could and should be satisfied with dispatch and simplicity. Dollie-LH interviews./ "In our family": 333./ "a man has to"; *ibid.*, 365.

Page 215 "When I was sounded out": *AO*, 34–35./ "Jewish boy": *ibid.*, 47.

Page 216 "In my autobiography": L, Oct. 14, 1932. US's mild answer, Oct. 31, 1932, admitted: "The problem of Jewish sensitiveness is a very difficult one to a Gentile."/ brief article: it appeared in German in a book, *Judenhass—Eine Anthologie*, compiled and published by Prometheus, an educational cooperative labor society in Vienna. In the Lilly Library there is no copy of US's original in English, remarkable when he saved so much else of less importance. The full text as translated from the German was published in *The Jewish Tribune*, June 11, 1926, 318./ When various Jews objected: Maximilian Hurwitz, "As Gentiles See It," the last of a three-part review of *Judenhass*, in *The Jewish Tribune*, May 28, 1926, 3. Also, "Mr. Sinclair's Error," editorial by Herman Bernstein, editor of *The Jewish Tribune*, June 11, 1926, 3. Also, L, Morris Kobacker to US, July 27, 1926, and attached unidentified newspaper editorial, and US's reply, July 31, 1926./ "I think that the Jewish race": L, US to editor, *The Jewish Tribune*, June 4, 1926, printed *The Jewish Tribune*, June 11, 1926, 3./ Godfrey Lowell Cabot: See L. Harris, *Only to God*, NY, 1967.

Page 217   Hutchins Hapgood: *The Spirit of the Ghetto*, NY, 1902./ Dreiser, for example: See F. Matthiessen, *op. cit.*, 224–226./ Upton, who was unable: US's anti-Semitism crops up from beginning to end. When in a L, June 5, 1918, ten New York Jews subscribed to *Upton Sinclair's* but questioned what made US "speak so cynically of Hebrew financiers?" he had replied (L, to Comrade Lefkowitz, June 13, 1918): "It is a fact that the international financiers are 75 per cent Jews. It is also a fact that the founders of the Socialist movement are 75 per cent Jews." Ls, US to Frank Harris, Jan. 21, 1921; US to Saul Scher, Nov. 1, 1929; US to William Salisbury, July 21, 1937./ "The Jewish bourgeoisie": Speech to the Council of Peoples' Commissars, Aug. 9, 1918.

XVIII. *MAMMONART, MONEY WRITES!*, WORLD CORRESPONDENT

Quotations in this chapter not identified in these notes, as well as ideas or scenes from *Mam* for which there are no notes, appear in that book on pages 48, 191, 187, 188, 179 and 183, 169, 352, 81–84, 63, 30, 303 and 353, 266, 267, 272.

Page 218   "Puritanism can only": "Erasmus, Faust & Co.," *The New Yorker*, Jan. 13, 1973, 90./ rejected . . . art: See *TJOAS*, 11./ *Collier's*: Oct. 8, 1904, 22–25./ "Some day I hope": L, US to Stewart Edward White, Apr. 23, 1906, University of Virginia Library. US's uses of this subject prior to *Mam* are too frequent to list every instance but include *LP*, 588–589; L, US to Christopher Morley, July 10, 1921.

Page 219   "the most perfect type": Karl Marx recognized Balzac as "remarkable for his profound grasp of reality" in *The Process of Capitalist Production as a Whole*, Vol. 3 of *Capital*, Unab. 39, NY, 1967, where he paraphrased at some length from *Les Paysans* on how the usurer abuses the peasant. See also, Vol. 1, 589. Regarding Lenin's advice that proletarian writers learn by studying the masters, see Aaron, *op. cit.*, 216–218./ "he is not writing": quoted in R. Gilman, *Common and Uncommon Masks*, NY, 1970, 313.

Page 220   "By all means": L, Sterling to US, July 2, 1924./ "it is some of the worst": L, Aug. 4, 1925./ Edmund Wilson: *NR*, April 22, 1925, 236–237. Reprinted in *The Shores of Light*, London, 1952, 212–216./ "He contradicts himself": *"Mammonart" Pro and Con*, n.d./ "Having just returned": NY *Telegraph*, July 12, 1925./ "I am not": L, Dec. 29, 1926.

Page 221   *Honeypots*: another tentative title was *Book Urchins*./ "I beg you": L, May 16,
1927. See also Ls, Dell to US, Aug. 9 and 22, 1927, and US to Dell, Aug. 31,
1927./ almost to tears: See Schorer, *op. cit.*, 496./ "I would advise": L, to US,
Jan. 3, 1928./ "dealing with our living artists": L, US to HLM, Jan. 8, 1927.

Page 222   "the fundamental fact": "The Settin' Down Job," *Writer's Year Book and
Market Guide*, 1931./ "the essence of art": *LP*, 588–589./ "The essence of a
self-reliant": *Prejudices*, Ser. III, 93./ "No artist desires": *Dorian Gray*./
"There are two ways": *The Critic as Artist*./ "I noticed one": Brooklyn *Eagle*,
Oct. 3, 1927, 13./ Correspondence with college students: Ls, E. Vollmer to
US, Oct. 25, 1926; US to Vollmer, Oct. 30, 1926; D. Clephane to US, Mar. 4,
1925; telegram, H. Fuller to US, May 14, 1925; Ls, Gregory to US, June 15,
1926; US to Gregory, June 21, 1926; L, Robert Fraser to US, Feb. 8, 1926./
subscribed to their newspapers: Ls, US to editor, *New Student*, CCNY, May
3, 1926; US to Harry Birdoff, Feb. 1, 1933.

Page 223   "Well, courage to you": L, Sept. 24, 1925./ "man will become a radical": L,
Feb. 5, 1926./ a young Chinese student: L, Feb. 24, 1927. See also, L, Yung
Ying Hau, The Stud'ts Soc'ty for Adv't of Sun-Yat-senism in Amer., to US,
Mar. 1, 1927./ "Young China awakening": draft DL, n.d./ A CCNY
student: L, Apr. 6, 1927./ "the way to be happy": L, Dec. 14, 1925.

Page 224   eating sand: "My Life and Diet," *Physical Culture*, Nov. 1924, 37–38, 82, 84,
86./ "The trouble with you": L, HLM to US, Aug. 21, [1926]./ compared
him to Aristotle: *American Mercury*, Mar. 1928, 281./ "until I find
somebody": L, US to HLM, Feb. 28, 1928./ "Is her arm worth pinching?" L,
HLM to US, n.d./ "I have never laid eyes": L, US to HLM, Aug. 23, 1926./
"My very best thanks": L, HLM to US, Sept. 1, [1926]./ Hollywood brothel:
W. Manchester, *Disturber of the Peace*, NY, 1951, 227–228./ "Was baptized
by Aimee": quoted in Manchester, *op cit.*, 228./ "An Evangelist Drowns":
June 30, 1926, 171.

Page 225   Pasadena Tennis Club: L, US to Ray Doerschlag, Sept. 28, 1926./ referred to
him as a "Communist writer": L, US to Portland *Telegram*, Nov. 28, 1926./
"will take her place": L, US to *NA*, Dec. 10, 1925. US also wrote defending
others. See L, US to *Time*, May 25, 1926, defending Bernarr Macfadden from
Time's "vicious" attack./ "and I therefore respectfully": Oct. 23, 1925./
advising Charlie Chaplin: Dec. 29, 1925./ giving Sergei Eisenstein: L, Feb.
16, 1927./ sending Bertolt Brecht: See L, Elizabeth Hauptmann to US, July
17, 1926./ "I understand an atheist": L, US to Woolsey Teller, Apr. 5, 1926.

Page 226   "black magic for sex purposes": L, Sept. 4, n.d./ "cannibal gypsies": L, Sept.
23, 1931./ "I am greatly shocked": L, US to Isaac Don Levine, June 29,
1925./ "I consider preservation": draft of telegram, US to International
Committee for Political Prisoners, Dec. 16, 1925./ Roger Baldwin believed:
He revealed in an interview with LH in 1971 that he still believed so./
dollars cabled from Moscow: L, Alexander S. Cowie, assistant cashier,
Hellman Bank, to US, Sept. 8, 1925. But US could become so annoyed at the
Russians as to inquire (L, US to Alexander Gumberg, July 16, 1925,
Collection of the State Historical Society of Wisconsin): ". . . if you know
anybody in Moscow who can go to the office of Gossisdat and punch the

manager once or twice for me I will be grateful."—perhaps the only reference to his wanting to do personal violence in all his vast correspondence./ "I think you cover": L, July 27, 1927./ write for *The Nation*: draft telegram, Oct. 26, 1926.

Page 227   Bennett Cerf: Ls, Cerf to US, May 7, July 14, 1926, Mar. 17, July 9, Sept. 1, Sept. 8, 1927. Modern Library never issued *TJ*./ "the prevailing sentiment": L, Nov. 5, 1926./ "The Comrades have no means": L, US to Sam Weisenberg, Nov. 9, 1926./ not plan to wage: L, US to Lincoln Steffens, June 10, 1926.

Page 228   "I enclose a small cheque": L, Lincoln Steffens to US, May 19, 1926./ He made clear: Ls, US to Richardson, Oct. 28, 1925, May 26, 1927; and Richardson to US, Oct. 31, 1925./ "I point out": L, US to Richardson, Nov. 4, 1925./ "This is a State of boosters": L, US to *NA*, Nov. 4, 1925./ Post Office threatened: Ls, R. C. Knox to US, Sept. 23 and Oct. 5, 1925./ pettish letters: US to Harris, Sept. 10, 1925./ and the Post Office: L, US to R. C. Knox, Sept. 28, 1925./ "the strongest combination": L, US to Michael Koway, Jan. 29, 1937./ Harris . . . views on Sinclair: *Contemporary Portraits: Third Series*, 1920, 15–30.

Page 229   enjoying ill health: Ls in this chapter from both US and MCS to Dollie are in her collection./ "You'll get well": July 3, 1925./ "my cheeks are swelled": L, US to Albert Rhys Williams, Oct. 12, 1925.

Page 230   canned by the hundreds: L, MCS to Dollie, Sept. 28, 1929./ an agreement undertaking: LH-Dollie interviews, 34./ "moved so near here": June 30, 1924./ raising hell with whomever . . . forbade her sister: LH-Dollie interviews, 40–41: "of course, if you love your dog more than you love your sister . . ."/ imaginary cancers: L, US to Liveright, Apr. 1926./ "my temper": L, MCS to Dollie, Sept. 28, 1929./ was becoming bankrupt: L, US to DS, Feb. 3, 1931, and *Auto.*, 276–277./ income for 1931: L, US to Galen H. Welch, collector IRS, Apr. 12, 1932./ Alamitos Bay: 43-57th Place; L, US to Ralph Jones, Oct. 29, 1926./ Boys' school: L, US to Wilshire, Feb. 28, 1927./ "the stream of people": L, US to Herbert A. Gold, Aug. 21, 1929.

Page 231   then unknown Halldór Laxness: not until 1955 did Laxness receive the Nobel Prize for Literature. (L, Laxness to LH, n.d., but c. July 15, 1970)/ "absolutely determined": L, US to Kate Crane Gartz, July 18, 1927./ "For many years": L, US to P. B. Wadsworth, 1928./ two years in Long Beach: L, US to his mother, July 1, 1929./ a separate bedroom: L, US to Dollie, Apr. 13, 1929; also, LS, US to Frank Case, Aug. 31, 1933, and Oct. 5, 1935./ "Craig has been": Nov. 4, 1929./ trip to Mississippi: L, US to MCS, Feb. 11, 1930./ move back to Pasadena: L, US to Dr. Greg Hoskins, Dec. 4, 1929.

XIX. DELL'S BIOGRAPHY AND *OIL!*

Page 232   "There are few": *Dreamthorp*, VII./ suggested to Floyd Dell: L, Mar. 5, 1926./ "there are things": L, Mar. 5, 1926./ "When I had": Mar. 16, 1926./ "You were brought up": L, Nov. 17, 1926.

Page 233   "My comments": L, Jan. 6, 1927, Newberry Library copy where L has US's

handwritten additions not found in Lilly Library copy./ "do not inform":
quoted in L, US to Dell, Dec. 4, 1926./ "My Dearest Floyd": Dec. 18, 1926./
"The fact is": L, Nov. 25, 1926.

Page 234   promoted the sale: L, US to Dell, Dec. 20, 1927./ "it is as one," "Modern
industrial America," and "The Voltairean": *FDB*, 11–14./ "I am not": *ibid.*,
181.

Page 235   reviewed by Walter Lippmann: *SRL*, Mar. 3, 1928. US's answer, *SRL*, Apr. 7,
1928.

Page 236   "And there sat": *Auto.*, 239./ "taken the trouble": US to Liveright, Nov. 6,
1925./ "there is no propaganda": US to FvE, May 6, 1926.

Page 237   not a *roman à clef*: See, however, Ls, US to John Beardsley, Nov. 11, 1926,
and US to A. and C. Boni, Jan. 18, 1927./ "Shuffle the cards": *Oil!*,
unnumbered page opposite copyright./ "a pretty boy" and "with sensitive
red lips": *ibid.*, 15 and 56./ His mother tries: *ibid.*, 78–79 and 142–145./ "As
the Indians": *ibid.*, 61.

Page 238   "I am not satisfied": Dec. 1, 1926.

Page 239   "use of the arts": *MW*, 21./ "The trouble was": Dec. 18, 1926./ "I wrote the
words": Nov. 16, 1926./ who turned down *Oil!*: L, Liveright to US, Jan. 27,
1926./ a womanizer: see W. Gilmer, *Horace Liveright*, NY, 1970./ "I wrote a
number": A. Boni-LH interview.

Page 240   issued bulletins: June 1, 1927./ sent wires: telegram, US to Boni, June 1,
1927./ wrote letters: L, US to EH-J, May 28, 1927./ hired a Boston lawyer:
telegram, George E. Roewer to US, May 31, 1927./ "manifestly tending":
NYT, June 1, 1927./ "Special Permit": No. 9788 issued by the Public Works
Dept., June 27, 1927./ To satisfy those: *NYT*, June 8, 1927.

Page 241   John Masefield: L, to US, n.d., Boar's Hill. "I read *Oil* with interest and
pleasure. It hasn't done *me* any harm, . . ."/ Havelock Ellis: L, to US, July
14, 1927, "the tendency of the book is Puritanical."/ Lewis Mumford: L, to
US, June 10, 1927. "To censor *Oil* because it is 'indecent' is ridiculous."/
Norman Thomas: L, to US, June 9, 1927./ "I read it": L, July 16, 1927./
Edith Wharton: L, Aug. 19, 1927.

Page 242   "a tremendously enlarged version": quoted in Q. Bell, *Virginia Woolf*, Vol.
II, NY, 1972, 61.

XX. *BOSTON*

The quotations from *B* in this chapter are from pages 24, 333, 498–499, 53,
155, 167, 101, 233, 349, 75.

Page 243   "I could never believe": quoted in Macaulay's *History of England*, Ch. I. See
also, Thomas Jefferson's message on the fiftieth anniversary of the
Declaration of Independence, July 4, 1826, the day he died./ precisely
nine-thirty: *B*, v. Carey McWilliams remembered (interview with LH): "I
had lunch with him in Long Beach, California, at some cafeteria he used
rather like his club because Mary Craig would not allow him to bring anyone
home. It was the day Sacco and Vanzetti were executed and he said the
execution would have a long, long, long term effect. . . . He was very vivid

about it . . . that a great injustice had been done."/ "I am no longer": L, US to Kate Crane Gartz, Aug. 5, 1927./ "apostolic succession": Kaplan, *op. cit.*, 20–21.

Page 244   interest among artists: According to Max Eastman, "Is This the Truth About Sacco and Vanzetti?" *National Review*, Oct. 21, 1961, 261–264, "A total of 144 poems, six plays and eight novels have been published dealing with the case . . ."/ *Justice Denied in Massachusetts*: L. Untermeyer, *Modern American Poetry*, NY, 1950, 466–467. Miss Milholland married Boissevain July 15, 1913, and died Nov. 25, 1916. He married Millay ten years later./ *Gods of the Lightning*: written with Harold Hickerson, NY, 1928./ *The Male Animal*: written with Elliot Nugent, NY, 1940./ "SV execution most shocking": draft of telegram, n.d./ "I can't recollect": L, Sept. 21, 1928./ he decided *Boston* would be published: actual publication date was Nov. 11, 1928./ "people who come": L, to Emmerich, Aug. 8, 1927./ "I would like": L, US to M. A. Musmanno, Feb. 23, 1928.

Page 245   He had sold: L, Collins to US, Nov. 10, 1927./ dozens of friends: list dated Jan. 24, 1928./ James Fuchs: an unknown scholar and sometime writer for *New Yorker Volkszeitung*. Many of the ideas he sent US were brilliant and learned and used by the muckraker./ he requested: Ls, US to Dell, July 30, 1928, and US to Fuchs, Apr. 24, 1928./ "I don't agree": Aug. 9, 1928./ "a hired liar" and "The plain truth": L, US to Minor, Mar. 26, 1928./ "All these matters": L, US to Creighton Hill, Aug. 9, 1928.

Page 246   "When I went East": L, US to Minor, Feb. 8, 1928./ "I know positively": L, US to A. and C. Boni, Aug. 28, 1928./ Max Eastman, would come: Eastman, "Is This the Truth About Sacco and Vanzetti?" *National Review*, Oct. 21, 1961, 261–264.

Page 247   "pageant play": Ls, Apr. 18, 1929, to NR and others./ "I have thought": July 29, 1931.

Page 249   even Army, Navy, and Secret Service: *Oil!*, 245–247./ Sinclair's three best novels: that two of these, *TJ* and *B*, dealt with immigrants is, I believe, no more than an interesting coincidence./ "What Fielding was": Dec. 5, 618–619.

Page 250   "deserves praise": Nov. 18, 1928./ "been perfectly captured": L, Nov. 27, 1928./ "It is not merely": L, n.d./ "I look upon Sinclair": *Our African Winter*, London, 1929, 229./ one of mankind's masterpieces: Henry Poulaille, *Le Peuple*, Apr. 30, 1928. When even for a third-rate book, such as *Our Lady*, US heard from Albert Einstein (L, Oct. 15, 1938) that it "is to be compared only with the greater works of Anatole France," small wonder if he had an exaggerated view of his literary ability./ Robert Herrick: L, Herrick to US, Dec. 18, 1928./ Upton confided to Lovett: L, Dec. 27, 1928./ chairman of the 1928 Pulitzer Prize Committee: *NYHT*, Apr. 17, 1929. Chairman Richard K. Burton denied his statements quoted in the Minneapolis *Star*, Apr. 13, 1929, that the prize would be awarded to Dr. John Rathbone Oliver for his *Victim and Victor* only because *B* had too many "socialistic tendencies." The prize established by Joseph Pulitzer was intended to be given "for the American novel published during the year which shall best present the wholesome atmosphere of American life and the highest standard of American manners and manhood."/ Charles Boni, wired: Apr. 13, 1929.

Page 251　"I should think": L, May 6, 1929./ In one of his printed letters: May 1929./ Leslie Fiedler: L, Fiedler to LH, Sept. 29, 1970. "Still, the one book of his that moved me as a kid, helped in fact to confirm my life long interest in problems of innocence & guilt & the 'demonstration trial' was his *Boston*."/ Frederic Morton: Interview with LH, Jan. 20, 1970. "Sinclair was the only American writer I had read before I left Vienna. His *Oil!* and *Boston* gave me and many Europeans a whole and exciting picture of the USA—top to bottom."/ "absolutely intolerable treatment" and "request that our relationship": L, US to Charles Boni, Feb. 21, 1928./ contributed toward their advertising: US's royalty statement for *B* for the period ending Nov. 30, 1928, shows a $3,000 contribution by him toward $9,558.06 of advertising, some fifty-six ads including eight in the *NYT*./ "that the propaganda": Dec. 12, 1928./ his British agent: L, US to Dakers, Sept. 1, 1928./ willing to spend time: L, US to Dakers, Jan. 4, 1928.

Page 252　"I will agree": L, US to Laurie, Dec. 9, 1927./ "I have grave doubts": L, US to Manuel Gomez, Mar. 31, 1928, in answer to Gomez' L, Mar. 13, asking to add his name to that of Darrow, W. E. B. Du Bois, and others on the National Executive Committee of the All-America Anti-Imperialist League./ "I will be pleased": L, US to Deputy Mayor Harold in Düsseldorf, Apr. 12, 1929./ But no matter how worthy: see L, US to George Barr Baker, Nov. 15, 1929./ his own translators: L, Editorial, B. Bauza, Barcelona, to US, Nov. 6, 1929.

Page 253　"the looting of the Nez Perces": L, Feb. 22, 1929./ "thousands of women": L, Aug. 23, 1930(?)./ Leonard Abbott: Apr. 22, 1928./ "I'm only a poor school girl": L, Sept. 2, 1928./ "I intent": L, Aug. 30, 1930./ whether sexual relations: L, July 22, 1929./ "All I can say": L, US to Kress, July 29, 1929./ Richard J. Neutra: Ls, Neutra to US, Feb. 9 and 24, 1930./ Trotsky wrote: L, to US, July 10, 1930. US's reply, July 30, 1930./ "There is, I know": L, Mar. 28, 1928./ "Some one wants": *Writers' Digest*, Mar. 1930, 21.

Page 254　"I hope your": Jan. 2, 1929./ "As always, you are right": Feb. 22, 1930./ released to the press: Mar. 3, 1928./ aware that his correspondence: L, A. R. Williams to US, Apr. 19, 1928./ "publicity list": see instructions to his secretary, draft of telegram re British American naval competition, Apr. 25, 1929./ "I used to live on nuts": L, Feb. 13, 1928./ "with the utmost extravagance": Broun, *It Seems To Me*, NY, 1935. "I really think": L, Jan. 5, 1928./ "If you want": L, Aug. 22, 1928.

Page 255　"with no results": L, US to DS, Apr. 2, 1927./ "Of course the doctors": L, US to DS, Mar. 4, 1927./ Bettina Mikol: Daughter of an old Socialist and union organizer, she was a reader for Simon & Schuster and a sometime literary agent especially for unsolicited manuscripts sent US and forwarded by him to her. L, US to M. Sante Bargellini, Apr. 18, 1929. She and DS had a daughter; they were divorced on June 28, 1939./ Upton promised: L, US to DS, Sept. 25, 1928./ fifty dollars at Christmas: L, US to Wilshire, Mar. 14, 1927.

Page 256　"I don't think": Oct. 25, 1928.

XXI. *AMERICAN OUTPOST, MENTAL RADIO,* AND THREE NOVELS

Page 257 "Biography is the only": *Journal,* Jan. 13, 1832./ "I had a right": Feb. 19, 1929./ "conceited and cheap": *ibid./* Floyd Dell: L, Feb. 22, 1929./ objections of his mother: L, US to Mrs. David Sinclair, Apr. 8, 1929./ "I have decided": L, US to Bonis, Apr. 18, 1929./ "the facts about": "Is It 'Scandal' to Invade the Private Life of Geniuses?" Unidentified review, but identical to US's review of *The Private Life of Henry Maitland,* "Genius and Privacy," Chicago *Evening Post,* Feb. 21, 1913, 1, 14.

Page 258 *The New Frontier*: draft of telegram to Farrar, Jan. 3, 1932./ "Your mind reminds me": L, Aug. 29, 1932./ "very mellow quality": May 1, 1932./ "most effective pamphleteer": 179–181. Comparing US to Jack London, Chamberlain concluded: "In every way London inspires considerably less respect than Sinclair. He was theatric where Sinclair was sincere."/ For thirty years: *Auto.,* 244.

Page 259 van Eeden, believed: L, FvE to US, Apr. 9, 1916./ Bernard M. L. Ernst: L, to US, Aug. 29, 1930./ Harry Houdini: L, Houdini to US, June 10, 1924./ Alone at Long Beach: *Auto.,* 243–244./ record of her dreams: see four pages of notes, Apr. 22, 1929./ until two in the morning: L, US to DS, Feb. 19, 1929./ Mrs. Winnie: 171–174./ Dad . . . married a spiritualist: 455–456, 464./ Lanny Budd series: *Between Two Worlds,* 801 and *passim./* allegations of nobility: L, US to Embassy of Poland, Washington, D.C., Aug. 30, 1927./ Upton wrote *The New Republic*: Feb. 11, 1929.

Page 260 "Let me introduce": Draft of an article, "Explain This to Me! An Account of Some Psychic Mysteries," 14. See also, L, James H. Ellis to US, Aug. 31, 1927./ "she smuggled": When US and MCS had taken Dollie to Europe on their honeymoon, they not only preached suffragist dogma to her, but let her practice it as well, for she took part in the slashing of the portrait of the Duke of Wellington./ Arthur Ford: *Auto.,* 245–246./ Theodore Dreiser: See Ls, Theodore Dreiser to US, Jan. 5, 1939, and Helen Dreiser, Jan 3 and 17, 1939. Another author interested in Ostoja was Hamlin Garland, Ls, to US, Apr. 14 and 17, 1939./ Dr. Walker Franklin Prince: L, US to Prince, Aug. 2, 1927. In addition to many Ls between Dr. W. F. Prince and US, there are many between the M.D. and psychiatrist Dr. Morton Prince, and US throughout the twenties, see esp. May 1, 1923.

Page 261 J. B. Rhine, whose ESP research: Ls, Rhine to LH, July 17, Sept. 10, 28, Oct. 5, 1970. "U.S. had planned . . . if he won the campaign for the governorship . . . setting up in the State University at Berkeley a department of psychical research with McDougall in charge and with me as his assistant." See also Rhine's *Extra-Sensory Perception,* Boston, 1934, 1, 21./ Sinclair dropped the Pole: Ostoja continued from time to time to try to reestablish the relationship without success, see L, Ostoja to US, n.d., on the stationery of the Institute of Infinite Science of which Ostoja was founder and president, having replaced his patents of nobility with "Rt. Rev., PhD., D.D., N.D., D.Sc., L. Hy."/ "Your wife must": Ls, Conan Doyle to US, Sept. 3, Nov. 16, and Dec. 21, 1929; and US to Conan Doyle, Dec. 4, 1929./ asked Bertrand

Russell: L, May 7, 1929./ "it is quite impossible": May 21, 1929./ "I am too much bothered": L, June 5, 1929./ "has with characteristic courage": *MR*, v–ix./ McDougall had visited: *Auto.*, 244–245.

Page 262   "The outcome was": *ibid.*, 245. See also, L, Rhine to LH, June 28, 1973./ *Ghost Stories*: Jan. and Feb. 1930./ "apparently patronized": Dec. 24, 1929./ a second letter: June 30, 1931./ Sigmund Freud: L, Aug. 14, 1933./ "I have just read": L, Nov. 13, 1930.

Page 263   an inscription Einstein wrote: *MLIL,* 356.

> *Wen fict der schmutz igste Topf nicht an?*
> *Wer klopf die Welt an den Lohlen Zahn?*
> *Wer verdachtet das Jetzt and schwoert auf das Morgen?*
> *Wen Macht kein "undignified" je Sorgen?*
> *Der Sinclair ist der tapfre Mann.*
> *Wenn einer, dan ich en bezeugen kann.*

See also, *Auto.*, 256. Almost twenty years later in a L to Van Wyck Brooks, Mar. 12, 1952, US quotes with pride Einstein's accolade as "who is never afraid of being undignified."/ Gandhi wrote: Oct. 30, 1960. See also, *MLIL*, 361–362./ "Mr. Sinclair's thinking": L, Indira Gandhi to LH, Oct. 6, 1970./ articles that took seriously: Brooklyn *Eagle*, Aug. 25, 1930./ "Because Upton Sinclair": May 1969.

Page 264   then to Pasadena: July 10, 1929./ mid-July he began: L, US to Karl Reeve, July 13, 1929./ "beyond the customary [bounds]": "Fiat Justitia! A Radical Seeks Justice in Denver," *New Leader*, Aug. 3, 1929, 4. See also, L, US to Charles A. Erwin, Sept. 6, 1927; Complaint, State of Colorado, City and County of Denver, In the District Court Fed. No. 8570, Div. 5., Sept., 1927./ "She was so furious": L, US to Kate Crane Gartz, June 28, 1929./ "T. J. Goodson, publisher": L, US to Albert Boni, Nov. 14, 1929.

Page 265   "I have to be": L, Oct. 16, 1929./ "What you write is": Sept. 30, 1929./ "Have just read yr/ Mountain City": L, Dec. 5, 1930./ "You are a very jolly fellow": Dec. 30, 1930./ "I shd. be delighted": L, Feb. 6, 1929.

Page 266   "with some trepidation": L, Mar. 1, 1929./ "Do you think an open argument": L, Mar. 24, [1929]./ offended his daughter-in-law: L, US to Betty Sinclair, Dec. 31, 1929./ "You ask me for": US to *National Magazine*, Nov. 19, 1929./ where "they" had got the money: L, Jan. 4, 1929./ "we have to go without": L, Apr. 6, 1931./ was either Greek to her: L, US to his mother, Aug. 14, 1929./ "If there were": Dec. 9, 1920; Nov. 22 and Dec. 19, 1929.

Page 267   Priscilla Sinclair died: Baltimore *Sun*, Oct. 20, 1931: *NYT*, Nov. 6, 1931./ manuscript of *The Jungle*: It has never been found./ Howard Bland . . . spurned: L, DS to US, Oct. 20, 1930. Also, telegrams Oct. 19, 1931, US to DS and US to Mrs. John R. Bland./ having refused to stay: Dollie-LH interviews./ "beyond anything": Sept. 19, 1930./ Edgar Lee Masters: Feb. 7, 1931./ William Lyon Phelps: Feb. 16, 1931./ Howard Fast: Interview, Fast-LH./ What apparently had moved: L, US to *NR*, June 13, 1930.

Page 268   "Prohibition will never": L, US to editor, *Monde*, Jan. 23, 1929./ Mencken:

L, US to HLM, Aug. 30, 1930./ Sinclair Lewis: L, US to Lewis, Sept. 16, 1930. Lewis refused, L, Sept. 20, 1930./ Darrow: L, US to Darrow, Sept. 16, 1930./ La Guardia: L, US to La Guardia, Dec. 16, 1930./ William Randolph Hearst and Al Smith: L, US to Al Rogell, Jan. 1931./ "When I finish": L, US to Charlie [probably Chaplin or Oursler], Feb. 27, 1931./ five or six in the morning: L, US to DS, Apr. 13, 1931./ "putting clothes on the outside": L, US to Oursler, June 5, 1931./ "all royalties & other income": Assignment, July 23, 1931. In a virtually identical assignment six months later, Jan. 6, 1932, MCS got all the rights and titles to *AO*./ "Mr. Sinclair undertakes" and "His cunning": *NA*, Sept. 23, 1931, 310./ "One of the reasons": July 29, 1932./ "do not ever restrain": L, May 16, 1932./ "For God's sake": Dec. 26, 1930.

Page 269   he urged Sid Grauman: L, Mar. 29, 1932./ debate on prohibition: L, US to Dr. Wilson, Mar. 29, 1932./ Billy Sunday: Ls, Sunday to US, Aug. 22 and 31, 1931. Nor was US displeased to learn that a capitalist price war between Macy's and Gimbel's had driven down the retail price of his book from $2.50 to $1.36, causing it to sell briskly, L, E. Greene to US, Oct. 21, 1931./ his earlier experience: *Screenland*, June 1930, 38, 93./ praised the actors: *NYT*, Apr. 23 and May 1, 1932./ "This is something": L to *NM*, Oct. 2, 1927./ "I refuse": L, US to Betty Sinclair, Nov. 21, 1932./ twenty thousand dollars: L, US to Betty Sinclair, Apr. 15, 1932./ "Upton went to dinner": L, n.d., collection of Mrs. John Kling.

Page 270   ten thousand dollars: Memorandum of Agreement, Aug. 31, 1932./ "The Gold Spangled Banner": L, US to Dell, Oct. 29, 1932./ mansion in Beverly Hills: 614 North Arden Drive./ "gone Hollywood": L, US to Betty Sinclair, Sept. 16, 1932./ "We have profited": L, Nov. 21, 1932./ "I suppose": L, Nov. 29, 1932./ "palatial residence": Sept. 20, 1934./ After he had been cheated: US even earlier had evidenced interest in getting a Nobel Prize for himself, L, US to Enise Ottesen Jensen, Nov. 12, 1921.

Page 271   "I know that you": L, Mar. 19, 1930.

Page 272   asked by Sinclair to serve: L, US to Leon L. Whipple, Jan. 27, 1931, was the standard request./ John Dewey: L, Dewey to US, Feb. 3, 1931./ William McDougall: See L, US to McDougall, Nov. 29, 1930./ Bertrand Russell: L, Russell to US, Feb. 14, 1931./ signatories rounded up: "Upton Sinclair Proposed by 770 for Nobel Prize," *NYHT*, Jan. 11, 1932./ George Bernard Shaw: L, GBS to US, Nov. 13, 1931, and same date, L, GBS to Greene./ "I can't imagine": HLM, *Books Abroad*, May, 1932, 373./ "When I was": L, July 16, 1931.

Page 273   his former wife had wired: Schorer, *op. cit.*, 545./ four additional Americans won it: O'Neill, 1936; Faulkner, 1949; Hemingway, 1954; John Steinbeck, 1962./ continued to imply: *Auto.*, 397, 305./ wrote the California Teachers: L, July 8, 1930./ "You said you would not": L, US to W. W. Busick, July 10, 1930.

Page 274   to borrow money: L, Stanley Rogers to US, Nov. 4, 1930, and attached notes./ certified Upton as the Republican: L, US to Hon. Frank G. Jordan, Sept. 23, 1930./ "A surprising result": clipped from the Los Angeles

Examiner and sent, straight telegram, US to *New Leader*, Nov. 5, 1930./ he wired the victor: Nov. 6, 1930./ "police brutality": L, US to Mayor Porter, published in *Open Forum*, July 2, 1932./ Heywood Broun wrote: L, Apr. 30, 1931./ delighted to be thought of: L, US to DS, May 7, 1932./ "the man who runs": L, May 6, 1931.

Page 275　daily front page articles: beginning Sept. 11, 1929, *The Record*, Los Angeles. Bathing suit picture, Sept. 12, 1929./ "Upton, why in hell": L, Carr to US, Aug. 23, 1931./ "Some time when": L, Aug. 25, 1931.

Page 276　He sold the list: L, *The Survey (Graphic)* to US, June 7, 1929./ If a clipping bureau sent: L, US to International Press Cutting Bureau, Jan. 6, 1930./ "you should certainly": July 19, 1930./ readers who lent him money: L, US to Hans Ejrnaes, Denmark, Feb. 14, 1929, in reply to L, Jan. 15, 1928./ "It amounts to $3": L, Jan. 9, 1931./ Interstate Commerce Commission: L, Mar. 3, 1933. US wrote *NR*, Sept. 12, 1933, that the New Deal needed "a sock on the nose" for working men at Boulder Dam sixteen hours a week longer than the NRA permitted./ when any newspaper: L, US to *American Spectator*, Mar. 14, 1933./ Governor Gifford Pinchot: *NYT*, July 10, 1931./ "to voice the need": Feb. 19, 1931.

Page 277　"Your protest": L, Kate Crane Gartz to Ralph Burton, National Patriotic Society, Feb. 26, 1931. Many letters in US's files are for Mrs. Gartz's signature. Both MCS and US prepared such letters and helped Mrs. Gartz rewrite her own letters in return for her financial support to them and their causes./ "I am grateful": L, US to R. Engler, Dec. 17, 1931./ "a reformer like me": L, US to George Sylvester Viereck, Dec. 15, 1930./ "pornographic postcards" and "Do you deny": L, June 23, 1931./ Diego Rivera: Ls, US to Farrar & Rinehart, Jan. 5, 1931, to Diego Rivera, Feb. 6, 1931./ "equal to the possibilities": L, US to Parriton Maxwell, June 2, 1931./ predicted it would be: L, US to Priscilla Sinclair, Apr. 24, 1931./ "no call": L, US to W. B. Conkey Co., Aug. 17, 1932. Written in late 1925 when both US and MCS were ill, *Judd* was published by the author in 1926. Had a demand for it suddenly arisen, there remained the 6,063 copies in paper listed in the June 15, 1932, inventory./ Harry F. Sinclair's photograph: Ls, US to *Le Quotidien*, Paris, Sept. 17, 1929, and US to *Journal D'Alsace-Lorraine*, Strasbourg, Mar. 4, 1930.

Page 278　"a common laborer": L, Feb. 3, 1931./ "ready to give up my business": L, May 23, 1931./ almost illiterate oil field worker: L, Aug. 4, 1931./ "a girl, 23 years old": L, [1931]./ penitentiary libraries: L, US to Rev. K. E. Wall, July 28, 1931./ prisoners preferred: L, Jan. 15, 1929./ "I decided": Printed newsletter, Jan. 1931./ "I read everything": L, Aug. 24, 1931./ "I am enraptured": L, May 12, 1931.

Page 279　"Mr. Sinclair still has": R. Blankenship, *American Literature: as an Expression of the National Mind*, NY, 1931, 553./ "told more of the crooked things": L, July 15, 1932./ "could write a biography": L, June 29, 1932./ W. E. Woodward: L and analysis, July 13, 1932. See also L, Woodward to US, July 26, 1932./ "Don't you think": Aug. 3, 1932./ paid twenty thousand: US Income Tax report for the year showed a total income of $32,923.11. Return examined Feb. 1, 1935.

Page 280   learned from Floyd Dell: *Auto.*, 260–261, and Gottesman interview, 214./ "Do your part": Feb. 1933./ "In order to prevent": Feb. 6, 1933./ "I didn't think": Nov. 9, 1932.

XXII. *QUE VIVA MEXICO!*

Page 281   *QUE VIVA MEXICO!*: The tragic story of Eisenstein's experience in the United States and Mexico is told in GG (H. Geduld and R. Gottesman, *Sergei Eisenstein and Upton Sinclair*, Indiana University, 1970)./ "It is worse than a crime": The *mot*, in Fouché's *Memoirs*, referring to the murder of the Duc d'Enghien by Bonaparte, has also been attributed to the Emperor (Emerson, *Essays, Second Series*, "Experience"), to Talleyrand, and to others./ "Oh, that is": L, Eisenstein to US, Sept. 8 [?], 1931; GG, 135./ mutual friends: Salka and Berthold Viertel, see L, US to Dear Comrade [Smirnov], Mar. 19, 1932.

Page 282   to senators and others: telegrams, US to Senators Blaine, Borah, Costigan, Couzens, Dill, Howell, Hiram Johnson, La Follette, Norris, Nye, Shipstead, and Walsh, Nov. 14, 1930. Also to Louis Brandeis, Nov. 16, 1930./ "make two or three hundred percent": L, US to Macfadden, Feb. 17, 1931./ mortgaging her beloved real estate: L, US to M. W. Daunbney, n.d./ Indeed the contracts drawn: Nov. 24, 1930, also modifying letter, MCS to Eisenstein, Dec. 1, 1930./ never earned much . . . problem: Dollie-LH interviews, 4, 19, 21. Upton and Craig claimed: L, US to Eisenstein, Jan. 7, 1932; GG, 263–264./ "like a negro": L, Oct. 21, 1931; GG, 180–182.

Page 283   "*most* of the time": L, Eisenstein to US, c. Nov. 13, 1931; GG, 200–204./ "There is one embarrassing matter": L, US to HK, Dec. 5, 1930; GG, 123–124./ almost a quarter of a million feet: See L, US to Dear Comrade [Smirnov], Mar. 19, 1932; GG, 305–310./ Edmund Wilson: "Eisenstein in Hollywood," *NR*, Nov. 4, 1931, 320–322./ "This is a mean insult": L, Eisenstein to US, c. Nov. 13, 1931; GG, 200–204./ Eisenstein had a plan: M. Seton, *Sergei Eisenstein*, NY, 1962, 198–199. Alexandrov in the U.S.S.R. has recently received a copy of the Eisenstein footage from New York's Museum of Modern Art (which held it prior to its transfer to the Library of Congress). If he completes his effort, there may finally come to be at least a closer approximation of what Eisenstein might have done than anything made to date.

Page 284   hernia operation: L, US to Prynce Hopkins, Aug. 28, 1931./ "some kind of pervert": L, HK to US, Oct. 9, 1931; GG, 170–173./ repeatedly ascribed: L, US to Seton, Apr. 5, 1950; and "Thunder Over Mexico," *Institute of Social Studies Bulletin*, Vol. 2, No. 4, Winter 1953, 42–43, 45–48./ Marie Seton: *op. cit.*, 515–516./ "was put in jail": L, Eisenstein to US, c. Nov. 13, 1931, GG, 200–204. Forty years later, HK in frank and generous interviews with LH obviously relished telling about those days and evidenced none of the youthful problems he may have had./ "Kimbrough question": L, Eisenstein to US, c. Nov. 22, 1931, GG, 214–217; and L, Eisenstein to US, Nov. 24, 1931, GG, 219–221: "I understand very well the sinecure character of

Hunter's presence here, but on the other hand I can take on myself only the responsibility of transforming your so hardly gathered money into film footage but not into cascades of vomit!"/ long letter to Stalin: Nov. 22, 1931; GG, 212–214./ more than fifty thousand dollars: Mexican Picture Trust Statement of Expenditures, Nov. 15, 1930, to Dec. 31, 1931./ making future pictures: L, HK to US, Nov. 15, 1931; GG, 205–206./ "STOP BEING DUPED": Feb. 8, 1932; GG, 289.

Page 285   stopped by immigration officials: NYT and NY Sun, Feb. 22, 1932./ plotted with Sinclair: Telegram, US to Peter Bogdanov, Apr. 21, 1932./ usefulness of a "Moviola": L, US to Dear Comrade [Smirnov], Feb. 27, 1932; GG, 294–295./ "and all it might bring in": L, US to Eisenstein, Dec. 2, 1931./ "The question then becomes": L, US to Betty Sinclair, Apr. 15, 1932; GG, 315–316.

Page 286   might buy the film: Ls, US to DS, Apr. 28, 1932; E. Greene to US, Apr. 30, 1932; and US to Dear Comrade [Smirnov], July 27, 1932./ "Russia does not want": L, MCS to Dreiser, Sept. 8, 1932; GG, 352–353. Dreiser was one of the very few to whom US confided the existence and substance of the Stalin cable. Others included Henri Barbusse, L, Nov. 3, 1932, and Edmund Wilson, L, Dec. 10, 1931./ "The Russian Government got": L, US to Harry Dana, July 26, 1933; GG, 392–396./ simply reneged: Mexican Picture Trust Report of Progress, Feb. 13, 1932.

Page 287   obscene drawings: L, US to Seton, Apr. 5, 1950. And Seton, op. cit., 224–225 and 253–255./ "it was the vilest stuff": L, US to Seton, Apr. 5, 1950./ railed non-stop: Dollie-LH interview./ an attack of hiccups: NY Evening Sun, Jan. 20, 1931./ film had been removed: L, A. J. Guerin to [US], May 17, 1932; GG, 332.

Page 288   sent Stalin a long cable: Aug. 15, 1932; GG, 347–349./ "At best we eat": L, Betty Sinclair to US, May 24, 1931./ "I slept": L, Betty Sinclair to US, June 15, 1931./ "The authorities don't care": L, DS Aug. 23, 1931./ rarely sent any: L, US to Gossisdat, Feb. 14, 1929.

Page 289   "I am telling": L, US to Victor Rosen, June 16, 1951. Also, Auto., 266./ "I want to express": L, US to Kahn, Dec. 12, 1927. Also, Ls, Kahn to US, Jan. 4, 1929, and Dec. 30, 1930.

Page 290   "I have known Hunter": L, Jan. 7, 1932; GG, 263–264./ "She does not doubt": L, Oct. 19, 1934./ "is as dependable": Form L to investors, Feb. 10, [1931], and US to Mrs. Payne, Dec. 16, 1930./ "There must be": L, Dec. 15, 1930.

Page 291   "We have been looking": L, Oct. 22, 1936./ the investors got back: GG, 422–423 and passim./ "the truth—is, as usual,": Jan. 22, 1971, reviewing GG.

Page 292   "is in a white fury": L, Sept. 16, 1933./ "I do not think": L, US to Leonard Abbott, Nov. 25, 1931./ "Somewhere about 1909": "The Masses," Institute of Social Studies Bulletin, Fall 1952, 74, 80–81.

Page 293   "What finished me": L, Feb. 16, 1935./ written European publishers: Form L, Oct. 23, 1930./ genuine horror of violence: L, US to editor, Call of Youth, Aug. 10, 1933.

XXIII. EPIC

Page 294   "It is difficult": *The Roosevelt Myth*, NY, 1961, 146./ "at least it was better":
L. Whiteman and S. Lewis, *Glory Roads*, NY, 1936, 203./ white native
Americans: C. McWilliams, *Factories in the Field*, Boston, 1939, 305.

Page 295   Food prices: Williams, Current, Freidel, *op. cit.,* 522./ one person in four:
Lillian Symes, "California There She Stands," *Harper's*, Feb. 1935, 360–363./
four dollars and a half: Los Angeles *Times*, June 20, 1934./ "southern
California was": G. Creel, *Rebel at Large*, NY, 1947, 208./ "bloody
Thursday": July 5, 1934./ at least the third power: See, C. McWilliams,
Southern California Country, NY, 1946, 369./ "the ultimate segregation":
quoted in Duncan Aikman, "California Vibrates to 'Little Causes,' " *NYT*,
Sept. 9, 1934./ "be declared incompetent": NY *World Telegram*, Nov. 22,
1938./ undergoing a nervous breakdown: Paul A. Samuelson, "U.S. Identity
Crises," *Newsweek*, June 21, 1971.

Page 296   "They do not want": L, MCS to Bradford, Jan. 27, 1933./ "Any title": May
1, 1933.

Page 297   "had come to feel": Schlesinger, *The Age of Roosevelt*, Vol. 3, *The Politics of
Upheaval*, Boston, 1960, 111–123. ". . . the amiable scourge of the capitalist
system. . . . The last of the prewar muckrakers, Sinclair somehow kept a
gentle but durable innocence while all around him . . . Steffens to his left,
Mark Sullivan and Hearst to his right—capitulated to images of power and
success. His books were brisk and sentimental, saturated with fact and
suffused with moral indignation. They possessed a transparent sincerity and a
sweetness of temper which distinguished them from the smart-aleck
debunking of the twenties and the overwrought proletarianism of the early
thirties. . . . Sinclair remained voluble without being aimless, self-centered
without being egotistical, and persistent without being finally unbearable.
. . . His ostensible creed was socialism. But it was a romantic, old-fashioned
socialism in the tradition which had sprinkled America with utopian
communities in the nineteenth century."/ rich Santa Monica capitalist: L,
Aug. 28, 1933./ picked up by the newspapers: *NYHT*, Sept. 15, 1933. NY
American, Sept. 16, 1933./ "GLAD LEND YOU": DL, Sept. 16, 1933./ to
advertise: L, US to *Wall St. Journal*, Apr. 22, 1933./ more expenses: L, US to
Whitaker, Apr. 15, 1933, courtesy of the USC Library./ "I cannot endorse":
L, US to N. Baker, Aug. 18, 1933. US's income was high. In 1932 he had a
total income of $22,203.57 (L, G. H. Welch, collector of Internal Revenue,
to US, Apr. 13, 1933), but his expenses were higher./ "It is a magnificent
idea": L, Sept. 16, 1933.

Page 298   "Words are symbols": L, Sept. 27, 1933./ "how very keenly": L, May 1,
1934. See also, L, Thomas to Peterson, Apr. 5, 1934./ "sublime naïveté": *The
Choice Before Us*, NY, 1934, 228; also, *Human Exploitation in the United States*,
NY, 1934./ happening to the Socialist Party: See, M. Seidler, *Norman
Thomas, Respectable Rebel*, Syracuse, 1967, 188–191; J. Weinstein, *The Decline of
Socialism in America*, NY, 1969; M. Harrington, *Socialism*, NY, 1972; and D.
Egbert and S. Persons, *Socialism and American Life*, Princeton, 1952./

Steffens: L, June 4, 1934./ Dos Passos: L, Oct. 1, [1934]./ "not a monomaniac": L, Pound to US, Jan. 30, 1935. Also, Ls, Nov. 7, 1933; Sept. 10 and Dec. 19, 1934; Sept. 26, 1936; and L, to US from H. L. Pound, Ezra's father, Apr. 5, 1934.

Page 299   Republicans being outnumbered: K. Stewart, "Upton Sinclair and His EPIC Plan for California," *Literary Digest*, Aug. 24, 1934./ eight other candidates: Creel, Justus Wardell, William H. Evans, Z. T. Malaby, William J. McNichols, James Wadell, Forrest E. Dewey, Milton K. Young.

Page 301   "Thus under another influence": Walter Davenport, "Sinclair Gets the Glory Vote," Oct. 27, 1934./ "moral passion": H. C. Herring, "California Votes for God," Oct. 31, 1934, 137./ "Political Prayer": *Christian Century*, Nov. 14, 1934; *NYT*, Nov. 1, 1934.

Page 302   an educational exercise: L, US to ER, Oct. 31, 1933./ "We do give": Sept. 12, 1934, 286–288./ "The real implication": *The Living Age*, 347, 276–277, Nov. 1934, quoting from Laski's "Pen Portraits," in the London *Daily Herald*./ asked Eleanor Roosevelt: telegram, Oct. 21, 1933./ sent her his EPIC program: Jan. 15, 1934./ "I have read": Jan. 26, 1934./ "1) Say nothing": quoted in Burns, *Roosevelt: The Lion and The Fox*, NY, 1956, 200–201. Also in Schlesinger, *op. cit.*, 120./ "to propagate impossible goals": *The Democratic Roosevelt*, Garden City, 1959, 298.

Page 303   "it looks as though": L, FDR to Pittman, Oct. 9, 1934, *F.D.R.—His Personal Letters*, NY, 1947–1950, Vol. II, 426–427./ to the candidate by telegram: DL, Marvin H. McIntyre to US, Aug. 29, 1934./ "in manifest elation": *NYT*, Sept. 5, 1934./ Whether or not Franklin Roosevelt: See, Burns, *op. cit.*, 200–201; Ls, US to ER, Aug. 24, 1956; ER to US, Sept. 11, 1956; Burns to LH, Oct. 30, 1970.

Page 304   had positively assured him: *Auto.*, 274./ he had also met: *NYT* and *NYHT*, Sept. 5, 1934./ "like so many others": Schlesinger, *op. cit.*, 115–117; also, F. Perkins, *The Roosevelt I Knew*, NY, 1946, 127./ quickly retreated: See J. Lash, *Eleanor and Franklin*, NY, 1971, 386 and 399; telegram, US to ER, Jan. 31, 1934; and L, ER to US, Feb. 6, 1934./ "I've been taken": NY *American*, Sept. 8, 1934./ that Coughlin would: Ls, US to Coughlin, Dec. 2, 1933, and Oct. 3, 1934. Also, *Auto.*, 273–274, and L, US to Joseph North, Nov. 18, 1939. There were some public figures and movements he repudiated such as Pelly's Silver Shirts (L, campaign manager to Horace Andrew Keefer, Jan. 16, 1934)./ ten million dollar campaign: Estimates varied wildly as to what was spent and no accurate figure is obtainable since efforts were uncoordinated and often secret, but: "According to Mr. Van Devander, over $10,000,000 was spent to defeat Sinclair." McWilliams, *Southern California Country*, 298./ It set a pattern . . . guided by southern Californians: during and after the EPIC campaign, as during and after the campaigns of Richard M. Nixon, journalists and scholars have speculated upon why political campaigns there are more savage and cruel than elsewhere. Eric Sevareid has suggested (June 7, 1973, CBS Evening News) that perhaps advertising and flackery are necessary for election in California because there are neither the older traditions nor the precinct organizations common in many other areas.

Distances preclude person-to-person contact and so only through the media can the candidate impress himself on the voters. Packaging is especially important when there is no way to know the product at first hand. See also, C. McWilliams, *California, The Great Exception*, NY, 1949, 182.

Page 305   "scared the hell out of": L, Wilder to LH, Feb. 25, 1971./ every employee at M-G-M: B. Crowther, *Hollywood Rajah*, NY, 1960, 198./ "Stenographers, technicians, writers,": *NYHT*, Oct. 23, 1934./ Charlie Chaplin: Gottesman interview, 207, 309–310, and *Auto.*, 273./ Dorothy Parker and Nunnally Johnson: L, Scully to US, Oct. 1934./ Jean Harlow, James Cagney, and Morrie Ryskind, who, with Gene Fowler: Schlesinger, *op. cit.*, 119./ court action: *NYT*, Nov. 1, 1934./ move to Florida: "California, Here I Run," *Time*, Oct. 15, 1934; *NYT*, Oct. 6, 1934./ "That's the biggest 'piece of bunk' ": *NYHT*, Oct. 23, 1934./ one out of seven people: California State Relief Administration, *Economic Trends in California, 1929–1934*, San Francisco, California Emergency Relief Administration, 1935./ Fake newsreels: *Auto.*, 275; Schlesinger, *op. cit.*, 118–119.

Page 306   "I made those shorts": B. Thomas, *Thalberg*, Garden City, 1969, 268–269; also Crowther, *op. cit.*, 199–200./ "a perfectly well-meaning" and "traipsing after": *NYT*, Sept. 2, 1934; also W. Swanberg, *Citizen Hearst*, NY, 1961, 448–449./ recognized as actors: US, *I, Candidate*, 151–152; Schlesinger, *op. cit.*, 119, and R. Cleland, *California in Our Time*, NY, 1947./ "We hired the scum": quoted in L, Hans Zeisel to LH, Oct. 14, 1974.

Page 307   every newspaper in California: C. Van Devander, *The Big Bosses*, NY, 1944, 291./ "the first all-out public relations *Blitzkrieg*": Schlesinger, *op. cit.*, 118; also, S. Morison, *The Oxford History of the American People*, NY, 1965, 973./ "We had one objective": Schlesinger, *op. cit.*, 118./ "It was one": quoted in Irwin Ross, "The Supersalesmen of California Politics—Whitaker and Baxter," *Harper's*, July 1959, 55–61./ "Of course I am vulnerable": L, US to R. O. Foote, June 23, 1934.

Page 308   "was but a minute sample": Davenport, *op. cit.*/ phones were tapped and EPIC mail was stolen: US, *The Lie Factory Starts*, 1–2./ "of course thousands": *ibid.*/ "proofs" of a direct link: *ibid.*/ huge sums of money: Whiteman and Lewis, *op. cit.*, 219./ "become the victim of": L, Mooney to US, Sept. 27, 1934./ Texas oilmen: Interview, LH with independent Texas oil operator, "Even running 'hot oil' there usually wasn't much cash money to be found in 1934, but I had no trouble at all raising eighty-four thousand to bust that son-of-a-bitch. We knew if he won there, we'd soon have another like him here."/ "How much money": Van Devander, *op. cit.*, 297–298.

Page 309   family atmosphere: Ls and conversations, LH with Lorna D. Smith, founder of EPIC Club No. 3, Glendale. Also, McWilliams, *NR*, Aug. 22, 1934, 39–41.

Page 310   now one archimandrite, now another: See, Aikman, *op. cit.*/ opponents induced Aimee Semple McPherson: "Future of EPIC," *NR*, 616–617, Nov. 28, 1934 / Upton's rewrite: Schlesinger, *op. cit.*, 48./ "The movement is going": L, Nov. 24, 1933.

PCHS Media Center
Grant, Nebraska

Page 311   "He of all is": Davenport, *op. cit.*/ "the appeal of the Sinclair": Aikman, *op. cit.*/ Sinclair never wrote out his speeches: L, Richard S. Otto to Al Albrecht, Nov. 15, 1963. Otto was EPIC's campaign manager, see *Auto.*, 269–270./ "Whatever else may happen": L, US to Robert O. Foote, June 23, 1934.

Page 312   when . . . hecklers appeared: Borough, "Upton Sinclair's EPIC, 1934," *The Occidental Review*, Vol. 4, No. 2, n.d., 29–41./ demonstration of fair play: *Auto.*, 271./ Communists were running their own candidate: Sam Darcy, who polled 5,826 votes. The Socialist Party candidate, Milan C. Dempster, polled 2,947 votes./ attacking Sinclair . . . even in the Soviet Union: *NYT*, Oct. 7, 1934, reported an editorial in *Izvestia* signed by Karl Radek attacking US and predicting the EPIC campaign "will end only in bankruptcy, but may give the masses a lesson."/ Earl Browder: Interview with LH. The EPIC campaign, according to Browder, taught the Communists a great deal. "Mother" Bloor agreed: "Upton Sinclair's EPIC movement had proven a good training ground. . . ." *op. cit.*, 286./ "we should see": US, *Immediate EPIC* (Los Angeles: End Poverty League, 1934), 11./ insurance companies . . . Fish and Game Commissioner: US, *The Lie Factory*, 11–12./ normally forbidden ice cream: L, US to R. Brownell, Sept. 11, 1946./ "I cannot tell you": L, Oct. 17, 1934.

Page 313   seven to five: Turner Catledge, *NYT*, Oct. 29, 1934./ suit to disqualify: *NYT*, Oct. 19 and Nov. 1, 1934, and Symes, *op. cit.*, 368./ half a dozen by-line writers: Chapin Hall, Turner Catledge, S. J. Woolf, George P. West, Douglas W. Churchill, Duncan Aikman./ "What will happen": Oct. 22, 1934.

Page 314   *Time* published Sinclair's: Nov. 5, 1934./ asked Theodore Dreiser: *Esquire*, Dec. 1934, 32–33, 178–179./ "I would like": L, to Arnold Gingrich, Sept. 14, 1934, R. Elias, ed., *Letters*, University of Pennsylvania, 1959, 693./ in *Literary Digest*: "Sinclair Behind in Digest Poll," Oct. 27, 1934./ "The error did us": *I, Candidate*, 172./ "take the wild beast": US quoted in *NYT*, Apr. 1, 1934.

Page 315   "when he was elected": Herring, *op. cit.*, and for another *Christian Century* view, see Tigner, 1275, Oct. 19, 1932./ "reached a daily average": *NYT*, Oct. 18 and 19, 1934./ *Time*: See Oct. 15, 1934./ enormous flight of investment capital: *NYHT*, Oct. 17, 1934./ real estate contracts: *NYT*, Oct. 19, 1934./ "a sense of Armageddon": *NYT*, Oct. 14, 1934./ A. P. Giannini: M. and B. James, *Biography of a Bank*, NY, 1954, 431; and Schlesinger, *op. cit.*, 121./ neither Harry Hopkins nor: *NYT*, Oct. 18, 1934./ Postmaster-General Farley: *ibid.*, Oct. 26 and 27, 1934./ Senator McAdoo: *ibid.*, Oct. 27, 1934.

Page 316   George Creel: NY *World Telegram*, Oct. 26, 1934./ in return, Roosevelt would not: Schlesinger, *op. cit.*, 121; also, Burns, *op. cit.*, 201: and Turner Catledge, *NYT*, Nov. 1, 1934./ two to one odds: Turner Catledge, Oct. 29, 1934./ two hundred thousand votes. His campaign "is more": Turner Catledge, Nov. 4, 1934./ 879,557 votes: *Statement of the Vote at the General Election Held on November 6, 1934, State of California* (Sacramento: California State Printing Office, 1934).

Page 317   To A. P. Giannini: James, *op. cit.*, 431./ to President Roosevelt: Flynn, *op. cit.*, 75–76; and Tugwell, *op. cit.*, 337./ In less than a year: June 19, 1935. See

W. Leuchtenburg, *Franklin D. Roosevelt and the New Deal: 1932–1940,*
Chicago, 1958, 114–115./ important citizens: L, Henry Commager to LH,
Nov. 2, 1971: "I had immense admiration for Sinclair's political courage;
hoped he would win the governorship of California; regarded him as a
pioneer in many social reforms and economic experiments." See also, L.
Friedman, *A History of American Law,* NY, 1973, 586./ White Paper: Feb.
15, 1934./ "your book 'The Jungle' ": L, Dec. 21, 1938./ a poll *The Literary
Digest* took: "They Stood Out," Dec. 29, 1934, 7./ Galbraith: See note for
Introduction of this book and L to LH, July 10, 1970./ Paul A. Samuelson: L,
Samuelson to LH, Mar. 22, 1971; and Samuelson's *Economics,* NY, 1961,
136–137./ Henry Hazlitt: L, Hazlitt to LH, Feb. 4, 1971: "I admired Sinclair
for many things—particularly his prolificness and his power as a pamphlet-
eer—but I found myself on the opposite side from him on nearly every
political and economic question."/ John W. Gardner: L, Gardner to LH,
Oct. 5, 1970, "the kind of critic every healthy society needs"; and *The
Recovery of Confidence,* NY, 1970./ "He clearly contributed": L, Friedman to
LH, Mar. 16, 1971.

Page 318   "there was undoubtedly": L, Walter W. Heller to LH, June 22, 1971: "In
your study of Sinclair, I hope you will draw some parallels and contrasts with
Ralph Nader and his consumer movement. The greater reliance on research,
group effort, and action on specific issues and institutions is quite different
from, though a logical extension of, the great contributions of Upton
Sinclair."/ one of the most successful experiments: See, McWilliams,
Southern California Country, 298./ "Sinclair got licked": Schlesinger, *op. cit.,*
121–122./ But good resulted: L, Senator John V. Tunney to LH, Mar. 4,
1971: "His influence can be seen in the progressive administrations of
Governors Warren and Brown and their efforts to make California a leader
among States in promoting effective welfare and employment programs."
Also, L, Saul David Alinsky to LH, Feb. 11, 1971./ State positions under
Civil Service: McWilliams, *California, The Great Exception,* 182./ "The EPIC
campaign thus": Schlesinger, *op. cit.,* 123. See also, L, Jerry Voorhis to LH,
Aug. 11, 1970.

Page 319   "Would Sinclair have done worse": quoted by O. G. Villard, "Come Laugh
at California," *NA,* 563, May 15, 1935./ Los Angeles reporter: Roy Ringer,
Los Angeles *Evening Mirror News,* Sept. 18, 1958.

XXIV. "ENLISTED FOR THE WAR"

Page 320   "The rights and interests": L, to W. F. Clark, Apr. 1, 1902./ "We are just
starting": Max Stern, "EPIC Is 'Enlisted for the War,' Sinclair Declares,"
NY *World Telegram,* Nov. 7, 1934./ "As I read": L, Nov. 23, 1934, printed
by US at the end of *I, Candidate,* 215./ had written his will: *Auto.,* 275–276,
and *SB,* 358./ "It was a relief": *Auto.,* 278/ papers all over the country: See
NY *Evening Post,* beginning Dec. 17, 1934./ "An important feature": L, US
to John Farrar and Stanley Rinehart, Nov. 8, 1934./ "What beat us": "The
Future of EPIC," *NA,* Nov. 28, 1934, 616–617.

Page 321   helped unknown writers: See L, George Soule to US, Sept. 15, 1933./ to sell
            the list: L, US to the *NA*, Mar. 28, 1934./ funeral of Horace Liveright: J.
            Schevill, *Sherwood Anderson*, Denver, 1951, 307–308./ "I have come":
            "Sinclair Salutes Steinbeck," *Common Sense*, May 1939, 22–23. Ls, US to
            Steinbeck, Apr. 4 and June 30, 1939; Steinbeck to US, Apr. 4 and n.d., 1939./
            deeply in debt: L, US to George D. James, June 1, 1935, and L, US to Stanley
            Rinehart, May 12, 1936, put the debt at $15,000, although to John Haynes
            Holmes US had given a figure of $10,000./ twenty thousand miles . . .
            seven thousand dollars: tax statement, Mar. 4, 1936./ Hamilton Fish: *NYT*,
            July 21, 1935, and *NYHT*, Oct. 30, 1935./ "white-haired ladies": "Why Not
            Tory-Baiting?" *Common Sense*, Aug. 1936, 12–15.

Page 322   "We have no objection": unsigned copy of a L, Sept. 7, 1935, to US's lecture
            manager./ *Depression Island* was refused: L, Harold Clurman to US, Aug. 15,
            1935./ "musical comedy": L, US to DS, Aug. 8, 1936./ "of having Cervantes
            also appear": L, Paul Muni to US, Apr. 29, 1938./ "personal appearances":
            contract, Jan. 12, 1935./ association with Mrs. Gartz: L, MCS to Dollie, n.d.,
            Collection of Mrs. John Kling./ her father's death in January 1935: L, US to
            Betty Sinclair, Jan. 30, 1935./ "Everyone who knows": L, MCS to Harry,
            n.d./ written promises: Feb. 5, 1936./ offered Stone his own papers: L, US to
            Stone, June 23, 1938.

Page 323   dropped the project: L, Stone to US, Jan. 27, 1939, and Stone-LH interview./
            stayed at home: the Sinclairs had moved back to Pasadena and were trying to
            sell the Beverly Hills house, L, MCS to Dollie, n.d., Collection of Mrs. John
            Kling./ "to the movies": *ibid.*/ "intellectual" dinner parties: *Letters of Aldous
            Huxley*, London, 1969, 427./ forbade visits at home: L, Malraux to US, n.d.,
            [1937]./ Einstein and J. B. Rhine: Aug. 19 and 23, 1937./ Upton refused to
            give: L, US to DS, Nov. 28, 1938./ a long tirade: L, Meta to DS, Nov. 28,
            1938, Collection of DS./ 1940 through 1944, David Sinclair was in
            psychoanalysis: DS-LH interviews./ outspoken in their opposition: L, US to
            DS, Feb. 14, 1939./ "I tell you plainly": June 25, 1940, Collection of DS./
            "Here is the letter": Aug. 7, 1940, Collection of DS./ Some of David's letters
            criticizing: One long and detailed L, DS to US, Aug. 26, 1940, exists at the
            Lilly Library.

Page 324   "I have . . . only sorrow": Nov. 13, 1942, Collection of DS./ "I love you":
            Mar. 1, 1943, Collection of DS./ Again and again, Craig demanded: Dec. 18,
            1940; Oct. 1942; Jan. 1944; Feb. 2, 1945; 1948./ "become the haunt": L, US
            to DS, Oct. 23, 1942, Collection of DS./ "we can see": L, US to I. O. Evans,
            Aug. 20, 1945./ "Watch out for spies": L, MCS to Martin Birnbaum, mailed
            July 1947./ "They find us": L, MCS to Birnbaum, mailed July 11, 1947.

Page 325   "I have not made": L, to McWilliams, Feb. 28, 1945./ "Every morning from
            9 to 12": L, US to Miss Brown, n.d., c. 1948./ "A Four-Year Plan":
            advertisement *NR*, July 10, 1935./ *Nation, New Republic, Christian Century*:
            identical Ls, Mar. 20, 1935./ "without consistency or substance": "Upton
            Sinclair Considers the Infinite," *NYT*, Feb. 2, 1936./ a man in Missouri: L,
            Nov. 18, 1935./ three thousand dollars: L, Willa Roberts to US, Apr. 10,
            1935.

Page 326   "and then write a full length novel": L, US to Stanley Rinehart, May 12, 1936./ In 1919 . . . Upton had tried: *Auto.*, 258, 285–288, 324–325; and "Henry Ford Tells," *Reconstruction*, May 1919./ "Upton Sinclair . . . helped found our union": L, Victor Reuther to US for US's eightieth birthday celebration. Also, L, V. Reuther to LH, Jan. 5, 1971./ two hundred thousand paperback copies: L, US to Betty Sinclair, Sept. 27, 1937./ suggested to the UAW: L, Oct. 15, 1937./ Edmund Wilson: L, Wilson to US, Aug. 10, 1938./ "it seems to me to be": L, May 20, 1938.

Page 327   "It is too bad": L, Apr. 21, 1954./ In his *Autobiography*: 287–288./ Mrs. Ford's threat: See also, C. Sorensen and S. Williamson, *My Forty Years With Ford*, NY, 1956, 268ff./ obscure publisher: Rodale./ "I think I love": L, US to Dave Randall, Nov. 12, 1963./ precisely opposite: See Lewis Gannett reviewing *Little Steel*, *NYHT*, Sept. 22, 1938, on US's character Clum Jinkins; vis-à-vis, Rose C. Feld, *NYT*, Oct. 16, 1938, on the same character./ to influence Franklin Roosevelt: US to FDR, telegrams, May 29, 1935, and May 11, 1938; L, Oct. 20, 1938. US to ER, Ls, Feb. 27, 1936, Jan. 5, 1937, July 7, 1937. Also, "An Open Letter to President Roosevelt," *Liberty*, Aug. 14, 1937./ favorite son candidate: *NYHT*, Feb. 24, 1936./ ."My belief is": *American Mercury*, May 1936, 1–11.

Page 328   "I think that is": June 1936, iv–vi./ "You protest": *American Mercury*, vii. See also *ibid.*, July 1936, L, HLM to US./ "take my remarks": L, Apr. 19, 1937./ "It was thru": L, Dec. 8, 1939./ "you have always": L, Mar. 28, 1938./ "I have come to think": L, n.d., [1938].

Page 329   "The capitalist-Fascist war": L, US to Eugene Lyons, Mar. 31, 1938./ "I cannot recall": L, Mar. 30, 1938. On Mar. 15, 1938, US had written almost the identical words to DS./ "only as naïve": *NYT Book Review*, July 9, 1972, 1. There were other intellectuals with US on the wrong side of the Moscow trials issue. See telegram, Herman Michelson to US, Mar. 16, 1938, inviting US along with Thomas Mann, Harold Laski, Langston Hughes, and others to a mass meeting at Carnegie Hall Mar. 24. Also, L, Corliss Lamont to US, Mar. 19, 1938, listing other sponsors. US addressed the meeting by long distance telephone from California./ "I think that": L, US to Abe H. Rifkind, Mar. 26, 1937./ whose leader he addressed: See Ls, US to Stalin, introducing friends, Jan. 4, 1935, and Aug. 6, 1936. Also, telegram urging Stalin to offer US's former German publisher political asylum, Oct. 9, 1938./ column for *Pravda*: Ls and telegrams, M. J. Olgin to US, Apr. 11, 15, June 6, 8, 18, 1938; and US to Olgin, Apr. 12, 18, 1938, and *passim*./ to write jointly: L, US to editor of *International Literature*, Apr. 16, 1938./ was not and never had been a Communist: US sought to appear before the House Un-American Activities Committee and when he was not allowed to, he sent an affidavit to be made a part of the committee's record. See NL, US to Dies, Oct. 26, 1938; Ls, Robert E. Stripling to US, Dec. 22, 1938, and US to Stripling and accompanying affidavit, Dec. 28, 1938.

Page 330   "All my differences": L to the editor, *Pacific Weekly*, n.d./ "has achieved a masterpiece": L, US to Woodward, Sept. 25, 1939./ "I am afraid": published in NY *Call*, Dec. 23, 1939./ "I feel about like": L, US to Kress, Jan. 27,

1940./ "I admit that if": "Upton Sinclair, Answering Max Eastman, 'Reconsiders' Socialism, Russia and EPIC," *Common Sense*, Apr. 1940, 30–31.

Page 331   America's alliance with the Soviet Union: draft of cable sent Dec. 29, 1944, in reply to cable of Dec. 22, 1944, from *Izvestia* editor-in-chief Illichif./ "a money grubbing careerist": *NYT*, Apr. 21, 1948./ His writings, along with: *The Star*, Dec. 17, 1948./ lying Fascist propagandist: NY, *Daily Worker*, Oct. 6, 1949, 12./ "Russia is a slave state": Apr. 15, 1949./ encouragement of Mrs. Roosevelt: L, ER to US, July 1, 1949./ "if I were asked": Douglas W. Churchill, "Upton Sinclair, Looks Back on His Crusades," *NYT Magazine*, Sept. 18, 1938.

Page 332   "All my life": L, US to Otto, May 15, 1940./ "I hope you won't": L, US to Woodward, Sept. 16, 1938./ "America should keep": L, US to V. F. Calverton, May 13, 1935, for a symposium conducted by Calverton's *The Modern Monthly* on "What I Will Do When America Goes to War," Collection of the University of Texas./ "My thoughts are entirely": L, US to George Seldes, Feb. 21, 1941./ "I got a big idea": L, US to Fulton Oursler, Dec. 7, 1938./ included Einstein: L, Dec. 24, 1938.

Page 333   rich young idealists: See Gottesman inverview, 76–77./ ruthless in his business: *A World to Win*, 20–21./ "The character of Lanny": Perry Miller, "Mr. Sinclair's Superman Carries On," *NYT Book Review*, June 2, 1946, 4./ Craig and her sister Dollie feared: L, US to Helen Woodward, Mar. 14, 1941./ "love story" between Lanny's mother: L, US to story editor, Warner Brothers, Mar. 20, 1940./ only two or three volumes: L, US to James Henle, Dec. 6, 1938.

Page 334   "a thousand letters": US, "Farewell to Lanny Budd," *SRL*, Aug. 13, 1949, 18–19, 38./ Eleanor Roosevelt: L, US to ER, June 18, 1945./ President Truman: L, HST to US, July 16, 1949. Courtesy of the Truman Library. Also, L, US to HST, Sept. 9, 1952./ J. Edgar Hoover: Ls, Hoover to US, Sept. 16 and Nov. 10, 1952./ Albert Einstein: Ls, Einstein to US, Oct. 22, Nov. 9, 1945; Sept. 18, 26, 1946./ Earl Browder's: L, Browder to US, Apr. 5, 1948./ unknown schoolgirl's: L, May 24, 1943./ Vice-President Henry A. Wallace and . . . Nelson A. Rockefeller: L, US to Wallace, Apr. 28, 1942 (US sent identical letters to Harry Hopkins, Librarian of Congress Archibald MacLeish, Rexford Tugwell, and Supreme Court Justice Frank Murphy)./ President Truman and General Douglas MacArthur: Ls, US to HST and MacArthur, both Apr. 12, 1948; MacArthur to US, Apr. 22, 1948; Secretary of the Army Kenneth C. Royall to US, Apr. 27, 1948; HST to US, Apr. 29, 1948./ in 1943 the Pulitzer Prize: The jury consisted, Heubsch wrote US confidentially, May 19, 1943, of Lewis Gannett, Maxwell Geismar, and John Chamberlain./ elected to the National Institute: Telegram, Henry S. Canby to US, Dec. 14, 1943, and L, Canby to US, Dec. 21, 1943.

Page 335   "It was the 'graces and refinements'": *Sketches in Criticism*, NY, 1932, 296–297./ "I have regarded you": L, GBS to US, Dec. 12, 1941; and also Jan. 6, 1949./ "gained a more vivid recollection": L, Helene Lindow, personal secretary to Mrs. Lyndon B. Johnson, to LH, Jan. 28, 1971./ "The Lanny Budd series": L, Hugh Sidey to LH, Sept. 14, 1970.

Page 336   "a sense of nostalgia": R. L. Duffus, " 'The Jungle' Revisited," *NYT Book
Review*, Oct. 13, 1946. See also, James T. Farrell's "Return to the Jungle,"
NR, Nov. 4, 1946, 601–603./ "a Rollo book" and "He also makes": *Time*,
reviewing *Between Two Worlds*, Mar. 24, 1941, 90. Charles Poore, reviewing
One Clear Call in the *NYT*, Sept. 2, 1948, called Lanny "the Tom Swift of
destiny."/ "The style is": "Lanny Budd Rides Again," *NYT*, Aug. 29, 1948,
a review of *One Clear Call*./ "Mr. Sinclair has grown": Duffus, "A New
Novel by Upton Sinclair," *NYT Book Review*, June 16, 1940, 1./ "As I look
back": "Upton Sinclair," *The Clipper, A Western Review*, Sept. 1940, 3–4.

XXV. SINCLAIR AND THE CRITICS

Page 338   Brooks, in *The Confident Years*: 387, 380, 376, 383; also, *Emerson and Others*,
209–217, and L, Brooks to US, Nov. 4, 1921.

Page 339   correspondence with Lewis Mumford: L, Brooks to Mumford, Feb. 7, 1955,
The Van Wyck Brooks–Lewis Mumford Letters, NY, 1970, 395./ "The problem
you raise": L, Mumford to Brooks, Feb. 20, 1955; *ibid.*, 396; also Mumford,
The Golden Day, 122–125./ the work of other writers: US to editor, *NR*, Mar.
17, 1942, "Glory hallelujah, what a story *[The Moon Is Down]*! Sacrifice's
cock for Steinbeck."/ "I got the book originally": Apr. 8, 1953./ "that
extraordinarily interesting letter": May 17, 1953.

Page 340   "I added two more pages": L, Brooks to US, Feb. 1, 1955./ "difficult to be
right about": See also Aaron, *op. cit.*, 46: "Upton Sinclair was completely *sui
generis* . . ."/ "you are one": L, Mar. 18, 1955./ "There is a phrase": L, Mar.
12, 1972./ "a sub-literary belligerance": "The Confused Case of Upton
Sinclair," Aug. 1946.

Page 341   " 'Wanted: American Radicals' ": James B. Conant, *Atlantic Monthly*, May
1943, 4145, also *Time*, May 31, 1943, 21./ In his reply: "Author to Critic,"
Oct. 1946, 29./ "I have tried": *An Upton Sinclair Anthology*, ed. I. O. Evans,
1934, Los Angeles, 6–7./ *Literary History of the United States*: R. Spiller *et. al.*,
NY, 1963, Vol. 11, 996–997.

Page 342   Carl Van Doren: "The social and industrial order": "Contemporary
American Novelists," *NA*, Sept. 28, 1921, 347 348. Reprinted in Van
Doren's *Contemporary American Novelists*, NY, 1922, 65–74. Two decades later
in *The American Novel*, 1789–1939, NY, 1940, 240–242, Van Doren's final
appraisal while less generous was still complimentary./ ". . . Sinclair's
innocence": "Lincoln Steffens and Upton Sinclair," *NR*, Sept. 28, 1932,
173 175. See L, Steffens to US, Sept. 24, 1932./ he and . . . Bliven
apologized: Ls, Wilson to US, Oct. 19, 1932; Bliven to US, Sept. 22, 1932;
and DS published *NR*, Oct. 12, 1932, 263–267./ "One of the characteristic
forms": Wilson, "Vienna: Idyll and Earthquake," *NR*, Aug. 26, 1940,
283–284, a review of Franz Hoellering's *The Defenders*./ As Wilson
acknowledged: L, Wilson to US, June 23, 1932.

Page 343   "For a writer": June 24, 1972, 96./ Sartre: John Gerassi, "Sartre Accuses the
Intellectuals of Bad Faith," *NYT Magazine*, Oct. 17, 1971, 38./ "what use is
art": Joyce Carol Oates, quoted in an interview by Walter Clemons,

Newsweek, Dec. 11, 1972, 77./ "tiresome and amateurish": *TJOAS*, 208–209./ Edward Dahlberg: L, Dahlberg to LH, July 8, 1970: ". . . [of] his own books, one in particular had a prodigious effect upon me . . . *Mammon Art* [sic]. I own the book . . . and prize it enormously. I am of the mind that every author, commonly bent upon making money rather than seeking an honest fame, should read and study this . . . [for] the writer who commences as an iconoclast and then goes out to that Sodom of lucre, Hollywood, I know of no work of such sovereign importance for the American writer or student save *Mammon Art*."/ S. N. Behrman: L, Mrs. Anne Grossman, secretary to Mr. Behrman, to LH, Oct. 29, 1970: "Mr. Behrman has asked me to write . . . he admired him tremendously. He read 'The Jungle' when he was very young and was greatly impressed by it, and feels that Sinclair had a great influence on him, as a lesser H. G. Wells."/ Budd Schulberg: L, Schulberg to LH, June 9, 1971: "I consider Upton Sinclair one of the major influences in my life. Whenever I speak in schools, I find myself saying that I believe American novelists have an obligation to go to the 'social sores,' and in trying to explain what I mean I begin with Mark Twain and then move on to Upton Sinclair. . . . He may not have been our most stylish novelist, but my very strong feeling is that his imperfect works are worth a score of Updikes."

Page 344 "Perhaps a writer" 80th birthday tributes, Sept. 1958./ "This pale and soft-voiced ascetic": R. Cantwell, "Upton Sinclair," *After the Genteel Tradition*, NY, 1937, 37–51; also in *NR*, Feb. 24, 1937, 69–71./ "he will remain": Kazin, *On Native Grounds*, Garden City, 1956, 116–121.

Page 345 "Because his behavior": "Warmakers and Peacemakers," *NR*, June 24, 1940, 863./ "The Survival of Upton Sinclair": *College English*, 1943, 213–220. See also, W. Rideout, *The Radical Novel in the United States*, Harvard, 1956.

XXVI. WHAT CAN ONE MAN DO?

Page 346 "He has been a burr": L, HST to Harry Laidler, Sept. 9, 1958./ Helen Keller: Telegram to US, Sept. 19, 1958./ "Upton Sinclair's writings": Telegram from James B. Carey, president of the International Union of Electrical, Radio, and Machine Workers, and United Automobile Workers President Walter Reuther wrote, L, Feb. 26, 1959: "I do not know of any other writer who has helped so many people."/ "Most of all": L, Aug. 4, 1958. "What you are," Lewis Mumford wrote, "is even more important than what you have done: for from your example others will learn once more how to hope."/ journalists: foreign as well as American journalists, including British cartoonist David Low, L, July 11, 1957: "you made an impression on my juvenile mind as one of the great writer reformers of our time with THE JUNGLE. That seems a good while ago and I have followed you ever since."/ "I wish I could see": L, Aug. 31, 1958./ "Upton Sinclair's life": L, Aug. 8, 1958.

Page 347 to find a history of America: A sampling includes: Williams, Current, Freidel, *op. cit.*, Vol. 11, 290–291, 316–317: Freidel, *America in the Twentieth*

Century, NY, 1960, 56, 77; Morison, Commager, *The Growth of the American Republic,* NY, 1969, Vol. 11, 82, 279, 306, 307; Morison, *The Oxford History of the American People,* 514, 819, 909, 973; Shannon, *Twentieth Century America,* Chicago, 1963–69, 33, 96, 114, 264, 338; Hofstadter, Aaron and Miller, *The American Republic,* Englewood Cliffs, 1959, Vol. 11, 368, 379, 469; Parkes and Carosso, *Recent America,* NY, 1963, Book I, 104, 112, 144; Link, *American Epoch,* NY, 1955, 401, 444./ influence on historians themselves: L, Perry Miller to US, Dec. 10, 1952: "I was brought up in Chicago, by a Socialist father, and I believe that almost the first writer beyond the kindergarten level to whom I was introduced was Upton Sinclair. You have been an important part of my intellectual and spiritual life, as you have been for thousands in my generation."

L, Arthur Schlesinger Jr., to US, Apr. 7, 1953: "I would also like to take this occasion to thank you in general for your writings over the last half century. I have read you from an early age . . . with gratitude for the part you have played in creating the climate of opinion which made the social changes of the last generation possible." And to the eightieth-birthday dinner: "You have spoken to the people of the world more directly perhaps than any American writer of our time."/ superbly healthy man: L, US to Aline Law, Mar. 30, 1946./ passed the California test: May 2, 1958.

Page 348   moved to Buckeye: L, US to H. Howard Bland, May 5, 1951./ heart attacks: L, US to Martin Birnbaum, Feb. 27, 1954./ the rice diet: L, US to Dr. Kempner, July 25, 1954./ ex-President Hoover: L, US to Librarian, Yale University, Oct. 3, 1956.

Page 349   "Upton is really putting": L, MCS to Birnbaum, envelope dated Mar. 17, 1946./ she at first refused: Ls, US to B. W. Huebsch, Feb. 3, 1951, and MCS to Doniger, n.d./ "None of it": L, June 26, 1958./ "my teacher and my great friend!": postcard to US, Apr. 3, 1946./ Ex-EPIC workers: to US, filed Dec. 29, 1957: "An old 'Epic' now a 'Technocrat.' "/ unknown authors sent: L, US to Rose Shapiro, May 22, 1944./ candidates for graduate degrees: L, US to E. W. Lockard, Mar. 1947./ "what did the reading": L, US to Victoria Pierce, July 18, 1937./ beneficiary: correspondence between US and the Penn Mutual Life Insurance Co., Sept. 19 through Dec. 14, 1946./ an advertisement in *The New Republic:* Nov. 19, 1951, 19./ Errol Flynn: Nov. 28, 1951./ a thoughtful correspondence: Ls, Jung to US, published in *NR,* Apr. 27, 1953, 18–19, and Feb. 21, 1955, 30–31.

Page 350   "My life will": The song was "The Side of the Angels" from the Pulitzer Prize play for 1956, *Fiorello!,* copyright 1959, Sunbeam Music Corp., quoted with the kind permission of Sheldon Harnick, L, to LH, Sept. 3, 1973. The book of *Fiorello!* is by DS's brother-in-law, Jerome Weidman, and George Abbott./ A retelling of the Faust legend: *A Giant's Strength,* see L, Maxwell Anderson to US, June 4, 1947./ a retelling of *Pamela: Another Pamela,* L, Robert E. Sherwood to US, Nov. 9, 1949./ praised by Albert Camus: L, Camus to US, June 26, 1959./ asked Marshal Tito: L, Feb. 3, 1951./ Adlai Stevenson: Ls, US to Stevenson, Sept. 9 and Nov. 12, 1952./ Ezra Pound: L, Feb. 18, 1957./ Margaret Sanger: L, Feb. 17, 1957./ President Nasser: L, US to Nasser, Sept. 6, 1961; also, L, Nasser to US, Sept. 9, 1961./ Caroline Kennedy: L, Letitia Baldrige to US, Nov. 28, 1962./ letters to the editor: L, US to *Time*, Apr. 23, 1934, 2./ "you used my question": L, US to Bill Slater, Mar. 22, 1947./ questions to quiz programs: Ls, US to Clifton Fadiman, Feb. 23 and May 29, 1940./ they stood out: L, US to *Time*, Sept. 7, 1959, 4, on the correct use of datum and data.

Page 351   "The American people": L, Sept. 25, 1951./ "Let's be friends!": Sept. 13, 1959, and, L, Packard to LH, Oct. 26, 1970: "I held Mr. Sinclair in awe from college days."/ "how impressed I am": Aug. 10, 1950./ from Meta's third husband: by her second husband, Lester Keene, Meta had had another son, also named Lester./ *"Be assured"*: L, US to Stone, Oct. 15, 1963./ "cleared up a dark corner": L, Dec. 30, 1963./ "she seems to have": Apr. 21, 1964./ "I am sorry indeed": Apr. 23, 1964. After Meta's death, Sept. 3, 1964, the correspondence between US and Stone continued, US urging that Meta's papers should become part of the Sinclair collection at the Lilly Library, which they did./ Upton married: Oct. 16, 1961. See *NYT.*/ confiding to a friend: The friend, when interviewed by LH, insisted on anonymity. The statement is not one likely to be invented and it seems even less likely that the puritan US would have invented the episode. US was, however, somewhat given to stressing that his sex life was "normal," as in L, to Howard Fast, n.d., regarding Fast's review of *Auto.* in *SRL.*/ "The last thing": *Newsweek*, Oct. 23, 1961.

Page 352   "You mean to say": "Personal Close-Up," Mike Wallace, Nov. 25, 1963./ slept in the same bed: Jean Sinclair–LH interviews: "Upton had a gallant Southern manner with women and was obviously a sensuous man."/ "indebted as I am": L, May 12, 1964. The SDS was the student department of the League for Industrial Democracy that US had founded./ television and radio shows: L, Abe Elkin to US, Oct. 16, 1963./ "done more for labor": postcard, US to DS and Jean Sinclair, Sept. 22, 1965, Collection of DS./ United Automobile Workers honored: L, Walter Reuther to US, Mar. 1, 1962./ New York Newspaper Guild: *NYT*, Apr. 28, 1962.

Page 353   lunched at the White House: L, Mrs. Lyndon B. Johnson to US, Sept. 8, 1966./ returned there to watch: Max Frankel, "Johnson Welcomes Upton Sinclair, 89, at Meat Bill Signing," *NYT*, Dec. 16, 1967./ "I sort of felt": quoted in C. McCarry, *Citizen Nader*, NY, 1972, 320–321./ social accounting: Business Section, *NYT*, Apr. 8, 1973, 16./ business atrocities: R. Heilbroner, *In the Name of Profit*, NY, 1972./ misrepresented foods: G. Marine and J. Van Allen, *Food Pollution*, NY, 1972, and *Harper's*, Sept. 1972, 81–88.

Page 354   "What Drew Pearson writes": Nov. 27, 1968.

Page 355   "Someone has remarked": *NR*, May 2, 1960, 24./ *"The Jungle* must renew": *Atlantic*, Dec. 1961. See also, Swados, *A Radical's America*, Boston, 1962./ "Upton Sinclair is": *NR*, Dec. 1, 1962, 23–24.

Page 356   "exuberant, still optimistic": L, Max Lerner to LH, July 9, 1970./ "You're cool, Mr. Sinclair.": *The Courier-News*, Plainfield, N.J., July 9, 1968, 1./ "The English Queen Mary": *Auto.*, 329

Books by Upton Sinclair

SPRINGTIME AND HARVEST 1901 (Reissued as KING MIDAS 1901)
THE JOURNAL OF ARTHUR STIRLING 1903
PRINCE HAGEN 1903
MANASSAS: A NOVEL OF THE WAR 1904 (Reissued as THEIRS BE
    THE GUILT 1959), 1969
A CAPTAIN OF INDUSTRY 1906
THE JUNGLE 1906, 1973
THE INDUSTRIAL REPUBLIC 1907
THE OVERMAN 1907
THE METROPOLIS 1908
THE MONEYCHANGERS 1908, 1969
SAMUEL THE SEEKER 1910
THE FASTING CURE 1911
LOVE'S PILGRIMAGE 1911
PLAYS OF PROTEST 1912, 1970
THE MILLENNIUM: A COMEDY OF THE YEAR 2000 1912
SYLVIA 1913, 1971
DAMAGED GOODS 1913
SYLVIA'S MARRIAGE 1914
THE CRY FOR JUSTICE 1915, 1975
KING COAL 1917
THE PROFITS OF RELIGION 1918, 1970
JIMMIE HIGGINS 1919, 1970
THE BRASS CHECK 1919, 1970
100%: THE STORY OF A PATRIOT 1920
THE BOOK OF LIFE 1921
THEY CALL ME CARPENTER 1922
THE GOOSE-STEP 1923, 1970

HELL: A VERSE DRAMA AND PHOTOPLAY 1923
THE GOSLINGS 1924, 1970
SINGING JAILBIRDS: A DRAMA IN FOUR ACTS 1924
THE POT BOILER 1924
MAMMONART 1925
BILL PORTER: A DRAMA OF O. HENRY IN PRISON 1925
THE SPOKESMAN'S SECRETARY 1926
LETTERS TO JUDD 1926
OIL! 1927
MONEY WRITES! 1927, 1970
BOSTON 1928 (Reissued as AUGUST TWENTY-SECOND 1965)
MOUNTAIN CITY 1930
MENTAL RADIO 1930, 1962, 1971
ROMAN HOLIDAY 1931
THE WET PARADE 1931
AMERICAN OUTPOST 1932, 1969
UPTON SINCLAIR PRESENTS WILLIAM FOX 1933, 1970
THE WAY OUT 1933
I, GOVERNOR OF CALIFORNIA—AND HOW I ENDED POVERTY
    1933
THE EPIC PLAN FOR CALIFORNIA 1934
I, CANDIDATE FOR GOVERNOR—AND HOW I GOT LICKED 1935
WE, PEOPLE OF AMERICA 1935
DEPRESSION ISLAND 1935
WHAT GOD MEANS TO ME 1936
CO-OP 1936
THE GNOMOBILE 1936, 1962
WALLY FOR QUEEN 1936
THE FLIVVER KING 1937
NO PASARAN 1937
LITTLE STEEL 1938
OUR LADY 1938
TERROR IN RUSSIA 1938
EXPECT NO PEACE 1939
LETTERS TO A MILLIONAIRE 1939
MARIE ANTOINETTE 1939
TELLING THE WORLD 1939
YOUR MILLION DOLLARS 1939
WORLD'S END 1940, 1973

BETWEEN TWO WORLDS 1941, 1973
PEACE OR WAR IN AMERICA 1941
DRAGON'S TEETH 1942, 1973
WIDE IS THE GATE 1943, 1973
PRESIDENTIAL AGENT 1944, 1973
DRAGON HARVEST 1945, 1973
A WORLD TO WIN 1946, 1973
PRESIDENTIAL MISSION 1947, 1973
A GIANT'S STRENGTH 1948
LIMBO ON THE LOOSE 1948
ONE CLEAR CALL 1948, 1973
O SHEPHERD, SPEAK! 1949, 1973
ANOTHER PAMELA 1950
THE ENEMY HAD IT TOO 1950
A PERSONAL JESUS 1952
THE RETURN OF LANNY BUDD 1953, 1973
WHAT DIDYMUS DID 1955
THE CUP OF FURY 1956
IT HAPPENED TO DIDYMUS 1958
MY LIFETIME IN LETTERS 1960
AFFECTIONATELY EVE 1961
THE AUTOBIOGRAPHY OF UPTON SINCLAIR 1962

Index

417